Jóhanna Barðdal
Oblique Subjects in Germanic

Studies in Language Change

Edited by
Cynthia Allen
Harold Koch
Malcolm Ross
Don Daniels

Volume 21

Jóhanna Barðdal
Oblique Subjects in Germanic

Their Status, History and Reconstruction

DE GRUYTER
MOUTON

ISBN 978-3-11-221509-8
e-ISBN (PDF) 978-3-11-107801-4
e-ISBN (EPUB) 978-3-11-107807-6
ISSN 2163-0992

Library of Congress Control Number: 2023938297

Bibliographic information published by the Deutsche Nationalbibliothek
The Deutsche Nationalbibliothek lists this publication in the Deutsche Nationalbibliografie; detailed bibliographic data are available on the internet at http://dnb.dnb.de.

© 2025 Walter de Gruyter GmbH, Berlin/Boston
This volume is text- and page-identical with the hardback published in 2023.
Cover image: iStockphoto/thinkstock
Typesetting: Integra Software Services Pvt. Ltd.
Printing and binding: CPI books GmbH, Leck

www.degruyter.com

Til Hans Heinrichs!

Icelandic
  Til míns ástkæra eiginmanns!

Danish
  Til min kærlige ægtemand!

Swedish
  Till min kärleksfulla make!

Norwegian
  Til min kjære mann!

Dutch
  Aan mijn liefhebbende man!

German
  An meinen liebenden Ehemann!

English
  To my loving husband!

Preface

Writing this book has been a sheer joy. Some of the data presented here were gathered during the last two and a half decades and parts of the content have been published in sundry versions in several different articles throughout the years.

As a graduate student, I wrote a term paper on oblique subjects in Old Norse-Icelandic as a part of a course on Old West Scandinavian in the fall of 1994. This term paper was written under the supervision of Christer Platzack who incidentally was also the editor of a journal, Arkiv för nordisk filologi, where an article had been published earlier on the issue of whether potential oblique subjects exhibit any syntactic subject properties in Middle Norwegian. This particular article in ANF, authored by Endre Mørck in 1992, sparkled my interest in this topic, an interest that has stayed with me ever since.

The goal of this monograph is to bring together not only the relevant historical and synchronic data, but also to communicate my conclusions and the cumulative knowledge that I have acquired through this research process in a coherent whole, a book. This entails producing a lengthy text to be made available in a book format to a wider audience than only the few souls taking interest in the diachronic syntax of Old West Scandinavian, or the few historical syntacticians who have engaged in the issue of whether oblique subjects existed or not in earlier periods of the Old West Scandinavian languages. In other words, my goal with this book is to invoke the interest of both students and established researchers in issues of relevance for not only historical Germanic linguistics, but also for theoretical linguistics, typology, and general linguistics alike. This includes both historical and synchronic approaches to subjecthood and the subject status of potential oblique subjects throughout the Germanic era, along the axis of both time and space.

The first part of this book was written in the spring semester of 2020 in Amsterdam, during an in-residence fellowship at NIAS, the Netherland's Institute for Advanced Study in the Humanities and Social Sciences. I am immensely grateful to NIAS for having granted me the opportunity to spend a semester in such an invigorating and stimulating interdisciplinary environment, while at the same time providing the solitude needed for intensive periods of academic writing. I also thank the audience of the Thursday seminar at NIAS, in particular Rens Bod, for extensive comments on the first version of Chapter 2.

Unfortunately, due to the sudden and unexpected outbreak of the Coronavirus, the NIAS Building at Korte Spinhuissteeg 3 in downtown Amsterdam was abruptly evacuated in mid-March, cutting short the semester-long book-writing period, with subsequent delays in finalizing the manuscript. Despite travels and various other commitments, one chapter of the book was written in the summer of 2020. Most of the remaining chapters were committed to paper in the fall of the same year, when back in Ghent at my home university, except for the last chapter which was written in the summer months of 2021. I am especially thankful to the Linguistics Department at Ghent University for providing me with the opportunity to write and finalize this book project.

Further funding bodies have contributed to my research throughout the years, including my research on the subject properties of oblique subjects in the Germanic and the Indo-European languages. These funding bodies include the European Research Council (EVALISA, Consolidator Project nr. 313461), Ghent University's Special Research Fund (BOF-STA, grant nr. 01N02116), the Norwegian Research Council (NonCanCase, grant nr. 205007), the Bergen Research Foundation (currently renamed as the Trond Mohn Foundation), the University of Bergen, STINT in Sweden, the Icelandic Research Council, The Nordic Research Councils for the Humanities, and Lund University, as well as several smaller funding bodies during my junior years in Sweden.

For help with some of the data analysis, especially in cases where my own language expertise failed, I particularly thank Giacomo Bucci, Steven Mark Carey, Brian Cluyse, Juliane Elter, Michael Frotscher, Peter Alexander Kerkhof, Svetlana Kleyner, Guus Kroonen, Leonid Kulikov, Hjalmar P. Petersen and Roland Pooth. Thank you guys for allowing me to pick your brains whenever I needed to. Without you and your input, I would not have been able to present as complete an analysis of the data in Ch. 3–5 below, as is indeed the case now. Special thanks also go to Torsten Leuschner, Roland Pooth and Joren Somers for providing me with feedback on the German data in Ch. 6.

In addition, I thank all my friends and colleagues who have contributed as co-authors to, or conversation partners of, the various publications from which this book volume benefits. This includes all of the above-mentioned from the previous paragraph, as well as Avery Andrews, Hans C. Boas, Laura Bruno, Eleonora Cattafi, Michela Cennamo, Bill Croft, Eystein Dahl, Serena Danesi, Tonya Kim Dewey, Chiara Fedriani, Spike Gildea, Mihaela Ilioaia, Cynthia A. Johnson, Ritsuko Kikusawa, Kristian Emil Kristoffersen, Esther Le Mair, Kirsten Middeke, Verónica Orqueda, Catrine Sandal, Ilja Serzant, Thomas Smitherman, Valentina Tsepeleva, and earlier in my research career, Ute Bohnacker, Eiríkur Rögnvaldsson, Christer Platzack, the late Cecilia Falk, Jan Terje Faarlund and Halldór Ármann Sigurðsson. My deepest gratitude also goes to Thórhallur Eythórsson who has co-authored several publications with me on this topic, and who critically discussed some of those issues with me back and forth and back again over extended periods of time during the last two decades.

I am especially grateful to the editors of this series, Cynthia Allen, Harold Koch, Malcolm Ross and Don Daniels, for welcoming this monograph into their series, the reviewers, in particular Bettelou Los, for their constructive comments, Bernat

Bardagil, Kirsten Middeke, Roland Pooth and Joren Somers for having read and commented on (parts of) the manuscript. My deepest gratitude also goes to Cindy Allen for having painstakingly read and commented on the final manuscript twice and for having saved me from several solecisms and analytical oversights. I also thank Andrew Winnard for invaluable support and Birgit Sievert and Kirstin Börgen at Mouton de Gruyter for swift and speedy work on first getting this book into production and then getting it out of the printers and into the hands of the individual members of the linguistic community.

Last but not least, I thank my loving and nurturing husband, Hans Heinrich Marxen, for his endless patience towards an ever-working wife. Without your daily support, this book would not have seen the light of day. Tack, älskling!

Contents

Preface —— VII

1	**Introduction —— 1**	
1.1	Aims and objectives —— 3	
1.2	Subject in a "normal" language —— 5	
1.3	Establishing a nominative subject baseline for case languages —— 9	
1.4	Construction Grammar and grammatical relations —— 17	
1.5	Overview —— 19	

2	**What is a subject? —— 22**	
2.1	Earlier approaches to subjecthood —— 22	
2.1.1	Traditional grammar and modern syntactic approaches to subjecthood —— 22	
2.1.2	Subject as a universal category: The empirical problems —— 25	
2.1.3	Subject as a language-specific category: The methodological problems —— 30	
2.2	The present approach to subjecthood —— 33	
2.2.1	Subject as a construction-specific category —— 34	
2.2.2	Defining subject: Top-down vs. bottom-up approaches —— 39	
2.2.3	Argument structure, event structure and force dynamics —— 40	
2.2.4	Modeling subject behavior —— 43	
2.3	Deviations from the subject canon —— 46	
2.3.1	Oblique subjects —— 47	
2.3.2	Icelandic vs. German —— 48	
2.3.3	Interpreting deviations —— 51	
2.3.4	Acceptability judgments —— 60	
2.4	Typological considerations —— 65	
2.5	Summary —— 67	

3	**Alternating Dat-Nom / Nom-Dat predicates —— 70**	
3.1	The concept of alternating predicates —— 70	
3.1.1	Event structure and construal —— 71	
3.1.2	Identifying alternating predicates —— 74	
3.1.3	Word order statistics —— 78	
3.2	Alternating Dat-Nom / Nom-Dat predicates in the Germanic languages —— 81	
3.2.1	Modern Icelandic —— 81	
3.2.2	Modern Faroese —— 94	

3.2.3	Old / Middle English —— **97**	
3.2.4	Old Swedish and Old Danish —— **99**	
3.3	Alternating Dat-Nom / Nom-Dat predicates in the early / archaic Indo-European languages —— **112**	
3.4	Modeling the argument structure of alternating predicates —— **121**	
3.5	The verbs 'like' and 'seem' as alternating verbs in Early Germanic —— **125**	
3.5.1	'like' —— **125**	
3.5.2	'seem' —— **129**	
3.6	The relative chronology of alternating vs. non-alternating predicates —— **133**	
3.7	Summary —— **137**	
4	**Oblique subjects in Early Germanic: Gothic, Old / Middle High German, Old / Middle English, Old Saxon, Old Norse-Icelandic, Old Swedish and Old Danish —— 140**	
4.1	Where do oblique subjects come from? —— **141**	
4.1.1	The Object-to-Subject Hypothesis —— **141**	
4.1.2	The Semantic Development Hypothesis —— **142**	
4.1.3	The Topicality Hypothesis —— **143**	
4.1.4	The Transimpersonal Hypothesis —— **145**	
4.1.5	The Free Dative Hypothesis —— **147**	
4.1.6	The Anticausative Hypothesis —— **149**	
4.1.7	The Oblique Subject Hypothesis —— **151**	
4.1.8	The Extended Intransitive Hypothesis —— **151**	
4.2	Subject behavior in Early Germanic —— **152**	
4.2.1	Conjunction reduction —— **153**	
4.2.2	Clause-bound reflexivization —— **156**	
4.2.3	Long-distance reflexivization —— **159**	
4.2.4	Raising-to-subject —— **162**	
4.2.5	Raising-to-object —— **167**	
4.2.6	Control infinitives —— **178**	
4.2.7	Word order —— **200**	
4.3	Summary and discussion —— **207**	
5	**Reconstructing oblique subjects for Proto-Germanic —— 211**	
5.1	Reconstructing syntax —— **212**	
5.2	Alleged problems with syntactic reconstruction —— **214**	
5.2.1	Lack of cognates —— **214**	
5.2.2	Lack of arbitrariness —— **216**	
5.2.3	Lack of directionality in syntactic change —— **217**	

5.2.4	Lack of continuous transmission —— 218	
5.2.5	Lack of form–meaning correspondences —— 219	
5.3	Reconstructing predicate and argument structure constructions —— 220	
5.3.1	Reconstructing verbs and predicates —— 221	
5.3.2	Reconstructing argument structure constructions —— 227	
5.4	Reconstructing subject behavior for Proto-Germanic —— 247	
5.4.1	Word order —— 248	
5.4.2	Raising-to-subject —— 252	
5.4.3	Raising-to-object —— 257	
5.4.4	Control infinitives —— 267	
5.4.5	Long-distance reflexivization —— 271	
5.5	Summary —— 273	
6	**Modern German: An anomaly?** —— 275	
6.1	Argument structure and subject status in German —— 276	
6.2	Arguments against subject behavior of oblique subjects in German —— 279	
6.3	Alternating Dat-Nom / Nom-Dat predicates in German —— 289	
6.3.1	Word order —— 289	
6.3.2	Conjunction reduction —— 295	
6.3.3	Clause-bound reflexivization —— 301	
6.3.4	Raising-to-subject —— 306	
6.3.5	Raising-to-object —— 311	
6.3.6	Control infinitives —— 315	
6.4	Modeling subject behavior in German —— 322	
6.5	Summary —— 324	
7	**Synthesis** —— 327	

References —— 357

Name Index —— 379

Language Index —— 385

Subject Index —— 387

1 Introduction

Of the Germanic languages, one language in particular was instrumental during the late 1970's and early 1980's in documenting that there may be syntactic subjects in other morphological cases than the nominative (Andrews 1976; Thráinsson 1979; Zaenen, Maling, and Thráinsson 1985; Sigurðsson 1989, 1992; among others). This language was Modern Icelandic. During the 1980s, research on Modern Faroese also demonstrated that only a subject analysis is viable for corresponding potential oblique subject arguments in that language (Barnes 1986). This argumentation is based on a host of subject properties, of which especially two became pivotal in the discussion:

Icelandic
Conjunction reduction
(1) a. Hann **kom** iðulega og ___ **varð** alltaf óglatt.
he.NOM came frequently and Ø.DAT became always queasy
'He came frequently and always felt queasy.'

Control infinitive
b. Hann kann ekki við **að** ___ **vera** óglatt,
he.NOM likes not with to PRO.DAT be.INF queasy
'He does not like to feel queasy.'

Example (1a) shows how a subject in a conjoined clause may be left unexpressed on the basis of identity with the subject of the first clause. This has been termed *conjunction reduction* in the literature. In (1b) the subject of the non-finite clause is left unexpressed on the basis of identity with the subject of the matrix clause. Infinitives of this type are called *control infinitives* in the syntactic literature. In both examples, the Icelandic predicate *vera óglatt* 'feel queasy' takes a dative subject, which is here left unexpressed. Syntactic objects, in contrast, are generally not left unexpressed in conjunction reduction and control infinitives (see examples in Section 3.1 below).

Syntactic research on Modern German during these early times was not able to establish subject behavior of corresponding potential oblique subject arguments in that language (Reis 1982; Zaenen, Maling, and Thráinsson 1985; Sigurðsson 1989: 349–356, 1992). The German examples (2a–b) below have the same structure as the Icelandic ones in (1a–b), yet they are ungrammatical.

German
Conjunction reduction
(2) a. *Er **kam** häufig und __ **würde** immer *übel.*
he.NOM came frequently and Ø.DAT became always queasy
Intended meaning: 'He came frequently and always felt queasy.'

Control infinitive
b. *Er mag es nich übel __ **zu sein.**
he.NOM likes it not queasy PRO.DAT to be.INF
Intended meaning: 'He does not like to feel queasy.'

Almost all later research by the German establishment devoted to this topic has followed suit, arguing against a subject analysis of corresponding potential oblique subjects in the German language (Fanselow 2002; Bayer 2004; Wunderlich 2009; Haider 2005, 2010; Pankau 2016), with the exception of Stepanov (2003).

This discrepancy between the three modern Germanic languages that have retained morphological case marking, Icelandic and Faroese, on the one hand, and German, on the other, raises the question of how corresponding potential oblique subjects behaved syntactically in the earlier stages of the Germanic languages. Or, in other words, does North Germanic preserve the original state of affairs or is this rather preserved by West-Germanic? Faarlund (1990, 1992, 2001), Askedal (2001), and Heltoft (2021) in their work on Old Norse-Icelandic and Old Danish, respectively, argue that there is no distinct subject category to be found in these languages; instead they argue that Old Norse-Icelandic and Old Danish were non-configurational languages without a clear phrase structure.

In fact, Faarlund argues that the situation in Modern Icelandic and Modern Faroese must be the result of a change in the grammar of North-Germanic from medieval to modern times, involving the development of a syntactic category of subject. His approach entails that the situation in Modern German represents the original state-of-affairs for Proto-Germanic. Faarlund's two primary motivations for assuming that the situation in North-Germanic, in Icelandic and Faroese, cannot represent the original state-of-affairs in Proto-Germanic are the following: a) the alleged lack of evidence for the subject status of oblique subjects in Old Norse-Icelandic (Faarlund 1990, 1992), and b) the typological rarity of oblique subjects in the world's languages (Faarlund 2001: 131).

Faarlund is certainly right that conjunction reduction in Old Norse-Icelandic does not single out subjects from objects, which in turn means that conjunction reduction is not a subject test in that language. He also argues against the validity of a set of control infinitives, claiming that either the relevant examples are not control infinitives or that they are ungrammatical "contaminations" of other structures (Faarlund 2001: 129, see further discussion in Section 4.2.6 below). A third argument Faarlund proposes is that there is no dedicated subject position in Old Norse-Icelandic, as nominatives may occupy four different positions in the clause. As a consequence, on his approach there cannot be any subject category in Old Norse-Icelandic (for a critical discussion of this last point, see Section 2.1.3 below).

However, during the 1990's, Rögnvaldsson showed in a series of articles (1991, 1995, 1996) that Old Norse-Icelandic truly is a configurational language, not only exhibiting a clear phrase structure but also a distinctive category of subject. In particular Rögnvaldsson shows that both noun and verb phrases may be fronted to initial position and both may also be pronominalized, i.e. referred to with pro-forms, which is an argument for internal structure and against non-configurationality.

Rögnvaldsson also demonstrates beyond doubt that exactly as in Modern Icelandic, there are structures in Old Norse-Icelandic involving oblique case marking of the potential subject, structures which without question call for a subject analysis and exclude an object analysis, contra Faarlund's earlier claims. Also, in 1995, Allen published a monograph on Old and Middle English arguing along the lines of Rögnvaldsson that there are indeed oblique subjects in the early stages of the English language. Allen's arguments are based on conjunction reduction and word order (see Chapter 4 below)

On the assumption that there are oblique subjects in both the early stages of Germanic, i.e. Old and Middle English and Old Norse-Icelandic, as well as in Modern Icelandic and Modern Faroese, the question arises as to how Modern German fits into this puzzle at all. Has West Germanic, aside from English, changed from having oblique subjects to a situation where such potential oblique subjects do not show subject properties? Or, were Old and Middle English perhaps different from Old and Middle German in this respect? In the remainder of this book, I argue against the perceived consensus in the German scholarship, claiming instead that there truly are oblique subjects in German, exactly as in Icelandic. In fact, German turns out to be the language that has changed throughout its history, with North Germanic representing the original state-of-affairs. As a consequence, oblique subjects are reconstructable for the grammar and syntax of Proto-Germanic.

1.1 Aims and objectives

As is already clear from the introductory text above, the foremost goal of this book-length study is to throw light on the issue of whether Modern Icelandic and Faroese represent the original state of affairs with regard to oblique subjects, or whether this is more correctly represented by Modern German. In other words, were there oblique subjects in Proto-Germanic or not? In order to address this issue, data from the earliest stages of the Germanic languages must be compared and evaluated. As for this, a substantial amount of data has already been presented in the literature, most notably from Old Norse-Icelandic, Old and Middle English, and some from Gothic.

Therefore, in Chapter 4 below, I present additional data from Old Saxon, Old Swedish and Old Danish, as well as some new material from Old Norse-Icelandic and Gothic, not published in the earlier literature. In combination, all these data present an overwhelming body of evidence in favor of a subject analysis of potential oblique subjects throughout the Germanic phylum. This bundle of evidence, in turn, supports a reconstruction of oblique subjects for Proto-Germanic, an enterprise carried out in Chapter 5 below.

However, a key concept for understanding and analyzing the linguistic material correctly, both historically and synchronically, is the concept of *alternating Dat-Nom / Nom-Dat predicates*. This involves verbs and compositional predicates which behave such that either argument, usually an animate dative and an inanimate nominative argument, takes on the syntactic role of subject, i.e. either argument passes the subject tests, although, self-evidently, not at the same time. When the dative argument occupies the first position in the argument structure of the clause, it takes on the behavioral properties of subject, while when the nominative argument occupies the same first position of the argument structure, it is this nominative that takes on the behavioral properties of subject. Notice that this does not mean that the arguments of a single verb may occupy two different positions within one and the same argument structure. Rather, one single verb may instantiate two different argument structure constructions which are diametrical opposites of each other, one being Nom-Dat and the other Dat-Nom.

This dual or alternating behavior of Dat-Nom / Nom-Dat predicates makes the Germanic data increasingly difficult to analyze, resulting, among others, in the subject behavior of the nominative being used as an argument against any potential subject analysis of the dative. This has happened in the case of Modern German (Bayer 2004: 56; Wunderlich 2009: 590) Old Swedish (Falk 1997: 26) Old Danish (Heltoft 2021: 267–268) and Gothic (Cole et al. 1980: 721–727). Still, such argumentation would only be relevant on a non-alternating analysis, i.e. on an analysis involving only one argument structure construction and not two.

In contrast, on an alternating analysis, which presupposes the existence of two distinct argument structure constructions, any argumentation based on the behavior of one of the arguments in one of the argument structures can naturally not be regarded as evidence for or against any syntactic analysis of the other argument in the other argument structure. The linguistic facts, moreover, speak for an alternating analysis over a non-alternating analysis which would involve only one argument structure for the relevant dataset. This, in turn, means that the concept of alternating predicates requires a proper explication in the present context. Due to this, the syntactic behavior of the two arguments in either of the two argument structures, Dat-Nom and Nom-Dat, is laid out in Chapter 3 below for two living languages, namely Modern Icelandic and Faroese, with additional examples provided for several early Germanic and Indo-European languages. An alternating analysis is also further discussed in Chapter 6 for Modern German.

Any analysis of subject behavior and subject properties raises the question of what the concept of subject really entails. Any engagement in that issue involves both a detailed description of the behavioral properties of subject and a theoretical discussion of the subject concept within and across languages, compatible at least with the behavioral subject properties of the language under investigation, if not for the study of any given language. This is the topic of Chapter 2 below, where I present the definition of subject used in this study, along with a problematization of existing definitions of subject which are either implicitly equated with the behavioral subject properties or based on theory-internal considerations. The following section gives a convenient example of the former, that is, of a textbook discussion of the subject properties in one of the most spoken languages in the world, English, where the reader is left without any proper definition of subject.

1.2 Subject in a "normal" language

In introductory textbooks on English grammar, for instance Börjars and Burridge (2010: 80–81), the reader learns that a basic sentence is divided into a subject and a predicate, and that the subject is a noun phrase, while the predicate contains a verbal element of some sort. We also learn that the subject has certain properties that distinguishes it from objects. Börjars and Burridge (2010: 82–86) list the following ones (recast in my terminology):
– Neutral Word Order
– Subject-Verb Inversion in Questions
– Subject-Verb Agreement
– Case Marking

Starting with neutral word order, the subject is generally placed in first position in an ordinary declarative clause in English, as is shown in (3a), although in some cases the subject may be preceded by an adverbial, as is shown in (3b–c):

First position in neutral word order
(3) a. *I smile now.*
   b. *This morning,* **he** *certainly kept the cat in his lap*
   c. *Surely,* **she** *held me in her arms.*

Reversing the order of subjects and objects yields not only marked structures but also ungrammatical ones:

(4) a. **This morning, the cat certainly kept* **he** *in his lap*
   b. **Surely, me held* **she** *in her arms.*

However, in *yes-no* questions in English, matters are slightly different. The subject inverts with auxiliary verbs, resulting in the auxiliary occurring in first position and the subject immediately following the auxiliary:

Yes-no questions
(5) a. *Can* **I** *smile now?*
   b. *May* **he** *keep the cat in his lap?*
   c. *Did* **she** *hold me in her arms?*

Note that exactly as with ordinary declarative clauses, reversing the order of subjects and objects yields ungrammatical structures in English:

(6) a. **May the cat keep* **he** *in his lap?*
   b. **Did me hold* **she** *in her arms?*

These examples therefore show, plain as day, that *yes-no* questions indeed distinguish between subjects and objects in the English language.

Agreement of the verb with the subject is a morphosyntactic property, not available for objects in English. Subject-verb agreement is limited to present tense, 3rd person singular, and is morphologically realized as an *-s*, as is shown in (7–8) below:

Subject-verb agreement
(7) a. **He** *keeps the cat in his lap.*
   b. *****They*** *keeps the cat in their lap.*

(8) a. **She** *holds me in her arms.*
   b. *****They*** *holds me in their arms.*

The b-examples above are ungrammatical since subject-verb agreement does not apply to subjects in the 3rd person plural, only in the 3rd person singular.

The fourth property that Börjars and Burridge (2010) mention as distinguishing between subjects and objects is case marking. This is shown in (9–10) below, where the subject forms in 1st person and 3rd person masculine are *I* and *he*, while the corresponding object forms are *me* and *him*, respectively.

Case marking
(9) a. *I keep **him** in my lap*
    b. **Him** *keep I in my/his lap*

(10) a. *He holds **me** in his arms.*
     b. ***Me** holds he in his/my arms.*

Examples (9a) and (10a) show the correct subject and object forms in their relevant positions, while corresponding structures with the object forms in subject position and the subject forms in object position in (9b) and (10b) are ungrammatical.

In addition to the four subject tests discussed above, Börjars and Burridge later on (2010: 115, 229) also mention the following constructions as distinctly separating subjects from objects:
- Imperatives
- Passives

It is certainly true that subjects in both imperatives and passives behave in a specific way, and this behavior is different from objects. First, one of the characteristics of imperatives in English is that they systematically occur without a subject, while, in contrast, an object is not systematically left unexpressed. Compare the following sets of examples containing declarative and imperative clauses, respectively:

Declaratives
(11) a. *I smile now.*
     b. *He keeps the cat in his lap.*
     c. *She holds me in her arms.*

Imperatives
(12) a. *Smile now!*
     b. *Keep **the cat** in your lap!*
     c. *Hold **me** in your arms!*

The examples in (11) above all contain a subject, *I*, *he* and *she*, given in boldface. In contrast, the corresponding examples in (12) are all subjectless, as the boldfaced arguments in (11) are missing from the examples in (12). At the same time, the objects in (11b–c), the non-italicized *the cat* and *me*, are both expressed in the imperatives in (12). Equivalent examples without the objects turn out to be ungrammatical, as is shown in (13a–b) below:

(13) a. **Keep in your lap!*
b. **Hold in your arms!*

The transitive verbs *keep* and *hold* are also ungrammatical in imperative clauses where the subject is present and the object not:

(14) a. ******You*** *keep in your lap!*
b. ******You*** *hold in your arms!*

These examples of imperatives in English show that subjects and objects behave differently in such constructions. For that reason, imperatives have been used to distinguish between subjects and objects in many languages (cf. also Section 2.1.2 below).

Turning to passives, it is also well known that subjects and objects behave differently in the active–passive alternation in English, as is shown in (15) below:

Active

(15) a. **The prisoner** killed the warden.

Passive

(15) b. *The warden was killed (by* **the prisoner***)*

In the active clause in (15a) the subject is *the prisoner* and the object is *the warden*. One of the properties of passives is that the object of a corresponding active clause is promoted to subject in the passive alternant, *the warden* in this case, while the subject of the active clause, *the prisoner*, is either left unexpressed or demoted to a *by* phrase. This is shown through the brackets around *by the prisoner* in (15b). Therefore, it is very clear from these examples that passivization deals differently with subjects and objects of transitive active clauses.

Despite the elementary discussion of the subject category and the subject properties in a language as widely spoken as the English language, no specific and accurate definition of subject is provided by Börjars and Burridge (2010). This is also the case for several other contemporary introductions to the grammar of

English, such as Tallerman (1998), Huddleston and Pullum (2005), van Gelderen (2010), Aarts (2011), Payne (2011), Aman and Tan (2018), Kim and Michaelis (2020), among others. Instead, the subject tests are implicitly used to define the subject in the English language. Clearly, even in textbooks where the goal is to teach undergraduate students to identify syntactic subjects, the need for providing a definition of subject should be obvious.

The reason for this lack of explicit subject definition in the literature, I believe, stems from the notorious difficulties in defining the subject concept in an adequate way, given the numerous theoretical frameworks of grammar that exist in the field, in which each and every framework provides its own definition of subject. Such subject definitions are often based on theory-internal assumptions and mechanisms, instead of highlighting the empirical core of subjecthood. This empirical core, as a matter of fact, consists of behavior that is common to subjects irrespective of the nature of the relevant theoretical framework.

In Chapter 2 below, I put forth a definition of subject, intended to capture the empirical core of subjecthood, valid across different theoretical frameworks. Prior to that, we must establish a baseline for nominative subjects in languages which still exhibit morphological case marking, as opposed to English where such morphological marking is minimal, only present with pronouns.

1.3 Establishing a nominative subject baseline for case languages

Icelandic is a language where case morphology is alive and well, even though some minor morphological mergers have taken place throughout its history (Þórólfsson 1925; Nilsson 1975; Þórhallsdóttir 1997; Bernharðsson 2004; Müller 2005; Axelsdóttir 2014). And given that oblique subjects in Icelandic play a pivotal role in the remainder of this book, it is appropriate to give examples of ordinary nominative subjects from that language here. Such examples further serve as a baseline for a comparison with oblique subjects in Icelandic to be extensively discussed in Chapter 3 below and further throughout this book.

The discussion below is confined to two different semantic verb types, the causative *drepa* 'kill', selecting for a nominative subject and an accusative object, i.e. the Nom-Acc case frame, and the stative *treysta* 'trust', selecting for a nominative subject and a dative object, i.e. the Nom-Dat case frame. Through this, two birds are killed with one stone, in that the two verbs not only represent two different semantic verb classes, but they also instantiate two different case frames. The goal here is to demonstrate that syntactic behavior is neither dependent on semantic verb classes nor on case frames.

Up to 19 different tests for grammatical relations (cf. Jónsson 1996) have been proposed in the literature to identify and distinguish between subjects and objects in Modern Icelandic. The discussion below is confined to only a subset of these, namely the ones that have been most prominent in the literature on subjects in Icelandic (Andrews 1976; Thráinsson 1979; Zaenen, Maling, and Thráinsson 1985; Sigurðsson 1989, 1992; among others). These are the following:
- Neutral Word Order
- Subject-Verb Inversion
- Clause-Bound Reflexivization
- Long-Distance Reflexivization
- Conjunction Reduction
- Raising-to-Subject
- Raising-to-Object
- Control Infinitives

Starting with neutral word order, consider the following examples with the two verbs *drepa* 'kill' and *treysta* 'trust', with the nominative subject in boldface and the object, accusative or dative, in normal style:

(16) a. **Lukku Láki** hefði ekki drepið Daldónana ...
Lucky Luke.NOM would.have not killed Daldons.the.ACC
'Lucky Luke would not have killed the Daldons ...'
b. **Lukku Láki** hefði ekki treyst Daldónunum ...
Lucky Luke.NOM would.have not trusted Daldons.the.DAT
'Lucky Luke would not have trusted the Daldons ...'

In the examples in (16) above, representing neutral word order, the nominative behaves syntactically as a subject in that it precedes the finite verb in both cases. The object, in contrast, be it accusative or dative, immediately follows the nonfinite verb, hence occupying an object position in Icelandic (cf. Thráinsson 2007: 21–22).

Moreover, the subject typically inverts with the verb in questions, topicalizations and narrative inversion (cf. Thráinsson 2007: 22). This subject-verb inversion is shown in the questions in (17) below for the verbs in (16):

(17) a. Hefði **Lukku Láki** ekki drepið Daldónana ...
would.have Lucky Luke.NOM not killed Daldons.the.ACC
'Would Lucky Luke not have killed the Daldons ...?'
b. Hefði **Lukku Láki** ekki treyst Daldónunum ...
would.have Lucky Luke.NOM not trusted Daldons.the.DAT
'Would Lucky Luke not have trusted the Daldons ...?'

The nominative argument of *drepa* and *treysta* also behaves differently with regard to reflexivization from their respective accusative and dative objects. Even though both subjects and objects may bind reflexives in Icelandic, there is a systematic difference in the behavior of the two (Thráinsson 1976, 2007: 462–464; Maling 1986; Jónsson 1996: 74–76).

Starting with subjects, these can only bind reflexives and not personal pronouns, as is shown in (18) below, where the accusative and dative reflexives, *sig* and *sér*, are bound by their subjects *hún* 'she'. The asterisk following the accusative and dative personal pronouns, *hana* and *henni*, as well as the difference in the indexation of the reflexives and the personal pronouns in both examples, demonstrates that the subject cannot bind personal pronouns in Icelandic, but only reflexives. That is, personal pronouns in such examples must refer to someone other than the subject referent.

(18) a. *Ógæfu Jóna$_i$ drap sig$_i$ /hana$_j$*$_i$ ekki.*
 Calamity Jane.NOM killed REFL.ACC /her.ACC not
 'Calamity Jane did not kill herself.'
 b. *Ógæfu Jóna$_i$ treysti sér$_i$ /henni$_j$*$_i$ ekki.*
 Calamity Jane.NOM trusted REFL.DAT /her.DAT not
 'Calamity Jane did not trust herself.'

Objects, in contrast, may bind both reflexives and personal pronouns in Icelandic, as shown in (19) below:

(19) a. *Ógæfu Jóna$_i$ drap indjánakonuna$_j$ með*
 Calamity Jane.NOM killed indian.woman.the.ACC with
 styttu af sér$_j$ / henni$_j$.
 statue.DAT of REFL.DAT her.DAT
 'Calamity Jane killed the Indian woman with a statue of herself.'
 b. *Ógæfu Jóna$_i$ treysti indjánakonunni$_j$ fyrir*
 Calamity Jane.NOM trusted indian.woman.the.DAT for
 styttu af sér$_j$ / henni$_j$.
 statue.DAT of REFL.DAT her.DAT
 'Calamity Jane trusted the Indian woman with a statue of herself.'

Here, the accusative and dative objects, *indjánakonuna* and *indjánakonunni* 'the Indian woman', respectively, bind a reflexive within their respective noun phrases, exactly as the subjects in (18) above bind reflexives. The difference between (18) and (19), however, is that the examples in (19) show that objects may also bind the personal pronoun *henni* 'her', in addition to binding reflexives. That is, both the reflexive and the personal pronoun may be bound by objects. These examples therefore show a very clear difference in the binding properties of subjects and objects in that subjects may only bind reflexives, while objects may bind both reflexives and personal pronouns.

In addition to clause-bound reflexivization of the type shown in (18–19) above, Icelandic also exhibits long-distance reflexivization. This involves binding into a subordinate clause, as shown in (20) below where the subject of the main clause, *Billi barnungi* 'Billy the Kid' binds the accusative and dative reflexive objects, *sig* and *sér*, in the subordinate clauses headed by the subordination *að* 'that'.

(20) a. **Billi barnungi**$_i$ segir [að Lukku Láki hafi ekki
Billy youngling.NOM says that Lucky Luke has not
drepið sig$_i$].
killed REFL.ACC
'Billy the Kid says that Lucky Luke had not killed him.'
b. **Billi barnungi**$_i$ segir [að Lukku Láki hafi ekki
Billy youngling.NOM says that Lucky Luke has not
treyst sér$_i$].
trusted REFL.DAT
'Billy the Kid says that Lucky Luke had not trusted him.'

In languages where long-distance reflexivization does not exist, like English and German, personal pronouns are found in subordinate clauses of the type shown in (20), bound by the subject of the matrix clause, not reflexives.

Turning to conjunction reduction, the subject in a coordinated clause may be left unexpressed on identity with the subject of the first clause. This is shown in (21) below for the nominative subject of both *drepa* 'kill' and *treysta* 'trust', where the subjects of the two conjuncts have a matching reference:

(21) a. **Lukku Láki** treystir ekki Daldónunum og
Lucky Luke.NOM trusts not Daldons.the.ACC and
__ drepur þá.
Ø.NOM kills them.ACC
'Lucky Luke does not trust the Daldons and kills them.'
b. **Lukku Láki** drepur Daldónana en __
Lucky Luke.NOM trusts Daldons.the.DAT but Ø.NOM
treystir þeim ekki.
kills them.DAT not
'Lucky Luke kills the Daldons but does not trust them.'

Objects, in contrast, cannot be left unexpressed in the second conjunct of coordinate clauses, irrespective of whether they match in reference to the subject of the main clause (22) or the object of the main clause (23):

(22) a. ***Lukku Láki** treystir ekki Daldónunum og
    Lucky Luke.NOM trusts not Daldons.the.ACC and
    Daldónanir drepa ___.
    Daldons.the.NOM kills Ø.ACC
    Intended meaning: 'Lucky Luke does not trust the Daldons and the Daldons kill (him).'

b. ***Lukku Láki** drepur Daldónana en
    Lucky Luke.NOM kills Daldons.the.DAT but
    Daldónanir treysta ___ ekki.
    Daldons.the.NOM trust Ø.DAT not
    'Intended meaning: 'Lucky Luke kills the Daldons, as the Daldons do not trust (him).'

(23) a. ***Lukku Láki** treystir ekki Daldónunum og
    Lucky Luke.NOM trusts not Daldons.the.ACC and
    (hann) drepur ___.
    he.NOM kills Ø.ACC
    Intended meaning: 'Lucky Luke does not trust the Daldons and (he) kills (them).'

b. ***Lukku Láki** drepur Daldónana og **(hann)**
    Lucky Luke.NOM kills Daldons.the.DAT and he.NOM
    treystir ___ ekki.
    trust Ø.DAT not
    'Intended meaning: 'Lucky Luke kills the Daldons and (he) do not trust (them).'

Observe that the examples in (23) are equally ungrammatical both with and without the second subject being left unexpressed, as is indicated with the use of brackets in these examples.

As is also shown in (23) above, objects cannot be left unexpressed in second conjuncts on identity with the object of the main clause. This also applies in cases where the order of the arguments is reversed, such that the object has been topicalized to first position, as in (24) below:

(24) a. *Kúrekanum treysta **Daldónanir** ekki og
cowboy.the.DAT trust Daldons.the.NOM not and
__ hjálpa **Daldónanir** ekki heldur.
ø.DAT help Daldons.the.NOM not either
Intended meaning: 'The Daldons do not trust the cowboy and the Daldons do not help (him) either.'
b. *Kúrekann drepa **Daldónanir** ekki en
cowboy.the.ACC kill Daldons.the.NOM not but
__ lemja **Daldónanir** í staðinn.
ø.ACC hit Daldons.the.NOM in stead
'Intended meaning: 'The Daldons do not kill the cowboy and the Daldons hit (him) instead.'

Raising-to-Subject may also be used to distinguish between subjects and objects in Icelandic, as shown in (25) below:

(25) a. **Billi barnungi** byrjaði að drepa kúrekann.
Billy youngling.NOM started to kill.INF cowboy.the.ACC
'Billy the Kid started to kill the cowboy.'
b. **Billi barnungi** byrjaði að treysta kúrekanum.
Billy youngling.NOM started to trust.INF cowboy.the.DAT
'Billy the Kid started to trust the cowboy.'

Here the nominative subjects of the lower verbs, *drepa* and *treysta*, occur as the subjects of the finite verb *byrja* 'start', an inceptive verb which does not select for a subject of its own (cf. Sigurðsson 1989: 65–67: Barðdal 2001a; Thráinsson 2007: 428–430, on complement choices of inceptive verbs in Icelandic). At the same time, the objects of *drepa* and *treysta*, i.e. *kúrekann* and *kúrekanum* respectively, remain in their canonical object positions following the verb.

Two other types of infinitive structures also distinguish between subjects and objects in Icelandic, namely raising-to-object (a.k.a. AcI and ECM in the literature) and control infinitives. Examples of raising-to-object are given in (26) below:

(26) a. *Lukku Láki sá* **Billa barnunga** *drepa*
Lucky Luke.NOM saw Billy youngling.NOM kill.INF
kúrekann.
cowboy.the.ACC
'Lucky Luke saw Billy the Kid kill the cowboy.'

b. *Lukku   Láki   sá   **Billa   barnunga**   treysta*
   Lucky   Luke.NOM   saw   Billy   youngling.NOM   trust.INF
   kúrekanum.
   cowboy.the.DAT
   'Lucky Luke saw Billy the Kid trust the cowboy.'

Here the main verb is the verb *sjá* 'see' which selects for an infinitival clause. The argument in the nominative case, corresponding to the subject of *drepa* and *treysta* in ordinary finite clauses, occurs here as the accusative object of *sjá*, hence the term *raising-to-object*. While the nominative subject of *drepa* and *treysta* turns up in the accusative here, the accusative and dative objects of the two verbs, *kúrekann* and *kúrekanum*, stay in their canonical object position, immediately following the nonfinite verb.

The final subject property to be illustrated here involves control infinitives, as exemplified in (27) below:

(27) a. ***Billi   barnungi***   *reyndi   að   __   drepa*
        Billy   youngling.NOM   tried   to   PRO.NOM   kill.INF
        kúrekann.
        cowboy.the.ACC
        'Billy the Kid tried to kill the cowboy.'
     b. ***Billi   barnungi***   *reyndi   að   __   treysta*
        Billy   youngling.NOM   tried   to   PRO.NOM   trust.INF
        kúrekanum.
        cowboy.the.DAT
        'Billy the Kid tried to trust the cowboy.'

The matrix verb *reyna* 'try' selects for an infinitive with which the subject is left unexpressed, since this subject is coreferential with the subject of *reyna*. This means that the subject of *drepa* in (27a) and *treysta* in (27b) are here left unexpressed on the basis of identity with *Billi barnungi*, the subject of *reyna* 'try'. Unlike the raising-to-subject verb *byrja* 'start' in (25) above, the agentivity of *reyna* 'try' is not in doubt. Control verbs come in a range from highly agentive, like *reyna*, to statives like *líka* 'like'. Two examples of stative predicates are given in (28a–b), *vera kúl* 'be cool' and *vera hægt* 'be possible', respectively:

(28) a. *Það   er   ekki   kúl   að   __   drepa   kúreka.*
        it   is   not   cool   to   PRO.NOM   kill.INF cowboys.ACC
        'It is not cool to kill cowboys.'

b. Það   er   ekki   hægt   að   ___   treysta   kúrekum.
   it   is   not   possible   to   PRO.NOM   trust.INF   cowboys.DAT
   'It is not possible to trust cowboys.'

Examples of this type are generic in nature (referred to as *arbitrary PRO* in the generative literature), meaning that the nominative subject of *drepa* and *treysta* is not left unexpressed on identity with the syntactic subject of the control predicate, since that subject is an inanimate non-referential *það* 'it'. Instead, the generic referent controlling the unexpressed subject of the lower verb must simply be retrieved from the context.

The divergence in the agentivity of different control verbs will be relevant in the chapters to come, as verbs and predicates selecting for oblique subjects can generally not be embedded under highly agentive control verbs (cf. Barnes 1986: 26; Rögnvaldsson 1991: 372, 1996: 50; Jónsson 2000: 76–77; Barðdal 2000a: 102, Barðdal 2006: 67–72; Barðdal and Eythórsson 2003a: 461, 2006: 158–163; Eythórsson and Barðdal 2005: 837–838), either in Icelandic, Faroese, or in any other language that I know of.

However, the ability of subjects of control infinitives to be unexpressed is not confined to structures where these are coreferential with either the subject of the matrix clause, as in (27) above, or on the basis of a generic reference as in (28) above. Instead, these may also be left unexpressed on identity with an object of the matrix clause, as is shown in (29) below where the dative object of the verb *hjálpa* 'help', i.e. *Ógæfu Jónu* 'Calamity Jane', controls the omission of the unexpressed nominative subject of the infinitives of both *drepa* and *treysta*:

(29) a. **Billi   barnungi**   hjálpaði   Ógæfu   Jónu   að
        Billy   youngling.NOM   tried   Calamity   Jane.DAT   to
        ___   drepa   kúrekann.
        PRO.NOM   kill.INF   cowboy.the.ACC
        'Billy the Kid helped Calamity Jane to kill the cowboy.'
     b. **Billi   barnungi**   hjálpaði   Ógæfu   Jónu   að
        Billy   youngling.NOM   tried   Calamity   Jane.DAT   to
        ___   treysta   kúrekanum.
        PRO.NOM   trust.INF   cowboy.the.DAT
        'Billy the Kid helped Calamity Jane to trust the cowboy.'

It should be emphasized here that differences in the verbal semantics of the matrix verb, and any subsequent differences in the syntactic relation of the antecedent of the unexpressed subject of the infinitive, are entirely irrelevant for the nature of this subject test. What is relevant, however, is the fact that the argument corresponding to the nominative subject of *drepa* and *treysta* in finite clauses is also the argument that is omitted in control infinitives. In other words, the omitted argument is always a subject. This is the essence of the control test.

I have now established a baseline for a comparison with oblique subjects, demonstrating how nominative subjects behave syntactically in a modern Germanic case language. This behavior of nominative subjects is the benchmark against which the syntactic behavior of oblique subjects will be compared in the following chapters. Prior to that, a few words are in order about the theoretical framework adopted in this study.

1.4 Construction Grammar and grammatical relations

Construction Grammar has become an important alternative to Generative Grammar with regard to modeling both synchronic grammar and language change. It was founded by West-Coast linguists, most notably George Lakoff, Charles J. Fillmore, Paul Kay, and their students and associates. Construction Grammar grew out of these scholars' interest in idioms and set phrases, i.e. the type of language material that was problematic for Generative Grammar (cf. Croft and Cruse 2004: Chapter 9), and which was to a large degree set aside by generativists as not belonging to the core of grammar, but to the periphery, or more specifically to the lexicon.

The founding fathers of Construction Grammar had serious conceptual problems with the fact that the generative enterprise shuffled off to the lexicon not only idioms and set phrases but also fixed expressions which could involve both regular and irregular grammar, as well as both regular and irregular semantics. In other words, Construction Grammar started off with the goal to attract attention to the fact that several multi-word expressions exhibiting non-compositional meaning were also relevant for grammar description and modeling.

One of the fundamental assumptions of Construction Grammar is that the basic unit of language is a form–meaning or a form–function pairing. This applies not only to the smallest morphemes and words, but also to larger syntactic units, which are traditionally not assumed to have a meaning of their own (Lakoff 1987; Fillmore, Kay and O'Connor 1988; Fillmore and Kay 1993; Jackendoff 1997; Kay and Fillmore 1999; Goldberg 1995, 2006; Michaelis 1998; Croft 2001). Such larger syntactic units may consist of idioms and collocations which are semantically irregular, like the English *kick the bucket* which means 'die', as well as of more schematic and grammatically regular, intransitive, transitive and ditransitive constructions (Croft 2003; Goldberg 1995; Boas 2003, 2010; Cappelle 2005; Barðdal 2007, 2008; among others).

Moreover, Construction Grammar is a monostratal theory which does not assume different levels of grammar, like deep structure and surface structure.

Instead, it assumes that constructions stand in systematic relations to one other, often notated with different kinds of links between constructions. For instance, it is not assumed that passives are syntactically derived from actives, but rather that these two are constructions in their own right, describing the same events from two different perspectives (cf. Barðdal and Molnár 2003; Gonzálvez García 2006; Puckica 2009; Colleman 2015; Giacalone Ramat 2017; Östman 2018).

It is not the intention here to give a full-fledged description of Construction Grammar, as this can be found in several current handbook articles and textbooks (Croft and Cruse 2004; Trousdale and Hoffmann 2013; Hilpert 2014; Kim and Michaelis 2020), but rather to outline why Construction Grammar is an important player in the field of grammatical frameworks, and more specifically to discuss the subject concept within this theoretical machinery (see Section 2.2 below).

One version of Construction Grammar, i.e. Radical Construction Grammar (Croft 2001, 2005, 2012; Barðdal 2006; Fischer and Alm 2013; Karlsson 2018), is a maximally non-reductionist theory of grammar, meaning that it takes the parts to be derived from the whole, instead of the whole being derived from the parts. This means that Radical Construction Grammar takes the basic assumptions of Construction Grammar to its logical conclusions, in that the parts are not assumed to exist outside of larger wholes, i.e. the constructions which are the basic building blocks of language.

Also, in Radical Construction Grammar, the claim is that grammatical relations are not only language specific, but also construction specific. This means that the subject relation is not regarded as a generalized relation within a language, holding for all verbs and predicates in that language. Rather, grammatical relations are regarded as roles within a specific construction, which is to say that grammatical relations are construction specific (see Chapter 2 below).

The assumption that grammatical relations like subjects and objects are not only language-specific but also construction-specific does, of course, not exclude a scholarly comparison of how subjects behave. This includes both subjects of language-specific constructions and subjects across languages. For closely related languages, like the Germanic languages, it is of course expected that subjects behave more similar to each other than for typologically diversified languages, as closely related languages share a common ancestry. This is further elaborated on in Chapter 4, where equivalent data from different Germanic languages are compared, as well as in Chapter 5, where the Construction Grammar formalism is used to reconstruct grammatical relations for Proto-Germanic.

These two views of grammatical relations, as either being roles within specific constructions or as being generalized relations holding for all verbs within a language, makes certain predictions about, for instance, the historical development of grammatical relations (cf. Barðdal and Gildea 2015: 30–31). On the first view, if a subject of a given construction acquires or loses a specific behavior, this is predicted to be confined to that construction, while on the second view, such a change in behavior should be found for all verbs and all constructions at the same time in the relevant language. These two complementary views of grammatical relations also make predictions about diversity in subject and object behavior across and within languages. That there are language-specific differences in behavioral properties across the early Germanic languages is discussed in Chapter 4. That there are construction-specific differences in coding properties within and across the Germanic languages is outlined in Chapter 2. These are the reasons why I have chosen Construction Grammar as a theoretical model in my investigation of grammatical relations in the remainder of this book.

1.5 Overview

This book volume brings to the fore the arguments that have been put forward in favor of a subject analysis of potential oblique subjects in the early and archaic stages of the Germanic languages, arguing against an object analysis. The relevant data and the analysis incontrovertibly show that potential oblique subjects were not only syntactic subjects in the early Germanic languages, but also that they must be reconstructed for Proto-Germanic. Additional historical data favoring a subject analysis of oblique subjects, not published in the earlier literature, are also introduced in Chapters 3–4.

Chapter 2 commences with an overview of earlier approaches to subjecthood in the field of linguistics, beginning with traditional Latin school grammar, before outlining the development of the subject concept in the latter part of the last century. The present approach to subjecthood is introduced and a definition of subject is given in terms of the first argument of the argument structure, based on a bottom-up approach, evolving from a generalization of the syntactic behavior of the arguments across the behavioral subject tests. Also, deviations from the subject canon are discussed, involving verbal arguments which behave syntactically as subjects but are not in the nominative case, i.e., so-called *oblique subjects*. On the subject definition argued for here, there are oblique subjects in German, exactly as in Icelandic, which in turn raises the question of why these do not pass all the same behavioral tests as nominative subjects do. A further comparison of the behavioral subject tests reveals a generalization, namely that the tests that oblique subjects do not pass in German all involve ellipsis. Thus, an analysis in terms of "restricted ellipsis" is proposed, as an alternative to the standard object analysis in German.

In Chapter 3 I introduce into the discussion the concept of *alternating predicates*, a concept which is of major relevance for the analysis of the subject properties of oblique subjects, not only in Germanic but in Indo-European in general. Alternating predicates select for two arguments, a dative and a nominative, and either argument may take on the subject role and the other the object role. This is manifested in two diametrically opposed argument structures for the same verb, i.e. Dat-Nom and Nom-Dat, respectively. Evidence for analyzing these as two distinct argument structures and not as one of the word orders being a topicalization of the other, is presented from Modern Icelandic, involving all the subject tests introduced in Section 1.3 above. Alternating verbs have also been shown to exist in Modern Faroese, Old English, Old Swedish and Old Danish, although the evidence for an alternating analysis is clearly not equally strong for the earlier corpus languages than for the modern languages. In addition, examples suggesting the same type of alternation are offered from several archaic and ancient Indo-European languages, in particular Gothic, Sanskrit, Hittite, Latin, Ancient (and Modern) Greek, Slavic and Baltic. In the earlier discussion of dative subjects in the literature, the subject properties of the nominative have, as a matter of fact, been used to argue against potential subject status of the dative. This is why alternating predicates are of major relevance for the current discussion, as clearly any subject properties found for the nominative in Nom-Dat constructions do not undermine a subject analysis of the dative in corresponding Dat-Nom constructions.

Chapter 4 is devoted to the subject tests in the earliest stages of the Germanic languages, Gothic, Old High German, Old English, Old Saxon, Old Norse-Icelandic, Old Swedish and Old Danish. The chapter starts with a short section on the possible origin of oblique subject constructions, presenting some of the most prevailing hypotheses that have been advanced in the earlier scholarship. These existing hypotheses mostly favor an analysis in terms of objects changing into subjects in the course of time. In contrast, the hypothesis argued for in the remainder of this book assumes instead that potential oblique subjects have not developed from objects but have been syntactic subjects all along, at least from the time of the common Germanic era, if not longer. A systematic overview of the subject tests reveals that those subject tests that are applicable for the earlier Germanic language stages unanimously speak for a subject analysis and exclude an object analysis of potential oblique subjects. These subject tests are i) conjunction reduction (for Old English) ii) long-distance reflexivization (for Old Norse-Icelandic and Gothic), iii) raising-to-subject, iv) raising-to-object, v) control infinitives and vi) word order. It is thus incontrovertible that potential oblique subjects behaved syntactically in the same manner as nominative subjects did in the earliest stages of the Germanic languages.

The primary goal of Chapter 5 is to reconstruct grammatical relations for Proto-Germanic, including oblique subjects. The chapter sets out with a brief overview of the history of syntactic reconstruction, before laying out the five main arguments against the viability of reconstructing syntax. These include i) lack of cognates in syntax, ii) lack of arbitrariness, iii) lack of directionality in syntactic change, iv) lack of continuous transmission, and v) lack of form–meaning correspondences in syntax. After having rejected the arguments against the viability of syntactic reconstruction, the actual reconstruction of grammatical relations commences. This involves, first, the reconstruction of verbs and predicates, in particular the verbs and predicates that select for non-canonical subject marking in Proto-Germanic, and second, the reconstruction of the constructions involving the subject tests. Then the interaction between the arguments of the argument structure and their behavior in the subject tests is modeled through indexing. Consequently, not only argument structure constructions turn out to be reconstructable for Proto-Germanic, but oblique subjects as well.

The final content chapter of this book, Chapter 6, focuses on oblique subject predicates in German selecting for the Dat-Nom case frame, which are here hypothesized to be alternating predicates. The syntactic behavior of Modern German Dat-Nom predicates is systematically compared with the behavior of both alternating Dat-Nom / Nom-Dat and non-alternating Dat-Nom predicates in Icelandic. This involves investigating and comparing word order, conjunction reduction, clause-bound reflexivization, raising-to-subject, raising-to-object and control infinitives across the two languages. The comparison confirms the hypothesis that Dat-Nom verbs in German are alternating predicates, exactly like their Icelandic Dat-Nom / Nom-Dat counterparts, and unlike non-alternating Dat-Nom verbs in Icelandic. In addition, the dative of the Dat-Nom alternant appears to pass all the subject tests in German.

Chapter 7 summarizes the main content and conclusions of this book-length study, drawing together the threads from all the preceding chapters, in order to present the object of study and the conclusions as a coherent whole.

2 What is a subject?

What is a subject? Where does subjecthood come from? Which factors determine which verbal argument takes on the subject role and which the object role? Can one use the subject properties (tests) as a stand-in definition for subject? How should one account for the fact that not all subjects behave in a uniform manner, not only cross-linguistically but also language internally? How can grammatical theory account for the fact that some subject-like arguments pass some subject tests but not others? Is there anything gained by adopting an approach to subject resulting in a subject-like argument being analyzed as more or less of a subject, say, for instance, a 50% or a 70% subject? Which are, if any, further fallacies of adopting a prototype approach to subjecthood?

These questions are addressed in the remainder of this chapter, starting with earlier approaches to the subject concept in linguistics (2.1), before introducing the present approach to subjecthood, namely that subject is regarded as not only a language-specific but also a construction-specific category (2.2). Here a definition of subject is introduced, applicable independently of the subject tests. Section 2.3 is devoted to the issue of how to analyze deviations from the subject canon, including oblique subjects in Icelandic and potential oblique subjects in German. Section 2.4 discusses the typological implications of the present proposal, while Section 2.5 summarizes the discussion and conclusions of this chapter.

2.1 Earlier approaches to subjecthood

In Section 2.1.1 a review of the subject concept in traditional grammar is given and the development from traditional grammar to modern syntactic approaches to subjecthood is outlined. The subject concept employed in universal grammar is presented in Section 2.1.2, along with a discussion of some major empirical problems associated with such a concept. In 2.1.3 the present approach to subject is introduced, including a discussion of some of the methodological problems that arise when defining a subject in and across languages.

2.1.1 Traditional grammar and modern syntactic approaches to subjecthood

The term *traditional grammar* refers to Latin and Ancient Greek school grammars, which were, and still are until the present day, used to teach students the grammars of these ancient Indo-European languages. Although modern linguistic approaches

to language are less descriptive and more theoretical, they have adopted a great amount of conceptual tools and terminology from traditional grammar. For the present purposes, there are in particular two aspects of traditional grammar that are relevant here:
i) the basic clause is divided into subject and predicate
ii) the subject is systematically defined as being in the nominative case

Starting with the first point, all approaches to subjecthood which take as its point of departure that the basic clause is divided into subject and predicate implicitly assume phrase structure. This means that a bipartite division into subject and predicate is ultimately based on the concept of *phrase*. A phrase, in turn, is a group of words that functions as a clause constituent; as a consequence, the concept of phrase means that there is internal structure within clauses. The subject is one of the phrases of a clause, the other being the predicate. Therefore, in traditional grammar, the subject concept is, as a matter of fact, relational, even though the notion of constituent, on the whole, is not very prominent in that tradition.

However, the second point is even more relevant for the present purposes, i.e. the fact that in Latin school grammar, the subject is invariably defined as being in the nominative case and agreeing in person and number with the verb. Compare the two following quotes, taken from a Latin grammar book, published around the mid-19th century:

> The subject of a finite verb is put in the nominative. (Harkness 1869: 81)

> A finite verb agrees with its subject in number and person. (Harkness 1869: 107)

These direct quotes are intended to demonstrate the nature of the descriptions of subject found in the 19th century. Such definitions of subject are not only confined to 19th century grammars; they are also well established in the 20th century and have even made their way into reference grammars of the 21st century, as is shown in the following quote:

> Das Subjekt wird morphologisch durch ein Substantiv (oder ein substantivisches Pronomen) im Nominativ repräsentiert. (Helbig and Buscha (2001: 455)

> The subject is morphologically represented by a noun (or a nominal pronoun) in the nominative. [translation, JB]

However, not only is subject generally defined in terms of being in the nominative case and controlling verb agreement, as the quotes from Harkness and Helbig and Buscha above show, but even approaches that are more up-to-date and typologically informed tend to define the subject as the argument that is in the nominative.

This is shown in the following quote from Hentschel (2011: 142–143) on the nominative case in Modern German:

> dabei gilt, dass der Nominativ das Agens bei auf ein Objekt gerichteten, also transitiven, Verben ebenso ausdrückt wie das bei intransitiven Verben, bei denen nur das Subjekt an der Handlung beteiligt ist. *Der Mann* steht sowohl in dem Satz *Der Mann joggt* als auch in *Der Mann beisst den Hund* im Nominativ. Dies ist typisch für sog. Nominativ- oder Subjektsprachen, wie das Deutsche eine ist, und macht zugleich die übereinzelsprachliche Definition des Nominativs aus. Anders sind die Verhältnisse z.B. in sog. Ergativsprachen ...
>
> this means that the nominative marking of the agent with verbs selecting for an object, i.e. transitive verbs, is also found for intransitive verbs with which only the subject is involved in the event. *The man* in the sentence *The man jogs* and in the sentence *The man bites the dog* is in the nominative case. This is typical for so-called accusative or subject languages like German and at the same time this makes up our single-language definition of the nominative. The situation is different in so-called ergative languages ... [translation, JB]

Thus, it appears that "the subject is nominative" has become an *axiom* in certain linguistics circles (cf. the discussion in Barðdal 2000a). This simple concept of the subject function, that the subject is in the nominative case and controls verb agreement, has remained at the core of grammatical description for centuries and, as is demonstrated above, is still very much alive today.

This pretheoretical notion of subject was later imported into the earliest versions of modern grammatical theory, as for instance in Chomsky (1957: 64). It was not until the quest for universal grammar began, that this pretheoretical notion of subject was called into question. Once linguists started describing languages outside of the Indo-European language family, it became evident that subjects behave differently in different languages (see next section).

These differences in subject behavior across languages raised the basic question of how to distinguish between subjects and topics in languages in general (Li 1976) and what characterizes subjects in particular (Comrie 1973, 1978; Anderson 1976; Keenan 1976; Sasse 1978). As a consequence, research started being carried out on languages with different alignment of subjects and objects, like accusative, ergative and active languages. Keenan (1976), as one of these early pioneers, attempted to provide an exhaustive list of subject properties cross-linguistically, dividing them into the following categories:
– Coding Properties
– Behavioral Properties
– Semantic Properties
– Pragmatic Properties

Of these, it is first and foremost coding and behavioral properties that have been applied in linguistic analyses of subjecthood, with coding properties defined as case marking, agreement and sometimes position, while behavioral properties comprise specific syntactic properties associated with subjects as opposed to objects. The reason is simple, as it is first and foremost behavioral properties, and perhaps to some extent coding properties, that are relevant for a subject concept defined in terms of syntax. In contrast, the semantic and pragmatic properties do not tease subjects and objects apart, but may be common to both of these.

The following behavioral properties are included in Keenan's (1976: 312–320) original description:
– Reflexivization
– Relativization
– Conjunction Reduction
– Control Infinitives
– Raising-to-Object
– Raising-to-Subject
– Control of Floating Quantifiers

These properties will be further elaborated on throughout this book. First, however, some of the problems raised by the conception that subject is a universal category merits a discussion.

2.1.2 Subject as a universal category: The empirical problems

Despite Keenan's attempt to provide a unified concept of subject, there are still several major problems with the assumption that the grammatical category of subject exists as a universal category, as Keenan of course also notes himself. This involves, in particular, the fact that not all subjects in all languages share all the subject properties that have been shown to function as subject tests in the languages of the world, as is well recognized today. Below I outline a few such problems that I have encountered in particular.

For instance, not all languages have case marking or agreement. While German has both of these, English has only partial 3rd person agreement (cf. Section 1.2 above), with the Scandinavian languages having neither morphological case nor any agreement between the subject and the verb:

German
(30) a. ich   *kaufe*   ein   Auto   aber Johannes   *kauft*   ein   Boot.
         I.NOM   buy.1SG   a.ACC   car   but   John.NOM   buys.3SG   a.ACC   boat
         'I buy a car while John buys a boat.'

Swedish

(b.) jag **köper** en bil men Johann **köper** ein båt.
    I   buy.1SG a car but John buys.3SG a boat
    'I buy a car while John buys a boat.'

The agreement of the subject with the verb in German is evident from the fact that the 1st person singular form is *kaufe* in (30a) above, while the 3rd person singular form is *kauft*. German generally distinguishes between different person and number forms in past and present tense, while only the 3rd person singular form in English, *buys*, differs from the remaining form, *buy*, and only so in the present tense. This is evident from the translations of (30a–b) above. In contrast, Swedish has the same form, *köper* in the present tense in (30b), for all person and number forms throughout the paradigm. As a consequence, there are no coding properties of subjects in a language like Swedish, as Swedish has neither case marking nor subject-verb agreement.

A second problem is that not all of Keenan's subject tests distinguish between subjects and objects, as he himself acknowledges. In the Germanic languages, relativization does not distinguish between subjects and objects, for instance, as either the subject or the object may be relativized, as shown in (31) below, with the subject being relativized in (31a), but the object in (31b):

(31) a. **The man who came** sent me the book
     b. The man sent me **the book that came**.

Since relativization does not tease apart subjects and objects in the Germanic languages, it is not a subject property in the sense that it is confined to subjects. Hence, it cannot be used as a subject test either in these languages.

Another example of a so-called subject test that cannot be universally applied is the imperative test (see discussion in Section 1.2 above). Modern Icelandic is a language where the pronominal form of the subject has been univerbated with the verb, as is shown in (32) below for 2nd person singular and plural:

Icelandic

(32) a. *Fær-ðu*   mér   bókina!
        bring-you.2SG me.DAT book.the.ACC
        'Bring me the book!'
     b. *Færið-i*   mér   bókina!
        bring-you.2PL me.DAT book.the.ACC
        'Bring me the book!'

Omission of the subject in imperative clauses in Icelandic is still possible despite the univerbation, although such examples sound quite stilted. Another problem with the use of the imperative as a subject test is that it generally targets subjects of agentive verbs and is thus considerably less felicitous with non-agentive verbs, although the actual linguistic manifestation of this, of course, varies from language to language.

With regard to word order distribution, in SO languages the subject occurs in first position in clauses with neutral word order. However, using position as a test for subject status can be difficult to apply in languages with so-called *free word order*. One example of such a language is Modern Czech, which is notorious for allowing several different word orders for the same linguistic string. The examples in (33) are taken from Sarkar and Zeman (2000: 692), representing SVO, OVS and SOV word order.

Czech
(33) a. *Martin   otvírá soubor.*   SVO
        Martin.NOM opens files.ACC
        'Martin opens the file.'
     b. *Soubor   otvírá Martin.*   OVS
        files.ACC opens Martin.NOM
        'Martin opens the file.'
     c. *Martin   soubor otvírá.*   SOV
        Martin.NOM files.ACC opens
        'Martin opens the file.'

However, it has been argued that word order in Czech is not random but rather that it is guided by certain communicative considerations along the lines of topic and focus (cf. Rysová, Mírovský, and Hajičová 2015). Such an analysis may be well motivated for a language like Czech, but the issue of freedom in word order becomes more difficult for languages only known from written corpora, like Latin and Ancient Greek, and for any historical studies of grammatical relations. To conclude, position in the clause cannot be uniformly applied to single out subjects from objects across languages.

A further problem with a universal subject concept involves omission in conjoined clauses (see Section 1.3 above), as a subset of the world's languages are pro-drop languages, where subjects are systematically left unexpressed if they are pronouns. Two such languages are Italian and Spanish, as is shown in (34–35):

Italian **1sg**
(34) a. *Parl-o* *inglese.*
      speak-1SG English
      'I speak English.'

Italian **3sg**
(34) b. *Parl-a* *inglese.*
      speak-1SG English
      'He/she speaks English.'

Spanish **1sg**
(35) a. *Habl-o* *inglés.*
      speak-1SG English
      'I speak English.'

Spanish **3sg**
(35) b. *Habl-a* *inglés.*
      speak-3SG English
      'He/she speaks English.'

It is generally assumed in the literature that a systematic omission of pronominal subjects, pro-drop, is allowed because of the subject-verb agreement found in these languages. That is, the agreement endings of the verb demonstrate whether the pro-dropped subject is 1st person or 3rd person, for instance. Nevertheless, phenomena like pro-drop may make it difficult to apply subject tests involving omission to pro-drop languages since this requires that the conditions governing ordinary pro-drop and omission in conjoined clauses be teased apart. If these conditions cannot be teased apart because they overlap in a given language, this means that either subject omission in conjoined clauses does not exist in that language or that subject omission in conjoined clauses is simply a subcategory of pro-drop.

    It has also been observed that in some languages the subject tests may "leak" and distribute across different arguments of the verb. One example is Dat-Nom verbs in Modern German, where the dative occupies the first position in clauses representing neutral word order, while the verb agrees with the nominative post-verbal argument.

Modern German
(36) *Mir* **gefallen** *diese* *Fotos* *nicht.*
     me.DAT.SG like.3PL these.NOM photos.PL not
     'I do not like the photos.'

Facts of this type have been dealt with differently for different languages, with some analyses appearing as more ad-hoc than others. For Icelandic it has been argued that such facts indeed demonstrate that agreement is not governed by the syntactic subject but by nominative case, irrespective of grammatical relations (Sigurðsson 1990–91, and later work). For German, in contrast, it is argued that subjects are generally the first arguments of all verbs, except for with Dat-Nom verbs like *gefallen* 'like, please' above. For such verbs, the subject is instead assumed to be the second argument, i.e. the nominative (Helbig and Buscha 2001: 46; Bayer 2004: 70;

Haider 2005: 23–24; Wunderlich 2009: 592).[1] For a further discussion of German, see Sections 2.3.2–2.3.3 and Chapter 6 below.

In addition, some languages make a morphological distinction between subjects of transitive and intransitive verbs, namely so-called ergative languages, which use an ergative case marker for subjects of transitive verbs but an absolutive case marker for subjects of intransitive verbs. The Basque examples below, here cited from Hualde (1986: 315), serve to illustrate this point:

Basque
(37) a. *Neska-k mutila-Ø ikusi du.*   Transitive
      girl-ERG boy.the-ABS see AUX
      'The girl saw the boy.'
   b. *mutila-Ø etorri da eskola-ra.*   Intransitive
      boy.the-ABS come AUX school-to
      'The boy came to school.'

In (37a) the subject, 'girl', is marked with a dedicated case marker *-k*, systematically found on subjects of transitive verbs in Basque. In contrast, the subject in (37b) 'the boy' is unmarked morphologically, formally exhibiting the same "marking" as the object of the transitive clause in (37a). This means that Basque uses different morphological cases for subjects, depending on whether the verb is a transitive or an intransitive one.

Moreover, even within the same language, subjects of different constructions may behave differently with regard to the subject tests. In Estonian, for instance, transitive subjects of active verbs may be left unexpressed in control infinitives, as is shown in (38a), while subjects of passives may not (see Metslang 2013: 223):

Estonian
(38) a. *Kogemus, mis ulatub ___ puudutama*
      experience that extends.3SG PRO.NOM touch.INF
      alateadvuse kihte.
      subconsciousness.GEN layer.PART.PL
      'An experience that has extended to touch the layers of subconsciousness.'
   b. **Arve läheb ___ makstud olema.*
      bill.NOM goes.3SG PRO.NOM paid get.INF
      Intended meaning: 'The bill will go to get paid.'

---

[1] See Falk (2018: 2) and Heltoft (2021: 258–259) for similar analyses of Old Swedish and Old Danish, namely that the potential oblique subject is regarded as being the first argument of the argument structure, yet not considered a syntactic subject according to their definitions.

The final problem to be mentioned here with Keenan's approach is that it does not take as its point of departure how subjects may be differentiated from, for instance, objects. In that sense, Keenan's approach is in essence a prototype approach to subjecthood, not even intended as a guide in teasing apart subjects and objects. For a further discussion and critical remarks of prototype approaches to subjecthood, see Section 2.3.3 below.

Despite all of this, there is no doubt that the concept of subject forged ahead in leaps and bounds from earlier traditional grammar to modern linguistic approaches to syntax. That is, the subject concept made major headway through the generative approach with its strong emphasis on developing syntactic tests of use to tease out subjects from objects. The generativists working on subjecthood at the time carried out important empirical work, evident from the fact these subject tests are still in use today and are applied by advocates of different theoretical frameworks, formalists, functionalists and typologists alike.

2.1.3 Subject as a language-specific category: The methodological problems

Even the assumption that a subject is a language-specific category is far from being unproblematic, as we saw above in relation to the Estonian examples in (38a–b). The problems are particularly apparent when comparing studies of two or more languages, especially with respect to methodological issues. For instance, when comparing grammatical relations in even as closely related languages as Icelandic and German, it turns out that only a small number of subject tests are assumed to be common to both languages.

In the early work of Andrews (1976), Thráinsson (1979), Zaenen, Maling, and Thráinsson (1985) and Sigurðsson (1989) for Icelandic and Reis (1982) and Zaenen, Maling and Thráinsson (1985) and Sigurðsson (1989) for German, only nine out of 13 potentially relevant subject tests were assumed to be subject tests in Icelandic, while seven were regarded as being subject tests in German. Furthermore, of these 13 tests, only three are common to both languages, as is shown in Table 1 with gray shading.

There are, of course, some empirical differences between the two languages. Long-distance reflexivization, for instance, does not exist in German and deletion in imperatives cannot be used in Icelandic since the pronominal subject and the verb have univerbated (see Section 2.1.2 above). Even if one ignores these two tests, the results in Table 1 for the two languages show a surprisingly little overlap. The question arises whether Icelandic and German are really so radically different from each other in terms of grammatical relations as Table 1 appears to suggest.

Table 1: Subject tests in Icelandic and German (from Barðdal 2006: 48).

	Icelandic	German
First Position in Declarative Clauses	√	*
Subject-Verb Inversion	√	*
First Position in Subordinate Clauses	√	*
Subject-to-Object Raising	√	*
Subject-to-Subject Raising	√	*
Long Distance Reflexivization	√	*
Clause-Bound Reflexivization	√	√
Control Infinitives	√	√
Conjunction Reduction	√	√
Deletion in Telegraphic Style	*	√
Deletion in Imperatives	*	√
Nominative Case	*	√
Verb Agreement	*	√

The problem is that when comparing the methodological choices that have been made when investigating grammatical relations in these languages, it turns out that a major inconsistency is found between the two early approaches to Icelandic and German, respectively. Yet, these approaches laid the foundation for almost all work on grammatical relations in the two languages for years to come.

Andrews (1976), Thráinsson (1979), Zaenen, Maling, and Thráinsson (1985) and Sigurðsson (1989) took the behavioral properties as their point of departure, as their aim was to demonstrate that potential oblique subjects in Icelandic behave syntactically in the same way as nominative subjects do, which they clearly succeeded in showing. Potential oblique subjects in Icelandic are indeed behavioral subjects despite the fact that they do not possess the coding properties of nominative subjects. In contrast, Reis (1982) took the coding properties, i.e. nominative case and verb agreement, as a point of departure in her work on German and argued in favor of a systematic exclusion of all properties shared by nominative subjects and potential oblique subjects, thus maintaining the traditional view that the subject is in the nominative case.

As is further discussed in Section 2.3.3 below, potential oblique subjects in German do, as a matter of fact, behave like nominative subjects with regard to the first five tests listed in Table 1, which also means that they behave in the same way as oblique subjects do in Icelandic. The reason that this is not shown in Table 1 is that this table only lists the tests that are *assigned the status of being a subject test* in each language. Reis (1982) argues against defining the first five as subject tests, hence they have been excluded as subject tests for the German language.

On the basis of the subject tests used in Icelandic and German and the behavior of potential oblique subjects in both languages, it has been concluded that there are oblique subjects in Icelandic but not in German (Zaenen, Maling, and Thráinsson

1985; Sigurðsson 1989, 2004; Fanselow 2002; Bayer 2004; Wunderlich 2009; Haider 2005, 2010; Pankau 2016). However, this conclusion is first and foremost based on two different behavioral properties across Icelandic and German, as manifested in coordinated clauses and control infinitives (see Section 2.3 below).

I believe that the methodological choices of the Icelandic school were sound, since their aim was to compare the syntactic behavior of nominative subjects and potential oblique subjects. This is also explicit in their work. I find Reis's methodological choices more questionable, because clearly when prioritizing coding properties over behavioral properties, the possibility of analyzing potential oblique subjects as syntactic subjects is excluded by definition.

The same view is also found in Faarlund (1990), in his work on Old Norse-Icelandic, although the argument is construed a bit differently. Faarlund argues that there is no subject category in Old Norse-Icelandic, basing his claims on the distribution of nominative arguments across four different positions in the clause. These are: i) clause-initial position, ii) inverted subject position, i.e. the position immediately following the finite verb, iii) position preceding the non-finite verb, and iv) position immediately following the non-finite verb. Faarlund's (1990: 115–116) examples are given in (39) below:

Old-Norse Icelandic
Clause-initial position
(39) a. **Hálfdan** **hvítbein** var konungr ríkr
Hálfdán.NOM whiteleg.NOM was.3SG king.NOM rich.NOM
'Hálfdan the Whiteleg was a powerful king' (Ynglinga saga, ch. 49)

Inverted subject position
b. hafið **þit** verit hér um hríð með mér.
have.2PL you.PL been here of while with me
'You guys have been here for a while with me' (Egils saga, ch. 22)

Position preceding the non-finite verb
c. Þótti honum **hon** vel hafa gert
seemed.3SG him.DAT she.NOM well have done
'He felt that she had done well'
(Saga Inga konungs og bræðra hans, ch. 29)

Position immediately following the non-finite verb
d. Var þeim gefinn **dagverður**
was.3SG them.DAT given breakfast.NOM
'They were given breakfast.' (Ólafs saga helga, Ch. 141)

When concluding the discussion after the examples in (39) above (his ex. 75–77), Faarlund (1990: 116) claims that either other arguments than nominatives are subjects in Old Norse-Icelandic or that the word order distribution of nominative arguments does not reflect subject status. Yet, later in the very same section of this monograph, Faarlund (1990: 129) states:

> For Old Norse, I defined "subject" pretheoretically as a nominative NP, and the study of subject properties in Old Norse above did not give us any reason to establish a subject category on any other basis.

In essence, Faarlund conflates nominative arguments of nominative subject verbs (39a–b) and nominative object-like arguments of Dat-Nom verbs (39c–d). Clearly nominative subjects occupy different positions in the clause from nominative objects, the former typically occurring in the pre- and midfield (39a–b), while the latter occur normally in the mid- and endfield (39c–d). Thus, by blending the two argument types into one, one can certainly draw the conclusions Faarlund draws, however unfounded they may be.

There is no doubt that the choices of subject tests made by the Icelandic school for Icelandic were based on clear and explicit goals, namely to compare the syntactic behavior of nominative subjects with that of potential oblique subjects. This is also methodologically sound. However, I find their conclusions on the differences between Icelandic and German, which are only based on two syntactic behaviors, conjunction reduction and control infinitives, less well motivated (see further the discussion in Sections 2.3.2–2.3.3 below). Reis's and Faarlund's conclusions on German and Old Norse-Icelandic, respectively, are a clear example of what Croft (2001: 30–32, 41–44) labels *methodological opportunism*. That is, different behaviors are used to define subject in different languages, without a principled discussion of how to choose between the different tests (see Barðdal 2000a for a further methodological criticism of Kristoffersen 1991 and Mørck 1992 for Old Norse-Icelandic and Falk 1997 for Old Swedish).

2.2 The present approach to subjecthood

To start with, a construction-specific approach to the subject concept is presented and its validity argued for, including how such a concept may be modeled within Construction Grammar, in particular within Radical Construction Crammar (2.2.1). Thereafter, the present definition of subject is introduced along with a comparison between top-down and bottom-up approaches to subjecthood (2.2.2). Then the relation between argument structure and clausal conceptual structure is explained, in particular in relation to force dynamics and event structure (2.2.3). Finally, it is shown how subject behavior may be modeled employing the formalism of Construction Grammar (2.2.4).

2.2.1 Subject as a construction-specific category

Due to empirical problems of the type discussed in Section 2.1.2 above, the consensus in the linguistic community today is that subject is a language-specific category and not a universal category (cf. Foley 1993; Sorace 1995; Culicover and Jackendoff 2005; Haspelmath 2007; Mel'čuk 2014; to mention a few). Several scholars have even taken a more radical approach to grammatical relations, arguing that they are not only language-specific, but also construction specific (Cf. Van Valin 1981; Foley and Van Valin 1984; Gamon 1997; Croft 2001; Barðdal 2006; Barðdal, Eythórsson, and Dewey 2019; García-Miguel 2007; Cristofaro 2009; Witzlack-Makarevich 2010; Metslang 2013; Dattner et al. 2019).

Most syntactic theories are reductionist in that they assume that the parts of a whole are the primitives of language and that the parts, when combined, build the whole. In contrast, Radical Construction Grammar is a non-reductionist theory assuming that the parts do not exist outside of the whole. That is, the construction itself is taken to be the primitive of language, with the parts being derived from the whole. Thus, on a Radical Construction Grammar approach to grammar and language (Croft 2001, 2012, 2022; Barðdal 2006; Tomasello 2006; Cristofaro 2009; LaPolla 2013; Metslang 2013), grammatical relations are regarded as part-whole relations, while on most other approaches to grammatical relations, these are viewed as part-part relations (cf. Kay 1997 on the differences between syntactic roles and syntactic relations). The difference between the two may be illustrated with Figure 1, where *a*, *b* and *c* stand for three different parts of a larger construction C, which is itself denoted with the box around the three parts.

Assuming that C is a transitive construction, then *a* is the subject, *b* the verb and *c* the object. On the traditional view, to the right in Figure 1, *a* stands in a syntactic relation with *b*; which is a global subject-predicate relation, a general syntactic relation holding irrespective of constructions within a language, as is indicated in Figure 1 by the lack of connections between the subject-predicate relation itself at the right-hand bottom of Figure 1 and the construction immediately above it. In contrast, to the left in Figure 1, the subject *a* is regarded as a role in the construction C, as is signaled by the extraction of *a* out of construction C in Figure 1. This is how the syntactic role of subject becomes specific for each construction, instead of being a generalized global relation holding across all constructions found in a language.

As such, this visualization shows the crucial difference between Radical Construction Grammar and other syntactic frameworks.

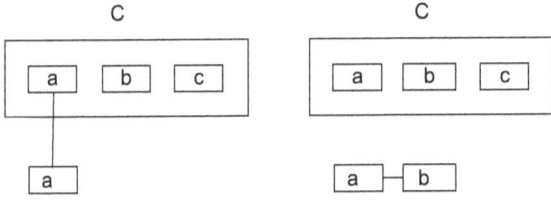

Figure 1: Part-whole relation vs. part-part relation.

Given the assumption that the subject function is a construction-specific relation, i.e. a *syntactic role*, syntactic relations, as a more technical term for a global relation irrespective of constructions, also become redundant in this framework. How can Radical Construction Grammar do away with syntactic relations, one may ask. In order to address that question, consider the following example:

Icelandic
(40)   ***Honum***   *er*   *óglatt.*
       him.DAT   is.3SG   unglad.NEUT
       'He feels queasy.

The syntactic subject in the Icelandic example in (40) is in the dative case *honum* 'him' and the predicate is *vera óglatt* 'feel queasy'. This simple sentence is shown in Figure 2. The outmost box stands for the construction as a whole, while the two horizontal inner boxes represent the syntactic elements and the semantic components, respectively, marked with the labels SYN and SEM. The dotted line between the syntactic element *honum* and the semantic component *HONUM* represents the symbolic relation between the two. The outer vertical box around *honum* and *HONUM* mark out the two as a lexical unit. Formally, *er óglatt* and *ER ÓGLATT* are two lexical units, but for ease of exposition, these are combined into one in Figure 2.

These outer vertical boxes are the Saussurian sign, an arbitrary form–meaning pairing, hence the *s* for *symbolic*. The same symbolic relation holds between *er óglatt* and *ER ÓGLATT*, again shown with dotted lines. The third dotted line, also marked *s*, shows that there is a symbolic relation between the SYN field as a whole and the SEM field as a whole. There is also a semantic relation between the two components of the SEM field, *HONUM* and *ER ÓGLATT*, given with a bold straight line, labeled *r* for *relation*. This last semantic relation is the thematic relation between the arguments and the predicate, here assumed to derive from event structure and

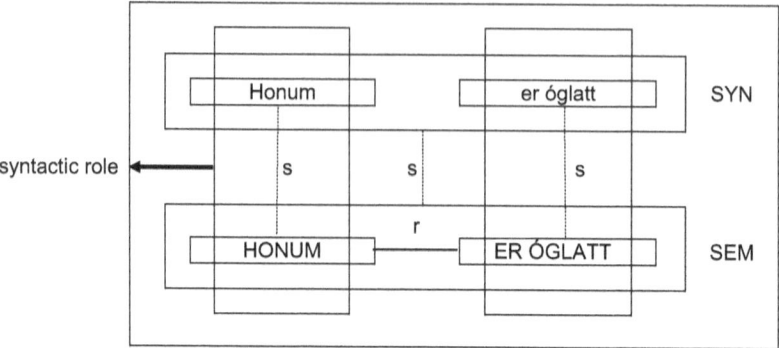

Figure 2: The internal structure of constructions.

the causal conceptual structure of verbs (see more on that in Section 2.2.3 below). Finally, there is a horizontal bold line from the lexical unit honum/HONUM to the outer part of the larger construction, signifying that this lexical unit has a syntactic role in the construction as a whole.

This means that given the proper modeling of semantic relations, symbolic relations and syntactic roles, syntactic relations are simply not needed. To explicate, there is a semantic relation between *HONUM* and *ER ÓGLATT*, linking those two components of the semantic structure together. The semantic component *HONUM* is also symbolically linked to the syntactic element *honum*. The same is true for *ER ÓGLATT* and *er óglatt*. Through this modeling, the hearer knows who the participants are, expressed in the event described by the utterance *honum er óglatt*, and how these participants relate to each other if there are more of them. This means, in essence, that syntactic relations are derivatives of semantic relations and symbolic relations combined. Further, adding syntactic roles to the equation, manifested through clause structure, it is not needed to assume a relation between the elements of the syntactic structure in Figure 2.

However, if syntactic relations were to be modeled in Figure 2, that would have been with a line between the two syntactic elements, *honum* and *er óglatt*. Yet, when taken together, the concepts of semantic relations, symbolic relations and syntactic roles, and the interaction between these, make the modeling of syntactic relations redundant. Also, in a theoretical model assuming these concepts, the syntactic behavior of subjects and objects in a given language falls out directly from the proper modeling of the constructions involving the behavioral properties of subjects (cf. Barðdal and Eythórsson 2012a). This will be modeled in Chapter 5 below.

In contrast, on a view adopting the part-part relations to the right in Figure 1 above, where syntactic relations are assumed to be generalized syntactic relations holding for all constructions within a language, syntactic relations are regarded as direct derivatives of clause structure, irrespective of semantic relations. By that I am not claiming that scholars adopting the generalized approach to syntactic relations (the part-part relation), do not relate syntactic relations to semantic roles, of course they do. But relating syntactic relations to semantic roles is not inherent to the part-part approach where the subject-predicate relation is viewed as a global syntactic relation. Instead, such a process involves semantic analyses of specific constructions in language and is as such an independent add-on to the generalized part-part approach to syntactic relations.

Also, when I reject the notion of syntactic relations as global part-part relations, which are taken to exist independently of the individual constructions in a language, I am of course not rejecting the notion of clause structure. I am also not claiming that there is no nexus relation holding between a subject and a predicate. Instead, I believe that this nexus relation comes into being through the interaction between semantic relations, symbolic relations and syntactic roles. As such, I am only arguing against a generalized notion of syntactic relations, assumed to exist irrespective of individual argument structure constructions in a language.

As is well known, Construction Grammar originally arose to deal with non-core language, i.e. idioms and set phrases which fell outside the "core" of language. This involves in particular semantically non-compositional parts of language, where the meaning of the whole cannot be derived from the meaning of the parts. Examples of that type have been used in the literature to argue for the superiority of Construction Grammar over other linguistic frameworks.

Regarding non-compositional meaning, it is the symbolic relation between the whole SYN and SEM fields that allows Construction Grammar to map non-compositional meaning to compositional syntax. This may involve a mismatch in the number of syntactic elements and semantic components or the semantic components may have a specific meaning only found in a given construction. On a further development of the constructional framework, it became clear that the mechanisms and formalisms used to account for semantically non-compositional language may also be used to account for semantically compositional languages, as I do in Figure 2. In this sense, Construction Grammar is not a theory confined to "non-core" language but may equally well be used to account for ordinary structures in our everyday language.

From an outside perspective, it may appear as if there is considerable redundancy in Figure 2, and perhaps particularly in the SYN and SEM fields. However, the different types of relations would only appear as redundant in the eyes of a viewer not adhering to Construction Grammar, i.e. a viewer assuming the part-part approach to grammatical relations where it seems that only one relation needs to be assumed. This, however, is an illusion, as all theoretical frameworks have to assume semantic relations to account for the combined meaning between the lexical items, all have to assume symbolic relations to account for the Saussurian sign, and all have to account for the nexus relation between the subject and the verb. There is therefore no redundancy in Table 2. And even if there were such a redundancy, recall that Radical Construction Grammar is a non-reductionist theory that does not shy away from representing redundant information if it is psychologically real in the minds of speakers.

Observe also that the two different approaches to grammatical relations, in terms of syntactic relations vs. syntactic roles, make different predictions about subject behavior within a given language. On the traditional view where grammatical relations are perceived of in terms of a generalized syntactic relation between a subject and a predicate, irrespective of constructions, it is expected that all subjects behave syntactically in the same way. On a Radical Construction Grammar account where grammatical relations are perceived of in terms of roles within a specific construction, one may expect different behavior for different subjects, depending on the construction they are subjects of. As will be evident in the remainder of this chapter, the predictions of the Radical Construction Grammar approach, that a subject is a role in a larger construction, are indeed borne out, as subjects turn out to behave differently, depending on which constructions they are subjects of. As a consequence, the predictions of the traditional approach, including modern linguistics approaches, that there is a generalized subject relation between a subject and its predicate, cannot be corroborated. This is because subjects of different constructions within a language do not behave in a uniform manner, as is discussed in Section 2.3 below.

A final issue to address, before turning to the present subject definition and the mapping of the arguments to grammatical relations, relates to the possibility of carrying out comparative work on subjecthood, given the assumption that grammatical relations are not only language specific but also construction specific. Alas, such basic assumptions do not rule out comparative work on subjecthood, no less than they rule out a comparison of subject behavior across the constructions subjects have a role in within a given language. Rather, the acknowledgment that subject is a construction-specific role only means that one cannot take a subject test from language A and apply it on language B without first establishing the validity of that test in language B. As its corollary, one cannot expect a property of the subject of one construction within a language to also be a property of another construction in that same language, without investigation.

2.2.2 Defining subject: Top-down vs. bottom-up approaches

The notion of subject has been defined in different ways depending on theoretical frameworks. In, for instance, classical government and binding theory, the subject is defined through its position in the tree-structure representation, while on optimality-theoretic accounts the subject is defined through the ranking of different constraints. In the minimalist program the subject is defined through the merging of certain EPP features in the specifier position of TP (tense phrase) in the stepwise derivation of the clause.

The definitions listed in the paragraph above are top-down definitions of subject; first the subject is defined as a part of the theoretical machinery, then the subject properties are derived from this definition. Falk (1997), for instance, in her work on Old Swedish defines the subject in terms of a specific position in the tree-structure representation and then argues that the subject properties in Old Swedish follow from this particular position in the tree.

In contrast, under a bottom-up definition of subject, the subject tests are applied first and then a generalization is made on the basis of the behavior of the arguments relative to the subject tests. An example of such a bottom-up approach is found in Eythórsson and Barðdal (2005), who argue that the subject tests systematically target the leftmost / first argument of the argument structure and not the rightmost / second argument. This fact leads them to suggest a definition of subject which they view as being theory-neutral, truly capturing the empirical core of subjecthood; this empirical core may then be recast into one's theory of choice. More specifically, Eythórsson and Barðdal's definition is as follows:

> The subject of a predicate is the leftmost argument of its subcategorization frame ... The internal order of the arguments is in turn determined by the causal conceptual structure of the predicate and the force-dynamic relations between the participants of the event denoted by each predicate. (Eythórsson and Barðdal 2005: 831)

The difference between top-down and bottom-up approaches to subjecthood may not have many practical consequences, since both approaches are ultimately rooted in linguistic reality and both capture the behavior of the subject argument relative to the object argument. However, a bottom-up approach is more in line with the aims of basic linguistic theory (cf. Dixon 1997: 128–138, 2009, 2010, 2012; Haspelmath 2004; Dryer 2006; Kibrik 2012), than the aims of explanatory formal theories. The former aims to describe language and structure in a uniform and a user-friendly manner, while the latter aim to contribute to a further theoretical discussion along with their linguistic descriptions.

A final question to ponder relates to whether the subject properties themselves may function as a subject definition. That is, can the subject tests act as a stand-in definition of subject in the lack of a clearly articulated subject definition? In point of fact, this is common practice within typology and descriptive work on grammatical relations. However, there is one major disadvantage of this "subject test stand-in" definition of subject, clearly surfacing in research on non-nominative subjects, namely the problem of how to prioritize among subject tests. This will be further discussed in Section 2.3.3 below.

2.2.3 Argument structure, event structure and force dynamics

Returning to the definition of subject presented in the preceding section, most earlier linguistic frameworks make use of the concept of subcategorization frames, a concept that has been reinterpreted in terms of *argument structure* in later work. The concept of argument structure has become an integral part of constructional approaches to language, as is evident from the formalizations in Figures 3–4 below, given through *Attributed Value Matrices*. On a constructional approach, argument structure constructions are assumed to exist in their own right, irrespective of the verbs that instantiate them (cf. Goldberg 1995; Goldberg and Bencini 2005; Allen et al. 2012; Croft 2012).

The linking of participant roles of verbs to the arguments in the argument structure is far from arbitrary. The factors which determine this order, and hence which argument is the subject and which the object, can be directly derived from *event structure*. Event structure, in turn, is made up of causal conceptual structure and the force-dynamic relations holding between the participants of any given event (Croft 1998, 2001, 2012).

For this purpose, Talmy's (1976, 1985, 1988) notion of force dynamics describes the dynamics between two entities when exposed to force, either physical force or emotional force. If one of the two entities puts greater force on the other, that entity is the causer, and thus the initiator of the event, while the other entity, the one acted upon, is a non-causer, and thus the endpoint of the force of that event. The notion of force-dynamics has been successfully applied in research on grammatical relations (Langacker 1991, 2008; Croft 1998, 2012; Barðdal 2001b; Eythórsson and Barðdal 2005; Barðdal, Eythórsson, and Dewey 2019), where it has been used to capture the relation between a verb and its arguments and, in particular, the interaction between the participants of an event denoted by that verb. Force-dynamics is thus a component of event structure, interacting with the lexical semantics and the causal conceptual structure of verbs.

For illustration purposes, consider the list of argument structure constructions below for three different verbs, *murder*, *trouble* and *like* in English and their translational equivalents in Icelandic, *myrða*, *angra* and *líka*:

(41) a. English *murder*   [ARG1, ARG2]
       Icelandic *myrða*   [ARG1$_{nom}$, ARG2$_{acc}$]
    b. English *trouble*   [ARG1, ARG2]
       Icelandic *angra*   [ARG1$_{nom}$, ARG2$_{acc}$]
    c. English *like*   [ARG1, ARG2]
       Icelandic *líka*   [ARG1$_{dat}$, ARG2$_{nom}$]

The verb 'murder' in (41a) selects for two arguments of which the first one refers to the entity carrying out the event, the initiator, and the second one refers to the entity being affected by the event, the endpoint. The first argument, the initiator of the causal chain, is labeled ARG1 in the argument structure listed above, while the second argument, the endpoint of the causal chain, is labeled ARG2. This is how the order of the arguments in the argument structure is a derivative of event structure, involving both causal conceptual structure, the causal chain, and the force-dynamic relation holding between the two participants of the event.

For the verb 'trouble' in (41b), the entity causing the trouble is the initiator, listed as ARG1, while the entity being troubled is the endpoint, listed as ARG2. Again, the initiator of the causal chain acts upon the endpoint of the same causal chain, which means that the initiator is assigned the first argument of the argument structure, while the endpoint is assigned the second argument of the argument structure, exactly as with 'murder' above; both verbs are causatives, although 'murder' is an example of *volitional causation*, while 'trouble' is an example of *affective causation* in Talmy's (1976) terminology.

The causal chain for murdering and troubling events may be represented as in (42) below, following the notational system suggested by Croft (2012: Ch. 6):

(42) The man murdered the taxidriver
     man   →   taxidriver
     ARG1   ARG2

In (42) there is a causer, *the man*, exerting physical force upon another entity, the endpoint of the event's causal chain, *the taxidriver*. The direction of the force is shown with the arrow in (42). The causer is thus higher in the causal chain of the event, and the endpoint is lower in the causal chain. This also follows directly from iconicity, as the initiator of the event certainly exists prior to the event, while the endpoint of the event does not exist in its altered state until after the event has taken place (cf. Croft 1998).

In the same manner, for the verb 'trouble' in (41b), there is a causer exerting affective force upon another entity, the endpoint. Hence, the causer is higher in the causal chain, while the endpoint is lower in the causal chain. As a consequence, the causer is assigned the first argument role of the argument structure, ARG1, and the endpoint is assigned the second argument role in the argument structure, ARG2. The participant roles come from the verb and these have to be compatible with the arguments of the argument structure, while the causal chain allows for the internal ranking between these arguments in the argument structure.

Note that there is one major difference between the present approach and Croft's (2012) approach and this difference lies in the current definition of subject as being the first argument of the argument structure and the object as being the second argument of the argument structure. Due to this definition, my notational system and formalism does not have to specify how the participant roles are assigned to grammatical relations like subjects and objects. It is enough that my notational system and formalism specifies how participant roles are assigned to the arguments in the argument structure, as is shown in (42) above. It is further laid out in Section 2.2.4 and Chapter 5 below how the behavior of the arguments of the argument structure with regard to the subject tests can be modeled, such that grammatical relations (syntactic roles) simply fall out from that mechanism.

Turning to the verb 'like' in (41c), the entity doing the liking is ARG1, construed as the initiator of the event, while the entity being liked is ARG2, construed as the endpoint of the event (I return to construal operations in Section 3.1.1 below). Observe that there is one major difference between the English and Icelandic 'like' though, namely that ARG1 in Icelandic is marked in the dative case while ARG2 is marked in the nominative case. Although English does not have case marking on nouns in the modern-day language, this case marking is the same as is found with *lician* in Old English, which is a cognate of Modern Icelandic *líka* (for a further discussion of *lician* in Old English, see Section 3.5 below).

Regarding psychological events in general, these are well known for being force-dynamically neutral in that the relation between the participants of the verb are not necessarily force-dynamic in the sense that one entity acts upon another. Instead, such events may be construed in two different ways, either as an experiencer directing his/her attention towards a stimulus (*fear* construal) or as the stimulus affecting the experiencer (*frighten* construal). Which type of event construal is found for which predicate is simply a lexical idiosyncrasy of each predicate (cf. Croft 1998). As will become evident in Section 3.2 below, the choice between two opposite construals is not only found for stative psychological events, but also for certain inchoative events, be they of a psychological nature or not.

In sum, event structure is a level of linguistic representation from which the mapping of event participants to argument structure is derived. For the three verbs listed in (41) above, the relevant event types involve causative events and stative psychological events. For causatives, like 'murder' and 'trouble', it is the initiator of the causation that is linked to the first argument of the argument structure, while the endpoint of the causation is linked to the second argument of the argument structure. The ranking between the arguments in the argument structure is further achieved through their relational status in the causal chain, following from their inner force-dynamic interdependence.

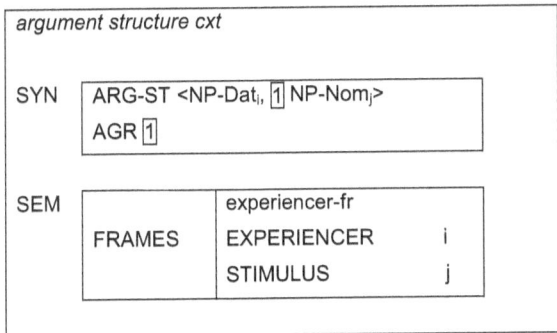

Figure 3: Dat-Nom argument structure construction.

For a formalization of the Dat-Nom argument structure construction of the verb 'like' in Icelandic, see Figure 3, where the first argument is in the dative case and the second in the nominative. The attributed value matrix consists of two fields, the SYN field and the SEM field, respectively. The argument structure (ARG-ST) in the SYN field contains an ordered list of arguments with the dative preceding the nominative in the relative order. The tag in the boxed numeral in the ARG-ST is co-indexed with the second argument, the nominative, showing that it agrees with the verb. The semantic information in the SEM field is rendered through semantic frames (cf. Fillmore et al. 2012), in this case an experiencer-frame, consisting of two participant roles, an experiencer and a stimulus. These two participant roles each map onto one of the two arguments in the ARG-ST, the experiencer onto the first argument in the dative case and the stimulus onto the second argument in the nominative case.

2.2.4 Modeling subject behavior

For the Icelandic verb *líka* from (41c) above, I suggest a lexical entry of the type shown in Figure 4. The difference between the lexical entry in Figure 4 and the argument structure construction in Figure 3 is first and foremost that the list of arguments in the lexical entry is unordered, hence the curly brackets in Figure 4, as opposed to the angled brackets in Figure 3. This means that it is only when the verb *líka* enters the argument structure that the order of the arguments becomes fixed. In the lexical entry in Figure 4, there is also a FORM field at the top, which is not found for the argument structure construction in Figure 3, here filled with the phonological form of the lexical verb for which the entry applies. This is one way of modeling the relation between lexical entries of verbs and their argument structure in construction grammar. For a further discussion of the different options, see Barðdal, Eythórsson, and Dewey (2019: 153–161) and Section 3.4 below.

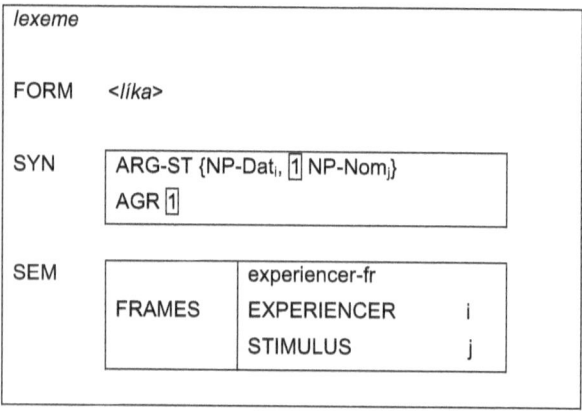

Figure 4: Lexical entry for Icelandic *líka* 'like'.

To conclude so far, the ordered structure of the arguments in Figure 3, compatible with the lexical entry of the verb *líka* in Icelandic in Figure 4, with the dative preceding the nominative, represents a specific event type construal, where ARG1 directs his/her attention towards ARG2. In one sense of the word, this can be viewed as a *thematic hierarchy*, although such a thematic hierarchy would be confined to a specific event type, here involving the experiencer-frame. The same can also be said about causatives, inchoatives, etc., in that the order of the arguments in the argument structure is a fixed one, again derived from event structure with the aid of causal conceptual structure and force dynamics. This approach, then, makes universal thematic hierarchies à la Jackendoff (1972, 1990), Van Valin (1990) and Grimshaw (1990) redundant; instead what needs to be captured is the relation of the participant roles relative to *each other*, and not relative to a hierarchy of generalized semantic roles (cf. Croft 1998, 2001, 2012, Barðdal 2001b).

In addition to lexical entries and argument structure constructions, the constructions that identify the subject properties also need to be modeled in order to properly account for the syntactic behavior of subjects within a given language. This is one of the topics of Chapter 5 below, but taking a head start on this matter, consider an example of one of the subject tests randomly chosen from Table 1 above, i.e. a subject's ability to be left unexpressed in control infinitives:

Icelandic
Control infinitive
(43) Kannski bara farnir að ___ líka   þetta   vel.
     perhaps just started to   PRO.DAT like.INF this.NOM well
     'Perhaps (they have) even started really liking it.'

The example in (43) consists of an incomplete matrix clause *kannski bara farnir* 'perhaps just started' and the infinitive clause, *að líka þetta vel* 'to really like this'. Recall that the verb *líka* selects for a dative subject and a nominative object in Icelandic, of which the first is left unexpressed in the control infinitive in (43), while the latter, the nominative *þetta*, is expressed. The case marking of the unexpressed argument is properly marked in the glosses, immediately before the nonfinite verb. The structure of this control construction in Icelandic is laid out in Figure 5; in particular the subject's ability to be left unexpressed is accounted for.

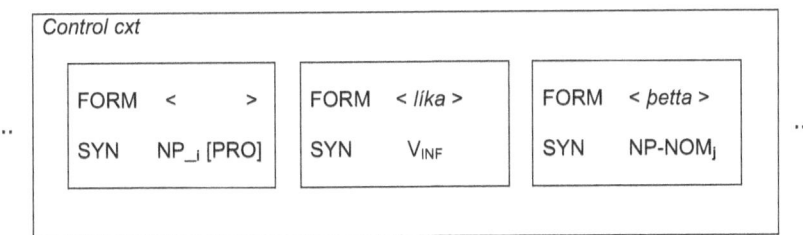

Figure 5: Subject behavior in control constructions.

Control infinitives in general are found with different types of matrix verbs, with the matrix subject, the matrix object or even an arbitrary controller providing the reference of the unexpressed subject of the infinitive. The example in (43) above instantiates the first type, with the dropped subject *þeir* 'they' controlling the reference of the unexpressed dative subject in the control infinitive. Due to the heterogeneous nature of the types of matrix clauses found with control infinitives, the modeling in Figure 5 is confined to the small clause itself, i.e. to the control infinitive.

The ellipsis to the left and to the right of the construction in Figure 5 shows that there may be material in front of the unexpressed subject as well as following the expressed object. In this sense, this model is only partial. The three boxes within the construction stand for the different syntactic elements of the control construction, namely the unexpressed dative subject, the nonfinite verb and the expressed nominative object. Each of these contains two fields, a FORM field and a SYN field. The SYN field of the verb is defined as V_{INF}, and the SYN field of the object contains the second argument of the argument structure, the nominative, indexed with a *j*, exactly like the second argument of the argument structure of *líka* in Figure 3 above. In contrast, the SYN field of the subject contains the unexpressed subject argument, here labeled PRO, following the norms of the generative tradition, a label going back decades in time. This unexpressed subject is here in the dative case and indexed with an *i*, exactly like the first argument of the argument structure of *líka* in Figure 3 above. The FORM fields of the second and third elements contain *líka* and *þetta*, respectively, while the FORM field of the first element is empty, since it represents the unexpressed subject.

It is through the co-indexing of the arguments in the argument structure with the arguments in the control infinitive that the mapping between argument structure and subject and object behavior takes place. ARG1 is indexed with an *i* in the argument structure while ARG2 is indexed with a *j*. Also, for each type of clause structure where the position of ARG1 and ARG2 is modeled relative to the other elements in the clause, this co-indexation is specified. From this mechanism, i.e. lexical entries, argument structure constructions and clause structure constructions, where the order of the arguments is systematically shown with indexes, the behavior of syntactic subjects directly falls out.

2.3 Deviations from the subject canon

Starting with a general introduction and examples of verbs and predicates selecting for (potential) oblique subjects in different languages in Section 2.3.1, the similarities and differences between oblique subject constructions in Icelandic and German are discussed in Section 2.3.2, in particular the two subject tests that give different results in the two languages. Section 2.3.3 is devoted to an analysis of the deviations from the nominative canon and the question of how it is best to account for such deviations. This further involves a comparison between prototype approaches and the present approach where a subject definition is applied independently of the subject tests themselves, and an argument is made for the superiority of the latter approach. The final section, 2.3.4, documents, through the use of questionnaire surveys, that grammaticality judgments vary for some of the attested data, both for Icelandic and German, in reality suggesting that the difference between the two languages is a difference in degree and not a difference in kind.

2.3.1 Oblique subjects

In the wake of research on subject status and grammatical relations during the 1970's (cf. Section 2.1.1 above), oblique subjects not only kindled interest among syntacticians, but also among typologists and historical linguists at the time. Some early work involves Andrews (1976) and Thráinsson (1979) on Icelandic and Masica (1976), Kachru, Kachru, and Bhatia (1976) and Klaiman (1980) on South Asian languages. Some examples instantiating this argument structure are given in (44) below, from different languages; the ones in (44a–c) are from three different Indo-European languages, Icelandic, German and Romanian, (44d) is from a Dravidian language, Malayalam, while (44e) is from Hebrew.

Icelandic
(44) a. **Henni** lék bros um varir.
she.DAT moved smile.NOM of lips
'She had a smile on her lips.' (Lögberg 48(19): 6, c.1935)

German
b. was **mir** gelang, gelang nicht **mir**
what.NOM me.DAT succeeded.3SG succeeded.3SG not me.DAT
allein.
alone
'What I succeeded with, I did not succeed with alone.'
(Philosophie: II. Existenzerhellung, 173, c.1956)

Romanian
c. **Îmi** este necesar să văd punctele de vedere
me.DAT is.3SG necessary that I.see points.the of view
ale candidaților.
of candidates.the
'I need to know the points of view of the candidates.'

Malayalam
d. **avaḷ-kkə** dukkham vannu
she.DAT sadness came
'She became sad.' (Nizar 2010: 8)

Hebrew

e. ... ʕattā kaʔăšer ṣar   **lā-kem**
         now   when   distressed to-you
'...now that you are distressed?' (Judg. 11:7, cited from Pat-El 2018: 161)

Since the insight that behavioral properties of subjects are not intrinsically tied to nominative case and agreement, oblique subjects have been argued to exist in language after language, on the basis of data from several language families across different continents. This includes Quechuan languages (Hermon 1985), Dravidian (Verma and Mohanan 1990), Dardic (Steever 1998), Japanese (Shibatani 1999), Greek (Anagnostopoulou 1999), Russian (Moore and Perlmutter 2000), Tibeto-Burman (Bickel 2004), Korean (Yoon 2004), Semitic (Landau 2009; Pat-El 2018), Cariban (Castro Alves 2018), Tsezic languages (Comrie, Forker, and Khalilova 2018), Romanian (Ilioaia 2021; Ilioaia and Van Peteghem 2021), in addition to several South-Asian languages (see, for instance, references in Hock and Bashir 2016).

2.3.2 Icelandic vs. German

One particularly problematic issue when addressing the question of whether potential oblique subjects exhibit behavioral subject properties is not only that languages may differ in this respect, but also that constructions which appear to be equivalent to each other may show different properties both across languages and within a language. This is, of course, unexpected on the assumption that subject is a universal category. But what is more, this is even unexpected on the assumption that subject is a language-specific category, as one would then expect all subjects in a language to behave uniformly with regard to the subject tests. To illustrate this point, consider the following facts about Icelandic and German.

In a systematic comparison between Modern Icelandic and Modern German, Zaenen, Maling, and Thráinsson (1985) show that potential oblique subjects do not behave in the same way with regard to omission in coordinated clauses and omission in control infinitives. Before turning to the Icelandic and German data, let me briefly outline the nature of these tests with the examples in (45–46) below from English (see also the discussion in Sections 1.1 and 1.3 above):

Conjunction reduction
(45) ***I spotted*** *Mary across the crowded room **and walked** over to her.*

Control infinitive
(46) *An older lady tried **to open** the door.*

2.3 Deviations from the subject canon — 49

The example in (45) contains two conjoined clauses, *I spotted Mary across the crowded room* and *walked over to her*. The omitted subject of the verb *walk* in the second conjunct is coreferential with the subject *I* in the first conjunct. For that reason, the subject of the second conjunct can be left unexpressed. The same is true for the control infinitive in (46); the subject of the nonfinite verb *open* has the same reference as *an older lady*, the subject of *tried* in the matrix clause.

Observe that there is a difference between omission in conjoined clauses and omission in control infinitives, in that omission in conjoined clauses can only take place when the omitted subject is coreferential with the subject of the first clause, while for omission in control infinitives, this is not the case. In control infinitives the omitted subject may be coreferential with any argument of the preceding clause, the subject or the object, or it may be recoverable from the context. This means that the relevant subject behavior found in control infinitives is not determined by the grammatical status of the argument of the preceding clause which is coreferential with the omitted subject, but rather by an argument's ability to be left unexpressed in the infinitive clause, as only subjects may be left unexpressed in control infinitives and not objects.

The differences between conjunction reduction and control constructions are illustrated in the examples below, where the relevant predicates are the Icelandic *vera óglatt* 'feel queasy' and its translational equivalent in German, *übel sein*, which both systematically select for a potential dative subject when occurring in finite clauses in their respective languages. Some of the examples below are cited directly from Zaenen, Maling, and Thráinsson (1985), while others are inspired by their discussion.

Icelandic
(47) a. því **mér** er svo óglatt.
because me.DAT is.3SG so queasy
'because I feel so queasy.'

German (cf. Zaenen, Maling, and Thráinsson 1985: 478 for a corresponding example)
b. dass **mir** so oft übel ist?
that me.DAT so often queasy is.3SG
'that I feel queasy so often?'

Having now shown that 'feel queasy' selects for a potential dative subject in both languages, consider the following examples of conjunction reduction and control infinitives.

Conjunction reduction
Icelandic
(48) a. *Hann* **kom** *iðulega* **og** ___ **varð** *alltaf óglatt.*
 he.NOM came frequently and Ø.DAT became always queasy
 'He came frequently and always felt queasy.'

German
 b. **Er* *kam* *häufig* **und** ___ **wurde** *immer übel.*
 he.NOM came frequently and Ø.DAT became always queasy
 Intended meaning: 'He came frequently and always felt queasy.'

The examples in (48) show, in sooth, that there is a difference between Icelandic and German in that the dative in Icelandic can be left unexpressed in conjoined clauses (48a), as opposed to in German (48b), where such clauses are ungrammatical. It should be added here that nominative subjects may be left unexpressed in conjoined clauses in both languages.

The aforementioned difference between Icelandic and German is also found in control infinitives, where the example in (50a) with the dative being left unexpressed in Icelandic is grammatical, while the corresponding structure in the German example in (50b) is ungrammatical. Again, verbs selecting for nominative subjects show a systematic omission of the nominative subject in control infinitives in both languages, as is shown in (49) below.

Control infinitives (unambiguous nominative subjects)
Icelandic
(49) a. *Það er gott að* ___ **fara** *heim.*
 it is.3SG good to PRO.NOM go.INF home
 'It is good to go home.'

German
 b. *Es ist gut, nach Hause* ___ **zu gehen.**
 it is.3SG good towards home PRO.NOM to go.INF
 'It is good to go home.'

Control infinitives (potential oblique subjects)
Icelandic
(50) a. *Það er ekki gott að* ___ **vera** *óglatt.*
 it is.3SG gott good to PRO.DAT be.INF queasy
 'It is not good to feel queasy.'

German
b. *Übel* ___ *to* *sein* *ist* *nicht* *angenehm.*
queasy PRO.DAT zu be.INF is.3SG not easy
Intended meaning: 'It is not good to feel queasy.'
(Zaenen, Maling, and Thráinsson 1985: 478)

Zaenen, Maling, and Thráinsson (1985) argue on the basis of the differences shown above that the dative is a syntactic subject in Icelandic but not in German. Note also that Zaenen, Maling, and Thráinsson systematically compare the behavior of potential oblique subjects across several possible subject tests in both languages. The same is true for Sigurðsson's subsequent work on Icelandic and German (1989, 1992, and later work), as well as the work of Fanselow (2002), Bayer (2004), Wunderlich (2009), Haider (2005, 2010) and Pankau (2016). As a consequence, certain subject tests have received a more privileged status than other subject tests.

However, no principled discussion is offered on why exactly these two subject tests, *conjunction reduction* and *control infinitives*, should rank higher than other tests when deciding on how to "define" subject. That is, no principled discussion on how to prioritize among the subject tests is given. Instead, the choice of "criterial" subject tests is left to the whims of the individual researcher. Note that, in this case, the choice of "criterial" singles out the two tests where Icelandic and German truly differ from each other. This is one of the clearest examples I have come across of Croft's (2001: 30–32, 41–44) methodological opportunism, where Zaenen, Maling, and Thráinsson (1985) set the agenda for decades to come.

2.3.3 Interpreting deviations

To summarize the present findings so far, potential oblique subjects clearly deviate from the subject canon. However, these deviations may be divided into two types, the self-evident deviations and the non-self-evident ones, as is laid out below:
- Self-evident deviations:
  - Lack of nominative case
  - Lack of agreement with the verb
- Not self-evident deviations:
  - Lack of occurrences in conjoined clauses
  - Lack of occurrences in control infinitives

It is self-evident when investigating the possible subject behavior of potential oblique subjects that these do not possess the coding properties of subjects, i.e. nominative case and verb agreement. It is perhaps less clear why agreement is self-evidently excluded, as opposed to nominative case marking, but the reason is that agreement in the Germanic and Indo-European languages is confined to nominative arguments, be they subject or object arguments (cf. Sigurðsson's 1990–91, 2004 work on Icelandic). That is, it is only nominative arguments that exhibit person and number agreement, while all non-canonical subjects occur with the default 3rd singular agreement form. This type of *default agreement* is found with clausal subjects, infinitival subjects, dummy subjects, and oblique subjects alike (Corbett 1991: 204).

In contrast, the fact that potential oblique subjects in German cannot be left unexpressed in either conjoined clauses or control infinitives is much less self-evident than the lack of nominative case and agreement. This has given rise to a major analytical difference between German and Icelandic, as Icelandic is a language where oblique subjects are indeed left unexpressed in such clause types. What is worse, however, is that present scholarship has simply left comparative research between German and Icelandic at this impasse.

Due to the "empirical differences" between Icelandic and German outlined above, the general consensus in the field has it that there are oblique subjects in Icelandic but not in German. Correspondingly, potential oblique subjects in German have been analyzed and labeled as objects, although no independent evidence has been provided for an object analysis, only the apparent lack of subject behavior. As such, the category of object has become a waste-paper-basket category, whose membership has been subjected to a much lower standard than the membership of the subject category.

Nevertheless, taking a further glance at the similarities and differences in the behavior of potential oblique subjects in the two languages reveals some interesting generalizations. This emerges clearly from Table 2 which shows that potential oblique subjects in German really behave similarly to oblique subjects in Icelandic in not only many, but actually in most respects, i.e. in a total of six out of nine behaviors. As will be demonstrated in Section 6.3 below, potential oblique subjects in German show the same word order distribution as their Icelandic cousins, they are raised to subject in subject-to-subject raising and to object in subject-to-object raising constructions, exactly like their Icelandic cousins, and they behave in a similar manner as their cousins in Icelandic with regard to (the intricacies of) reflexivization (cf. Barðdal, Eythórsson, and Dewey 2019).

The logical question certainly arises as to why these six common properties are not sufficient to analyze potential oblique subjects in German as syntactic subjects. The answer to this question has already been alluded to in Section 2.1.3 above. First there is the theoretical possibility that there may be grammatical differences found between the two languages, such that a subject behavior in one language is not a subject behavior in the other. Second, it was argued by Reis, as early as in 1982, that the coding properties should be given priority over the behavioral prop-

Table 2: Similarities and differences in the behavior of potential oblique subjects across Icelandic and German (from Barðdal 2006: 83).

	Icelandic	German
First Position in Declarative Clauses	√	√
Subject-Verb Inversion	√	√
First Position in Subordinate Clauses	√	√
Subject-to-Object Raising	√	√
Subject-to-Subject Raising	√	√
Clause-Bound Reflexivization	√	√
Control Infinitives	√	*
Conjunction Reduction	√	*
Deletion in Telegraphic Style	√	*
Deletion in Imperatives	*	*

erties, seemingly only to preserve the traditional view of subject that it must be in the nominative case. Third, Reis also argued for the exclusion of the six behaviors common to German and Icelandic, claiming that they do not distinguish between subjects and objects in German. For further data and counterarguments to Reis's and Zaenen, Maling, and Thráinsson's arguments, see Chapter 6 below which is devoted to the situation in Modern German.

There is, moreover, a fourth reason for why potential oblique subjects have been analyzed differently across Icelandic and German, and that is an utter and complete lack of an independent subject definition, or at least a lack of a subject definition that can be independently applied. Instead, the subject properties themselves have acted as a stand-in definition of subject. This turned out not to be a problem for Icelandic since oblique subjects exhibit all the same behavioral properties as nominative subjects do. The situation in German, however, is different since the behavior of potential oblique subjects in that language only aligns partially with the behavior of nominative subjects.

There are several analytical ways of dealing with the kind of situation described above for German, one being a total rejection of a subject analysis and adopting a waste-paper-basket object analysis instead, while another way is to adopt a prototype approach to subjecthood, which in turn presupposes a "gradient" view of the subject concept. The first option has been exercised by the German scholarship when analyzing the status of potential oblique subjects in German (Reis 1982; Zaenen, Maling, and Thráinsson 1985; Sigurðsson 1989, 1992, 2004; Fanselow 2002; Bayer 2004; Wunderlich 2009; Haider 2005, 2010; Pankau 2016), while the second option has been exercised by the Lithuanian scholarship when analyzing the status of potential oblique subjects in Baltic (Holvoet 2013, 2016; Seržant 2013; Bjarnadóttir 2014a).

The disadvantages of the first approach have already been laid out above, namely methodological opportunism and inconsistencies, while the disadvantages of the second approach have not. One major problem with a prototype approach to subjecthood is the concomitant "gradience" of the subject concept it entails. On such an approach, an argument may be analyzed as a "partial" subject, instead of being or not being a subject. This has resulted in terminology like "semi-subject", "pseudo-subject" or "quasi subject" being invented in the literature (Elmer 1981; Bremmer 1986; Farrell 2005; Conti 2008, 2009; Conti and Luraghi 2014; Benedetti 2013a, 2013b; Holvoet 2013, 2016; Seržant 2013; Bjarnadóttir 2014a).

Another problem with a prototype approach is that no principled "answer sheet" exists on how many behaviors are enough for an argument to qualify as a subject and how many are not enough. In the same vein, there is no principled "answer sheet" on how to rank the different subject behaviors internally, thus allowing some behaviors to be considered as more important than others. For this reason, a prototype approach to subjecthood can only result in a view that an argument is a "partial" subject, say 30% subject, 50% subject or a 70% subject. Such an approach is not only absurd, when taken to its logical conclusion, but also explanatorily inadequate, without any predictive power.

Contrariwise, on the approach adopted here, an argument is either a subject or it is not a subject. It cannot be a partial subject, nor should it necessarily be analyzed as an object if it shows deviations from the subject canon. This, however, involves employing an independent definition of subject, i.e. a definition which may be applied independently of the subject tests themselves. On the definition of subject suggested in Section 2.2.2 above, that *the subject is the first argument of the argument structure*, potential oblique subjects in German should clearly be regarded as subjects. Of course, this does not free the analyst from explaining any "partial" subject behavior that may be found in German, like the inability of potential oblique subjects to pass the conjunction reduction and the control infinitive tests. Note, however, that it is only on an analysis where a subject definition is employed that questions like that are raised. Without an independent subject definition, the research community has so far been content with either the wastepaper-based object analysis or the bland and innocuous "semi-subject" analysis.

Returning to the differences between Icelandic and German with regard to the behavior of potential oblique subjects, these involve only three out of ten behavioral tests, as is evident from Table 2 where these are shaded in gray. These are control infinitives, conjunction reduction and telegraphic style. Observe that these three subject tests all share a common feature, i.e. they all involve ellipsis. This raises the question of whether the difference between Icelandic and German is really best described as a difference in grammatical relations, as opposed to a difference with regard to restrictions on ellipsis. As a matter of fact, Barðdal (2002,

2006) and Barðdal and Eythórsson (2018) have argued for the latter approach and against the former, referring among others to data presented by Bayer, Bader, and Meng (2001) which show that datives in German are generally much less inclined to be elliptic than accusatives.

One kind of argument for a "restricted ellipsis" analysis, as opposed to a "non-subject" analysis of German may be found in the grammaticality of examples like (51–52) below. All three examples involve conjunction reduction; the potential accusative subjects of *ekeln* 'feel discussed' and *dürsten* 'thirst' (51a–b) and the potential dative subject of *grauen* 'worry' (52), in the second conjuncts, are indeed left unexpressed on identity with the potential accusative subjects of *schaudern* 'feel horrified' and *hungern* 'hunger' and the potential dative subject of *schlecht werden* 'feel sick' in the first conjuncts.

German
Accusative
(51) a. **Mich** schauderte und __ **ekelte**.
me.ACC felt.horrified.3SG and Ø.ACC felt.disgusted.3SG
'I felt horrified and disgusted.'
b. **Mich hungert** nach Süßigkeiten und __
me.ACC hungers.3SG for sweets and Ø.ACC
dürstet nach Flüssigkeiten.
thirsts.3SG for fluids
'I hunger for sweets and thirst for liquids.'

Dative
(52) **Mir wird('s)** schlecht **und** __ **graut('s)** vor der
me.DAT is.3SG.it bad and Ø.DAT worries.3SG for the
Zukunft.
future
'I feel sick and worry about the future.'

The fact that examples like those are entirely grammatical in German undeniably suggests that the reason examples like (48b) above are ungrammatical is because of the mismatch in case between the subjects of the two conjoined clauses. That is, (48) has a nominative subject in the first conjunct but a dative subject in the second conjunct, while the potential subjects of the examples in (51–52) share the same morphological case.

Consider now the following examples of control infinitives from Early Modern German (Eythórsson and Barðdal 2005: 853):

German
Control infinitive
(53) a. *Hier sind wir noch halb sinnlich, und es ist äusserst naturwidrig, hier alles verleugnen wollen, was Gott dem physischen Menschen zum Labsal und zur Erfrischung hie und da am Pfade unserer Wallfarth aufgetischt hat: aber den Lebensweg darum pilgern, um an diesen Erquickungsorten zu schmausen,*

das ist so verächtlich, dass man das Auge davon
this is.3SG so disgusting that one the eye there.from
abwenden muss um ___ nicht **übel**
turn.INF must.3SG in.order.to PRO.DAT not sick
zu werden.
to become.INF

(J.H. Jung-Stilling *Rede über den Werth der Leiden*, c.1789)

'Here we are still half sensuous, and it is very much against nature to abstain from everything here that the Lord has served the physical person for comfort and refreshment here and there on the path of our pilgrimage: but to take a pilgrimage on the path of life in order to feast at these rest places, that is so disgusting that one has to turn (the eye) away *in order not to feel sick*.'

b. *Denn ein Teil dieser Erkenntnisse, die mathematischen, ist im alten Besitze der Zuverlässigkeit, und gibt dadurch eine günstige Erwartung auch für andere, ob diese gleich von ganz verschiedener Natur sein mögen. Überdem, wenn man über den Kreis der Erfahrung hinaus ist, so ist man sicher,*

durch Erfahrung nicht **widersprochen** ___ **zu**
through experience not contradicted PRO.DAT to
werden.
become.INF

(gutenberg.spiegel.de/kant/krva/krva003.htm, c.1791)

'Because a part of this knowledge, the mathematical one, has always possessed reliability, and by means of this it provides a favorable expectation for others, even though these may be of a quite different nature. Besides, if one is beyond the sphere of experience, one can be certain *not to be contradicted* by experience.'

The two examples above are the oldest examples of this type that I have so far come across in German. The first one in (53a) is from Prof. J.H. Jung Stilling's *Rede über den Werth der Leiden* 'Lecture on the Significance of Suffering', while (53b) comes from Immanuel Kant's earlier edition of *Kritik der reinen Vernunft* 'Critique of pure reason'. Kant was one of the most influential philosophers of his time, while his contemporary, Jung Stilling, was a writer and a scholar, who held academic positions at colleges and universities in Kaiserslautern, Heidelberg and Marburg. Thus, the examples in (53) do not stem from non-native speakers of the German language, nor do they stem from "illiterate" speakers of the community. In contrast, these examples come from published texts, written by grave and learned penmen who undoubtedly reviewed and edited their texts before publication. These examples can therefore not be brushed aside as irrelevant, as they were produced by members of the academic and literary elite at the time.

The two examples in (53a–b) above show different types of predicate and argument structure. The first one involves a control infinitive of a Dat-only predicate, i.e. the intransitive *übel sein/werden* 'feel/get queasy'. Observe that this is an attested example exactly corresponding to the one in (49b) above, which is supposedly ungrammatical in German. The latter example is a control infinitive containing a Dat-only passive, the intransitive *widersprochen werden* 'get contradicted, which in turn is formed by the transitive Nom-Dat verb *widersprechen* 'contradict'. In both (53a–b) the unexpressed subject corresponds to a dative argument, showing that not only datives of so-called "impersonal" verbs but also datives of passives behave syntactically as subjects at least during this period of the German language. For similar examples in Modern German, see Section 6.3.6 below.

A scrutiny of Jung Stilling's and Kant's texts also reveals that they systematically use these predicates with datives, and not, say, with nominatives. That is, in all four finite examples found with *übel sein/werden* in this text, Jung Stilling consistently uses it with a potential dative subject and not a nominative subject. One of those examples is given in (54a).

German
(54) a. *daß **der Frauen** von dem vielen und*
that the.DAT woman.DAT by the much and
*ungewohnten Essen etwas **übel geworden**.*
uncommon food somewhat sick become
'that the woman felt somewhat sick because of the large amount of rare food' (www.buecherquelle.com/jungstil/stjugend/stjugen4.htm, c.1777)
b. ***Ihnen** ist aber nicht ohne Grund von anderen*
you.DAT is.3SG but not without reason by others
***widersprochen worden** ...*
contradicted be(come)
'You are not being contradicted by others without a reason...'
(gutenberg.spiegel.de/kant/kuk/Druckversion-kukp421.htm, c.1790)

The same is true for Kant's use of the active voice *widersprechen* 'contradict' and the passive voice *widersprochen werden* 'be contradicted'. A careful examination of a randomly selected extract of Kant's texts reveals a consistent use of the dative with both the active and the passive alternants of *widersprechen* in German. Further, no examples are found with nominatives with these predicates in Kant's texts.

There is one additional explanation that might be available for the existence of examples like those in (53a–b), namely that the unexpressed argument really is in the nominative case and not in the expected dative case. However, assuming that the examples in (53a–b) above from Jung-Stilling and Kant somehow represent a covert unattested nominative use, instead of the attested dative use in (54), simply goes against scientific methods. The reason is straightforward:

i) no examples of nominative subjects are found with these predicates in the preserved and published texts by Jung-Stilling and Kant
ii) all the attested examples consistently document the use of potential dative subjects with these verbs

Thus, only a dative analysis is possible for the unexpressed argument in (53a–b) above, as a nominative analysis is unfounded.

Hence, the data in (54) above show that it is incontrovertible that potential dative subjects in German behave in the same way as ordinary nominative subjects do with respect to both conjunction reduction and control infinitives. That is, potential dative subjects in German exhibit the same ability as nominative subjects to be left unexpressed in such constructions. What is important here is that these are the two behavioral tests that have been systematically used by the scholarly community to reject a subject analysis of potential oblique subjects in German, on the basis that such examples are ungrammatical (recall the discussion around examples like 48b above).

One might now ask the question whether there is a systematic difference between the ungrammatical control infinitives in German in (49) above and the attested German control infinitives in (52), as both are found with potential oblique subject verbs as lower verbs. In Barðdal (2006: 86) I compare a whole range of attested examples of control infinitives involving oblique subject verbs across Icelandic and German, on the basis of which I propose the control construction's identity relation hierarchy given in (55) below:

(55) **The control construction's identity relation hierarchy:**
rel. pron. > PP > noun > generic pron. > unexpr. ref. > nom. pers. pron.

The controllers found in the dataset are relative pronouns, prepositional phrases, nouns, generic pronouns like *man* 'one', unexpressed generic referents retrieved from the context, and personal pronouns in the nominative case.

This implicational hierarchy specifies that it is easiest to embed oblique subject verbs in control infinitives in the Germanic languages if the controller is a relative pronoun, while it is most difficult if the controller is a personal pronoun in the nominative case. Observe that the ungrammatical example in (50b), repeated here for the sake of convenience, occupies a relatively low position on this implicational hierarchy, i.e. immediately above personal pronouns in the nominative case. This is the least favored category of controllers in terms of the implicational hierarchy. In other words, examples in which the controller is unexpressed should be deemed worse than examples in which the controller is a generic pronoun of the type *man* 'one'. These predictions are also borne out by the ungrammaticality of (50b) above where the controller is unexpressed. Compare (50b) with the apparent grammaticality of the attested examples in (53) above, where the controller is the generic pronoun *man* 'one'.

German
(50) b. Übel   __   **to** **sein** ist   nicht   angenehm.
         queasy   PRO.DAT   zu   be.INF   is.3SG not   easy
         Intended meaning: 'It is not good to feel queasy.'
                                        (Zaenen, Maling, and Thráinsson 1985: 478)

Whether the implicational hierarchy in (55) above holds for more languages than only the Germanic languages remains to be verified.

To sum up, it is clear that without a subject definition which can be applied independently from the subject tests, potential oblique subjects become less subject-like if they have fewer behavioral properties. This, in turn, raises the question of where to draw the limit between how many properties may be sufficient for an argument to qualify as being analyzed as a subject and how many are not sufficient. This is exactly the kind of methodological problems that prototype approaches to subjecthood face, as on such approaches subject becomes a gradient concept, perhaps resulting in a 70% subject analysis or a 50% subject analysis, to mention only a few possibilities resulting from this unconstrained approach. Therefore, when the prototype approach is taken to its logical conclusions, major analytical problems are uncovered. Taken together, a gradient notion of subject has no explanatory power at all, and should, as such, be dispensed with from grammatical theory.

Finally, the comparison above between Icelandic and German has shown that even when setting aside both nominative case and agreement, subjects do not behave uniformly even within one and the same language, further supporting the construction-based approach to subjecthood, suggested in Section 2.2.1 above and adopted throughout this study. In contrast, with an independent definition of subject as being the first argument of the argument structure, we may, as expected, analyze potential oblique subjects in German as exactly that, oblique subjects. The more exciting task then remains to explain why these oblique subject arguments deviate from the nominative canon. One explanation has been suggested here, namely that there are restrictions on ellipsis in German, the "restricted ellipsis" approach, which may exclude oblique subject verbs in German from occurring in constructions involving ellipsis.

At this juncture, the more alert reader may pose the question of how a scholar who rejects the idea of a subject being needed at a language-specific level may be able to use the subject tests to argue that potential oblique subjects are syntactic subjects. The reason is simple; rejecting the idea that subject exists as a language-specific category *does not mean doing away with subject and object altogether*, as is explained in Section 2.2.1 above. It only means that subjects and objects are taken to be construction specific instead of language specific, that is, they are taken to be specific for each construction. This, in turn, means that applying the subject tests on different constructions may yield different results, depending on which construction is being examined. In this section I have shown that on a language-specific approach to the grammatical relations of subject and object, the fact that oblique subjects behave differently from nominative subjects is unexpected, as such an approach entails that all subjects should behave in the same manner within a language, irrespective of the constructions they occur in. On a construction-specific approach, in contrast, it is expected that oblique subjects may behave differently from nominative subjects in some respects.

2.3.4 Acceptability judgments

Examples like (50b) above are generally regarded as ungrammatical in the literature on oblique subjects in German, despite the fact that such examples are being produced by native speakers. Given that, it is important to evaluate the validity of the assumed "ungrammaticality" of such examples. In this section I report on an acceptability study with examples of potential oblique subjects being left unexpressed in control infinitives in German. As a comparison, corresponding Icelandic examples are also included.

While languages like Icelandic and Faroese may have a special position within the Indo-European language family in that oblique subjects in these languages generally pass all the behavioral subject tests, finding examples of oblique subject verbs in conjunction reduction and control infinitives in these languages is not as easy as it may sound from the general discussion in the field. For instance, examples of oblique subject verbs in control infinitives in Icelandic have been presented in publication after publication without any caveat from the relevant researchers that such examples may not readily be found in texts (with the exception of early publications by Thráinsson 1979; Barnes 1986; and Rögnvaldsson 1996).

The most famous examples of oblique subject predicates occurring in control infinitives, introduced by Andrews (1976: 174), Thráinsson (1979: 469) and Zaenen, Maling, and Thráinsson (1985: 457), are undoubtedly collocations involving the control verb *vonast til að* 'hope to':

Icelandic
(56) a. *Ég   vonast   til   að   __   verða   bjargað.*
         I.NOM   hope   til   to   PRO.DAT   be(come).INF   saved
         'I hope to be saved.'
     b. *Ég   vonast   til   að   __   vanta   ekki   efni*
         I.NOM   hope   til   to   PRO.ACC   lack.INF   not   material
        í   ritgerðina.
         in   thesis.the
         'I hope not to lack material for the thesis.'
     c. *Ég   vonast   til   að   __   verða   hjálpað.*
         I.NOM   hope   til   to   PRO.DAT   be(come).INF   helped
         'I hope to be helped.'

However, as pointed out by Eythórsson and Barðdal (2005: 852–853), examples of oblique subject verbs embedded under *vonast til að* 'hope to' in Icelandic are not very natural. In fact, the only examples of that type that can be retrieved from online texts are constructed examples occurring in linguistic publications. No attested occurrences are found involving either *vanta* 'lack' or *vera hjálpað* 'be helped' in online texts, embedded under *vonast til að*, thus confirming Eythórsson and Barðdal's earlier claim that such examples are not idiomatic Icelandic.

Surely, with the birth and expansion of the World Wide Web, finding examples of oblique subject verbs in control infinitives has become considerably less time consuming. This includes examples which sound a great deal more natural than the examples with *vonast til að* 'hope to' above. Two such naturally occurring examples are given in (57) below, again with *vanta* 'lack' and *vera hjálpað* 'be helped', as a point of comparison:

Icelandic
(57) a. *Að   __   vanta   salt   í   blóðið,   hvað   þýðir   það?*
         to   PRO.ACC   lack.INF   sodium   in   blood.the   what   means   that
         'To lack electrolytes in the blood, what does that mean?'

b. ... þessi   maður   ætti   það   ekki   skilið   að __
       this   man   had   it   not   deserved   to PRO.DAT
   vera   hjálpað.
   be.INF   helped
   '... that this man did not deserve being helped.'

Nevertheless, despite the fact that perfectly good examples may be found in contemporary online texts, not all speakers of Icelandic agree on the quality of such occurrences. Some examples appear as being highly unidiomatic. One such is given in (58) below, involving the dative subject verb *líða illa* 'feel bad', embedded under the highly agentive matrix verb *hætta* 'stop':

Icelandic
(58) *Ég   veit!   hættu   bara   **að** __   **líða**   illa*
     I   know   stop.you   just   to PRO.DAT   feel.INF   badly
     'I know! Just stop feeling bad'

An entirely idiomatic version of this example would involve the causative *láta* 'let', as in *láta sér líða illa* 'let oneself feel badly'. Also, in a study on acceptability judgments of oblique subject verbs in control infinitives, based on a questionnaire survey with 31 participants, all native speakers of Icelandic, Barðdal and Eythórsson (2006: 160–163) document that only 6.5% of the participants found the example in (58) acceptable. A total of 29% of the participants found it strange or marginal, while as many as 64.5% found it entirely unacceptable (see Table 3). This stands in stark contrast to the felicitousness of the examples in (57), according to my judgment as a native speaker. Thus, the inevitable conclusion is that it varies from speaker to speaker and from instance to instance how examples involving oblique subject verbs in control infinitives are evaluated in Icelandic, the language in which examples of this type have hitherto been assumed to be rock solid.

Table 3: Acceptability judgments for Icelandic and German control infinitives with dative subject predicates.

	Good/OK		Strange		Bad/wrong		Total
	N	%	N	%	N	%	N
að líða illa	2	6.5	9	29.0	20	64.5	30
widersprochen zu werden	6	21.4	5	17.9	17	60.7	28

Returning to the situation in German, Barðdal and Eythórsson (2006: 151–156) also carried out a questionnaire survey equivalent to the Icelandic one, involving 28 native speakers of German, a study which generated acceptability judgments for several German examples involving oblique subject verbs in control infinitives. One of the examples they used was, as a matter of fact, Kant's example in (53b) above with *widersprochen werden* 'be contradicted'. Unexpectedly, given the standard story of German that such examples are ungrammatical, ca. 21.5% of the participants found this utterance completely grammatical, ca. 18% found it questionable or marginal, while ca. 67.5% found it unacceptable (see Table 3).

Note, also, that the acceptability of Kant's German example is, in fact, rated higher by German speakers than the acceptability of the Icelandic example with *líða illa* 'feel bad' in (28) by Icelandic speakers. That is, six of 28 participants fully accepted Kant's German example, while only two of 30 participants accepted the Icelandic example with *líða illa* 'feel bad'. However, these are only two examples, one from Icelandic and one from German. In general, what Table 3 reveals is that there is a great variation in the acceptability of oblique subject verbs embedded under control infinitives across Icelandic and German, considerably more variation than expected given the assumed dichotomy between the two languages, with control infinitives allegedly being grammatical in Icelandic but ungrammatical in German.

Further statistics, corroborating the observed variation in acceptability found in Table 3, are given in Table 4, where three additional examples of German *widersprochen zu werden* 'be contradicted' are presented. Table 4 shows that even one and the same lexical string, in this case *widersprochen zu werden* 'be contradicted', may be subjected to highly varied acceptability judgments. In Barðdal (2006: 71–72) I argue that this is due to the linguistic context and differences in the nature of the controller of the unexpressed oblique subject (recall the discussion of the control construction's identity relation hierarchy in 55 above).

Table 4: Acceptability judgments for further Icelandic and German control infinitives with dative subject predicates.

	Good/OK		Strange		Bad/wrong		Total
	N	%	N	%	N	%	N
German							
widersprochen zu werden	5	16.7	8	26.7	17	56.6	30
widersprochen zu werden	2	6.7	3	10.0	25	83.3	30
widersprochen zu werden	4	14.3	4	14.3	20	71.4	28
assistiert zu werden	11	34.4	5	15.6	16	50.0	32
Icelandic							
að þykja	16	57.1	7	25.0	5	17.9	28
að þykja	5	17.8	8	28.6	15	53.6	28

Observe, moreover, that exactly the same variation is documented for Icelandic in Table 4, with the acceptability judgments for two different examples of the same dative subject verb, *þykja* 'find, think, feel'. While 57% of the participants accepted the first instance of the infinitival *þykja*, only 18% of the same participants accepted the second example of the infinitival *þykja* in Icelandic. Again, this may well be because of the linguistic context, as I discuss in Barðdal (2006) and in the preceding section. Either way, the variation found for *líða illa* 'feel bad' and *widersprochen zu werden* 'be contradicted' in Table 3 is confirmed by a similar variation found with more examples of that string, as well as with acceptability judgments of another control infinitive in German, *assistiert zu werden* 'be assisted.'

To give some further background of these acceptability judgment studies, they all involved university students studying German or Icelandic. Also, all participants were native speakers of German or Icelandic, respectively. The acceptability judgment tasks were set up at the students' home universities in Iceland, on the one hand, and Germany and Austria, on the other. The acceptability judgment tasks were supervised by the students' instructors, their Icelandic instructors in Iceland and their German instructors in Germany and Austria. Moreover, for both languages, a control group was set up with university students in Iceland and Germany studying English, also native speakers of German and Icelandic.

An intra-control group comparison between German speakers studying German and English revealed that the native German students studying German assigned much lower acceptability scores to the German examples than their German peers studying English. The same results were obtained for the Icelandic students in that the ones studying English were much more acceptable of the relevant Icelandic control infinitives than their peers studying Icelandic. Whether this has something to do with the Icelandic and German students possibly being "tested" in their university subject (Icelandic and German), as opposed to those studying English who were not being tested in their university subject (English), is hard to know.

Note that the students studying Icelandic and German were second- and third-year students, while the ones studying English were first-year students. Whether the lower acceptability rankings of the students studying Icelandic and German is due to these individuals having a greater depth of understanding for the subtleties of their language than the students studying English is difficult to know. Also, no statistical difference was obtained between the German students in Germany and Austria. For further examples from both Icelandic and German and more detailed descriptions of the questionnaire surveys, see Eythórsson and Barðdal (2005) Barðdal (2006) and Barðdal and Eythórsson (2006).

Thus, to conclude, what this examination has shown, first of all, is that not all examples of oblique subject predicates instantiating control infinitives are regarded as grammatical in Icelandic, contrary to what is claimed in the literature. Second, this examination has demonstrated that German speakers are equally divided in their evaluation of corresponding examples in German, with some deeming them as fully acceptable, contrary to what is claimed in the literature on German.

Falling out from this is the fact that the black-and-white picture of Icelandic and German painted in the literature so far is neither realistic nor true. Examples of oblique subject verbs instantiating control infinitives in Icelandic are not unanimously accepted by Icelandic speakers. In the same manner, not all examples of corresponding examples in German are unanimously rejected by native German speakers. Thus, the alleged dichotomy between Icelandic and German assumed in the field turns out to be a difference in degree, but not a difference in kind.

2.4 Typological considerations

Further questions that arise at this point are the following:
i) To which degree does the subject definition suggested in Section 2.2.2 above have a wider typological validity?
ii) Is the subject also the first argument of the argument structure in languages with OS word order, as opposed to the Germanic languages discussed above which are all SO languages?
iii) How do ergative languages in which intransitive subjects seem to align with objects of transitive verbs and not their subjects fare in this respect?

Below I start with the first set of questions regarding languages that are generally treated as SO vs. OS, before dealing with the issue of ergative languages.

An immediate option would be to assume that the subject is the second argument of the argument structure in OS languages where the object systematically precedes the subject in clauses with neutral word order. The difference between SO and OS languages is shown in Figure 6, with SO to the left and OS to the right. This analysis entails a direct mapping between argument structure and word order. Whether this is an adequate way of modeling the mapping between grammatical relations and word order depends entirely on one's assumptions of the nature of the relation between these two.

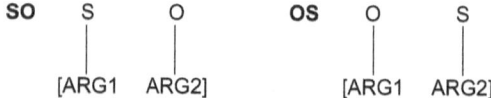

Figure 6: Direct relation between grammatical relations and word order: SO vs. OS.

However, on the present approach, the link between word order and the order of the arguments in the argument structure is indirect, determined by the iconic relation between the members of the event chain (force-dynamics), where initiators act upon endpoints; hence initiators precede endpoints in the order of the arguments in the argument structure (cf. Sections 2.2.3–2.2.4 above). In other words, the order of the arguments of the argument structure is here assumed to be the same across languages, determined by the iconicity principle, while the mapping from argument structure (or grammatical relations) to word order is language-specific, as is shown in Figure 7.

The mapping between grammatical relations and word order, in turn, will be modeled in Chapter 5 below for the Germanic languages, more specifically for Proto-Germanic which was an SO language. This involves reconstructing word order constructions for Proto-Germanic, with SO word order, shown to the left in Figure 7. As its corollary, word order constructions with OS word order may be modeled in the same fashion, except with the reverse word order, as is shown to the right in Figure 7.

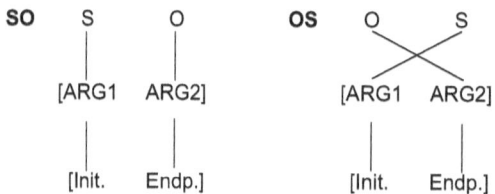

Figure 7: Indirect relation between grammatical relations and word order: SO vs. OS.

Turning now to the issue of ergative languages, the most basic concept of ergativity entails that the case marking of transitive objects is the same as the case marking of intransitive subjects, while transitive subjects have a different morphological marking. This is different from accusative languages where the transitive and the intransitive subject share case marking, while the transitive object has a different morphological marker.

However, ever since, at least, Dixon (1972, 1979), Anderson (1976), Comrie 1978), and others, ergative languages have been divided into syntactically ergative and morphologically ergative languages. To explain the difference between the two in very simple terms, morphologically ergative languages behave syntactically as accusative languages with regard to the subject tests. That is, the subject tests target the two subjects, transitive and intransitive ones alike, irrespective of case marking. In syntactically ergative languages, in contrast, the subject tests instead target intransitive subjects and transitive objects alike, in conformity with case marking.

Therefore, one may argue that case marking is simply a surface phenomenon in morphologically ergative languages, as it does not affect grammatical relations. For syntactically ergative languages, however, where intransitive subjects and transitive objects pattern together syntactically, in conformity with case marking, one may argue that the relevant tests are simply case tests and not subject tests. However, it should be noted that some of these concepts have been contested in the literature and some remain controversial up until today (Anderson 1976; Naylor 1995; Legate 2005; Anand and Nevins 2006; among others).

Irrespective of the type of analysis adopted for the so-called "syntactic ergativity" in languages like Dyirbal, the behavior of the relevant arguments is certainly not a problem for the present definition of subject as being the first argument of the argument structure. The reason is simple in that not all so-called subject tests must behave in the same way across all languages. On a constructional approach where grammatical relations are not only language-specific but also construction specific, any restrictions on each of the relevant subject tests must be properly modeled for that language.

A final question to ponder is whether there are subjects in all languages. If all languages have some type of distinction between subject and object, is it then possible to claim that subject is a universal category? In my opinion, there is no rightful place for such a manifold subject concept in universal grammar. Instead, it is most likely the need to distinguish between subjects and objects that is universal. Thus, on the present approach, subjects exist only as language-specific and construction-specific categories.

2.5 Summary

The traditional notion of subject as being in the nominative case and controlling verb agreement has been adopted into several current linguistic frameworks. As a matter of fact, this axiom is still alive and well in certain traditional linguistic circles. It was not until the quest for a universal subject concept began that this traditional notion of subject developed into a multi-faceted concept, involving both coding and behavioral properties. Nevertheless, due to several empirical problems and generally the verifiable differences between languages, all attempts to establish a uniform subject concept in universal grammar were bound to fail. What is more, even the assumption that subject exists as a language-specific category is far from unproblematic, as definitions of subject vary from one language to the other and so do the methodological choices underlying these language-specific definitions. Instead, it is argued here that a construction-specific approach to grammatical relations is considerably more fruitful, involving a definition of subject in terms of the order of the arguments in the argument structure. This order, in turn, is taken to be derived from causal conceptual structure and the force-dynamic relation holding between the participants of a given verbal event. In particular, it is the causal chain and the exertion of force of one participant on the other that decides on the ranking between the participants in the argument structure. It is briefly demonstrated how subject behavior may be modeled with the aid of the Construction Grammar formalism, a topic recurrent in Chapter 5 below.

Turning to the issue of oblique case marking and subject status, a review of the early literature on Icelandic and German actually reveals major discrepancies and inconsistencies in these initial attempts at investigating whether potential oblique subjects show subject behavior or not in the two languages. By focusing on the two subject tests that differ between Icelandic and German, conjunction reduction and control infinitives, Zaenen, Maling, and Thráinsson (1985) laid the first stone towards a major dichotomy between the two languages, according to which potential oblique subjects behave syntactically as subjects in Icelandic, but not in German. By prioritizing the coding properties at the cost of the behavioral properties, Reis (1982) authoritatively asserted the legitimacy of an analysis of potential oblique subjects in German as not being (syntactic) subjects.

To avoid the problem of having to prioritize among the subject tests, I have here argued for the need to implement an independent definition of subject into our theory and our methodology. Only on such an approach does the more interesting question arise, as to how to analyze any deviations from the subject canon. In contrast, on a prototype approach to subjecthood the researcher is simply left with the conclusion that a potential candidate for subject status may be analyzed as a 30% subject, 50% subject, or 75% subject, as unsatisfactory as that may be. It is also intrinsic in the "object approach" to German that no further questions be asked about the nature of the differences between Icelandic and German.

In contrast, analyzing potential oblique subjects in German as syntactic subjects, exactly as in Icelandic, truly prompts the researcher to dive deeper into the differences between the two languages. Thus, a further scrutiny of the situation in German has revealed that linguistic examples may actually be found, showing that oblique subject verbs do occur in both conjunction reduction and control infinitives in that language. Such a scrutiny of German, or any other language for that matter, had not been undertaken on a prototype approach, in which the scholarship seems to be content with deeming a subject-like argument as being, say, a 75% subject, nor had it been undertaken on an "object approach" to German. Instead, the scrutiny carried out here presupposes a subject definition that may be applied independently of the subject tests. Only on this last approach have questions been asked as to why only some examples of oblique subject predicates are felicitous in conjunction reduction and control infinitives in German.

3 Alternating Dat-Nom / Nom-Dat predicates

Chapter 4 below focuses on the application of the relevant subject tests on the early Germanic languages, including representative languages from all three Germanic subbranches, East, West and North Germanic. Prior to that, however, the concept of alternating predicates or alternating verbs must be introduced into this discussion, since such verbs and predicates complicate the syntactic analysis considerably. This is especially true for any historical investigation, based on corpus languages where no native speakers are available to confirm or disconfirm one's analysis. That is the topic of this chapter.

Section 3.1 provides an introduction to this concept of alternating predicates, which happen to instantiate two argument structures involving a nominative and a dative argument. The internal order of the two arguments varies, corresponding to two diametrically opposed argument structures, namely Dat-Nom and Nom-Dat, respectively. Also, statistics of word order distribution in Modern Icelandic are presented, which corroborate the alternating analysis, based on a comparison with ordinary Nom-Dat verbs and non-alternating Dat-Nom verbs. In Section 3.2 data from different Germanic languages are presented, including subsections on Modern Icelandic (3.2.1) and Modern Faroese (3.2.2), the languages from which it is easiest to retrieve the relevant evidence. Subsections on Old/Middle English (3.2.3), Old Swedish and Old Danish (3.2.4) then follow, as well as a subsection presenting data from several early / ancient Indo-European languages (3.3). Then, in Section 3.4 I suggest a way to formalize this alternation based on the formalism introduced in Chapter 2 above. Section 3.5 is devoted to the most infamous oblique subject verbs in the history of English, 'like' and 'seem', and the standard story is reviewed, originally suggested by Jespersen in 1927 and iterated by the scholarship in large. The standard story is then juxtaposed against a story involving alternating verbs, based on evidence from several (early) Germanic languages, all to the detriment of the standard story. Finally, Section 3.6 discusses the diachrony of the two constructions, alternating vs. non-alternating, including a suggestion of a relative chronology for the two types.

3.1 The concept of alternating predicates

In the following three subsections, I first introduce the general concept of alternating predicates, their event structure and their internal lack of a causal chain. This makes alternating predicates force-dynamically neutral, which in turn means that they are compatible with two types of event construals. I then, in Section 3.1.2

present criteria to identify alternating predicates, examining in particular the word order distribution found between these and non-alternating Dat-Nom verbs. Finally, in Section 3.1.3, further large-scale statistical evidence is presented from Modern Icelandic corpora, undeniably corroborating the alternating analysis for that language.

3.1.1 Event structure and construal

In Section 2.2.3 above, it is argued that grammatical relations are a derivative of argument structure, while argument structure is a derivative of causal conceptual structure of verbs and their force dynamics. Three examples are offered, namely 'kill', 'trouble' and 'like'. What is true for both 'kill' and 'trouble' is that the initiators of the killing and troubling events exert force on the endpoints, in this case physical and emotional force, while the endpoints are being subjected to this force. Thus, the initiator ranks higher than the endpoint in the causal chain, which in turn means that the initiator is mapped to the first argument of the argument structure, while the endpoint is mapped to the second argument of the argument structure.

On the present approach to grammatical relations where subject is defined as being the first argument of the argument structure, all that is needed to map participant roles to argument structure is the type of causal chain described in Section 2.2.3 above. And, as is shown in Chapter 5 below, by properly modeling the behavior of the two arguments in different clausal constructions, namely the clausal constructions that contain the subject tests, grammatical relations (syntactic roles) simply fall out from that.

In contrast, for psychological events such as 'like', two *construals* are found governing the mapping between the two arguments, the experiencer and the stimulus, both cross-linguistically and language internally. This is, of course, well known in the literature, with the two construals usually associated with 'fear' and 'frighten' verbs (Belletti and Rizzi 1988; Grimshaw 1990; Croft 1993, 1998, 2012; Pesetsky 1995; Wechsler 1995; Barðdal 2001b; among others). The difference between the two construals is the following:
a) *fear*: the experiencer directs his or her attention towards a stimulus, hence the experiencer is equated with the initiator, while the stimulus is equated with the endpoint
b) *frighten*: the stimulus affects a patient, hence the stimulus is equated with the initiator and the patent with the endpoint

As a consequence, the "causal chains" of such psychological events may be represented as in Figure 8 (inspired by Croft 2012: 233):

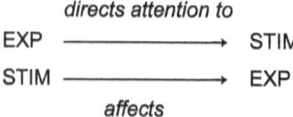

Figure 8: Force-dynamic neutrality of psychological verbs.

In the first case, it is the experiencer participant who is the first argument of the argument structure, while the stimulus participant is the second argument of the argument structure, as this construal entails that the experiencer is perceived of as the initiator and the stimulus as the endpoint in the causal chain. In the second case, it is the stimulus participant who is the first argument of the argument structure, while the experiencer participant is the second argument of the argument structure. This follows from the construal that the stimulus participant is perceived of as the initiator and the experiencer as the endpoint in the causal chain.

Regarding the 'frighten' construal, defined under the alphabetically-ordered list above, I use the label *patient*, instead of *experiencer*, since the verbal event only expresses that the initiator affects the endpoint, and not what the endpoint may feel as a consequence of this affecting event. Therefore, I believe, the label *patient* is more appropriate than that of *experiencer* (cf. Barðdal 2001c: 57–74 for a problematization of the whole concept of semantic roles, as well as a thorough discussion of the ontological status of this concept in linguistic theory, including being a derivative of verbal semantics, cf. also Croft 1998, 2012).

Moreover, I concur with Croft (1998) who claims that it is a lexical idiosyncrasy of each psychological verb, whether it conveys the 'fear' or the 'frighten' construal. In other words, neither argument structure nor grammatical relations can be derived from any semantic property of the verb, as there is no causation involved with verbs expressing psychological events. Instead, with *frighten* verbs, one may argue that the event is indeed construed as a causative event, with the stimulus linked to subject and the patient to object, even though no causation is involved. With *fear* verbs, however, the event is construed as a stative event with the experiencer directing his/her attention to a stimulus, hence the experiencer is linked to subject and the stimulus to object.

Now, ordinary 'fear' and 'frighten' verbs typically select for the Nom-Acc case frame in Icelandic. That is, the subject is in the nominative case and the object in the accusative for both 'fear' and 'frighten' verbs, irrespective of construal. This is shown in (59) below with the 'fear' construal in (59a) and the 'frighten construal' in (59b):

Icelandic
(59) a. **Ég** hræðist **hunda**.
I.NOM fear.1SG dogs.ACC
'I fear dogs.'
b. **Hundar** hræða **mig**.
dogs.NOM frighten.3PL me.ACC
'Dogs frightens me.'

Observe, now, that the alternating predicates under discussion here show a different case frame from ordinary 'fear' and 'frighten' verbs. The case frames found with alternating verbs are the Dat-Nom and Nom-Dat case frames (and possibly the Acc-Nom and Nom-Acc case frames). This entails that the animate argument is always in the dative case and the inanimate argument in the nominative case, as shown in the following two examples from Modern Icelandic:

Dat-Nom
(60) a. **Fólki** hefur fallið **íslenskt** **skyr** vel
people.DAT has.3SG fallen Icelandic.NOM milk.curds.NOM well
í geð.
in liking
'People have taken a liking to Icelandic skyr.'

Nom-Dat
b. **íslenskt** **skyr** hefur fallið **fólki** vel
Icelandic.NOM milk.curds.NOM has.3SG fallen people.DAT well
í geð.
in liking
'Icelandic skyr has been to people's liking.'

One might now ask the question of why some verbs typical of the first construal in Figure 8 above, where the animate subject directs his or her attention towards a stimuli, show up in the nominative case, as in (59a) above, while other verbs, also with animate subjects, show up with their subjects in the dative case, as in (60a) above. As has repeatedly been noted in the literature on verbal semantics and case marking in Icelandic, this is because verbs occurring with animate subjects in the nominative are perceived of as being more "agentive" than verbs with animate subjects in the dative case (cf. Jónsson 1997–98, 2003; Barðdal 2004). In other words, verbs expressing psychological events and occurring with their animate subjects in the nominative case adhere strictly to the force-dynamic construal that the animate subject is the initiator of the causal chain, acting upon an endpoint, irrespective of non-linguistic reality.

3.1.2 Identifying alternating predicates

Having now explained why alternating predicates are compatible with two diametrically opposed argument structure constructions, i.e. Dat-Nom and Nom-Dat, I now continue to demonstrate how such alternating predicates may be identified syntactically.

Starting with the attested examples in (61) below, the relevant predicate is a compositional one, *falla í skaut* 'fall in sb's lap', which assigns dative case to the animate argument, the receiver, and nominative to the inanimate argument, the item being received. This case assignment takes place irrespective of the internal order of the two arguments in the argument structure and, hence, irrespective of the order of the arguments in constructions exemplifying neutral word order. For a formalization of this alternation, see Section 3.4 below.

Dat-Nom

(61) a. **Jóhannesi** úr Kötlum hafa bæði fallið í skaut
John.DAT from Katlar.DAT have.3PL both fallen in lap
færri krónur og skemmri ferðalög en ...
fewer krones.NOM and shorter trips.NOM than
'Jóhannes úr Kötlum has had both less money and fewer trips fall in his lap than ...'   (*Þjóðviljinn*, 1951)

Nom-Dat

b. **Bókaverðlaun** barnanna hafa sex sinnum fallið
book.award.NOM children.GEN have.3PL six times fallen
honum í skaut.
him.DAT in lap
'The children's book award has fallen in his lap six times.'
(https://www.forlagid.is/vara/draumatjofurinn)

These examples have been chosen particularly because they involve both a finite and a non-finite verb, *hafa fallið í skaut* 'have fallen in sb's lap', where the temporal auxiliary *hafa* is finite, while the main predicate, *falla í skaut*, is nonfinite. Therefore, these examples clearly demonstrate the subject and object positions in Icelandic. The subject occurs in front of the finite verb in clauses with neutral word order. The object, in contrast, follows the verb in clauses with neutral word order, either the finite verb with simple tenses or the nonfinite verb, when the tense is expressed periphrastically, as it is here. Again, it is exactly for that reason that the examples in (61) above have been chosen; they are in the perfective, which requires both a finite and a non-finite verb. As a native speaker of Icelandic, I also confirm that both examples in (61a–b) exhibit neutral word order. Thus, one of the orders is not a topicalization of the other.

Notice that in (61a) the dative argument, *Jóhannesi úr Kötlum*, occurs in first position immediately preceding the finite verb *hafa* 'have', which is the subject position in Icelandic. The nominative, however, *færri krónur og skemmri ferðalög* 'less money and shorter trips', follows the nonfinite *fallið í skaut* 'fallen in sb's lap', which is the object position in Icelandic. Recall the discussion in Section 1.3 above where it is shown that syntactic objects in Icelandic systematically occur in the position following the verb, thus they behave differently from subjects. Hence, this word order shows that the dative is the subject and the nominative the object in (61a).

In contrast, in (61b) the order is exactly the opposite, the nominative *bókaverðlaun* 'book award' occupies the preverbal position, while the dative, *honum* 'him', occupies the position following the non-finite verb. This word order shows that the nominative is the subject and the dative the object in (61b). As stated above, both examples are neutral with regard to information structure, topicalization is ruled out, as this would involve subject-verb inversion, which is not found here, and no topicalization intonation is found either. Cf. further the discussion about neutral word order in Icelandic in Section 1.3 above, in particular ex. (16–17).

In addition to the subject occurring in first position in Icelandic and preceding the finite verb, as is shown in (61) above the subject may also immediately follow the finite verb in structures involving subject-verb inversion. This inversion of the subject and the verb is found with certain clause types like questions and topicalizations. It is also possible to use verb-subject orders in ordinary declarative clauses, a phenomenon generally referred to as *narrative inversion* in the literature on Icelandic (Sigurðsson 1983, 2018, 2019; Platzack 1985; Thráinsson 2007; Franco 2008), also found in Germanic in general (Platzack 1987; Önnerfors 1997; Lindström 2001; Mörnsjö 2002; Lindström and Karlsson 2005; van Kampen 2020).

Dat-Nom
(62) a. *Hafa* **Jóhannesi** *úr Kötlum bæði fallið í skaut*
have.3PL John.DAT from Katlar.DAT both fallen in lap
***færri krónur** og **skemmri ferðalög** en ...*
fewer krones.NOM and shorter trips.NOM than
'Has Jóhannes úr Kötlum had both less money and fewer trips fall in his lap than ...?'

Nom-Dat

b. *Hafa* **bókaverðlaun** *barnanna sex sinnum fallið*
have.3PL book.award.NOM children.GEN six times fallen
honum *í skaut?*
him.DAT in lap
'Has the children's book award fallen in his lap six times?'

Note that the position of the object is not affected by subject-verb inversion, as the object continues to occupy the position immediately following the nonfinite verb, as is shown in (62) above.

In (62a) the dative *Jóhannesi* inverts with the finite verb, while the nominative *færri krónur* 'less money' remains in the object position. In contrast, in (61b) it is the nominative *bókaverðlaunin* 'the book awards' that inverts with the verb, while the dative remains in the object position following the nonfinite verb. This shows, as a matter of fact, that the first position of the dative in (61a) and the nominative in (61b) is not due to topicalization, but represents neutral word order.

The conclusion to draw at this point is that the word order in the two examples in (61) above reflects the argument structure in each of the two examples. That is, *falla í skaut* 'fall in sb's lap' instantiates two diametrically opposite argument structure constructions, namely either Dat-Nom or Nom-Dat, although, of course, not both at the same time (cf. Barðdal 2001b; Barðdal, Eythórsson, and Dewey 2014, 2019). This will be further elaborated on in Section 3.2.1 below which deals with alternating predicates in Icelandic).

Consider the option to analyze one of the orders as representing neutral word order, while the other might be a topicalization of the first one, as is briefly argued against above. The problem with such an analysis is that an alternating analysis for predicates like *falla í skaut* is corroborated by a host of subject tests, which clearly demonstrate that the first argument behaves syntactically as a subject, while the second argument behaves syntactically as an object, valid for both the Dat-Nom and the Nom-Dat orders (Bernódusson 1982: 37–38; Jónsson 1997–98: 14–15; Barðdal 1999a, 2001b; Platzack 1999; Thráinsson 2007: 162–163; Rott 2013, 2016; Wood and Sigurðsson 2014; Barðdal, Eythórsson, and Dewey 2014, 2019). Again, further evidence in favor of this alternating analysis is presented in Section 3.2.1 below.

The more observant reader may have noticed that my terminology has shifted from *experiencer* and *stimulus* to *animate* and *inanimate argument*, as the stimulus is inanimate in most cases. Another reason is that alternating predicates are not confined to verbs expressing psychological events, but are found with several semantic classes of Dat-Nom verbs, including inchoatives of the type in (61–62) above (cf. Section 3.2.1 below). As a matter of fact, this is not only true for alternating predicates in Icelandic, but for oblique subject predicates in general in the Germanic languages, as well as in the early and archaic Indo-European languages (cf. Barðdal 2001b, 2004; Barðdal et al. 2012; Barðdal et al. 2016; Möhlig-Falke 2012; Viti 2017; Middeke 2021).

Verbs and compositional predicates of this type, i.e. showing the ability to alternate between two diametrically opposed argument structure constructions, were first discussed in an Icelandic master's thesis by Bernódusson (1982), where it is shown that both word orders are equally neutral. This stands in stark contrast with "ordinary" Dat-Nom verbs in Icelandic which do not show this alternation. One such example is found with the verb *skiljast* 'gather', as is evident from (63) below, where the dative precedes the finite verb in (63a), while the nominative follows the nonfinite verb. In turn, the opposite order of the arguments is ungrammatical, as is shown in (63b), where the nominative is in first position and the dative follows the nonfinite verb:

Dat-Nom

(63) a. *Hún sagði að **þeim** hefði loksins skilist **það**.*
she said that them.DAT had.3SG finally gathered it.NOM
'She said that they had finally gathered it.'

*Nom-Dat

b. **Hún sagði að **það** hefði loksins skilist **þeim**.*
she said that it.NOM had.3SG finally gathered them.DAT
Intended meaning: 'She said that it had finally been understandable to them.'

Observe that if *skiljast* 'gather' were an alternating verb, both word orders in (63) should be grammatical, exactly as with *falla í skaut* 'fall in sb's lap' in (61) above. Instead, what the examples in (63) show is that only the Dat-Nom argument structure is allowed with *skiljast* 'gather' in Icelandic.

Consider now the following examples involving verb-subject orders, also with *skiljast* 'gather'.

Dat-Nom

(64) a. *Hafði **þeim** loksins skilist **það**?*
had.3SG them.DAT finally gathered it.NOM
'Had they finally gathered it?'

***Nom-Dat**
b. *Hafði **það** *loksins skilist* **þeim?**
had.3SG it.NOM finally gathered them.DAT
Intended meaning: 'Had it finally been understandable to them?'

It is the dative in (64a) that behaves syntactically as a subject in that it inverts with the finite verb when the verb occupies the first position, The nominative argument, in contrast, continues to follow the nonfinite verb, exactly as it does in (63a). Thus, the nominative in (64a) behaves syntactically as an object, while the example in (64b) is ungrammatical in Icelandic, exactly as (63b) above. This word order distribution shows beyond doubt that *skiljast* is not an alternating verb in Icelandic but only a Dat-Nom verb.

At this juncture it is appropriate to mention that subjects may of course occur later in the clause in both Icelandic and the Germanic languages in general. This is typically found for indefinite and heavy subjects, which again means that such structures do not represent neutral word order. Such examples will not be discussed further here.

To sum up so far, the Dat-Nom verb *skiljast* 'gather' is syntactically different from the Dat-Nom predicate *falla í skaut* 'fall in sb's lap', in that the former only instantiates the Dat-Nom argument structure construction, while the latter may instantiate both the Dat-Nom and the Nom-Dat constructions. Section 3.2.1 below documents further syntactic differences between the two predicates, taking as a point of departure the established subject tests in Icelandic, presented in Section 1.3 above. The remainder of Section 3.2 is, subsequently, devoted to documenting that alternating predicates of this type are not confined to Icelandic but are found across the Germanic languages. Further, Section 3.3 focuses on data from the early and archaic Indo-European languages that are also consistent with an alternating analysis.

3.1.3 Word order statistics

Before diving into the data in the subsequent sections, it is appropriate to introduce some statistical evidence to corroborate the alternating analysis argued for here, in this case on the basis of Modern Icelandic (for corresponding statistics for German, see Section 6.3.1 below). For this purpose, Table 5 introduces word order statistics for verbs selecting for three types of argument structure constructions in Icelandic, namely Nom-Dat, non-alternating Dat-Nom, and alternating Dat-Nom / Nom-Dat in Modern Icelandic texts (cf. Somers and Barðdal 2022). The relevant verbs in the three categories are the following:

Nom-Dat

i) *hjálpa* 'help' *líkjast* 'resemble', *mótmæla* 'contradict', *þakka* 'thank' *treysta* 'trust',

Dat-Nom

ii) *áskotnast* 'receive', *blöskra* 'be shocked', *leiðast* 'be bored', *líka* 'like', *þykja* 'think, find, seem'

Dat-Nom / Nom-Dat

iii) *duga* 'suffice', *dyljast* 'fail to notice, be hidden', *endast* 'last', *henta* 'suit', *nægja* 'suffice'

The data have been gathered from the Icelandic Ten Ten 20 corpus which contains 518 million running words retrieved from the World Wide Web (for general information about the Ten Ten corpus family, see Jakubíček et al. 2013).[1] As much as 10,000 instances of each verb have been extracted from the Ten Ten corpus, of which the first 200 eligible tokens have been annotated for different variables including case marking. These 200 tokens all involve active clauses, both main clauses and subordinate clauses, excluding relative clauses, with one of the two arguments occurring in first position, immediately preceding the finite verb, while the other argument occurs post-verbally, either immediately following the finite verb in simple clauses or immediately following the non-finite verb in complex clauses. Examples with reflexive objects are excluded, although both nominal and pronominal fillers are otherwise included in the eligible tokens.

Table 5 only includes examples involving two full NPs, in order to avoid pronominal influence. Starting with ordinary Nom-Dat verbs like *hjálpa* 'help' which are unambiguous Nom-Dat verbs in the sense that the nominative is the subject and the dative the object, it turns out that neutral word order (Nom-Dat) is found in 98% of the cases, while topicalizations (Dat-Nom) are only found in 2% of the cases. These numbers contribute to establishing a baseline for how common topicalization is in Icelandic when the two arguments are full NPs.

The proportions for non-alternating Dat-Nom verbs like *líka* 'like', where the dative behaves syntactically as a subject and the nominative as an object, are specified under B in Table 5. As a matter of fact, the relevant numbers turn out to be the exact converse of what is found with *hjálpa* verbs, with Dat-Nom found in 96% of the cases, although this time it represents neutral word order, while the Nom-Dat word order is found in 4% of the cases, involving topicalization. These numbers

---

[1] https://www.sketchengine.eu/isTenTen-Icelandic-corpus

further corroborate the baseline for how common topicalizations are, namely ranging from 2–4% in the texts found in the Icelandic Ten Ten corpus when both arguments are full NPs.

Table 5: Dat-Nom and Nom-Dat linear order with three classes of verbs.

	Dat-Nom		Nom-Dat	
	N	f	N	f
A: Nom-Dat *hjálpa* verbs				
hjálpa 'help'	0	0%	25	100%
líkjast 'resemble'	0	0%	125	100%
mótmæla 'contradict'	2	2%	98	98%
treysta 'trust'	0	0%	31	100%
þakka 'thank'	0	0%	55	100%
B: Dat-Nom *líka* verbs				
líka 'like'	28	100%	0	0%
áskotnast 'receive'	48	100%	0	0%
blöskra 'be shocked'	68	100%	0	0%
leiðast 'be bored'	26	100%	0	0%
þykja 'think, find, seem'	23	96%	1	4%
C: Dat-Nom/Nom-Dat *nægja* verbs				
henta 'suit, befit'	0	0%	86	100%
duga 'suffice'	9	21%	33	79%
dyljast 'be hidden'	6	75%	2	25%
endast 'last'	22	70%	9	30%
nægja 'suffice'	23	46%	27	54%

Consider now the word order statistics for alternating Dat-Nom / Nom-Dat verbs, where far more variation is found than with either Nom-Dat or Dat-Nom verbs. The proportions between the two word orders with alternating verbs range from 75–25% to 21–79% for Dat-Nom vs. Nom-Dat linear orders. This excludes the numbers for the verb *henta* 'suit', which appears to systematically occur with the Nom-Dat word order, despite the fact that native speakers find both word orders, Dat-Nom and Nom-Dat, equally neutral (cf. Barðdal 2001b). I will not dwell further on the issue of *henta* here, but let it suffice to point out that alternating Dat-Nom / Nom-Dat verbs deviate considerably from the baseline established for Nom-Dat *hjálpa* verbs, a baseline which was further confirmed for non-alternating Dat-Nom *líka* verbs. This baseline for topicalizations vs. neutral word order involves 2–4% topicalizations vs. 96–98% neutral word order for these two verb classes, which is considerably less than 21% vs. 79% for alternating verbs, in its most extreme case with *duga* 'suffice', but ranging from there to 46% vs. 54% with *nægja* 'suffice'.

In other words, the verb *nægja* 'suffice', shows almost a 50–50 distribution between the two word orders, Dat-Nom and Nom-Dat, which is unexpected on the assumption that one of the word orders represents neutral word order and the other a topicalization thereof. Rather, this 46%–54% distribution, to be accurate, can only be explained on the assumption that *nægja* is an alternating verb which may instantiate two diametrically opposed argument structure constructions, namely the Dat-Nom and Nom-Dat argument structure constructions.

3.2 Alternating Dat-Nom / Nom-Dat predicates in the Germanic languages

I start below with data from two modern languages, Icelandic (3.2.1) and Faroese (3.2.2), where relevant evidence may easily be extracted from internet texts and native speakers. The historical material is, of course, much more uncertain, but there are data, I believe, which speak for an alternating predicate analysis in the history of English (3.2.3), the history of Swedish and Danish (3.2.4), as well as in the history of the Germanic and Early and Ancient Indo-European languages in general (3.3).

3.2.1 Modern Icelandic

In addition to word order distribution, further tests that distinguish between subjects and objects in Modern Icelandic involve conjunction reduction, reflexivization, both clause-bound and long-distance, raising-to-subject, raising-to-object and control infinitives, as already discussed in Section 1.3 and Chapter 2. I now compare the behavior of the two predicates, *skiljast* 'gather' and *falla í skaut* 'fall in sb's lap', in Modern Icelandic in order to document with robust evidence that *skiljast* is a non-alternating Dat-Nom verb, while *falla í skaut* is an alternating Dat-Nom / Nom-Dat verb. Before this comparison, however, a few words on the semantics of the Dat-Nom construction are in order.

Oblique subject constructions are generally discussed in the literature as being experiencer constructions cross-linguistically, with the dative holding the semantic role of an experiencer (Belletti and Rizzi 1988; Haspelmath 2001; Rákosi 2006; Fedriani 2014; Serzant 2015; among others). This is, of course, a gross simplification of the empirical facts, as a wide array of verbal semantics are found with not only the oblique subject construction in general but also the dative subject construction. For Modern Icelandic, for instance, I have analyzed as many as 111 verbs and compositional predicates as belonging to the alternating type, out of ca. 650–700 dative subject predicates in general (cf. Barðdal 2001b: 53–58). The simple verbs, which are in a minority, are the following:

(65) *berast* 'receive', *birtast* 'appear', *bragðast* 'taste', *duga* 'suffice', *dyljast* 'be not aware of sth', *endast* 'last', *falla vel* 'like, please', *fara vel* 'suit', *fylgja* 'accompany', *gagnast* 'be of use to', *glatast* 'be lost to', *henta* 'please, suit', *hverfa* 'be lost to sby', *hæfa* 'suit', *nýtast* 'be of use to', *nægja* 'suffice', *opinberast* 'appear in a vision', *passa* 'please, suit', *reynast* 'prove, turn out to', *smakkast* 'taste', *sóma* 'be proper, suit', *sækjast vel* 'go well/badly', *sæma* 'be proper, suit', *vitrast* 'appear in vision', *þóknast* 'please, suit'

In addition to these full verbs, several compositional predicates are also found, either with the verbs *vera/verða* 'be/become' or with other light verb constructions like *bera* 'carry', *falla* 'fall', *fara* 'go', *hrjóta* 'jump' *koma* 'come', *líða* 'glide', *liggja* 'lie', *leika* 'dance, hop', *rata* 'find', *renna* 'run', *standa* 'stand', *stíga* 'rise', *svella* 'swell' and *vaxa* 'grow'. The predicative part itself can either consist of a nominative noun, an adverbialized adjective (in the neuter), or a prepositional phrase. Some of the compositional predicates are composed from the lexical verbs given in (65) with further modifying manner elements or attributes specifying bodily location. These are listed in (66) below, according to the semantic classification suggested in Barðdal (2004) and further elaborated on by Somers (2021) for Modern German, Barðdal, Smitherman, et al. (2012) for the early Indo-European languages, and Barðdal, Arnett, et al. (2016) for the early Germanic languages):

(66) **Gain:** *berast í hendur* 'receive', *falla í hlut* 'fall in sb's lot' *falla e-ð í skaut* 'fall in sb's lap', *koma að gagni* 'be of use to'

Emotion: *falla í geð* 'like, please', *liggja e-ð á hjarta* 'be anxious', *renna til rifja* 'cut to the quick', *renna kalt vatn milli skinns og hörunds* 'be terrified', *reynast erfitt* 'find sth difficult', *vera e-ð á móti skapi* 'dislike', *vera e-ð fjarri skapi* 'dislike', *vaxa e-ð í augum* 'find sth more difficult than it really is', *veitast auðvelt* 'find sth easy', *vera auðvelt* 'find easy', *vera erfitt* 'find difficult', *vera e-ð í lófa lagið* 'be easy for sby', *vera kært* 'be dear', *vera e-m (mikil) kvöl* 'be painful for sby', *vera ljúft* 'be a pleasure', *vera (ó)gerlegt* 'find (im)possible', *vera (ó)mögulegt* 'be (im)possible for sby', *vera til ama* 'be disturbing', *vera þvert um geð* 'dislike'

Cognition: *festast í minni* 'stick in sby's memory', *greypast í minni* 'stuck in sby's mind', *hverfa veröldin* 'sleep for a while', *koma á óvart* 'surprise', *líða ekki úr hug/minni* 'be unable to forget', *koma spánskt fyrir sjónir* 'find sth strange', *koma við* 'be of sby's business', *stíga til höfuðs* 'go to sby's head', *vera augljóst* 'be obvious', *vera efst í huga* 'think of sth more than anything else', *vera e-ð fyrir mestu* 'be most important for sby', *vera framandi* 'be alien to sby', *vera hugleikið* 'be important to sby', *vera í fersku minni* 'remember vividly', *vera í sjálfsvald sett* 'have the authority to decide for oneself', *vera ljóst* 'be obvious', *vera mikilvægt* 'be important for sby', *vera minnisstætt* 'remember vividly', *vera e-ð mótfallið* 'be against sth, *vera ókunnur* 'be unknown to sby', *vera ókunnugt* 'be unknowing about sth', *vera óskiljanlegt* 'be incomprehensible', *vera e-m ráðgáta* 'be a mystery to sby', *vera til efs* 'doubt sth', *vera uppörvun* 'be an encouragement'

Enabling: *standa til boða* 'be offered sth', *verða að góðu* 'be good for sby', *vera að kostnaðarlausu* 'be without cost', *vera frjálst* 'be free', *vera fyrir bestu* 'be best for sby', *vera hollt* 'be healthy for sby', *vera kærkomið* 'be welcome', *vera velkomið* 'be welcome to', *verða til happs* 'be of luck', *verða til lífs* 'facilitate survival'

Success: *fara e-ð vel úr hendi* 'do sth well', *leika í lyndi* 'go well', *vera allir vegir færir* 'be able to do anything', *vera ekkert að vanbúnaði* 'be fully prepared', *vinnast e-ð vel* 'make good progress'

Failure: *falla verk úr hendi* 'fail to do sth'

Hindrance: *koma í koll* 'get in trouble', *standa fyrir þrifum* 'be hampered by sth', *vera allar bjargir bannaðar* 'be in a hopeless situation', *vera glatað* 'be lost to sby', *vera dýrkeypt* 'suffer, pay dearly for sth', *vera ofraun* 'be too difficult', *vera ofvaxið* 'be beyond sby's power', *vera ofviða* 'be too difficult', *vera (ó)heimilt* 'be prohibited/allowed', vera *ókleift* 'be impossible', *vera um megn* 'be too overwhelming for sby', *verða að falli* 'cause a downfall', *verða að fótakefli* 'be a hindrance', *vera þyrnir í augum* 'be a thorn in sby's side/flesh'

Natural Disposition: *vera eðlislægt* 'sth comes naturally for sby', *vera eiginlegt* 'sth comes naturally for sby', *vera í blóð borið* 'have a natural talent for sth', *vera tamt* 'be natural for sby', *vera til lista lagt* 'have a talent'

Accidental Speaking: *hrjóta af vörum* 'let words slip', *ratast á munn* 'accidentally speak', *svella í munni* 'be verbally exaggerated'

Regarding the semantics of these verbs and compositional predicates, it is generally assumed in the literature that oblique subject verbs are experiencer verbs with a stative meaning. This, however, is not true. A generalization falling out from the semantics of the narrowly circumscribed verb subclasses above pertains to aktionsart or aspect. It so happens that these predicates are not only stative but also inchoative, i.e. expressing change of state (cf. Barðdal 2001b). Some examples of inchoatives are *berast* 'receive, *birtast* 'appear', *openberast* 'appear', *vitrast* 'appear in vision', *koma á óvart* 'surprise', *koma í koll* 'get in trouble' and *hrjóta af vörum* 'let words slip, to mention only a few of the relevant inchoative predicates.

Turning now to the syntactic behavior of the two arguments, the nominative and the dative, of *falla í skaut* 'fall in sb's lap' and *skiljast* 'gather', I have already shown in 3.1 above that *falla í skaut* allows for both Dat-Nom and Nom-Dat word order in clauses expressing neutral word order and in clauses containing questions, while *skiljast* only allows for the Dat-Nom word order under the same conditions. The remaining subject tests of relevance are the following:
- Conjunction Reduction
- Clause-bound reflexivization
- Long-distance reflexivization
- Raising-to-subject
- Raising-to-object
- Control infinitives

For a documentation of how ordinary nominative subjects and ordinary accusative and dative objects in Modern Icelandic behave with regard to these tests, see Section 1.3 above, where the baseline for nominative subjects vs. accusative and dative objects is established. There it is shown that the behavioral tests in the bulleted list above clearly tease apart nominative subjects, on the one hand, and accusative and dative objects, on the other.

In the remainder of this section, I show how the two arguments, the dative and the nominative, of alternating *falla í skaut* 'fall in sb's lap' and non-alternating *skiljast* 'gather' behave. Starting with Conjunction Reduction, consider the following examples which again illustrate the asymmetry between *falla í skaut* 'fall in sb's lap' and *skiljast* in Icelandic, established in 3.1 above:

Dat-Nom
(67) a. *Einleikarinn   stóð   sig   frábærlega   og   ___   féll*
       solo.player.NOM stood REFL fantastically and   Ø.DAT   fell
       sá   heiður   í   skaut   að   ...
       the.NOM   honor.NOM in   lap   to
       'The solo player performed incredibly well and had the honor fall into his lap to ...'

Nom-Dat

> *Verkið   var   boðið   út   og   __   féll*
> job.the.NOM was   put.up.for.tender out   and Ø.NOM fell
> ***öðrum   í   skaut.***
> another.DAT in   lap
> 'The contract was put up for tender and fell in somebody else's lap.'

In (67a) the dative of *falla í skaut* is left unexpressed in the second conjunct on the basis of identity with *einleikarinn* 'solo player' in the first conjunct. The nominative *heiður* 'honor' is expressed and occupies the object position following the finite verb *féll* 'fell'. In (67b), the opposite is found in that the nominative of *falla í skaut* is left unexpressed in the second conjunct on the basis of identity with *verkið* 'job' in the first conjunct. The dative *öðrum* 'others' is expressed and occupies the object position following the finite verb *féll* 'fell'. These examples show that the behavior of the two arguments with regard to conjunction reduction supports the conclusion from Section 3.1 above that *falla í skaut* may instantiate two diametrically opposed argument structures, namely both Dat-Nom and Nom-Dat. This is not true for *skiljast* 'gather' as is shown in (68) below:

Dat-Nom

(68) a. *Ég   þekki engan   í   fjarnámi   og   __*
         I.NOM know   nobody.ACC in   distance.learning and   Ø.DAT
         skilst að   það sé   ekki í   boði.
         gather that it   is.3sg   not   in   offer
         'I know nobody [studying] through distance learning and [I] understand that it is not offered.'

*****Nom-Dat**

> **Fjarnám*   getur   verið   erfitt   og   __   hefur*
> distance.learning.NOM can   been   difficult and   Ø.NOM has
> ***mér   alltaf   skilist.***
> me.DAT   always   gathered
> Intended meaning: 'Distance learning can be difficult and [that] I have always gathered.'

These examples show that the nominative of *skiljast* 'gather' cannot be left unexpressed in conjoined clauses, but only the dative, evident from the contrast in grammaticality between (68a) and (68b). This means that *skiljast* can only instantiate the Dat-Nom argument structure construction and not the Nom-Dat construction, while *falla í skaut* 'fall in sb's lap' can instantiate either one.

Turning to clause-bound reflexivization, the examples in (69) below show that either the dative in Dat-Nom structures or the nominative in Nom-Dat structures with *falla í skaut* 'fall in sb's lap' may bind a reflexive, indeed speaking for a subject analysis of the dative in (69a) and the nominative in (69b).

Dat-Nom
(69) a. **Skáldkonunni**$_i$ *féll í skaut þessi* **gáfa** **sín**$_i$
poetess.the.DAT fell in lap this.NOM gift.NOM REFL.NOM
/***hennar**$_i$ *að geta skrifað ljóð.*
hers to be.able.to written poetry
'The poetess had this gift of hers fall in her lap, to be able to write poetry.'

Nom-Dat
b. **Eiginmaðurinn**$_i$ *féll þessari* **konu** **sinni**$_i$ /***hans**$_i$ *í*
husband.the.NOM fell this.DAT wife.DAT REFL.DAT his in
skaut alveg óvænt.
lap quite unexpectedly
'The husband fell in his wife's lap, quite unexpectedly.'

In addition, these examples also show that subject binding does not involve a choice between a reflexive and a personal pronoun, as is the case with object binding in Icelandic, but is instead confined to reflexives. In Section 1.3 above, where the baseline for nominative subjects was established, it was shown that subjects only bind reflexives, while objects have a choice between binding reflexives and personal pronouns.

I return to object binding below, but prior to that, let us examine how binding works with the verb *skiljast*.

Dat-Nom
(70) a. **Henni**$_i$ *skildist á sínu* **fólki**$_i$ *að* ...
her.DAT gathered on REFL.DAT people.DAT that
'She understood from her people that...'

***Nom-Dat**
***Það**$_i$ *skildist á* **fólkinu**$_i$ *sínu að* ...
it.NOM gathered on people.the.DAT REFL.DAT that

It turns out that of the two arguments with *skiljast*, only the dative may bind a reflexive while the nominative cannot. Of course, one might now argue that the ungrammaticality of (70b) is due to the inanimacy of the nominative argument. This may well be the case, although the remaining examples in this section show that *skiljast* does not instantiate a Nom-Dat construction at all. I therefore interpret these examples as demonstrating that there is an asymmetry between *falla í skaut* and *skiljast* in that the former may instantiate two argument structures, Dat-Nom and Nom-Dat, while the latter can only instantiate the Dat-Nom argument structure construction.

As stated above, object binding differs from subject binding in Icelandic in that only subjects may bind reflexives while objects have a choice between binding reflexives and personal pronouns. To demonstrate this for object binding, two examples are provided in (71) with *falla í skaut* 'fall in sb's lap'.

Dat-Nom

(71) a. *Honum   féll   ákveðin   kona$_i$ í   skaut   með   öllu*
        him.DAT fell   certain.NOM   woman.NOM   in lap   with all
        sínu$_i$ / hennar$_i$ hafurtaski.
        REFL   her   impedimenta
        'He had a certain woman fall in his lap with all her impedimenta.'

Nom-Dat

b. *Eiginmaðurinn   féll   eiginkonunni$_i$ í   skaut   með   öllu*
    husband.the.NOM   fell   wife.DAT   in   lap   with   all
    sínu$_i$ / hennar$_i$ fylgdarliði.
    REFL   her   retinue
    'The husband fell in his wife's lap with all her retinue.'

Observe that the nominative *ákveðin kona* 'certain woman' in (71a) may bind both a reflexive and a personal pronoun in the adjunct phrase, and the same is true for the dative *eiginkonunni* 'the wife' in (71b). In other words, the examples in (71) demonstrate that the nominative in (71a) and the dative in (71b) behave syntactically as objects, and not as subjects, with regard to clause-internal binding.

Issues are more complicated with the verb *skiljast* 'gather' since its nominative object cannot be animate, making it difficult to illustrate the object behavior of this argument with respect to binding. However, *skiljast* may also occur with an animate prepositional object, as is evident from (70a) above, and, to be sure, this animate prepositional object behaves syntactically as an object with respect to binding, as is shown in (72) below.

Dat-Nom

(72) a. *Henni   skildist   á   manninum$_i$ með   allt   hafurtaskið*
        her.DAT gathered   on   man.the.DAT   with   all   impedimenta
        sitt$_i$ / hans$_i$ að   ...
        REFL   his   that
        'She understood from the man with all his impedimenta that . . .'

However, since the object in (72) is not in the nominative case, this example cannot serve as evidence for the object behavior of the nominative of *skiljast* 'gather'. This example does, however, corroborate the subject analysis of the dative argument of the verb *skiljast* 'gather', established with respect to binding in (70a) above.

Long-distance reflexivization entails that the subject of the main clause binds a reflexive in a subordinate clause, an *að* 'that' clause in (73a) but an adjunct clause in (73b).

Dat-Nom

(73) a. **Eiginkonunni**$_i$ *féll það í skaut að gera*
wife.the.DAT fell it.NOM in lap to do.INF
eiginmanninum það ljóst að hann skyldi ekki
husband.the.DAT it clear that he.NOM should not
svíkja **sig**$_i$.
betray.INF REFL
'The wife had it fall into her lap to make it clear to her husband not to betray her.'

Nom-Dat

b. **Undirsáti**$_i$ *féll embættinu í skaut sem vildi*
underling.NOM fell office.the.NOM in lap who wanted
láta koma vel fram við **sig**$_i$.
let.INF come.INF well forward with REFL
'An underling fell into the office's lap who wanted to be treated well.'

In (73a) the dative *eiginkonunni* 'the wife' in the main clause binds the reflexive *sig* in the subordinate *að* 'that' clause. The nominative subject *hann* 'he' in this subordinate clause does not bind the reflexive *sig*, so this is not clause-bound reflexivization, but instead long-distance reflexivization. In (73b), moreover, the nominative subject *undirsáti* 'underling' binds the reflexive object *sig* in the relative clause. These examples therefore show that either the dative or the nominative of *falla í skaut* may bind long-distance reflexives, a behavior that is confined to subjects in Icelandic.

Turning now to the non-alternating verb *skiljast* 'gather', the example in (74) shows that the dative *eiginkonunni* 'the wife' in the matrix clause indeed controls the reflexive *sig* in the subordinate *að* 'that' clause, exactly as is expected by a subject:

(74) a. **Eiginkonunni**ᵢ skildist   á   eiginmanninumⱼ   að   hann
         wife.DAT   gathered   on   husband.the.DAT that he
         myndi   ekki   svíkja   **sig**ⱼ.
         would   ekki   betray.INF   REFL
         'The wife gathered from the husband that he would not betray her.'

The problem with the verb *skiljast* 'gather' is that its nominative in Dat-Nom constructions is usually a clause-anticipating *það* 'it' which does not bind a reflexive anyway. Hence, exactly as with clause-bound reflexivization it is impossible to demonstrate that this nominative does not bind long-distance reflexives. However, the remaining evidence presented in this section shows that *skiljast* 'gather' cannot instantiate a Nom-Dat construction.

In raising-to-subject constructions, either argument of *falla í skaut* 'fall in sb's lap' may take on the subject behavior of the matrix verb, as is shown in (75) below with the modal verb *geta* 'can, be able to' as a raising-to-subject verb:

Dat-Nom
(75) a. Þá   gat   **verktakanum**   ekki   fallið   **samningurinn**
         then   could   entrepreneur.the.DAT   not   fallen   contract.the.NOM
         í   skaut.
         in   lap
         'Then the entrepreneur could not have the contract fall in his lap.'

Nom-Dat
     b. Þá   gat   **samningurinn**   ekki   fallið   **verktakanum**
         then   could   contract.the.NOM   not   fallen   entrepreneur.the.DAT
         í   skaut.
         in   lap
         'Then the contract could not fall into the entrepreneur's lap.'

Exactly as with neutral word order, shown in (61–64) in Section 3.1.2 above, either argument of *falla í skaut* 'fall in sb's lap' can take on the subject behavior of *geta* 'can', the dative in (75a) and the nominative in (75b), immediately following the finite verb *gat* 'could' when the adverb *þá* 'then' occupies the first position in the clause. At the same time, the other argument, the nominative in (75a) and the dative in (75b) behave syntactically as objects in that they occupy the position immediately following the non-finite verb *fallið* 'fallen'.

This, in contrast, is not the situation found with *skiljast* 'gather', as is shown in (76) below:

Dat-Nom

(76) a. *Þá   gat   **honum**   ekki   skilist   **þetta**.*
then   could him.DAT   not   gathered this.NOM
'Then he could not fathom this.'

*****Nom-Dat**

b. **Þá   gat   **þetta**   ekki   skilist   **honum**.*
then   could this.NOM   not   gathered him.DAT
Intended meaning: 'Then this could not be fathomable to him.'

In (76a) it is the dative *honum* 'him' that takes on the subject behavior of *geta* 'can', while the nominative *þetta* 'that' immediately follows the non-finite verb, *skilist* 'gathered'. The opposite word order, with the nominative in subject position and the dative in object position is ungrammatical for *skiljast*, demonstrating once again that while *falla í skaut* is an alternating predicate, *skiljast* does not demonstrate that behavior, but can only instantiate the Dat-Nom argument structure construction in Icelandic.

Turning now to raising-to-object, the penultimate test to be discussed here, this behavior is found with four verb classes in Icelandic, i.e. verbs of believing, verbs of saying, verbs of perception, like 'see' and 'hear', and causatives, which in Icelandic typically involves the verb *láta* 'let' (cf. Kristoffersen 1996: Ch. 5; Sigurðsson 2002; Thráinsson 2007: 436–439; Barðdal and Eythórsson 2012a: 380–383). In (77) below, this behavior is exemplified with the perception verb *sjá* 'see':

Dat-Nom

(77) a. *Ég   sá   **verktakanum**   aldrei   falla*
I.NOM   saw   entrepreneur.the.DAT   never   fall.INF
***samningurinn**   í   skaut.*
contract.the.NOM   in   lap
'I never saw the entrepreneur have the contract fall in his lap.'

Nom-Dat

b. *Ég   sá   **samninginn**   aldrei   falla   **verktakanum***
I.NOM   saw   contract.the.ACC   never   fall.INF entrepreneur.the.DAT
í   skaut.
in   lap
'I never saw the contract fall into the entrepreneur's lap.'

One characteristic of raising-to-object, also labeled AcI or ECM in the literature, is that in cases where the lower verb is a nominative subject verb, this nominative subject is the argument which takes on the object behavior of the matrix verb, occurring in the accusative case in such structures. The assumption is that this accusative case is assigned by the matrix verb to its object. This is clear from the example in (77b) where the nominative subject of the lower verb, *samningurinn* 'contract', occurs in the accusative, *samninginn*. However, this behavior is only found for nominative subjects, and not for oblique subjects, accusative, dative or genitive. Instead, oblique subjects maintain their oblique case in the raising-to-object construction, as is evident from (77a) where *verktakanum* occurs in the dative case, despite occupying the object position of *sjá* 'see'. To conclude, also with regard to raising-to-object does either argument of *falla í skaut* 'fall in sb's lap' show subject behavior while the other argument behaves as object, be it the dative or the nominative argument.

Turning to the verb *skiljast* 'gather', only the Dat-Nom order is grammatical when embedded under *sjá* 'see', not the Nom-Dat order, as is evident from the asterisk in (78b) below.

Dat-Nom
(78) a. *Ég   sá   **honum**   aldrei   skiljast   **þetta**.*
        I.NOM   saw   him.DAT   never   gather.INF this.NOM
        'I never saw him fathom this.'

***Nom-Dat**
    b. *Ég   sá   **þetta**   aldrei   skiljast   **honum**.*
        I.NOM   saw   this.ACC   never   gather.INF him.DAT
        Intended meaning: 'I never saw this be fathomed by him.'

This contrast between (78a) and (78b), on the one hand, and between (77) and (78), on the other, shows that *skiljast* 'gather' is not an alternating verb, as opposed to *falla í skaut* 'fall in sb's lap' in Icelandic.

Finally, consider *falla í skaut* 'fall in sb's lap' in the two control constructions in (79) below, where the dative is left unexpressed on identity with a nominative subject in the matrix clause in (79a) and the nominative is left unexpressed, also on identity with a nominative subject in the matrix clause in (79b):

Dat-Nom
(79) a. *Þá   fór   þessi   maður   ekki   varhluta   af því*
        then   went   this.NOM   man.NOM   not   miss.DAT   of it
        *að   ___   falla   í   skaut   **allur**   **hugsanlegur***
        to   PRO.DAT   fall.INF   in   lap   all.NOM   possible

	heiður	sem	fremstu	vísindamönnum	í	læknisfræði
	honor.NOM	which	headmost	scientists	in	medicine
	getur	hlotnazt.				
	can	received				

'Then this man did not miss out on having all possible honor fall in his lap, which the headmost scientists in medicine may receive.' (http://www.kirkju.net/index.php/sir_william_liley_avi_hans_og_storf_ae_r?blog=10, 1992)

Nom-Dat

b. *Arðurinn af sjálfbærri auðlindanýtingu með virðingu*
   dividend.NOM of sustainable resource.use with respect
   *fyrir landinu verður að falla __ **þjóðinni** í*
   for land.the must to fall.INF PRO.NOM nation.the.DAT in
   skaut.
   lap

'The dividend from sustainable usage of natural resources, respecting the land, must fall into the nation's lap.'

(https://saevarh.blog.is/blog/saevarh/entry/1077559, 2010)

As its corollary, the nominative *allur hugsanlegur heiður* 'all possible honor' behaves syntactically as an object in (79a), immediately following the whole compositional non-finite predicate, *falla í skaut* 'fall in sb's lap', while the dative *þjóðinni* 'nation' in (79b) takes on the object behavior of immediately following the non-finite verb *falla* 'fall'. Observe that the nominative *allur hugsanlegur heiður* 'all possible honor' in (79a) is indefinite, hence it is located further back in the sentence than otherwise. However, the nominative *allur hugsanlegur heiður* 'all possible honor' may as well occur immediately following the non-finite verb, as is shown in (80), instead of clause-finally, without that jeopardizing its grammaticality.

Dat-Nom

(80) a. *Þá fór þessi maður ekki varhluta af því að*
       then went this.NOM man.NOM not miss.DAT of it to
       __ *falla **allur hugsanlegur heiður** í skaut.*
       PRO.DAT fall.INF all.NOM possible honor.NOM in lap

'Then this man did not miss out on having all possible honor fall in his lap.

The two examples in (79a–b) are attested examples, the first from the year 1992 and the second from 2010, and they show beyond doubt that either argument of *falla í skaut* 'fall in sb's lap', the dative in Dat-Nom constructions and the nominative in

Nom-Dat constructions, may take on subject behavior. At the same time, the second argument of these two argument structures, Dat-Nom and Nom-Dat, behaves syntactically as an object, and this takes place irrespective of whether the second argument is in the nominative or in the dative case.

A search for attested examples of *skiljast* 'gather' in control infinitives has only yielded examples of the following type where the dative is left unexpressed and the nominative is expressed through an *að* 'that' clause:

Dat-(Nom)
(81) a. Við   þurfum   ekki   nema   heyra   þessar   raddir
        we.NOM   need   not   except   hear   these.ACC   voices.ACC
        til   að __   skiljast   **að**   **senn** ...
        for   to PRO.DAT gather.INF that   soon
        'We need not but to hear these voices in order to understand that soon...'   (Læknablaðið 104: 200, 2018)

The attested example in (81) documents that structures in which the dative of the Dat-Nom argument structure may be left unexpressed in control infinitives with *skiljast* 'gather' are readily found in online texts. The lack of control examples in which the nominative of *skiljas*t 'gather' is left unexpressed speaks for the infelicitousness of such examples. Also, as a native speaker of Icelandic, I am unable to construct grammatical examples of this type, which further corroborates the present claim that *skiljast* 'gather' is not an alternating predicate in Icelandic, but may only instantiate the Dat-Nom argument structure construction.

To sum up so far, in this section I have systematically demonstrated for Icelandic that there are two types of Dat-Nom predicates in that language: those that can only instantiate the Dat-Nom construction, like *skiljast* 'gather', here referred to as non-alternating Dat-Nom verbs, and those that can instantiate either one of the two argument structure constructions, Dat-Nom and Nom-Dat, like *falla í skaut* 'fall in sb's lap', here referred to as alternating verbs. This has been shown through a methodical investigation based on how the two arguments of these two predicates behave with regard to the subject properties that have already been established for Icelandic.

Further, an examination of the compositional predicate, *falla í skaut* 'fall in sb's lap', has shown that either argument of this predicate, the dative or the nominative, passes the subject tests, but only one at the time, of course. The argument that passes the subject tests is the argument that occupies the first position of the argument structure, the dative in the case of Dat-Nom and the nominative in the case of Nom-Dat. In contrast, only the dative of *skiljast* 'gather' behaves syntactically as a subject in Icelandic, while the nominative behaves as an object.

3.2.2 Modern Faroese

The language which is genealogically most closely related to Modern Icelandic is Modern Faroese, as both are West-Scandinavian languages of the North-Germanic branch. Already as early as in 1986, it was established by Barnes that Faroese also has predicates selecting for subjects in the oblique cases. This includes Dat-Nom, Dat-Acc, Acc-Acc, Dat-only, Acc-only, etc. Barnes (1986) shows that the potential oblique subject behaves syntactically as a subject in Modern Faroese. In addition to this, Barnes also documents the existence of alternating predicates in this language.

In Modern Faroese the nominative argument of Dat-Nom verbs has already been replaced by an accusative as a default object case, while the dative has generally maintained its case marking in such constructions (cf. Barnes 1986; Petersen 2002), although some speaker-internal variation seems to exist (Thráinsson et al. 2012: 229, 314). At the same time, the dative of intransitive verbs in Faroese is less stable, showing considerable variation in case marking. The following examples from Barnes (1986: 34, 36) illustrate the case marking patterns for the older Dat-Nom construction, while their corresponding Nom-Dat alternants have kept the nominative in preverbal position, i.e. when the nominative behaves syntactically as a subject.

Dat-Nom (currently realized as Dat-Acc)
(82) a. ***Honum*** tókti ***skattin*** ov litlan.
him.DAT thought tax.the.ACC too small.ACC
'He felt that the tax was too low.' (Barnes 1986: 34)

Nom-Dat
b. ***Skatturin*** tókti ***honum*** ov lítil.
tax.the.NOM thought him.DAT too small.NOM
'The tax seemed too low to him.' (Barnes 1986: 36)

Note that *ov litlan* 'too small' in the accusative in (82a) is an object predicative complement, while *ov lítin* 'too small' in the nominative case in (82b) is a subject predicative complement. This supports an object analysis of the accusative *skattin* 'the tax' in (82a) and a subject analysis of the nominative *skatturin* 'the tax' in (82b). As its corollary, the dative in (82a) is the syntactic subject, while it is a syntactic object in (82b). Another example of an original alternating Dat-Nom / Nom-Dat predicate presented by Barnes (1986: 36) is given in (83):

3.2 Alternating Dat-Nom / Nom-Dat predicates in the Germanic languages

Dat-Nom (currently realized as Dat-Acc)
(83) a. *Tá   kom   mær   ommu   knappliga í   hug.*
        then came   me.DAT   grandma.ACC   suddenly   in mind
        'Then all of a sudden I remembered grandma.'

Nom-Dat
   b. *Tá   kom   omma   mær   knappliga í   hug.*
        then came   grandma.NOM   me.DAT   suddenly   in mind
        'Then all of a sudden grandma came to my mind.'

These examples are even more telling than the ones in (82) above, as here the preverbal position is occupied by an adverb *tá* 'then', while the two arguments immediately follow the verb, *kom* 'came', the dative in (83a) and the nominative in (83b). In this respect, these examples are an exact parallel to the Modern Icelandic examples in (62a–b), where both arguments follow the finite verb, due to the unavailability of the preverbal position.

In the Faroese example in (83a) above, it is the dative *mær* 'me' that immediately follows the finite verb *kom* 'came', while the accusative *ommu* 'grandma' follows the dative subject, here preceding the sentence adverbial *knappliga* 'suddenly'. By the same token, it is the nominative subject *omma* 'grandma' in (83b) that immediately follows the finite verb, *kom* 'came', while the dative object *mær* 'me' precedes the sentence adverb *knappliga* 'suddenly'. Hence, word order properties attest to the subject properties of the dative in (83a) and of the nominative in (83b).

Barnes (1986: 36–37) provides a short list of predicates in Modern Faroese which alternate between Dat-Nom and Nom-Dat. The relevant verbs are:

(84) *sýnast* 'think, seem', *hóva* 'like, please', *falla væl/illa* '(dis)like', *renna í huga* 'come to mind' and *koma fyrir* 'seem'

All five predicates occurred with a dative and a nominative in Old Norse-Icelandic. For a further discussion of oblique subject constructions in Modern Faroese, see Petersen (2002), Eythórsson and Jónsson (2003), Barðdal (2004), Jónsson and Eythórsson (2005) and Thráinsson et al. (2012).

The chances of finding examples of control infinitives containing alternating Dat-Nom / Nom-Dat verbs in written Faroese are seriously hampered by the rarity of these verbs in that language, and the rarity of control infinitives in general. However, I have come across the following two examples in contemporary Faroese texts, representing two related compositional predicates: *koma í hug* 'come to mind, remember' and *renna í huga* 'go through mind':

Dat-Nom (currently realized as Dat-Acc)

(85) a. *At halda hvíldagin heilagn, er vœl tað at ___*
to hold rest.day holy is well it to PRO.DAT
koma **Guð** *í hug.*
come.INF God.ACC in mind
'To keep the rest day holy, that's remembering God.'
(https://nordlysid.fo/tidindi/57364/halgidagar-harrans-dagur, 2018)

Nom-Dat

b. *Sjógangurin har niðri fekk so mangt at ___*
rough.see.the there down got so much to PRO.NOM
renna **honum** *í huga.*
run.INF him.DAT in mind
'The rough sea down under got so many things to go through his mind.'
(Lesibók III; til tridja real, p. 229, 1974)

In (85a) the dative of the original Dat-Nom construction is left unexpressed, while the accusative *Guð* 'God' is found in the position immediately following the non-finite verb, *koma* 'come', which is a dedicated object position. At the same time, the nominative of the Nom-Dat construction in (85b) is left unexpressed, while the dative *honum* 'him' is located in the object position immediately following the non-finite verb, *renna* 'run'. These Faroese examples are parallel to the examples in (79a–b) above from Modern Icelandic, even though the lexical material of this family of verbal constructions is not identical, with *koma* 'come' vs. *renna* 'run', respectively, in the verb slots in (85a–b).

Note that this family of constructions, [to V.motion 'in mind'], is not confined to Faroese but is also found in Icelandic. What characterizes this constructional family is that the verb slot can be filled with different motion verbs like *koma* 'come', *renna* 'run', *falla* 'fall' *detta* 'fall' and *skjóta* 'shoot' in both languages. Also in Modern Swedish the variant with 'come' still exists, *komma i håg* in the meaning 'remember'. Examples of this type also exist in Latin (cf. Barðdal and Smitherman 2013: 48–49).

To conclude, word order facts suggest that alternating predicates of the Dat-Nom / Nom-Dat type are also found in Faroese, exactly as in Modern Icelandic. The problem with Modern Faroese is that structures of this type, alternating and non-alternating, are generally falling into disuse, making it difficult to find examples of the alternation in current texts. Here I have also presented control infinitives involving two related predicates, *koma í hug* 'come in mind' and *renna í huga* 'go through mind', documenting that either the dative or the nominative may be left unexpressed in control examples with this constructional family. Further, it appears that several Dat-Nom verbs in Modern Faroese do not alternate between the two constructions. This is parallel to Modern Icelandic where both non-alternating and alternating Dat-Nom predicates exist. These facts raise the question of whether corresponding predicates in Modern German also divide across alternating Dat-Nom / Nom-Dat and non-alternating Dat-Nom predicates. This is the topic of Chapter 6 below.

3.2.3 Old / Middle English

In addition to the evidence from Modern Icelandic and Modern Faroese, Allen (1995: 114–117) observes that one type of oblique subject constructions in Old English appears to be of the alternating type. Consider the following examples with *lician* 'like', instantiating the Dat-Nom and the Nom-Dat constructions in Old English:

Dat-Nom
(86) a. **Đam**   wife   þa   word   wel   licodon.
         the.DAT   woman.DAT   those.NOM   words.NOM   well   liked.3PL
         'The woman liked those words well.'   (Beowulf 639)

Nom-Dat
  b. **ge**   noldon   **gode**   lician   on   godum
     you.NOM.PL   not.would.3PL   God.DAT   please   in   good
     ingehyde   . . .
     understanding
     'You would not please God with good understanding . . .'
                        (ÆCHom II, 44 332.160, cited from Allen (1995: 146–147)

In (86a) it is the dative *ðam wife* 'the woman' that occupies the first position, while the nominative *þa word* 'those words' occupies the second position. In contrast, in (86b) the nominative *ge* 'you' occupies the preverbal position, while the dative *gode* 'God' occupies the position preceding the non-finite verb. The order of the two arguments above also coincides with the two meanings suggested for *lician*, namely as meaning 'like' when occurring with the Dat-Nom word order, but 'please' when the word order is Nom-Dat (cf. Fischer and van der Leek 1983).

Notice that the verb in (86a), *licodon*, is in the plural, agreeing with the nominative 'those words'. As is already discussed in Section 2.3.3 above, this is not a problem for an object analysis of the nominative, as the verb consistently agrees with nominatives in Icelandic, Germanic and the Indo-European languages, irrespective of grammatical relations.[2] In essence, this means that the agreement is not subject-verb agreement but nominative-verb agreement (cf. Sigurðsson 1990–91, 2004, and later work).

Returning to Old English, the following predicates are listed as alternating verbs by Allen (1995: 114):

(87) *eglian* 'bother, ail', *gelician* 'like', *hreowan* 'pity', *laþian* 'loathe', *lician* 'like', *losian* 'lose, be lost', *mislician* 'dislike', *ofhreowan* 'pity', *oflician* 'dislike', *ofþyncan* 'regret', *þyncan* 'think, seem'

Allen also specifically notices that either argument may control the deletion of the subject in a second conjunct with these verbs. However, the dative may only be the controller when it is the first argument of the argument structure, but never when it is the second argument, as I interpret Allen's descriptions of the facts. In the same vein, Allen claims that the nominative can only control subject ellipsis in a second conjunct if it is the first argument of the argument structure. The following two examples illustrate this (provided by Allen through personal communication).[3]

Dat-Nom

(88) a. Þa   gelicode   **þam**   **gedwolum**   þæs   bisceopes
       then   liked   them.DAT   heathens.DAT this.GEN   bishops.GEN
       dom,   and   ___   wacodon   þa   þreo niht
       ruling.NOM   and   Ø.NOM   watched.3PL then   thee nights
       'Then the heathens liked the ruling of the bishop and [they] watched for three nights'
       (ÆlS (Basil) 338)

Nom-Dat

b. þæt   **he**   on   godum   þeowum   **Gode**   gelicode, &
   that   he.NOM   on   good   virtues   God.DAT   pleased   and
   ___   to   Godes   wegum   awend   hine   sylfne
   Ø.NOM   to   God's   path   turend   him   self
   'that he pleased God with good virtues and [he] turned himself to God's paths'
   (ÆHom 18 113)

---

[2] During my research projects on oblique subject constructions in the early Indo-European languages, funded by the Bergen Research Foundation (2008–2012), The Norwegian Research Council (2011–2015) and the European Research Council (2013–2018), I have come across hundreds of examples of this type where the verb agrees with the nominative plural object-like argument.

[3] I am particularly grateful to Cindy Allen for sharing these examples with me.

The example in (88a) shows that the dative *þam gedwolum* 'the heathens' in the position immediately following the finite verb *gelicode* 'liked' controls the deletion of the nominative plural form 'they' in the second conjunct, while (88b) shows that the nominative *he* 'he', and not the dative *Gode* 'God, controls the deletion of the nominative subject 'he' in the second conjunct. These examples are therefore entirely compatible with an alternating analysis of *gelician* 'like' in Old English.

It should, however, be mentioned here that while subject deletion in conjoined clauses mostly happens on the basis of identity with the subject of the first conjunct, it does happen that such subject deletion in the second conjunct takes place on identity with an object of the first conjunct in Old English. Still, Allen (1995: 52–59, 113–117) argues that there is a major statistical difference between subject deletion in second conjuncts on identity with subjects or objects in first conjuncts. Allen demonstrates that subject deletion in second conjuncts takes place in 80% of the cases on identity with nominative subjects in the first conjunct and 50–60% of the cases on identity with oblique subjects in the first conjunct. In contrast, subject deletion on identity with an object in the first conjunct takes place in 1% of the cases. While Allen's statistics are based on a limited subset of Old English material, she still documents a certain tendency for that language.

Allen's example in (88b) is one of four Nom-Dat examples involving conjoined clauses with *gelician* 'like' in the first conjunct. Of those four examples, it is only in this one that deletion in the second conjunct is found. In other words, in 25% of the attested cases, the nominative subject controls deletion in the second conjunct, when this nominative is preverbal. Since this figure, 25% of nominative subjects controlling deletion in second conjuncts, is based on only four examples, drawing any major conclusions on the basis of these would not comply with scientific method. However, the fact that the nominatives that are second arguments in Dat-Nom constructions do not control deletion in the second conjunct, indeed speaks for the object status of nominatives in Dat-Nom constructions.

In sum, while the data presented here in favor of the existence of alternating Dat-Nom / Nom-Dat verbs in Old English are not as strong as the evidence from Modern Icelandic or Modern Faroese, the evidence offered still speaks for the existence of such alternating Dat-Nom / Nom-Dat predicates in Old English.

3.2.4 Old Swedish and Old Danish

I have argued earlier (Barðdal 1998) that alternating predicates also existed in Old Swedish and Old Danish. Several examples from the history of these languages attest to such a claim. I start with examples from earlier Swedish, before proceeding to the Old Danish ones. For three of five Swedish examples and one of three Danish examples, I show that a cognate verb in Modern Icelandic is also an alternating verb. Further evidence from the modern languages is then introduced, illustrating variation in argument structure across these languages. This variation indeed attests to an earlier Dat-Nom / Nom-Dat alternation within Swedish, Danish and Norwegian, of which different alternants, the Dat-Nom or Nom-Dat, have survived into the contemporary languages.

The following examples of *nöghia* 'suffice', *smaka* 'taste' *söma* 'befit', *þykkia* 'think, seem' and *þäkkias* 'like, please', documented in older Swedish texts occur with either a Dat-Nom or a Nom-Dat word order (Old Swedish source abbreviations are adopted from Söderwall's 1884–1918 Old Swedish Dictionary):

Old Swedish
Dat-Nom
(89) a. ey   nögdhe   **henne**   thetta
         not   sufficed her.DAT   this.NOM
         'She did not find that sufficient.'   (Su 161, c.1475–1500)

Nom-Dat
   b. **thz**   nöghdhe   **them**   **allom**   wel
       it.NOM   sufficed   them.DAT   all.DAT   well
       'This sufficed them all well.'   (ST 17, c.1420)

In (89a), the dative *henne* 'her' occurs immediately following the finite verb *nögdhe* 'sufficed', while the nominative *thetta* 'this' immediately follows the dative. In contrast, in (89b), the order is exactly opposite; the nominative *thz* 'it' occurs in preverbal position, while the dative *them allom* 'all of them' shows up in the position following the finite verb *nöghdhe* 'sufficed'. These examples may therefore be taken as documenting alternation between Dat-Nom and Nom-Dat with *nöghia* 'suffice' in Old Swedish.

There is no doubt that the example in (89a) is unambiguous, as the dative shows up in an inverted position, which is a clear-cut subject position, and the nominative occurs in a clear-cut object position, following the inverted subject. The example in (89b), however, is not as clear-cut, as it is an analytical possibility that the nominative *thz* 'it' has been topicalized to the preverbal position. In Modern Icelandic however, the cognate verb *nægja* 'be sufficient' is an alternating predicate, as shown in (90) below and in Table 5 in Section 3.1.3 above. Therefore, the comparative evidence also speaks for an alternating analysis.

Icelandic
Dat-Nom
(90) a. Þá   nægir   henni   þetta.
       then suffices her.DAT this.NOM
       'Then she found this sufficient.'

Nom-Dat
   b. Þá   nægði   það   þeim   öllum.
      then sufficed it.NOM   them.DAT all.DAT
      'Then this was enough for them.'

Returning to Old Swedish, generally subjects occur in first position in subordinate clauses (see, however, Falk 1997: 35 for some very marked exceptions to this). In (91a) the dative *os* 'us' precedes the finite verb *smakar* 'tastes', while the nominative *alt* 'everything' follows the finite verb. This word order is reversed in (91b) where the nominative *vathn* 'water' occurs in preverbal position, with the dative *honom* occurring in postverbal position.

Old Swedish
Dat-Nom
(91) a. then   sötme   ... j   hulkom   som   **os**   smakar
        the   sweetness   in   such.DAT which us.DAT   tastes
        alt   got
        all.NOM   good
        'The sweetness ... in such which we find all very tasteful'
                                                               (Bir 1: 126, c.1390)

Nom-Dat
   b. **vathn**   smakadhe   **honom**   bätir   en   nokor   annar
      water.NOM   tasted   him.DAT   better   than any   other
      drykker
      drink
      'Water was more to his taste than any other drink'
                                                           (Lg 785, c.1400–1450)

In principle, both of these examples may be interpreted as containing a topicalized object, the dative *os* 'us' in (91a) and the nominative *vathn* 'water' in (91b). But these examples can also be interpreted as representing neutral word order in which the preverbal argument is the subject and the postverbal one the object. On the latter analysis, the verb *smaka* 'taste' is an alternating verb in Old Swedish.

In Icelandic, moreover, the cognate verb *smakkast* 'taste' is an alternating verb, as is documented in (92) below:

Icelandic
Dat-Nom
(92) a. Þá   smakkaðist **okkur**   **allur**   **maturinn**   mjög   vel.
         then   tasted   us.DAT   all.NOM   food.the.NOM   very   well
         'Then we found all the food very tasteful.'

Nom-Dat
   b. Þá   smakkaðist **vatnið**   **okkur**   betur   en   nokkur
       then   tasted   water.NOM   us.DAT   better   than   any
       annar   drykkur.
       other   drink
       'Then the water was more to our taste than any other drink.'

Therefore, in addition to the word order variation in the Swedish examples in (91) above, the comparative evidence also speaks for an alternating analysis of the verb *smaka* 'taste' in Old Swedish.

Consider now the following examples of the verb *söma* 'befit' in Old Swedish:

Old Swedish
Dat-Nom
(93) a. sömpde   **honu[m]**   **ey**   **swa**   **fwl**   **oc**   **oreen**   **gärning**
         befitted   him.DAT   not   so   foul   and   unclean   act.NOM
         'It was not befitting for him [to carry out] such a fowl and unclean act'
                                                                       (MB 1: 111, c.1275–1300)

Nom-Dat
   b. **the**   **pina**   sömde   **honom**   väl
       that   torment.NOM   befitted   him.DAT   well
       'That torment befitted him well.'   (KL 250, c.1385)

The examples in (93) are exactly parallel to the ones in (89) above, with i) both arguments following the finite verb in (93a), the dative first and the nominative to the right of the sentence adverbial *ey* 'not', and ii) with the nominative in preverbal position in (93b) and the dative in postverbal position. The example in (93a), with both arguments following the finite verb, truly speaks for a subject status of the dative, while the one in (93b) may either be interpreted as instantiating neutral word order or involving a topicalized nominative object in first position.

In Modern Icelandic, *sæma* 'befit', is also an alternating predicate, as is shown in (94) below:

Icelandic
Dat-Nom
(94) a. *Ekki sæmir* **honum** *svo* **fúll og óhreinn gjörningur**.
not befits him.DAT such foul and unclean act.NOM
'It is not befitting for him [to carry out] such a fowl and unclean.'

Nom-Dat
b. *Ekki sæmir* **sú** *kvöl* **honum** *vel*.
not befits that.NOM torment.NOM him.DAT well
'That torment does not befit him well.'

Therefore, the comparative evidence indeed corroborates an alternating analysis for *söma* 'befit' in Old Swedish.

The examples in (95) below of the verb *þykkia* 'think, seem' are different from the ones above in that both arguments follow the finite verb in both cases, the dative and the nominative in (95a) but the nominative and the dative in (95b). These examples, therefore, show beyond doubt that an alternating analysis is called for for the verb *þykkia* 'think, seem' in Old Swedish.

Old Swedish
Dat-Nom
(95) a. *ä thokte* **hanom** *thät*
not thought him.DAT it.NOM
'He did not think that.' (Bil 801, c.1400–1450)

Nom-Dat
b. *skulu* **the** *os thikkia vara stora*
shall they.NOM us.DAT think.INF be.INF big
'They shall appear as big to us.' (Bo 20, c.1375–1400)

One of the interesting features of the examples in (95) is that both arguments occur in the midfield immediately following the finite verb, and both arguments are pronouns. Delsing (1999: 208–209), in a very extensive study of the word order variation between OV and VO in the history of Swedish, a study which includes the word order within the midfield, observes that subjects always precede objects in the linear order, unless the object is a pronoun and the subject a full NP. In those cases, the pronominal object may precede the subject in the linear order. If both arguments are pronouns, the subject precedes the object in the midfield. The same tendency has also been observed for Old Norse-Icelandic (Haugan 2001: 174–184; Jónsson 2018: 140–148).

Turning to the comparative evidence, note that the cognate verb *þykja* in Modern Icelandic is not an alternating predicate, but can only instantiate the Dat-Nom argument structure construction in that language.

Icelandic
Dat-Nom
(96) a. *Ekki þótti* **honum** **það**.
not thought him.DAT it.NOM
'He did not think that.'

***Nom-Dat**
b. **Ekki þótti* **það** **honum**.
not thought it.NOM him.DAT
Intended meaning: 'He did not think that.'

This comparison shows that there is not a one-to-one correspondence between alternating predicates across the Germanic languages, even though many cognate verbs display the same argument structure options. Still, a complicating factor here is that (95b) contains an infinitive clause, selected for by *þykkia*, which may further distort the order of the arguments in this example.

The last Old Swedish examples to be discussed here involve the verb *þäkkias* 'like, please', given in (97) below:

Old Swedish
Dat-Nom
(97) a. *huru mykyt* **gudhi** *thäkkias ödhmiuka manna*
how much God.DAT likes.3PL humble.GEN men.GEN
böne
prayers.NOM
'How well God likes the prayers of humble men.' (Bir 2: 32, c.1390)

Nom-Dat
b. *at* **man** *... hällir thäkkis* **creature** *... än*
that man.NOM rather pleases creature.DAT than
skaparenom
creator.the.DAT
'That a man ... will rather please a creature ... than the creator.'
(Bo 18, c.1375–1400)

Both examples in (97) above consist of subordinate clauses, a *wh*-clause in (97a) and a *that*-clause in (97b). In (97a) the dative occurs in preverbal position and the nominative in postverbal one, while in (97b) the word order is exactly opposite, the nominative occurs in preverbal position and the dative in postverbal one. Recall from the discussion above that the first position in subordinate clauses is a dedicated subject position, meaning that the two examples in (97) may be taken to represent neutral word order. Note also that both arguments are full NPs and no pronouns are involved. As such, these examples suggest that *þäkkias* is an alternating Dat-Nom / Nom-Dat verb in Old Swedish.

This particular verb, *þekkjast* 'suit', is also found with a dative and a nominative in Old Norse-Icelandic, as is shown in (98) below, which incidentally stems from a translated text where the original is in Latin:

Old Norse-Icelandic
Dat-Nom
(98) megi þer   mitt   lif   þekkjast ok
     may you.DAT my.NOM life.NOM suit   and
     'May you find my life suitable and'   (*Barl.* 148[32])

This verb *þekkjast* also occurs with a Nom-Acc frame with the meaning 'consent to' in Old Norse-Icelandic:

Old Norse-Icelandic
Nom-Acc
(99) ef þú   vill mína   umsjá   þekkjast, þá
     if you.NOM will my.ACC care.ACC accept   then
     'If you will consent to my care, then'   (*Fm.* VI, 104[21])

It is unclear whether *þekkjast* in Old Norse-Icelandic was an alternating verb or not, given that a) the Dat-Nom example is from a translated text, and b) the other case frame found with this verb in Old Norse-Icelandic is Nom-Acc and not Nom-Dat. What appears to be clear from these examples, however, is that the meaning also varies between 'find suitable' and 'consent to, accept', which could be interpreted as attesting to the type of alternation found with alternating predicates. But even so, notice that the nominative in (99) is animate, which deviates from the pattern generally found with alternating predicates, where the dative is animate and the nominative is inanimate.

For more verbs of this type in older Swedish, cf. Barðdal (1998). Consider now the following examples from Old Danish, this time with the verbs *angre* 'pain', *gaghne* 'be of use' and *fortryde* 'regret' (Old Danish source abbreviations are adopted from Kalkar's (1886–1982) Old Danish Dictionary):

Old Danish
Dat-Nom
(100) a. **hannem** angrede **hans hane**, han haffde mist.
him.DAT pained his cook.NOM he had lost
'He was pained by the fact that he had lost his cock.'
(Herm. Weigere. 48v, c.1555)

Nom-Dat
b. **thet** angrær **mek**, at thu ...
it.NOM pains me.OBL that you
'It pains me that you ...' (Romant. Digtn. II. 251, c.1500)

Note that the accusative and dative pronouns underwent a functional merger during the Old Swedish and Old Danish periods, with the dative forms *hannem / hanom / honom* 'him' and *henne / hende* 'her' surviving in 3rd person singular, while the accusative forms *mik* 'me' and *þik* 'you' survived in 1st and 2nd person singular.

Turning to the examples in (100), in (100a) the dative *hannem* 'him' occurs in preverbal position and the nominative *hans hane* 'his cock' in postverbal position. Exactly the opposite order of the arguments is found in (100b) with the same verb *angre* 'pain'. That is, the nominative *thet* 'it' is in preverbal position and the oblique *mek* 'me' in postverbal position. It is an analytical possibility that one of the two examples in (100) involves topicalization, which one, we would not know at this stage of inquiry, but on the assumption that the two examples represent neutral word order, (100) shows that *angre* 'pain' alternated between the Dat-Nom and Nom-Dat argument structure construction in the history of Danish.

In Modern Icelandic, in contrast, the cognate verb *angra* does not exist with the meaning 'pain', but only with the meaning 'bother', selecting for a Nom-Acc argument structure. This verb does, therefore, not alternate between Dat-Nom and Nom-Dat in Icelandic.

Turning now to the Old Danish *gaghne* 'be of use', there is no doubt that this verb was an alternating Dat-Nom / Nom-Dat verb in Old Danish, as evidenced by the word order variation in (101) below, where the oblique *mik* 'me' occupies the inverted subject position in (101a), while the nominative *thet* 'it' occupies the same inverted subject position in (101b). At the same time, the nominative *førræ fødelsen* 'first birthright' in (101a) and the dative *oss* in (101b) follow the preceding dative and nominative, respectively, hence occupying the typical object position in Old Danish.

Old Danish
Dat-Nom

(101) a. *Hwat gaffwnær **mik** **førræ fødelsen**?*
how   is.of.use   me.OBL   former   birth.the.NOM
'How can I make use of my birthright?'   (Mos I 25:32, c.1475–1500)

Nom-Dat

b. *Hwat gaffnær **thet** **oss**, at*
how   is.of.use   it.NOM   us.OBL   that
'How is it of use to us that ...'   (Mos I 37:26, c.1475–1500)

As a clinching argument, consider the following examples of the cognate verb *gagnast* 'be of use' in Modern Icelandic, which, as a matter of fact, is also an alternating verb in that language:

Icelandic
Dat-Nom

(102) a. *Ekki gagnast **mér** **frumburðarréttur minn**.*
not   is.of.use   me.DAT   birthright.NOM   mine.NOM
'I cannot make use of my birthright'

Nom-Dat

b. *Ekki gagnast **þetta** **öllum**.*
not   is.of.use   this.NOM   all.DAT
'This is of no use to everybody.'

The word order in (102) is exactly the same as the word order in (101), with both arguments following the finite verb, with the Dat-Nom word order in the (a) examples, and a Nom-Dat word order in the (b) examples. Again, the position immediately following the verb is the inverted subject position, while the next position is the object position. Hence, the comparative evidence indeed corroborates an alternating analysis for *gaghne* 'be of use' in Old Danish.

The last Old Danish example pair to be discussed here involves the verb *fortryde* 'regret', shown in (103) below:

Old Danish
Dat-Nom

(103) a. *tha for trød **hanum** **thet** ganze sare, ath*
then   re gretted   him.DAT   this.NOM   rather   sorely   that
'Then he regretted it sorely that'   (Romant. Digtn. II. 92, c.1500)

Nom-Dat

b. ***det***   *fortrød*   ***hannem***,   at de
    this.NOM   regretted   him.DAT
    'It was to his regret that they' (2. Makk. 7.39 c.1550)

Interestingly, the internal order of the pronouns in (103a), with a dative *hanum* 'him' and a nominative *thet* 'it' immediately following the finite verb, shows that the dative must be analyzed as the subject in this example, as it occupies the inverted subject position. In the same vein, in this particular example (103a), the nominative must be analyzed as the object, as it occupies the object position immediately following the inverted subject position. In (103b) in contrast, the nominative *det* 'it' occurs in preverbal position, while the dative *hannem* 'him' is found in postverbal position. It is of course an analytical possibility that the nominative *det* 'it' has been topicalized to the preverbal position in (103b), in which case the dative occupies the inverted subject position, although it cannot be excluded that the word order in (103b) represents neutral word order. On such an analysis, the examples in (103) attest to an alternating status of *fortryde* 'regret' in Old Danish.[4]

In Icelandic, in contrast, a verb cognate to *fortryde* does not exist, and not surprisingly so, as this particular verb is a low German borrowing into Mainland Scandinavian, *vordreeten*. Yet, a non-prefixed variant of this verb *þrjóta* 'lack' exists both in Icelandic and in the other North-Germanic languages. However, *þrjóta* 'lack' in Icelandic does not occur with a dative and a nominative argument but is consistently found in the Acc-Nom argument structure in both Old and Modern Icelandic. Therefore, it seems that no comparative evidence may be adduced in favor of an alternating analysis of *fortryde* 'regret' in Old Danish.

That said, Dunn et al. (2017) reconstruct the argument structure of Proto-Germanic **þreutan* with an accusative subject on the basis of the earliest attested evidence from both North and West Germanic, where this verb consistently occurs with an accusative subject. That is, an accusative, and not a dative, is found with this verb in Old Norse-Icelandic, Old English and Old High German. This might even be considered an argument against analyzing *fortryde* as an alternating verb in Old

---

4 An anonymous reviewer claims that the order of the pronouns in the midfield in (103a), with the dative preceding the nominative, is the only grammatical order of weak pronouns in the midfield in Old Danish, irrespective of grammatical relations. However, exactly the opposite order of pronouns is observed in (103b), also from Old Danish, speaking against this claim. Recall also from the discussion above that the order of subject and object pronouns in the midfield in both Old Norse-Icelandic and Old Swedish is fixed to the subject preceding the object. It would be very surprising if Old Danish behaves differently from Old Swedish and Old Norse-Icelandic in this respect and I am not aware of any studies confirming such a difference.

Danish. However, Acc-Nom verbs in Icelandic also alternate between two diametrically opposed argument structures, in this case Acc-Nom vs. Nom-Acc, as is shown for the Modern Icelandic verb *henda* 'happen' in (104) below:

Icelandic
Acc-Nom
(104) a. *Aldrei   hefði   **mig**   hent   **þetta**.*
          never   would.have   me.ACC   happened   this.NOM
          'I would never have to experience this.'

Nom-Acc
    b. *Aldrei   hefði   **þetta**   hent   **mig**.*
        never   would.have   this.NOM   happened   me.ACC
        'This would never have happened to me.'

It therefore seems that *fortryde* 'regret' in Old Danish may very well have been an alternating predicate, irrespective of whether this is due to a contemporary Dat-Nom / Nom-Dat case frame or whether it is due to an earlier Acc-Nom / Nom-Acc case frame, which would then have existed in the earlier history of the Danish language.

Consider now the following pairs of examples which show that even in the modern North-Germanic languages, remnants of the older alternating behavior still exists for certain verbs. The first three sample pairs, involving *lyckas/lykkes* 'succeed' stem from Modern Swedish, Modern Danish and Modern Norwegian, respectively:

Swedish
Dat-Nom (currently realized as Nom-PP)
(105) a. *när   **jag**   lyckades   **med**   det   här   receptet* ...
          when   I.NOM   succeeded   with   this   here   recipe.the
          'When I succeeded with this recipe...'

Nom-Dat (currently realized as Nom-Obl)
    b. *Även   om   **det**   lyckades   **mig**   att* ...
        even   if   it.NOM   succeeded   me.OBL   to
        'Even if it was a success for me to...'

The example in (105a) is the modern equivalent of an older Dat-Nom construction, with the animate dative having changed into an animate nominative, *jag* 'I', most likely due to it being a syntactic subject. The nominative object, however, has been replaced by a prepositional object, headed by the preposition *med* 'with'. The example in (105b), in contrast, is the modern equivalent of the older Nom-Dat, with the inanimate nominative subject *det* 'it' maintaining its subject status and the (earlier dative) object *mig* 'me' maintaining its object status.

The following examples from Modern Danish and Modern Norwegian are structurally exact parallels to the Swedish examples in (105) above:

Danish
Dat-Nom (currently realized as Nom-PP)
(106) a. *Jeg håber at **jeg** lykkedes **med det**.*
      I hope that I.NOM succeeded with this
      'I hope that I succeeded with it.'

Nom-Dat (currently realized as Nom-Obl)
    b. *og **det** lykkedes **mig** at ...*
      and it.NOM succeeded me.OBL to
      'And it was a success for me to ...'

Norwegian
Dat-Nom (currently realized as Nom-PP)
(107) a. *og følte at **jeg** lyktes **med jobben** ...*
      and felt that I.NOM succeeded with job.the
      'And felt that I succeeded with the job ...'

Nom-Dat (currently realized as Nom-Obl)
    b. *Og **det** lyktes **meg** ganske fort ...*
      and it.NOM succeeded me.OBL relatively quickly
      'And it was a success for me relatively quickly ...'

Engberg-Pedersen (2018) notes that the alternation with *lykkes* has been around for centuries in the history of Danish.

The second example set stems from South Swedish, containing the verb *fela* 'lack' (here cited from Falk 1997: 157):

South Swedish
Dat-Nom (currently realized as Nom-Acc)
(108) a. ***Jag** felar **en krona**.*
      I.NOM lack one krone.ACC
      'I lack one krone.'

Nom-Dat (currently realized as Nom-Obl)
    b.   ***Det***   *felar*   ***mig***   *en*   *krona.*
       it.NOM   lack   me.OBL   one   krone.ACC
       'There is one krone lacking for me.'

The verb *fela* 'lack, miss' is a very early borrowing from middle low German into the Scandinavian languages. It shows a systematic alternation between two argument structure constructions in the South Swedish dialects of today. It is reasonable to assume that an older Dat-Nom construction lies behind the Nom-Acc examples of the type shown in (108a), with the older dative animate subject changing into a nominative. In contrast, the argument structure in (108b) most likely represents an older Nom-Dat construction which is now reanalyzed as a Nom-Obl construction.

The very final set of examples to be presented here involves the verb *angre* 'regret' from Modern Norwegian:

Norwegian
Dat-Nom (currently realized as Nom-Acc)
(109) a. *Nakenbilder*   *og*   *chatt* *på* *nettet* – ***jeg***   *angrer*
         nude.pictures and chat on online   I.NOM regret
       det ***hele.***
       the   whole.ACC
       'Nude pictures and chat online – I regret the whole thing.'

Nom-Dat (currently realized as Nom-Obl)
    b. MHM, ***det***   *angrer*   ***meg***   *sånn* *at*   *jeg* *glemte*...
       hmm   the   regret   me.OBL such that I   forgot
       'Hmm, it really regrets me that I forgot...'

The examples in (109) show that the modern variant of the verb *angre* 'regret' indeed turns up in Modern Norwegian with two opposite linear word orders which correspond to earlier Dat-Nom and Nom-Dat argument structure constructions of the type documented in (100) for Old Danish.

To summarize, there are several examples of Dat-Nom verbs in the history of Swedish and Danish that may be interpreted as speaking for an alternating analysis of the relevant verbs during earlier periods of these languages. Comparative evidence involving cognate alternating verbs in Modern Icelandic also strengthens the alternating hypothesis for these verbs in Old Swedish and Old Danish. The same alternations in argument structure found for some of these verbs in the modern Mainland Scandinavian languages also speaks for such an analysis. However, my goal here has not been to argue for an alternating analysis of specific verbs, but rather to argue that it is reasonable to assume that alternating verbs existed in the history of Old Swedish and Old Danish, irrespective of the details of analysis for each and every verb. I believe that the data presented above shows that alternating Dat-Nom / Nom-Dat verbs most likely existed in the history of the Mainland Scandinavian languages.

Before leaving the sphere of the medieval and modern Germanic languages, it should be mentioned that alternating predicates of the type discussed in this chapter are also the topic of investigation in Chapter 6 below, although there with a focus on Modern German.

3.3 Alternating Dat-Nom / Nom-Dat predicates in the early / archaic Indo-European languages

I now turn to examples from several different early and ancient Indo-European languages, which attest to an alternating Dat-Nom / Nom-Dat nature of the relevant verbs. This involves sets of examples from Gothic, Sanskrit, Hittite, Latin, Ancient Greek, Old Russian and Lithuanian. I have included Gothic here, even though it is a Germanic language, as it is also an *ancient* Indo-European language, exactly like Sanskrit, Hittite, Ancient Greek and Latin.

Starting with the verb *ganahan* 'suffice' in Gothic, cf. the examples below, of which (110a) shows that the Dat-Nom argument structure existed in that language, as the dative *þamma swaleikamma* 'such a man' occurs in the inverted subject position immediately following the finite verb. At the same time, the nominative *andabeit þata* 'this punishment' occurs in the object position following the inverted subject, confirming the analysis that (110a) instantiates a Dat-Nom argument structure construction.

Gothic
Dat-Nom
(110) a. *ganah* ***þamma swaleikamma andabeit** þata*
sufficient them.DAT such.one.DAT blame.NOM that.NOM
fram managizam
from many
'Sufficient to such a man is this punishment [inflicted] by many.'
(Cor. II 2:6)

3.3 Alternating Dat-Nom / Nom-Dat predicates in early / archaic Indo-European — 113

Nom-Dat
b. **jah**   *ganah*   *unsis*
    it.NOM.and sufficices us.DAT
    'And it is sufficient for us.'   (John 14:8)

In (110b), in contrast, the nominative *jatuh* 'and it' occurs in preverbal position, while the dative *unsis* 'us' occurs in postverbal position. It is, of course, possible that the nominative *jathu* 'and it' has been topicalized to first position, but it is equally likely that (110b) represents neutral word order, an analysis under which *ganahan* 'suffice' is an alternating predicate in Gothic. Observe also that Gothic *ganahan* 'suffice' is cognate with the Icelandic *nægja* and the Old Swedish and Old Danish *nöghia* and *nøghje*, even though the first one is a preterite-present verb and the latter are *jan*-verbs. All four verbs have the same meaning 'suffice' and at least the Modern Icelandic verb (90), and most likely also the Old Swedish one (89) are alternating predicates as well (see further Sections 5.3.1–5.3.2 below where this verb is reconstructed for Proto-Germanic with different argument structures).

Turning now to an even older stratum of the Indo-European languages, i.e. Vedic Sanskrit, consider the examples in (111a–b) below:

Vedic Sanskrit
Dat-Nom
(111) a. *tébhya*   *eṣá*   *lokò*   '*chandayat*
     them.DAT this.NOM world.NOM seemed.good.3SG
     'They found the world good.'   (ŚB, 8, 3, 1, 2)

Nom-Dat
b. __   *ácchānta*   *me*
    you.NOM.PL seemed.good.3PL me.DAT
    'You guys seemed good to me.'   (RV, I, 165, 12)

The root *chad-* 'like, please' is used in two diametrically opposed argument structure constructions in (111) above, the Dat-Nom construction in (111a), but the Nom-Dat construction in (111b). In (48a) the dative *tébhya* 'them' precedes the nominative *eṣá lokò* 'this world, while the verb occurs in final position. In contrast, in (111b) the dative *me* 'me' follows the finite verb, while the nominative plural form is prodropped from clause-initial position, as is evident from the form of the finite verb, which is conjugated in the 2pl form.

It could now be argued that these examples do not show anything, since the word order in Sanskrit is relatively free (cf. Speijer 1886; Delbrück 1888; Staal 1967; Gillon and Shaer 2005; among others). This is, of course, true. However, the goal here is not to show beyond doubt that Sanskrit had alternating predicates or that *chad-* is such an alternating verb, but rather to introduce into the discussion examples from the early and ancient Indo-European languages that might qualify as potential alternating verbs. These Sanskrit examples, as well as all the examples in the remainder of this section, may well be interpreted as testifying to the existence of alternating predicates in general, particularly when considered in conjunction with the Germanic data. Further research on the early and Indo-European languages is, of course, needed to establish this beyond doubt.

Proceeding to Hittite, (112–113) below contain two sets of examples consisting of a compositional predicate, *āššiyan- ēš* 'like, be to sb's liking' (112), and the related simple verb *āššiya-* 'like, please' (113), respectively.

Hittite
Dat-Nom
(112) a. ᴰ*UTU-i*   =kan   **kuiš**   *aššiyattari*
sungod.DAT =PTCL who.NOM likes.3SG.MID
'The sun god likes whom' (KUB XXIV 7 IV 37, Puhvel)

Nom-Dat
b. *parā*   **ḫandanzaš** =a   =kan   **antuḫwaḫḫaš**   *tuk*
forth   just.NOM   =CONN =PTCL man.NOM   you.DAT
=pat   ANA   ᴰUTU   ᵁᴿᵁArinna   āššiyanza
=PTCL   DAT/LOC   sungod.DAT   Arinna   liking.PTCP
'the just man is to your liking, sungod of Arinna'
(KUB XXIV 3 I 40-1, Puhvel)

First of all, the word order in Hittite is generally SOV and this word order is relatively fixed, according to Hoffner and Melchert (2008: 406). The example in (112a) contains a dative ᴰ*UTU-i* 'sungod' preceding the nominative *kuiš* 'who', while the order of the arguments is reversed in (112b), with the nominative *ḫandanzaš antuḫwaḫḫaš* 'just man' preceding the dative *tuk* 'you'. In both cases, the verb is in clause-final position.

There is one difference between the two examples, namely that the verb is in the middle form in (112a), but is an active present participle in (112b). Yet, there does not seem to be any difference in the argument structure of this verb, depending on whether it occurs in the middle diathesis or not, as both actives and middles occur systematically with a dative and a nominative argument. What is difficult to know, however, is whether the examples in (112a–b) represent neutral word order or not, but at least, without any further knowledge, these examples may be

3.3 Alternating Dat-Nom / Nom-Dat predicates in early / archaic Indo-European — 115

taken to show that *āššiyan- ēš* 'like, be to sb's liking' was an alternating predicate in Hittite.

Hittite
Dat-Nom
(113) a. [AN]A ᵈUTU-ŠI kuiški āššuš
DAT/LOC storm-god.DAT/LOC someone.NOM dear.NOM
'The storm god finds him dear' (KUB XXVI 12 iii 25)

Nom-Dat
b. *kuiš*=a *antuwaḫḫšaš* ITTI LUGAL SAL.LUGAL
who.NOM=CONN man.NOM DAT king queen
āššuš
dear.NOM
'Which man is dear to the king and the queen?'
(KUB XIX 26 I 17-8 Puhvel)

Nom-Dat
c. *ḫandanza*=kan *antuḫšaš tuk*=pat āššuš
just.NOM=PTCL man.NOM you.DAT/ACC=PTCL dear.NOM
'The just man is dear to you' (KUB XXXI 127 I 8-9 Puhvel)

The last set of examples from Hittite also illustrates that the related simple verb, *āššiya-* 'like, be to sb's liking' occurs with two different word orders, which, again, may be taken as evidence of two different, diametrically opposed, argument structures, Dat-Nom in (113a) and Nom-Dat in (113b–c). In (113a) the dative [AN]A ᴅUTU-ŠI 'storm god' occurs in first position, while the nominative *kuiški* 'someone' occurs in second position, both immediately preceding the predicate, āššuš 'likes'. In (113b), in contrast, *kuiš*=a *antuwaḫḫšaš* 'which man' occurs in first position, immediately followed by the dative, ITTI LUGAL SAL.LUGAL 'king and queen', with the verb in final position. The same word order is found in (113c), *ḫandanza*=kan *antuḫšaš* 'just man' is in first position, followed by the pronoun *tuk* 'you', with the verb in final position. Again, it is difficult to know whether these examples represent neutral word order or not, but on such an assumption, these examples may be taken to show that Hittite also had alternating verbs, exactly like Germanic.

Turning to Latin, the two verbs in (114–115) below, *sufficit* 'suffice' and *placet* 'like, please', serve to illustrate the point that the two word orders exemplify two diametrically opposed argument structures:

Latin
Dat-Nom

(114) a. in   omnia   enim   ***illis***   ***natura***   ***sua***
         in   everything.ACC because them.DAT   nature.NOM   their.DAT
         sufficit
         suffice.3SG
         'because they find their nature sufficient in everything'

(Sen. Ben. 4,3,2)

Nom-Dat

   b. Si   ***res***   ***tua***   ***tibi***   non *sufficit*
      if   thing.NOM your.NOM   you.DAT   not suffice.3SG
      'If this is not sufficient for you'

(Balbus 238)

In (114a) the dative argument, *illis* 'them', precedes the nominative *natura sua* 'their nature', while in (114b) it is the nominative *res tua* 'your things' that precedes the dative *tibi* 'you'. The structure of the two examples is otherwise quite parallel, except for the internal order of the two arguments. Both examples start with a conjunction / subjunction, both have the finite verb immediately following the two arguments, the dative is a pronoun in both cases and the nominative a two-word nominal phrase.

Latin
Dat-Nom

(115) a. ***Nobis***   ***quartus***   ***eius***   ***locus***   maxime   *placet.*
         us.DAT   forth.NOM   it.GEN   place.NOM   most   pleases.3sg
         'We find the fourth place most pleasing.'

(Quint. Inst. 3.3)

Nom-Dat

   b. Nam si   ***Octavius***   ***tibi***   *placet,*   . . .
      for if   Octavius.NOM   you.DAT   pleases.3sg
      'For, if Octavius is to your liking, . . .'

(Cic. Ad Brut. 1.16)

In both examples in (115) the verb is in final position, the dative is a pronoun in both cases, while the nominative is a noun phrase. The only difference between the two examples is the internal order of the arguments, with the dative *nobis* 'us' preceding the nominative *quartus eius locus* 'fourth place' in (115a) and the nominative *Octavius* preceding the dative *tibi* 'you' in (115b). Both sets of Latin examples in (114–115) are therefore parallel to the examples from Gothic, Vedic Sanskrit and Hittite above in that either argument may occur before the other, which in fact may

3.3 Alternating Dat-Nom / Nom-Dat predicates in early / archaic Indo-European

be interpreted as this verb instantiating two argument structure constructions, the Dat-Nom and the Nom-Dat constructions.

Consider now the Ancient Greek examples below with the verb *aréskō* 'like, please' and corresponding Modern Greek examples with its modern descendant, *arésō* also meaning 'like, please':

Ancient Greek
Dat-Nom
(116) a. oúte   gár   **moi**   **Polukrátēs**   éreske
       and.nor   because   me.DAT   Polycrates.NOM   liked.3SG
       despózōn
       mastering.PTCP.NOM
       'because nor did I like Polycrates, bossing men'   (Hdt. 3, 142, 12)

Nom-Dat
  b. eì   mḕ   **taũta**   **humĩn**   aréskei
      if   not these.NOM   you.DAT   likes.3SG
      'if these things do not please you'   (Lys. 30.21f.).

In (116a) both the dative *moi* 'I' and the nominative *Polycrates* precede the finite verb *éreske*, in this order. In (116b), in contrast, the nominative *taũta* 'these' occurs before the dative *humĩn* 'you', with both arguments preceding the finite verb, *aréskei*. Notice that the nominative is in the plural in (116b) while the verb itself is in the singular. This is allowed in Ancient Greek only in cases where the nominative is neuter plural, as it is here (van Emde Boas et al. 2019: 322). In light of the comparative evidence, these examples may indeed speak for an alternating analysis of the verb *aréskō* 'like, please' in Ancient Greek.

A corroborating evidence for an alternating analysis of *aréskō* in Ancient Greek stems from Modern Greek where the modern descendant of *aréskō*, i.e. *arésō*, is also well known for instantiating two different argument structure constructions, Dat-Nom and Nom-Dat, respectively. Two such examples are shown in (117) below, here cited from Anagnostopoulou (1999: 69):

Greek
Dat-Nom
(117) a. **Tu   Pétru**   **tu**   arési   **to   krasí**.
        the   Peter.DAT   CL.DAT   likes.3SG   the   wine.NOM
        'Peter likes the wine.'

Nom-Dat

b. ***to   krasí   tu   arési   tu   Pétru***
    the wine.NOM CL.DAT likes.3SG the Peter.DAT
    'The wine pleases Peter.'

In (117a) the dative *tu Pétru* precedes the verb, while the nominate *to krasi* 'the wine' follows it. The order of the argument is exactly the opposite in (117b), with the nominative *to krasi* 'the wine' preceding the finite verb and the dative *tu Pétru* following it. According to Anagnostopoulou (1999: 69), both word orders are equally neutral in Modern Greek, although perhaps with a slight preponderance for the Dat-Nom construction.

The penultimate set of examples to be discussed here comes from Russian. The examples in (118) are from Old Russian, while the ones in (119–120) are Modern Russian. Starting with the Old Russian examples, observe that the dative *mi* 'me' precedes the finite verb, *mьrzitь* 'detests' in (118a), while the nominative *životъ ixъ* 'their life' immediately follows it. In contrast, in (118b) the nominative *ničto* 'nothing' precedes the same finite verb, while the dative *emu* 'him' follows it. These examples may therefore be taken to suggest that alternating predicates are also found in Old Russian.

Old Russian
Dat-Nom

(118) a. *Zělo   **mi**   mьrzitь   **životъ**   **ixъ**.*
      strongly me.DAT detests.3SG life.NOM their
      'I feel strongly disgusted by their life.' (Izbornik of Sviatoslav, c. 1076)

Nom-Dat

b. ***Ničto***   *že*   *tako*   *merzitь*   ***emu***   ...
    nothing.NOM indeed so detests.3SG him.DAT
    'Nothing disgusts him so ...'
            (Cyril of Turov, Pritcha o chelovecheskoj dushi i o telesi
            [Parable of the soul and body] 142, c. 1160)

The more observant reader may have noticed that the dative *mi* 'me' in (118a) might be a second position Wackernagel clitic, in which case this example does not truly document a Dat-Nom word order with *mьrzitь* 'detests' in Old Russian. For this reason it is important to consider material from different time periods within a language, if such material is available.

Unfortunately, the verb *mьrzitь* 'detests' has fallen into disuse in the history of Russian, but two other compositional predicates that are cognates to *mьrzitь*

3.3 Alternating Dat-Nom / Nom-Dat predicates in early / archaic Indo-European — 119

exist, showing exactly the same alternation in argument structure, as they may instantiate both the Dat-Nom and the Nom-Dat argument structure constructions in Modern Russian. Both orders, the Dat-Nom and Nom-Dat, are equally neutral with these verbs in Modern Russian, according to my native speaker informants, which shows that one of the orders is not a topicalization of the other. Instead, these are two separate argument structure constructions.

Russian
Dat-Nom

(119) a. *Ibo* **Gospodu** *merzok* **nash smrad**.
for Lord.DAT disgusting.M our stink.NOM
'Because the lord finds our stink disgusting.'
(cited from D. Merezhkovskij, Peter and Aleksij)

Nom-Dat

b. *Ibo* **nash smrad** *merzok* **Gospodu**.
for our stink.NOM disgusting.M Lord.DAT
'Because our stink disgusts the lord.'

The predicative participle *merzok* 'disgusting' in (119) occurs in the Dat-Nom construction in (119a), but the Nom-Dat construction in (119b). In (119a) the dative *Gospodu* 'Lord' precedes the predicative participle *merzok* 'disgusting', while the nominative *nash smrad* 'our stink' immediately follows it. In contrast, in (119b) it is the nominative *nash smrad* that precedes the predicative participle *merzok*, while the dative *Gospodu* follows it.

Russian
Dat-Nom

(120) a. **Mne** *omerzitel'na* *ix* **žizn'**.
me.DAT disgusting.F their life.NOM
'I find their life disgusting.'

Nom-Dat

b. **Ix žizn'** *omerzitel'na* **mne**.
their life.NOM disgusting.F me.DAT
'Their life is disgusting to me.'

The same word order distribution is found in the Modern Russian examples in (120) above, involving another predicative participle, *omerzitel'na* 'disgusting', which is also cognate to *mьrzitь* 'detests' in Old Russian. In (120a) the dative *mne* 'me' precedes the predicative participle, while the nominative *ix žizn'* 'their life' follows it. In contrast, in (120b), it is the nominative *ix žizn'* that precedes the predicative participle while the dative *mne* immediately follows it. As is evident from these examples, *omerzitel'na* 'disgusting' is also an alternating predicate, exactly like its cognate *merzok* 'disgusting' in Modern Russian and *mьrzitь* 'detests' in Old Russian. Again, the fact that both word orders in (119–120) are equally neutral confirms that the word order differences here represent two different argument structure constructions.

The final set of examples discussed here comes from Baltic, more specifically from Lithuanian, which is generally regarded as being one of the most archaic modern Indo-European languages:

Lithuanian
Dat-Nom
(121) a. **Vaikams   patinka   ryškios   spalvos**.
children.DAT   please.3PL   lively.NOM   colors.NOM
'Children like lively colors.'   (cited from Holvet 2013: 265)

Nom-Dat
b. **Ryškios   spalvos   patinka   vaikams**.
lively.NOM   colors.NOM   please.3PL   children.DAT
'Lively colors are pleasing to children.'   (cited from Holvoet 2013: 266)

In (121a) the dative *vaikams* 'children' occurs in clause initial position while the nominative *ryškios spalvos* 'lively colors' occupies the postverbal position. In (121b) the order of the arguments is exactly the opposite, with the nominative in clause-initial position and the dative in postverbal position. Both word orders are equally neutral in Modern Lithuanian.

To briefly summarize the content of this section, I have presented here example sets from Gothic, Vedic Sanskrit, Hittite, Latin, Ancient Greek, Old and Modern Russian and Lithuanian involving two word orders found with the same predicate. According to the traditional analysis of the early and ancient Indo-European languages, examples of this type are generally taken to represent freedom in word order. However, I have argued that together with the comparative evidence, as well as with evidence found in the modern descendant languages, like Modern Greek and Modern Russian, an alternating analysis is equally likely. On such an analysis, these predicates instantiate two diametrically opposed argument structure constructions, the Dat-Nom and the Nom-Dat constructions, in the early and archaic Indo-European languages. On such an account, alternating predicates are not specific for Germanic but may be of Indo-European origin. As a matter of fact, alternating predicates have recently been reconstructed for Proto-Indo-European (cf. Pooth et al. 2019). I return to this issue in Section 3.6 below, but prior to that an explication of how to formalize the behavior of alternating predicates within Construction Grammar is in order, in particular the difference between alternating Dat-Nom / Nom-Dat predicates and non-alternating Dat-Nom predicates.

3.4 Modeling the argument structure of alternating predicates

Several linguistic frameworks are forced to assume that since alternating predicates like *falla í skaut* 'fall in sb's lap' may instantiate both the Dat-Nom and the Nom-Dat argument structures, there must be two different entries for *falla í skaut* in the lexicon, one associated with each of the two alternating case frames. However, following Barðdal (2001b) and Barðdal, Eythórsson, and Dewey (2014, 2019), I suggest an analysis in terms of only one verbal predicate, *falla í skaut*, which can then instantiate either of the two argument structure constructions. For a verb like *skiljast* 'gather', in contrast, this verb would only occur in one of the two argument structures, i.e. only in the Dat-Nom one.

Making use of the constructional formalism introduced in Sections 2.2.3–2.2.4 above, the first step is to model lexical entries for both predicates, *falla í skaut* and *skiljast*. One way of carrying out such modeling is shown in Figures 9–10, where the two arguments of the argument structure are given in an unordered list. This is signaled with the curly brackets around the arguments in the argument structure in the SYN field. This means that at the level of the lexical entry, there is no difference between *falla í skaut* 'fall in sb's lap' and *skiljast* 'gather', as both select for one dative and one nominative argument.

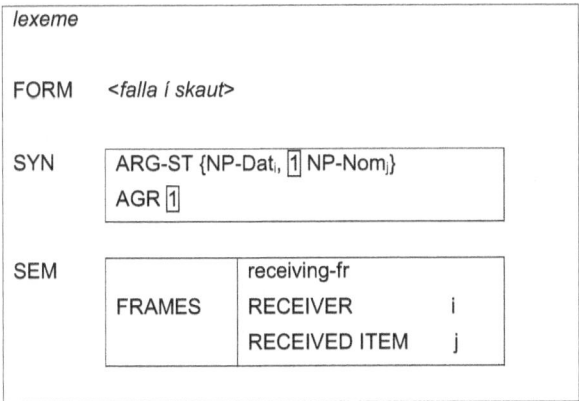

Figure 9: Lexical entry for Icelandic *falla í skaut* 'fall in sb's lap'.

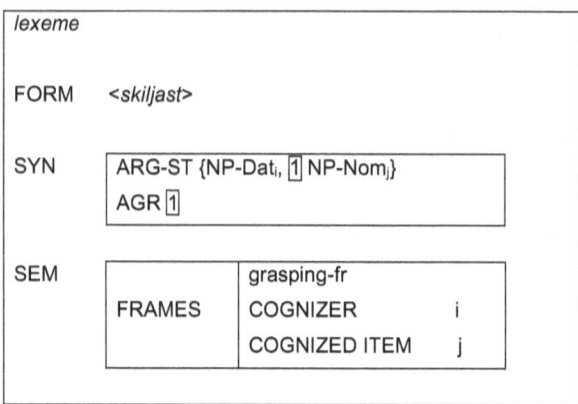

Figure 10: Lexical entry for Icelandic *skiljast* 'gather'.

The difference between the two predicates, *falla í skaut* 'fall in sb's lap' and *skiljast* 'gather', is instead found in how the two lexical entries interact with their respective argument structure constructions, which are introduced in Section 2.2.4 above. While *skiljast* can only instantiate the Dat-Nom argument structure construction, *falla í skaut* can instantiate both the Dat-Nom and the Nom-Dat argument structure constructions. This is modeled for *skiljast* in Figure 11 and *falla í skaut* in Figure 12.

In essence, this kind of modeling means that the locus of explanation is moved from the lexicon to the lexicon–syntax interface, as both predicates are modeled in the same way in the lexicon itself, namely through only one lexical entry each. There are several different ways to model this within the Construction Grammar machinery, depending on one's theoretical choices.

As is pointed out by Barðdal, Eythórsson, and Dewey (2019: 154–161), there are three theoretical options available regarding whether the list of arguments in the lexical entry is ordered or not. These are the following:

a. All predicates have an ordered list of arguments
b. All predicates have an ordered list of arguments, except alternating predicates which have an unordered list of arguments
c. All predicates have an unordered list of arguments

There are two problems with the first option, namely that if the list of arguments in the lexical entry are ordered, the argument structure has simply been moved into the lexical entry, making argument structure constructions entirely superfluous in the model. On a modular approach where syntax and lexicon are separate modules, this amounts to moving syntax into the lexicon. The second problem with this approach is that it has already been shown by existing research that argument

3.4 Modeling the argument structure of alternating predicates — 123

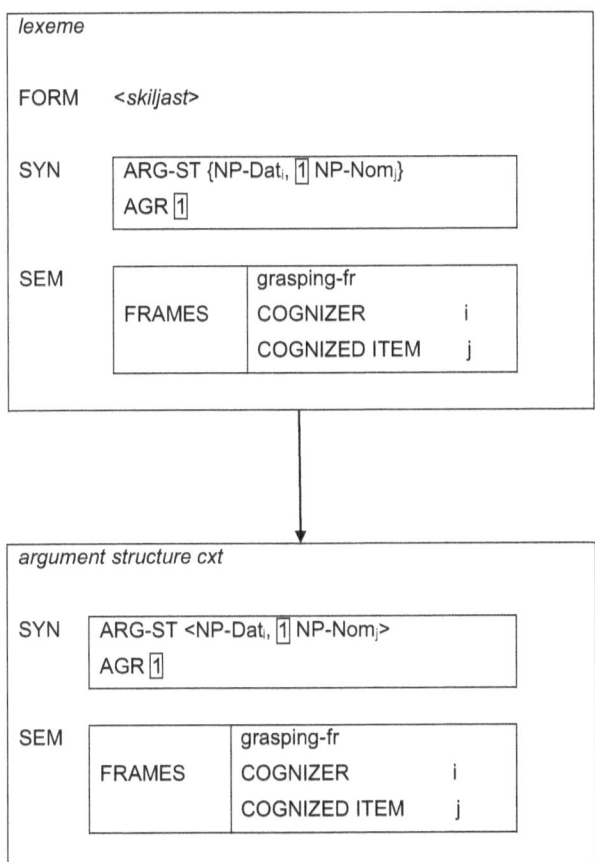

Figure 11: The interaction between the lexeme *skiljast* 'gather' and its Dat-Nom argument structure.

structure constructions are needed independently of lexical entries, as verbs may instantiate several different argument structures.

Turning to the second option, that all predicates have an ordered list of arguments, except alternating predicates, is not unproblematic either. The first problem is that one would still be moving the syntax into the lexicon for all verbs, except for alternating verbs. Again, this would be problematic for verbs that may instantiate different argument structure constructions, like the verb *kick* in English which is well known for its ability to occur in several different argument structure constructions (cf. Goldberg 1995: 11). The second problem is that offering different solutions for different verb classes eliminates the option of providing consistency in the structure of the lexicon. This would, for instance, make argument structure constructions

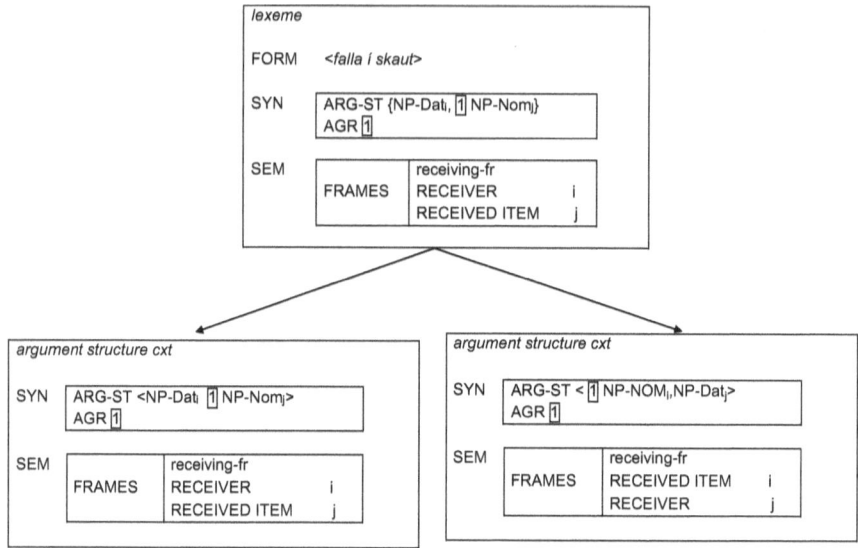

Figure 12: The interaction between the lexeme *falla í skaut* 'fall in sb's lap' and its two Dat-Nom and Nom-Dat argument structures.

redundant for all verbs except for alternating ones, again resulting in differences in the structure of the constructional networks for different verbs and verb classes.

The third option, that all lexical entries contain an unordered list of arguments, while the order of the arguments is instead ordered in the argument structure, is, in fact, conceptually most compatible with the constructional framework in general, as it has been repeatedly shown that argument structure constructions are needed, irrespective of the verbs instantiating them. As a matter of fact, the sheer existence of alternating verbs calls for a solution like this. Otherwise, there would have to be two lists of argument structures in the lexical entry for these predicates, as opposed to only one for non-alternating predicates, in addition to the fact that all other argument structure constructions each verb may instantiate would have to be listed in the argument structure field of the lexical entry. Again, as is already stated above, this amounts to moving the syntax into the lexicon for all verbs.

Instead, on this third option, alternating predicates are linked with both the Dat-Nom and the Nom-Dat argument structure constructions, while non-alternating predicates are only linked with the Dat-Nom argument structure construction. Furthermore, on this third option, consistency throughout the constructional network is achieved across different types of predicates.

A further consideration to take into account relates to the fact that it is not only verbs like *kick* that may occur in several different argument structure constructions. Rather, some of the oblique subject verbs discussed here may also occur in intransitive constructions without either the dative or the nominative, like German *gelingen* 'succeed' and Icelandic *takast vel upp* 'do well', as I discuss in Section 6.3.6 below. Again, these supplementary argument structures are also linked to the relevant lexical entries, instead of being located in the lexical entries themselves.

In the next chapter, I turn to the subject properties of potential oblique subjects in the early Germanic languages. Prior to that, however, a few tangles from the history of English must be untwisted, in fact, on the basis of the concept of alternating predicates.

3.5 The verbs 'like' and 'seem' as alternating verbs in Early Germanic

In the following two subsections, I zoom in on two verbs in the history of the English language, *lician* and *sēme*, and show how an alternating analysis yields a far more parsimonious account of the changes in the argument structure of these two verbs than accomplished by the standard analysis found in the historical syntactic literature.

3.5.1 'like'

A famous example, often cited in historical research on Old and Early Middle English, is the example of the "king liking pears" originally brought to the fore by Jespersen in 1927, iterated by Lightfoot (1981), Fischer and van der Leek (1983), and still considered to be part and parcel of the the standard story in the syntactic history of English, for instance by Loureiro-Porto (2010), Malchukov (2018), van Gelderen (2018: 147) and Shariatmadari (2019: 30–31), to mention only a few. For an extensive overview of early research on this alleged change in English, see Denison (1993: Ch. 5).

The example in (122a) is Jespersen's original reconstructed example, while (122b) shows the same verb in Modern English after a reanalysis of its argument structure, a reanalysis which is concomitant with a change in meaning from 'please' to 'like'.

(122) a. Þam cynge licodon peran.
 the.DAT king.DAT liked.3PL pears.NOM
 'The pears pleased the king.'
 b. **The king** liked **the pears**.

The nominative *peran* 'pears' in (122a) is traditionally analyzed as the subject of this verb in Old English, first and foremost because of the nominative case marking, while the dative *þam cynge* 'the king' is analyzed as the object, again because of the case marking. The alleged dative object, *þam cynge* 'the king', is assumed to occur in preverbal position due to freedom in word order. Hence the argument structure of (122a) is traditionally assumed to be Stim-Exp, mapping onto a Nom-Dat case frame, only showing Dat-Nom surface word order due to information structure. In contrast, the order of the semantic roles in the argument structure of the Modern English example in (122b) is clearly not Stim-Exp, but rather Exp-Stim, mapped on a Nom-Obl (earlier Nom-Dat) case frame.

Thus, the standard story purports that the arguments of the verbs in question have been "swapped" within their argument structure, from Stim-Exp to Exp-Stim. The analysis assuming such "swapping" of the arguments in the argument structure was a child of its time and it is generally not supported by what is now known about how argument structures change over time, as opposed to almost hundred years ago when this analysis was first proposed by Jespersen. At that time, the concept of oblique subjects simply did not exist, hence it was beyond the bounds of conceptual possibility to even imagine analyzing the dative as anything but an object.

Turning to the comparative evidence, from what is known about the syntactic behavior of 'like' in Gothic, there is no doubt that the cognate verb *galeikan* 'like' in that language shifted semantically between the two meanings, 'like' and 'please', concomitant with variation in argument structure (see Eythórsson and Barðdal 2005: 832–833 for a discussion). According to Snædal's (1998) concordance of the Gothic Bible, there are 26 instances of the verb *galeikan* in the Gothic Bible, of which three are ambiguous, while 13 have the meaning 'please', all occurring with Nom-Dat word order (see Table 6). Another seven examples have the meaning 'like', occurring either with a single argument, the dative, or with Dat-PP, i.e., with the Stimulus occurring as a prepositional object instead of being in the nominative case.

Table 6: Argument structures of Gothic *galeikan* (Eythórsson and Barðdal 2005: 832).

N	Argument Structure	Gloss
13	Nom-Dat	'be pleasing to, please'
7	Dat-(PP)	'like'
3	Nom-(PP)	'like'
3	ambiguous	

Since the Gothic Bible is a translation from Greek, it may also be instructive to gauge into which Greek verbs are being translated with *galeikan* into Gothic. It turns out that *galeikan* is used to translate three different verbs in the Greek original, namely *areskein* 'please/like', *dokein* 'seem/find (good)', and *eudokein*, meaning to 'be pleased with' (cf. Eythórsson and Barðdal 2005: 833). I suggested in Section 3.2.3 above that *areskein* 'please/like' is an alternating predicate in Ancient Greek, while both *dokein* 'seem/find (good)' and *eudokein* 'be pleased with' appear to be of the 'like' type, as opposed to the 'please' type. The fact that *galeikan* is a translation of the Ancient Greek verb *areskein* 'please, like' may be interpreted as a further support for an alternating Dat-Nom / Nom-Dat analysis for *galeikan* in Gothic.

For Old English, Fischer and van der Leek (1983: 352) argue that *lician* had the meaning 'please' when the nominative preceded the dative, but the meaning 'like' when the dative preceded the nominative. This suggests, indeed, that the two meanings are coupled with two different argument structures, namely Nom-Dat with the 'please' meaning and Dat-Nom with the 'like' meaning, even though Fischer and van der Leek did not explicitly make that assumption. This analysis is corroborated by the facts in Gothic, mentioned above, where the meaning 'please' is found with Nom-first word orders and the meaning 'like' with Dat-first word orders.

In Modern Icelandic, however, *líka* can only have the meaning 'like', as it does in Modern English, but then again, in Modern Icelandic *líka* can only occur in the Dat-Nom construction and not in the Nom-Dat construction (cf. the systematic examples of Modern Icelandic *líka* with regard to the subject tests in Section 6.3 below). There is, however, another verb in Modern Icelandic, *falla í geð* 'like, be pleasing to', already mentioned in Section 3.1.1 above, that may instantiate both argument structure constructions with exactly the same difference in meaning: 'please' when occurring with the Nom-Dat argument structure, but 'like' when occurring with the Dat-Nom structure. The examples from 3.1.1 above are repeated here as (123):

Icelandic
Dat-Nom
(123) a. **Fólki**   hefur   fallið   **íslenskt**   **skyr**   vel
         people.DAT has.3SG fallen   Icelandic.NOM milk.curds.NOM well
         í   geð.
         in   liking
         'People have taken a liking to Icelandic skyr.'

Nom-Dat
     b. **íslenskt**   **skyr**   hefur   fallið   **fólki**   vel
         Icelandic.NOM milk.curds.NOM has.3SG fallen   people.DAT well
         í   geð.
         in   liking
         'Icelandic skyr has been to people's liking.'

Therefore, even though the modern Icelandic cognate verb *líka* 'like' does not show alternating behavior, there are synonymous compositional predicates in Modern Icelandic which do. Observe, also, that *falla í geð* 'like, be pleasing to' in Icelandic is cognate to Modern German *gefallen*, a Dat-Nom predicate which will be further discussed in Chapter 6 below.

Returning to the argument structure of 'like', evidence from the Old Norse-Icelandic sagas suggests that *líka* could only mean 'like'. However, there are some documented examples in Old Norse-Icelandic which show an unambiguous Nom-Dat order. Two such examples are given in (124) below:

Old Norse-Icelandic
Nom-Dat
(124) a. Þá   líkar   **hon**   **mér**   yfir   allar   þœr   er
       then   likes   she.NOM   me.DAT   over   all   those   those
       er   ek hefi   fyrr   sét   ok   heyrt
       whom   I   have   earlier   seen   and   heard
       'her I like best of all those I have seen or heard'

(Barlaams ok Josaphats saga, ch. 68,
here cited from Kristoffersen 1991: 88)

Nom-Dat
   b. ok   líkaði **þat**   öllum   vel.
      and   liked   it.NOM   everyone.DAT   well
      'and everyone was at ease with that.'   (Brennu-Njálssaga, ch. 6)

In both cases the two arguments are in the midfield, following the finite verb. It is generally assumed that the argument immediately following the finite verb is the subject, because of subject–verb inversion in Icelandic, while the second argument, immediately following the first one, is generally taken to be the object. Note, however, that the two arguments in the two examples are pronouns and the order of pronouns in the midfield in Old Norse-Icelandic is a poorly researched topic (see, however, Haugan 2001: 174–184 and Jónsson 2018: 140–148). For a further discussion of these examples, see Barðdal (2001b).

Recently, Sigurðsson and Viðarsson (2020) have uncovered more Old Norse-Icelandic examples of *líka* with the Nom-Dat word order and they argue that *líka* means 'please' in such cases. The problem with their examples is that they all stem from translated texts. They argue, however, that these translated texts, which are mostly of religious nature, may represent an older layer of Icelandic than the one found in the sagas, as they were, in fact, written down before the sagas. This may or may not be a valid argument.

Having now examined the known facts about Old English *lician* and two of its cognates in early Germanic, I return to the traditional analysis of the changes in the argument structure of *lician* in the history of English. As already stated in the beginning of this section, the standard story asserts that the nominative stimulus was the subject and the dative experiencer the object in Old English, while the argument structure in Modern English is Exp-Stim (earlier Dat-Nom). This means that first the arguments of the argument structure must have "swapped" from Stim-Exp to Exp-Stim and then the case marking of the arguments within the Exp-Stim case frame changed from Dat-Nom to Nom-Acc (for further arguments debunking the standard story of the changes in argument structure of 'like' in the history of English, see Allen 1986).

In contrast, on the assumption that *lician* was an alternating verb in Old English, any analysis involving "swapping" of arguments remains uncalled for, as on an alternating analysis, *lician* could instantiate either the Dat-Nom or the Nom-Dat argument structure construction. The change from Old English to Modern English would simply involve the loss of one of the two alternants, the Nom-Dat construction, and a change in the case marking of the surviving Dat-Nom construction, from Dat-Nom to Nom-Acc, a change which must be assumed anyway. An alternating analysis of *lician* in Old English would thus yield a much more parsimonious diachronic analysis than that provided by the standard story.

3.5.2 'seem'

The second example to be discussed in this section stems from Harris and Campbell (1995: 88–89) and involves the verb *sēme* 'seem, be fitting', which appears to have been borrowed into Middle English from Early Scandinavian. Harris and Campbell argue that *sēme* 'seem, be fitting', was in the process of undergoing a change from dative experiencer object to nominative experiencer subject verb in Middle English. This would involve a change from Nom.$_{Theme}$-Dat.$_{Exp}$ to Nom.$_{Exp}$-Obj.$_{Theme}$, i.e. a development from Stage 1 to Stage 2a in Figure 13, constructed on the basis of Harris and Campbell's description of events. They, then, argue that this development was reversed, meaning that the new construction disappeared (Stages 2a–3), while the old construction continued its life, with the dative experiencer maintaining its morphological case in a postverbal position, later becoming a PP (Stage 2b in Figure 13), like other postverbal dative experiencers in Modern English (it seems *me* → it seems *to me*).

(1) Nom.Th-Dat.Exp ⟨ (2a) Nom.Exp-Obj.Th → (3) ∅
                    (2b) Nom.Th-PP.Exp

Figure 13: Harris and Campbell's (1995) chronology of the development of the argument structure of *sēme* 'seem' in the history of English.

There are several problems with Harris and Campbell's analysis, the most serious one, in my opinion, is that their development from Stage 1 to Stage 2a is oversimplified. This is because in order to convincingly argue for a development from Nom-Dat to Nom-Obj, where the experiencer goes from being the second argument of the argument structure (the Dat in Nom-Dat) to becoming the first argument of the argument structure (the Nom in Nom-Obj), one must first document how the Nom-Dat argument structure has developed into the Dat-Nom one. This omitted intermediate step is shown in the more thorough version of the schema in Figure 13, presented here as Figure 14.

(1) Nom.Th-Dat.Exp ⟨ (2a) Dat.Exp-Nom.Th → Nom.Exp-Obj.Th → (4) ∅
                    (2b) Nom.Th-PP.Exp

Figure 14: Revised version of Harris and Campbell's chronology of the development of the argument structure of *sēme* 'seem' in the history of English.

In essence, this means that the arguments of the argument structure must "swap" places in order for the Nom-Obj construction to arise, as this means that now the experiencer is the first argument of the argument structure, a prerequisite for it developing into a nominative. Since Harris and Campbell do not discuss this intermediate stage, it is unclear whether they assume that the development from Nom-Dat to Dat-Nom takes place before Dat-Nom develops into Nom-Obj, or whether these two changes happen simultaneously. In any case, the only way for Harris and Campbell's analysis to work is on the assumption that the two arguments, the Theme and the Experiencer, "swapped" places in the argument structure, either before the changes in case marking or at the same time as the changes in case marking took place.

Moreover, Harris and Campbell give the following examples as a documentation of their claims, in this order:

Nom-Dat
(125) a. **hit**   semit   **me**   for   certayn
         it.NOM   seemed.3SG   me.DAT   for   certain
         'It seemed to me for certain'   (Destruction of Troy, 198, c.1636)

Dat-Nom

b. | *me* | -seem | *my* | *head* | doth | swim |
    |---|---|---|---|---|---|
    | me.DAT | -seem.1SG | my | head.NOM | does | swim |

'I think my head swims.' (Damon and Pythias, 79 c.1564)

Nom-subject

c. | *do* | *as* | *ye* | | *seems* | *best* |
    |---|---|---|---|---|---|
    | do | as | you.NOM.PL | | seems.3SG | best |

'Do as you guys find best.' (Generydes, 6007, c.1440)

Unfortunately, Harris and Campbell give no dates for their examples above; yet when locating their examples in time, it turns out that they are not even documenting their stages properly. Instead, the original construction on their account, Nom-Dat in (125a), is the latest example they present, from 1636, while the example representing the final stage of their development, the one where the experiencer has changed into nominative, is the earliest of their examples, from 1440.

It is, of course, entirely possible that it is not Harris and Campbell's intention to have these examples document their chronology. Still, the least one can expect is that the examples they present do not go against the chronology that they argue for, as these examples do. What is more, a simple search in the OED reveals that all three constructions certainly existed even some centuries earlier than the examples from Harris and Campbell (1995) suggest:

Nom-Dat

(126) a. | *righte* | *so* | *it* | | *semethe* | **hem**, | | *that* |
    |---|---|---|---|---|---|---|---|
    | right | so | it.NOM | | seemed | them.DAT | | that |

'right so it seemed to them that'
(Mandeville's Trav. (1839) xvii. 184, c.1400)

Dat-Nom

b. | *Yf* | *so* | *be* | *that* | *the* | | *semeth* | *to* | *longe* | *a* |
    |---|---|---|---|---|---|---|---|---|---|
    | if | so | be | that | you.DAT | | seemed | too | long | a |

tarieng	*to*	*abide*	*until*...
delay	to	wait	until

'If it is so that you find the delay too long to wait for until...'
(G. Chaucer Treatise on the Astrolabe 2.25.30, c.1390)

Nom-only

c. *as **al the peple** semed.*
    as all the people.NOM seemed
    'As all the people thought.' (G. Chaucer Squire's Tale 193, c.1386)

The two constructions, Nom-Dat in (126a) and the Dat-Nom in (126b), turn out to be contemporaneous, which does not support the chronology suggested by Harris and Campbell, but is instead consistent with an alternating analysis of *sēme* in Early Middle English. As is outlined above, Harris and Campbell assume that the Nom-Dat construction is original, that the arguments got "swapped", resulting in a Dat-Nom construction, whose subject then starts occurring in the nominative and the object in an objective case, as the accusative and the dative had merged at the time.

Turning to the comparative material, it so happens that the Icelandic verb *sæma* 'befit', cognate to English *seem*, is also an alternating verb (Barðdal 2001b: 54–55), and this may also be true for the Old Swedish *söma* with the same meaning. Examples documenting this in Old Swedish and Modern Icelandic are given in (93–94) in Section 3.2.4 above. Observe, however, that the Modern Icelandic examples in (94), are constructed examples, showing a matching structure to the Old Swedish ones. Therefore, I provide below attested examples which demonstrate the alternating behavior of *sæma* in contemporary Icelandic:

Icelandic
Dat-Nom

(127) a. *Síst   hefði **munkinum** sæmt   illa   **herklæði***
         at.worst had   monk.the.DAT befitted   badly   armor.NOM
         *landvinningamannsins, **herðaslá** og   **fimur**   **hestur***
         conqueror.the.GEN   cape.NOM   and skillful.NOM horse.NOM
         bófaforingjans.
         chief.bandit.the.GEN
         'At worst, the monk had neither found the conqueror's armor unbefitting, nor the cape or the chief bandit's skillful horse.'

Nom-Dat

b. ***Markið***   ... *hefði sæmt   hverju   Úrvalsdeildarliði*
    goal.the.NOM   had   befitted every.DAT premier.division.DAT
    sem er.
    as   is
    'The goal ... had been befitting for every potential premier division.'

In (127a) the dative *munkinum* 'the monk' occupies the inverted subject position immediately following the finite verb *hefði* 'had', as an adverb *síst* 'at worst' is found in clause-initial position. The nominative *herklæði* 'armor', in contrast, is located in the postverbal position, immediately following the non-finite *sæmt* 'befitted'. Hence, the argument structure of (127a) is, without a doubt, Dat-Nom. In (127b) the nominative *markið* 'the goal' occupies the clause-initial position, while the dative *hverju úrvalsliði* 'whatever premier division' is in postverbal position, immediately following the non-finite *sæmt* 'befitted. Hence, the argument structure in (127b) is Nom-Dat.

Having now shown that the cognate verb *sæma* in Icelandic is an alternating verb, let us return to Middle English *sēme* and the alleged changes in its argument structure, as postulated by Harris and Campbell. On the assumption that *sēme* is an alternating verb in Middle English, it is most reasonable to assume that both constructions, Nom-Dat and Dat-Nom, existed from early on and that it was indeed the Dat-Nom construction which had its subject case marking changed from dative to nominative, before it fell into disuse. The Nom-Dat construction, in contrast, continued to exist in English, realized as Nom-PP in Modern English. This development is schematically laid out in Figure 15.

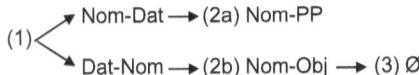

Figure 15: On an alternating analysis of the development of the argument structure of *sēme* 'seem' in the history of English.

Given these facts, Harris and Campbell's analysis, which involves swapping of the arguments before the experiencer changed its case from dative to nominative, need not be invoked, since all that happened was a short-lasting change from dative experiencer subject to nominative experiencer subject before the Dat-Nom construction fell into disuse with *sēme*.

3.6 The relative chronology of alternating vs. non-alternating predicates

To conclude, the data presented in this chapter show, beyond all reasonable doubt, that there are Dat-Nom / Nom-Dat alternating predicates in not only Icelandic, but also in several other Germanic languages, including Faroese, Old/Middle English, Gothic, and the Scandinavian languages. I have also argued for the existence of such alternating predicates in several early / archaic Indo-European languages in general. While further research on potential alternating predicates in the early Indo-European languages is needed to firmly determine the existence of such systematic alternations in the early layers of the Indo-European languages, the material presented here certainly speaks for such systematic alternations.

Establishing the existence of alternating Dat-Nom / Nom Dat predicates in Icelandic, and even Germanic and the Indo-European languages in general, is important because the subject behavior of the nominative argument has consistently been used as an argument against a subject analysis of the dative argument (Cole et al. 1980; Falk 1997; Bayer 2004; Wunderlich 2009). This subject behavior of the nominative, however, is only an argument against a subject analysis of the dative if the relevant predicate is not an alternating predicate, like with Icelandic *skiljast* 'gather', *líka* 'like', and others of that type. If, in contrast, the relevant predicate is an alternating predicate, like Icelandic *falla í skaut* 'fall in sb's lap', such argumentation falls lightweight, as the behavior of one of the arguments does not bear witness of the behavior of the other, since we are, in fact, dealing with two different argument structure constructions, the Dat-Nom and the Nom-Dat argument structure constructions.

The facts presented in this chapter also raise certain questions about diachrony, namely whether the two types of predicates, alternating and non-alternating ones, are original for Germanic, and even Indo-European, or whether one of the two represents an original stage of affairs, while the other may be a later development. Two scenarios are foreseeable:

i) Alternating predicates are original and the non-alternating Dat-Nom predicates in Icelandic are a later development, having most likely arisen through the loss of the Nom-Dat structure with the relevant verbs.
ii) Non-alternating verbs represent the original situation in Germanic, and perhaps even in Indo-European, and they have developed into alternating verbs through the addition of one of the argument structures.

A follow-up question that arises for the second scenario is then which of the two argument structures is original, the Dat-Nom or the Nom-Dat one, and, consequently, which one is an addition to the existing structure.

Haspelmath (2001) argues for the second scenario, suggesting that the Nom-Dat argument structure construction of the alternating type is the one that is original and that the Dat-Nom construction grew out of the Nom-Dat construction due to a systematic fronting of the dative argument, on the basis of its animacy and topicality (cf. also Section 4.1.3 below). There is one major problem with this explanation, however well it may otherwise sound, namely that experiencer objects of 'frighten' verbs are not known for being systematically fronted due to their animacy. If the Dat-Nom construction really developed from the Nom-Dat construction, due to the animacy of the dative object, one might expect to find the same development for accusative animate objects of 'frighten' verbs in the languages of the world.[5] As a native speaker of Icelandic, I confirm that no such systematic fronting of the accusative object of 'frighten' verbs exists in that language, nor in any of the other languages that I have near-native speaker knowledge of, which are Swedish, Danish, Norwegian and English.

In addition, there is a long way from an animate object being fronted and to it being reanalyzed as a subject by speakers. Such a reanalysis would, as a matter of fact, mean that the older object becomes to exhibit all the behavioral properties of subjects. This entails a major change resulting in a topicalization construction being reanalyzed as exhibiting neutral word order. And, even though such a reanalysis may be conceivable, it does not automatically entail that the preverbal argument all of a sudden acquires all the behavioral properties of subjects overnight; like – poof! –, now that you are a preverbal argument, you are instantly licenced to occur in all the constructions exhibiting the behavioral properties of subjects. I know of no such development documented in the literature, although I am aware of one serious suggestion to this end, put forward by Haspelmath and Caruana (2000) for the history of Maltese, in which they assume a gradual acquisition of the subject properties over time. The problem with their analysis is that it is a reconstruction, instead of being a documentation of historically attested changes.

Another explanation for the existence of Dat-Nom predicates, going back as far as to the neogrammarians, is that the dative was a free dative (cf. Havers 1911; Blosen 1972; Boon 1979), inserted into existing argument structures, and thus does not represent an argument structure construction of its own (cf. Barðdal and Eythórsson 2009 for arguments against this view). This free-dative explanation has recently been iterated by Serzant (2013; see also Falk 1997: 157), although the developmental path that Serzant outlines is purely hypothetical, not documented with historical data (cf. also Section 4.1.5 below). Also, no explanation is offered for the systematic alternation between the Dat-Nom and Nom-Dat constructions instantiated by the same predicates.

Pooth et al. (2019) also address the issue of alternating predicates, arguing that these emerged through a development from semantic alignment to accusative alignment (cf. Section 4.1.8 below). More specifically, the assumption is that an anti-

---

5 Verhoeven (2015) claims that animate objects of 'frighten' verbs are more often fronted in German than ordinary accusative objects. The problem with her analysis is that even though she distinguishes between causative structures with verbs like *erschrecken* 'frighten', *ärgern* 'bother', etc. and potential accusative subject verbs like *wundern* 'wonder' and *ekeln* 'feel disgusted', it is not clear that the verbs she investigates are correctly assigned to each class, as she illustrates no verb-class internal structure.

passive-like construction was reanalyzed as an active construction, with the active endings which are found in the earliest Indo-European layers representing older middle endings. In particular, Pooth et al. are able to explain the case marking of alternating predicates, namely why there is a nominative argument accompanying a dative argument, and not, say, an accusative argument. On the present assumption that datives of Dat-Nom argument structures are syntactic subjects, how come that the object argument is marked as a nominative, which is typically used to mark subjects?

Pooth et al.'s explanation for the case marking of the nominative is straightforward. First of all, the dative of Dat-Nom structure originates in an extended experiencer argument (see, also, Kotin 2021), most likely a locative with the ending *-i, later replaced by a purposive-benefactive *-ei, which then developed into the IE dative. This extended experiencer argument was found in the intransitive antipassive-like construction before its reanalysis into an active construction. Second, the only core argument of this intransitive antipassive construction was zero marked, i.e. it was in the absolutive case. Since this argument was typically inanimate and neuter, the extended experiencer argument could either precede or follow this zero-marked argument, depending on how the event expressed might have been construed (see Section 2.2.3). This, in turn, would result in *converse-lability* for Proto-Indo-European

Through the reanalysis of the antipassive as the new active, zero absolutive marking was generally replaced with the *-s marker, which became the new nominative case in the accusative system, inherited into the Indo-European daughter languages. It is through this combination of factors, namely the extended experiencer in the locative, later dative, occurring in intransitive constructions where the only intransitive argument was in the absolutive case, zero-marked, which was later replaced by the *-s marker, the new nominative, that the inherited Dat-Nom / Nom-Dat argument structures arose. The original case marking of these structures was Loc-Abs / Abs-Loc in the transition period from semantic to accusative alignment. This hypothesis is rooted not only in syntactic factors, as is the hypothesis suggested by Barðdal and Eythórsson (2009), but it is also rooted in the reconstructed morphology of the early Indo-European languages (see Pooth et al. 2019 for details), as well as in existing typological knowledge of how antipassives behave with regard to extended arguments.

To recapitulate, Pooth et al. (2019) reconstruct the alternation between Dat-Nom and Nom-Dat back to Proto-Indo-European, having its roots in the transition from semantic to accusative alignment. They further assume that the key to this alternation between the two diametrically opposed argument structure constructions is found in the fact that the original zero-marked argument, which later developed into a nominative, occurring as -*s* when it was animate, was generally represented by inanimate neuter nouns which are, anyway, unmarked for case.

I concur with the analysis suggested in Pooth et al. (2019) which entails that the first scenario above is the original scenario for Proto-Indo-European, and, subsequently, that alternating predicates must be reconstructed for prehistoric stages of the Indo-European languages. Under this scenario, verbs like *líka* 'like' must have developed from being alternating Dat-Nom / Nom-Dat verbs to becoming non-alternating Dat-Nom verbs. What must then have happened in the history of Icelandic is that the Nom-Dat alternant of verbs like *leiðast* 'be bored and *líka* 'like' has simply fallen into disuse.

3.7 Summary

In this chapter I have introduced the concept of alternating Dat-Nom / Nom-Dat verbs into the current discussion, as opposed to the concept of non-alternating Dat-Nom verbs, which is generally well known in the literature. The distinction between these two types of verbs is particularly important for any historical analysis of potential oblique subject constructions, as either argument, the dative or the nominative, may take on the subject vs. the object role.

When the dative is the first argument, i.e. in Dat-Nom constructions, it behaves syntactically as a subject, while the nominative is the second argument, behaving syntactically as an object. In contrast, when the nominative is the first argument, i.e. in Nom-Dat constructions, it behaves syntactically as a subject, while the dative is the second argument, behaving syntactically as an object. However, not all Dat-Nom verbs necessarily show this alternating behavior; for these verbs the dative is always the subject and the nominative is always the object. These are, therefore, non-alternating Dat-Nom verbs.

I started out in Section 3.1 demonstrating the word order differences between alternating and non-alternating predicates in Modern Icelandic, in particular making use of two different predicates, *falla í skaut* 'fall in sb's lap' and *skiljast* 'gather'. The former verb alternates between the Dat-Nom and the Nom-Dat constructions, while the latter only occurs in the Dat-Nom construction. A comprehensive comparison of how the two arguments, the dative and the nominative, behave in the constructions that make up the subject tests in Icelandic further reveals that either argument of *falla í skaut* 'fall in sb's lap' behaves syntactically as a subject, while the other argument behaves as an object. In contrast, for the two arguments of *skiljast* 'gather', only the dative takes on the syntactic behavior of subjects, while the nominative behaves systematically as an object.

In order to provide independent evidence for the existence of alternating predicates, I have compared the word order distribution of alternating predicates with both ordinary Nom-Dat verbs like *hjálpa* 'help' and unambiguous non-alternating Dat-Nom verbs like *líka* 'like'. The control group of *hjálpa* verbs yielded the baseline of 2% topicalizations vs. 98% neutral word order in a web-based corpus of Modern Icelandic, the Icelandic Ten Ten 20 corpus, when both arguments are full NPs. Non-alternating *líka* verbs corroborated this baseline with 4% topicalizations (Nom-Dat) and 96% neutral word order (Dat-Nom). However, alternating predicates, i.e. *nægja* verbs, showed a much greater variation in their word order distributions, ranging from 21% Dat-Nom word order (vs. 79% Nom-Dat order) to 75% Dat-Nom (vs. 25% Nom-Dat order), depending on the verb. This variation clearly deviates from the established baseline for topicalizations, meaning that the statistical differences in word order distribution neither pattern with *hjálpa* verbs nor with *líka* verbs. Instead, the word order statistics support the analysis that *nægja* verbs may either instantiate the Dat-Nom argument structure construction or the Nom-Dat argument structure construction, again conforming with the definition of alternating predicates.

Moreover, Modern Icelandic is not the only language having Dat-Nom predicates which alternate between Dat-Nom and Nom-Dat argument structure constructions. Barnes (1986) has also documented the existence of such alternating verbs in Modern Faroese, even though these appear to be substantially fewer than in Icelandic. Still, this is not surprising since there are considerably more oblique subject constructions in Modern Icelandic than in Modern Faroese anyway. Also, Allen (1995) claims that a subset of Dat-Nom verbs in Old English are alternating verbs. She shows that either the dative or the nominative of such verbs may control subject deletion in second conjuncts, but only when the relevant datives and nominatives are the first arguments of the argument structure and not when they are the second argument of the argument structure.

Similar material is easily retrievable from both Old Swedish and Old Danish, indeed supporting an alternating analysis of the relevant verbs in the earlier stages of the Mainland Scandinavian languages. Still, many of the alternants have fallen into disuse during the course of time, leaving only one of the alternants intact in the modern languages. In spite of that, some of the relevant verbs still exist in the modern Scandinavian languages, showing argument structure alternations which correspond to earlier Dat-Nom and Nom-Dat constructions, thus providing further evidence for the alternating analysis in the earlier stages of Germanic. Similar examples of verbs and compositional predicates showing the same word-order variation in several early and archaic Indo-European languages are also presented, including examples from Gothic, Sanskrit, Hittite, Latin, Ancient Greek, Old Russian and Lithuanian. Corresponding examples from Modern Greek and Modern Russian further corroborate an alternating analysis for earlier stages of these languages.

Two verbs in the history of English, *like* and *seem*, have been subjected to the standard story involving a "swap" of the arguments of the argument structure from Nom-Dat to Dat-Nom. This "swapping" analysis has its roots in Jespersen's early analysis of the development of *like* in the history of English. I have here reviewed some of the problems posed by the standard story and juxtaposed it with a story involving alternating predicates. On an alternating analysis, no swapping of arguments needs to be assumed as both verbs could instantiate either argument structure, Dat-Nom and Nom-Dat, from the very beginning. A story involving alternating predicates is thus considerably more parsimonious than the standard story with its alleged argument "swapping".

The final issue discussed in this chapter is the relative chronology of alternating predicates in the history of the Indo-European languages. Two scenarios are possible, namely a) that non-alternating predicates developed from alternating ones, or b) that alternating predicates developed from non-alternating ones. I have here argued for the first scenario, especially given the fact that alternating predicates have already been reconstructed for Proto-Indo-European by Pooth et al. (2019) in relation to their reconstruction of a change from semantic alignment to accusative alignment. On this approach, the nominative has developed from an earlier zero-marked absolutive of an intransitive antipassive-like construction which was later reanalyzed as an active construction, while the dative is a development of a locative, later benefactive, extended argument. This extended experiencer argument could either precede or follow the zero-marked intransitive argument, due to the lack of agentivity of the latter, which was generally both inanimate and neuter. This is how the alternation between Dat-Nom and Nom-Dat arose during the transition from an earlier period of semantic alignment to accusative alignment and handed down to posterity as such.

Investigations that fail to take the distinction between alternating and non-alternating verbs into account may lead to Nom-Dat word orders of alternating verbs being incorrectly analyzed as topicalizations of the Dat-Nom construction instead of being regarded as an argument structure in its own right. As its corollary, Dat-Nom word orders of alternating verbs may also be analyzed as topicalizations of the Nom-Dat construction instead of being viewed as argument structures of their own. In particular, the subject behavior of the nominative of the Nom-Dat construction has been used to argue against a subject analysis of the dative in the Dat-Nom construction (cf. Cole et al. 1980: 721–727; Falk 1997: 27–28, 37; Bayer 2004: 56; Wunderlich 2009: 590). For this reason, it is important to not only recognize the existence of alternating vs. non-alternating verbs to begin with, but also to know whether any relevant Dat-Nom verb under analysis is an alternating verb or not.

4 Oblique subjects in Early Germanic: Gothic, Old / Middle High German, Old / Middle English, Old Saxon, Old Norse-Icelandic, Old Swedish and Old Danish

The goal of this chapter is to systematically examine oblique subject constructions in the early Germanic languages and their behavior with regard to the subject tests that have been used to establish subject behavior in the modern languages. This is needed in order to lay out the argument that oblique subjects existed in the early Germanic languages and should thus be reconstructed for Proto-Germanic. In Section 1.3 above, I established a baseline for nominative subjects in a modern case language, showing how a nominative argument of Nom-Acc and Nom-Dat constructions behaves with regard to the subject tests. In Section 3.2.1 above, I also showed how both alternating Dat-Nom / Nom-Dat and non-alternating Dat-Nom predicates behave with regard to this baseline, with either argument of alternating predicates, the dative or the nominative, passing the subject tests, while only the dative of non-alternating predicates demonstrates this same behavior. These findings, however, are based on modern languages, while this chapter is dedicated to earlier stages of the Germanic languages.

To start with, Section 4.1 below is devoted to the description of some proposed hypotheses within historical linguistics on how potential oblique subjects have arisen. This is despite the fact that there is no real compelling and persuasive story out there on how such structures may have emerged. But one of those stories, and among the oldest ones, is the Object-to-Subject Hypothesis, proposed by Cole et al. (1980). They discuss data from three different language families, Germanic, Polynesian and Georgian, arguing that the data at their disposal attest to a change from object status to subject status within these language families in the course of time. With that said, there are severe empirical problems with Cole et al.'s claims regarding the Germanic languages, first and foremost due to their lacking knowledge of alternating predicates in Germanic (see Chapter 3 above), and, subsequently, their misanalysis of the relevant data of importance to this issue.

In addition, setting the Object-to-Subject Hypothesis aside, seven additional hypotheses have been put forward on how oblique subjects may emerge, also discussed in Section 4.1 below. These are the Topicality Hypothesis advanced by Haspelmath (2001), the Transimpersonal Hypothesis advanced by Malchukov (2008, 2018), the Anticausative Hypothesis advanced by Barðdal et al. (2020), the Free Dative Hypothesis advanced by Seržant (2013), the Oblique Subject Hypothesis proposed by Eythórsson and Barðdal (2005), and finally the Extended Intransitive Hypothesis, launched by Pooth et al., as recently as in 2019.

The remainder of this chapter, Section 4.2, focuses on the subject properties of potential oblique subjects in the early Germanic languages, pivoting in particular on long-distance reflexivization, raising-to-subject, raising-to-object, control infinitives and word order. The data presented in this section all speak for a subject analysis of potential oblique subjects in the early Germanic languages, and exclude an object analysis.

4.1 Where do oblique subjects come from?

In the following subsections, I provide an overview of the most prominent approaches in the literature on the birth of oblique subjects (cf. also the overview in Barðdal and Eythórsson 2009). This includes a discussion of the Object-to-Subject Hypothesis, the Semantic Development Hypothesis, the Topicality Hypothesis, the Transimpersonal Hypothesis, the Null Subject Hypothesis, the Anticausative Hypothesis, the Free Dative Hypothesis, as well as their antithesis, namely the Oblique Subject Hypothesis and its continuation, the Extended Intransitive Hypothesis. The Oblique Subject Hypothesis will be further pursued in subsequent sections of this chapter.

4.1.1 The Object-to-Subject Hypothesis

In a seminal paper from 1980, Cole and his colleagues argue for the earliest Germanic languages that oblique subject constructions did not exhibit any behavioral properties of subjects, in the sense of Keenan (1976). Instead, they claim that oblique subjects in languages like Icelandic and Faroese started out as objects in Proto-Germanic, a stage at which they also place Gothic and Modern German (see Table 7). Gradually, according to them, these object arguments acquired behavioral subject properties in the course of the centuries, with Icelandic having fully developed such behavioral properties by the time of Modern Icelandic. They also argue that this change from object to subject status has already taken place in Old English and Old Swedish. Also, they place Old Norse-Icelandic at an intermediate stage between, on the one hand, Proto-Germanic, Gothic and Modern German, and on the other hand, Modern Icelandic. This claim is based on their assumption that the relevant object arguments have acquired some subject properties in Old Norse-Icelandic, although they have not acquired all the behavioral properties found in Modern Icelandic.

Table 7: Stages in the development of subject properties of objects, according to Cole et al. (cited from Eythórsson and Barðdal 2005: 826).

A	A -> B	B	B -> C	C
Object Behavior		**Subject Behavior**		**Subject Coding**
PGmc.	Old N-I.	Mod. Icel.	Mod. Far.	Mod. Sw.
Goth.		Old Sw.		Mod. Engl.
Mod. HG		Old Engl.		

Cole et al. base their syntactic analysis on the following five behavioral properties of subjects:
– Reflexivization
– Conjunction reduction
– Control infinitives
– Subject-to-object raising
– Subject-to-subject raising

However, it is not only Cole et al. (1980) who view oblique subject-like arguments in the earlier stages of Germanic as syntactic objects. This is, of course, the position taken in traditional (Latin) school grammar, as well as in the majority of historical studies from the 20th century, like van der Gaaf (1904), Jespersen (1927), Butler (1977), Sigurðsson (1983), Smith (1994, 1996), Faarlund (1990, 2001), Kristoffersen (1991, 1994), Juntune (1992), Mørck (1992), Falk (1997) and Askedal (2001). Some notable exceptions to this are Harris (1973), Elmer (1981), Seefranz-Montag (1983, 1984), Allen (1986, 1995, 1996) and Fischer (2010).

The whole Object-to-Subject Hypothesis is most likely based on the case marking of oblique subjects, that is on the fact that these arguments are not in the typical subject case, the nominative, but show instead the same case marking as objects, i.e., accusative, dative and genitive. This approach, that oblique subjects have developed from objects, turns out still to be alive and well (cf. Seržant and Kulikov 2013), despite a fundamental lack of historical evidence supporting it.

4.1.2 The Semantic Development Hypothesis

Several motivations of the Object-to-Subject Hypothesis exist in the literature, including the Semantic Development Hypothesis, which is basically a conceptualization of the semantic changes accompanying the standard story, assumed in the early 20th century (cf. Jespersen 1927; Lightfoot 1979), and briefly discussed in Section 3.4.1 above.

The general assumption is that the verb *like* developed from the predicative adjective 'like' in uses such as "A is like B", with the adjective assigning dative case to its object, as it still does in, for instance, Icelandic, cf. *Hún er lík honum*, meaning 'she is like him'. There is also a verb having the meaning 'liken' in the early Germanic languages, cf. ON-I *líkja* 'liken', from Proto-Germanic **līkōjan-*, a ditransitive verb selecting for a dative indirect object. The Icelandic *líkja* and German *gleichen* still select for a dative object in the modern languages.

On the Semantic Development Hypothesis the process is assumed to have proceeded from 'be like sb', to 'be agreeable to sb' and ended with 'be likable to sb' (see discussion in Barðdal and Eythórsson 2009; Barðdal and Smitherman 2013). The general logic here is that *we like what is like us*, although the exact steps in this development, and the exact nature of each step, are not very clear. In addition, this semantic development story is purely hypothetical, with no documentation corroborating it, a fact that seems to be generally overlooked in current research.

Contrariwise, the Norwegian etymologists, Bjorvand and Lindeman (2000: 523–524), argue that 'like' is a primary verb, inherited from Proto-Germanic and neither derived from the noun **leika-* 'body', nor from the adjective **ga-leika-* 'same, similar'. They suggest instead that the Proto-Germanic verb **leikōn* developed from the root **leik-*, meaning 'move', 'hop' or 'dance'. A development from hopping and dancing to liking is conceptually plausible on the assumption that human beings manifest their mental states, liking or being happy, in a physical manner, with hopping and dancing. While Bjorvand and Lindeman's suggestion is also hypothetical, exactly like the alleged semantic chain of 'be like –> 'be agreeable' –> 'like', but if sustainable, their etymology certainly knocks the legs out of the arguments of the standard story.

4.1.3 The Topicality Hypothesis

In more recent times, Haspelmath (2001) has brought forward an approach, labeled the *Topicality Hypothesis* by Barðdal and Eythórsson (2009), as it assumes that accusative and dative subjects originate in structures where these arguments are syntactic objects (cf. also 3.6 above). These must therefore have been Nom-Acc or Nom-Dat structures of the type shown in (117) and discussed in Section 3.3 above. This example set, repeated here for convenience, stems from Modern Greek (also cited by Haspelmath):

Greek
Dat-Nom
(117) a. ***Tu   Pétru   tu   arési   to   krasí.***
  the Peter.DAT CL.DAT likes.3SG the wine.NOM
  'Peter likes the wine.'

Nom-Dat
  b. ***to   krasí   tu   arési   tu   Pétru***
  the wine.NOM CL.DAT likes.3SG the Peter.DAT
  'The wine pleases Peter.'

In (117a) the verb *arésō* 'please' occurs with a nominative stimulus subject *to krasí* 'the wine' and a dative experiencer object *tu Pétru*. In (117b), in contrast, the verb means 'like', occurring with a dative subject *tu Pétru* and a nominative stimulus object *to krasí* 'the wine'. Therefore, on the Topicality Hypothesis, the animate and topical object was consistently topicalized to first position and, thus, reanalyzed as a subject. The attractiveness of this approach is that it may perhaps explain the existence of alternating predicates of the type discussed in Chapter 3 above, although the discussion in Section 3.5 above favors another type of explanation for the existence of such structures (see also 4.1.8 below). Needless to say, there is a long way from an argument being systematically topicalized to it being reanalyzed as a syntactic subject exhibiting the behavioral properties of subjects, as Haspelmath also acknowledges.

Despite the conceptual attractiveness of the Topicality Hypothesis, such a development remains unattested in historical linguistics. Haspelmath and Caruana (2000) present an attempt to document this development in Maltese, but their description is essentially a reconstruction and not a documentation of an historically attested process.

Table 8: Case frames in Old Germanic.

Nom	Acc	Dat	Gen
Nom-only	Acc-only	Dat-only	Gen-only
Nom-Acc	**Acc-Nom**	**Dat-Nom**	Gen-Nom
Nom-Dat	Acc-Acc	Dat-Gen	Gen-PP
Nom-Gen	Acc-Gen	Dat-PP	Gen-S
Nom-PP	Acc-PP	Dat-S	
Nom-S	Acc-S		

Another problem with the Topicality Hypothesis is that it only explains the existence of two argument structure constructions in the early Germanic and Indo-European languages, namely Acc-Nom and Dat-Nom, and not the existence of other case frames where no nominative is present. But what is worse, this approach does not even explain the existence of Gen-Nom structures, since genitive subjects are very seldom animate. Given the existence of Gen-Nom structures, which are found in both Old Norse-Icelandic (Barðdal 2009) and Old High German (Seefranz-Montag 1983: 171–189), one would ultimately want an explanatory model that could satisfactorily take into account all three Acc/Dat/Gen-Nom constructions and not only the first two.

In addition, as is evident from Table 8, this approach excludes one-place predicates like Acc-only, Dat-only and Gen-only, as well as two place-predicates like Acc-Acc, Acc-Gen and Dat-Gen. All the case frames in Table 8 are inherited into Germanic, except for perhaps the Acc-Acc case frame, which may be secondary in Icelandic (although a few Acc-Acc verbs are also documented in Old High German).

It should now be evident to the reader that I have major conceptual problems with the Topicality Hypothesis, since being a subject is not a theoretical primitive, as I discuss at great length in Chapter 2 above. Rather, analyzing an argument as a subject is a theoretical acknowledgment of the fact that this argument behaves syntactically as a subject with regard to a series of subject tests within a given language. Thus, in order to show that an argument has developed from an object to subject, it is not enough to claim that through a simple word order change, an object is reanalyzed as a subject. Instead, one has to show how this change to clause-initial position is followed by a step-for-step development of the "topicalized object's" ability to start passing one subject test after the other in the history of a given language.

I assume that as a first step, the "topicalized object" would also start occupying clause-initial position in subordinate clauses. From there, for languages like the Germanic languages, one would have to show that this "topicalized object" has started inverting with the verb in questions, for instance. This would cover some of the different word order distribution of subjects, as opposed to objects. But, additionally, one has to document newly acquired behaviors like passing the subject-to-subject raising test, the subject-to-object raising test and the control test, just to mention the most important behavioral tests. Whether this newly acquired ability to pass the different subject tests is something which happens in a piecemeal fashion or whether it is an abrupt and an instantaneous change also needs to be established. Without such a proper documentation of the development, the Topicality Hypothesis simply remains unconvincing.

4.1.4 The Transimpersonal Hypothesis

Malchukov (2008, 2018), in his research on how split-S systems arise across languages, reintroduces the concept of *transimpersonal* verbs, following Sapir (1917), as an influential factor in this development. Transimpersonal verbs are verbs selecting for an experiencer object and a stimulus subject, typically corresponding to 'it'. The idea is that this stimulus 'it' gradually becomes vacuous and, hence, is left out of the utterance, resulting in a reanalysis of the relevant argument structure as being intransitive. For the Germanic languages, Malchukov (2008: 93) refers to Jespersen's and Lightfoot's standard story of the "king liking the pears" (some of the problems related to this analysis are already discussed in Sections 3.4.1 and 4.1.2 above), see (128 below):

(128) a. **Þam cynge** licodon **peran**.
b. **The king** liked **the pears**.

It is not clear whether Malchukov assumes that structures of this type exist for a period as "subjectless" (cf. Falk 1995), before the "object experiencer" is promoted to subject or whether the experiencer object is immediately promoted to subject upon the reanalysis of the argument structure as intransitive. Either way, the main problem with this analysis for the Germanic data, and corresponding Indo-European data, for that matter, is that there is no documentation whatsoever in the earliest documented stages of Germanic or Indo-European of an 'it' ever being a part of the argument structure of oblique subject constructions. In a database containing more than 3,500 entries of oblique subject constructions from all 11 branches of the Indo-European languages, including examples from Avestan, Sanskrit and Hittite, there are no examples found of this type.[6]

In this context, it is worth pointing out that the Indo-European languages are documented as going at least as far back as 3500–4500 years in time, and perhaps even longer, according to scholars using phylogenetic methods, or 8000–10000 years (cf. Gray and Atkinson 2003 and later work). This lack of 'it' in the argument structure of oblique subject constructions is all the more surprising given the fact that the Indo-European language family is one of the best documented language families in the world, both in breadth and time.

Malchukov (2008: 77) also argues that there is a formal similarity between his transimpersonal constructions and oblique subject constructions, namely agreement. That is, one finds the same agreement pattern with transimpersonal constructions as with objects in the languages that have object agreement, and this similarity cannot be overlooked, according to Malchukov. However, I disagree with

---

[6] The NonCanCase Database (https://www.evalisa.ugent.be/noncancase) was funded by the Bergen Research Foundation (2008–2012), the Norwegian Research Council (2011–2015) and the European Research Council (2013–2018) through three different grants to PI Jóhanna Barðdal.

Malchukov on this point, since 3rd person singular agreement is *neutral agreement*, i.e. it is the agreement pattern one finds with all non-prototypical subjects, as is confirmed by the following quote to Corbett (1991: 204):

> The range of non-prototypical [agreement] controllers vary from language to language ... It may include clauses, infinitive phrases, nominalization, interjections and other quoted phrases, noun phrases in particular cases (for example, **subject noun phrases in an oblique case**), dummy elements and certain null elements. [emphasis added, JB]

Therefore, 3rd person singular agreement, found with oblique subject constructions, does not in any way attest to an earlier 'it' ever having been a part of the argument structure of oblique subject verbs.

The most serious problem with the Transimpersonal Hypothesis when it comes to Germanic and Indo-European is already alluded to above, namely the lack of attestation of the alleged 'it'. It is both contrary to common sense and against scientific method to assume an argument structure for a given verb or predicate, if this argument structure cannot be documented at all in any of the material handed down to us by our forefathers during the last 3500 years (cf. Smitherman and Barðdal 2009: 263). For this reason, the Transimpersonal Hypothesis has to be rejected for the Germanic and Indo-European languages.

4.1.5 The Free Dative Hypothesis

Havers (1911), in his work on the dative case in the Indo-European languages, analyzes potential oblique subjects as being instances of the *dativus sympatheticus*, which is a free dative, not considered a part of the argument structure of specific verbs (cf. Hole 2014). Instead, free datives are generally analyzed as having an adverbial function, for instance in German. Havers' analysis raises the question of whether potential oblique subjects may have its origins in so-called "free datives" (cf. Seržant 2013). An example of such free datives is given in (129b) below from German:

German
(129) a. Das   ist   eine   grosse   Ehre.
         this.NOM is   a. NOM   great. NOM   honor
         'This is a great honor.'
      b. Das   ist   **mir**   eine   grosse   Ehre.
         this.NOM is   me.DAT   a. NOM   great. NOM   honor
         'This is a great honor for me.'

The fact that the dative is not obligatorily selected for by the predicate *eine grosse Ehre sein* 'be a great honor' is generally taken as evidence for the "free" status of the dative in (129b). However, verbs and predicates may occur in many different argument structures, without that necessarily entailing that one of the nominals is not an argument but an adverbial. To demonstrate this, consider the following examples, again from German.

German
(130) a. *Es   ist   warm.*
         it.NOM is   warm
         'It is warm.'
      b. ***Mir***   *ist   es   warm.*
         me.DAT   is   it.NOM   warm
         'I feel warm.'
      c. ***Mir***   *ist   warm.*
         me.DAT   is   warm
         'I feel warm.'

On the basis of pairs like (130a–b), one might conclude that the dative is not obligatory with *warm sein* 'be warm'. Still, it might be argued that *warm sein* has two different meanings in these examples, namely that 'it is warm outside' in (130a), vs. 'feeling warm' in (130b), potentially even yielding the comparison between (130a–b) as meaningless. Given that, consider pairs like (130b–c) instead, on which basis one might argue that *es* 'it' is not obligatory with this predicate in the meaning 'feel warm'. This is certainly true, but this further raises the question of whether *es* in (130c) is an adverbial "free *es*" or whether it should be considered an argument.

Recall from the discussion in 3.2.1 above that the verb *skiljast* 'understand' in Icelandic takes a dative subject, as in examples like (131a) below:

Icelandic
(131) a. ***Mér***   *skildist   það.*
         me.DAT   understood   it.NOM
         'I understood it.'
      b. *Það   skildist.*
         it.NOM   understood
         'It got understood.'

However, a comparison between (131a–b) reveals that the dative is not obligatory with the verb *skiljast* in Icelandic, which means 'understand' in both (131a) and (131b), although (131a) has an active reading, while (131b) is an anticausative.

Therefore, these examples show that the optionality of a nominal is not equal to non-argument status, as the dative of *skiljast* in (131) passes all the subject tests in Icelandic (see Section 3.2.1 above). Also, taking Construction Grammar to its logical conclusion means that "free datives" would simply represent an argument structure of its own. However, going deeper into the adjunct–argument debate would take us too far from the issue of whether oblique subjects originate in "free datives" or not, which is what is at stake here.

While there is no reason *a priori* to exclude the possibility that some potential oblique subjects might originate in "free datives", this would of course not be a valid Hypothesis for the origin of all potential oblique subjects, certainly not the ones that are case marked in the accusative or the genitive in the Germanic languages.

4.1.6 The Anticausative Hypothesis

The Anticausative Hypothesis, originally put forward by Barðdal and Eythórsson (2009), assumes that oblique subjects may arise through an anticausativization process, labeled *oblique anticausativization*. More specifically, this process entails that oblique subjects emerge through a systematic alternation between transitives and intransitives, involving valency decrease in which the case marking of the transitive object is maintained on the subject of the intransitive verb. A synchronic alternation of this type is shown in (132) below:

Icelandic
(132) a. ***Hann*** kastar ... *þungum steini á suma*
he.NOM throws haeavy.DAT stone.DAT on some
'He throws ... a heavy stone at some' (Þjóð 28(41), c.1876)
b. ***Honum*** kastaði ofan á skeiðina ...
him.DAT got.thrown top on ship.the
'He got thrown on top of the ship ...' (JsJsRit II, 183 c.1947–1949)
c. ***húsum*** ... kastaði um koll
houses.DAT got.thrown over top
'Houses ... got toppled over [in the hurricane]' (Þjóð. 34(68), c.1882)

The verb *kasta* 'throw' in (132a) selects for a Nom-Dat case frame, i.e. it occurs with a nominative subject *hann* 'he' and a dative object *þungum steini* 'heavy stone.' In contrast, in (132b–c) we find an intransitive use of *kasta*, in which the intransitive subject corresponds semantically to the transitive object; hence the case marking. There is also a change in meaning from active to middle, i.e. from 'throw' to 'get thrown', without this change in diathesis being marked on the verb. Instead, the verb continues to be marked as active. As a consequence, this type of anticausativization is dependent marking, with the anticausative marker found on the arguments, as opposed to the well-known head-marking type, where the anticausative marker is an affix on the verb (cf. Barðdal et al. 2020).

Synchronic alternations of this this type are well known from research on Icelandic under different labels: *unaccusative derivation* (Zaenen and Maling 1984) *ergative derivation* (Sigurðsson 1989: 216–218), *impersonal detransitivization* (Ottósson 2013: 368–369) and *oblique anticausativization* (Barðdal 2014; Barðdal et al. 2020, Bjarnadóttir 2014b; Cennamo, Eythórsson, and Barðdal 2015). See also Matasović (2013) on alternations of this type in Classical Latin.

A first serious attempt at putting flesh to the bones of the Anticausative Hypothesis in a diachronic context was published in an article only very recently (Barðdal et al. 2020). Synchronic alternations of the type discussed in (132) above are uncovered in language after language throughout different Indo-European branches. In addition to Germanic, examples are presented from Baltic, Slavic, Italic, Greek, Anatolian and Indo-Aryan. Oblique anticausatives turn out to be easily documentable in the North-Central branches of Indo-European, i.e. Germanic, Baltic, Slavic and Italic, while only sporadic examples are found in South-Eastern branches, like Greek, Anatolian and Indo-Aryan.

Observe that there is a very distinct semantic restriction on this kind of oblique anticausativization, at least in the Northern Indo-European branches, namely that it targets first and foremost verbs that may be used to describe natural processes, like weather phenomena, as in (132b–c) above. For this particular reason, it is unclear whether oblique anticausativization is confined to this one semantic field, or whether such a process has been productive at different times in different languages and branches, across different semantic fields. This latter scenario may perhaps be the case, given that the Latin data which Matasović (2013) documents mostly involve experiencer predicates.

Note that oblique subject verbs come in several different guises, as is evident from Table 8 above. It is therefore not a given that different subconstructions have emerged in the same manner. The Anticausative Hypothesis may account for the emergence of oblique subject predicates which correspond systematically with equivalent transitive structures in the language, while the Extended Intransitive Hypothesis accounts for the emergence of alternating Dat-Nom / Nom-Dat predicates (see Section 4.1.8 below).

4.1.7 The Oblique Subject Hypothesis

Together with Thórhallur Eythórsson, I have argued earlier that evidence for the subject status of potential oblique subjects in the earliest Germanic languages is indeed available to us (cf. Barðdal 2000b; Barðdal and Eythórsson 2003a, 2009, 2012a; Eythórsson and Barðdal 2005). As a consequence, the Object-to-Subject Hypothesis should naturally be rejected. On the basis of the evidence known to us at the time, we proposed a contrasting hypothesis, the Oblique Subject Hypothesis, which assumes that potential oblique subjects have exhibited subject properties at least since Proto-Germanic, if not as long as such structures have existed in the Indo-European languages.

4.1.8 The Extended Intransitive Hypothesis

The last hypothesis to be discussed here is the Extended Intransitive Hypothesis, which is a continuation of the Oblique Subject Hypothesis. Given that all of the earliest Proto-Indo-European daughter languages, except for Anatolian, are accusative languages, it comes as no surprise that the majority view is that Proto-Indo-European was an accusative language at the time of the split into the daughter languages (cf. Drinka 1999; Keydana 2018). However, Pooth et al. (2019) assume instead that Proto-Indo-European had semantic alignment (in the sense of Donohue 2008 and Wichmann 2008) and that the transition from semantic to accusative alignment took place during the period when the daughter languages branched off and formed a post-Proto-Indo-European dialect continuum (cf. Pooth et al. 2019, and the discussion in 3.6 above).

The assumption that Proto-Indo-European had semantic alignment is based on morphological and syntactic reconstruction of alignment in Proto-Indo-European. More specifically, there are some morphological intricacies found in the earliest branches of Indo-European, which motivate the assumption of a change from semantic alignment to accusative alignment already during pre-historical periods (the Proto-Middle-Antipassive to Neo-Active Shift Hypothesis, cf. also Pooth 2004, 2014; Pooth and Orqueda 2021). This is related to the morphology of the verb and an older proto-middle marker, *-o-*, developing into an active marker, due to a reanalysis of an intransitive antipassive-like construction to a new active construction. Regarding case marking, the assumption is that there was an agentive marker, *-s*, marking agentive subjects and a zero-marked anti-agentive marker, marking non-agentive subjects. Through the proto-middle-antipassive to neo-active shift, the agentive *-s* marker developed into a general subject marker with animate nouns, a form which later came to be called nominative.

It is well known from the typological literature that antipassive constructions can occur with additional arguments, so-called *extended* arguments, labeled *E* in alignment typology. With an experiencer as the extended argument, this experiencer would most likely have been marked in the locative case, *-i. This, in turn, would result in structures involving two arguments, a zero-marked stimulus, i.e. the original non-agentive subject, and a locative experiencer. Due to the non-agentive nature of the stimulus, which is typically inanimate and neuter, the locative experiencer could either occur pre- or post-verbally, depending on the construal of the event (see Section 2.2.3 above). A similar behavior has been documented for the verb *juṣ-* 'enjoy, please' in Early Vedic (cf. Pooth 2021). As a consequence, Pooth et al. (2019) reconstruct socalled *converse-lability* for Proto-Indo-European, a typological concept identified by Letuchiy (2009), involving converse structures, in our case stimulus-experiencer vs. experiencer-stimulus constructions.

Regarding case marking, the earlier locative later merged with the benefactive dative *-ei, yielding dative experiencers, while the zero-marker was reanalyzed as a nominative, in relation to the general change from semantic to accusative alignment, occurring as -s in the rare cases of animate stimuli, but zero-marked with inanimate neuter nouns. That is, this *s*-marker was reanalyzed as a generalized nominative case, thus expanding to non-agentive subjects, including the earlier absolutive zero-marker on anti-agentive intransitive subjects. This explains the existing alternation between Dat-Nom and Nom-Dat in the Indo-European daughter languages of the type discussed in Chapter 3, where the nominative stimulus is, in any case, most frequently an inanimate neuter noun or a pronoun, still unmarked for case (see also Section 6.3.1 below).

4.2 Subject behavior in Early Germanic

In the remainder of this chapter, I present evidence showing that potential oblique subjects behaved syntactically as subjects in the earliest stages of the Germanic languages, and subsequently, that they have never behaved syntactically as objects in Germanic, at least not during the times of the written era. The presentation below draws in part on data and analyses already suggested in the earlier literature, and in part on newly discovered data that have thus far not been disclosed to the scholarly community, at least not in this context.

Several of the established subject tests pertinent to the modern Germanic languages may be, and have been, successfully applied to the earlier stages of Germanic. However, two of the established subject tests discussed in Section 1.3 and in the bulleted list in 4.1.1 above, are more difficult to apply for the earlier stages than the others, as is discussed in the following two subsections, 4.2.1 and 4.2.2 below.

These are conjunction reduction and clause-bound reflexivization. The remaining tests that can be successfully applied to the early material are discussed in the following subsections.

Before proceeding towards a discussion of the early Germanic material, it is appropriate to mention that the subject tests used here on the Germanic languages are well attested cross-linguistically and have been applied on languages from various different language families. This includes Hermon's work (1985) on Quechuan languages, Verma and Mohanan's work (1990) on Dravidian, Steever's work (1998) on Dardic, Shibatani's work (1990) on Japanese, Hiietam's (2003) and Metslang's (2013) work on Estonian, Bickel's (2004) work on Tibeto-Burman languages, Yoon's (2004) work on Korean, Rákosi's (2006) work on Hungarian, Landau's (2009) and Pat-El's (2018) work on Semitic, Casto Alves' (2018) work on Cariban, and Comrie, Forker and Khalilova's (2018) work on Tsezic languages. This is in addition to research on other branches of the Indo-European language family, such as Anagnostopoulou's (1999) work on Modern Greek, Moore and Perlmutter's (2000) work on Modern Russian, Mathieu's (2006) work on Old French, Ilioaia's (2021) and Ilioaia and Van Peteghem's work on Romanian, and Barðdal et al.'s (2023) work on Latin and Ancient Greek.

In the languages where these tests are applicable, they are unambiguous subject tests and do not single out objects, nor are they sensitive to discourse prominence. And as a final point, even though the established subject tests were originally developed within formal approaches, they have, since then, been adopted by functionalists, typologists and anthropological linguists alike.

4.2.1 Conjunction reduction

Conjunction reduction has been successfully used as a subject test cross-linguistically, including in the modern Germanic languages, as is shown in the English examples in (133) below, where the subject of the second conjunct is left unexpressed on identity with the subject, *Europe,* of the first conjunct. In (133b) the subject of the second conjunct is also left unexpressed on identity with the subject of the first conjunct, *the coronavirus pandemic*. In other words, since the two subjects of these two conjoined clauses share the same reference, the second mention may be left unexpressed.

English
(133) a. **Europe**$_i$ *is a world leader in offshore renewable energy and* ___$_i$ *can become a powerhouse for its global development.*
   b. **The coronavirus pandemic**$_i$ *is destroying Europe's reputation for good governance and* ___$_i$ *is accelerating the economic decline.*

What restricts conjunction reduction in the modern languages is that the two arguments must be of the same syntactic category, i.e. they must both be subjects. In some Germanic languages, like Modern German, examples can be found involving objects being left unexpressed but of course only on identity with other objects. In Modern Icelandic, moreover, objects may only be left unexpressed in second conjuncts provided that the subject is also left unexpressed (Rögnvaldsson 1990; Thráinsson 2007: 479). This is shown in (134) below where only (134a) is grammatical:

Icelandic
(134) a. **Ég**ᵢ náði í **súpuna**ⱼ og ___ⱼ setti í pottinn
I.NOM fetched in soup.the.ACC and Ø.NOM put in pot.the
'I got the soup and put [it] into the pot.'
b. ??Ég náði í **súpuna**ⱼ og ég setti í pottinn
I.NOM fetched in soup.the.ACC and I.NOM put in pot.the

In (134a) both arguments of the second conjunct are left unexpressed on identity with the two corresponding arguments of the first conjunct. The example in (134b), in contrast, where only the object is left unexpressed in the second conjunct, while the subject is spelled out, is ungrammatical.

However, it is of considerable concern in this context that in the early Germanic languages arguments in general, and not only subjects, may be left unexpressed on identity with coreferential arguments earlier in the clause or even in the preceding context. This phenomenon is usually referred to as *argument drop* in the literature, or more specifically *topic drop* (cf. Thráinsson and Hjartardóttir 1986; Hjartardóttir 1987; Sigurðsson 1993, 2019). Two such examples are shown in (135) below where an object of a conjoined clause is left unexpressed on identity with an object of the first conjunct, while the subject in the second conjunct is phonologically and morphologically expressed:

Old Norse-Icelandic
(135) a. er Egill sá **skipið**ᵢ, þá kenndi hann
when Egill.NOM saw ship.the.ACC then recognized he.NOM
___ᵢ þegar
Ø.ACC instantly
'when Egil saw the ship, he recognized (it) immediately'
(Egils saga Skallagrímssonar, ch. 58, here cited from Hjartardóttir 1987: 57)

b. var   þar   tréborg   um   **staðinn**ᵢ,   settu
   was   there   wooden.fort   around place.the.ACC   put
   þeir   þar   menn   til   að   verja   __ᵢ
   they.NOM   there   men. ACC   for   to   defend.INF Ø.ACC
   'There was a wooden fort around the place, they placed men there to
   guard (it).'   (Egils saga Skallagrímssonar, ch. 47)

Similar examples are readily found in the other early Germanic languages (cf. Falk 1997: 30–31; Axel 2007; Heltoft 2012; Lander and Haegeman 2014). For this particular reason, evidence involving conjunction reduction will not be called upon here in favor of a subject analysis of potential oblique subjects in the early Germanic languages.

Nevertheless, there is a vast statistical difference between subjects and objects being left unexpressed, as object drop is considerably less common than subject drop in the early Germanic languages. For instance, Ferraresi and Lühr (2010: 3) claim that the ancient Indo-European languages are general subject-drop languages but only partial object-drop languages. Allen (1995: 50–59, 113–114) capitalizes on the statistical difference between the argument drop of subjects in conjoined clauses, based on identity with the subject or the object of the first conjunct.

According to Allen's counts (cf. also 3.2.3 above), subjects of second conjuncts are only left unexpressed on identity with an object in a preceding main clause in ca. 1% of the cases, while nominative subjects are left unexpressed in ca. 80% of the cases on identity with other nominative subjects in the preceding main clause. In contrast, nominative subjects in second conjuncts are left unexpressed on identity with potential oblique subjects in ca. 50–60% of the cases where such omission is possible. These numbers show that potential oblique subjects indeed pattern with nominative subjects in this respect, and not with objects, even though the statistics for nominative subjects and potential oblique subjects are not identical. Clearly, as long as we have not identified the factors that prevent subject drop in the 20% of the cases when it does not take place, it is impossible to know to which degree the same factors are at work when it comes to subject drop on the basis of potential oblique subjects.

In conclusion, conjunction reduction will not be used here as a subject test for the early Germanic languages, even though its use in Old and Early Middle English speaks for a subject analysis of potential oblique subjects in that language. Hence, I now proceed to clause-bound reflexivization and why it cannot be used either as a test for the subject status of potential oblique subjects in the early Germanic languages.

4.2.2 Clause-bound reflexivization

In the modern Germanic languages, it is incontrovertible that subjects bind reflexives within their minimal clause, as shown in (136) below for Icelandic and German:

Icelandic
(136) a. **Hann**$_i$ á styttu af **sér**$_i$ / *honum$_i$.
  he.NOM has statue.ACC of REFL.DAT him.DAT
  'He has a statue of himself.'

German
 b. **Er**$_i$ hat eine Statue von **sich**$_i$ / *ihm$_i$.
  he.NOM has one.ACC statue of REFL.DAT him.DAT
  'He has a statue of himself.'

What these examples also show is that only a reflexive may be bound by the subject of a clause, while a non-reflexive pronoun cannot be bound by the subject. This is of course well known in both general linguistics and theoretical syntax, as non-reflexive pronouns must be free within their minimal clause.

However, as discussed in Sections 1.3 and 3.2.1 above, objects may also bind reflexives in Icelandic, although only optionally, as is shown in (137a). The same seems to be true for German (see 137b).

Icelandic
(137) a. Ég gaf **honum**$_i$ styttu af **sér**$_i$ / honum$_i$.
  I.NOM gave him.DAT statue.ACC of REFL.DAT him.DAT
  'I gave him a statue of himself.'

German
 b. Ich gab **ihm**$_i$ eine Statue von **sich**$_i$ / ihm$_i$.
  I.NOM gave him.DAT one.ACC statue of REFL.DAT him.DAT
  'I gave him a statue of himself.'

In other words, an object may bind either a reflexive or a non-reflexive pronoun. As a consequence, it is certainly possible to distinguish between subject binding and object binding, as in the following examples involving an oblique subject construction:

Modern Icelandic
(138) a. **Honum**$_i$ kemur styttan   af **sér**$_i$ /   *honum$_i$ spánskt
him.DAT comes statue.NOM of REFL.DAT him.DAT Spanish
fyrir sjónir.
for sights
'He perceives the statue of himself as being strange.'

Modern German
b. **Ihm**$_i$ kommt die   Statue von **sich**$_i$ /   *ihm$_i$.
him.DAT comes the.ACC statue of REFL.DAT him.DAT
spanisch vor.
Spanish for
'He perceives the statue of himself as being strange.'

Since the dative subject in (138a) above can only bind a reflexive and not a non-reflexive pronoun, it patterns with syntactic subjects and not with objects. The same appears to be true for German. Hence, examples like these show that the dative subjects of Icelandic *koma spánskt fyrir sjónir* and the German *spanish vorkommen* 'find sth strange' indeed behave as syntactic subjects with respect to clause-bound reflexivization in the modern languages.

For the earlier Germanic languages, matters are more complicated. Reflexive pronouns may also be bound by objects during these early stages, as in the modern languages. This is shown in the following examples from Gothic, Old Norse-Icelandic, Old Swedish and Old Danish:

Gothic
(139) a. jam **þamma**$_i$ wiljandin af þus leihvan   **sis**$_i$
and the.one.DAT wanting of you borrow.INF REFL.DAT
ni   uswandjais
not turn.away
'And do not turn away the one wishing to borrow for himself from you.'
(Mat. 5.42, cited from Harbert 1978: 46)

Old Norse-Icelandic
b. Þá   bauð   Ketill að flytja **hana**$_i$ til **frænda**
then offered Ketill to move her.ACC to relatives.GEN
sinna$_i$.
REFL.GEN
'Then Ketil offered to take her to her relatives'
(Landnámabók, ch. 76, Rögnvaldsson 2007: 4)

Old Swedish
c. *at   thu   **minom   son**$_i$ i   geen   skipadhe   **sina**   **hustru**$_i$*
   that   you   my.DAT   son   a   gain   appointed   REFL.ACC   wife
   'that you again arranged his wife for my son.'

   (Siälinna tröst, 386, c.1401, Falk 1997: 29)

Old Danish
d. *Item   thil   bynder   iæck   meg   oc   myne   arfuinge   ath   frii*
   item   to   bind   I   me   and   my   hairs   to   free
   oc   frelsse   for^{de} hederligh   capitell
   and   release   aforementioned   honorable   priest
   ***for**^{de} **gaard   oc   gotz**$_i$ meth   **alle   syn**$_i$*
   aforementioned   farm   and   goods   with   all   REFL
   ***tiill   legelsse**   tiill   ewindelig   eyæ*
   abutting   contingencies for   eternal   possession
   'After that, I commit myself and my heirs to free and release to the aforementioned honorable priest the aforementioned farm and goods with all its contingencies for his eternal possession.'

   (ÅrhusB. 923, c.1438)

In (139a–c) the reflexives *sis* 'oneself', *frænda sinna* 'her relatives' and *sina hustru* 'his wife' are bound by objects, i.e. the direct objects *þamma* 'the one' in (139a), *hana* 'her' in (139b) and the indirect object *minom son* 'my son' in (139c). In (139d), the direct object *gaard oc gotz* 'farm and goods' binds the reflexive *syn* 'self' in the modifying adverbial phrase.

While binding of reflexives by objects is optional in Old Swedish (Falk 1997: 29), exactly as in Modern Icelandic and Modern German, subjects may also bind non-reflexive pronouns, which in turn means that subject binding is not confined to reflexives, as it is in the modern languages. Examples of that type have also been documented for Old Norse-Icelandic (Rögnvaldsson 2007), as is shown in the following example:

Old Norse-Icelandic
(140) a. ***konungur**$_i$ ...   býður   þeim   að   taka   við   skírn*
         king.NOM   orders   them   to   take   with   christening
         *eftir   **boði   hans**$_i$.*
         after   order   his
         'the king ... orders them to be christened according to his orders.'

         (Ólafs saga Tryggvasonar, ch. 56, cited from Rögnvaldsson 2007: 7)

Old Swedish

b. ***han**$_i$ wart   konunghir   æpthir **hans**$_i$ **fadhir**   dødan*
   he.NOM   became   king.NOM   after   his   father.ACC   dead.ACC
   'He became king upon his father's death'
   (Fem moseböcker på fornsvenska: 14, c.1275–1300,
cited from Falk 1997: 29)

Falk also reports, citing Ljunggren (1901), that considerably more variation is found for subject binding in the oldest Swedish legal texts, with subjects binding either reflexives or non-reflexive pronouns, while later texts are more in line with the situation in the modern languages. Turning to Old English and Old Saxon, these languages do not have simple reflexives at all, and it seems that reflexive and non-reflexive possessives, at least in the Heliand, are subject to metrical restrictions (Sapp 2010).

To conclude, too much variation is found in and across the early Germanic languages with regard to subject and object binding of reflexives and non-reflexives for clause-bound reflexivization to be a usable subject test for these early stages. However, the same is not true for long-distance reflexivization.

4.2.3 Long-distance reflexivization

A characteristic of long-distance reflexives is that they are bound by the subject of an earlier clause, either a matrix clause or a preceding clause earlier in the context. In other words, a reflexive of a subordinate clause may be controlled by the syntactic subject of the main clause and is not necessarily controlled by the syntactic subject of its own subordinate clause. Of the earlier Germanic languages, however, long-distance reflexives have only been documented in Gothic and Old Norse-Icelandic. The following examples illustrate this with nominative subjects as antecedents:

Gothic

(141) a. ***Jains**$_i$ skal   wahsjan   iþ   ik   minznan.   Eiþan*
        that.one.NOM   shall   grow.INF   but   I.NOM   lessen.INF   since
        *nu   siponjam   **seinaim**$_j$,   þeim   bi   swikneim*
        now   disciples.DAT   his.DAT   those.DAT   about   cleansing.DAT
        *du   Judaium   sokjandam   jah   qiþandam   **sis**$_i$*
        for   jews.DAT   disputing.DAT   and   saying.DAT   REFL.DAT
        'He shall grow and I shall shrink. Since now his disciples, disputing with the Jews about the cleansing and saying to him:'
        (Skeireins 4:2, cited from Ferraresi 2005: 95)

b. akei [is$_i$]   was kunnands þatei swaleikamma waldufnja
   and   he   was knowing   that   such.DAT   authority.DAT
   mahtais   **sei[na]izos**$_i$ nauþs   ustaiknida wesi[7]
   power.GEN REFL.GEN   force.NOM shown   would.be
   'He knew, nevertheless, that by such authority, the force of His power
   would be revealed'   (Skeireins 1:4, cited from Harbert 1978: 38)

Old Norse Icelandic
   c. hafði **hann**$_i$ uppi orð   **sín**$_i$ og   bað   Snorra
      had   he.NOM   up   words REFL   and asked Snorri
      goða   að   hann gifti   **sér**$_i$ Þuríði systur sína
      Goði   that he   would.marry REFL   Þuríur sister REFL
      'He brought up his errand and asked Snorri the Chieftain to marry off
      Þuríð, his sister, to him'
                     (Eyrbyggja saga, ch. 29, cited from Rögnvaldsson 2007: 7)

In (141a) the subject *jains* 'the one' in the first main clause conjunct binds a reflexive object in a participle clause, *sis* 'self' which is the object of *qiþandam* 'saying'. This is despite the fact that two other subjects intervene between *jains* and *sis*, i.e. *ik* 'I', the subject of the second main clause conjunct, and *siponjam seinaim* 'his disciples', the subject of the relevant participle clause. In (141b) the pro-dropped nominative subject of *was kunnands* 'be knowing' in the main clause binds a reflexive in the subject phrase *mahtais sei[na]izos nauþs* 'force of his power' of the subordinate clause.

The two Gothic examples differ in that the reflexive is found in a participial clause in (141a), which is not unheard of, according to Ferraresi, but in a subordinate 'that' clause in (141b). Harbert (1978: 38) claims that this is the only such example that he has come across, where a subject in a subordinate clause is bound by the subject of a main clause.

In this context, Ferraresi (2005: 95–97) suggests a diachronic development involving the loss of long-distance reflexivization in the "history" of Gothic, as later texts, like the Skeireins, she claims, appear to use non-reflexive pronouns instead of reflexive pronouns to a greater degree than earlier texts. Without frequency figures, it is difficult to take a position on such a claim, especially considering the fact that both examples in (141a–b) are from the Skeireins.

In the Old Norse-Icelandic example in (141c), the subject of the first main clause conjunct, *hann* 'he', binds the object, *sér* 'self', of the finite verb *gifta* 'marry' in the

---

[7] The reflexive in this example is located far to the right in the manuscript margin and is heavily bleached, yet identified by Bennett (1950: 1268) through means of ultraviolet radiation.

subordinate clause, despite the intervening subject *hann*, which in this case refers back to Snorri Goði, the object of the preceding matrix clause. For more examples of this type in Old Norse-Icelandic, see Rögnvaldsson (2007).

Therefore, the examples in (141) above attest to the existence of long-distance reflexivization in two early Germanic languages, Gothic and Old Norse-Icelandic. However, given the scarcity of such structures, it might not be all that easy to find examples involving oblique subject constructions in the earliest texts. This is certainly true for Gothic, which is not at all surprising given the meagreness of the Gothic corpus. Still, Bucci and Barðdal (2023) report on one such example, shown in (142) below:

Gothic
(142) *þugkeiþ* **im**$_i$ *auk ei in filuwaurdein* **seinai**$_i$
thinks.3SG them.DAT then that in many.words their.REFL
andhausjaindau.
would.be.heard.MP.3PL
'then they think that due to their extensive speech, they would be heard.'
(Matthew 6:7)

The reflexive is found in the adverbial phrase *in filuwaurdein seinai* 'in their many words' in the subordinate clause headed by *ei* 'that', bound by the potential dative subject *im* 'them' in the matrix clause.

Examples of this type have *also* been reported for Old Norse-Icelandic in the literature (cf. Rögnvaldsson 1991, 1995, 2007: 12):

Old Norse-Icelandic
(143) a. *dreymdi* **hann**$_i$ *að* **Bárður faðir sinn**$_i$ *kœmi til hans*
dreamt he.ACC that Bard father REFL came to him
'he dreamt that his father Bard came to him'
(Bárðar saga Snæfellsáss, Ch. 21)

b. *þá líkar* **honum**$_i$ *eigi þarvist þeirra og þykir eigi*
then likes he.DAT not stay their and finds not
örvænt að þeir muni þar eflast ætla til
impossible that they will there strengthen intend to
móts við **sig**$_i$.
against with REFL
'he does not like their stay there and does not find it impossible that they intend to gain strength and turn against him.'
(Geirmundar þáttur heljarskinns)

In (143a) above, the potential accusative subject *hann* 'he' with the verb *dreyma* 'dream' binds the reflexive *sinn* 'self' in *Bárður faðir sinn* 'his father Bard' in the subordinate clause. In the same manner, the reflexive *sig* in the subordinate clause in (143b) is bound by the potential dative subject *honum* 'he' in the first main clause.

This particular behavior, to bind reflexives outside a minimal clause is indeed confined to subjects. In other words, the examples in (142–143) above show that potential accusative and dative subjects behave syntactically as nominative subjects with regard to long-distance reflexivization in both Gothic and Old Norse-Icelandic.

I now turn to subject-to-subject raising in the early Germanic languages.

4.2.4 Raising-to-subject

The inventory of subject-to-subject raising verbs varies from language to language; these are typically verbs which do not select for a subject of their own, like for instance modal verbs, aspectual verbs expressing beginning phases or end phases, verbs of seeming and other verbs with "impoverished" lexical semantic meaning (cf. Polinsky 2013; Landau 2013; Kim and Michaelis 2020: Ch. 7). Examples from Modern English can be used to illustrate this syntactic behavior:

(144) a. *It* rains.
       b. *He* runs.

(145) a. *It* started to **rain**
       b. *He* started to **run**.

In both examples in (145) above, it is clear that the subjects, *it* and *he*, respectively, come from the lower verbs, *rain* and *run*, since *rain* selects for an expletive subject like *it*, as is shown in (144a) and *run* when involving physical activity selects for an animate subject like *he*, as is shown in (144b).

Structures involving raising-to-subject are found in all the early Germanic languages (cf. Denison 1990; Harbert 2007: 259–261; Demske 2008; Barðdal and Eythórsson 2012a). The examples in (146) demonstrate their existence with a nominative subject in Gothic, Old High German, Old English, Old Norse-Icelandic, Old Swedish and Old Danish:

Gothic
(146) þanuh **dags** juþan dugann **hneiwan**
         but   day.NOM already began.3SG droop.INF
         'and when the day began to droop'   (Luke 9: 12)

Old High German
(147) dáz **er**... ne-dúnche   hônen   námen   **bréiten**
     that he   not-seems.3SG   honorable.ACC   name.ACC   spread.INF
     'that he ... does not seem to spread his honorable name.'
                           (Notker, Boeth.Cons. II 133.27, cited from Demske 2008: 152)

Old English
(148) þæt   ðæt   **fýr**   ongon   **sweðrian**   syððan
     that this fire.NOM   began.3SG   weaken.INF   after.that
     'that this fire began to weaken after that'   (Beowulf 2701–2702)

Old Norse-Icelandic
(149) en   er   **hún**   tók   að   **brenna**
     but   when she.NOM   started.3SG   to   burn.INF
     'but when it started to burn'   (Egils saga Skallagrímssonar, ch. 22)

Old Swedish
(150) **wädhrit**   matte   **bläsa**   them   badhe   hiit
     weather.the.NOM   could.3SG   blow.INF   them   both   hither
     oc   thiit
     and   thither
     'the weather could blow them both hither and thither'
                                                       (Siälinna tröst, 419, c.1401)

Old Danish
(151) tha   bwrdhe   **Erich**   marken   ath   **fly**
     then   started.3SG   Erich.NOM   field.the   to   flee. INF
     'then Erich started to flee from the field.' (Den danske Rimkrønike, c.1495)

The nominative arguments, *dags* 'day', *er* 'he', *fýr* 'fire', *hún* 'she' *wädhrit* 'weather' and *Erich*, bold-faced in the examples in (146–151) above, behave syntactically as the subjects of the finite verbs, Go. *duginnan* 'begin', OHG *thunken* 'seem', OE *onginnan* 'begin', ON-I *taka* 'begin, OSw. *magha* 'may, can', and ODa. *byrje* 'begin. At the same time, a corresponding nominative subject is missing from the relevant non-finite verbs, which otherwise occur with a nominative subject when these verbs are finite.

To the more theoretically oriented reader, I would like to point out that structures of this type qualify as evidence for subject status, irrespective of whether one assumes a monostratal framework like Construction Grammar, or a multistratal framework like Generative Grammar. On a classical Generative Grammar analysis, the subject of the lower verb is assumed to move or raise from the subject position of the lower verb to the subject position of the higher verb, leaving a trace in the lower subject position.

In contrast, on a constructional account no literal, nor metaphorical raising or movement, is assumed to take place in subject-to-subject raising constructions. What matters is that it is only the subject of a corresponding finite verb, and not its object, that takes on the behavioral properties of the finite modal or aspectual verbs in (146–151) above. To be sure, those are the empirical facts relevant for the subject behavior of raising-to-subject constructions. Although I do not adhere to analyses involving the type of raising assumed in the generative literature, the label *raising-to-subject* is and will be used here due to how established it is in the syntactic and typological literature.

The following examples demonstrate that potential oblique subjects behave in the same manner as nominative subject do, with respect to subject-to-subject raising in the early Germanic languages:

Old High German
(152) a. **ímo   sélbemo** nesúle   **dúnchen** scône
         him.DAT self.DAT not.shall.3SG think.INF beautiful
         'he shall not deem himself beautiful'   (Notker, Boeth.Cons. II, 81.18)
     b. Sô **ímo**   dára   nâh   **nôten**   gestât
         so him.DAT there after trouble.NOM stood.3 SG
         'and then he began to get into trouble.'   (Notker, Boeth.Cons. III, 138.9)

Old English
(153) a. þa   ongan   **hine**   eft   **langian** on   his   cyþþe
         then began.3SG him.ACC after long.INF for his kith
         'then he started to long for his family.'
                              (Blickling Homilies, c. 971, cited from Cole et al. 1980: 729)
     b. Þonne mæg   **hine**   scamigan   þære
         then may.3SG him.ACC shame.INF the
         brædinge   his   hlisan
         spreading.GEN/DAT his fame.GEN
         'Then he may be ashamed of the extent of his fame'
                              (Boethius 46.5, c. 850–950, here cited from Denison 1990: 153)

Old Saxon
(154) a. *that* **ina** *bigan bi thero mennisko*
 then him.ACC began.3SG by that.DAT humanity.DAT
 môses **lustean**
 meat.GEN lust.INF
 'Then he started to lust for meat due to his humanity'
 (Heliand 13: 1060)
 b. *"ni tharf* **iu** *wiht* **tregan**,*" quathie*
 not need.3SG you.DAT.PL anything regret.INF said.he
 '"you guys need not regret anything", he said' (Heliand 65: 5520)

Old Norse-Icelandic
(155) a. **honum** *kvaðst það illa* **þykja** *að...*
 him.DAT said.REFL.3SG it.NOM badly feel.INF
 'He said that he felt that it was bad that...' (Reykdæla saga, Ch. 13)
 b. *og lést* **honum** *sú sending*
 and acted.REFL him.DAT that.NOM consignment.NOM
 þykja *ágæt og...*
 find.INF good and
 'and he acted as if he liked the consignment and...'
 (Króka refs saga, Ch. 12)

Old Swedish
(156) a. **them** *matte* **förtryta** *at the...*
 them.DAT should.3SG regret.INF that they
 'they should regret that they...' (Karlskrönikan, c. 1452)
 b. **drotningenne** *took ok dygert* **langa**...
 queen.the.DAT took.3SG also fiercely long.for.INF
 'The queen started to long fiercely for...' (Erikskrönikan, c.1330)

Old Danish
(157) a. **hanum** *kwnne æy rodh tiil* **ryndhe**
 him.DAT knew.3SG not advice.NOM to run.INF
 'he could not think of any solution'
 (Den danske Rimkrønike I, 77:2394, c.1495)
 b. *at* **them** *icke skal offtere* **lystæ** *at...*
 that them.DAT not shall.3SG oftener lust.INF
 'That they shall not more often want to...'
 (Diplomatarium Danicum, c.1464)

Note that Old High German *thunken* is the lower verb in (152a), while it is used as the finite raising-to-subject auxiliary in (147) above. Such syntactic behavior is also found for its Icelandic cognate *þykja*, as shown in (158) below:

Modern Icelandic
(158) a. og   sumum   **fór**   að **þykja**   hún   ómissandi
         and some.DAT began to   find.INF she.NOM indispensable
         'and some people started finding it indispensable'
      b. Hann   **þykir**   líklegur   til   að   **verða**   öflugur
         he.DAT appears.3SG likely   for   to   become.INF forceful
         og   framsýnn   leiðtogi.
         and visionary   leader
         'He appears to have the ability to become a forceful and a visionary leader.'

Note that examples involving potential oblique subjects with raising-to-subject verbs have not been documented in Gothic. Needless to say, this is not surprising given the small size of the Gothic corpus. Apart from that, such examples have been documented in all the other early Germanic languages, as (152–157) shows.

Moreover, the arguments behaving as syntactic subjects of the finite verbs in (152–157) are potential oblique subjects, belonging to the lower verbs. These are *ímo* 'him', *ímo* 'him', *hine* 'him', *ina* 'him', *iu* 'you', *honum* 'him', *honum* 'him', *them* 'them', *drotningenne* 'the queen', *hanum* 'him' and *them* 'them', respectively. The forms *hine* and *ina* are older accusative forms, while the remaining forms are datives. The verbs *langian* 'long for', *scamigan* 'be ashamed' and *lustean* 'desire' in Old English and Old Saxon (153a–b and 154a), and their cognates throughout the other early Germanic languages, select for potential accusative subjects, while the remaining verbs, OHG *dúnken* 'think', OHG *nôten* 'be in trouble', OS *tregan* 'regret', ON-I *þykja* 'think', OSw *förtryta* 'regret' and ODa *rodh tiil ryndhe* 'have advice', select for potential dative subjects. Observe that the OSw *langa* in (156b) occurs here with a dative, but the comparative evidence suggests that *langa* was originally constructed with an accusative (cf. its Old English cognate in 153a). The same is true for ODa *lystæ* in (157b, cf. its Old Saxon cognate in 154a), where the form *them* is ambiguous between an accusative and dative reading.

Examples like the ones in (152–157) therefore demonstrate that potential oblique subjects behave syntactically as nominative subjects with respect to raising-to-subject in the early Germanic languages, while an object analysis is excluded. As such, the data presented in this section speak for a subject analysis of these arguments during the earliest stages of Germanic and against an object analysis.

Before leaving this issue, it should be mentioned that Heltoft (2021: 263–264) argues, in one of his latest articles, that there is no raising-to-subject in Old and Middle Danish. Instead, he views examples like (157a–b) as involving "[relocation] in the relevant string", denying any nexus relation between *hanum* 'him' and *them* 'them' with the modals *kunne* 'can, be able to' and *skulle* 'should'.

There are two problems with Heltoft's "relocation hypothesis": The first problem is that it leaves the structure of the meaning found in examples (157a–b) unaccounted for, as then clearly these examples cannot mean 'he could' and 'they shall', respectively, if they do not instantiate the raising-to-subject construction. Instead, the Old Danish strings in (157a–b) would be meaningless word salads, as it is not clear how *hanum* and *them* should be interpreted. However, given that these examples are attested examples from Old Danish texts, it is clear that they are not meaningless word salads, but did instead serve a communicate purpose, where the dative *hanum* is the referent that did not have the ability to 'think up a solution' in (157a) and the dative *them* is the referent that should not have the desire expressed in (157b). The only way to account for that nexus relation is through a raising-to-subject analysis.

The second problem with Heltoft's analysis is that it leaves unaccounted for the fact that structures involving modal verbs and aspectual verbs of the type found in (146–157) above always have the potential oblique subject, as well as nominative subjects in general, immediately preceding the finite verb or immediately following it in both Old West and Old East Norse. It thus seems that Heltoft would have to assume an obligatory "relocation" to either one of these positions, which would be a problem as there is no motivation for such obligatory "relocation". In contrast, on a raising-to-subject analysis, both these problems go away and the meaning is accounted for.

I now turn to raising-to-object in the early Germanic languages.

4.2.5 Raising-to-object

Raising-to-object constructions are known to occur with four types of verbs in the Germanic languages, namely causatives like 'let', perception verbs like 'see' and 'hear', verbs of saying and *believe*-type verbs (Kristoffersen 1996: 128; Harbert (2007: 262–263, Thráinsson 2007: 436). Specifically, Harbert (2007: 262–263) documents that Gothic has raising-to-object with all four verb types, while he maintains that the other Germanic languages only have raising-to-object with 'let'. Harbert cites Fischer (1990) in this respect who argues that raising-to-object with verbs of saying and believing is a calque from Latin into English, which again leads Harbert to speculate that the West-Germanic situation represents the original state-of-affairs for Germanic.

However, as is discussed in Barðdal and Eythórsson (2012: 382–383), what militates against the scenario postulated by Harbert is the fact that all four types are found in native texts in Old Norse-Icelandic (cf. Kristoffersen 1996: 128). Since raising-to-object occurs with all four verb types in both East and North-Germanic, this may be taken to suggest that it is in fact West-Germanic that has innovated here. Supporting evidence for this hypothesis is provided in Section 5.4.3 below where perception verbs and verbs of saying are documented in raising-to-object constructions in native Old High German texts.

When verbs of letting, saying, believing and perception are found with an embedded infinitive, these are called *raising-to-object* constructions, *AcI*, or *ECM* in the literature. The main characteristic of these constructions is that the argument corresponding to the subject of the lower verb, when it is finite, behaves syntactically as the object of the matrix verb, including occurring in the accusative case. The following examples from Modern English demonstrate this, the first with the perception verb *hear* and the second with *believe*:

(159) a. *He heard **her** come through the door.*
      b. *She believes **him** to be a revolutionary.*

The trademark of such structures is that the nominative of nominative subject verbs shows up in the accusative case, evident by the forms *her* and *him* in (159a–b), as is also shown for Modern Icelandic in Section 1.3 above, where I establish a baseline for nominative subjects with regard to the subject tests.

Raising-to-object constructions also exist in the early Germanic languages, as is shown in (160–166) below for nominative subject verbs. Note that the bold-faced arguments, *þans* 'those', *iz* 'it', *hildebord* 'battle boards', *thene man* 'this man', *þá suma* 'some of the them', *mik* 'me' and *them* 'them', all correspond to the nominative subjects of the lower verbs when they are finite, here showing up in the accusative case. These examples are given here as a documentation that raising-to-object constructions existed in the earliest layers of Germanic and how nominative subjects fare when embedded under such structures.

Gothic
(160) *letiþ*   **þans**   *gaggan.*
      let.2PL   those.ACC   go.INF
      '[you] let them go.'   (John 18:8)

Old High German
(161) *Laz* ***iz*** sús thuruh gán
      lets.3SG it.ACC so through go.INF
      'So let it go through' (Otfrid I, 25, 11)

Old English
(162) ... *laétað* ***hildebord*** *hér* *onbidan*
      lets.3SG battle.boards.ACC here wait.INF
      '... lets battleboards wait here' (Beowulf 397)

Old Saxon
(163) *than* *lât* *thu* ***thene*** ***man*** *faren*
      then let.2SG you.NOM this.ACC man.ACC go.INF
      'Then you let this man go.' (Heliand 40: 3237)

Old Norse-Icelandic
(164) *Hann* ... *kvað* ***þá*** *eigi* *mundu* *sjást*
      he.NOM said.3SG them.ACC not would.INF see.REFL.INF
      oftar ***suma***
      oftener some.ACC
      'He ... said some would not see each other again.' (Njáls saga, ch. 149)

Old Swedish
(165) *antighi* *lät* ***mik*** *thässa* *bytning* *behalda* *älla* *scolom*
      either let.2SG me.ACC this.ACC gain.ACC keep.INF or shall
      wi *ther* *vm* *slas*
      we there of fight
      'either you let me keep this gain or we shall fight about it.' (Bil 865, c.1420–50)

Old Danish
(166) *hin* *late* ***them*** *swæria* *ofna* *thy* *samma*
      other.NOM lets.3SG them.ACC swear.INF on.top the same
      thingi
      assembly
      'the other had them swear [an oth] at that same parliament.' (SkL. HolmB74, c.1250)

At this juncture, it is important to mention that on a constructional analysis, there can be no "raising" from the position of the subject of the lower verb to the object position of the higher verb. What matters instead is the empirical fact that the argument corresponding to the subject of the lower verb in finite clauses shows up in structures of this type, behaving syntactically as the object of the lower verb. Since this label, *raising-to-object*, is well established in the literature, I continue to use it here. Albeit, it has no bearing, whatsoever, on the present analysis whether one assumes that the accusative case is assigned by the matrix verb, as is taken for granted in most current theoretical frameworks, or whether the accusative case is taken to be assigned by the construction itself, as is entailed by the current constructional analysis.

Further, observe that the case marking of the "raised" subject does not turn up in the accusative if the embedded verb is, for instance, a dative subject verb. In such cases, the "raised" subject maintains the same case marking as it has in finite clauses. This is shown in (167–168) below for *falla í hug* and *einfallen* 'come in mind' in Modern Icelandic and German, respectively.

First, the examples in (167) demonstrate that the two compositional predicates, *falla í hug* and *einfallen* 'come to mind', occur with a (potential) dative subject in the two languages, namely *honum* and *ihm* 'him'.

Icelandic
(167) a. Samt   fellur   **honum**   ekkert   áhugavert   í   hug.
          yet   falls.3SG   him.DAT   nothing.NOM   interesting in   mind
          'Yet, he cannot think of anything interesting.'

German
      b. Doch   fällt   **ihm**   nichts   Interessantes   ein.
          yet   falls.3SG   him.DAT   nothing.NOM   interesting   in
          'Yet, he cannot think of anything interesting.'

Second, this dative is maintained in the raising-to-object constructions in (168) below:

Icelandic
(168) a. Þú   lætur   **þér**   ekki   **falla**   í   **hug**   að...
          you.NOM   let.2SG   you.DAT   not   fall.INF   in   mind   to
          'You will not let it enter your mind to...'

German

    b.   Du   lässt   **dir**   nicht   **einfallen**   zu ...
        you.NOM let.2SG you.DAT not   come.to.mind.INF to
        'You will not let it enter your mind to ...'

For verbs which select for accusative subjects in Modern Icelandic, the "raised" subject shows up in the accusative case, as is shown in (169) below for *gruna* 'suspect':

Icelandic

(169) a.   **Mig**   grunaði   að   eitthvað ...
          me.ACC   suspected.3SG that something.ACC
          'I suspected that something ...'
     b.   en   lét   **sig**   **gruna**   að   eitthvað ...
          but   let.3SG REFL.ACC suspect.INF that something.ACC
          'but let himself suspect that something ...'

The example in (169a) shows that the verb *gruna* occurs with an accusative subject in Icelandic, while (169b) documents that this same verb also occurs with an accusative in raising-to-object constructions. It is impossible to know whether the accusative in (169b) comes from the construction itself or whether it is assigned by the lower verb. Either way, accusative subject verbs may be embedded under raising-to-object verbs in Icelandic.

Returning to the early Germanic languages, examples like the one in (169b) above, involving potential accusative subject verbs, may also be found there:

Old Saxon

(170) a.   Sô   he   **ina**   thô   **gehungrean**   lêt
          since he.NOM REFL.ACC then hunger.INF   lets.3SG
          'Since he then lets himself hunger.'   (Heliand 13:1059)

Old Norse-Icelandic

    b.   Þórir   kvað   **sig**   eigi   **saka**   mundu
        Þórir.NOM said.3SG REFL.ACC not be.harmed.INF would.INF
        'Þórir said that he would not be harmed.'   (Gull-Þóris saga, Ch. 12)
    c.   Kolur   kvað   **sig**   **dreymt** hafa   Hákon
        Kolur.NOM said.3SG REFL.ACC dreamt have.INF Kákon.ACC
        jarl   um   nóttina
        earl.ACC of   night
        'Kolur said that he had dreamt Earl Hákon during the night'
                                                (Brennu-Njáls saga, Ch. 82)

The verb 'hunger' selects for a potential accusative subject in all the early Germanic languages and this accusative shows up behaving syntactically as the object of 'let' in the Old Saxon example in (170a). Likewise, the verb *saka* 'be harmed' occurs consistently with a (potential) accusative subject in both Old Norse-Icelandic and Modern Icelandic. In (170b) above, this accusative behaves syntactically as the object of *kveða* 'say'. In (170c) the non-finite verb *dreyma* 'dream' selects for a potential accusative subject in Old Norse-Icelandic, here occurring with its accusative argument in this raising-to-object construction.

What is particularly interesting about (170a–b) is the fact that a sentence adverbial occurs between the "raised" subject and the verbal complex, *thô* 'then' and *eigi* 'not', respectively. It is generally assumed that sentence adverbials demarcate the beginning of the verb phrase, thus showing that the two potential accusative subjects occupy a position in the structure which is to the left of the verb phrase. The only possible position is the object position of the matrix verb. This means that the placement of *thô* 'then' and *eigi* 'not' may indeed be taken to show that the accusative *ina* and *sik* in (170a–b) occupy the object position of the matrix verbs 'let' and 'say'.

In addition, several examples of potential dative subject verbs may be found in raising-to-object constructions in the early Germanic languages. As mentioned above, the dative case is maintained in such constructions (see Rögnvaldsson 1996 for more examples of this type in Old Norse-Icelandic; Falk 1997: 26–28 for some examples in Old Swedish; and Demske 2008 for at least one more Old High German example):

Old High German
(171) a. *laz*   ***thir***   *quéman*   *iz*   *in*   *múat*
           let.2SG   you.DAT   come.INF   it.NOM   in   mind
           'let yourself get this in mind'   (Otfr., Ev.2, 21, 43)
       b. *laz*   ***dir***   *zorn*   *sîn*
           let.2SG   you.DAT   thorn   be.INF
           'let yourself be angry'   (Notker, Psalter 78 (289, 2, 22))

Old Saxon
(172) a. *lâtit*   ***im***   *is*   *[bittrun]*   *dâd*   *an*   *is*   *hugie*
           lets.3SG   him.DAT   his   bitter   deed   at   his   heart
           hrewan
           regret.INF
           'let him regret his bitter deed in his heart'   (Heliand 42: 3479–80)

b. *ef he **im** than lâtid is **môd twehon***
   if he.NOM him.DAT then lets.3SG his mind doubt.INF
   'If he lets himself have doubts in his mind' (Heliand 16: 1374)

Late Middle English
(173) a. *þat ye **me** cause so to **smerte***
      that you me.OBL cause so to pain.INF
      'that you cause me to hurt so much'
      (G. Chaucer Troilus and Criseyde Book IV, 1448,
      c.1374, cited from Zeefranz-Montag 1983: 132)

Old Norse-Icelandic
(174) a. *Konungur lét **þeim** það víst betur **henta**.*
      king.NOM lets.3SG them.DAT it surely better suit.INF
      'The king let them surely have what suited them better.'
      (Grænlendingaþáttur, ch. 1)
   b. *... láta **sér** nú **sóma** að fara til Íslands*
      let.INF REFL.DAT now befit.INF to go.INF to Iceland
      '... [they] let themselves now find it befitting to go to Iceland.'
      (Vatnsdæla saga, ch. 10)
   c. *Eiríkur ... kvað **þeim** ekki mundu **duga** að*
      Eiríkur.NOM said them.DAT not would.3SG avail that
      'Eiríkur ... said they would not find it sustainable that'
      (Grettis saga, ch. 7)

Old Swedish
(175) *lät **thik** äkke **ledhas** vidh at thänkia*
      let.2SG you.OBL not be.saddened.INF with to think
      thz som ...
      that which
      'Don't let yourself get sad thinking about that which ...'
      (Bo 183, c.1380–1400)

Old Danish
(176) *schulæ wy ladæ **oss** ... **nøghæ** meth thet*
      shall.1PL we let us.OBL find.sufficient.INF with it
      'We shall let ourselves ... find it sufficient' (D. Mag. IV. 364, c.1407)

Starting with the two Old High German examples in (171a–b), these involve the compositional predicates *quéman in múat* 'come in mind' and *zorn sîn* 'be angry, be heated'. Both of these occur with a potential dative subject in Old High German, as the following examples show:

Old High German

(177) a. int   imo   in   múat   quámi
         and   him.DAT in   mind   would.come.3SG
         'And he would get [an idea] in mind.'   (Otfr., Ev.2, 4, 84)
     b. theiz imo   filu   zórn   was
         thus him.DAT   much   thorn was.3SG
         'Thus, he was very angry'   (Otfr., Ev.4, 19, 59)

I have come across a few examples of *quéman in múat* 'come' in mind' with a potential dative subject in Old High German (and none with the animate argument in the nominative). For *zorn sîn* 'be angry, be heated', I have found one example with a potential dative subject in Old High German, in addition to (177b) above, but more examples are readily found in later stages of German, for instance, Middle High German.

The Old Saxon examples in (172) are instantiated by the verbs *hrewan* 'regret' and *twehon* 'doubt'. As is documented by Allen (1995: 114), *hreowan* 'regret' and its prefixed variants, *gehreowan* and *ofhreowan*, occur consistently with a potential dative subject in Old English. Even though the Old Saxon corpus is not the largest one, there are still seven examples of the verb *hrewan / hrewen* 'rue' in the Heliand, all occurring in the infinitive. In other words, none of these attested examples is finite. Instead, three are raising-to-object examples of the type discussed in this section, one is a raising-to-object example with the matrix verb 'see', discussed in Section 5.4.2 below, two examples instantiate the raising-to-subject constructions of the type discussed in the previous section, and one example will be further discussed in the following section on control infinitives. Nevertheless, the two raising-to-subject examples and the three raising-to-object examples with 'let' all testify to the use of *hrewan* 'regret' with a potential dative subject in the Old Saxon language.

Regarding the second Old Saxon example *môd twehon* 'doubt in one's mind', when the verb *twehon* 'doubt' occurs on its own, it selects for a nominative subject, while when *twehon* occurs with *môd*, as in (172b) above, it selects for a potential dative subject. With the compositional variant, *tweho sîn* 'be of doubt', it is only found with a potential dative subject.

Old Saxon

(178) **Mi**   nis   an   mînumu   môde   tweho
       me.ACC/DAT   not.is.3SG   at   my.DAT   mind.DAT doubt
       'I have no doubts in my mind'   (Heliand 57: 4780)

Thus, it is indisputable that the dative of *môd twehon* 'doubt in one's mind' in (172b) above is the "raised" argument in this raising-to-object example, a behavior confined to syntactic subjects in the Germanic languages.

The Late Middle English example in (173) involves the verb *smerten* 'pain' which selects for a potential oblique subject, here instantiating a raising-to-object structure with the borrowed verb *causen* 'cause' as a matrix verb. The example in (173) is from Chaucer and so is the following example which shows a finite usage of *smerten* 'pain', attesting to its use with potential oblique subjects, *hym* 'him' in this case.

Late Middle English
(179) He   may   not   wepe   al   thogh   **hym**   soore   smerte
      he   may   not   cry   all   though   him.OBL   sorely   pains
      'He may not cry, although he is in great pain'
      (G. Chaucer CT Prologue, 230, c.1374)

It needs to be emphasized here that structures involving raising-to-object are extremely rare in Old English, which in turn means that the absence of such examples with oblique subject verbs comes as no surprise. A brief glance at both Völundarkviða and Hamðismál, two of the earliest Eddic poems composed in Old Norse-Icelandic in the 9th century and contemporaneous with Old English, reveals one example of raising-to-object in Völundarkviða and two in Hamðismál. Needless to say, none of these examples involves oblique subject verbs.

Of the Old Norse-Icelandic examples in (174) above, all three verbs occur systematically with a potential dative subject at this language stage, as is shown in examples (180) below. What is more, these verbs are not found with the animate argument occurring with any other case marking than the dative during this early language stage:

Old Norse-Icelandic
(180) a. hvað   **mönnum**   hentar   því   að...
          what   men.DAT   suits.3SG   therefore   at
          'what people find suitable, due to...'   (Þorleifs þáttur jarlaskálds, ch. 4)
      b. og   sómir   **yður**   það   vel   að   eigi...
          and   befits.3SG   you.DAT   it.NOM   well   that   not
          'and it befits you well that not...'   (Ljósvetninga saga, ch. 22, C-variant)
      c. Dugir   **honum**   það   er   hann   er...
          sustains.3SG   him.DAT   it.NOM   as   he   is
          Does he find it sustainable that he is...'
          (Finnboga saga ramma, ch. 129)

Thus, the examples in (180a–c) show that it is uncontroversial that the Old Norse-Icelandic raising-to-object examples in (174) above involve verbs which systematically occur with potential dative subjects at this early language stage.

In the Old Swedish example in (175) above, the relevant oblique subject verb is *leþas* 'be bored', which may occasionally occur with a nominative subject instead of the potential dative one. However, in this particular text, *leþas* is only found with a dative, as is evident from the sentence in the text following the one in (175) above:

Old Swedish
(181) a. thz som **herranom** leddes äkke at thola
that which lord.the.DAT saddened not to tolerate.INF
'that which the lord is saddened not to tolerate.' (Bo 183, c.1380–1400)

However, Falk (1997: 27) presents two examples which she argues do show that potential dative subjects behave syntactically as objects and not as subjects with respect to raising-to-object. These examples are the following, with 'say' and 'know' as raising-to-object verbs:

Old Swedish
(182) a. the sighia syndena ... ey swa mykit mistäkkias
they.NOM say.3PL sin.the.acc not so much dissent.INF
gudhi
god.DAT
'they say that the sin ... was not so much dissenting from God'
(Bir 1: 140, c.1380)
b. vm the hafdo vitat haua thäktz **mik**
if they.NOM had known have.INF consented.to me.OBL
'If they had known that it was to my consent.' (Bir 2: 201, c.1380)

The relevant verb in both these examples is the verb *thäkkas*. Yet, according to the information in Söderwall's Old Swedish dictionary, this verb could be construed both personally and impersonally, as is shown in (183) below:

Old Swedish
(183) a. huru han mahge **allom** thäkkias
how he.NOM would.may.3SG all.DAT consent.to.INF
'how he may please everybody' (Bir 3: 64, c.1380)
b. **henne** thectis hälder gudhlik **gipta** ... en
her.DAT liked.3SG rather godly than
'she liked godly marriage ... rather than' (Bil 109, c.1440–1450)

The example in (183b), analyzed by Söderwall as an "impersonal" variant, is a Dat-Nom verb, while the example in (183a) is a Nom-Dat verb where the nominative is the subject and the dative the object. This also explains why the dative in the Old Swedish examples in (182a–b) above follows the verb, occurring in the typical object position, the reason being that *thäkkias* is an alternating Dat-Nom / Nom-Dat verb in Old Swedish. Therefore, Falk's examples do not constitute a counterargument against a dative subject analysis of potential dative subject verbs in Old Swedish, as her alleged counterexamples are not examples of potential dative subject verbs to begin with.

Turning to the last example of raising-to-object in (176), the Old Danish one, this example contains the verb *nøghje* 'suffice', which occurs systematically with a potential dative or oblique subject in Old Danish, of which one such example is shown in (184) below:

Old Danish
(184)   som   **hannem**   nogher   med
        which   him.DAT   suffices   with
        'which he finds sufficient'   (KøbStL, c.1415)

Heltoft (2021: 263–264) argues that raising-to-object constructions in Old Danish are not a subject test, even though one would go along with a raising-to-object analysis for structures of the type in (176). Instead, Heltoft claims that raising-to-object constructions certainly target the first argument of the argument structure but that the first argument of the argument structure is not the syntactic subject. According to him, there are no syntactic subjects in Old and Middle Danish, as word order is motivated by information structure and not clause structure, and because Old and Middle Danish are non-configurational languages (following Faarlund's 2004 analysis for Old Norse-Icelandic). Regarding a non-configurational analysis of Old Norse-Icelandic, I refer the reader to Rögnvaldsson (1995) where it is shown that there is a clear and distinct phrase structure in Old Norse-Icelandic, exactly as in Modern Icelandic. As a consequence, a non-configurational analysis of Old Norse-Icelandic is simply unattainable.

It is writ large that Heltoft approaches the issue of Old and Middle Danish syntax from a very different perspective than I am. While I certainly believe that certain word orders in Old West and Old East Norse are motivated by information structure, that does not exclude the existence of grammatical relations (syntactic roles) in those languages. The fact that Old Danish has structures like raising-to-subject, raising-to-object and control, structures which are well known for targeting subjects cross-linguistically, speaks, as a matter of fact, for the existence of grammatical relations (syntactic roles) in Old and Middle Danish. Therefore,

Heltoft's analysis that the oblique argument *oss* 'us' in examples like (176) is the first argument of the argument structure simply appears to be a notational variant of my own analysis.

Before leaving the issue of raising-to-object, it should be mentioned here that the morphological case system in both Old Swedish and Old Danish was in the process of collapsing in the nominal and adjectival declensions. The pronouns kept their case marking much longer, but also for the pronominal paradigms were case forms lost, with other forms taking over their functions. For instance, for 1st and 2nd person singular pronouns, the accusative forms took over the dative forms, while for 3rd person singular, the dative pronouns took over the functions of the accusative forms. This makes it difficult to distinguish between accusative and dative forms and functions after 1400 in Swedish and somewhat earlier in Danish (Delsing 1991, 1995).

To conclude, I have here presented examples of raising-to-object from Old High German, Old English, Old Saxon, Old Norse-Icelandic, Old Swedish and Old Danish. These examples show beyond doubt that oblique subject verbs in these languages may be embedded under raising-to-object verbs and that it is indeed the potential oblique subject that is "raised" in such constructions, thus behaving syntactically as nominative subjects do. For accusative subject verbs, the "raised" subject occurs in the accusative case, making it difficult to know whether the accusative comes from the construction itself or from the lower verb. However, for dative subject verbs, the "raised" subject maintains the dative case of the potential subject of the lower verbs. As such, the data presented here speaks for a subject analysis of potential oblique subjects and excludes an object analysis.

I now turn to control infinitives in the early Germanic languages.

4.2.6 Control infinitives

After having discussed both raising-to-subject and raising-to-object, it is pertinent to mention that freedom in word order, in particular the variation between OV and VO within the verb phrase, has been adduced as detracting from the validity of both raising-to-subject and raising-to-object constructions in corpus languages like Old Swedish (Falk 1997: 27–28), and Old Danish (Hrafnbjargarson 2004: 64). Such objections are based on the generative view that the subject of the lower verb is literally "raised" to the object position in raising-to-object and to the subject position in raising-to-subject constructions.

As already touched upon in the previous two sections, on a monostratal approach like the Construction Grammar one, no literal "raising" takes place in these constructions. The empirical facts are that the subject of the lower verb takes on the syntactic properties of subjects in raising-to-subject constructions and the syntactic properties of objects in raising-to-object constructions. For raising-to-subject constructions, for instance, if the "raised" subject is a potential oblique subject, then the verb is always in 3rd person singular, irrespective of whether the potential oblique subject is in the singular or plural. Lack of number agreement here indeed corroborates that such potential oblique subjects behave syntactically as subjects of the relevant finite verbs, despite being assigned by the lower verbs. Examples of that type are found in (154b) from Old Saxon, (156a) from Old Swedish and (157b) from Old Danish, and more examples are readily found in texts if searched for. In addition, "raised" subjects occur either in preverbal position or postverbally in inversion structures, as is also seen in all the examples in (152–157) above.

The same is true for raising-to-object, as potential dative subjects maintain their case marking in raising-to-object constructions despite them behaving syntactically as objects of raising-to-object verbs. This object behavior of the subject of the lower verbs is certainly manifested in word order distribution, namely that the "raised" object usually occurs immediately following the finite verb verb, unless it is a very light pronoun, then it may even occur earlier in the clause. The same is true if the finite verb occurs in clause-final position, as in West-Germanic, or if metric factors dictate otherwise, as in the Heliand. Generally, the "raised" object behaves syntactically as other objects do, for instance in following the subject of the finite verb, if it is inverted with the verb, as in (163) above.

Therefore, generative assumptions based on "raising" to a specific position in the tree structure representation, be it the subject position in raising-to-subject or the object position in raising-to-object, are not the criteria being used here for determining whether a potential oblique subject has been "raised" to either subject or object position. Rather, it is the overall behavior of the arguments in these constructions that constitute the subject test, compared to how the same arguments behave in corresponding finite clauses.

This aforementioned potential counterargument against perfectly valid raising-to-subject and raising-to-object constructions, namely freedom in word order due to OV-VO variation, is not relevant for control infinitives, since the subject is simply left unexpressed there, instead of showing up in the matrix clause. As a consequence, data involving control infinitives cannot be brushed aside in the same manner as data involving raising constructions. For this reason, scholars of historical linguistics, like Rögnvaldsson (1996: 49–51), Falk (1997: 38) and Faarlund (2001), (see also Moore and Perlmutter 2000 for Russian), have emphasized the role of control infinitives as being an indisputable subject test for the historical Germanic languages.

Before diving into the early Germanic data, a few words explaining the nature of control infinitives are in order. Certain verbs and predicates select for infinitive complements that differ from both raising-to-subject and raising-to-object above in that the argument corresponding to the subject of the lower verbs in finite clauses is simply not expressed at all. This is in opposition to raising constructions where this subject argument either takes on the behavior of the "raised" subject or the "raised" object of the matrix verb. A simple set of examples from Modern English is given in (185) below to illustrate this:

(185) a. *I keep my word*
 b. *I intend **to** ___ **keep** my word.*
 c. **I intend **to keep**.*

The example in (185a) is a simple finite clause with the verb *keep*, the subject *I*, and the object *my word*. In (185b) this subject is left unexpressed on identity with the subject of *intend*, while the object immediately follows the nonfinite verb, as it does in (185a). Hence, since the subject of the lower verb is the same as the subject of the matrix verb, the latter subject may be left unexpressed, resulting in a control infinitive. In this case, the subject of the matrix verb controls the identity of the subject of the infinitive. What is important about infinitives of this type is that the object cannot be left unexpressed in such constructions, evident by the fact that *I intend to keep* in (185c) is not a grammatical sentence in English.

Subjects of control infinitives may also be left unexpressed on the basis of identity with an object of the matrix clause or on identity with no argument at all in case of a generic reference, as is shown in some of the examples below. It is a worthwhile exercise to consider the empirical evidence for assuming that there is an unexpressed subject in control infinitives in the first place, instead of simply postulating that such an unexpressed subject must be assumed.

There are several syntactic behaviors that call for an analysis involving an unexpressed subject of control infinitives (cf. Landau 2013: Ch. 3), of which three are discussed here. These involve:
i) reflexives
ii) secondary predication
iii) floating quantifiers

Starting with reflexives, it is long known that control infinitives may contain reflexives which appear to be bound by the unexpressed subject (cf. Postal 1970). Consider first the following examples from Modern Icelandic:

Icelandic
(186) a. **Honum**_i þykir vænt um **sjálfan** **sig**_{i.}
him.DAT.M thinks good of self.ACC.M REFL.ACC
'He cares for himself.'
b. **Hana**_i dreymir **sjálfa** **sig**_{i.}
her.ACC.F dreams self.ACC.F REFL.ACC
'She dreams about herself.'

The two predicates in (186) are *þykja vænt um* 'care for' and *dreyma* 'dream'. As is evident from the examples above, the first one selects for a dative subject in Modern Icelandic and a prepositional accusative object, while the second occurs with an accusative subject, as well as with an accusative object.

When embedding the structures in (186) under control verbs, the following happens: a) the reflexives are bound by the unexpressed subject of the control infinitive, and b) the emphatic reflexive *sjálf-* agrees in gender with the unexpressed subject. In (187a) below *sjálfan* is in the masculine form, while *sjálfa* in (187b) is in the feminine form. This gender agreement reflects the gender of the oblique subjects in (186a–b) above, which are left unexpressed in (187).

Icelandic
(187) a. Það er gott [að ____i þykja vænt um **sjálfan**
it is good að PRO.DAT think.INF good of self.ACC.M
sig_i].
REFL.ACC
b. Það er ömurlegt [að ____i dreyma **sjálfa**
it is sucking að PRO.ACC dream.INF self.ACC.F
sig_i]. veika
REFL.ACC ill. ACC.F
'It sucks to dream about oneself being ill.'

In addition, (187b) also demonstrates how secondary predication agrees with the unexpressed subject in gender, as the adjectival subject predicate, *veika* 'ill', also shows up in the feminine form. The reflexive pronoun *sig*, in contrast, can only be declined in case, not in gender.

Turning now to floating quantifiers, consider the following nominative and dative passives, *vera kosnir* 'be elected' and *vera boðið* 'be invited', in (188a–b), respectively, which are embedded under the matrix verbs in (189), *líka* 'like' and *óska* 'wish' (examples inspired by Sigurðsson 2008: 210):

Icelandic
(188) a. **Þeir** voru **báðir** kosnir.
they.NOM.PL were.3PL both.NOM.PL.M elected.NOM.PL.M
'They were both elected.'
b. **þeim** var **báðum** boðið.
them.DAT.PL was.3SG both.DAT.PL.M invited.N
'They were both invited.'

The floating quantifiers, *báðir* and *báðum* 'both', so called since they are separated from the subjects with which they agree, *þeir* and *þeim* 'they', in (188a–b), occur instead immediately before the participles *kosnir* 'elected' and *boðið* 'invited'. The same is true for the control infinitives in (189a–b). As such, these floating quantifiers are situated close to the right periphery of the control infinitives themselves, far removed from the unexpressed subjects, the nominative *þeir* in (189a) and the dative *þeim* in (189b):

Icelandic
(189) a. *Tvíburunum líkaði illa* [*að* __ *vera ekki*
twins.the.DAT.PL liked badly to PRO.NOM.PL be.INF not
báðir *kosnir*].
both.NOM.PL elected.NOM.PL
'The twins disliked not being both elected.' (Sigurðsson 2008: 210)
b. *Tvíburarnir óskuðu þess* [*að* __ *vera*
twins.the.NOM.PL wished.for it.GEN to PRO.DAT.PL be.INF
báðum *boðið*].
both.DAT.PL invited.N
'The twins wished to be both invited.'

The clinching evidence here for the assumption that the unexpressed syntactic subject of control infinitives must somehow still be assumed to exist in the structure, in spite of being unexpressed, stems from the case agreement between the unexpressed subject and the quantifier. In (189a) the unexpressed subject corresponds to a nominative plural argument *þeir* (see 188a), hence the quantifier *báðir* is in the plural nominative case, while the subject of the matrix clause in (189a), *tvíburunum*, is in the dative case. This shows that the floating quantifier, *báðir* 'both', does certainly not agree with the subject of the matrix clause, but with *þeir*, the unexpressed nominative subject of the control infinitive. In the same vein, the quantifier *báðum* in (189b) is in the dative case, agreeing in case with *þeim*, the unexpressed dative subject of the passive *vera boðið* (see 188b), and not with the nominative subject *tvíburarnir* in the matrix clause.

Having presented three empirical arguments above, based on: i) reflexives, i) secondary predication and iii) floating quantifiers for the existence of the unexpressed subject in control infinitives in general, I return to the early Germanic data and the control infinitives involving oblique subjects in these language stages. Consider first the following example from Gothic, presented here to demonstrate that structures involving control infinitives indeed existed at the earliest Germanic stage.

Gothic

(190)   *hvaiwa*   *mag*   *sa*   *unsis*   *leik*   *giban*   **du**
       how   may.3SG   the.one.NOM   us.DAT   flesh.ACC   give.INF   to
       __   ***matjan?***
       PRO.NOM   eat.INF
       'How can he give us flesh to eat?'   (John 6:52)

In this particular example, the infinitive is *du matjan* 'to eat'. The subject reference is controlled by the indirect object *unsis* 'us' of the verb *giban* 'give' in the matrix clause, i.e. the unexpressed subject has the same reference as this indirect object. In this example, the verb *matjan* 'eat' does not occur with any object, since the eating has a generic reference, customarily referring to food and edibles. The unexpressed subject is marked in the example itself with a lower line "__", and glossed as PRO in the glossing line. The case marking of the unexpressed subject, i.e. its case marking in ordinary finite clauses, is provided in the glossing line, in this case a nominative, since the verb 'eat' selects for a nominative subject in Gothic.

I let it suffice to document the existence of control infinitives in general for early Germanic with the Gothic example in (190) above, and turn instead directly to control infinitives involving accusative and dative subject verbs in the early Germanic languages. This includes examples from Gothic, Old Saxon, Early Middle English, Old Norse-Icelandic, Old Swedish and Old Danish.

Gothic

(191)   *hvazuh*   *saei*   *saihviþ*   *qinon*   ***du***   __   ***luston***
       whoever   who.NOM   sees   woman.ACC   to   PRO.ACC   lust.INF
       izos]
       her.GEN
       'whoever looks at a woman in order to lust for her.'
                (Matthew 5:28, cited from Barðdal and Eythórsson 2012a: 386)

Old Saxon
(192) a. *gi   ni   thurƀun   [__   an   ênigun   sorgun*
       you.NOM not   need.2PL   PRO.DAT at   any   sorrows
       ***wesan** an   ... hugi   hwergin]*
       be.INF   on   mind   nowhere
       'You need not feel any sorrows in [your] ... heart anywhere'
       (Heliand 22: 1897–98)

   b. *bethiu   ne   thurƀun   ...   [__   thius   werk*
       thus   not   need.2PL   PRO.DAT these.NOM deeds.NOM
       ***tregan]**, [__   **hrewan** mîn   hinfard]*
       regret.INF   PRO.DAT rue.INF   my.NOM departure.NOM
       'therefore, you need not ... regret these deeds, nor rue my departure'
       (Heliand 57: 4730–31)

Early Middle English
(193) a. *good is, quaþ Joseph, [**to** __   **dremen**   of   win*
       good   is   said   Joseph   to   PRO.OBL dream.INF of   wine
       'It is good, said Joseph, to dream about wine.'
       (Gen. & Ex. 2067, c. 1250, cited from Cole et al. 1980: 730)

   b. *Him   burþ   [**to** __   **liken**   well his lif].*
       him.OBL ought to   PRO.OBL like.INF   well his life
       'He ought to like his life well.'
       (Dame Sirith: 82, c.1275, cited from Cole et al. 1980: 729)

Old Norse-Icelandic
(194) a. *Þorvaldur   kvaðst   [__   ólíklegt   **þykja]**   að   hún*
       Þorvaldur.NOM   said   PRO.DAT   unlikely   think.INF   that she
       'Þorvaldur said he found it unlikely that she ...'   (Fljótsdæla saga, ch. 5)

   b. *Þorsteinn   kvaðst   [þá   betra   __   **þykja]**   ef   hann*
       Þorstein.NOM   said   then   better   PRO.DAT   think.INF   if   he
       'Þorsteinn said he found it better if he ...'   (Laxdæla saga, ch. 61)

   c. *Snorri   kvaðst   [__   einsætt   **þykja]**   að*
       Snorri.NOM   said   PRO.DAT   obvious   think.INF   that
       'Snorri said that he found it obvious that ...'   (Laxdæla saga, ch. 67)

   d. *Glúmur   kvaðst   [__   því   betur   **þykja]**   er*
       Glúmur.NOM   said   PRO.DAT   the   better think.INF   which
       'Glúmur said that he found it better, which'   (Reykdæla saga, ch 18)

e. *Þorbergur   kvaðst   [__   þetta   þykja]*
   Þorbergur.NOM said   PRO.DAT   this.NOM   think.INF
   féfrekt]   en ...
   cost.consuming   but
   'Þorbergur said that he found this cost-consuming but ...'
   (Reykdæla saga, ch. 28)

f. *Mun   þeim   eigi   þykja   [__   þungt   falla*
   will   them.DAT   not   think.INF PRO.DAT   grievous   find.INF
   að   svo ...
   at   such
   'They will not find this grievous, at this ...'
   (Ljósvetninga saga (C), ch. 24)

g. *að   Gunnhildi   þótti   [__   hyggjuleysi*
   that Gunnhildur.NOM   thought   PRO.DAT   thoughtlessness.NOM
   til ganga   eða   öfund]   ef ...
   til go.INF   or   envy.NOM   if
   'that Gunnhildur thought that [people's] intentions were colored by thoughtlessness or envy, if ...'
   (Laxdæla saga, ch. 19)

Old Swedish
(195) a. *Os   duger   ey   [thar   effter   __   langa]*
         us.DAT   suffices   not   there   after   PRO.OBL long.INF
         'It is useless for us to long for that.'
         (Hertig Fredrik av Normandie, c.1308, cited from Falk 1997: 25)

   b. *Huath   hiælper   idher   [ther   æpter   __   langa]*
      what   helps   you.OBL there   after   PRO.OBL long.INF
      'How does it help you to long for that?'
      (Herr Ivan 1229, c.1303, cited from Falk 1997: 25)

   c. *Än   huat   är   at   til   ryggia   ganga   [vtan   __*
      but   what   is   to   to   back   go.INF   without   PRO.OBL
      angra   j   frestilsom   at   haua
      regret.INF in   temptation   to   have.INF
      'But what is it to retreat and instead regret to have, in temptation'
      (Heliga Birgittas uppenbarelser IIII (Holm A 5a), ch. 20, c.1400–1425)

Old Danish
(196) *Aldrigh   listær   mek   [fran   ether   at   __   langæ]*
      never   lusts   me.ACC   from   you   to   PRO.OBL long.INF
      'I never want to long away from you'
      (Ivan Løveridder (K4), 210, c.1485)

In addition to these examples from six different early Germanic languages, two additional control infinitives from Middle Danish have also been reported by Hrafnbjargarson (2004: 67). These control infinitives contain the verbs *undre på* 'wonder about' and *lide* 'like', documented in the years 1534 and 1638, respectively. The problem with both of these examples, however, is that a short glance at the two relevant texts reveals that both of these verbs have started occurring with a nominative subject at this late medieval stage in the history of Danish. One can therefore not be sure that the two verbs in Hrafnbjargarson's examples unambiguously occur with oblique subjects rather than with nominative subjects. Recall that only oblique subject constructions embedded under control verbs, and not nominative subject constructions, constitute evidence for the subject status of potential oblique subjects.

However, I have been able to locate one example of a control infinitive in Old Danish, where the embedded infinitive contains an oblique subject verb, shown in (196) above. What is interesting about this example is that the matrix verb is itself an oblique subject verb, i.e. 'lust', as is evident from *listær mek*, where *mek* is in the accusative case. This verb 'lust' selects here for in infinitive containing the verb *langæ* 'long for' which otherwise occurs with a potential accusative subject, as is shown in (197) below from the same text.

Old Danish
(197) *Af   thet   godz   henne   effter   **langæ***
       of   this   goods   her.OBL after   longs.3SG
       'Of the goods that she longs for'   (Ivan Løveridder (K4), 4719, c.1485)

The potential accusative subject with *langæ* 'long for' in (196) is left unexpressed on identity with the potential accusative subject of 'lust'. This is a clear case of subject behavior, showing that potential oblique subjects in Danish behave syntactically as nominative subjects do. Observe also that all examples of *langæ* 'long for' in this particular text occur with a potential oblique subject and not one example is found with a nominative subject. There is thus no doubt that the unexpressed subject in the control infinitive in (196) is in the accusative case.

Now, this Old Danish control infinitive in (196) comes from a text which is a medieval translation of a corresponding Swedish text. The Danish text exists in two manuscripts, an earlier one in the Zealand dialect, K4, from the latter part of the 15th century, and an later one in a Jutlandic dialect, K47, most likely from the end of the 15th century. The language is certainly somewhat older than the manuscripts and it is generally assumed that the earlier K4 text is closer to the Swedish original, since the later K47 text has very distinct Jutlandic traits (see Brandt 1870). However, the line in (196) is non-existent in the later Jutlandic text and is nowhere to be found in the original Swedish text. It therefore seems that the control infinitive in

(196) represents a real Old Danish example. And note, moreover, that even though a similar line had been in the Swedish original, the scribe in Zealand surely had the freedom to change it whichever way he or she may have found fitting, if it did not accord with his or her native speaker intuition.

Heltoft (2021: 264) argues against a control analysis of Old Danish examples like the one presented in (196) above, claiming that Barðdal and Eythórsson (2003a, 2012a) and Eythórsson and Barðdal (2005) do not "add anything empirical here in support of the assumed subject PRO". In the beginning of this section, I have discussed three empirical facts which show that one must assume that the unexpressed subject is a part of the clause structure of control infinitives. These three empirical facts relate to gender and number agreement with reflexive objects, gender and number agreement in secondary predication and gender and number agreement found with floating quantifiers (see Landau 2013: Ch. 3 for a discussion of further empirical issues supporting the analysis that one has to assume an unexpressed argument in control infinitives).

In addition, we know from the structure of the modern Germanic languages, as well as from further cross-linguistic comparisons, that there are in essence three types of infinitive clauses found in our languages. These are raising-to-subject, raising-to-object and control infinitives. Raising-to-subject structures may be recognized by the fact that the matrix verb does not take a subject of its own, but receives it from the lower verb. This involves aspectual verbs and many modal verbs. Raising-to-object structures may be recognized by the fact that the subject of the lower verb occurs further to the left in the structure, outside of the verb phrase, and it generally occurs in the accusative case, unless the lower verb selects for potential dative subjects. If so, the subject of the lower verb occurs in the dative case. This kind of structure is found with four types of matrix verbs, causatives like 'let', perception verbs like 'see' and 'hear', verbs of saying and verbs of believing. In contrast, what is typical for the third type of infinitive clauses is that the subject of the lower verb is neither found in a nexus with the finite verb, nor does it occur further left in the structure and outside the verb phrase. Instead, the subject simply appears to be missing. Therefore, identifying control infinitives in the Germanic languages, including earlier Danish, is far from being an intractable task, as Heltoft (2021) avers.

Let us therefore have a closer look at the Old Danish example in (196), repeated here for convenience:

Old Danish
(196) *Aldrigh listær mek   [fran ether at   __   langæ]*
      never   lusts me.ACC   from   you   to   PRO.OBL   long.INF
      'I never want to long away from you'   (Ivan Løveridder (K4), 210, c.1485)

The accusative *mek* 'me' is selected for by the matrix verb 'lust', evident by the fact that it inverts with the verb when the temporal adverb *aldrigh* 'never' occurs in first position. Further examples of the verb 'lust' from Old High German, Old Saxon, Old English, Old Dutch and Old Norse-Icelandic are given in (213) below, demonstrating beyond doubt that 'lust' selects for a potential accusative subject in the Germanic languages. The phrase *fran ether* 'from you' in (196) is an adverbial phrase modifying *langæ* 'long', specifying in particular the direction of the longing sensation, in this case away from the second person addressee. This leaves no candidate left for being raised to subject in a putative raising-to-subject construction or for being raised to object in a putative raising-to-object construction. As a consequence, the only analytical option, and the only viable analysis, left available for (196) is that it is a control infinitive, which is in turn confirmed by the lack of the expressed accusative subject, as is typical of control infinitives. With this explication I hope to have laid out, once and for all, the logic behind the control infinitive analysis, as opposed to the two other available analyses for infinitive clauses, raising-to-subject and raising-to-object.

Turning to Old Swedish, a total of three examples of oblique subject verbs being embedded under control verbs have hitherto been reported in the literature (Falk 1997: 25). These three examples are with the verbs *lepas vidh* 'sadden by' and *langa æpter* 'long for'. Falk notes that *lepas vidh* 'be saddened' has already started occurring with a nominative subject at the production time of this example. However, the remaining two examples, both with *langa æptir* 'long for', are very early examples, produced long before this verb started occurring with a nominative subject. These two examples of control infinitives, here given in (195a–b), are therefore philologically good examples which show that accusative subject verbs could be embedded under control verbs in Old Swedish.

Observe that in (195a) the control predicate is *dugha* 'suffice', which itself occurs consistently with a potential dative subject in the early Germanic languages (cf. Dunn et al. 2017). This potential dative subject is here manifested as *us* in initial position, controlling the reference of the potential accusative subject of *langa*. This is therefore structurally similar to the situation with the Danish example, as the matrix verb there, 'lust', also selects for its own potential oblique subject. The other Old Swedish control infinitive in (195b) above is embedded under the verb *hiälpa* 'help', with its object *idher* 'you' controlling the reference of the potential accusative subject of the lower verb, *langa*. Therefore, these two examples of control infinitives are not only philologically good examples, but are also structurally good examples, showing that accusative subject verbs may be embedded under control verbs in Old Swedish.

A 4th example of a control infinitive in Old Swedish involving a potential oblique subject predicate, is given in (195c) above and repeated here for convenience. This example, with the verb *angra* 'regret', has not been discussed so far in the earlier literature. The subjunction *vtan* 'without' selects for an infinitive, here represented by the accusative subject verb *angra* 'regret', with the potential accusative subject being left unexpressed on identity with a generic controller, retrievable from the context.

(195) c. Än   huat   är   at   til   ryggia   ganga   [vtan   ___
       but   what   is   to   to   back   go.INF without PRO.OBL
       angra   j   frestilsom   at   haua
       regret.INF   in   temptation   to   have.INF
       'But what is it to retreat and instead regret to have, in temptation'

All unambiguous examples of *angra* from this particular manuscript, Cod. Holm. A 5a, show *angra* occurring with an accusative, as in (198) below:

Old Swedish
(198) O   herra   gudh   **mik**   **angra**   aff   allo   hjärta
      o   lord   god   me.ACC   regrets   of   all   heart
      'O dear Lord, I regret from all my heart'
                    (Heliga Birgittas uppenbarelser VIII [Holm A 5a], ch. 48, c.1400–1425)

There can thus be no doubt that the unexpressed subject of *angra* 'regret' in (195c) is in the accusative case.

Against an analysis assuming that Old Swedish has oblique subjects, Falk (1997: 26) presents one example in which it is not the potential oblique subject that is left unexpressed in a control infinitive, but the nominative argument instead. This example is shown in (199) below:

Old Swedish
(199) vm   han   astunda   [at   ___   thäkkias   **minum**
      if   he.NOM   practices   to   PRO.NOM   consent.to.INF   my.OBL
      son   **ok**   **mik**
      son   and   me.OBL
      'if he practices to consent to my son and me'
                                      (Birgittas uppenbarelser, c.1380)

However, recall from Section 4.2.5 above that this verb, *thäkkias*, appears to be an alternating Dat-Nom/Nom-Dat verb in Old Swedish. It is clear from this example that the nominative is the subject and the dative the object; thus the usage in (199) is an instance of a Nom-Dat verb, not a Dat-Nom verb, as Falk alleges. This verb also existed in Old Norse-Icelandic and still exists in Modern Icelandic; in Old Norse-Icelandic it was constructed either with an accusative or a dative object, while in Modern Icelandic, it only exists with an accusative object. This is shown in the attested Modern Icelandic control infinitive in (200) below where the nominative subject of the non-finite *þekkjast* 'consent to' is left unexpressed on identity with the underlying agent of the clause-initial nominal, *í tilraun minni* 'in my attempt':

Icelandic
(200) a. *Í   tilraun   minni   til   [að   ___   þekkjast   þessa*
       in   attempt   mine   for   to   PRO.NOM   consent.to.INF   this.ACC
       heimspeki]   sem   ...
       philosophy   which
       'In my attempt to consent to this philosophy which ...'

Therefore, Falk's Old Swedish Nom-Dat verb in (199), and others of this type for that matter, cannot be used as arguments against a subject analysis of Dat-Nom verbs or other oblique subject verbs in Old Swedish.

Turning now to Old Norse-Icelandic, six examples of control infinitives have so far been documented in the literature, three by Rögnvaldsson (1996) and three by Barðdal and Eythórsson (2003a: 458–459). In (194a–g) above I introduce to the scholarship seven more examples of control infinitives in Old Norse-Icelandic, where the unexpressed subject of the infinitive is in the dative case.

Observe that the first five examples involve the matrix verb *kveðast* 'say' and all five have a nominative subject with this matrix verb, namely *Þorvaldur, Þorsteinn, Snorri, Glúmur* and *Þorbergur*, which are all unambiguous nominatives. Note also that in all five cases, the non-finite verb is *þykja* 'seem, think, find' which occurs systematically with a potential dative subject. One such example is shown in (201) below:

Old Norse-Icelandic
(201) *ef **þér**   **þykir**   það   betra.*
       if   you.DAT   finds.3SG   it.NOM   better
       'if you think it is better.'   (Kjalnesinga saga, ch. 14)

The last two Old Norse-Icelandic control infinitives in (194f–g) involve two different lower verbs, which both occur consistently with a potential dative subject, namely *falla þungt* 'find grievous' and *ganga til* 'have intentions':

Old Norse-Icelandic
(202) a. *Fellur* **mönnum** *þungt.*
falls men.DAT heavy
'The men find this grievous.' (Hænsna-Þóris saga, ch. 4)
b. *Eigi gekk* **mér** *það til heldur hitt að ...*
not went me.DAT it.NOM til rather other that
'Not did I have that intention, rather the other one that ...'
(Þorsteins saga hvíta, ch. 7)

Given these facts, it is inconceivable that the unexpressed subjects in the Old Norse-Icelandic control infinitives in (194f–g) above are anything but potential dative subjects.

Against the Old Norse-Icelandic examples in (194a–e) above, one might perhaps argue that the verb *kveðast* 'say' is not a control verb but a raising-to-object verb in Old Norse-Icelandic, as the last morpheme, the *-sk* (here represented with Modern Icelandic spelling *-st*), could be regarded as a cliticized reflexive pronoun attached to the verbal stem, *kveða* (cf. Faarlund 2001: 106). If so, *kveðast* would mean 'say of oneself' instead of 'say'. Such an analysis, however, would predict that *kveðast* and *kveða sig* select for the same type of complements in both Old Norse-Icelandic and Modern Icelandic. This, however, is not borne out, as is shown in the following attested Old Norse-Icelandic examples of *kveðast* and its predicative complements in (203a–b) below:

Old Norse-Icelandic
(203) a. *Hann ... kvaðst* **vera sekur maður.**
he.NOM said.3SG be.INF guilty.NOM.SG man.NOM.SG
'He ... said that he was a guilty man.' (Finnboga saga ramma, ch. 51)
b. *Þeir kváðust* **vera húskarlar** *Þorvalds.*
they.NOM said.3PL be.INF housecarls.NOM.PL Þorvaldur.GEN
'They said that they were Þorvaldur's housecarls' (Grettis saga, ch. 9)

These examples show that *kveðast* selects for a subject predicate, where the predicative complement is in the nominative case, agreeing in case and number with the nominative subjects of *kveðast*, *hann* 'he' and *þeir* 'they', respectively; the first example is in the nominative singular, agreeing with *hann* 'he' and the second is in the nominative plural, agreeing with *þeir* 'they'. In other words, *-sk* is not a clitic attached to the verbal stem, but is instead a derivational suffix in Old Norse-Icelandic, exactly as in Modern Icelandic (cf. Ottósson 1992: 68; Rögnvaldsson 1996: 61).

In contrast, if *kveðast* really were structurally equivalent to *kveða sig* 'say of oneself', it would select for an object predicate of the type illustrated in (204a–b) below, for the simple reason that the relevant predication must agree with the object, the accusative *sik* 'self' in this case:

Old Norse-Icelandic
(204) a. *En   Svási   kvað   **sig**   vera   þann*
          but   Svási.NOM.SG said.3SG   REFL.ACC be.INF that.ACC.SG
          Finninn   *er*   . . .
          Finn.the.ACC.SG   who
          'But Svási said himself to be that Finlander who . . .'
                                                                (Haraldar saga hárfagra, ch. 26)
     b. *Hrolleifur   kvað   **sig**   eigi   **skyldan**   að* . . .
        Hrolleifur.NOM said.3SG   REFL.ACC   not   obliged.ACC   to
        'Hrolleifur said himself not to be obliged to . . .'   (Vatnsdæla saga, ch. 22)

Note that the object predicates in (204), *vera þann Finninn* 'be that Finlander' and *skyldan* 'obliged', show a different case and agreement pattern than the subject predicates in (203), with the object predicate agreeing in case and number with the object, *sik* 'self', thus showing up in the accusative, as opposed to being in the nominative in subject predicates.

This pattern, moreover, is not only confined to *kveðast* but is found with *-sk* verbs in general in Old Norse-Icelandic, as is shown with the verbs *nefnast* 'be named' and *nefna sig* 'call oneself' in (205) below:

Old Norse-Icelandic
(205) a. *Hún   nefndist   **Hallgerður**   og   kvaðst   vera* . . .
         she.NOM   was.named.3SG   Hallgerður.NOM   and   said   be.INF
         'She was named Hallgerður and said that she was . . .'
                                                                (Brennu-Njáls saga, ch. 33)
     b. *Hann   nefndi   sig   **Óla***   . . .
        he.NOM   named.3SG   REFL.ACC   Óli.ACC
        'He named himself Óli . . .'   (Ólafs saga Tryggvasonar, ch. 32)

In (205a) *Hallgerður* is a subject complement, thus turning up in the nominative case and agreeing with the subject *hún* 'she'. If the *-sk* of *nefnast* were a cliticized reflexive object, *nefnast* would be equal to *nefna sik* 'name oneself', and it would select for an object predicate showing up in the accusative case, instead of the attested nominative. That is, if V-*sk* equals V *sik*, both *kveðast* and *nefnast* should select for object predicates instead of the attested subject predicates in Old Norse-Icelandic:

(206) a. *Hann ... kvaðst **vera sekan mann.**
       he.NOM   said.3SG be.INF guilty.ACC.SG man.ACC.SG
   b. *Þeir   kváðust **vera húskarla** Þorvalds
       they.NOM said.3PL be.INF housecarls.ACC.PL Þorvaldur.GEN
   c. *Hún   nefndist **Hallgerði**
       she.NOM was.named.3SG Hallgerður.ACC

Instead, the constructed examples in (206) are unattested in Old Norse-Icelandic and ungrammatical in Modern Icelandic.

Before we leave Old Norse-Icelandic, it is worthy of being pointed out that *kveðast* appears to be able to occur either as a raising-to-subject verb, as already shown in Section 4.2.4 above, or as a control verb, as demonstrated in this section. I repeat a subset of the relevant data here for ease of exposition:

Raising-to-subject
(207) a. **Honum** kvaðst það illa **þykja** að ...
       him.DAT said.REFL.3SG it.NOM badly feel.INF
       'He said that he felt that it was bad that ...' (Reykdæla saga, ch. 13)

Control infinitive
   b. *Snorri* kvaðst [__ einsætt **þykja]** að
      Snorri.NOM said   PRO.DAT obvious think.INF
      'Snorri said that he found it obvious that ...' (Laxdæla saga, ch. 67)

The difference between these two examples is that *kveðast* occurs with a potential dative subject in (207a), which is selected for by the lower verb, *þykja* 'think, feel, seem'; hence it is a raising-to-subject construction. In contrast, in (207b) *kveðast* occurs with a nominative subject, *Snorri*, thus selecting for a subject of its own. As a consequence, the resulting infinitive must be analyzed as a control infinitive.

This is in line with the situation in Modern Icelandic where *kveðast* and *segjast* 'say (of oneself)' are assumed to select for control infinitives (cf. Anderson 1990: 265–266). However, it appears that, at least, *segjast* in Modern Icelandic may have the same choices as *kveðast* in Old Norse-Icelandic in that it also occurs as a raising-to-subject verb (cf. Andrews 1990: 206; Barðdal and Eythórsson 2003a, 2006: 165–166). Consider the following attested examples from Modern Icelandic:

Icelandic
(208) a. **Honum segist** vera létt og hann viti ...
       him.DAT says.REFL.3SG be.INF relieved and he knows
       'He says that he is relieved and he knows ...'

b. *Og þegar **honum   segist   líða   illa   vegna***
   and   when   him.DAT   says.REFL.3SG   be.INF   badly   because
   þess   að   hann   sé   nakinn...
   of   that   he   is   naked
   'And when he says that he feels bad because he is naked ...'

c. ***Honum   segist***   *ekki   hafa   verið   um   sel*
   him.DAT   says.REFL.3SG   not   have.INF   been   of   ease
   eftir   þetta.
   after   this
   'He says that he has not felt at ease after this.'

The non-finite verbs in (208) above, *vera létt* 'be relieved', *líða illa* 'feel bad' and *vera um sel* 'be at ease', all select for a dative subject in Modern Icelandic. As already discussed in Section 4.2.4 above, the subject of the lower verb in raising-to-subject constructions takes on the behavioral properties of the subject of the matrix clause. Thus, the dative subjects of the lower verbs behave syntactically here as the subjects of the matrix verbs, while corresponding dative subjects of the lower verbs are missing. Therefore, the fact that *kveðast* 'say' can occur either as a raising-to-subject or a control verb does not invalidate either the raising-to-subject or the control analysis of the examples presented above. This is simply an idiosyncrasy of these two verbs.

Turning to Early Middle English, the examples in (193a–b) above are well known from the literature, and they are also relatively straightforward. They involve the verbs *dremen* 'dream' and *lician* 'like', which both select for potential oblique subjects at this stage of the English language. Originally, 'dream' selected for a potential accusative subject, as it still does in Modern Icelandic, while 'like' selected for a potential dative subject (cf. Section 3.4 above). In (193a), however, the potential accusative subject of *dremen* is left unexpressed in a control infinitive, on identity not with a subject nor with an object of the matrix clause, but rather on identity with a generic reference, retrievable from the context. In (193b), the potential dative subject of *lician* is left unexpressed on identity with the dative *him*, which is itself a potential dative subject of *biren* 'be obliged' in Early Middle English. In that respect, this Early Middle English example is comparable with the Old Norse-Icelandic examples in (194f–g), the Old Swedish example in (195a) and the Old Danish one in (196). More importantly, however, both of the Early Middle English control infinitives in (193) above are attested from a period before both *dremen* and *lician* started occurring with a nominative subject (Cole et al. 1980: 729, fn. 16; Allen 1986: 381).

Consider now the three Old Saxon control infinitives involving potential oblique subjects in (192a–b) above. The first example in (192a) occurs with the compositional predicate *an sorgun wesan* 'be in grief'. This predicate occurs systematically with a potential dative subject in Old Saxon, as is demonstrated with three examples from the Heliand in (209) below:

Old Saxon
(209) a. *Was*   ***im***   *thoh* *an* *sorgun*   *hugi*
         was.3SG   them.DAT   yet   in   sorrows.DAT   heart.NOM
         'Yet they grieved in their heart'   (Heliand 1: 85)
      b. *Warð*   ***Mariun***   *thô*   *môd*   *an*   *sorgun*
         became.3SG   Mary.DAT   then   heart.NOM   in   sorrows.DAT
         'Then Mary grieved in the heart'   (Heliand 10: 803)
      c. *swîðo*   *warð*   ***imu***   *an*   *sorgun*
         very   became.3SG   him.DAT   in   sorrows.DAT
         'He grieved very much'   (Heliand 59: 4996)

There are no examples in the Heliand with the animate argument in the nominative case, only in the dative case. This, in turn, demonstrates that the unexpressed subject in the control infinitive in (192a) must involve a potential dative subject. The matrix verb is *thurƀan* 'need', which occurs here with a subject of its own, the nominative plural *gi* 'you'. The form of the verb, *thurƀun* 'need' is 2nd person plural, thus agreeing in number with the nominative plural subject *gi*. All of this shows that *thurƀan* 'need' occurs here as a control verb, selecting for its own subject, which in turn means that the embedded infinitive must be regarded as a control infinitive, in this case with a potential dative subject being the unexpressed argument.

While the Old Saxon example of the control infinitive in (192a) is relatively simple, the second and third Old Saxon examples, the ones in (192b), pose a few challenges. I reproduce these examples here, due to the complicated nature of the argument.

Old Saxon
Control infinitive
(192) b. *bethiu*   *ne*   *thurƀun*   ...   [__]   *thius*   *werk*
         thus   not   need.2PL   PRO.DAT   these.NOM   deeds.NOM
         tregan],   [__]   ***hrewan***   *mîn*   *hinfard]*
         regret.INF   PRO.DAT   rue.INF   my.NOM   departure.NOM
         'therefore, you need not ... regret these deeds, nor rue my departure'
                                                                    (Heliand 57: 4730–31)

First of all, there is a lacuna in this particular example, immediately following the finite verb *thurƀun* 'need', and preceding the first control infinitive and its nominative object, *thius werk tregan* 'regret these deeds'. This lacuna is very small, yielding space for perhaps a couple of letters. All the more important in this context is the fact that the nominative subject of *thurƀun* 'need' is lacking in this example, suggesting that *ge* 'you' may be the missing text. A very strong argument for such an assumption stems from the form of the verb *thurƀun*, which is the 2nd person plural, indeed requiring a nominative subject like *ge* 'you'.

Another possibility, however, is that it is the dative plural form *iu* 'you' which is the missing pronoun in the lacuna in this example. If so, the example in (192b) is a raising-to-subject example and not a control infinitive. However, in Section 4.2.4 above, an Old Saxon example of raising-to-subject is given, also containing the verb *thurƀan* 'need'. This example is reproduced here for the sake of the argument:

Old Saxon
Raising-to-subject
(154) b. "ni   tharf   **iu**   wiht   **tregan**," quathie
     not need.3SG you.DAT.PL anything regret.INF said.he
     '"you guys need not regret anything", he said'   (Heliand 65: 5520)

Observe that the form of the finite verb is 3rd person singular *tharf* in this raising-to-subject example, and not 2nd person plural *thurƀan*, due to the nexus between the finite verb and the potential dative subject. This qualifies as a major argument against a raising-to-subject analysis for (192b) and for a control analysis, because if (192b) were a raising-to-subject example, one should expect *thurƀan* 'need' to show up as *tharf*, with default agreement which is third person singular, which it does not do. Assuming that the lacuna in (192b) contains the second person dative plural *iu* 'you' is therefore altogether out of the question.

This means that *thurƀan* 'need' can either be a raising-to-subject verb or a control verb in Old Saxon. This variation in complementation is also found for *kveðast* 'say of oneself' in Old Norse-Icelandic and its synonym *segjast* in Modern Icelandic, as is clear from the examples and the discussion above (see also Barðdal and Eythórsson 2003a, 2006). Furthermore, this variation in complementation found with specific auxiliary verbs has also been observed in Italic. Barðdal et al. (2023) document exactly the same complement variation for the Latin auxiliary *possum* 'can', which occurs either as raising-to-subject or a control verb in the Latin language. Clearly, some verbs are borderline examples between the two categories, showing the ability to instantiate both structures.

Setting this issue aside, I now turn to the control infinitives themselves in (192b). These consist of the oblique subject verbs *tregan* and *hrewan*, both meaning 'regret'. The first one, *tregan*, only occurs three times in the Heliand, two of which are presented above as (154b) and (192b). The third example is also a raising-to-subject example, given in (210) below:

Old Saxon
Raising-to-subject
(210) ôðo   [beginnad]   **imu**   than   is   werk   **tregan**
       easily begins.3SG   him.DAT   then   his   deeds   regret.INF
       'He then easily begins to regret his deeds.'   (Heliand 40: 3233)

The two examples of *tregan* occurring outside of a control construction reveal that this verb selects for a potential dative subject and not a nominative subject. This means that the unexpressed subject in (192b) cannot be anything but the potential dative subject of *tregan*.

Turning our attention to *hrewan* 'rue', the second and conjoined control infinitive in (192b), this verb occurs seven times in the Heliand, in addition to the occurrence in (192b). Four of those seven are raising-to-object constructions, two are raising-to-subject constructions and one is finite. The problem with the finite example, shown in (211) below, is that there is, again, a lacuna in the text where the reference to the animate argument is located, hence the case marking cannot be determined. As luck would have it though, the two raising-to-subject examples demonstrate clear-cut morphological datives of the animate argument, as is shown in (212) below:

Old Saxon
finite *hrewan*
(211) hrau   [im]   sô   hardo
       rues.3SG   them.DAT   so   hard
       '[they] regret so much.'   (Heliand 59: 5022)

Old Saxon
non-finite *hrewan*
(212) a. thô   bigan   **imu**   thiu   dâd   after   thiu
         yet   began.3SG   him.DAT   the.NOM   deed   later   these.ACC
         an   is   hugea   hrewan
         in   his   mind   rue.INF
         'yet he began thereafter to regret the deed in his heart'
                                                              (Heliand 61: 5147)
      b. ôðo   [beginnad]   **imu**   ...   an   [is]   hugi   hrewan
         easily   begins.3SG   him.DAT   in   his   heart   rue.INF
         'he then begins easily ... to rue in his heart'   (Heliand 40: 3234)

These examples therefore show that the unexpressed argument of *hrewan* 'rue' in (192b) is a potential dative subject, and not a nominative subject. This analysis is further supported by the fact that *mîn hinfard* 'my departure', the expressed object in (192b) is an unambiguous nominative. This nominative case marking of *mîn hinfard* 'my departure', indeed restricts the case marking of the unexpressed subject to either accusative or dative, i.e. to either a Dat-Nom or an Acc-Nom case frame.

This concludes the discussion of the three Old Saxon control infinitives involving *an sorgun wesan* 'feel sorrow', *tregan* 'regret' and *hrewan* 'rue', in which the unexpressed subject clearly is a potential dative subject and not a nominative subject. These examples therefore corroborate a subject analysis of potential oblique subjects in the Old Saxon language.

Finally, turning our attention to the Gothic control infinitive in (191), this example contains the verb *luston* 'lust' which selects for a potential accusative subject and a genitive object. Alas, note that this is the only example of 'lust' in the Gothic material, hence it cannot be corroborated with data from Gothic that the unexpressed subject corresponds to an accusative found with this verb in finite clauses. Instead, let us consider the comparative material. Not surprisingly, 'lust' consistently selects for a potential accusative subject and a genitive object in the early Germanic languages in general, as is shown in (213) below (cf. Barðdal and Eythórsson 2012a: 386–387):

Old High German
(213) a. nu **dih** es so wel lustit
now you.ACC it.GEN so well desires.3SG
'now that you desire it so well.' (Hildebrandslied 59)

Old Saxon
b. that **ina** bigan bi thero mennisko
that him.ACC began.3SG because.of that.DAT humanity.DAT
môses lustean
meat.GEN desire.INF
'that because of his humanity, he began to desire meat.' (Heliand 1060)

Old English
c. **Hine** nanes þinges ne lyste on ðisse
him.ACC no.GEN thing.GEN not desired.3SG on this
worulde
world
'He desired nothing in this world.' (Boethius Cons.Phil. 35,6)

Old Dutch
   d. **Mich**   *nelusted*   *niewehtes*
      me.ACC   not.lusted.3SG   nothing.GEN
      'I desired nothing'   (LW 85,8, here cited from van der Horst 2008: 241)

Old Norse-Icelandic
   e. *er*   **þig**   *lysti*   **þessa**
      when   you.ACC   desired.3SG   that.GEN
      'when you desired that.'   (Ljósvetningasaga, ch. 19)

In addition, the object *izos* 'her' in the Gothic example in (191) is in the genitive case, which is consistent with 'lust' selecting for Acc-Gen in Gothic, exactly as this verb does in all the other early Germanic languages.

However, since the Gothic Bible is a translation, the question arises which verb is used in the Greek original, i.e. which verb does 'lust' translate. Inspecting the Greek Bible reveals that the verb used there is *epithumeō* 'desire', which is a Nom-Dat verb, also occurring in a control infinitive in the original Bible text with the nominative subject left unexpressed (cf. Barðdal and Eythórsson 2012a). Hence, the case frame used with 'lust' in Gothic, Acc-Gen, is not a calque from Greek, but is instead the inherited Germanic Acc-Gen case frame. What is equally important, is that when Wulfila translated *epithumeō* 'desire' into Gothic, it was clearly not an obstacle for him that 'lust' does not occur with a nominative subject in Gothic. This means that Wulfila equated the Acc-Gen case frame of 'lust' with the Nom-Dat case frame of the Greek original. In other words, Wulfila treated the potential accusative subject of 'lust' as a syntactic subject by leaving it unexpressed in a control infinitive.

Before leaving the issue of control infinitives altogether, it needs to be mentioned here that Cole et al. (1980: 721–727) provide arguments against a subject analysis of potential dative subjects in Gothic on the basis of the following example:

Gothic
(214) a. *inuþ-þis*   *usdaudjam*...   *[waila*   ___   *galeikan*
         because-of.this   strive.1PL   well   PRO.NOM   please.INF
         imma].
         him.DAT
         'Because of this we strive ... to please him well.'   (II Corinthians 5:9)

There is no doubt that the dative behaves syntactically as an object in (214) and that the nominative is the unexpressed argument in this control infinitive. Thus, the nominative takes on the behavioral properties of subject here. Nevertheless, examples like this are no counter-arguments against a subject analysis of potential dative subjects in Gothic; they can only be used as arguments for the subject status of the nominative of *galeikan* 'please, like' in Gothic.

As I discuss to considerable length in Section 3.4.2 above, it appears that Old and Early Middle English *lician* and Gothic *galeikan* are alternating predicates which may instantiate either the Dat-Nom or the Nom-Dat argument structure construction. Clearly, in (214) above, it is the Nom-Dat argument structure that is being used with *galeikan*, and not the Dat-Nom argument structure. As such, the example in (214) has no validity for this discussion.

To summarize the content of this section, I have here presented control infinitives involving oblique subject verbs from six different early Germanic languages, Gothic, Old Saxon, Early Middle English, Old Norse-Icelandic, Old Swedish and Old Danish. These control infinitives show that only a subject analysis is viable for potential oblique subjects in those languages and that an object analysis is ruled out entirely.

4.2.7 Word order

The reason that potential oblique subjects are consistently referred to as "psychological" subjects in the earlier philological literature (von der Gabelentz 1869; Jespersen 1894; Lindqvist 1912; among others) is that these verbal arguments behave syntactically as subjects when it comes to word order distribution. That is, they typically occupy the first position of the clause and invert with the subject in questions and topicalizations. Hence, it seems that the only reason that potential oblique subjects were not analyzed as subjects at the time is their oblique or non-nominative case marking.

These word order properties are demonstrated in (215–221) below: the a) examples are instances of clause-initial position and the b) examples show subject-verb inversion.

Gothic
(215) a. iþ   sundro **þaimei** þuhta,
            but   only   these.DAT thought.3SG
          'but only these ones thought' (Galatians 2:2)
      b. aftra   þugkeiþ   **izwis**   ei
            again   thinks.3SG you.DAT that
          'Again, you think that' (Corinthians II 12:19)

Old High German
(216) a. *sosǫ* **imu** *rát thunkit*
so.that him.DAT advise.NOM thinks.3SG
'So that he finds [it] it advisable' (Otfr., Ev.2, 12, 42)
b. *uuaz thunkit* ***úuuih*?**
what thinks.3SG you.ACC
'What do you think?' (Tat., Ev.Harm., 191, 2)

Old Saxon
(217) a. *sô* **mi** *thes wundar thunkit*
so me.ACC/DAT that.GEN wonder.GEN thinks.3SG
'So I find this a wonder' (Heliand 2: 157)
b. *"ni thunkid* **mi** *thit [sômi] thing" quað he,*
not thinks.3SG me.ACC/DAT that seemly thing said he
'He said: "I do not find this a seemly thing"' (Heliand 54: 4508)

Old English
(218) a. *þe* **him selfum** *ðincð þæt . . .*
then him.DAT self.DAT thinks.3SG it
'Then he himself thinks that . . .'
(Alfredian Boethius (Otho) xxix. 66, c.890–950)
b. *Þinceð* **him** *to lytel*
thinks.3SG him.DAT too little
'He finds this too little' (Beowulf 1748)

Old Norse Icelandic
(219) a. *. . . hvort* **mér** *þykir vel eða illa*
whether me.DAT thinks.3SG well or badly
'. . . whether I find this good or bad.' (Íslendings þáttur sögufróða)
b. *Svo þykir* **mér** *sem . . .*
then thinks.3SG me.DAT as.if
'Then I feel as if . . .' (Brennu Njáls saga, ch. 3)

Old Swedish
(220) a. *ty* **honom** *tikkie got wara*
because him.DAT would.think.3SG good be.INF
'because he would not find this good'
(Konungastyrelsen 29 (74, 31), c.1350)

b. väghin   thötte   **them**   ey   vara   lang
   road.the thought.3SG them.DAT not be.INF long
   'They didn't find the road long'
                                   (Hertig Fredrik av Normandie 1599, c.1308)

Old Danish
(221) a. vm   **oss**   thycker   thet   nuttelicht wære
         if   us.DAT   thinks.3SG   this.NOM   useful   be.INF
         'If we find this useful.'   (Skråer II. 114, c.1443)
      b. tha   thatæ   **hannum**   skam   oc   wanhæther
         then thought.3SG him.DAT   shame.NOM and disgrace.NOM
         wære   at...
         be.INF   at
         'Then he finds it to be a shame and disgrace that...' (RydÅrb. I, c.1314)

While word order in the early Germanic languages was certainly much freer than it is in the modern languages, there are still very clear tendencies for the potential oblique subject to occur either clause-initially or immediately following the verb in cases where some other sentence element occupies the first position.

However, word order facts have also been used as arguments against assuming a subject analysis for potential oblique subjects during earlier periods. For instance, Falk (1997: 37) presents a set of Old Swedish examples which demonstrate, in her view, that potential dative subjects occupy the object position and not the subject position:

Old Swedish
(222) a. at   thz   wæl   behaghadhe   **iudhomen**
         that   it.NOM well   suited.3SG   jews.the.DAT
         'That it suited the Jews'   (Herr Ivan 2561, c.1303)
      b. thekkis   thz   **idher**
         cosents.to.3SG it.NOM you.DAT
         'Is this to your approval?'   (Siälinna tröst, 72, c.1401)
      c. oc   täktos   ordhen   **minum**   **brödhrom**
         and   consented.to.3SG   words.the.NOM   my.DAT   brothers.DAT
         'and the words were to my brothers' approval'
                                                (Leg 3: 462, c.1450–1500)

Observe that the first example is with *behaga* 'suit' which I analyze, in Section 3.2.4 above, as an alternating verb in Old Swedish. And the latter two examples contain the verb *thekkias* 'consent to', which Söderwall in his Old Swedish dictionary mentions as having the ability to be constructed either personally or impersonally, as is discussed in Sections 4.2.5 and 4.2.6 above. Examples of this type do not therefore testify to object behavior of potential oblique subjects, since the datives in these examples are clear-cut objects of Nom-Dat verbs anyway.

Faarlund (2001) also presents examples which he believes should invalidate word order as an argument for the subject status of potential oblique subjects. More specifically, Faarlund argues that there is a major difference between word order distribution in Old Norse-Icelandic and Modern Icelandic in that objects can occupy all the same positions in Old-Norse Icelandic as subjects can, while this is not so in Modern Icelandic. It follows from this, Faarlund argues, that position cannot be used as an argument for a subject analysis of potential oblique subjects for that language stage. The following two examples are here cited from Faarlund (2001: 117–118, 121–122):

Old Norse-Icelandic
(223) a. *Mundu* **það** *sumir menn mæla í mínu landi*
 would.3PL it.ACC some men.NOM say in my country
 'Some men would say so in my country.' (Finnboga saga, ch. 9)
 b. *Þá skal* **sínum húsum** *hver ráða*
 then shall.3SG REFL.DAT houses.DAT each.NOM rule.INF
 'Then each shall decide over his own house.'
 (The Law of Magnús lagabætir)

Examples like the one in (223b) are dealt with by Barðdal and Eythórsson (2003a: 446–447) who point out that this word order, i.e. with the object preceding the subject, is typical for complex distributive pronouns involving the reflexive possessive pronoun *sinn* 'self, own' and the indefinite pronoun *hver* 'each'. The following attested example from the Modern Icelandic Gigaword Corpus documents this (see Barkarson, Steingrímsson, and Hafsteinsdóttir 2022):

Icelandic
(224) *Hrepparnir haga svo til að þeir skipta smjörflutningum niður á bændur eftir ítölu í rjómabúum þeirra*
 og fer þá **sína ferðina** *hver,   eru jafnvel*
 and goes then REFL.ACC trip.ACC each.NOM are even
 3–4 um hverja ferð.
 3–4 of each trip
 'The rural districts have the arrangement that they divide the butter transports across the farmers, depending on number of allowed sheep in their creameries, and *each [farmer] takes on his own trip*, [they] may even be 3–4 [farmers] on each trip.' (Samvinna á Suðurlandi, c.2020, IGC-2022)

Here too does the possessive reflexive object *sína ferðina* 'own trip' precede the indefinite subject *hver* 'each' in the order of the clausal constituents in (224). In this respect, Old Norse-Icelandic does not differ from Modern Icelandic, as opposed to Faarlund's claims.

Turning to examples like the one in (223a), Jónsson (2018) makes a convincing argument for a process in Old Norse-Icelandic, which he labels *pronominal object scrambling*. This entails that pronominal objects may precede the subject if they are light pronouns (cf. also Haugan 2001: 174–184). This type of weak pronominal scrambling with which the object precedes the subject is also well known from Old English (Wallenberg 2008) and Modern Swedish (Josefsson 1992; Hellan and Platzack 1995). For more types of word order examples presented by Faarlund (2001) and arguments against their validity, cf. Barðdal and Eythórsson (2003a).

All in all, Jónsson (2018) argues that subjects always precede objects in Old Norse-Icelandic, except for under three conditions, namely with: i) pronominal object scrambling, ii) complex distributive pronouns, and ii) heavy or indefinite subject shift. This last condition is well known from the modern Germanic literature as involving a subject occurring late in the clause, if it is heavy or indefinite (cf. Ottósson 1989; Bobaljik and Jonas 1996; Wallenberg 2015; among others). Needless to say, these three conditions are always identifiable as such in Old Norse-Icelandic texts, meaning that subjects and objects can always be teased apart.

I conclude this section with a summary of Barðdal and Eythórsson's (2012a) quantitative study on word order distribution in the history of Icelandic, first and foremost comparing the distribution of nominative and oblique subjects. The numbers in Table 9 are slightly revised from the 2012a study due to a later qualitative scrutiny of some of the smaller categories, although this does not affect the overall tendencies documented in the data set.

Table 9: Word order distribution of nominative and oblique subjects in the history of Icelandic.

	SOV		SVO		VSO		OSV		OVS		VOS	
	N	f	N	f	N	f	N	f	N	f	N	f
Nominative	0	0	2327	66.9%	554	16.0%	0	0	578	16.6%	17	0.5%
Oblique	0	0	96	64.9%	42	28.4%	0	0	6	4.0%	4	2.7%

The frequencies are extracted from the IcePaHC corpus, compiled by Wallenberg et al. (2011). This corpus contains Icelandic texts dating back to the late 12th century and almost ten centuries forward, up to the present. Quite unexpectedly, the proportions between nominative and oblique subjects remain the same across the different word order combinations over the centuries (cf. Ingason, Sigurðsson, and

Wallenberg 2011). For this reason, our numbers are conflated into only two categories, nominative and oblique subjects, irrespective of time intervals.

The statistics in Table 9 are based on main clauses only. All possible combinations of S, V and O are given. Observe that two of the word order combinations, SOV and OSV are not found in Icelandic, neither Old Norse-Icelandic nor Modern Icelandic. The remaining word order combinations, valid for Icelandic, are SVO, VSO, OVS and VOS.

The order SVO represents neutral word order in Icelandic, with the subject occurring in clause-initial position, the verb occurring in second position and the object following the verb. This is also the most frequent word order found in the corpus. Nominative subjects are found in this word order constellation in 67% of the cases. Oblique subjects also show up in this word order in 65% of the cases. The second valid word order constellation, VSO, is found in questions, narrative inversion and other structures involving subject-verb inversion. Nominative subjects thus invert with the verb in 16% of the cases, while corresponding figures for oblique subjects are higher, namely 28% of the cases.

This difference between nominative and oblique subjects in VSO structures, 16 vs. 28%, is entirely in line with an observation made by Rögnvaldsson (1991) that experiencer subjects show a greater tendency than agentive subjects to follow the verb, instead of preceding it. This tendency, Rögnvaldsson notes, is valid across all case-marked subjects, i.e. it is found for nominative, accusative and dative subjects alike. However, since a considerable portion of oblique subject verbs are experiencer verbs, and a much greater portion than that found for nominative subject verbs (Barðdal 2001c: 100–101), it is expected that oblique subjects at large are affected by this tendency to a greater extent than nominative subject verbs.

The third word order combination, OVS, represents structures where the object is topicalized, also resulting in subject-verb inversion, exactly as with VSO structures. Here nominative subjects outnumber oblique subjects proportionally, with accusative, dative and genitive objects being topicalized in 16.6% of the cases, while corresponding figures for nominative objects are only 4%. In fact, the mismatch in numbers here is inversely correlated with the mismatch in numbers for VSO, with a 12% difference for both word order combinations, as oblique subjects occur in VSO structures in 28.4% of the cases, while nominative subjects do so in only 16% of the cases. Conversely, nominative subjects occur in OVS structures in 16.6% of the cases, while oblique subjects do so in only 4% of the cases.

Finally, VOS structures are found when the subject is either heavy or indefinite. This takes place in .5% of the instances with nominative subjects and 2.7% of the instances with oblique subjects. This is clearly a minority word order combination for both nominative and oblique subjects in the history of Icelandic.

Table 10: Analyzing the potential oblique subject as a syntactic object.

	SOV		SVO		VSO		OSV		OVS		VOS	
	N	f	N	f	N	f	N	f	N	f	N	f
Nominative	0	0	2327	66.9%	554	16.4%	0	0	578	16.6%	17	0.5%
Oblique	0	0	6	4.0%	4	2.7%	0	0	96	64.9%	42	28.4%

Let us now, for the sake of the argument, analyze potential oblique subjects as objects and the nominative of Acc-Nom and Dat-Nom predicates as a subject. The statistics for such an analysis are given in Table 10. On the analysis that the nominative of Dat-Nom and Acc-Nom is a subject, this alleged subject only occurs in SVO structures in 4% of the instances, which is certainly not what ordinary nominative subjects do, as they otherwise occur in SVO structures in 67% of the instances. For VSO structures, the nominative of Dat-Nom and Acc-Nom only inverts with the subject in questions and narrative inversion in 2.7% of the cases, as opposed to 16% of the cases for ordinary nominative subjects. Also, potential oblique subjects, on an object analysis, are topicalized in 65% of the cases, as opposed to ordinary objects being topicalized in 16,6% of the cases. The same disproportions are found in VOS structures where the subject is either heavy or indefinite. On a subject analysis of the nominative in Dat-Nom and Acc-Nom constructions, as many as 28% of such nominative subjects are placed following the object, as opposed to .5% of ordinary nominative subjects.

Taken together, analyzing the nominative of Dat-Nom and Acc-Nom constructions as a syntactic subject leads to major inconsistencies between these two types of "nominative subjects", basically ruling out an object analysis of potential oblique subjects. Instead, all the evidence suggests that potential oblique subjects show the same word order distribution as nominative subjects do in the history of Icelandic, even though the proportions for these categories are not exactly the same. In other words, potential oblique subjects show the same statistical tendencies as nominative subjects do in texts dating all the way back to the late 11th century.

To conclude, I have presented examples in this section from Gothic, Old High German, Old Saxon, Old English, Old Norse-Icelandic, Old Swedish and Old Danish showing that potential oblique subjects typically occupy the clause-initial position in these languages, and invert with the verb when other elements are topicalized to first position. I have also presented quantitative data from the history of Icelandic, documenting that potential oblique subjects behave in the same way as nominative subjects do.

4.3 Summary and discussion

Of the eight different hypotheses introduced in Section 4.1 above on the origin of the oblique subject construction, only two are supported by the data presented in the previous section. These are the Oblique Subject Hypothesis, which was originally argued for by Barðdal (2000b), Barðdal and Eythórsson (2003a) and Eythórsson and Barðdal (2005), and its continuation, the Extended Intransitive Hypothesis, suggested by Pooth et al. (2019). On this hypothesis, potential oblique subjects were already syntactic subjects in Proto-Germanic, if not in Proto-Indo-European. This means that oblique subjects have been syntactic subjects since such structures arose (cf. in particular the discussion in 3.6 above)

Of the subject behaviors that have here been used as tests to distinguish between syntactic subjects and objects in the modern Germanic languages, two cannot be reliably applied in the early languages, namely clause-bound reflexivization and conjunction reduction, for different reasons. The problem with clause-bound reflexivization is that while Harbert (1978: 37–38, 1991: 34) argues, following Streitberg (1920), that only subjects may bind reflexives in Gothic, examples of subjects binding personal pronouns, and not reflexives, have been reported for both Old Norse-Icelandic and Old Swedish. Given that, binding of reflexives has not been used here to tease apart subject and object behavior. A similar problem is found with conjunction reduction, caused by the fact that the early Germanic languages are argument-drop languages, resulting in both subjects and objects' ability to be dropped if they are recoverable from the preceding text or the context. For this particular reason, it may be difficult to distinguish between topic-drop and conjunction reduction in the early Germanic languages.

Allen (1995: 112–115), however, argues that conjunction reduction may be used in Old English as a subject test, not on the basis of specific examples, but on the basis of frequencies. She shows that potential dative subjects control deletion of nominative subjects in second conjuncts in 50–60% of the cases, while objects control deletion of nominative subjects in second conjuncts in 1% of the cases. The relevant statistics for nominative subjects controlling the deletion of other nominative subjects in second conjuncts is ca. 80% of the cases. On the basis of these numbers, Allen argues, and quite convincingly so, in my opinion, that potential oblique subjects indeed behave syntactically as subjects and not as objects in Old English. For this reason, conjunction reduction is listed in Table 11 as a viable subject test for Old English.

Long-distance reflexivization exists in both Gothic and Old Norse-Icelandic, but has not been documented in the remaining early Germanic languages. There is no doubt that potential oblique subjects in Old Norse-Icelandic exhibit this behavior, and examples of long-distance reflexives bound by nominative subjects are found in abundance in that language. For Gothic, however, Harbert (1978: 38) only documents one example of a main clause nominative subject controlling a reflexive in a subordinate 'that'-clause. Still, despite the rarity of such examples in Gothic, one example of a potential oblique subject controlling a reflexive in a subordinate clause has been reported on here. Thus, long-distance reflexivization is listed in Table 11 as a viable subject test for both Gothic and Old Norse-Icelandic.

Table 11: Syntactic behavior of oblique subjects in the Early Germanic languages.

	Go	O/ME	O/MHG	OS	ON-I	OSw	ODa
Conj. Reduction	n/a	√	n/a	n/a	n/a	n/a	n/a
Long-Dist. Refl.	√	n/a	n/a	n/a	√	n/a	n/a
Subject raising	–	√	√	√	√	√	√
Object raising	–	√	√	√	√	√	√
Control	√	√	–	√	√	√	√
Word Order	√	√	√	√	√	√	√

The remaining four subject properties involve raising-to-subject, raising-to-object, control infinitives and word order, as is shown in Table 11. Starting with word order, it is clear that potential oblique subjects occupy first position and invert with the verb exactly as nominative subjects do in all seven early Germanic languages. In addition, an existing investigation of word order in Icelandic, ranging from the late 12th century to the present, where frequencies for nominative and oblique subjects are compared, reveals the same statistical tendencies for the word order distribution of nominative and oblique subjects throughout the history of Icelandic. In contrast, analyzing potential oblique subjects in Icelandic as objects would yield absurd frequencies, in no accordance with word order distribution of objects in the language. Therefore, word order distribution speaks for a subject analysis, and against an object analysis, not only in Icelandic but in the early Germanic languages in general.

Examples of raising-to-subject and raising-to-object with oblique subject verbs are found in all the earliest documented Germanic languages, except for Gothic. However, there are generally not very many examples of these constructions in the Gothic material anyway, making it even more unlikely to come across oblique subject verbs in such constructions. The absence of such examples in Gothic is therefore no argument against a subject analysis of potential oblique subjects in the Gothic language. The presence of raising-to-subject and raising-to-object in the other early Germanic languages, including Old/Middle English and Old High German, also speak for a subject analysis of potential oblique subjects and against an object analysis.

Finally, control infinitives with oblique subject verbs have so far been found in several early Germanic languages, including six in Old Norse-Icelandic, two in Old Swedish, two in Early Middle English and one in Gothic. To this, I have here added three examples from Old Saxon, seven examples from Old Norse-Icelandic, one from Old Swedish and one from Old Danish, a total of twelve examples which have not figured in the earlier literature on this topic.

It has been argued by several historical linguists that control infinitives are the best type of evidence for the subject status of potential oblique subjects in corpus languages where word order freedom may obscure the analysis of both raising-to-subject and raising-to-object constructions. Freedom in word order, however, does not impinge on control constructions since the relevant subject property is the ability to be left unexpressed, a syntactic behavior confined to subjects. Therefore, the control infinitives that have been discussed here show, once and for all, that potential oblique subjects behave syntactically as subjects and that an object analysis for such structures is altogether excluded.

As a highly relevant side point, I would like to emphasize that examples of oblique subject verbs being embedded under control verbs are extremely rare even in Modern Icelandic, the archetype of all languages which exhibit structures involving oblique subjects. It was not until the birth of the World Wide Web that it started becoming easier to find such control constructions in the modern language, which in turn entails that huge amounts of texts are needed to uncover such structures, not to mention with the right lexical types. Therefore, it is all the more astounding that the few examples documented so far across the early Germanic languages have even been detected at all in the earliest Germanic tests.

Taken together, the abundance of evidence discussed in this chapter shows, once and for all, that potential oblique subjects behaved syntactically as subjects in the early Germanic languages. That is, the data and evidence presented here, some new and some long-established, are only compatible with a subject analysis of potential oblique subjects. As such, this evidence bundle completely invalidates the Object-to-Subject Hypothesis proposed by Cole et al. (1980) for Germanic. See, also, Eythórsson and Barðdal (2005) for a discussion of additional problems with the Object-to-Subject Hypothesis, pertaining to facts that are straightforwardly accounted for by the Oblique Subject Hypothesis.

Cole et al. also draw on data from both Polynesian and Georgian, in favor of their Object-to-Subject Hypothesis. However, on a closer inspection, there is no evidence that the Georgian oblique subjects that they discuss ever were syntactic objects, as they acknowledge in fn. 27 (1980: 741). Facts of Polynesian are considerably more complex, but involve in essence a totally different type of language change, namely from accusative to ergative languages, instead of a change from objects to subjects with a set of given verbs. Moreover, later research has also refuted the validity of the Polynesian evidence, showing instead that the development was most likely the exact opposite, namely from ergative to accusative in Polynesian (cf. Kikusawa 2002, 2003). Given this, together with the Germanic evidence discussed in 4.2 above, I avow that the bottom has, once and for all, been knocked out of Cole et al.'s (1980) Object-to-Subject Hypothesis.

5 Reconstructing oblique subjects for Proto-Germanic

As is distinctly shown in the previous chapter, potential oblique subjects behave syntactically as subjects in the earliest Germanic languages with respect to all the relevant linguistic properties that are available for teasing apart syntactic subjects and objects during these early stages. These subject behaviors include conjunction reduction in Old English, long-distance reflexivization in Gothic and Old Norse-Icelandic, and raising-to-subject, raising-to-object, control infinitives and word order in the other early Germanic languages. At the same time, these potential oblique subjects also demonstrate a behavior which unquestionably excludes an object analysis of the relevant argument. It is therefore not only such that the syntactic behavior of potential oblique subjects is compatible with a subject analysis, rather their behavior also requires a subject analysis in order to account for the wide range of data relevant for this issue. That is, only on a subject analysis may the whole array of data from the early Germanic languages, pertinent to this discussion, be explained.

After having established beyond doubt that potential oblique subjects behave syntactically as subjects in the earliest Germanic languages, it appears to be a timely task to demonstrate how this syntactic behavior may be accounted for in the grammar of Proto-Germanic. This entails i) a reconstruction of the relevant parts of the grammar of Proto-Germanic, and ii) a reconstruction of the lexical verbs and predicates selecting for non-canonical case frames, as well as iii) the interaction between these two types of constructions. This is the primary goal of the present chapter.

Section 5.1 starts with a brief account of the history of syntactic reconstruction, starting with the neogrammarians and their tentative reconstructions of syntactic structures, until the present-day. Section 5.2 further outlines the five major arguments against syntactic reconstruction put forward in the literature. These are i) lack of cognates, ii) lack of arbitrariness, iii) lack of directionality in syntactic change, iv) lack of continuous transmission, and finally v) lack of form–meaning correspondences. After having argued against the validity of these five arguments, I turn to how grammatical relations may be reconstructed, starting with the reconstruction of verbs and their argument structures in Section 5.3 and then continuing in Section 5.4 towards reconstructing the subject behaviors that are reconstructable for Proto-Germanic.

5.1 Reconstructing syntax

Syntactic reconstruction has been frowned upon in the domain of historical linguistics for a long time, and for various reasons. Originally, the Comparative Method was designed as a tool to compare and reconstruct sounds and morphemes, including words. This may perhaps, to some degree, be a consequence of the fact that the neogrammarians, and the structuralists following them, were simply not that interested in syntax, as Fox (1995: 104) rightfully points out in his book-length introduction to linguistic reconstruction.

A further issue of major relevance for the insignificant status of syntactic reconstruction during the neogrammarian period relates to the common view, shared by the neogrammarians, the structuralists and generative grammarians alike, that sentence meaning is compositional. This entails that sentence meaning is regarded as the sum of the meanings of all the lexical parts which make up a sentence, and, hence, that syntactic objects were not deemed as simple form–meaning correspondences (cf. Klein 2010). This, in turn, excludes syntactic reconstruction, since morphological and lexical reconstructions are based on such form–meaning correspondences. Without form–meaning correspondences, there can be no reconstruction.

Nevertheless, some specific syntactic issues clearly excited the curiosity of the neogrammarians, for instance the issue of word order variation in the early Indo-European languages (Jolly 1872; Jacobi 1897; Wackernagel 1892; Thommen 1905; Fischer 1924). Another topic of considerable interest and debate was the relation between main and subordinate clauses, with a special focus on whether subordinate clauses existed in the proto-language or not (Avery 1881; Hermann 1895; Brugmann 1925; Porzig 1932). A third topic of some importance was case syntax, in particular the function of the cases across the early Indo-European languages (Winkler 1896; van der Meer 1901; Delbrück 1907; Havers 1911). The neogrammarians also paid considerable heed to syntactic comparisons of certain verbal moods, like the imperative, optative and conjunctive across the archaic Indo-European languages (Jolly 1872; Thurneysen 1885; Delbrück 1893–1900).

As a consequence, the earliest syntactic reconstructions suggested by the neogrammars dealt with topics like word order, the position of the verb and the position of clitics and particles (Delbrück 1893–1900; Wackernagel 1892). Interest in the nature of alignment in Proto-Indo-European also resulted in a tentative reconstruction of an ergative alignment system for this proto-stage (Uhlenbeck 1901; Pedersen 1907; Vaillant 1936). Despite these initial provisional reconstructions, the neogrammarians did not further improve their methodology to adequately deal with syntactic reconstruction, leaving the syntactic side of their enterprise underdeveloped for decades to come.

During the 1970's, syntactic reconstruction appeared to be bolstered through the materialization of three word order studies, all published around the same time: Lehmann (1974), Friedrich (1975) and Miller (1975). The first of these, Lehmann (1974), was based on Greenberg's (1966) typological universals. Lehmann argued, along the same line as Delbrück (1878), among others, that Proto-Indo-European was an SOV language on the basis of an interrelation between OV word order in simple clauses and possible OV correlates within other areas of syntax. Unfortunately, there are major methodological problems with Lehmann's proposal. The most important one is that his reconstruction is not based on attested linguistic structures, but on an assumption that certain syntactic features go hand in hand with each other (cf. Harris 1985; Hale 1987b; Mendoza 1998; Drinka 1999; Gildea 2000; Wichmann 2008; Barðdal and Eythórsson 2012a). In this sense, Lehmann's reconstruction does not follow the procedures of the Comparative Method, making his reconstructions on the basis of typological insights highly fallible. There is no doubt, however, that Lehmann was a pioneer in his field, being an original and progressive thinker, willing to apply new methods on old problems.

The two other publications came out the following year, also dealing with word order. Friedrich (1975) argued for SOV as being the most basic word order in Proto-Indo-European, this on the basis of word order statistics revealing that SOV was the most common pattern in the earliest Indo-European texts, and especially so in Homer. Thus, Friedrich's argumentation and reconstruction was based on the majority pattern. In contrast, Miller took the variation found in later texts as his point of departure, arguing that the three word order constellations, SOV, SVO and VSO, must all have been basic in Proto-Indo-European.

These reconstructions by Lehmann, Friedrich and Miller were sharply criticized, especially by Watkins (1976), and, following him, by Jeffers (1976), Lightfoot (1979), and Winter (1984), among others. Watkins, in particular, fiercely lambasted Lehmann's typological approach to syntactic reconstruction, while also pointing out the methodological problem of how three different approaches to word order reconstruction may straight and smoothly reach not only different but diametrically opposite conclusions as to what to reconstruct for the same proto-language.

After the massive trouncing of these three attempts at reconstructing syntax by Watkins and his like-minders during the 1970's, it was not until fairly recently that crucial methodological breakthroughs were made within the field of syntactic reconstruction. The first scholars to actively argue for the feasibility of reconstructing syntax were Harris and Campbell (Harris 1985, 2008; Harris and Campbell 1995; Campbell and Harris 2003), who effectively developed their own research program for reconstructing syntax. Instead of basing their program on the concept of *cognate sentences*, a concept that had been severely criticized by Jeffers (1976) and others, they suggest that syntactic reconstruction may be carried out on the basis of *syntac-*

tic patterns, i.e. cognate patterns found across genetically related languages. With the term *pattern*, Harris and Campbell (1995) refer to sentence structures which may or may not be filled with cognate lexical material across related languages.

Several historical syntacticians have followed in the footsteps of Harris and Campbell, among them Gildea (1992, 1998, 2000) and Kikusawa (2002, 2003). Gildea's reconstruction of the Proto-Cariban alignment system, focusing on morphosyntax, has only been achieved through a rigorous methodological approach on how to distinguish between linguistic innovations and relics in the grammar of the Cariban languages. Moreover, Kikusawa (2002, 2003) introduced into the field of historical syntax the concept of *cognate structures* in her reconstruction of the alignment system of Proto-Central Pacific. Somewhat later, Eythórsson and Barðdal (2011) and Barðdal and Eythórsson (2012a, 2012b) proffered the concept of *cognate argument structure constructions*, a concept which serves as part and parcel of the more complicated reconstruction of grammatical relations. For a further discussion of these issues, cf. Sections 5.3–5.4 below where argument structure constructions are reconstructed for a proto-stage, as a part of the more general enterprise of reconstructing grammatical relations, including oblique subjects, for a common prehistoric stage of Germanic.

For an extensive and considerably more detailed overview of the history of syntactic reconstruction within general linguistics, cf. Gildea, Luján, and Barðdal (2020), and in particular for the history of syntactic reconstruction within Indo-European linguistics, see Eythórsson and Barðdal (2016). I now turn to some of the issues that have been raised in the literature, both in the 1970s and more recently, as arguments against syntactic reconstructions and why these arguments are of limited validity.

5.2 Alleged problems with syntactic reconstruction

There are five major arguments that have been launched against the feasibility of syntactic reconstruction. These are i) lack of cognates, ii) lack of arbitrariness, iii) lack of directionality in syntactic change, iv) lack of continuous transmission, and, v) lack of form–meaning correspondences. I now discuss each of these in a subsection of its own (see also discussion in Eythórsson and Barðdal 2011, 2016, Barðdal and Eythórsson 2012a, 2012b, 2020, Barðdal 2013, 2014).

5.2.1 Lack of cognates

Jeffers (1976), followed by Lightfoot (1979, 1981), and Winters (1984), argued that there is a qualitative difference between syntax, on the one hand, and phonology, morphology and the lexicon, on the other, making syntactic reconstruction impossible. Since there exists no finite set of sentences for the proto-language, he argues, there can be no input for potential correspondence sets, which are needed to carry out a reconstruction. This entails, in turn, that there are no cognates in syntax, according to Jeffers. He is right, of course, that syntactic reconstruction cannot be based on a potential finite set of sentences, even though comparable sentences may be reconstructed consisting of cognate lexical material, as is shown in (225) below:

Icelandic
(225) a. *Jóhannes sá grasið í garðinum.*
John.NOM saw.3SG grass.the.ACC in garden.the.DAT
'John saw the grass in the garden.'

German
b. *Johannes sah das Gras in dem Garten.*
John.NOM saw.3SG the.ACC gras in the.DAT garden
'John saw the grass in the garden.'

English
c. *John saw the grass in the garden.*

The three example sentences from Icelandic, German and English have the same meaning, the same structure and they are composed of cognate lexical material. The subject nouns *Jóhannes*, *Johannes* and *John* are cognate names in the Germanic languages, the verbs *sá*, *sah* and *saw* are also cognate, the object nouns *gras*, *Gras* and *grass* are also cognate, the locative prepositions *í*, *in* and *in* are cognates, and *garði*, *Garten* and *garden* are also cognates. The preposed definite articles in German and English are also cognate, *das* and *the* vs. *dem* and *the*. The Icelandic postposed definite article has developed from another demonstrative pronoun, namely *hinn/hitt* 'that one'. It is implicit in Jeffers' account that even though the input material is like that in (225), entailing that a reconstruction could be carried out, such a reconstruction would be meaningless, since one cannot reconstruct all possible sentences for the proto-language. This view has been the dominant one within historical linguistics circles for decades, tainting every attempt at reconstructing syntax ever since.

Be that as it may, Jeffers is still wrong about one key part, namely that the goal of syntactic reconstruction should not be to reconstruct a finite set of utterances for the proto-language anyway, as if utterances were lexeme-like units stored in a finite lexicon. Instead, syntactic reconstruction should be a reconstruction of the grammar of the proto-language, including the properties of syntax and syntactic structures. And this may well be achieved, as I demonstrate in Sections 5.3–5.4 below. See also Gildea, Luján, and Barðdal (2020: 16–23), on some procedural steps and guidelines for identifying cognates in syntax, as well as the articles in that same volume (Barðdal, Gildea and Luján, eds., 2020).

5.2.2 Lack of arbitrariness

It is an essential requirement for lexical reconstruction that the form–meaning pairing is an arbitrary pairing in the sense that one cannot derive from the meaning how the form is, and vice versa, that one cannot derive from the form what the meaning is. This follows directly from the Saussurian view that words are signs, i.e. arbitrary form–meaning pairings. One would only expect to come across systematic arbitrary form–meaning pairings in related languages where such pairings are inherited from an earlier proto-stage. Therefore, only through the attestation of such arbitrary pairings can the etymologist be certain that repeated lexemes found across languages are cognate lexemes.

With regard to syntax, consensus has it that since there is no arbitrariness found in syntax, one can not reconstruct syntactic structures in the same secure manner as one reconstructs lexical items. This is certainly true, but at the same time, arbitrariness is first and foremost needed to establish genetic relatedness (Harrison 2003: 225), which has usually already been established when potential syntactic reconstruction begins. Therefore, the arbitrariness requirement is simply superfluous for syntactic reconstruction and as such it is irrelevant.

Nevertheless, in the view that there is no arbitrariness in syntax, it is implicit that syntax is both regular and compositional. By now, it is well known from research within Construction Grammar that this is not true. First, ordinary syntactic structures are not devoid of meaning, cf. Goldberg's (1995) research on the ditransitive in English and the polysemy she observes there between different subconstructions of the ditransitive construction. Also, countless examples may be found in the Construction Grammar literature of syntactic structures that are semantically noncompositional in the sense that the meaning of the whole cannot be derived from the meaning of the parts. To give an example from my own work, consider the following ditransitive examples from Modern Norwegian, which exemplify a specific variant of the ditransitive construction, expressing an extra amount of comfort, enjoyment or pleasure, according to Barðdal, Kristoffersen and Sveen (2011: 86–93):

Norwegian

(226) a. *Thomas* **gikk** **seg** *en* **kveldstur** *mens de andre*
Thomas walked REFL an evening.walk while the others
koste *seg* *med beskyldninger, løgn og svik.*
enjoyed REFL with accusations lies and betrayals
'Thomas treated himself to a late walk, while the others enjoyed themselves with accusations, lies and betrayals.'

b. *Han måtte alltid* **ha** **seg** *en* **støyt** *etter jobb.*
he must always have REFL a swig after work
'He always had to treat himself to a swig after work.'

While there is no doubt that the "form" of these examples is ditransitive, i.e. the examples contain a verb and two objects, an animate indirect one and an inanimate direct one, the meaning expressed here and in similar examples is not directly that of transfer, intended, metaphorical, or any other, as Goldberg's (1995) analysis of the ditransitive construction would predict. Note, also, that the verb in (226a) is an intransitive one, *gå* 'walk', here occurring with a content object, *tur* 'walk'. Further, the verb in (226b) is stative, *ha* 'have', when used outside of this construction. Due to the meaning involving an extra dose of comfort, enjoyment and pleasure, the best translation of these examples is 'treat oneself to sth', instead of with potential ditransitive uses of 'walk' or 'have'.

To conclude, the examples in (226) are real documented utterances, attesting to a form and meaning discrepancy, where the meaning of the whole is not derivable from the meaning of the parts. As such, they show that there is also arbitrariness in syntax, despite claims to the contrary in the literature. For a detailed discussion and analysis of both the syntactic and semantic irregularities of the "pleasurable" ditransitive subconstruction in Norwegian, see Barðdal, Kristoffersen and Sveen (2011: 83–93), and for a reconstruction of the general ditransitive construction in Proto-Germanic, see Vázquez-González and Barðdal (2019).

5.2.3 Lack of directionality in syntactic change

One of the main reasons that lexical reconstruction has been as successful as it has is because of the sound laws established by the neogrammarians. The sound laws have been used to determine the directionality of phonological change, under the assumption that the sound laws are regular. But since there are no corresponding "laws" in syntax, that rules out syntactic reconstruction (cf. Miranda 1976; Lightfoot 1979, 2002; Campbell and Mithun 1980). However, the assumption that the sound laws are regular is a misconception. The sound laws are only regular *by definition*, as observed by Hoenigswald as early as in 1978. That is, the sound changes that are not entirely regular were simply excluded from the definition of being sound laws.

Moreover, as Harrison (2003) has pointed out, what is needed to confirm cognacy is a similarity metric, i.e. a way to measure similarity in order to decide whether two items are similar enough to be deemed cognates. Since no such similarity measures exist, nor have any been developed since the neogrammarian period, the sound laws have simply functioned as a stand-in for such a similarity metric. Thus, it is implicit in Harrison's argumentation that the issue of directionality of phonological change is primarily needed in order to decide on cognacy.

Returning to syntax, another of Jeffers' (1976) main objections against syntactic reconstructability is that syntactic change does not necessarily entail small changes in inherited structures, which he claims is what is needed to ascertain which structures are inherited across daughter languages. Instead, he argues that syntactic change takes place through pattern replacement and it is not in any way inherent for pattern replacement which of the patterns are an innovation and which are inherited.

Jeffers' assumptions about the nature of pattern replacement are certainly true, except for the fact that many syntactic changes do not involve pattern replacement, but inherited constructions which have developed in different ways in different daughter languages. For such cases, see Gildea, Luján, and Barðdal (2020: 23–31), for some procedures on how to determine directionality, and the relevant articles in that volume (Barðdal, Gildea, and Luján, eds., 2020). Also, Willis (2011) argues for a distinction between *universal* and *local* directionality. Local directionality involves the direction of syntactic changes of a given reconstruction problem and the linguistic data relevant for that problem. Only through careful scrutiny of the relevant data and the mechanisms of change found for that dataset may prior language stages be identified and thus the directionality of change (cf. also Harris and Campbell 1985; Campbell and Harris 2003; Barðdal and Eythórsson 2012a; Dunn et al. 2017; Gildea, Luján, and Barðdal 2020).

5.2.4 Lack of continuous transmission

Lightfoot (1979 and later work), Hale (1998), and Janda (2001), among others, have argued that due to a principled distinction between the lexical word and the clause, lexical words and clauses are not transmitted in the same way to coming generations. Lightfoot claims that words, or lexical items, are inherited from one generation to the other. For clauses, in contrast, these are not inherited from one generation to the other, he argues. Instead, the language learner abduces the rules of grammar and syntax from the input clauses that he or she is exposed to.

Observe that the assumption that lexical words are inherited directly from one generation to the other, while grammar and clausal syntax is not, surely presupposes that lexical words are assumed to be less abstract and, thus, somehow more easily transmitted to coming generations than syntax and syntactic structures. However, as Barðdal and Eythórsson (2012a) point out, this view of lexical items is quite a simplistic one, since lexical words are also complex form–meaning pairings, and thus they are also abstract units. In other words, lexical words are Saussurian signs, composed of both abstract morphophonological properties, and lexical meaning, as well as the mapping between the two.

Therefore, the process that language learners go through, pairing form with meaning through repeated exposure, is a cognitive process, indeed no less complex than the one in which grammar is extracted from the input present in the linguistic environment of language learners. In both cases, abstract units are acquired, one involving learning form and meaning and the mapping between these on the basis of the lexical items learners are exposed to, while the other involves schematizing sentence structure. The fact that lexical words are abstract units has been acknowledged within several contemporary paradigms, both generative ones (cf. Adger 2003), and constructional ones (cf. Tomasello 2003; Goldberg 2006: Ch. 4).

As a consequence, there is no major qualitative difference between the transmission of smaller lexical words and larger syntactic clauses from one generation to the next. It follows directly from the basic assumptions of construction grammar that larger units than lexical words are also form–meaning pairings, exactly like words. This further entails that syntactic structures may be transmitted from one generation to the next, exactly like lexical words (Eythórsson and Barðdal 2011, 2016; Barðdal and Eythórsson 2012a, 2012b, 2020; Barðdal 2013, 2014; Barðdal and Smitherman 2013; Barðdal et al. 2013; Danesi, Johnson, and Barðdal 2017; Johnson et al. 2019; Pooth et al. 2019; Vázquez-González and Barðdal 2019; Barðdal et al. 2020; Gildea, Luján, and Barðdal 2020).

5.2.5 Lack of form–meaning correspondences

As already mentioned in Section 5.1 above, one major argument against syntactic reconstruction is the traditional view of syntax as being semantically compositional (cf. Klein 2010). In other words, since sentence meaning is assumed to be derived from the sum of the relevant lexical meanings, there can not be any simple sentence meaning mapped to the form of a sentence. Ergo, there can not be any cognates in syntax, and hence no material to be used as input for correspondence sets.

Many current theoretical models do not assume that syntactic structures themselves have any meaning, including Chomskyan Generative Grammar. On such models, therefore, syntactic reconstruction, i.e. a reconstruction based on form–meaning pairings, is intrinsically ruled out. This, however, has not prevented generativists from reconstructing syntax, as is evident from the reconstructions by Hale (1987a, 1987b, 2014), Garrett (1990), Willis (2011) and Walkden (2013, 2014). On a closer inspection, it turns out that at least Willis' (2011) reconstruction of free relative clauses in Common Brythonic and Walkden's (2014) reconstruction of the reflexive middle construction for Proto-Northwest-Germanic are, as a matter of fact, based on both form and function, even though there is no place for function in the formalism they use for reconstruction.

This criticism, however, does not apply to syntactic reconstructions carried out within Construction Grammar, as it is assumed within that research program that constructions, the basic building blocks of language, are form–meaning correspondences (Fillmore, Kay and O'Connor 1988; Goldberg 1995; Croft 2001; among others). Not only does this mean that the leap from synchronic form–meaning pairings to historical form–meaning pairings is nanoscopic, but also that syntactic reconstruction falls out directly from the basic assumptions of Construction Grammar. As such, syntactic reconstruction is fully achievable (cf. Eythórsson and Barðdal 2011, 2016; Barðdal and Eythórsson 2012a, 2012b, 2020; Barðdal 2013, 2014; Barðdal and Smitherman 2013; Barðdal et al. 2013; Barðdal and Gildea 2015; Danesi, Johnson, and Barðdal 2017; Daniels 2015, 2017, 2020; Johnson et al. 2019; Pooth et al. 2019; Vázquez-González and Barðdal 2019; Barðdal et al. 2020; Gildea, Luján, and Barðdal 2020; Frotscher, Kroonen, and Barðdal 2022).

Moreover, in addition to form–meaning pairings being at the core of the constructional program, the formalization of such pairings includes both form and meaning through dedicated fields in the notational formalism of Construction Grammar, as is already discussed in Section 2.2.4 above, and will be further elaborated on in the sections to follow. This contributes to the status of Construction Grammar as the best possible research program for syntactic reconstruction, clearly surpassing other contemporary frameworks which disavow the status of form–meaning correspondences as basic building blocks of language.

5.3 Reconstructing predicate and argument structure constructions

Despite the fact that Watkins (1976) successfully emasculated Lehmann's, Friedrich's and Miller's attempts at reconstructing word order for Proto-Indo-European, he still put forward some useful suggestions on how to carry out syntactic reconstruction in his 1976 article. More concretely, Watkins argued that any viable syntactic reconstruction should be based on morphosyntactic considerations (cf. Barðdal and Eythórsson 2020: 202–203). Furthermore, in his book from 1995, Watkins put forward his own research program on how syntactic reconstruction should be carried out. His work is based on formulaic expressions and identical collocations in early texts containing poetic language from within the same genre. Through innumerable examples, Watkins was able to demonstrate how bits and pieces of the morphosyntax of Proto-Indo-European could be fruitfully reconstructed. The reconstructions carried out in this section are based on exactly this methodology, i.e. they are based on the comparative method and involve morphological flags that aid in the identification of cognates in syntax.

The remainder of this chapter is devoted to reconstructing syntax. I focus in particular on how to reconstruct grammatical relations and argue, in part following Barðdal and Eythórsson (2012a), that this involves four steps:

i) the morpho-phonological reconstruction of the relevant verbs
ii) reconstructing argument structure constructions for the proto-language
iii) reconstructing the syntactic behaviors that have been identified as distinguishing between subjects and objects
iv) reconstructing the interaction between the two

Upon a successful reconstruction of all four, grammatical relations fall out directly. I start with a short discussion of the morpho-phonological reconstruction and reconstructability of oblique subject predicates in Proto-Germanic. I then reconstruct argument structure constructions, before going forward to reconstructing the behavioral properties of subjects in Section 5.4.

5.3.1 Reconstructing verbs and predicates

When reconstructing argument structure constructions, one first has to reconstruct the relevant verbs or predicates instantiating the argument structure constructions, as these make up the relevant morphological flags. By good fortune, the form and meaning of these verbs and predicates have already been reconstructed by Germanic and Indo-European etymologists and these reconstructions are available in the etymological dictionaries of the last century and the beginning of the present one (cf. Pokorny 1956–1969; de Vries 1957; Blöndal Magnússon 1989; Bjorvand and Lindeman 2000; LIV2 2001; Kluge 2012; and Kroonen 2013).

Approximately two thirds of the early Germanic vocabulary is assumed to be inherited (Venneman 2003: 1), including predicates which select for oblique subjects. Barðdal and Eythórsson (2012a: 370–371) list the following oblique subject predicates as reconstructable for Proto-Germanic on the basis of attestations in all three Germanic branches, North, West and East Germanic:

North, West and East Germanic
Dat-(Nom):
- *líka* (ON-I), *galeikan* (Goth), *lician* (OE), *(gi)lîhhên* (OHG) 'like'
- *þykja* (ON-I), *þugkjan* (Goth), *þyncan* (OE), *thunken* (OHG) 'feel, seem'
- *nægja* (ON-I), *ganah* (Goth), *geneah* (OE), *ginah* (OHG) 'suffice'
- *vera gott* (ON-I), *goþs wisan* (Goth), *god beon* (OE) 'be of good'
- *vera (ó)kunnleiki á* (ON-I), *(swi)kunþ wisan* (Goth), *cuð beon* (OE) 'be known'
- *verða vei* (ON-I), *wai wisan* (Goth), *wá beon* (OE) 'be woe'

Acc-(Gen/PP):
- *hungra* (ON-I), *huggrjan* (Goth), *hyngran* (OE), *hungaran* (OHG) 'hunger'
- *þyrsta* (ON-I), *þaursjan* (Goth), *þyrstan* (OE), dursten '(OHG) 'thirst'
- *lysta* (ON-I), *luston* (Goth), *lystan* (OE) 'desire'

It is a general requirement in historical-comparative linguistics that attestations are needed from at least three branches in order to motivate a reconstruction. However, since Germanic only has three branches altogether, and since one of the branches, East Germanic, only exists in limited biblical and religious translations, it is reasonable to loosen the three-branch requirement for Germanic, especially if the two cognates share both predicate structure and argument structure. Barðdal and Eythórsson (2012a) list the following predicates as reconstructable on the basis of attestations in two branches, North and West Germanic, East and West Germanic, and finally North and East Germanic:

North and West Germanic
Dat-(Nom):
- *leiðast* (ON-I), *lêdian* (OS), *laþian* (OE) 'dislike'
- *vera þörf á* (ON-I), *þearf(lic) beon* (OE), *thurft sîn* (OHG) 'need'
- *vera ljúft* (ON-I), *leof beon* (OE), *liep sîn* (MHG) 'be pleasant, dear'
- *duga* (ON-I), *dugan* (OS), *dugan* (OE) 'be sufficient'
- *vera nauðsyn* (ON-I), *neod beon* (OE), *niud wesan* (OS), *not sîn* (OHG) 'be necessary'
- *sofnast* (ON-I), *swefnian* (OE) 'fall asleep'
- *ganga vel/illa* (ON-I), *wel/yfle (ge)gan* (OE) *wel/yfle agan* (OE) 'have success/failure'
- *skæmmes* (OSw), *sceamian* (OE) 'shame'
- *tima* (OSw), *getimian* (OE) 'happen'
- *falla (í geð)* (ON-I), *gevallen* (MHG) 'like/be pleased'

Dat-(Gen/PP)
- *batna* (ON-I), *bazên* (OHG) 'get better (of illness)'
- *bresta* (ON-I), *brestan* (OS), *brestan* (OHG) 'lack'

Variable case frames
- *kala* (ON-I), *calan* (OE) 'feel cold'
- *lengjast* (ON-I), *langa* (OSw), *langôn* (OS), *langian* (OE) 'long'
- *forthryta* (OSw) 'regret', *þrjóta* (ON-I), *þreotan* (OE) 'lack'

East and West Germanic
Dat-(Nom)
- *agljan* (Goth), *eglian* (OE) 'be hurting'
- *wulþus (wisan)* (Goth), *wuldor beon* (OE) 'be glorified'

North and East Germanic
Dat-(Nom)
- *raþs wisan* (Goth) *vera ráð* (ON-I) 'be advisable'

To these twenty-eight or so cognate predicates, listed by Barðdal and Eythórsson (2012a), I append the following additional twenty-seven ones, of which the last five are compositional predicates which only share a part of their lexical material with each other.

North, West and East Germanic
Dat-(Nom)
- *vera sorg* (ON-I), *saurga wisan* (Goth), *sorg beon* (OE) 'be sorrowful'
- *vera väl* (OSw), *waila wairþan* (Goth), *wel beon* (OE), *wola sîn* (OHG) 'be(come) well'

Variable Case Frame:
- *tíma* (ON-I), *gatiman* (Goth), *gizeman* (OHG) 'happen, fit'

North and West Germanic
Dat-(Nom)
- *byrja* (ON-I), *(ge)byrian* (OE), *boren* (MD), *giburren* (OHG) 'start, happen'
- *grämia* (OSw), *gramian* (OE) 'be vexed'

- *verða heitt* (ON-I), *wesa hete* (OFr), *heiz sîn* (OHG) 'be(come) warm, eager'
- *verða kalt* (ON-I), *wesa kalde* (OFr) 'be cold, freeze'
- *verða leyft* (ON-I), *alyfed beon* (OE) 'be allowed'
- *vera von* (ON-I), *wana beon* (OE) 'expect'
- *vera bót* (ON-I), *bot beon* (OE) 'have remedy, feel relief'
- *vera mál* (ON-I), *mæl beon* (OE) 'have an emergency'
- *vera óvant* (ON-I), *ungewunelic beon* (OE) 'be unaccustomed to'
- *verða auðið* (ON-I), *eaðe beon* (OE) 'be possible'
- *vera um* (ON-I), *umbi uuesan* (OS) 'care for'
- *þverra* (ON-I), *zwiron* (OHG) 'dwindle'

Variable case frames
- *dreyma* (ON-I), *dromen* (MD), *troumen* (OHG) 'dream'
- *minna* (ON-I), *minna(s)* (OSw), *mynegian* (OE), *gimanon* (OS) 'recollect, remember'
- *sundla* (ON-I), *giswinten* (OHG) 'feel dizzy'
- *svíða* (ON-I), *swedan* (OHG) 'smart, feel pain'
- *trega* (ON-I), *träga* (OSw), *tregan* (OS) 'sadden, regret'
- *þrjóta* (ON-I), *aþreotan* (OE), *irthriazan* (OHG) 'lack, tire'

North and East Germanic
Dat-(Nom)
- *vera kært* (ON-I), *kara wisan* (Goth) 'be dear'

Of the twenty-one predicates above, three are found in all three branches, seventeen are shared across both North and West Germanic, while one is shared across North and East Germanic. Consider also the following five example sets representing compositional predicates of which only parts of the lexical material are cognate, while the predicate structure is the same, as well as the meaning.

North and West Germanic
Dat-(Nom)
- *koma í hug* (ON-I), *koma i hug* (OSw), *in githahti koman* (OHG), *an hugi fallan* (OS), *falla í hug* (ON-I) 'come in mind'
- *vera í huga* (ON-I), *zi muote sîn* (OHG) 'be on one's mind'
- *hrjóta tár, hrynja tár, fella tár* (ON-I), *thrahni fallan* (OS) 'have tears fall down one's check'
- *hrjóta af munni, verða á munni, koma af munni* (ON-I), *uuord faran fan mûðe* (OS) '(accidentally) speak'
- *snúast hugur* (Icel.), *hugi giuuendid uuerðan* (OS) 'change one's mind'

For the first compositional Dat-Nom predicate above, 'come in mind', in three of five cases the lexical verb is *koma / koman* 'come', while in Old Saxon the verb is *fallan* 'fall', a collocation which is also documented in Old Norse-Icelandic. In Modern Icelandic, furthermore, at least three different verbs may instantiate this compositional predicate, i.e. *koma* 'come', *falla* 'fall' and *detta* 'fall'. The remainder of this predicate consists of *í hug / i hug / an hugi* 'in mind', found for three of the predicates, while in Old High German the relevant lexical element is *in githahti* 'in thoughts'.

The second compositional predicate is 'be on one's mind', with the shared lexical material consisting of the verb 'be', while the remainder of the predicate uses two different words for 'mind', *huga* vs. *muote*, as well as two different prepositions, *í* 'in' vs. *zi* 'to'. The structure of the predicate, however, and the meaning is the same.

For the third predicate, *tár* and *thrahni* 'tears' are cognate, while the four relevant verbs are all motion verbs and partly synonymous, *hrjóta* 'slip', *hrynja* 'fall, collapse', *fella* 'fell' and *fallan* 'fall'. The same is true for the two remaining predicates. For the first one, '(accidentally) speak' the verbs are *hrjóta* 'slip', *verða* 'become', *koma* 'come' and *faran* 'go', while *munni* and *mûðe* 'mouth' are cognates. For the second and last predicate, 'change one's mind', *snúast* and *uuendean* are synonymous, meaning 'turn', while *hugur* and *hugi* 'mind' are cognates.

Each of these last five sets of compositional predicates only share a part of their cognate lexical material, but they otherwise show up with the same predicate structure, the same argument structure and the same or similar meaning. I, therefore, believe that these may all be reconstructed and that they stem from the same ancestral source.

To demonstrate how a reconstruction of oblique subject verbs may be carried out on the basis of one of the cognate sets above, consider first the Gothic and Old English examples in (227–228) below. This cognate set involves the verb 'suffice', which Barðdal and Eythórsson (2012a) list as being attested in all three branches of Germanic. Note that some of the attested instances below occur with potential oblique subjects and some do not:

Gothic
(227) a. *Ganah* **siponi** *ei* ...
suffices.3SG disciple.ACC that
'The disciple finds it sufficient that...' (Matthew 10: 25)
b. *ganah* **þamma swaleikamma andabeit**
suffices.3SG that.DAT such.DAT punishment.NOM
'such a man finds punishment sufficient' (Corinthians II 2: 6)

c. *ganah*   **þuk**   *ansts*   *meina*
   suffices.3SG you.ACC grace.NOM my.GEN
   'and you find my grace sufficient'   (Corinthians II 12: 9)

Old English
(228) a. *guma*   *þæs*   *on* *heahsetle* *geneah*
         man.NOM it.GEN on hight.seat suffices.3SG
         'the man on the throne has enough of it'   (Maxims 1: 69–70)
      b. *gif* **us**   *on* *ferðe* *geneah*   *ond* *we* ...
         if us.ACC/DAT on mind suffices.3SG and we
         'if we have enough in our minds and we ...'
                                    (The Exeter book, The Order of the World, 35)

It turns out that this verb, (Go) *ganah* and (OE) *geneah*, is not attested in North-Germanic, as the Old Norse-Icelandic cognate verb *nægja*, listed above, involves a different stem formation. Nevertheless, the form *ginah* is also documented in Old High German, but unfortunately it is only documented in two sets of glossaries, where it is given as a translation of the Latin verbs *sufficit* 'suffice' and *abundat* 'be abundant.' Sad to say, no usage examples have been passed down from Old High German, as the two glossaries give no examples. However, on the basis of attestations from two branches, both East and West Germanic, it is indeed possible to reconstruct this verb for Proto-Germanic.

Table 12: Lexical correspondence set for the verb 'suffice' in early Germanic.

	FORM	MEANING	RECONSTRUCTED FORM
Gothic	*ga-nah*	'suffice'	
Old English	*ge-neah*	'suffice'	*ga-nah
Old High German	*gi-nah*	'suffice'	

Consider the correspondence set in Table 12, which shows a clear lexical unity across the three daughter languages, Gothic, Old English and Old High German, in that the form is the same and the meaning is also the same. On the basis of such form–meaning correspondences, this verb *ga-nah* may be reconstructed, as 3rd person singular present tense of the preterite-present verb *ga-nahan- (cf. Kroonen 2013: 392). In the next section, I proceed to the reconstruction of an argument structure for this verb.

Walkden (2009, 2013) discusses one particular requirement for general reconstruction, *the double cognacy condition*, arguing that such a requirement cannot be fulfilled in syntax. Walkden bases his argumentation on the interaction between sounds and lexical items. His point is that a sound cannot be reconstructed for a common stage, unless it is found in inherited form–meaning correspondences which are also cognates. Or, in other words, one cannot reconstruct a sound unless it occurs in the "same" words in the daughter languages. This is, of course, about nothing else than identifying regular phonological correspondences in the lexicon (cf. Gildea, Luján, and Barðdal 2020: 18–19). While Walkden is certainly right that in syntax where specific slots may be empty, establishing cognacy can perhaps not be carried out in the same manner, as in cases where slots are occupied by lexical or morphological material.

Despite all of this, the double cognacy condition can easily be met when reconstructing argument structure. As I have argued elsewhere (Barðdal and Smitherman 2013; Barðdal and Eythórsson 2020), there are several levels of cognacy involved, including the following:

i) cognate case markers
ii) cognate case frames
iii) cognate predicate structure
iv) cognate lexical material

It is well known, for instance, that the case markers in the Germanic languages are cognate (Krahe 1969a, 1969b; Ringe 2006; Barðdal and Kulikov 2009). I have further argued that case frames are cognates in the sense that they are inherited from a common ancestor (Barðdal and Eythórsson 2012b). This involves case frames like Dat-Nom, Dat-Gen, Acc-Gen, Dat-Gen, among others, i.e., the combination of two or more case categories and the internal order between them, co-occurring with specific lexical verbs. Differences in predicate structure may involve whether the relevant predicate is a simple verb, prefixed verb, a compound verb or a compositional predicate with several elements and the same internal structure between the elements of the composition. In several cases, this means not only double cognacy, but triple or quadruple cognacy, as i) the lexical verbs are cognate, ii) the morphological cases are cognate, iii) the argument structures are cognate and iv) the predicate structures are cognate.

5.3.2 Reconstructing argument structure constructions

I now turn to reconstructing argument structure constructions for Proto-Germanic. I continue with the verb 'suffice' from above and reconstruct the argument structure of this verb for an earlier proto-stage. This is a particularly thorny issue and the extra complications are brought about by the existence of several different word formation patterns, as well as a large array of different case frames, seemingly randomly distributed across verbs and languages.

5.3.2.1 The Dat-Nom / Nom-Dat alternation

As a second step in the reconstruction process, recall the examples from Gothic and Old English in (227–228) above, listed in the correspondence set in Table 13 below. It is unclear at this point which argument structure to reconstruct for this verb, given the discrepancies found between Gothic and Old English and the amount of variation, even within each language. As is shown in the correspondence set in Table 13, on the basis of the examples in (227–228), Gothic shows three different argument structure constructions, Acc-only, Acc-Nom and Dat-Nom, while the attested argument structures in Old English are Nom-Gen and Acc/Dat-only. In other words, the Old English form, *us*, in (228b) above is ambiguous between the accusative and the dative case.

Table 13: Predicate-specific correspondence set for the argument structure of the Germanic verb *ga-nah*.

	ALT1	ALT2	ALT3	ALT4
Gothic	Acc-	Acc-Nom	Dat-Nom	
Old English	Acc-/Dat-			Nom-Gen[a]

[a] Note that the animate argument is always in the accusative or the dative case here, except for in the Old English example in the 4th alternant where it is in the nominative.

There is another major problem here, namely that the Gothic text is a translation from Greek, making it difficult to know to which degree the three different case frames are inherited or not. Therefore, it is imperative to compare these case frames with the case frames of the verbs used in the Greek original. It turns out that the three Gothic examples are translations of three different Greek verbs, *árketòn*, *hikanòn*, and *árkeî*, all meaning 'suffice' and all selecting for a dative subject, not an accusative one. This means that the third alternative, Dat-Nom, is true to the Greek syntax, while the first and the second alternatives, Acc-only and Acc-Nom, indeed deviate from the Greek original. Whether this shows that *ganah* could occur both with accusative and dative subjects in Gothic, or whether the dative is a calque from Greek is difficult to know at this point.

For the sake of precision, it should be added here that there is one more type of example found both in the Gothic Bible and Old English, with yet another argument structure, not included in Table 13. This is the Nom-Acc/Dat argument structure, shown in (229) below:

Gothic
(229) a. **þatuh   ganah   unsis**
this.NOM.and   suffices.3SG   us.ACC/DAT
'And this is sufficient for us'   (John 14: 8)

Old English
  b. *Ac*   **þas**   **bysna**   **us**   *magon   to*
     but   these.NOM   examples.NOM   us.ACC/DAT   may.3PL   till
     genogon   þæt . . .
     suffice.INF   that
     'But these examples may be enough for us to . . .'
                                    (Chrodegang of Metz 1:79.82.991)

The existence of examples like the Nom-Acc/Dat ones in (229), together with the unambiguous Dat-Nom example from Gothic in (227b) in the preceding section, clearly suggests that *ganah* in Gothic was an alternating verb, exactly as the cognate verbs *nægja* in Old Norse-Icelandic and *nöghia* in Old Swedish, as is documented in Chapter 3 above. However, it should be mentioned here that in the Greek original of (229a) where the verb *árkeî* is found, the nominative subject is pro-dropped, while the dative occurs in the normal object position. Therefore, this alternation in Gothic could be a translation effect. Either way, it would, as a matter of fact, speak for an alternating analysis of the Ancient Greek verb *árkeî* instead.

On an alternating analysis of *ganah* in Gothic, one might want to argue that *unsis* in (229a) must be dative since the alternating verbs discussed in Chapter 3 are, in fact, Dat-Nom / Nom-Dat verbs. However, as the more retentive reader may recall, alternating verbs may also show up with the Acc-Nom / Nom-Acc alternation, as I document in Section 3.2.4 above (ex. 104a–b). Therefore, an alternating analysis of *ganah* in Gothic does not favor a dative interpretation of (229a) over an accusative interpretation. We are therefore still left in uncertainty about which of the two argument structures to reconstruct for Proto-Germanic **ganah* on the basis of the Gothic material.

Turning to the Old English case frames documented in (228) and (229b) above, on the assumption that *us* in (228b) is accusative, it seems reasonable to reconstruct, at least the Acc-only case frame for Proto-Germanic, since it would be attested in both Old English and Gothic, in addition, of course, to the fact that the Gothic accusative deviates from the Greek original. The Nom-Acc/Dat case frame in (229b) may also be taken to support a reconstruction of the Dat-Nom / Nom-Dat alternation for Proto-Germanic, together with the Gothic material.

Turning to the Nom-Gen case frame in (228a), it is not unreasonable to assume that already in Old English, several common Germanic oblique subject verbs had already lost their oblique case marking (cf. Smirnicka 1972), by the time the first Old English texts were written in the Latin alphabet around 800 AD. Such a development, from oblique to nominative, is well known in the history of the Germanic languages (cf. Cole et al. 1980; Seefranz-Montag 1983, 1984; Allen 1995; Falk 1995, 1997; Eythórsson 2001, 2002; Petersen 2002; Jónsson and Eythórsson 2003, 2005; Barðdal 2011; Thráinsson et al. 2012; Jónsson 2013; and Dunn et al. 2017). Given that, the Nom-Gen case frame could have developed from either Acc-Gen or Dat-Gen into Nom-Gen (see further the discussion below on Old and Middle High German).

However, there is more to harvest from the early Germanic languages than only the examples from Gothic and Old English. Consider the following examples from Old Norse-Icelandic, Old Swedish, Old Danish, Old High German, Middle High German, Middle Low German, Middle Dutch and Old Frisian:

Old Norse-Icelandic
(230) a. *Bóndi   lét   **sér**   **þetta**   vel   nægja*
        yeoman.NOM let.3SG REFL.DAT this.NOM well suffice.INF
        'The yeoman let this be sufficient for him' (Grettis saga, ch. 88)
    b. *að   **það**   mátti   **honum**   eigi   nægja*
        that   it.NOM   might.3SG   him.DAT   not   suffice.INF
        'That it might not be sufficient for him ...' (Gríms saga loðinkinna, ch. 2)

Old Swedish
(231) a. *swa   at   **mik**   wäl   at   nögher*
        so   that me.ACC   well at   suffices.3SG
        'So that I have enough' (Svenskt diplomatarium, ny serie, 1: 91, c.1401)
    b. *thz   nöghdhe   **them**   **allom**   wel*
        it.NOM   sufficed.3SG them.DAT   all.DAT   well
        'This sufficed them all well.' (Siælinna Thröst 13, c.1420)
    c. *ey   nögdhe   **henne**   **thetta***
        not   sufficed.3SG her.DAT   that.NOM
        'She did not find that sufficient.' (Su 161, c.1475–1500)

Old Danish
(232) a. *swa   at   **hanum**   wel   meth   nøgdes*
        so   that   him.DAT   well   with   sufficed.3SG
        'So that he was satisfied (with that)' (Runekrøniken, c.1300)
    b. ***Honum**   nøghathe   ey   **thæs**   hældir*
        him.DAT   sufficed.3SG   not   it.GEN   either
        'He was not satisfied with that either.' (Sjæla trøst, c.1425)

c. at   **thæt**   nøghathe   **thøm**   **allum**   væl
    that it.NOM   sufficed.3SG them.DAT   all.DAT   well
    'that this sufficed them all well.'   (Sjæla trøst, c.1425)

d. *lade*   **oss**   ... *nøye*   *meth*   **thæt**
    let.3SG us.OBL   suffice.INF   with   it
    'let us ... find this sufficient'   (Roskilde diplom, c.1407)

e. *swa* *at*   **megh**   *nøyær*   *i*   *alle* *maadhe*
    so   that   me.ACC   suffices.3SG   in   all   way
    'so that I be satisfied in every way'   (diplom, Odense, c.1418)

Old High German

(233) a. *thaz* **mínna**   **sie**   *ginúage*,
          that   love.NOM   them.ACC   suffices
          'that love is enough for them,'   (Otfried Evangelium 3.7)

Middle High German

(234) a. **des**   *genüeget*   **mich**   *von*   *dir*
          that.GEN   suffices.3SG me.ACC   from   you
          'I will be satisfied with that from you'   (Der arme Heinrich, 936, c.1190)

b. *daz* **im**   **des**   *wol*   *genüeget*
    that   him.DAT   that.GEN   well   suffices.3SG
    'that he finds this sufficient'   (Alexander U.v.E, 26279, c.1270–84)

c. **ez**   *het*   **im**   *kûme*   *genüeget* *wol*
    it.NOM   would.have.3SG   him.DAT   hardly   sufficed   well
    'it would hardly have satisfied him' (Alexander U.v.E, 21472, c.1270–84)

d. *daz* **im**   *daz*   **guot**   *niht*   *mac*   *genüegen*
    that   him.DAT   the.NOM   goods   not   may.3SG   suffice.INF
    'that he would not find the goods sufficient'
                                       (Der Welsche Gast, 13827, c.1215)

e. *lâ*   **dir**   *genüegen*   *an*   *dem*   *dînen*
    let.3SG you.DAT   suffice.INF   on   the   yours
    'you be satisfied with your own'   (Die Heidin, 1533, c.1285)

Middle Low German

(235) a. *vnde* **syneme**   **sone**   *ofte*   **siner**   *dochter*   *mit*
          and   REFL.DAT   son.DAT   or   REFL.DAT   daughter   with
          ereme **vormunde**   *noget*   *uppe*   *de*   *tyd*
          his   legal.guardian   suffices   upon   that   time
          'and his son or his daughter are satisfied with their legal guardian, at
          that time'   (Hamburgische Rechtsaltertümer IV, Art 6, c.1292)

b. *Dat* **dĭ** *minsche heuet dan genůgt* **ůme**
that the.NOM people.NOM have then sufficed him.DAT
'That these people have then been sufficient for him.'

(Nr. MoralB. Spr., c.1270/1290)

c. *is sulik. dat* **ůme** *genůge dat hĭ heuet*
is such that him.DAT suffices that.NOM he has
'is such that he finds what he has sufficient'

(Nr. MoralB. Dogma, c.1270/1290)

d. **brodes** *ne noget* **en** *nicht dat dar* ...
bread.GEN not suffices the.ones.DAT not which there
'The ones who did not find the bread sufficient there ...'

(Buxteh. Ev., c.1480)

e. *vnde dat* **my** *nicht en nōgede an* **den ding** ...
and that me.DAT not PTCL sufficed at the thing
'and that I did not find these things sufficient ...'

(Lüb. Birg. Openb. c.1496)

Middle Dutch

(236) a. **den bisscop** *genoechde hier af*
the.OBL bishop sufficed here of
'the bishop found [this] sufficient from now on'

(Spiegel Historiael, II (6), p. 6, l. 98, c.1300)

b. *want dat* **Gode** *genoecht alsoe wel* **de meensamheit**
because that God.DAT suffices all.so well the.NOM coexistence
'as God found the coexistence sufficient, that is'

(Het boek van Sidrac, c.1320)

c. *dat genoecht* **den lichame**
that.NOM suffices the.OBL body
'that is sufficient for the body'

(Het boek van Sidrac, c.1320)

d. **Desen raet** *genoechde* **hem allen** *ende*
this.GEN advice sufficed them.DAT all.DAT and
'This advice was sufficient for all of them and'

(Vier Heemskinderen c.1400)

5.3 Reconstructing predicate and argument structure constructions — 233

Old Frisian

(237) a. nowet allena **tha** **keningge** and **thisse** **bode**
         not   alone   the   king.DAT   by   this   command
         nogade
         sufficed.3SG
         'the king alone did not find this command satisfying'
         (Fon Alra Fresena Fridome, 85, c.1300, cf. Bremmer 1986: 76)

   b. **ws** ... noeget   ende billiaeft   te   ontfaen
      us.OBL suffices.3SG and   pleases.3SG   to   receive.INF
      'We ... are satisfied and pleased to receive'   (O I 514, 39, c.1506)

The problem with the examples in (230–237) above is that they are not descendants of Proto-Germanic *ga-nahan*, as the Gothic and Old English examples in (227–229) are. Instead, they stem from the Proto-Germanic verb *ga-nōgjan-*, which is a deadjectival *jan*-verb, having the same meaning as *ga-nahan*, i.e. 'suffice'. This verb, *ga-nōgjan-*, is most likely derived from a corresponding adjective *ga-nōga* 'enough' (cf. de Vries 1957: 181). The lexical form–meaning correspondences for this verb are set up in Table 14, yielding the form *ga-nōgjan-*, as reconstructed by de Vries.

Table 14: Lexical correspondence set for the verb 'suffice' in early Germanic.

	FORM	MEANING	RECONSTRUCTED FORM
Old Norse-Icelandic	(g)nœgja	'suffice'	
Old Swedish	nöghia	'suffice'	
Old Danish	nøghje	'suffice	
Old Frisian	nogia	'please'	*ga-nōgjan
Middle Low German	nügen	'suffice'	
Middle Dutch	genoegen	'suffice'	
Middle High German	genüegen	'suffice'	
Old High German	ginuogen	'suffice'	

The question that now arises is whether one should reconstruct the same argument structure for these two verbs, *ga-nahan* and *ga-nōgjan-*, for Proto-Germanic or not. It is very common indeed that synonymous verbs share argument structure constructions, although it is not a given, as I have shown in my earlier work on this topic (Barðdal 1999b, 2001c, 2008, 2012; Barðdal and Eythórsson 2020). In order to address this issue, consider the correspondence sets in Tables 15–16 for the argument structure constructions documented for the descendants of *ga-nōgjan-*, as attested in the medieval Germanic material in (230–237) above. For reasons of space and clarity, I set up two different correspondence sets, one for potentially alternating Dat-Nom / Nom-Dat constructions and the other for instances without a nominative.

It is clear from Table 15 that the alternation between Dat-Nom and Nom-Dat is found in all three branches of Germanic. Note, however, that the alternation in Gothic is found with the extinct *ga-nahan-, but with the extant *ga-nōgjan- in the later Germanic languages, both North- and West-Germanic. Thus, it seems reasonable to assume that this alternation should be reconstructed for Proto-Germanic, at least with *ga-nahan-. It is unclear whether the extant verb, *ga-nōgjan-, also existed with this argument structure originally or whether it was somehow taken over from the earlier *ga-nahan-.

Table 15: Predicate-specific correspondence set for the argument structure of the Germanic 'suffice', with nominative in the argument structure.

	ALT1$_a$	ALT1$_b$	ALT2$_a$	ALT2$_b$
Gothic	Dat-Nom	Acc-Nom	Nom-Dat/Acc	
Old English	Acc/Dat-Nom			
Old High German				Nom-Acc
Old Norse-Icelandic	Dat-Nom		Nom-Dat	
Old Swedish	Dat-Nom		Nom-Dat	
Old Danish	Dat-Nom			
Middle Dutch	Dat-Nom		Nom-Obl	
Middle Low German	Dat-Nom		Nom-Dat	
Middle High German	Dat-Nom		Nom-Dat	

Following Barðdal and Eythórsson (2012a, 2012b, 2020), Barðdal (2013, 2014), Barðdal and Smitherman (2013), Barðdal, Bjarnadóttir et al. (2013), Barðdal, Kulikov et al. 2020, Eythórsson and Barðdal (2016), Danesi, Johnson, and Barðdal (2017), Johnson et al. (2019), Vázquez-González and Barðdal (2019) and Frotscher, Kroonen and Barðdal (2022), I use the notational formalism of Construction Grammar, the Attributed Value Matrix introduced in Section 2.2.3, to flesh out the details of the suggested reconstructions. This formalism has been successfully used to model both the grammar of synchronic languages and to model language change (Kay and Fillmore 1999; Michaelis and Ruppenhofer 2001; Fried and Östman 2005; Sag 2012; Michaelis 2010, 2012; Kim and Michaelis 2020, Gildea and Barðdal 2022).

Thus, on the basis of the correspondence set in Table 15, I suggest reconstructions as in Figures 16–17, which specify two alternating verb-specific argument structure constructions for the two-place preterite-present verb *ga-nahan- in Proto-Germanic, Dat-Nom and Nom-Dat. The notational formalism consists of three fields, a FORM field, a SYN field and a SEM field. The FORM field is in this instance filled with the form of the verb, as it is reconstructed in Table 12 above, namely *ga-nōgjan-. The SYN field specifies the argument structure, which is here reconstructed as Dat-Nom in Figure 16, but Nom-Dat in Figure 17. The SEM field contains the reconstructed suffice_frame for both argument structure constructions.

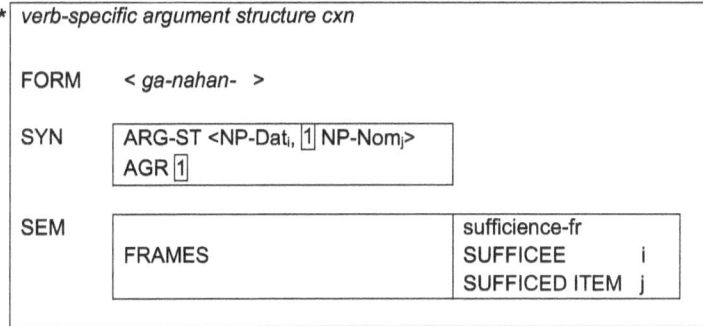

Figure 16: A Proto-Germanic reconstruction of a verb-specific Dat-Nom argument structure construction for *ga-nahan-*.

This suffice_frame only has two arguments, the predicate-specific participants, Sufficee, i.e. the person being satisfied, and the Sufficed Item. The difference between the two reconstructions in Figures 16 and 17 is thus not only the order of the arguments in the SYN field, but also the order of the semantic participants in the SEM field. In other words, Sufficee is indexed with i and Sufficed Item with j in Figure 16, while the order of the two participants is the opposite in Figure 17, where the Sufficed Item is indexed with i and the Sufficee with j.

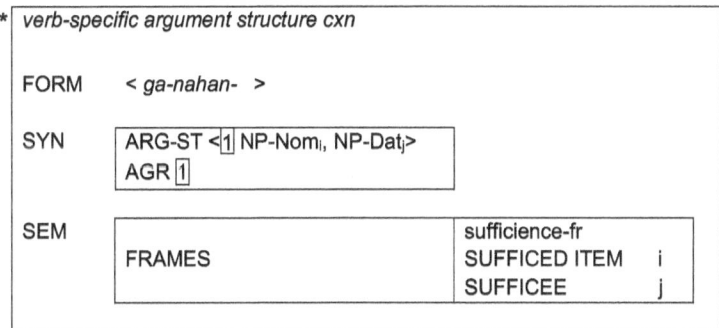

Figure 17: A Proto-Germanic reconstruction of a verb-specific Nom-Dat argument structure construction for *ga-nahan-*.

The more observant reader may have noticed that the formalism in Figures 16–17 above deviates to a certain extent from the formalism introduced in Sections 2.2.3–2.2.4 above, where both lexical entries and argument structure constructions are introduced. The differences between these two are twofold: a) the order of the arguments in lexical entries is unordered, given with curly brackets, while the order of the arguments in argument structure constructions is instead ordered, given with angled brackets, and b) argument structure constructions exist irrespective of lexical entries. The assumption is that lexical entries then merge with argument structure constructions, resulting in verb-specific argument structure constructions, where the order of the arguments is specified. This will be further discussed in Section 6.4 below, although in the remainder of this section, and for the simplicity of the presentation, I take a shortcut past lexical entries and argument structure constructions and illustrate instead the merged verb-specific argument structure constructions for the relevant verbs and argument structure constructions discussed above.

Before we leave the issue of alternating predicates for now, recall from Section 5.3.1 above that Gothic also occurs with an Acc-Nom argument structure construction, also listed in the correspondence set in Table 15. Observe that the Nom-Acc argument structure is also documented in Old High German, albeit with the more recent *jan*-verb. The problem here is that this is the only two-place occurrence of OHG *ginuogen*, although a few more occurrences are found, all of which are either one-place anticausatives of the type shown in (238) below, or are zero-place occurrences. While this might count as a motivation for reconstructing the Acc-Nom / Nom-Acc alternation for 'suffice' in Proto-Germanic, the Old High German data, due to their sparsity, do not reveal anything about whether *ginuogen* may also have instantiated the Acc-Nom alternant, making it difficult to carry out such a reconstruction.

Table 16: Predicate-specific correspondence set for the argument structure of the Germanic verb *ga-nōgjan-*, without nominative in the argument structure.

	ALT1	ALT2	ALT3	ALT4
Old Norse-Icelandic	Dat-			
Old Swedish	Dat/Acc-			
Old Danish	Dat/Acc-	Dat-PP	Dat-Gen	
Old Frisian	Obl-	Dat-PP		
Middle Dutch	Obl-		Dat-Gen	
Middle Low German		Dat-PP	Dat-Gen	
Middle High German		Dat-PP	Dat-Gen	Acc-Gen

Turning to the correspondence set in Table 16 for the remaining argument structure constructions, notice that the morphological accusative and dative categories are in the process of merging into a general oblique or non-nominative category in both Swedish and Danish already around 1400, as is already discussed in Section 4.2.5 above. This is at the time to which the oldest Swedish and Danish examples with *nöghia* and *nøghje* may be traced. This is the reason we find both dative and accusative with these verbs in Old Swedish and Old Danish. The same process has also taken place in Middle Dutch (cf. Weerman and de Wit 1999; Hendriks 2012; among others), hence Table 16 gives *Obl* for Middle Dutch examples of the type shown in (236a, 236c). However, there are two Middle Dutch examples, (236b, 236d), that speak for a dative analysis over an accusative one. First, the noun *Gode* 'God' in (236b) is clearly in the dative case and the same is true for the indefinite pronoun *allen* 'all' in (236d).

In addition, the Old Frisian example in (237a) shows an unambiguous dative, despite the fact that the case system is also in the process of breaking down in Old Frisian (Sherman 1969; here cited by de Haan 2001). Nevertheless, this case frame in Old Frisian, Dat-PP, may well be a development from Dat-Gen, since it is well known that genitive objects change to prepositional objects in the history of Germanic, as is discussed by Allen (1995: 217–219) for Old and Early Middle English. The Middle Low German example in (235a) also testifies to an unambiguous dative, selecting for a prepositional object as the second argument.

The Dat-PP construction is further documented in both Middle High German, Middle Low German and Old Danish, in addition to Old Frisian. Note that the PP is headed by the same preposition in Old Danish and Middle Low German, *meth* and *mit* 'with', respectively. The same is also true for the Old Frisian and Middle High German, in that the PP is headed by *and* and *an* 'on', respectively. For these reasons, I do not reconstruct Dat-PP for Proto-Germanic, as it is equally likely that this argument structure reflects a development from Dat-Gen, internal for West-Germanic and borrowed to Old Danish from Middle Low German.

Of the argument structures in Table 16, only two alternatives are left to discuss, namely, Dat-only and Acc-Gen. The first-mentioned, Dat-only, is attested in Old Norse-Icelandic, Old Swedish, Old Danish, and potentially in Old Frisian and Middle Dutch. There is, however, no need to reconstruct Dat-only *per se*, because this usage may simply be regarded as an intransitive use of the Dat-Nom argument structure construction, which has already been reconstructed for Proto-Germanic above. The second argument structure, Acc-Gen, is discussed in the following subsection.

5.3.2.2 The Acc-Gen vs. Dat-Gen conundrum

To start with, consider one of the Old Danish examples above, (232b), where we find the first and only documented example of Dat-Gen in North Germanic, namely with *honum* 'him' in the dative case and *thæs* 'its' in the genitive case. This example comes from the Danish version of Sjæla trøst, also existing in a Swedish version, which in turn is assumed to be a translation from German. Therefore, the fact that the only early example of the Dat-Gen construction documented with 'suffice' in the North-Germanic stratum is found in a medieval translation from German does not speak for the authenticity of this argument structure with this verb in North Germanic. Instead, it suggests that the argument structure may have been borrowed with the source verb during the translation process (cf. Barðdal 1999b, 2001c; and Barðdal and Eythórsson 2020, for a discussion of such a process).

Furthermore, it is well known from the history of Icelandic that there exists a variation between Dat-Gen and Dat-Nom (Barðdal 2009: 147–149), in the sense that these two are often instantiated by the same verbs and that the Dat-Nom construction generally attracted items from the Dat-Gen construction in the course of history. This, however, does not entail that all Dat-Nom verbs have developed from Dat-Gen verbs. On the contrary, it seems that both constructions existed side-by-side in the earlier layers of Germanic, even though some Dat-Gen verbs have certainly developed into Dat-Nom verbs over time. It should also be mentioned here that I have only come across one example of Dat-Gen in Middle Low German and so far only three in Middle Dutch. Of the Middle Dutch examples, one is a Dat-Gen and the two others are ambiguous between a dative or an accusative reading of the first argument, and hence between Dat-Gen and Acc-Gen readings.

Turning now to Acc-Gen, this argument structure is only found in Middle High German with 'suffice', not in any other medieval Germanic language. A further consideration to keep in mind is that there is a certain degree of variation found for accusative and dative subjects in the history of German, mostly in Middle High German, but also in Old High German to a certain extent. Seefranz-Montag (1983: 162–163) observes that many accusative subject verbs start occurring with a dative, and vice versa, many dative subject verbs start occurring with an accusative in early Middle High German. Dewey and Carey (2018) also show that there is a massive invasion of accusative subjects into the morphosyntactic sphere of dative subjects, starting already in Old High German, but becoming considerably more pronounced in Middle High German.

To give some examples of this interchangeability of accusative and dative subjects in earlier German, even fairly high-type-frequent verbs like *thunken* 'think, seem' are found with accusative subjects in Old High German, despite being originally constructed with a dative subject. The assumption that the dative is original with 'think, seem' is supported by the fact that this is the only subject case found for this verb in both Gothic and Old Norse-Icelandic. Another example from Old High German of this variation between accusative and dative is found with compositional predicates like *wola sîn* 'be well', which select for dative subjects, and not accusative subjects, throughout the Germanic and Indo-European languages. Note that an invasion of the accusative into the sphere of the dative is also documented with Avestan compositional predicates of this type (cf. Danesi 2014). This, in fact, confirms the analysis that the dative is the original subject case with 'be well' and that the accusative is an innovation.

The fact that the accusative was productive as a subject case in the history of German might make one averse to assuming that the Acc-Gen case frame is original for *ga-nōgjan-. To complicate matters even further, consider the following examples from Old High German, also with the more recent weak *jan*-verb, *ginuogen*, and not with the older preterite-present verb, *ginah*.

Old High German
(238) a. **mînes   uuillen**   negenûoget   darazûo
           my.GEN   will. GEN   not.suffices.3SG thereto
           'My will is not sufficient for that'   (Notker Psalmen 219: 35 [Hs. 2681])
       b. Vbe   **des**   negnuôget.   Sô ...
           if   this.GEN   not.suffices.3SG   then
           'If this is not sufficient, then ...'   (Notker Psalmen 6: 19–21)

Observe, however, that these examples are different from the examples in (227–237) above, as the genitive subject represents a different event-type participant than the experiencer subjects in (227–237). The examples in (238a–b) represent an anticausative variant of an unattested two-place predicate in Old High German, corresponding most likely either to Acc-Gen or Dat-Gen. This alternation is of the same type as the one found with the verb *lack* in English, as in *I lack money* vs *Money is lacking*, where the subject of the intransitive alternant corresponds to the object of the transitive one. This process, in which objects of transitive verbs become subjects of corresponding intransitive alternants, while at the same time maintaining their object case marking, has been labeled *oblique anticausativization* (see Section 4.1.6 above), and is by now relatively well documented in the international literature on Germanic and Baltic (Sandal 2011; Ottósson 2013; Barðdal 2014, 2015; Bjarnadóttir 2014b). Also, very recently, oblique anticausativization has been shown to be at work in several early and ancient Indo-European languages, such as Latin, Ancient Greek, Hittite and Sanskrit, in addition, of course, to Germanic, Baltic and Slavic (see Barðdal et al. 2020).

Returning to the Old High German examples in (238), as already stated, these attestations speak for either an Acc-Gen or a Dat-Gen two-place verb in Old High German, both of which are compatible with the argument structure constructions found in Middle High German, as is shown in the correspondence set in Table 16. There is also a third possibility, namely that *genûogen* in Old High German selected for the Nom-Gen case frame, as Old English *geneah* in (228a). Recall, however, that *geneah* is a different verb than the *jan*-verbs which are currently under discussion, making the Nom-Gen option less attractive to reconstruct than the Acc-Gen or Dat-Gen variants with this particular verb.

Given the upsurge in productivity of accusative subjects in the history of German, it might seem reasonable to assume that the Dat-Gen construction is the original one and that the dative was replaced with an accusative, yielding the following process Dat-Gen –> Acc-Gen. Furthermore, there does not seem to be a difference in the attestation dates of the two case frames, both found to exist in early Middle High German texts. This, in turn, might be taken to suggest that the variation between accusative and dative subjects with *ginuogen* existed already in Old High German.

It should also be mentioned in this context that these two case frames, Acc-Gen and Dat-Gen, are commonly found in Germanic with morphologically derived verbs, in particular denominal and deadjectival ones. Recall the verb 'lust' in the early Germanic languages which selects for the Acc-Gen case frame, as is discussed in Section 4.1.6 above; 'lust' is a denominal verb, derived from the Proto-Germanic noun *lustu-. Another such example involves the verb *batna* 'get well' in Old Norse-Icelandic which occurs with a Dat-Gen case frame, also a denominal or deadjectival verb, derived either from the noun *batan- 'recovery' or from a corresponding adjectival stem *bat-. In fact, there are a few more verbs in Old Norse-Icelandic, all denominal, including *minna* 'remember', *vilna* 'hope', *varða* 'matter' and *vænta* 'expect', which select for the Acc-Gen case frame.

The fact that the Acc-Gen and Dat-Gen case frames in Germanic are commonly found with deadjectival and denominal verbs raises the question of whether one or both of these case frames might not be reconstructed for *ga-nōgjan in Proto-Germanic. The answer to that question is in the negative since Acc-Gen and Dat-Gen with the medieval manifestations of *ga-nōgjan are only attested in West-Germanic, but are unattested in Gothic and North-Germanic, except for the one example of Dat-Gen in Old Danish, stemming from a translation from German. A reconstruction based on attestations in only one subbranch of three appears as unmotivated, unless of course there are good reasons to assume that the relevant structures have disappeared from the other two branches.

These considerations motivate a further investigation into the early Germanic material, as well as a search for additional examples with the verb 'suffice'. This supplementary investigation has uncovered the existence of three additional examples, shown in (239–240) below, of which (239) is from the Gothic Skeireins, while (240a–b) are from Old Norse-Icelandic texts.

Gothic
(239) a. jah   swa   **managai**   ganohjands   **ins**
          and   so   much.DAT.F   satisfying.NOM.SG.M   them.ACC.M
          wailawiznai
          nourishment.DAT.F
          'and then [he] satisfied them with much nourishment'   (Skeireins 7: 4)

Old Norse-Icelandic
(240) a. Dróttinn   mun   þik   gnægta   **öllum**   **góðum**
          lord.the.NOM   will.3SG   you.ACC   satisfy.INF all.DAT   good.DAT
          hlutum
          things.DAT
          'The lord will endow you with all good things'   (Stjórn 421, c.1350)
      b. hvé   hann   **urþjóð**   **auði**   gnægir
          how   he.NOM   men.ACC   riches.DAT   satisfies.3SG
          'How he endowed men with riches'   (Egils saga, ch. 80, c. 962)

To complicate matters even further, observe that the examples in (239–240) are ditransitive examples of the derived *jan*-verb 'suffice'. This discovery indeed attests to an undocumented oblique anticausative alternation for this verb in these languages, as I elaborate further on below.

The Gothic example in (239) instantiates the Nom-Acc-Dat argument structure construction. The subject, here unexpressed, is in the nominative, as is evident from the nominative masculine form of the predicative present participle, *ganohjands* 'satisfying', referring to Jesus Christ on the mountain sating the hunger of 5,000 men with five loaves of bread and two fish. The second argument *ins* 'them' is in the accusative case and the discontinuous third argument *managai wailawiznai* 'much nourishment' is in the dative case.

Turning to the two Old Norse-Icelandic examples, the one in (240a) instantiates exactly the same argument structure as the one found in the Gothic example in (239), namely Nom-Acc-Dat. The subject *dróttinn* 'lord' is in the nominative case, the second argument *þik* 'you' in the accusative case, while the third argument *öllum góðum hlutum* 'all good things' is in the dative case. The source text, Stjórn, is also a religious text, like the Gothic Skeireins, and it is a relatively free rendering of the Old Testament, compiled in Iceland in the middle of the 14th century (cf. Tómasson 2012).

The example in (240b), however, is from Arinbjarnarkviða by Egill Skallagrímsson, a skaldic poem in kviðuháttur meter, composed during the latter part of the 10th century. Exactly as in (239) and (240a), the subject *hann* 'he' is in the nominative, the third argument *auði* 'riches' is in the dative, while the form *urþjóð* 'men' of the second argument is ambiguous between an accusative and a dative reading. As it happens, Þ. Sigurðsson (2019: 234) points to a similar use of *gnægja* from the Book of Homilies, presented in (241) below:

Old Norse-Icelandic
(241) a. en   þeir   gnéogþo   **hana**   at ollo   goþo
           but   they.NOM   endowed.3PL   her.ACC   at all.DAT good.DAT
           (Book of Homilies, Holm. Perg. 15 4to 59v12–13, c.1200)

The subject *þeir* 'they' is in the nominative case, the second argument in (240–241), *hana* 'her', is in the accusative case, while the third argument in (240–241), *ollu goþu* 'all good' is here governed by a preposition *at* 'at'. The example in (241) indeed supports the reading of the ambiguous form *urþjóð* 'men' in (240b) as being in the accusative, as rendered by the interlinear glosses for this example.

Note that this causative three-place alternant of 'suffice' in (239–241) has the meaning 'satisfy, satiate' in Gothic, but 'endow with' in Old Norse-Icelandic. These are both very reasonable three-place meanings of a two-place verb with the meaning 'suffice, have enough'. The existence of these examples may indeed suggest that the two-place oblique subject occurrences of 'suffice' with Acc-Gen and Dat-Gen in Middle High German may be anticausatives, exactly like the Old High German examples in (238) above, except that here we are discussing a reduction in valency from three arguments to only two, as opposed to a reduction from two arguments to only one in the Old High German examples in (238). Assuming oblique anticausativization would only be required for West Germanic, as Acc-Gen and Dat-Gen are confined to this branch of the Germanic languages.

Before returning to the issue of reconstructing further argument structures for the verbs 'satisfy' and 'suffice' in Proto-Germanic, I would first like to draw the reader's attention to a difference in form between *gnægja* in (240b) and *gnægta* in (240a). The latter, *gnægta*, is deverbal, derived from *gnægja* with the intensifying suffix *-atjan* (cf. Kluge 1913: 183; and Marckwardt 1942 on the nature of this suffix). As the examples in (240) attest to, this difference in form between *gnægja* and *gnægta* clearly does not affect the argument structure of the two verbs. A parallel in Old Norse-Icelandic is found with the pair *væna* and *vænta*, both meaning 'expect'. Since the form *gnægta* is only documented in Old Norse-Icelandic, as far as the discussion above has shown, this verb will not be reconstructed for Proto-Germanic.

To illustrate the exact nature of oblique anticausativization with ditransitive verbs, consider the following pair of examples, cited from Barðdal (2014: 361), involving the verb *fýsta* which means 'spur' when used as a three-place predicate (242a), but 'yearn for' when used as a two-place predicate (242b):

Old Norse-Icelandic
(242) a. *fýsta   ek   þik   ...   fararinnar*
        spurred.1SG   I.NOM   you.ACC   trip.GEN
        'I urged you ... on the trip'   (Egils saga, Ch. 25)
    b. *fýsti   Ólaf   þess   at ...*
        get.spurred.3SG   Ólafur.ACC it.GEN   to
        'Ólafur yearned (for it) to ...'   (Ólafs saga Tryggvasonar, Ch. 31)

Through the reduction in valency, the nominative subject of the causative three-place predicate in (242a) is omitted from the event structure in (242b), while the two remaining arguments, the accusative and the genitive, keep their case marking. The accusative becomes the subject, while the genitive remains an object. In this particular case, the argument structure is reduced from Nom-Acc-Gen to Acc-Gen.

However, oblique anticausativization of 'satisfy, satiate' to 'suffice' would yield a different case frame, Acc-Dat, as in the hypothetical Gothic example in (243b):

Gothic
(243) a. *jah   swa   managai   ganohjands   ins*
         and   so   much.DAT.F   satisfying.NOM.SG.M   them.ACC.M
         wailawiznai
         nourishment.DAT.F
         'and then [he] satisfied them with much nourishment'   (Skeireins 7: 4)
    b. **swa   managai   wailawiznai   ins   ganohida*
         so   much.DAT.F   nourishment.DAT.F   them.ACC.M   sufficed.3SG
         Intended meaning: 'they were satisfied with so much nourishment'

In other words, a process of oblique anticausativization affecting the causative three-place *jan*-verb 'satisfy, satiate, endow with', selecting for the case frame Nom-Acc-Dat, would clearly result in an Acc-Dat case frame, i.e. with an accusative subject and a dative object.

Now, as its corollary, a prerequisite for the existence of an anticausative two-place verb with the Acc-Dat case frame is that there also exists a corresponding ditransitive verb with Nom-Acc-Dat. Such a ditransitive verb is documented in Gothic and Old Norse-Icelandic, but not in West-Germanic, as already stated above. Note also that the Old Norse-Icelandic example in (240b) stems from skaldic poetry in one of the oldest Icelandic sagas, Egils saga, composed in the latter part of the 10th century. So even though the Gothic example from the Skeireins and the Old Norse-Icelandic example from Stjórn are both translations, the example in (240b) from Egils saga clearly speaks for the authenticity of this case frame in the early Germanic languages.

Returning to the German data, there is no doubt that the direct object of a potential anticausative two-place 'suffice' in West-Germanic was in the genitive, and not in the expected dative, as is evident from the Old High German Gen-only structure for the one-place 'suffice' in (238a–b), and the Old English Nom-Gen example in (228a), albeit with a different 'suffice' verb, the *ga-nahan verb and not the *ga-nōgjan verb.

How can all of these case facts from the different early Germanic languages be reconciled? In order to address that issue, let us compare the case frames in Table 17 for indirect and direct objects of ditransitive verbs in Old Norse-Icelandic (cf. Barðdal, Kristoffersen, and Sveen 2011: 70), Old English (Allen 1995: 29) and Old High German (Dal and Eroms 2014: 8–49). Note that the case marking of the subject is not included in Table 17, only the case frames of the indirect and the direct object.

Table 17: Ditransitive (object) case frames in Early Germanic.

Old Norse-Icelandic	Old English	Old High German
Dat-Acc	Dat-Acc	Dat-Acc
Acc-Gen	Acc-Gen	Acc-Gen
Dat-Gen	Dat-Gen	(Dat-Gen)
Acc-Dat	Acc-Dat	
Dat-Dat	Acc-Acc	Acc-Acc

Both Old Norse Icelandic and Old English have five case frames each for ditransitives, of which four are the very same. The difference between the two subbranches is the last case frame listed in Table 17, namely Dat-Dat for North-Germanic, but Acc-Acc for both Old English and Old High German. This, however, is not the main point here, but rather the fact that the Acc-Dat case frame, which is the case frame found for the ditransitive *jan*-verb 'satisfy, satiate, endow with' in both Gothic and Old Norse-Icelandic, happens to exists in both Old Norse-Icelandic and Old English, as is highlighted in gray in Table 17.

Turning to German, according to the information in Dal and Eroms (2014), there are only three case frames attested with ditransitive verbs in Old High German. These are the canonical Dat-Acc case frame (first row), as well as Acc-Gen (second row) and Acc-Acc (last row). The case frame, Dat-Gen (third row), is listed in Table 17 within brackets, as all Dal and Erom's examples are from Middle High German, and not from Old High German. Pay heed to the shining absence of the Acc-Dat case frame in Old High German. As a consequence, any ditransitive use of the *jan*-verb 'satiate, be endowed with', cannot have occurred with the Acc-Dat case frame in the recorded history of German, as opposed to in Gothic and Old Norse-Icelandic.

5.3 Reconstructing predicate and argument structure constructions — 245

Before continuing this discussion, it is timely to reconstruct a ditransitive jan-verb *ga-nōgjan- 'satiate, satisfy' for Proto-Germanic, as it occurs in two out of three Germanic branches, namely East and North Germanic, with the argument structure Nom-Acc-Dat. Such a reconstruction is presented in Figure 18 and the relevant correspondence set in Table 18. Again, observe that the case marking of the nominative subject has been omitted from the correspondence set in Table 18, which otherwise contains only two alternants, the documented Acc-Dat and the internally reconstructed *Acc-Gen for Old High German.

Table 18: Predicate-specific correspondence set for the causative three-place argument structure of *ga-nōgjan.

	ALT1	ALT2
Gothic	Acc-Dat	
Old High German		*Acc-Gen
Old Norse-Icelandic	Acc-Dat	

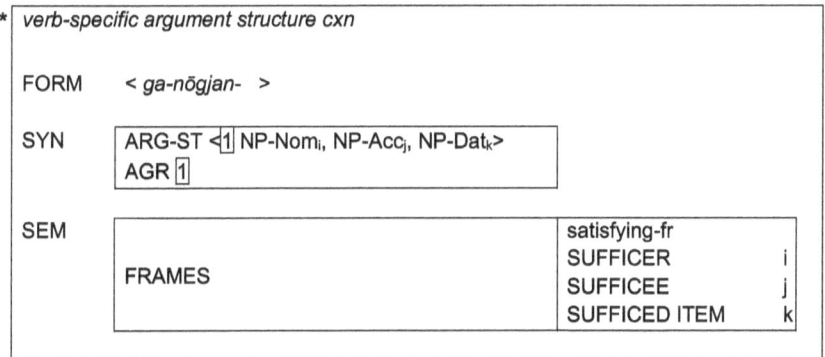

Figure 18: A Proto-Germanic reconstruction of a verb-specific argument structure construction for the causative three-place *ga nōgjan-.

Again, the reconstruction of a verb-specific argument structure construction for the ditransitive use of *ga-nōgjan- in Proto-Germanic is given in Figure 18. Like before, the notational formalism consists of three fields, a FORM field, a SYN field and a SEM field. The FORM field is in this instance filled with the form of the verb, as it was reconstructed in Table 13 above, namely *ga-nōgjan-. The SYN field specifies the argument structure, which is here reconstructed as Nom-Acc-Dat, nominative for the subject, accusative for the second argument and dative for the third argument, on the basis of Gothic and Old Norse-Icelandic.

The SEM field is set up in terms of semantic frames and here I suggest a satisfying_frame, consisting of a Sufficer, Sufficee and a Sufficed Item, i.e. the Sufficer provides the Sufficee with the Sufficed Item. The mapping between the semantic roles and the cases is done through indexing, with the Sufficer and the nominative co-indexed, the Sufficee and the accusative co-indexed, as well as the Sufficed Item and the dative being co-indexed with each other (for a reconstruction of the canonical Dat-Acc ditransitive construction in Proto-Germanic, cf. Vázquez-González and Barðdal 2019).

Observe that there is a connection between the semantic frame and the participants of the verb in Figures 16–17 above for the two-place *ga-nahan-* and the semantic frame and participants in Figure 18 for the causative three-place *ga-nōgjan-*. The suffice_frame is a partial instance of the satisfying_frame, in that the Sufficee and Sufficed Item of the suffice_frame correspond to the Sufficee and Sufficed Item of the satisfying_frame. This is, of course, a consequence of the fact that the two-place alternant is an anticausative of the causative three-place construction.

I now return to the Acc-Gen vs. the Dat-Gen conundrum with 'suffice' in the history of German. I hypothesize that sometime in the prehistory of Old High German but after the common Germanic period, the ditransitive *jan*-verb 'satiate, be endowed with' changed its case frame from Nom-Acc-Dat to Nom-Acc-Gen. This has most likely been a general development ousting all uses of the Nom-Acc-Dat case frame in the prehistory of German, since no ditransitive verbs occur with Acc-Dat in Old High German at all, as is shown in Table 18.

Thus, I conjecture that the Nom-Acc-Gen construction attracted all verbal types instantiating the earlier Nom-Acc-Dat construction, leading to the Nom-Acc-Dat construction falling into disuse in at least the *Irminonic branch* of West Germanic. I find this a more likely scenario explaining this gap in ditransitives in Old High German, as opposed to assuming that the Nom-Acc-Dat construction arose independently in Old Norse-Icelandic and Old English. The existence of the ditransitive Nom-Acc-Dat in Gothic further speaks against such a scenario.

Furthermore, I surmise that in the prehistory of German, oblique anticausativization was at work, deriving the two-place Acc-Gen 'suffice' from the corresponding three-place Nom-Acc-Gen 'satisfy'. The three-place verb 'satisfy' then fell into disuse, leaving behind in the German language only the two-place Acc-Gen construction. There is, in fact, a parallel found in the history of Icelandic, as the three-place 'endow with' in (240–241) above has disappeared from the living language. This scenario would clearly explain why the Acc-Gen construction is found with 'suffice' in Middle High German, as opposed to the Acc-Dat case frame.

Seefranz-Montag (1983: 171–189) observes that both genitive subjects and genitive objects with the form *es* 'it', get assimilated to nominative and accusative *ez* 'it' during the 13th century due to a phonological merger, causing Acc-Gen and Dat-Gen verbs to become Acc-Nom and Dat-Nom verbs. Whether this might explain the Dat-Nom case frame in the Middle High German example in (234d) above, I leave unsaid, as it is equally likely that the alternation between Dat-Nom and Nom-Dat is inherited from Proto-Germanic. The fact remains, however, that examples of the *jan*-verb 'suffice' with the Dat-Nom case frame are much rarer in Middle High German than corresponding Acc-Gen and Dat-Gen are.

Unfortunately, the evidence does not support a reconstruction of the two-place *jan*-verb 'suffice', with an Acc-Dat case frame, since there is no attestation of this case frame with that same two-place *jan*-verb 'suffice' in any of the daughter languages. Despite this, it is clear that, at least in the prehistory of German, the process of oblique anticausativization must have given rise to a two-place Acc-Gen *jan*-verb 'suffice' in Old High German, as there is no other way to explain the surviving Acc-Gen and Dat-Gen in Middle High German. I assume that this oblique anticausativization process took place after the common Germanic period, since its reflexes only exist in German. Further, the Dat-Gen case frame in Middle High German can easily be explained due to the general exchangeability between accusative and dative subjects, as documented both by Zeefranz-Montag (1983) and Dewey and Carey (2018), as reported on above.

This concludes the present section on how to reconstruct argument structure constructions for a proto-stage. The aim here has been to show that even in complicated instances where the attested case frames are not in concert with each other, it may still be possible to disentangle systematic alternations, to suggest a reasonable developmental path and a sound relative chronology for the various case frames and how they may have interacted with each other. For further reconstructions of argument structure constructions in both Proto-Germanic and Proto-Indo-European, cf. Barðdal and Eythórsson (2012a, 2012b, 2020); Barðdal (2013, 2014); Barðdal and Smitherman (2013); Barðdal, Bjarnadóttir et al. (2013); Eythórsson and Barðdal (2016); Danesi, Johnson, and Barðdal (2017); Dunn et al. 2017; Johnson et al. (2019); Vázquez-González and Barðdal (2019); Barðdal, Kulikov, et al. (2020); and Frotscher, Kroonen and Barðdal (2022).

5.4 Reconstructing subject behavior for Proto-Germanic

Having now shown how one can reconstruct predicate and argument structure constructions for Proto-Germanic, it is time to demonstrate how grammatical relations may be reconstructed not only as language-specific but also as construction specific categories. This requires the reconstruction of both nominative subjects as well as oblique subjects. In essence, this requires that the constructions that distinguish between subjects and objects be reconstructed and the behavior of the arguments fleshed out.

As discussed in Section 4.2 above, not all the subject tests in the modern Germanic languages may be used to distinguish between subjects and objects in the early stages of Germanic. One of these tests is conjunction reduction, involving the ellipsis of a conjoined subject, provided that the two have the same reference. The problem with the early Germanic languages is that they are argument drop languages, meaning that the subject or the object may be left unexpressed if it is recoverable from the preceding text. However, Allen (1995) convincingly shows that there is a major statistical difference between subject ellipsis in second conjuncts, depending on whether the ellipsis is on identity with the subject or the object of the first conjunct. Even so, as long as there is no good method to distinguish between conjunction reduction and topic drop, this particular subject behavior will not be reconstructed for Proto-Germanic here.

With regard to binding of reflexives, not only subjects but also objects may bind reflexives in some of the early Germanic languages. In addition, subjects may also bind non-reflexive pronouns. A further complication arises from the situation in Old English and Old Saxon, where there are no simple reflexives to bind. For this reason, no reconstruction of binding of reflexives in simple clauses will be carried out here.

In the following sections I focus on the clear-cut subject properties, common for all three branches of Germanic. These are word order, raising-to-subject, raising-to-object, control and long-distance reflexivization, each discussed in a subsection of its own.

5.4.1 Word order

Starting with word order, it is indisputable that there is a clear tendency in the early Germanic languages for the subject to precede the verb, as is demonstrated in Section 4.2.7 above. Of course, some deviations from that generalization exist, deviations which are generally motivated by either different clause functions or by information structure (Eythórsson 1995; Haugan 2001; Fuss 2003; Axel 2007; Harbert 2007; Los 2009; Viðarsson 2009; Hinterhölzl and Petrova 2010; Hinterhölzl and van Kemenade 2012; Barðdal, Bjarnadóttir et al. 2013; Jónsson 2018). Such deviations, however, do not exclude a reconstruction of neutral word order for Proto-Germanic, which is the current task.

The examples from Section 4.2.7 above are reproduced below since they provide the input for the correspondence set on which basis one reconstructs. Recall that the a) examples show subject-verb word order, while the b) examples instantiate subject-verb inversion. Since the comparative data are identical, as the verb 'think' consistently occurs with a dative subject and both word orders are possible, SV and VS, it is not necessary to set up a correspondence set for this reconstruction.

Gothic
(244) a. *iþ   sundro   **þaimei**   þuhta,*
        but   only   these.DAT   thought.3SG
        'but only these ones thought, ...'   (Galatians 2:2)
   b. *aftra   þugkeiþ   **izwis**   ei*
      again   thinks.3SG you.DAT   that
      'Again, you think that ...'   (Corinthians II 12:19)

Old High German
(245) a. *sosọ   **imu**   rát   thunkit*
        so.that him.DAT   advise.NOM   thinks.3SG
        'So that he finds [it] it advisable'   (Otfr., Ev.2, 12, 42)
   b. *uuaz   thunkit   **úuuih**?*
      what   thinks.3SG   you.ACC
      'What do you think?'   (Tat., Ev.Harm., 191, 2)

Old Saxon
(246) a. *sô   **mi**   thes   wundar   thunkit*
        so   me.ACC/DAT   that.GEN   wonder.GEN   thinks.3SG
        'So I find this a wonder'   (Heliand 2: 157)
   b. *"ni   thunkid   **mi**   thit   [sômi]   thing"   quað   he,*
      not   thinks.3SG   me.ACC/DAT   that   seemly   thing   said   he
      'He said: "I do not find this a seemly thing"'   (Heliand 54: 4508)

Old English
(247) a. *þe   him   **selfum**   ðincð   þæt ...*
        then him.DAT   self.DAT   thinks.3SG   it
        'Then he himself thinks that ...'
                                  (Alfredian Boethius (Otho) xxix. 66, c.890–950)
   b. *Þinceð   **him**   to   lytel*
      thinks.3SG   him.DAT   too   little
      'He finds this too little'   (Beowulf 1748)

Old Norse Icelandic
(248) a. *...   hvort   **mér**   þykir   vel   eða   illa*
            whether   me.DAT   thinks.3SG   well   or   badly
        '... whether I find this good or bad.'   (Íslendings þáttur sögufróða)
   b. *Svo   þykir   **mér**   sem ...*
      then   thinks.3SG   me.DAT   as.if
      'Then I feel as if ...'   (Brennu Njáls saga, ch. 3)

Old Swedish
(249) a. ty   **honom**   tikkie   got   wara
          because   him.DAT   would.think.3SG   good   be.INF
          'because he would find this good'
                                        (Konungastyrelsen 29 (74, 31), c.1350)
     b.   väghin   thötte   **them**   ey   vara   lang
          road.the thought.3SG them.DAT   not   be.INF   long
          'They didn't find the road long'
                                        (Hertig Fredrik av Normandie 1599, c.1308)

Old Danish
(250) a. vm   **oss**   thycker   thet   nuttelicht   wære
          if   us.DAT   thinks.3SG this.NOM   useful   be.INF
          'If we find this useful.'   (Skråer II. 114, c.1443)
     b.   tha   thatæ   **hannum**   skam   oc   wanhæther
          then   thought.3SG him.DAT   shame.NOM   and   disgrace.NOM
          wære   at
          be.INF   at
          'Then he finds it to be a shame and disgrace that'   (RydÅrb. I, c.1314)

On the basis of what is generally known about word order in Early Germanic, as well as on the basis of examples like those in (243–250) above, I suggest, following Barðdal and Eythórsson (2012a), two reconstructions of word order for Proto-Germanic, a reconstruction of the subject-predicate construction in Figure 19 and a reconstruction of the subject-verb inverted word order in Figure 20. For this purpose, I continue to use the Attributed Value Matrix employed in Construction Grammar, already introduced in Section 2.2.4 above, also used to model the behavior of alternating predicates (Section 3.4) and successfully applied in the previous subsection when modeling lexical entries and argument structure constructions.

The first of the two reconstructions proposed here, the one in Figure 19, models the internal order between the subject and the predicate in a neutral setting, namely with the subject preceding the verb. This is captured with the two inner boxes in Figure 19, of which the first represents the subject and the second represents the verb. This is modeled through the specifications of the SYN fields, which is NP_{-i} in the first box but V_{FIN} in the second box. The specification NP_{-i} then yields a coindexation with the first argument of verb-specific argument structures, as in Figures 16–18 above, be it nominative, accusative or dative. The FORM field in Figure 19 is empty because this is a schematic reconstruction with no lexical material.

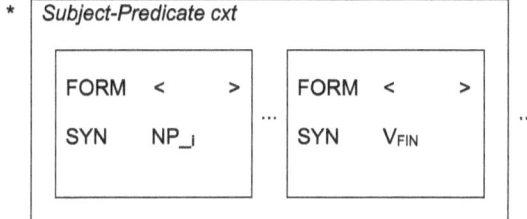

Figure 19: A reconstruction of the subject-predicate word order construction for Proto-Germanic.

Note also the ellipsis between the subject and the finite verb, which shows that V2, i.e. verb second, is not being reconstructed for Proto-Germanic, as other lexical material may intervene between the subject and the finite verb. There is also an ellipsis immediately following the finite verb, again showing that the verb is not in final position and that other sentence elements may follow the finite verb.

Furthermore, Figure 20 gives the specifications of the reconstructed subject-verb inverted word order, where the subject follows the verb, instead of preceding it. There is no ellipsis between the finite verb and the subject, showing that the two must be adjacent. However, there is an ellipsis immediately before the finite verb, as other lexical material may occur in first position, for instance time and place adverbials and topicalized material which would trigger subject-verb inversion in all the early Germanic language. But then again, the reconstruction in Figure 20 does not demand that any other lexical material precedes the verb, as would be the case in questions and narrative inversion, for instance. There is also a second ellipsis immediately following the subject in Figure 20, as other material may well follow the subject, all depending on the argument structure of the verb, as well as on other choices made by speakers.

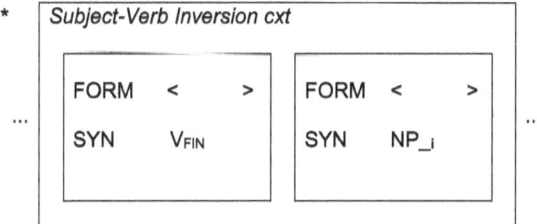

Figure 20: A reconstruction of the subject-predicate inverted word order for Proto-Germanic.

This concludes the reconstruction of neutral word order, i.e. the word order where the subject precedes the verb in Proto-Germanic, as well as the reconstruction of the inverted subject-verb construction where the subject follows the verb. The first argument of the argument structure of each lexical verb is indexed with an *i*, thus it is coindexed with the subject in both word order constructions. As a consequence, both nominative and oblique subjects will occur in first position in clauses with neutral word order, and the same is true for the inverted subject-verb word order. The subject can certainly have a wider distribution in Proto-Germanic than this, with for instance heavy and indefinite subjects occurring further to the right, but reconstructing neutral word order and subject-verb inversion will suffice for the present purposes.

5.4.2 Raising-to-subject

As already documented in Section 4.2.4 above, raising-to-subject not only exists in all the early Germanic languages, but examples involving oblique subjects have also been found in all the earliest stages of these languages except for Gothic. I repeat these examples here, since it is on the basis of these that raising-to-subject may be reconstructed for Proto-Germanic:

Old High German
(251) a. **ímo   sélbemo** nesúle   **dúnchen** scône
         him.DAT   self.DAT   not.shall.3SG   think.INF   beautiful
         'he shall not deem himself beautiful'   (Notker, Boeth.Cons. II, 81.18)
    b. Sô   **ímo**   dára   nâh   **nôten**   gestât
        so   him.DAT   there   after   trouble.NOM   stood.3 SG
        'and then he began to get into trouble.'   (Notker, Boeth.Cons. III, 138.9)

Old English
(252) a. þa   ongan   **hine**   eft   **langian**   on   his   cyþþe
         then   began.3SG   him.ACC   after   long.INF   for   his   kith
         'then he started to long for his family.'
                          (Blickling Homilies, c. 971, cited from Cole et al. 1980: 729)
    b. Þonne   mæg   **hine**   **scamigan**   þære
        then   may.3SG   him.ACC   shame.INF   the
        brædinge   his   hlisan
        spreading.GEN/DAT   his   fame.GEN
        'Then he may be ashamed of the extent of his fame'
                          (Boethius 46.5, c. 850–950, here cited from Denison 1990: 153)

Old Saxon

(253) a. *that* **ina** *bigan bi thero mennisko*
 then him.ACC began.3SG by that.DAT humanity.DAT
 môses **lustean**
 meat.GEN lust.INF
 'Then he started to lust for meat due to his humanity' (Heliand 13: 1060)

 b. *"ni tharf* **iu** *wiht* **tregan**,*" quathie*
 not need.3SG you.DAT.PL anything regret.INF said.he
 '"you guys need not regret anything", he said' (Heliand 65: 5520)

Old Norse-Icelandic

(254) a. **honum** *kvaðst það illa* **þykja** *að* ...
 him.DAT said.REFL.3SG it.NOM badly feel.INF
 'He said that he felt that it was bad that ...' (Reykdæla saga, Ch. 13)

 b. *og lést* **honum** *sú sending*
 and acted.REFL.shou him.DAT that.NOM consignment.NOM
 þykja *ágœt og* ...
 find.INF good and
 'and he acted as if he liked the consignment and ...'
 (Króka refs saga, Ch. 12)

Old Swedish

(255) a. **them** *matte* **förtryta** *at the* ...
 them.DAT should.3SG regret.INF that they
 'they should regret that they ...' (Karlskrönikan, c. 1452)

 b. **drotningenne** *took ok dygert* **langa** ...
 queen.the.DAT took.3SG also fiercely long.for.INF
 'The queen started to long fiercely for ...' (Erikskrönikan, c.1330)

Old Danish

(256) a. **hanum** *kwnne æy rodh tiil* **ryndhe**
 him.DAT knew.3SG not advice.NOM to run.INF
 'he could not think of any solution'
 (Den danske Rimkrønike I, 77:2394, c.1495)

 b. *at* **them** *icke skal offtere* **lystæ** *at* ...
 that them.DAT not shall.3SG oftener lust.INF
 'That they shall more often want to ...'
 (Diplomatarium Danicum, c.1464)

These examples represent a healthy mix of aspectual verbs meaning 'begin', modal verbs like 'shall', 'need', 'may' and 'can', as well as the Old Norse-Icelandic 'say' and 'act as if'. It must, however, be noted here that not all 'begin' verbs are raising-to-subject verbs, and neither are all modal verbs. Modern Icelandic, for instance, has five different 'begin' verbs of which some are raising-to-subject verbs and others are control verbs (cf. Barðdal 2001a). An example of a modal verb that is also a control verb is found in Section 4.2.6 above with Early Middle English *biren* 'be obliged' and its cognates in North Germanic, Old Norse-Icelandic *bera* and Old Swedish *böra* with the same meaning. An example of a modal verb that can either be a control verb or a raising-to-subject verb is the Old Saxon verb *thurban* 'need', as is documented in Sections 4.2.4 and 4.2.6 above.

We know that the finite verbs in (252–256) above are raising-to-subject verbs because they occur with a behavioral subject in the accusative or the dative case and this case marking happens to coincide with the case marking of the subject of the lower verbs, as is already discussed in Section 4.2.4 above. That is, the Old English verb *langian* 'long for' in (252a) and the Old Saxon verb *lustean* 'lust for' in (253a) select for accusative subjects, and so does the Old Swedish *langa* in (255a) although it occurs here with a dative due to the general functional merger between accusatives and datives in the history of the Mainland Scandinavian languages (see the discussion in 4.2.5 above). The remaining verbs all occur with a dative subject in their respective languages.

Raising-to-subject also exists in Gothic with both 'begin' verbs and modal verbs, even though no such examples have been documented with oblique subjects. This, in turn, is not surprising given the rarity of such constructions in Gothic texts. However, one example of raising-to-subject with aspectual 'begin' and one with modal 'shall' from Gothic are given in (257) below:

Gothic
(257) a. þanuh **dags** juþan **dugann** hneiwan
       but day.NOM already began.3SG droop.INF
       'and when the day began to droop' (Luke 9: 12)
   b. hvadre **sa** **skuli** gaggan
       whereto the.one.NOM should.3SG go.INF
       'Whereto would he go ...' (John 7: 35)

In (257a) the nominative *dags* 'day' is assigned by the lower verb *hneiwan* 'droop', yet it takes on the behavioral properties of the finite verb *dugann* 'begin'. The same is true for the nominative *sa* 'the one' in (257b); it is selected for by the lower verb *gaggan* 'go', but behaves syntactically as the subject of the modal *skulan* 'shall'.

It is incontrovertible that raising-to-subject constructions may be reconstructed for Proto-Germanic, given their existence in all the Germanic daughter languages. For such a reconstruction to be meaningful, one must both model the behavior of the arguments of the lower verb in relation to the finite verb and reconstruct a lexical entry for the finite verb itself. For the form of the relevant finite verbs 'begin' and 'shall', I refrain from setting up correspondence sets for a reconstruction of the form, since these verbs have already been reconstructed by Germanic etymologists. The reconstructions below are thus confined to the relevant lexical entries of these verbs.

As a part of such an enterprise, consider first the reconstructions of the lexical verbs 'begin' and 'shall' for Proto-Germanic, shown in Figures 21–22. Figure 21 represents the reconstruction of the aspectual verb 'begin' for Proto-Germanic, here represented only with the stem *-ginnan- (cf. Kroonen 2013: 178), irrespective of the nature of the prefix, which is *du-* in Gothic, *be-* in Old English and *bi-* in Old High German. What is most noteworthy about this reconstruction are the selectional properties of the auxiliary 'begin', which does not select for a subject of its own, and secondly, is specified in the semantic frame of the reconstruction in Figure 21 for the begin_frame.

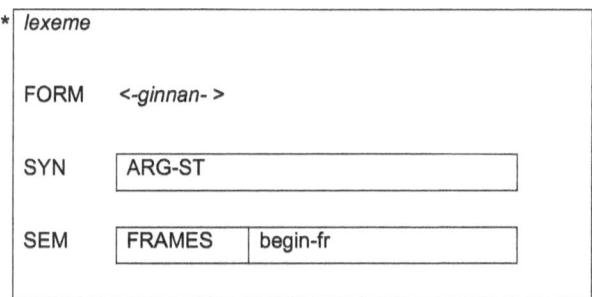

Figure 21: A Proto-Germanic reconstruction of the aspectual verb * *ginnan* and its verb-specific properties.

Turning to Figure 22, this reconstruction of the modal verb 'shall' for Proto-Germanic, is here represented through the lexical entry of the preterite-present verb *skulan-* (cf. Kroonen 2013: 450), which, exactly like 'begin', does not select for a subject of its own. Thus, the semantic frame, given in the SEM field in Figure 22, is the shall_frame.

Figure 23, moreover, fleshes out the details of the reconstructed raising-to-subject construction in Proto-Germanic, which in this case is confined to instances of the aspectual verb 'begin' and the modal verb 'shall' as finite verbs. Note that the

*	lexeme		
	FORM	< skulan- >	
	SYN	ARG-ST	
	SEM	FRAMES	shall-fr

Figure 22: A Proto-Germanic reconstruction of the modal verb *skulan- and its verb-specific properties.

ellipsis before the subject argument, here marked as NP_i, suggests that the subject is not necessarily the first element in the sentence. The same goes for the following ellipses in Figure 23, as there may be elements intervening between the subject and the finite verb, as well as between the finite verb and the infinitive.

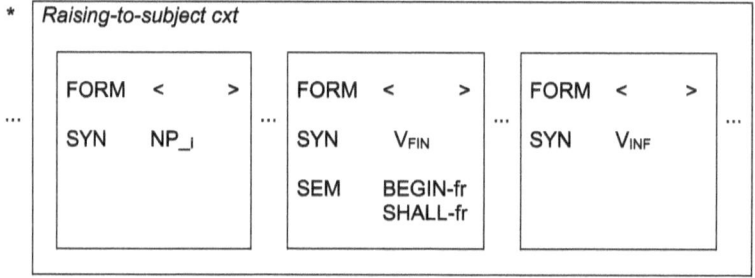

Figure 23: A reconstruction of the raising-to-subject construction in Proto-Germanic.

Observe that the lexical entries for *begin* and *shall* only provide the raising-to-subject construction with the relevant finite verb, limiting the construction to beginning events and events that are somehow required, thus occurring with the modal 'shall'.

The subject of the raising-to-subject construction is here indexed with i, which entails a coindexation of the first argument of the argument structure constructions of lexical verbs, be they dative as in Figure 16 above, or nominative as in Figure 17. This means that the case marking of the subject does not need to be specified, as it comes from the first argument of the argument structure, indexed i, in the lexical entry for each verb. This is how subject behavior in raising-to-subject constructions may be modeled and reconstructed for Proto-Germanic. The lower verb, here marked V_{INF}, is also provided by the main verb's lexical entry.

I now turn to the reconstruction of raising-to-object constructions (AcI) for Proto-Germanic.

5.4.3 Raising-to-object

In Section 4.2.5 above, examples are provided showing that raising-to-object constructions existed in all the earliest Germanic languages, including Gothic. However, while oblique subjects are found instantiating raising-to-object constructions in the earliest stages of both North and West Germanic languages, no such examples have been documented for Gothic. As already pointed out in the previous section, this is not surprising given the rarity of oblique subject predicates in the Gothic corpus and given the small size of the Gothic corpus in general. Below I reproduce the examples involving oblique subjects from the early West and North Germanic languages, since these form the basis for the reconstruction of raising-to-object for Proto-Germanic:

Old High German
(258) a. *laz* **thir** *quéman iz in múat*
let.2SG you.DAT come.INF it.NOM in mind
'let yourself get this in mind' (Otfr., Ev.2, 21, 43)
b. *laz* **dir** *zorn sîn*
let.2SG you.DAT thorn be.INF
'Let yourself be angry' (Notker, Psalter 78 (289, 2, 22))

Old Saxon
(259) a. *lâtit* **im** *is [bittrun] dâd an is hugie*
lets.3SG him.DAT his bitter deed at his heart
hrewan
regret.INF
'let him regret his bitter deed in his heart' (Heliand 42: 3479–80)
b. *ef he* **im** *than lâtid is môd twehon*
if he.NOM REFL.DAT then lets.3SG his mind doubt.INF
'If he lets himself have doubts in his mind' (Heliand 16: 1374)

Late Middle English
(260) a. þat ye **me** cause so to smerte
that you me.OBL cause so to pain.INF
'that you cause me to hurt so much'
(G. Chaucer Troilus and Criseyde Book IV, 1448,
c.1374, cited from Zeefranz-Montag 1983: 132)

Old Norse-Icelandic
(261) a. Konungur lét **þeim** það víst betur henta.
king.NOM lets.3SG them.DAT it surely better suit.INF
'The king let them surely have what suited them better.'
(Grænlendingaþáttur, ch. 1)
b. ... láta **sér** nú sóma að fara til Íslands
let.INF REFL.DAT now befit.INF to go.INF to Iceland
'... [they] let it now befit them to go to Iceland.' (Vatnsdæla saga, ch. 10)
c. Eiríkur ... kvað **þeim** ekki mundu duga að
Eiríkur.NOM said them.DAT not would.3SG avail that
'Eiríkur ... said they would not find it sustainable that ...'
(Grettis saga, ch. 7)

Old Swedish
(262) lät **thik** äkke ledhas vidh at thänkia
let.2SG you.OBL not be.saddened.INF with to think
thz som ...
that which
'Don't let yourself get sad thinking about that which ...'
(Bo 183, c.1380–1400)

Old Danish
(263) schulæ wy ladæ **oss** ... nøghæ meth thet
shall.1PL we let us.OBL find.sufficient.INF with it
'We shall let ourselves ... find it sufficient' (D. Mag. IV. 364, c.1407)

To this I add a Gothic raising-to-object example, in order to demonstrate the existence of this construction in Gothic, despite the lack of such examples with oblique subjects in the Gothic language.

Gothic
(264)   letiþ   **þans**   gaggan.
        let.2PL those.ACC go.INF
        '[you] let them go.'   (John 18:8)

All the examples in (258–264) above involve the raising-to-object verb 'let', except for the Old Norse-Icelandic one in (261c), *kveðast*, which means 'say about oneself'. All the lower verbs in (258–261) select for dative subjects, while the corresponding verbs in Old Swedish and Old Danish in (262–263) occur with a generalized oblique subject, since accusative and dative subjects are in the process of merging at that time.

The examples in (258–261) all involve dative subject verbs, although raising-to-object constructions have also been found with accusative subject verbs in Old Saxon and Old Norse-Icelandic, as is shown in (265–266) below. These verbs are *gihungrjan* 'hunger', *saka* 'be harmed' and *dreyma* 'dream'.

Old Saxon
(265) a. Sô   he   **ina**   thô   **gehungrean**   lêt
          since   he.NOM REFL.ACC   then   hunger.INF   lets.3SG
          'Since he then lets himself hunger.'   (Heliand 13:1059)

Old Norse-Icelandic
(266) a. Þórir   kvað   **sig**   eigi   **saka**   mundu
          Þórir.NOM   said.3SG   REFL.ACC   not   be.harmed.INF   would.INF
          'Þórir said that he would not be harmed.'   (Gull-Þóris saga, Ch. 12)
      b. Kolur   kvað   **sig**   **dreymt**   hafa   Hákon
          Kolur.NOM   said.3SG   REFL.ACC   dreamt   have.INF   Hákon.ACC
          jarl   um   nóttina
          earl.ACC   of   night.the
          'Kolur said that he had dreamt Earl Hákon during the night'
                                                       (Brennu-Njáls saga, Ch. 82)

Observe that the accusative subjects of OS *gihungrjan* 'hunger', ON-I *saka* 'be harmed' and ON-I *dreyma* 'dream' maintain their accusative case in raising-to-object constructions, thus yielding in essence the same case as is assigned by the matrix verb or the construction itself, namely accusative. This is different for oblique subject verbs that occur with dative subjects, as when these verbs are embedded under raising-to-object constructions, the dative case is actively seen in the raising construction, as is evident from the dative case of the "raised" subjects in (258–261) above.

Turning now to the raising-to-object verbs themselves, well known raising-to-object verbs in the Germanic languages involve not only the causative 'let', but also perception verbs like 'see' and 'hear, as well as verbs of saying and believing (cf. the discussion in Section 4.2.5 above). All these four verb classes are found in AcI constructions in Old Norse-Icelandic texts, i.e. in native texts which are not translations (cf. Kristoffersen 1996: Ch. 5). Note that with the term *AcI* or *raising-to-object*, I only refer to bare infinitives and not *to*-infinitives.

Harbert (2007: 261–264) discusses the state-of-affairs in Gothic where causatives like 'let' and perception verbs are documented in the raising-to-object construction. Harbert also reports that verbs of saying and believing may instantiate the raising-to-object construction, of which one example of a *believe*-type verb is particularly interesting, as it deviates from the Greek original, where the control verb *elpizō* 'hope' is used instead:

Gothic
(267) a. [ik] wenja **mik** hvo hveilo **saljan** at izwis
 I hope me.ACC one while stay.INF with you
 '[I] hope to stay with you for a while' (Cor I. 16: 7)

Even though most of the examples in (258–264) above are with the verb 'let', it is well known that perception verbs are also found in this construction in Old English (cf. Los 1998; Fischer 1999; among others), as is evident from the following examples of both 'see' and 'hear' from Old English and Old Saxon.

Old English
(268) a. Ic **seah** wrætlice wuhte feower samed
 I.NOM saw.1SG wonderful creatures.ACC four.ACC together
 siþian
 travel.INF
 'I saw four wonderful creatures travel together' (Riddle 49, c.960–980)
 b. Ic ðæt londbúend, leóde míne, **secgan**
 I.NOM it.ACC land.inhabitants.ACC people.ACC my.ACC say.INF
 hýrde
 heard.1SG
 'I heard the landowners, my people, ... say it' (Beowulf 1346, c.900)

Old Saxon
(269) a. *That ... mannes sunu mêr **gisâhi** is selbes*
that man.GEN son.DAT more saw.3SG his own
*word sêrur **hrewan**,*
words sorely rue.INF
'That [he] ever saw the son of mankind sorely rue his own words'
(Heliand 59: 5009–5010)
b. *sô hwat sô siu **gihôrda** thea mann*
so what so she.NOM heard.3SG these.ACC men.ACC
sprekan
speak.INF
'Whatever she heard these men speak of' (Heliand 6: 437)

The lower verbs in these examples are the infinitives *siþian* 'travel', *secgan* 'say', *hrewan* 'rue' and *sprekan* 'say'. The "raised" subjects, *wuhte feower* 'four creatures' in (268a), *londbúend, leóde míne* 'the landowners, my people' in (268b) and *thea mann* 'these men' in (269b) are all in the accusative case, as is expected when a verb selecting for a nominative subject is embedded in raising-to-object constructions in Germanic.

Note, however, that the form *sunu* 'son' in (269a) is ambiguous between an accusative and a dative reading here. Nevertheless, since all other examples of *hrewan / hrewen* 'rue' in the Old Saxon Heliand unambiguously show that its subject is in the dative case, as is also discussed in Section 4.2.5 above, there is simply no corroborating evidence for assuming that *sunu* is anything but a dative. For that reason, *sunu* in (269a) is glossed as a dative and not as an accusative.

Leaving Old English and Old Saxon aside for the time being and turning to Old High German, Diewald and Smirnova (2010: 48) observe the existence of perception verbs in raising-to-object constructions already in the Old High German period. I have come across one such example with 'hear', given in (270a) below. Notice that the form of the "raised" subject in the manuscript is *sîa*, an unambiguous accusative form, as Notker consistently uses *sie* or *si* for the nominative.

Old High German
(270) a. *Álle natûrliche léicha únde álle rártâ hábet*
every natural body.ACC and every voice.ACC has.3SG
*tiu sêla in íro. Sô sîa **síngen hôret**.*
the.NOM soal.NOM in herself.DAT so her.ACC sing.INF hears.3SG
'every natural body and every voice the soul has within. When [one] hears her sing ...' (Notker, Boeth.Cons. V 258.5)

b. Sô   skînet   óuh   táz   tu   **chîst.**   tia
   so   evident also that you.NOM say.2SG   the.ACC
   uuênegheít ...   **háldên.**
   misery   hold.INF
   'It is also evident that you say the misery ... hold.'
   (Notker, Boeth.Cons. IV, 206.27)

Despite the fact that perception verbs occur in raising-to-object constructions in Old High German, Wolf (1981: 85) claims that structures involving raising-to-object are borrowed and do, for instance, not exist with verbs of saying during the earliest stages of German. Wolf's claims are, however, not entirely true, as (270b) above shows. Here the contracted form of *quedan*, *chîst* 'says' selects for a bare infinitive *haldên* 'hold', whose "raised" subject occurs in the accusative case, *tia uuênegheít* 'the misery'. This particular example is not a translation from the Latin original, as it belongs to Notker's further elaborations of the Latin text, meaning that this is not a calque from Latin. The same is true for the example with 'hear' in (270a), as neither of these have corresponding clauses in the Latin original.

Demske (2008: 157), however, analyzes the string *táz tu chîst* 'that you say', as an insertion in this example. She argues that the infinitival complement, *tia uuênegheít ... háldên* is instead the complement of *scînan* 'shine, appear' in the main clause in (270b). There are three problems with Demske's analysis. The first problem is that on an insertion analysis, *táz* is not a subordinating conjunction, 'that', as I analyze it in (270b) above, but is instead the object of 'say', and should thus be rendered as 'it'. However, the word order of the string, *táz tu chîst* 'that you say', does not suggest that *táz* is the object of *chîst* 'say', because if it were a topicalized object in this string, the word order would be different, namely *táz chîst tu*, as a topicalization of the object should trigger subject-verb inversion in Old High German.

The second argument against Demske's analysis is that *tia uuênegheít* 'the misery' is clearly in the accusative case, which speaks against a raising-to-subject analysis of *scînan* in this example, where a nominative would have been expected instead. To be accurate, Demske does not mention the term *raising-to-subject* for this example either, but proposes instead that *scînan* selects here for "non-finite verbal complements assigning accusative case to the subject argument *in situ*". Observe that a non-finite verbal complement in this case is the infinitive *háldên* 'hold'. The problem with this account is that i) it is unheard of in terms of its structural properties, and ii) that if the subject of the lower verb is staying *in situ*, i.e., in the position where it is base generated, there is no rationale behind it occurring in the accusative case, on Demske's account. Again, a nominative would have been expected instead. There is only one reason for why one would expect accusative assignment to the subject of the lower verb, and that is on a raising-to-object (AcI) account. Such an analysis is, in fact, motivated by the occurrence of one particular verb of saying, namely *chîst* 'say', located immediately before the non-finite complement in (270b), again corroborating an AcI analysis of the example.

The third problem with Demske's argument is that *scînan* does not select for infinitives in Old High German, either 'to'-infinitives or bare infinitives. Instead *scînan* exists i) as a main verb with the meaning 'shine', ii) as a copular verb, and iii) selecting for a subordinate clause headed by *dass* 'that' or *als ob* 'as if'. In contrast, the raising-to-subject pattern with *scînan* is not documented until the late 17th century (Diewald and Smirnova 2010: 252–255).

In order to support her analysis, Demske refers to the fact that corresponding structures with *apparent* 'appear' show up with the subject in the accusative. However, this particular example does not have a model in the original Latin text, either with *apparent* or with any other verb, for that matter. In other words, this example is not a translation. Therefore, on Demske's analysis, Notker would have imposed the general structure of Latin *apparent* 'appear' onto this example, even though this example is not a direct translation of *apparent*, as Demske admits herself.

In essence, all of this means that not only 'let' verbs can be reconstructed as selecting for raising-to-object infinitives in Proto-Germanic, but also perception verbs, verbs of saying and even verbs of believing. That is, 'let' is found in raising-to-object constructions in all three branches of Germanic, perception verbs are also found in all three branches, verbs of saying are found in native texts in both North and West-Germanic in addition to Gothic, while verbs of believing are found in two branches, North and East Germanic, of which the North Germanic examples are all found in native texts.

On the basis of the facts discussed above, I now turn to the relevant reconstructions for Proto-Germanic. I let it suffice to reconstruct four raising-to-subject verbs, namely 'let', 'see', 'hear' and 'say' on the basis of evidence from at least two Germanic branches in which the data stem from native texts. This excludes the reconstruction of verbs of believing for Proto-Germanic, at least for the time being. Since the phonological forms of the verbs 'let', 'see', 'hear' and 'say' have been reconstructed for Proto-Germanic by Germanic etymologists, I refrain from presenting correspondence sets for these forms here, and let it suffice instead to reconstruct lexical entries for these verbs, when occurring in the raising-to-object construction.

Consider now Figures 24–27 which demonstrate the reconstruction of the lexical entries of the four raising-to-object verbs 'let', 'see', 'hear' and 'say' for Proto-Germanic. The structure of each lexical entry is the same throughout, the only difference is the form of the verb itself and the semantic frame that the relevant verb invokes. This is the cause_frame for 'let', the see_frame for 'see', the hear_frame for 'hear' and the say_frame for 'say'.

```
*  lexeme

   FORM    < lētan- >

   SYN     ARG-ST {[1]NP-Nomᵢ}
           AGR [1]

   SEM     FRAMES   cause-fr
                    CAUSER              i
```

Figure 24: A Proto-Germanic reconstruction of the raising-to-object verb */lētan-* 'let' and its verb-specific properties.

I also let it suffice to only reconstruct here the properties needed for the instantiations of these verbs in the raising-to-object construction. Since these four verbs occupy the slot for the finite verb in the raising-to-object construction, it is essential that their nominative subjects also be reconstructed as a part of this enterprise. The remainder of the relevant morphosyntactic properties is, in fact, provided by the raising-to-object construction itself, shown in Figure 28 below.

```
*  lexeme

   FORM    < sewan- >

   SYN     ARG-ST {[1]NP-Nomᵢ}
           AGR [1]

   SEM     FRAMES   see-fr
                    SEEER               i
```

Figure 25: A Proto-Germanic reconstruction of the raising-to-object verb *sewan- 'see' and its verb-specific properties.

Figure 28 specifies the details of the reconstructed raising-to-object construction itself. This reconstruction is partial as it only involves the finite verb, the "raised" subject and the infinitive, while the subject of the finite verb is immaterial to the raising-to-object construction, as this subject comes from the finite verb itself. This is fleshed out in Figures 24–27 above.

5.4 Reconstructing subject behavior for Proto-Germanic

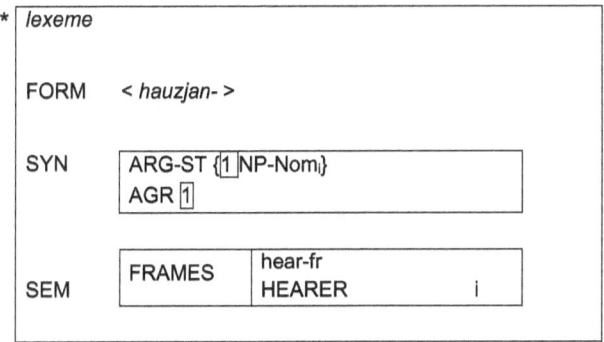

Figure 26: A Proto-Germanic reconstruction of the raising-to-object verb **hauzjan-* 'hear' and its verb-specific properties.

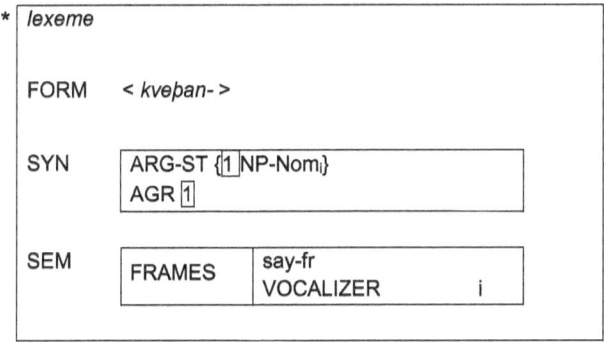

Figure 27: A Proto-Germanic reconstruction of the raising-to-object verb **kveþan-* 'say' and its verb-specific properties.

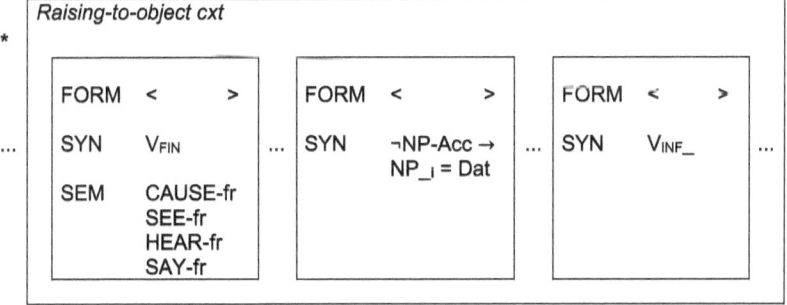

Figure 28: A reconstruction of the raising-to-object construction in Proto-Germanic.

The SEM field of the finite verb specifies that the construction is compatible with events involving causation, seeing, hearing and saying. This, in turn, secures that the four verbs in Figures 24–27, *lētan 'let', *sawan 'see', *hauzjan 'hear' and *kveþan 'say', can occupy the slot for the finite verb in individual instantiations of the raising-to-object construction in Proto-Germanic.

The middle box in the reconstruction in Figure 28 represents the "raised" subject, which is here specified as being in the accusative case, unless the first argument of the argument structure, NP_{-i}, is in the dative case. Now, one could argue that the accusative case marking need not be specified here, since all four verbs instantiating the finite verb slot of the construction, *lētan 'let', *sawan 'see', *hauzjan 'hear' and *kveþan 'say', assign accusative case to their objects. This is absolutely true. However, given that the dative overrides the accusative in cases where the lower verb selects for a dative subject, at least the override of the dative would have to be specified for the "raised" subject. This, in turn, means that the default accusative case might as well be defined here, as opposed to in the four lexical entries in Figures 24–27 above. Finally, the right-most box of the reconstruction in Figure 28 specifies that the lower verb is an infinitive. Exactly as with the raising-to-subject construction in the previous section, the properties of the infinitive verb itself come from the relevant lexical entry, including complement restrictions, etc.

Through the sequence of reconstructions presented in this section, not only the behavior of nominative subjects of the lower verbs turning up in the accusative, but also the behavior of dative subjects of the lower verbs, here turning up in the dative, may be reconstructed for Proto-Germanic. This means, in essence, that nominative subjects show up in the accusative case in raising-to-object constructions, while dative subjects maintain their dative case in that very same construction. More specifically, if the oblique subject is in the accusative, the case specifications of the "raised" subject and the case specifications of the object of the finite verb are in harmony, whereas if the subject case marking of the lower verb is in the dative, this dative will override the accusative case marking of the object slot. This is spelled out with the logical operators ¬ 'unless' and → 'then', meaning that the relevant "raised" subject should be in the accusative case, unless the subject of the lower verb is in the dative. If so, this argument should be case marked in the dative as well.

Another option would be to reconstruct two raising-to-object constructions for Proto-Germanic, one with accusative marking of the "raised" subject and the other with dative marking of the "raised" subject. However, given that the default marking of the object slot of the finite verb is accusative, and that the dative only occurs in cases where it has an overriding function over the accusative, the solution to only reconstruct one raising-to-object constructions instead of two, seems closest to the empirical facts, and, hence, closest to the linguistic reality at stake.

Before concluding this section, a question that arises is whether one should perhaps be reconstructing the full entries for both the raising-to-subject and the raising-to-object verbs discussed in Figures 21–22 and 24–27 above. That is, should one reconstruct all the specifications for these verbs, irrespective of whether these occur in the raising-to-subject constructions, the raising-to-object constructions, or as main verbs in their own right? My answer to that question is in the negative for the simple reason that this would require considerably more thorough reconstructions of the complement patterns of these verbs, complement patterns that are out of the scope of the present research. To be sure, within an enterprise involving the general reconstruction of verbs and their complementation patterns, one should definitely reconstruct the verbs 'begin', 'shall', 'let', 'see', 'hear' and 'say', both as auxiliary verbs and main verbs. However, a research exercise of the type conducted here focusing on grammatical relations in general and oblique subjects in particular, indeed restricts the goals of this study to the auxiliary uses of these raising-to-subject and raising-to-object verbs.

To conclude, the behavior of the subject of the lower verb in raising-to-object construction in Proto-Germanic may be modeled as described above, irrespective of whether this subject is in the nominative case or in the oblique case. I now turn to the penultimate reconstruction section, namely how to reconstruct control infinitives for Proto-Germanic.

5.4.4 Control infinitives

In Section 4.2.6 above, I present seventeen examples from the early Germanic languages of oblique subject verbs being embedded in control infinitives. Of these, one example comes from Gothic, three come from Old Saxon, two from Early Middle English, seven from Old Norse-Icelandic, three from Old Swedish and one from Old Danish. Of these, twelve examples are being documented here for the first time in the literature. These examples are repeated below, as they provide the input for the correspondence set on which basis control infinitives may be reconstructed for Proto-Germanic.

Gothic
(271) *hvazuh   saei   saihviþ   qinon   du   __   luston*
       whoever   who.NOM   sees   woman.ACC   to   PRO.ACC   lust.INF
       izos]
       her.GEN
       'whoever looks at a woman in order to lust for her.'
                    (Matthew 5:28, cited from Barðdal and Eythórsson 2012a: 386)

Old Saxon
(272) a. *gi   ni   thurƀun [__   **an   ênigun   sorgun   wesan** an*
         you.NOM not   need.2PL PRO.DAT at   any   sorrows be.INF   on
         ... *hugi   hwergin]*
             mind   nowhere
         'You need not feel any sorrows in [your] ... heart anywhere'
                                                     (Heliand 22: 1897–98)
     b. *bethiu ne   thurƀun ... [__   thius   werk*
         thus   not   need.2PL   PRO.DAT these.NOM   works.NOM
         tregan], [__   **hrewan** *mîn   hinfard]*
         regret.INF   PRO.DAT rue.INF   my.NOM   departure.NOM
         'therefore, you need not ... regret these deeds, nor rue my departure'
                                                     (Heliand 57: 4730–31)

Early Middle English
(273) a. *good   is,   quaþ   Joseph, [to   __   **dremen**   of   win*
         good   is   said   Joseph   to   PRO.OBL   dream.INF   of   wine
         'It is good, said Joseph, to dream about wine.'
                     (Gen. & Ex. 2067, c. 1250, cited from Cole et al. 1980: 730)
     b. *Him   burþ   [to   __   **liken**   well   his   lif]*.
         him.OBL ought   to   PRO.OBL like.INF   well   his   life
         'He ought to like his life well.'
                     (Dame Sirith: 82, c.1275, cited from Cole et al. 1980: 729)

Old Norse-Icelandic
(274) a. *Þorvaldur   kvaðst   [__   ólíklegt   **þykja]**   að   hún*
         Þorvaldur.NOM   said   PRO.DAT   unlikely   think.INF   that she
         'Þorvaldur said he found it unlikely that she'   (Fljótsdæla saga, ch. 5)
     b. *Þorsteinn   kvaðst   [þá   betra   __   **þykja]**   ef   hann*
         Þorstein.NOM   said   then   better   PRO.DAT think.INF   if   he
         'Þorsteinn said he found it better if he'   (Laxdæla saga, ch. 61)
     c. *Snorri   kvaðst   [__   einsætt   **þykja]**   að*
         Snorri.NOM   said   PRO.DAT   obvious   think.INF
         'Snorri said that he found it obvious that'   (Laxdæla saga, ch. 67)
     d. *Glúmur   kvaðst   [__   því   betur   **þykja]**   er*
         Glúmur.NOM   said   PRO.DAT   the   better   think.INF   which
         'Glúmur said that he found it better, which'   (Reykdæla saga, ch 18)

e. Þorbergur   kvaðst   [___   þetta   **þykja**]
    Þorbergur.NOM said   PRO.DAT   this.NOM   think.INF
    féfrekt]   en ...
    cost.consuming   but
    'Þorbergur said that he found this cost-consuming but ...'
                                                    (Reykdæla saga, ch. 28)

f. Mun   þeim   eigi   þykja   [___   **þungt**   **falla**
    will them.DAT   not   think.INF PRO.DAT grievous   find.INF
    að   svo
    at   such
    'They will not find this grievous, at this'
                                              (Ljósvetninga saga (C), ch. 24)

g. að   Gunnhildi   þótti   [___   hyggjuleysi
    that   Gunnhildur.NOM thought   PRO.DAT   thoughtlessness.NOM
    til **ganga** eða   öfund] ef ...
    til   go.INF   or   envy.NOM if
    'that Gunnhildur thought that [people's] intentions were colored by thoughtlessness or envy, if ...'   (Laxdæla saga, ch. 19)

Old Swedish

(275) a. Os   duger   ey   [thar   effter   ___   **langa**]
         us.DAT suffices   not   there   after   PRO.OBL   long.INF
         'It is useless for us to long for that.'
                         (Hertig Fredrik av Normandie, c.1308, cited from Falk 1997: 25)

      b. Huath   hiælper   idher   [ther   æpter   ___   **langa**]
         what   helps   you.OBL   there   after   PRO.OBL   long.INF
         'How does it help you to long for that?'
                                   (Herr Ivan 1229, c.1303, cited from Falk 1997: 25)

      c. Än   huat   är   at   til   ryggia   ganga   [vtan   ___
         but   what   is   to   to   back   go.INF   without   PRO.OBL
         angra   j   frestilsom   at   haua
         regret.INF   in   temptation   to   have.INF
         'But what is it to retreat and instead regret to have, in temptation, ...'
                  (Heliga Birgittas uppenbarelser IIII (Holm A 5a), ch. 20, c.1400–1425)

Old Danish

(276) Aldrigh   listær   mek   [fran   ether   at   ___   **langæ**]
      never   lusts   me.ACC   from   you   to   PRO.OBL   long.INF
      'I never want to long away from you'   (Ivan Løveridder (K4), 210, c.1485)

In addition to these examples involving oblique subjects, there are copious examples of nominative subjects being left unexpressed in control infinitives in the early Germanic languages. There is thus no doubt that this construction is inherited in Germanic and that only arguments corresponding to the subject of the lower verb in finite structures may be left unexpressed in constructions of this type. As such, a reconstruction of control infinitives for the grammar of Proto-Germanic is clearly well motivated.

The examples in (271–276) differ with respect to the nature of the finite verbs and who the controller of the unexpressed argument is. In the Gothic example in (271), in all three Old Saxon examples in (272), in the second Early Middle English example in (273b), six of the seven Old Norse-Icelandic examples in (274), the first Old Swedish example in (275a), and the only Old Danish example in (276), the unexpressed argument of the embedded verb is controlled by the subject of the finite verb. In five of these 14 examples, the subject of the matrix verb is itself an oblique subject. This is true for the Early Middle English example in (273b), the Old Norse-Icelandic examples in (274f–g), the Old Swedish example in (275a) and the Old Danish one in (276).

In contrast, it is the object of the finite verb that controls the unexpressed argument of the infinitive in the second Old Swedish example in (275b), whereas the unexpressed argument of the infinitive in the first Early Middle English example in (273a), the last Old Norse-Icelandic example in (274g) and the third Old Swedish example in (275c) are retrieved on the basis of the context, as these examples express generic statements. Thus, one may argue that the controller is arbitrary in these examples.

Since the predicate structure of the finite verb may vary as much as is found here, also resulting in differences with regard to which of the arguments of the finite verb, if any, is the controller, I suggest only a partial reconstruction of the control test for Proto-Germanic. This reconstruction involves only the structure of the control infinitive itself, i.e. the unexpressed argument and the nonfinite embedded verb, as is shown in Figure 29.

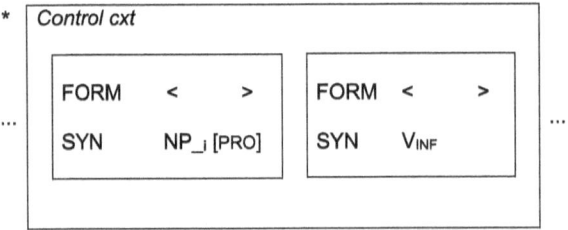

Figure 29: A partial reconstruction of control constructions in Proto-Germanic.

Since this is a schematic reconstruction involving no lexical material, the FORM fields in Figure 29 are both empty. The SYN field for the embedded verb to the right is specified as being in the infinitive form. In contrast, the SYN field for the subject of the embedded verb to the left specifies that this argument is unexpressed, marked as [PRO]. It is through the index *i*, that the matching of the unexpressed argument with the subject argument of the relevant lexical entry takes place, also indexed with *i*, of whichever verb it is that is the embedded verb occurring in this construction. For a comparison, see the modeling of the control infinitive with the verb 'like' in Modern Icelandic in Section 2.4.2 above.

5.4.5 Long-distance reflexivization

The last subject behavior to be discussed here is long-distance reflexivization which has been documented with nominative and oblique subjects in both Gothic and Old Norse-Icelandic (see Section 4.2.3 above). The examples involving oblique subject predicates are given below, since they provide the basis for the reconstruction of oblique subjects with this subject property in Proto-Germanic:

Gothic

(277) *þugkeiþ* **im**$_i$ *auk ei in filuwaurdein* **seinai**$_i$
 thinks.3SG them.DAT then that in many.words their.REFL
 andhausjaindau.
 would.be.heard.MP.3PL
 'then they think that due to their extensive speech, they would be heard.'
 (Matthew 6:7)

Old Norse-Icelandic

(278) a. *dreymdi* **hann**$_i$ *að* **Bárður faðir sinn**$_i$ *kæmi til hans*
  dreamt he.ACC that Bard father REFL came to him
  'he dreamt that his father Bard came to him'
  (Bárðar saga Snæfellsáss, Ch. 21)
 b. *þá líkar* **honum**$_i$ *eigi þarvist þeirra og þykir eigi*
  then likes he.DAT not stay their and finds not
  örvænt að þeir muni þar eflast ætla til
  impossible that they will there strengthen intend to

móts   við   **sig**_i_.
against with REFL
'he does not like their stay there and does not find it impossible that they intend to gain strength and turn against him.'

(Geirmundar þáttur heljarskinns)

What is typical for long-distance reflexivization is that the reflexive in a subordinate clause is bound by the subject of the matrix clause. The reflexive element itself may be a part of the subject of the subordinate clause, the object of the subordinate clause or it may be found in an adverbial phrase.

The reconstruction of long-distance reflexivization is given in Figure 30, which is a schematic reconstruction with no lexical material. Hence, the FORM field is empty in all the boxes in Figure 30. The first internal box represents the matrix subject, defined as NP_i, while the second box consists of the subordinate clause. This is, in turn, divided into two elements, the one containing the subjunction, defined as SUBJ, marking that this is a subordinate clause, and the one containing the reflexive, defined as REFL, in the SYN fields.

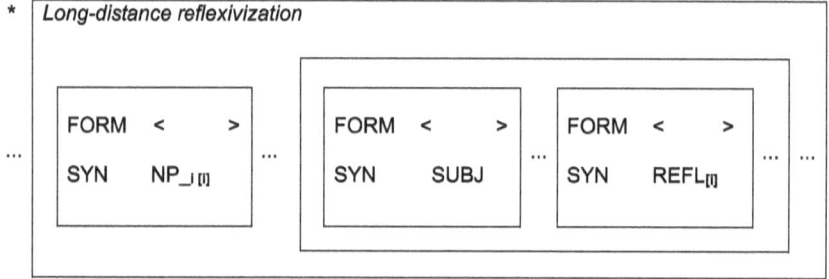

Figure 30: A reconstruction of long-distance reflexivization in Proto-Germanic.

The binding relation itself is given with an index, _i_, here occurring in square brackets to differentiate it from the co-indexing between the arguments in the ARG-ST and the semantic roles in the SEM field of lexical entries and the relevant argument structure constructions (cf. the discussion in 2.2.3–2.2.4 above). Since the reflexive in the subordinate clause is not confined to any specific syntactic argument, the only formalization that is needed is the binding of the reflexive with the subject of the man clause. This is given with the index _i_ in the square brackets in Figure 30, shown with a co-indexation of the subject of the matrix clause and the reflexive in the subordinate clause.

Having now demonstrated how the subject tests may be reconstructed for Proto-Germanic, i.e. through reconstructing the constructions relevant for these

subject tests and how the arguments behave with regard to the tests, it should be obvious how grammatical relations fall out from this. That is:
i) from the modeling of the subject as being the first argument of the argument structure, irrespective of its case marking
ii) from the reconstruction of lexical entries of verbs
iii) from the reconstruction of the constructions that make a distinction in the behavior of subjects and objects
iv) through proper coindexing of each argument across lexical entries and clausal constructions
v) grammatical relations fall out directly

This completes my reconstruction of grammatical relations for Proto-Germanic, including the reconstruction of oblique subjects.

5.5 Summary

Initially, in this chapter, I laid out the main arguments that have been put forward in the literature within historical syntax against syntactic reconstruction. These are i) lack of cognates, ii) lack of arbitrariness, iii) lack of directionality in syntactic change, iv) lack of continuous transmission, and finally v) lack of form–meaning correspondences. I claim that these objections have a limited validity and then go on to show, instead, how syntactic reconstruction may be carried out.

It is a general rule in historical-comparative linguistics that one should not reconstruct for a common proto-stage unless there is material supporting such a reconstruction from at least three of the daughter branches. There are several verbs and compositional predicates, selecting for oblique subjects, found across two or three of the branches, which lend themselves to syntactic reconstruction. In order to demonstrate how the comparative method may be applied to syntax, first a correspondence set was set up for the verb 'suffice' to show how the form of the verb itself may be reconstructed. Then examples were provided to document the relevant argument structure constructions found for this verb in the earliest stages of Germanic. This comparison reveals that there are two different, but etymologically related verbs that are found in the daughter languages with the meaning 'suffice', reconstructable as *ga-nahan and *ga-nōgjan.

The first of these two verbs, *ga-nahan, is a preterite-present verb, documented in Gothic, Old English and to a limited extent in Old High German. The case frames found in the individual usage examples of this verb show a considerable diversity, Acc-only, Acc-Nom and Dat-Nom in Gothic, and Nom-Gen and Obl-only in Old English. The second verb, *ga-nōgjan, is deadjectival and occurs with three different case frames in Middle High German, of which Acc-Gen and Dat-Gen are the most prominent ones. In Old Norse-Icelandic, in contrast, the argument structure of this verb appears to be limited to Dat-Nom. These case frames are not particularly compatible with each other, thus the chances of a successful reconstruction appear to be limited.

Nevertheless, a supplementary study reveals that the *jan*-verb could also occur as a ditransitive, instantiating the Nom-Acc-Dat case frame in both Gothic and Old Norse-Icelandic. This case frame is still not compatible with the case frames listed above, found for the two etymologically related verbs, **ga-nahan* and **ga-nōgjan*. This is where the concept of oblique anticausativization comes into play. Since the case frame Acc-Gen can not be a valency-reduced alternant of Nom-Acc-Dat, which is what is attested in Gothic and Old Norse-Icelandic, the only viable option is to internally reconstruct a causative ditransitive for the prehistory of German as having been Nom-Acc-Gen, which eventually ousted the earlier prehistoric Nom-Acc-Dat case frame in the Irminonic branch of West Germanic. Such a reconstruction is, in fact, supported by the case frames found for ditransitive verbs in Old High German, where Nom-Acc-Dat is not documented, whereas Nom-Acc-Gen is. Hence, through a reduction in valency from three arguments to two arguments, i.e. from Nom-Acc-Gen to Acc-Gen, the Acc-Gen case frame documented with the *jan*-verb may have arisen.

Finally, the methodological steps for reconstructing grammatical relations are the following. First, one must identify the relevant subject tests applicable for the earliest stages of the daughter languages. During this process, one also establishes which of the subject behaviors are reconstructable for a proto-stage. These methodological steps were taken in Chapter 4 above. In this chapter, the latter part of the procedure has been carried out, namely a) through setting up correspondence sets for, and reconstructing, some of the lexical verbs which one may with good reason assume existed in the proto-language, b) through setting up correspondence sets for the argument structure of verbs and, following that, through reconstructing these argument structures, c) through actually reconstructing the constructions which function as subject tests in Proto-Germanic. These subject tests involve neutral word order, raising-to-subject, raising-to-object, control infinitives and long-distance reflexivization in Germanic.

Through this process of reconstructing the argument structure constructions for lexical verbs and of reconstructing subject behavior, it is also defined, through co-indexation for each subject test, how the relevant arguments behave in that construction. Through this methodological procedure, the subject relation falls out. This is all it takes to reconstruct grammatical relations for a proto-stage.

6 Modern German: An anomaly?

In the two previous chapters it is shown that a) potential oblique subjects behave syntactically as subjects in the early Germanic languages, and b) that oblique subjects may even be reconstructed for Proto-Germanic. The first of those, that there are oblique subjects in the early Germanic languages, is established on the basis of several subject tests that have been shown to be valid for the modern Germanic languages, of which a subset is also valid for the earlier stages of Germanic. These syntactic behaviors involve long-distance reflexivization, word order, raising-to-subject, raising-to-object and control infinitives. As such, the behavior of oblique subjects in the earliest Germanic strata conforms to the subject definition suggested in Section 2.3.3 above, with the subject being the first argument of the argument structure.

In the preceding chapter, I demonstrate how each of these syntactic behaviors may be reconstructed for Proto-Germanic, using the Attributed Value Matrix of Construction Grammar, already introduced in Chapter 2 above in relation to how to model subject behavior in the grammar of modern languages. In addition to reconstructing these five syntactic behaviors, long-distance reflexivization, word order, raising-to-subject, raising-to-object and control infinitives, I also reconstruct lexical entries and argument structure constructions for verbs and demonstrate how grammatical relations fall out from these reconstructions, including the behavior of oblique subjects in Proto-Germanic.

This brings us to the final piece of this puzzle, namely Modern German, and whether that language conforms to the overall story drawn up in the previous chapters. This is especially pertinent given the fact that it is generally assumed that oblique subjects are syntactic objects in German (cf. Reis 1982), resulting in a major divide between the two languages, Modern Icelandic and Modern German, in this respect. I repeat *for emphasis*: potential oblique subjects have been analyzed as syntactic subjects in Icelandic, while their equivalents in German are analyzed as syntactic objects (cf. Zaenen, Maling, and Thráinsson 1985; Sigurðsson 1989, 1992, 2004).

Section 6.1 below starts with a short discussion of argument structure and subject status in German, underlining an inconsistency in the German scholarly literature, namely that the first argument of the argument structure (see 2.2.3 for criteria) is assumed to be the subject of all verbs except Dat-Nom and Acc-Nom verbs (cf. Bayer 2004: 70; Wunderlich 2009: 592; Schlesewsky and Bornkessel 2006). For those, the subject is taken to be the second argument of the argument structure, as *ad hoc* as that may sound. Thereafter, in Section 6.2, a presentation is given of the main arguments put forward in the existing literature against analyzing oblique subjects as syntactic subjects in Modern German.

Then, Section 6.3 outlines the arguments for analyzing dative subject verbs in Modern German as alternating predicates of the type introduced in Chapter 3 above. This means that these verbs instantiate two different argument structure constructions, Dat-Nom and Nom-Dat, which in turn explains the subject behavior of both the dative and the nominative, hitherto a paradox within German linguistics. Section 6.4 lays out the most optimal way to model the behavior of alternating predicates in German with the constructional formalism employed here.

6.1 Argument structure and subject status in German

Starting with argument structure, there is a general consensus in the scholarship on German that verbs like *gefallen* 'like, please' in (279a), *gelingen* 'succeed' in (279b), and others of that type are Dat-Nom verbs in that language. In essence, this means that the dative is the first argument of the argument structure, while the nominative is the second argument of the argument structure (cf. Bayer 2004; Haider 2005; Schlesewsky and Bornkessel 2006; Wunderlich 2009), as is outlined in Figure 31 below.

German
(279) a. ***Mir*** *gefällt die **neue Version*** *vom Huawei*
me.DAT likes the.NOM new version of Huawei
Browser nicht.
browser not
'I do not like the new version of the Huawei browser.'
b. ***Dem*** *FCW gelingt eine **Reaktion**.*
the.DAT FCW succeeds a.NOM reaction
'The FC Winterthur succeeded with a good reaction.'

The same is true for verbs like *interessieren* 'enthuse, be enthused', which select for an accusative for the animate argument but a nominative for the inanimate one, shown in (280) below. Such verbs are generally assumed to be Acc-Nom verbs, with the accusative being the first argument of the argument structure and the nominative the second argument of the argument structure.

German
(280) a. ***Mich*** *interessiert **die Stadt** und **ihr Wandel**.*
me.ACC is.enthused the.NOM city and her change
'I am enthused by the city and its change.'

This analysis of the order of the arguments in the argument structure is entirely in line with that of verbs like *líka* 'like' in Icelandic, as is discussed in Section 2.3.3 above, where the argument structure of *líka* 'like' and the relevant lexical entry are modeled, both of which are repeated here, as they appear to be equally applicable to verbs like *gefallen* 'like' and *gelingen* 'succeed' in German. The same is, of course, true for *interessieren* 'enthuse, be enthused', except that the dative would be replaced with an accusative in Figures 31–32 below.

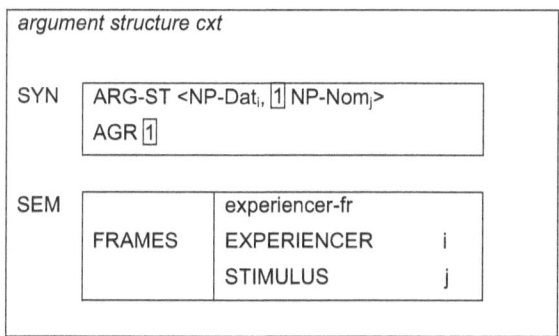

Figure 31: Dat-Nom argument structure construction.

First, the argument structure construction in Figure 31 contains two fields, a SYN field and a SEM field, as has been repeatedly discussed in Chs. 2, 3 and 5 above. Second, the argument structure (ARG-ST), as defined in the SYN field, contains two arguments, a dative and a nominative, of which the nominative agrees with the verb. What is most important here is that the internal order of the two arguments is fixed in the argument structure, with the dative preceding the nominative. This stands in stark contrast to the lexical entry, where the order of the arguments is not fixed, as is indicated with curly brackets in Figure 32, as opposed to angled brackets in Figure 31. Therefore, it is not until the verb *gefallen* 'like, please' from the lexical entry in Figure 32 enters the argument structure in Figure 31 that the order of the dative and the nominative becomes fixed.

Given the common consent in the German scholarship that the argument structure of verbs like *gefallen* 'like, please' and *gelingen* 'succeed' is Dat-Nom, it appears that the modeling in Figures 31–32 should indeed suffice for accounting for the facts in German as well as in Icelandic. This, however, is not the case, as will become evident in Section 6.3 below. As it happens, there is a major difference between *líka* 'like' in Icelandic and *gefallen* 'like, please' in German, as *líka* is a non-alternating Dat-Nom verb in Icelandic, while *gefallen* turns out to be an alternating Dat-Nom /

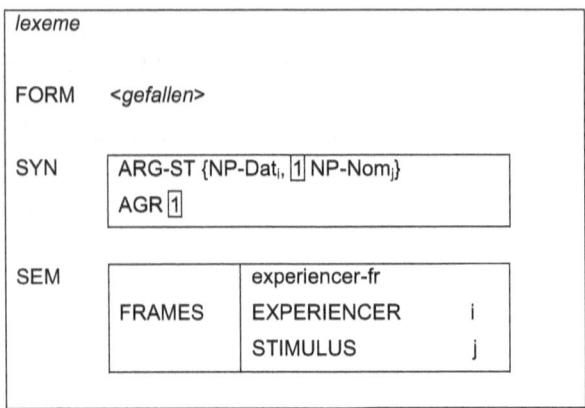

Figure 32: Lexical entry for German *gefallen*.

Nom-Dat verb in German (cf. Barðdal and Eythórsson 2003b; Barðdal, Eythórsson, and Dewey 2014, 2019, Somers and Barðdal 2022, 2023).

Turning now to subject status, it is generally assumed that the subject in German is in the nominative case and agreeing with the verb (cf. Reis 1982, and the references cited in Section 2.1.1). Hence, the first argument of all Nom-Acc verbs in German is also the subject. The same is true for all Nom-Dat verbs and Nom-Gen verbs in German. However, the situation is different for Dat-Nom and Acc-Nom verbs in German, i.e. for *gefallen*, *gelingen* and *interessieren*, as for such verbs the subject is not taken to be the first argument of the argument structure, but instead the subject is implicitly defined as being the second argument of the argument structure.

As a consequence, there is a major discrepancy across argument structures in German with regard to which argument of the argument structure is taken to be the subject; for Nom-**X** verbs the subject is defined as the first argument of the argument structure, while for **X**-Nom verbs, the subject is defined as the second argument of the argument structure (with **X** equalling accusative, dative or genitive). Differently put, the subject is generally taken to be the first argument of the argument structure for all German verbs, except with these two verb classes, Dat-Nom and Acc-Nom verbs. This appears not only as gravely *ad hoc*, but also as unnecessarily complicating the analysis of grammatical relations in German.

In Section 6.3 below, I show how the definition of subject suggested in Chapter 2, namely as equating the first argument of the argument structure, may be upheld for all verbs in German and not only for Nom-Acc, Nom-Dat and Nom-Gen verbs. As a consequence, not only are there oblique subjects in Modern Icelandic, Modern Faroese, Gothic, Old English, Old Saxon, Old High German, Old Norse-Icelandic, Old Swedish and Old Danish, but there are also oblique subjects in Modern German.

6.2 Arguments against subject behavior of oblique subjects in German

As is discussed in Section 4.2.6 above, Cole et al. (1980: 721–727) present examples from Gothic showing that the nominative of *galeikan* 'like, please' takes on the behavioral properties of subjects, since it is the unexpressed argument in control infinitives. Equivalent examples have also been presented in the scholarship on Modern German, cited as evidence against analyzing the potential oblique subject as a syntactic subject.

German
(281) a. *Diese   Damen   versuchten,   __   mir   zu*
         these   ladies.NOM tried.3PL   PRO.NOM   me.DAT to
         gefallen
         like/please.INF
         'These ladies tried to please me.'   (Cole et al. 1980: 727)
      b. *Der   Roman   wurde   besprochen,   ohne   __*
         the.NOM   novel   was.3SG   discussed   without PRO.NOM
         *jemanden   ernsthaft   **interessiert**   zu   **haben***
         anyone.ACC   seriously   enthused   to   have.INF
         'The novel was discussed without it having seriously enthused anybody'
                                                            (Bayer 2004: 56)
      c. *Ich   hoffe,   __   ihm   zu   **gefallen***
         I.NOM   hope   PRO.NOM   him.DAT   to   like/please.INF
         'I hope to please him/to be liked by him'   (Wunderlich 2009: 590)

In (281a) it is the nominative of *gefallen* 'like, please', which is left unexpressed in the control infinitive on identity with *diese Damen* 'these ladies' in the matrix clause, while the dative *mir* 'me' behaves syntactically as an object. The same is true for the nominative of *gefallen* 'like, please' in (281c), which is left unexpressed on identity with the subject of the matrix clause, *Ich* 'I', whereas the dative *ihm* 'him' is expressed in this control infinitive, thus behaving as an object. Likewise, in (281b) it is the nominative of *interessieren* 'enthuse, be enthused', that is left unexpressed, thus behaving syntactically as a subject, while the accusative *jemanden* 'anyone' takes on the object role.

In addition to the subject behavior of the nominative with the Dat-Nom and Acc-Nom verbs above, another type of argument has also been cited as evidence against a subject analysis, namely *oblique subject's lacking ability to be left unexpressed* in conjunction reduction and control constructions in German. Consider first some examples of conjunction reduction, shown in (282) below:

German
(282) a. **Er   kam   und   __   **wurde   geholfen.**
       he.NOM   came   and   ø.DAT   was   helped
       Intended meaning: 'He came and received help.'   (Cole et al. 1980: 728)

   b. **Der   Mann   mag   die   Bibel   und   __   **gefällt**
       the.NOM man   likes   the.ACC Bible   and   ø.DAT   pleases
       der   Koran.
       the.NOM   Koran
       Intended meaning: 'The man likes the Bible and is pleased by the Koran.'
                                                             (Fanselow 2002: 239)

   c. **Mir   war   schlecht   und   __   **konnte   nicht**
       me.DAT   was   bad   and   ø.NOM   could   not
       aufstehen.
       up.stand
       Intendend meaning: 'I felt sick and could not get up.'   (Bayer 2004: 57)

   d. **Ich   konnte   nicht   aufstehen   und   __   **war   schlecht**
       I.NOM   could   not   up.stand   and   ø.DAT   was   bad
       Intended meaning: 'I could not get up and feelt sick'   (Bayer 2004: 57)

In (282a) it is the dative subject of *geholfen werden* 'be helped' that is left unexpressed on identity with the nominative subject *er* 'he' in the first conjunct, apparently resulting in ungrammaticality. In (282b), which is equally ungrammatical, the dative subject of *gefallen* in the second conjunct is left unexpressed on identity with the nominative subject of the first conjunct, *der Mann* 'the man.' In (282c) it is the nominative subject of *aufstehen können* 'be able to get up' that is left unexpressed on the basis of identity with the dative subject *mir* 'me' in the first conjunct, also resulting in ungrammaticality. And, finally, in (282d) it is the dative subject of *schlecht sein* 'feel bad' that is left unexpressed on identity with the nominative *ich* 'I' in the first conjunct, also yielding an ungrammatical sentence. The ungrammaticality of these examples does not appear to be due to semantic incompatibility of the two conjuncts, as it is perfectly logical that if one is feeling bad, one may have problems getting out of bed, as in (282c), and that one cannot get out of bed because one is feeling bad, as in (282d).

Consider now the examples in (283) below which show that the relevant dative subjects cannot be left unexpressed either in control infinitives in German.

German
(283) a. *Ich   versuchte, ___   diese   Damen   zu gefallen
            I.NOM   tried.3SG   PRO.DAT these   ladies.NOM to like.INF
            Intended meaning: 'I tried to like these ladies.'   (Cole et al. 1980: 727)
       b. *Ihr   gelang   es,   ___   nicht **gefolgt** **zu**
            her.DAT managed.3SG it   PRO.DAT not   followed   to
            werden.
            be(come).INF
            Intended meaning: 'She managed not to be followed.'
                                                          (Wunderlich 2009: 606)
       c. *Ich   versuche,   ___   nicht   Geld   zu **fehlen**.
            I.NOM   try.3SG   PRO.DAT not   money.NOM   to lack.INF
            Intended meaning: 'I try not to lack money.'   (Fanselow 2002: 242)
       d. *Sie   hoffte   ___   das   Buch   **zu** **gefallen**
            she.NOM hoped   PRO.DAT the.NOM book   to   like/please.INF
            Intended meaning: 'She hoped to like the book.' (Haider 2010: 38)
       e. *Ich   hoffe   ___   nicht   **übel**   **zu** **sein**.
            I.NOM   hope   PRO.DAT not   queasy   to   be.INF
            Intended meaning: 'I hope not to feel sick.'
                                              (Zaenen, Maling, and Thráinsson 1985: 478)
       f. *___   **Übel**   **zu**   **sein**   ist   unangenehm.
            PRO.DAT queasy   to   be.INF   is.3SG uncomfortable
            Intended meaning: 'It is not comfortable to feel queasy.'
                                              (Zaenen, Maling, and Thráinsson 1985: 478)

In (283a) it is the dative subject that is left unexpressed, while the nominative *diese Damen* 'these ladies' is spelled out, behaving syntactically as an object, yielding an ungrammatical example. In (283b) the dative subject of the passive *gefolgt werden* 'be followed' is left unexpressed on identity with a dative subject of the matrix clause *ihr* 'her', yet this example is ungrammatical. The same is true for (283c) where the dative subject of *fehlen* 'lack' is left unexpressed on identity with the nominative subject of the matrix verb, *ich* 'I', while the nominative *Geld* 'money', behaves syntactically as an object.

The same is true for the remaining examples in (283). In (283d) the dative subject of *gefallen* 'please, like' is the unexpressed argument of the infinitive, while the nominative *das Buch* 'the book' is spelled out, behaving syntactically as an object, also yielding ungrammaticality. Finally, in (283e–f) the dative subject of *übel sein* 'feel queasy' is left unexpressed, first on identity with a nominative subject, *ich* 'I', of the matrix clause, and second in a generic statement with the controller being retrievable from the context, again resulting in two ungrammatical examples. Notice, however, that on a subject analysis of the dative, examples like these should be grammatical, which they turn out not to be.

Regarding the ungrammaticality of *übel sein* 'feel queasy' in the control infinitives in (283e–f), consider an example already presented in Section 2.3.3 above, repeated here for convenience:

Control infinitives

(284) a. *Hier sind wir noch halb sinnlich, und es ist äusserst naturwidrig, hier alles verleugnen wollen, was Gott dem physischen Menschen zum Labsal und zur Erfrischung hie und da am Pfade unserer Wallfahrt aufgetischt hat: aber den Lebensweg darum pilgern, um an diesen Erquickungsorten zu schmausen,*

das	ist	so	verächtlich,	dass	man	das	Auge
this	is.3SG	so	disgusting	that	one	the	eye
davon	abwenden	muss	um		nicht	
therefrom	turn.INF	must.3SG	in.order.to	PRO.DAT	not	
übel	**zu**	**werden.**				
sick	to	become.INF				

(J.H. Jung-Stilling *Rede über den Werth der Leiden*, c.1789)

'Here we are still half sensuous, and it is very much against nature to abstain from everything here that the Lord has served the physical person for comfort and refreshment here and there on the path of our pilgrimage: but to take a pilgrimage on the path of life in order to feast at these rest places, that is so disgusting that one has to turn (the eye) away *in order not to feel sick.*'

In this example the control infinitive is, in fact, *übel zu werden* 'to become sick', with its dative subject being left unexpressed on identity with the indefinite *man* 'one' in the matrix clause. Observe that this is exactly the same *übel sein/werden* as in the ungrammatical examples in (283e–f) above.

While I do not question the ungrammaticality of the constructed examples in (283d–f) above, the one in (284) is an attested example coming from an Early Modern German philosophical text, *Rede über den Werth der Leiden* 'Lecture on the Significance of Suffering'. This text was published in the year 1789 and the author, Prof. Jung-Stilling, held academic positions at three different universities during his professional years, in Kaiserslautern, Heidelberg and Marburg. Thus, it is entirely

6.2 Arguments against subject behavior of oblique subjects in German — 283

out of the question to argue that the native speaker producing the example in (284) must have been unlettered, not monitoring his own writing.

As already discussed in Section 2.3.3 above, a scrutiny of Jung-Stilling's texts reveals a consistent use of a dative subject with this predicate and no examples of a nominative subject are documented. Therefore, there can be no doubt that the dative subject of *übel sein/werden* is the unexpressed argument in the control infinitive in (284), thus behaving syntactically as a subject. This shows that matters are not as clear-cut as the earlier scholarship on German has let us believe. While Zaenen, Maling, and Thráinsson (1985) claim that examples like (283e–f) with *übel sein/werden* are ungrammatical in control infinitives in German, such examples may, nevertheless, be documented in texts, in this case in a text from more than 200 years ago.

Compare, now, the examples of conjunction reduction in (282) above, which are ungrammatical in German, with the examples below which are entirely natural, according to my native speakers' judgments (here repeated from Section 2.3.3).

German
Accusative
(285) a. ***Mich*** schauderte und __ ekelte.
me.ACC felt.horrified.3SG and Ø.ACC felt.disgusted.3SG
'I felt horrified and disgusted.'

b. ***Mich*** hungert nach Süßigkeiten und __
me.ACC hungers.3SG for sweets and Ø.ACC
dürstet nach Flüssigkeiten.
thirsts.3SG for fluids
'I hunger for sweets and thirst for liquids.'

Dative
c. ***Mir*** wird('s) schlecht und __ graut('s) vor der
me.DAT is.3SG.it bad and Ø.DAT worries.3SG for the
Zukunft.
future
'I feel sick and worry about the future.'

In (285a) the accusative subject of *ekeln* 'feel disgusted' is left unexpressed on identity with the accusative subject of *schaudern* 'feel horrified'. In (285b) the accusative subject of *dürsten* 'thirst' is left unexpressed on identity with the accusative subject of *hungern* 'hunger'. In (285c) the dative subject of *grauen* 'worry' is left unexpressed on identity with the dative subject of *schlecht sein/werden* 'feel/become bad'. Observe that this is the same *schlecht sein/werden* 'feel/become bad' as in (282c) above, where it is presented as being ungrammatical in clauses containing conjunction reduction. Clearly, in (285c) it is not ungrammatical at all. Note also the identity in case marking between the unexpressed subject in the second conjunct and its controller, i.e. the subject of the first conjunct.

The final set of examples to be discussed here as arguments against a subject analysis of oblique subjects in German comes from Fanselow (2002: 240) and Haider (2005: 26–27). Haider claims that examples like those in (285) above cannot be regarded as conclusive evidence for a subject analysis of oblique subjects, since topicalized objects may also be left unexpressed in conjoined clauses in German, provided that the topicalized objects in both conjuncts have the same case marking. This is shown in (286a–b) below, from Fanselow (2002) and Haider (2005), respectively. In (286a) the two conjoined verbs are *helfen* 'help' and *assistieren* 'assist', which both select for a nominative subject and a dative object, while in (286b) the two conjoined predicates are *geholfen haben* 'be helped' and *werden schaden können* 'will be able to harm', also selecting for a nominative subject and a dative object. The structure of the two examples is exactly parallel.

German
(286) a. **Dem Arzt** hilft Hans und ___ assistiert Maria.
the.DAT doctor helps Hans.NOM and ø.DAT assists Maria.NOM
'Hans helps the doctor and Maria assists [the doctor].'
(Fanselow 2002: 240)

b. **Ihm** hat kein Rat geholfen und ___ wird keiner schaden können.
him.DAT has no advice.NOM helped and ø.DAT will no.one.NOM hurt can
'No advice has helped him and nobody will be able to harm [him].'
(Haider 2005: 26–27)

Needless to say, the order of the arguments in each of the two conjuncts in (286a–b) above deviates from neutral word order, as the dative objects occur in preverbal position in both conjuncts, followed by the finite verbs *hilft* 'helps' in the first conjunct and *assistiert* 'assists' in the second conjunct in (286a). Immediately following the two finite verbs, we find the nominative subjects *Hans* and *Maria*. This word order distribution is typical of subject-verb inversion, which takes place, for instance, when an object has been topicalized to preverbal position. Thus, the argument left unexpressed in the second conjunct in (286a) is the object of *assistieren* 'assist', here coreferental with the topicalized dative object of *helfen* 'help', *dem Arzt* 'the doctor'.

In the example in (286b), the two datives also occur in preverbal position, followed by the finite verbs *hat* 'has' in the first conjunct and *wird* 'will' in the second conjunct. Immediately following the two finite verbs, there are the two nominative subjects *Rat* 'advise' and *keiner* 'nobody', again with subject-verb inversion. There is no doubt that the dative object of *schaden* 'harm', which is coreferential with the topicalized dative object of *helfen* 'help', *ihm* 'him' in clause-initial position, is being left unexpressed.

Therefore, Haider argues, only examples where the subject occurs in an inverted position qualify as arguments for a subject analysis, since examples like (286) above where a topicalized object is left unexpressed in a conjoined clause on identity with a topicalized object of the first conjunct are also grammatical in German. Hence, on Haider's argumentation, the examples in (285) above may equally well be analyzed as involving two topicalized dative objects.

Haider gives the following examples as evidence that only nominative subjects may be left unexpressed in structures where the subject of the first conjunct occurs in inverted position in German (Haider's 33a and 33c):

German
(287) a. In   den   Wald   ging   **der**   **Jäger**   und   __   schoss
         in   the   woods went   the.NOM   hunter   and   Ø.NOM shot
         einen Hasen
         a.ACC hare
         'Into the woods the hunter went and shot a hare.'
      b. *Im   Zoo   schauderte **mir**   vor   Bären   und   __
         in.the zoo   shuddered   me.DAT   for   bears   and   Ø.DAT
         würde auch im   Wald   davor   schaudern.
         would also in.the woods   for.it shudder
         Intended meaning: 'In the Zoo I shuddered at bears and would also shudder at them in the woods.'

However, there are four problems with a topicalized object analysis of the examples in (285), also relevant for the examples in (287). The first problem is that the examples in (286) with topicalized objects in conjoined clauses represent marked structures in German, to say the least, while the examples in (285) represent neutral word order. This simply rules out a topicalization analysis of (285), only leaving a subject analysis available for examples of this type.

The second problem with Haider's claims is that structures like in (287b) above are not entirely good in Icelandic either, as the following examples show:

Icelandic
(288) a. Inn   í   skóginn   fór   **veiðimaðurinn**   og   __
          in   to   woods.the went   hunter.the.NOM   and   Ø.NOM
          skaut   héra.
          shot   hare.ACC
          'Into the woods the hunter went and shot a hare.'
     b. ??En   gengur   **þér**   raunverulega   vel   með   þetta   og
          but   goes   you.DAT   really   well   with   this   and
          __   mun   ganga   vel   með   þetta   seinna   líka,
          Ø.DAT   will   go   well   with   this   later   also
          heldurðu?
          believe.you
          Intended meaning: 'But are you really doing well with this and will you continue to do well with this later on as well, you think?'
     c. ??En   leiðist   **þér**   þetta   virkilega   og   __
          but   be.bored   you.DAT   this.NOM   really   and   Ø.DAT
          mun   leiðast   þetta   seinna   líka,   heldurðu?
          will   be.bored   this.NOM   later   also   believe.you
          Intended meaning: 'But are you really bored by this and will you continue to be bored by this later on as well, you think?

Note that the English translations of (288b–c) are also not entirely grammatical either if the subject is left unexpressed in the second conjunct, exactly like their Icelandic translational equivalents and the German example in (287b):

English
(289) a. ??But are **you** really doing well with this and __ will continue to do well with this later on as well, you think?
     b. ??But are **you** really bored by this and __ will continue to be bored by this later on as well, you think?

The examples in (288b–c) and (289) include inverted structures because these are questions, but there is no a priori reason to believe that questions are more inclined to disallow the subject of the second conjunct to be left unexpressed than ordinary statements. This is confirmed by the Icelandic example below where a nominative subject of the second conjunct is left unexpressed in a question, without that resulting in ungrammaticality:

Icelandic
(290) a. Fer   **veiðimaðurinn** inn   í   skóginn   og   __
          goes   hunter.the.NOM   into   to   woods.the   and   Ø.NOM
          mun   skjóta   héra?
          will   shoot   hare.ACC
          'Does the hunter go into the woods and shoot a hare?'

The third problem is that, despite Haider's agnosticism, some examples involving an inverted oblique subject in the first conjunct appear to be entirely grammatical in German:

German
(291) a. *Deswegen*   **hungert**   **mich**   *nach   Süßigkeiten   und*
          therefore   hungers.3SG   me.ACC   for   sweets   and
          und __   **dürstet**   *nach   Flüssigkeiten.*
          and   Ø.ACC   thirsts.3SG   for   fluids
          'That's why I hunger for sweets and thirst for liquids.'
     b. *Deswegen*   **wird('s) mir**   *schlecht   und* __
          therefore   is.3SG.it me.DAT   bad   and   Ø.DAT
          graut('s)   *vor   der   Zukunft.*
          worries.3SG   for   the   future
          'That's why I feel sick and worry about the future.'

The German conjunction *deswegen* 'therefore' triggers subject-verb inversion, resulting in the accusative subject *mich* 'me' in (291a) and the dative subject *mir* 'me' in (291b) occurring immediately following the finite verbs *hungern* 'hunger' and *wird('s)* 'is (it)', respectively. This inverted position of the accusative subject in the first conjunct in (291a) has no consequences with regard to whether or not the accusative subject in the second conjunct may be omitted or not, as (291a) and (285b) are equally grammatical. The same is true for (291b) and (285c). Therefore, examples like the ones in (291) not only exclude an object analysis of the accusatives in (291a) and the datives in (291b), but are also only compatible with a subject analysis.

Fourth, if Haider is correct that dative subjects are not subjects but objects, they should align with topicalized objects in conjunction reduction. That is, a dative subject in second conjunct should be omissible on identity with a topicalized object in the first conjunct. Such examples, however, are ungrammatical, as is shown in (292a).

German
(292) a. *__Dem   Arzt   hilft   Hans   und ___   wird('s)__
the.DAT doctor helps Hans.NOM and ∅.DAT is.3SG.it
schlecht.
bad
Intended meaning: 'Hans helps the doctor and (the doctor) feels bad.'
b. ??__Mir   wird('s)__   schlecht   aber ___   hilft   keiner
me.DAT is.3SG.it bad but ∅.DAT helps no.NOM
Artzt
doctor
Intended meaning: 'I'm feeling sick but no doctor helps (me).

As its corollary, a topicalized dative object in second conjunct should be omissible on identity with a dative subject in the first conjunct, on Haider's analysis that oblique subjects are objects. Such examples are also ungrammatical, as is shown in (292b).

The ungrammaticality of the examples in (292) show that restrictions on omissibility in second conjuncts in German is not only tied to morphological case identity of the omitted argument and its controller in the first conjunct, but also that identity in grammatical relations is required. The examples in (292) are ungrammatical because the datives with *schlecht werden* are oblique subjects and not preposed objects, as Haider conjectures.

In Section 2.3.3 above, I suggest a "restricted ellipsis" analysis, as opposed to a "non-subject" analysis of oblique subjects in German, on the basis of the ungrammaticality of examples like the ones in (282–283) above and the unexpected grammaticality of corresponding examples of the type in (284–285) above. This "restricted ellipsis" analysis presupposes an independent definition of subject, or at least a definition that can be independently applied, in this case that the subject is regarded as the first argument of the argument structure. On such a subject definition, there are indeed oblique subjects in German, while the more interesting question arises as to why at all ellipsis is restricted in the way it is in German (see Barðdal 2006 for suggestions).

Having now dealt with the ungrammaticality of the German examples in (282–283) above, thus having dealt with the arguments against a subject analysis of oblique subjects in German, I use the remainder of this chapter to demonstrate that the reason that the examples in (281) above are grammatical is because Dat-Nom predicates in German are, in fact, alternating predicates of the type introduced in Chapter 3. This involves two argument structure constructions instead of only one, namely both Dat-Nom and Nom-Dat.

6.3 Alternating Dat-Nom / Nom-Dat predicates in German

The remainder of this chapter is devoted to showing that Dat-Nom verbs in German are alternating verbs, exactly like the Icelandic *falla í skaut* 'fall in lap', as opposed to Icelandic *skiljast* 'gather', which is a non-alternating Dat-Nom verb, as discussed in Section 3.1 above. In other words, I suggest that Icelandic has both alternating and non-alternating verbs and predicates, while German may only have verbs and predicates of the alternating type.

In the following subsections, I discuss word order (6.3.1), conjunction reduction (6.3.2), clause-bound reflexivization (6.3.3), raising-to-subject (6.3.4), raising-to-object (6.3.5) and control infinitives (6.3.6).

6.3.1 Word order

The German language is well known for having restrictions on word order within the midfield, with weak pronouns occurring before full NPs, nominative pronouns occurring before dative pronouns, etc. (Hawkins 1986; Lenerz 1992; Primus 1994; among others). For this reason, all word order examples presented here only involve full NPs.

It has also been acknowledged in the literature on German that there are some verbs for which both the Dat-Nom and the Nom-Dat word order appear to be equally neutral (Lenerz 1977: 112–116; Primus 1994: 67–68, 2012: 396; Haspelmath 2001; Eythórsson and Barðdal 2005; Barðdal, Eythórsson and Dewey 2014, 2019; Rott 2016), even though some individual differences between verbs may of course be found. Consider the following examples consisting of three pairs of German verbs, namely *behagen* 'be satisfied' (293), *gelingen* 'succeed' (294), and *genügen* 'find sufficient, have enough' (295) below:

German
Dat-Nom
(293) a. *Behagt* **den** **Bauern** *nicht* *der* **Augentrost** *auf*
 suits.3SG the.DAT farmers not the.NOM eyebright on
 den Wiesen?
 the meadows
 'Are the farmers not satisfied with the eyebright plants in the meadows?'

Nom-Dat

    b. *Behagen **fetter** und nasser **Boden** nicht den*
        suit.3PL fatty and wet.NOM soil.NOM not the.DAT
        ***empfindlicheren** Pflanzen?*
        sensitiver.DAT plants
        'Is nutritious and wet soil not satisfactory for the more sensitive plants?'

Dat-Nom

(294) a. *Gelingt **dem** Künstler nicht die **Relief-***
           succeeds.3SG the.DAT artist not the.NOM relief-
           ***Säule** aus 1981 an der Möllner Landstraße?*
           column from 1981 at the Möllner Land.street
           'Does the artist not succeed with the relief column from 1981 at Möllner Landstraße?'

Nom-Dat

    b. *Gelang **dieses Vorhaben** den Ruswilern*
        succeeded.3SG these.NOM endeavors the.DAT Ruswilers
        nun vollumfänglich und konnten sie ihren Vorsatz
        now completely and could they their intention
        umsetzen?
        realize
        'Were these endeavors of major success for the Ruswil research team and were they able to realize their intention?'

Dat-Nom

(295) a. *Genügt **dem** Wissenschaftler nicht die*
           suffices.3SG the.DAT scientist not the.NOM
           ***nackte Wahrheit**, will er auch ihr Röntgenbild sehen?*
           naked truth wants he also her X-ray see
           'Doesn't the scientist find the naked truth sufficient, does he also want to see her X-rays?'

Nom-Dat

    b. *Müssen **sechs Sekunden** dem Betrachter nicht*
        must.3PL six.NOM seconds the.DAT viewer not
        genügen…?
        suffice
        'Mustn't six seconds be enough for the viewer…?'

The (a) examples all show Dat-Nom word order with the dative preceding the nominative. All examples are construed as questions with the verb in first position and the dative immediately following the inverted verb, while the nominative follows the dative. In the (b) examples, in contrast, the word order is Nom-Dat. The (b) examples are also formulated as questions with the verb in first position. But this time, it is the nominative that follows the inverted verb, while the dative immediately follows the nominative.

The general syntax of German is no different from the remaining (non-English) Germanic languages in that the subject precedes the finite verb in neutral word order, but inverts with it if another constituent occurs in first position and in V1 structures like questions. The (a) examples in (293–295) above therefore show that it is the dative that behaves syntactically as a subject, inverting with the finite verb, while the (b) examples in (293–295) above show that it is the nominative that behaves as a subject, inverting with the finite verb. In other words, these word order facts support an alternating Dat-Nom / Nom-Dat analysis for *behagen* 'be satisfied', *gelingen* 'succeed' and *genügen* 'find sufficient, be enough' in German, as both word orders are equally neutral.

In order to compare the examples above with ordinary Nom-Dat verbs in German like *ähneln* 'resemble', consider the following examples.

German
Dat-Nom
(296) a. Wird   ein   "Inventor"   einem   Erfinder   ähneln?
         will.3SG a.NOM   inventor   a.DAT   discoverer   resemble.INF
         'Will an "inventor" resemble a discoverer?'

??Nom-Dat
    b. ??Wird   einem   Erfinder   ein   "Inventor"   ähneln?
        will.3SG a.DAT   discoverer   a.NOM   inventor   resemble.INF
        Intended meaning: 'Will a discoverer resemble an "inventor"?'

Dat-Nom
(297) a. Hat   das   Weibchen   dem   Männchen   geähnelt?
         has.3SG   the.NOM   female   the.DAT   male   resembled
         'Did the female resemble the male?'

?Nom-Dat
    b. ?Hat   dem   Männchen   das   Weibchen   geähnelt?
        has.3SG   the.DAT   male   the.NOM   female   resembled
        Intended meaning: 'Did the male resemble the female?'

This comparison, between the Nom-Dat and Dat-Nom linear word order with *ähneln* 'resemble' shows that only (296a) and (297a) are fully acceptable. These are the examples in which the nominative precedes the dative in inverted position, while the examples in (296b) and (297b) where the dative precedes the nominative in inverted position are quite marked. This means that the examples in (296–297) show that *ähneln* is a Nom-Dat verb, which cannot instantiate the Dat-Nom argument structure construction in German, although it may of course instantiate a dative-before-nominative order if that involves topicalized linear order. Observe, however, that the alternation between Dat-Nom and Nom-Dat in German has hitherto neither been systematically investigated with regard to word order (from a processing perspective, see, however, Schlesewsky and Bornkessel 2006 and later work) nor from a corpus-based perspective of word order statistics (although, see Somers et al. 2023, for an ongoing investigation).

Let us now compare these German verbs with two Icelandic verbs, *geðjast* 'like, please' and *leiðast* 'be bored'. It is known from the Icelandic literature that *geðjast* is an alternating Dat-Nom / Nom-Dat verb, while *leiðast* does not participate in this alternation, instead only instantiating the Dat-Nom construction:

Icelandic
Dat-Nom
(298) a. *Geðjast* **mönnum** **þessi** **þróun**, *eða hvað?*
likes.3SG people.DAT this.NOM development.NOM or what
'Do people like this development, or what?'

Nom-Dat
b. *Geðjast* **þessi** **þróun** **mönnum**, *eða hvað?*
likes.3SG this.NOM development.NOM people.DAT or what
'Is this development to people's liking, or what?'

Dat-Nom
(299) a. *Leiðist* **Íslendingum** **meðalmennska**, *eða hvað?*
bores.3SG Icelanders.DAT mediocrity.NOM or
'Are Icelanders bored with mediocrity, or what?'

*****Nom-Dat**
b. **Leiðist* **meðalmennska Íslendingum**, *eða hvað?*
bores.3SG mediocrity.NOM Icelanders.DAT eða hvað?
Intended meaning: 'Is mediocrity boring to Icelanders, or what?'

The examples in (298–299) confirm the assumption in the literature that *geðjast* 'like, please' is an alternating verb in Icelandic, as both (298a–b) are grammatical, with the dative inverting with the verb in (298a), and the nominative occurring in the same inverted position in (298b). The same cannot be said about *leiðast* 'be bored' in (299). This verb cannot have the nominative inverting with the verb, hence the ungrammaticality of (299b), as only the dative can invert with the verb, hence the grammaticality of (299a).

This means that *geðjast* 'like, please' in Icelandic behaves in the same way as *behagen* 'be satisfied', *gelingen* 'succeed' and *genügen* 'find sufficient, be enough' in German, namely as an alternating verb, at least with regard to word order. Note, moreover, the contrast in grammaticality between Icelandic *leiðast*, on the one hand, and German *ähneln*, on the other, as *leiðast* may only instantiate the Dat-Nom construction in Icelandic, while *ähneln* may only instantiate the Nom-Dat construction in German. It should be noted here that the Icelandic equivalent of *ähneln*, i.e. *líkjast* 'resemble', also only instantiates the Nom-Dat construction in that language. Thus, the difference between Icelandic and German only relates to verbs like *leiðast* which are exclusively Dat-Nom verbs in Icelandic, while the German Dat-Nom verbs investigated so far appear to be of the alternating type. Whether all Dat-Nom verbs in German are alternating needs to be further explored (cf. Somers et al. 2023).

A study of word order properties of four alternating and four non-alternating verbs in Icelandic has been carried out by Rott (2013), although that study compares word orders irrespective of whether the arguments are nouns or pronouns. Rott establishes a clear difference in the frequencies of alternating and non-alternating verbs, while the comparison presented below is confined to full NPs in German in order to steer away from whatever effects pronouns may have on word order.

As a first step in the investigation of the word order properties of alternating verbs in German, consider the frequencies presented in Table 19 (cf. Somers and Barðdal 2023). These were obtained through the same methodological procedures as the Icelandic frequencies presented in Table 5 in Section 3.1.3 above, only this time the relevant corpus is the German Ten Ten 13 corpus, containing 16 billion lemmatized words. In order to compare the German frequencies with the Icelandic ones, the following three sets of verbs are used, which are either cognate to the Icelandic verbs or (near)-synonymous with them:

i) *helfen* 'help', *ähneln* 'resemble', *danken* 'thank' *vertrauen* 'trust', *widersprechen* 'contradict'
ii) *gefallen* 'like, please', *dünken* 'seem, appear', *grauen* 'dread', *leidtun* 'be sorry', *zufallen* 'receive'
iii) *geziemen* 'befit', *entgehen* 'fail to notice, be hidden' *genügen* 'suffice', *nützen* 'be of use', *reichen* 'suffice'

The *helfen* verbs are unambiguous Nom-Dat verbs with the subject in the nominative case and the object in the dative case. These verbs are included as a control set

Table 19: Dat-Nom and Nom-Dat linear order with three classes of verbs.

	Dat-Nom		Nom-Dat	
	N	f	N	f
A: Nom-Dat *helfen* verbs				
helfen 'help'	2	4%	53	96%
ähneln 'resemble'	0	0%	129	100%
danken 'thank'	2	4%	49	96%
vertrauen 'trust'	1	2%	46	98%
widersprechen 'contradict'	10	10%	95	90%
B: Dat-Nom *gefallen* verbs				
gefallen 'like,please'	8	53%	7	47%
dünken 'seem, appear'	12	55%	10	45%
grauen 'dread'	–	–	–	–
leidtun 'be sorry'	–	–	–	–
zufallen 'fall to, be awarded'	44	38%	77	62%
C: Dat-Nom/Nom-Dat *geziemen* verbs				
geziemen 'suit, befit'	16	44%	20	56%
entgehen 'fail to notice'	36	61%	23	39%
genügen 'suffice'	29	45%	35	54%
nützen 'be of use'	11	17%	53	83%
reichen 'suffice'	24	62%	15	38%

to establish a baseline for how frequent topicalizations are with full NPs in German. As the numbers in Table 19 show, topicalizations range from 0% to 10% with *helfen* verbs, depending on the verb. These numbers also show that topicalization is more frequent in German than in Icelandic where only 4% of the examples were topicalizations (see Table 5 in Section 3.1.3).

Another striking difference between Icelandic and German is that *gefallen* verbs, under B in Table 19, do not behave as unambiguous Dat-Nom verbs, like *líka* verbs do in Icelandic. For the verb *gefallen* 'like, please' itself, this does not come as a surprise, as it has been established by Barðdal, Eythórsson, and Dewey (2019) that *gefallen* is an alternating verb. However, for *dünken* 'seem, appear' and *zufallen* 'fall to, be awarded', the ratio between Dat-Nom and Nom-Dat word orders is 55% vs. 45% and 38% vs. 62%, respectively. These numbers certainly do not align with the numbers for topicalization under A in Table 19, but are instead aligned with the numbers for alternating verbs under C, where two distinct argument structure constructions are available, the Dat-Nom and the Nom-Dat argument structures.

For the last class of verbs, *geziemen* verbs under C in Table 19, the ratio between the Dat-Nom and Nom-Dat word orders ranges from 17% vs. 83% with *nützen* 'be of use' to 62% vs. 38% with *reichen* 'suffice'. All verbs in this class, except for *nützen* 'be of use', show a fairly even distribution across the two word orders, which again speaks for an alternating analysis of these verbs. These verbs therefore pattern with *gefallen* verbs and not with *helfen* verbs, except for perhaps *nützen*. This raises the question of whether frequencies may be used to distinguish between alternating predicates, on the one hand, and neutral word order and topicalizations, on the other, when the numbers are so skewed. It also raises the question of at which frequency to draw the line between the two, which clearly is a topic for further study.

To conclude this section, it appears that several Dat-Nom verbs in German are alternating verbs, exactly as in Icelandic, as several such verbs seem to occur in both the Dat-Nom and the Nom-Dat argument structure constructions in German without any difference regarding the neutrality of the two word orders. Whether all Dat-Nom verbs in German are alternating or not awaits further research. I now turn to the second subject behavior to be discussed in the context of German, namely conjunction reduction

6.3.2 Conjunction reduction

Consider, first, the Modern German examples in (300–302) below, involving the verbs *gelingen* 'succeed, turn out well', *gefallen* 'like, please' and *gut gehen* 'do well, have things turn out well':

German
Dat-Nom
(300) a. Angola hat sich endgültig und unwiderruflich für den Sozialismus entschieden. Das erklärte der Vorsitzende des MPLA-Partei der Arbeit und Präsident der Volksrepublik Angola, Agostinho Neto, in einem Interview.

Dem internationalen Imperialismus und der inneren
the.DAT international imperialism and the.DAT inner
Reaktion ist es nicht gelungen und ___ wird
reaction is it.NOM not succeeded and ø.DAT will
***es** nicht gelingen, Angola in die Knie zu zwingen, betonte Neto.*
it.NOM not succeed

'Angola has finally and irrevocably decided in favor of socialism. This was declared by the Chairman of the MPLA Party of Labor and President of the People's Republic of Angola, Agostinho Neto, in an interview. International imperialism and domestic reaction have not succeeded *and will not succeed* in bringing Angola to his knees, Neto stressed.' (*Neues Deutschland*, 23.01.1978)

Nom-Dat

b. *Es   ist   mir   nicht   gelungen   und   ___   wird*
   it.NOM is me.DAT not   succeeded and   ø.NOM will
   ***mir*   nicht gelingen. Ich   hab   die   Idee   aufgegeben.**
   me.DAT not   succeed   I   have the   idea   up.given
   'I have not succeeded *and will not succeed*. I have given up on the idea.'

Dat-Nom

(301) a. *Das   zieht   sich   die   Gesellschaft   hin,   mir*
        this   drags   REFL   the   society   onward me.DAT
        persönlich   kann   es   nicht   gefallen   und   ___   wird
        personally   can   it.NOM not   like.INF   and   ø.DAT will
        ***es*   nicht   gefallen,   weil   . . .**
        it.NOM not   like.INF   because
        'This drags on the company, I personally can not like it *and will not like it*, because . . .'

Nom-Dat

b. *Ja.   Aber   das   ist   etwas   kompliziert   und*
   yes   but   this.NOM is   somewhat   complicated   and
   *___   wird   **Ihnen**   nicht   gefallen,*
   ø.NOM will   you.DAT   not   please.INF
   'Yes. But this is somewhat complicated *and will not be to your liking*.'
                                        (SC Paderborn 07' facebook, October 2020)

Dat-Nom

(302) a. *Um meinetwillen beunruhige Dich nicht. Du weisst, die Geschäfte gehen niemals glatt; aber ich versichere Dir, Du sollst gute Nachrichten von unseren Kriegsoperationen erhalten.*
        Mir   geht   es   gut   und   ___   wird   es   gut
        me.DAT   goes   it.NOM   well   and   ø.DAT will   it.NOM   well
        gehen   wenn Ich nur von Deiner Besserung höre. Erhalt ich aber
        go.INF
        schlechte Nachrichten aus Bayreuth

        'For my sake, do not worry. You know business never goes smoothly; but I assure you, you shall receive good news about our war operations. I am doing well *and will be doing well*, if I only hear of your improvement. But if I receive bad news from Bayreuth . . .'
                                        (*Briefe*, Friedrich der Große, c.1758)

Nom-Dat

b. Es   geht ***mir*** gut   und   ___   wird ***mir*** gut
   it.NOM goes me.DAT well and   ∅.NOM will me.DAT well
   gehen wenn Ich   nur   von   deiner Besserung   höre
   go.INF if   I   only from your   improvement hear
   'Things are working out well for me *and will be working out well for me,
   if I only hear of your improvement*.

It is expected, of course, that the nominative of *gelingen* 'succeed', *gefallen* 'like, please' and *gut gehen* 'do well, have things go well for one' may be left unexpressed in conjoined clauses, as is evident from (300b), (301b) and (302b). In the first example, the nominative *es* in the second conjunct with *gelingen* is left unexpressed on identity with the nominative *es* with *gelingen* in the first conjunct. In the second example, (301b), the nominative of *gefallen* in the second conjunct is left unexpressed on identity with the nominative subject of the first conjunct. In the third example (302b), the nominative *es* of *gut gehen* in the second conjunct is left unexpressed on identity with the nominative *es* of *gut gehen* in the first conjunct. Observe that all the examples in (300–302) above are attested examples, except for (302b), which is a flip version of (302a). I have been unable to locate attested examples with this structure, but native speakers confirm the felicitousness of this example in German.

What is more surprising, however, is that the dative of *gelingen* 'succeed', *gefallen* 'like, please' and *gut gehen* 'do well, turn out well', may also be left unexpressed in second conjuncts, while the nominative *es* 'it' with these verbs is left expressed instead (boldfaced in the examples above). This is shown in (300a), (301a) and (302a) above. In (300a) the dative of *gelingen* is left unexpressed on identity with the dative of the same predicate, *gelingen*, in the first conjunct, while the nominative *es* 'it' with *gelingen* in the second conjunct is expressed. In (301a) *gefallen* 'like, please' occurs in both conjuncts. Hence, the dative of *gefallen* is left unexpressed in (301a) on identity with the dative of *gefallen* in the first conjunct, while the nominative *es* 'it' is left expressed in the second conjunct. In (302a) the dative of *gut gehen* 'do well, turn out well', is left unexpressed in the second conjunct on identity with the dative of *gut gehen* in the second conjunct, while the nominative *es* of the second conjunct is expressed on identity with the nominative *es* in the first conjunct.

Not only the acceptability of the examples in (300a), (301a) and (302a) where a dative of the second conjunct is left unexpressed on identity with the dative of the same verb in the first conjunct, but also the sheer existence of such examples, goes against the non-subject analysis of oblique subjects in German. That is, examples of this type should be both unacceptable and non-existent, according to the standard story in German (Zaenen, Maling, and Thráinsson 1985; Sigurðsson 1989, 1992; Fanselow 2002; Bayer 2004; Haider 2005, 2010; Wunderlich 2009; Pankau 2016).

What is more, these three pairs of examples extensively show that *gelingen*, *gefallen* and *gut gehen* are alternating predicates, which have the possibility of instantiating either the Dat-Nom or the Nom-Dat argument structure construction in German. It is interesting that in all three examples of the Dat-Nom constructions (300a, 301a, 302a), the verb is the same in both conjuncts. That is, the dative of the second conjunct is left unexpressed on identity with a corresponding dative in the first conjunct, and the same is, of course, true for the nominative in (300b) and (301b).

Note, moreover, that the examples in (300a, 301a, 302a) are reminiscent of the examples in (285) above where accusative subjects are left unexpressed in conjunction reduction on the basis of identity with accusative subjects in the preceding clause, and dative subjects on identity with dative subjects in the preceding clause. Recall also from Section 2.3.3 above, that there seems to be a restriction on ellipsis in German, with ellipsis being confined to arguments having not only the same morphological case, but also the same syntactic function, labeled the Restricted Ellipsis Analysis in 2.3.3. above. This would explain why native speakers of German find examples like (300–302) above grammatical, as both the datives and the nominatives in the second conjuncts are left unexpressed on identity with arguments in the first conjunct which, in fact, share their case marking. This, in addition to the fact that these arguments share grammatical relations. Hence, the only viable analysis for the examples in (300–302) above is that the subject of the second conjunct is left unexpressed on identity with the subject of the first conjunct, be it a nominative or a dative subject.

I now turn to corresponding examples in Modern Icelandic, featuring the translational equivalents of *gelingen*, *gefallen*, and *gut gehen*, namely *reynast kleift* 'find sth doable', *falla í geð* 'like, please' and *ganga vel* 'go well, do well'. Notice that the exact translational equivalents of *gelingen* in Icelandic, *takast*, *heppnast* and *lukkast* 'succeed, manage', may only instantiate the Dat-Nom construction and not the Nom-Dat construction. That is, these three verbs are not alternating in Icelandic. However, the near synonym, *reynast kleift* 'find sth doable' is. For this reason, I use that predicate here instead.

Icelandic
Dat-Nom
(303) a. *Angóla hefur loksins og óafturkallanlega tekið afstöðu sósíalisma í hag.*
Þessu lýsti formaður MPLA Verkamannaflokksins og forseti Alþýðulýðveld-
isins Angóla, Agostinho Neto, yfir í viðtali.

Alþjóðlegri	heimsvaldastefnu	og	innri	viðbrögðum	hefur
international	imperialism.DAT	and	inner	reactions.DAT	has

> ekki   reynst   **það**   kleift   og   __   mun   ekki
> not   turn.out it.NOM   doable   and   Ø.DAT will   not
> reynast **það**   kleift   að knésetja Angóla, lagði Neto áherslu á.
> turn.out it.NOM   doable   to

'Angola has finally and irrevocably decided in favor of socialism. This was declared by the Chairman of the MPLA Party of Labor and President of the People's Republic of Angola, Agostinho Neto, in an interview. International imperialism and domestic reactions have not managed it *and will not manage* to bring Angola to his knees, Neto stressed.'

Nom-Dat

> b. Það   hefur   ekki   reynst   **mér**   kleift   og   __
>   it.NOM has   not   turn.out me.DAT   doable   and   Ø.NOM
>   mun   ekki   reynast **mér**   kleift.   Ég   hef   gefið
>   will   not   turn.out me.DAT   doable   I   have   given
>   hugmyndina   upp   á   bátinn.
>   idea.the   up   on   boat.the
>
>   'It has not been doable for me and it *and will not be doable for me*. I have given up on the idea.'

Dat-Nom

(304) a. Samfélagið   drattast   áfram,   mér   persónulega   getur
         society.the   drags   onward   me.DAT   personally   can
         ekki   fallið   þetta   í   geð   og   __   mun   ekki
         not   fallen   this.NOM   in   mind   and   Ø.DAT will   not
         falla þetta   í   geð,   vegna   þess ...
         fall   this.NOM in   mind   because of

         'The society is dragging on, I personally can not like it *and will not like it*, because ...'

Nom-Dat

> b. Já.   En   það   er   svolítið   flókið   og   __
>   yes   but   it.NOM   is   somewhat   complicated and   Ø.NOM
>   mun   ekki   **falla**   yður   í   geð.
>   will   not   fall.INF   you.DAT   in   mind
>
>   'Yes. But this is somewhat complicated *and will not be to your liking*.'

These examples show that Icelandic *reynast kleift* 'find sth doable' and *falla í geð* 'like, please', behave in the same way as German *gelingen* and *gefallen* with regard to conjunction reduction. Either the dative or the nominative may be left unexpressed in second conjuncts, on identity with either a dative or a nominative in the first conjunct.

However, the translational equivalent and cognate predicate of German *gut gehen*, i.e. *ganga vel* in Icelandic, may only instantiate the Dat-Nom construction in that language, and not the Nom-Dat construction. This is shown in (305a–b) below where the Dat-Nom construction passes the conjunction reduction test, while the Nom-Dat construction does not.

Dat-Nom

(305) a. *Mín vegna, ekki hafa áhyggjur. Þú veist að viðskipti ganga aldrei greiðlega; en ég fullvissa þig um að þú munt fá góðar fréttir af stríðsaðgerðum okkar.*
Mér   gengur   þetta   vel   og   ___   mun   **ganga**
me.DAT   goes   this.NOM   well   and   Ø.DAT   will   go
þetta   vel,   *ef ég aðeins heyri um framfarir þínar. En ef ég fæ*
this.NOM   well
slæmar fréttir frá Bayreuth . . .

'For my sake, do not worry. You know business never goes smoothly; but I assure you, you shall receive good news about our war operations. I'm doing well in life *and will be doing well in life* if I only hear of your improvement. But if I receive bad news from Bayreuth . . .'

***Nom-Dat**

  b. **Það   hafði   gengið   mér   vel   og   ___   myndi
it.NOM   had   gone   me.DAT   well   and   Ø.NOM   would
ganga   mér   vel   ef   aðeins   ég   fengi   fréttir
go   me.DAT   well   if   only   I   would.receive   news
af   bata   þínum.*
of   recovery your
Intended meaning: 'Things would be going well for me *and would continue to go well for me,* if only I received news of your recovery.'

One possible reason for the ungrammaticality of the Nom-Dat example in (305b) may be because *ganga vel* in Icelandic can also occur with a PP instead of the nominative. This Dat-PP construction may well have ousted the Nom-Dat construction from the language, making it difficult for the remnants of the Dat-Nom construction to undergo productive operations. This comparison simply shows that not all alternating predicates in German are necessarily alternating in Icelandic.

Before concluding this section, observe that the fact that examples of the type shown above involve neutral word order, as is documented in the previous section, indeed rules out a topicalization analysis of these examples in general, contrary to the standard story found in the literature on German.

To summarize the content of this section, the examples presented here from German can only be interpreted such that Dat-Nom verbs in German are alternating predicates, as either the dative or the nominative can be left unexpressed in structures involving conjunction reduction. Two types of Icelandic examples have been introduced, two of which are alternating predicates in Icelandic, while one is a non-alternating one. The alternating predicates, *reynast kleift* and *falla í geð* show the same behavior as the German verbs, while occurrences with *ganga vel* suggest instead that *ganga vel* is a non-alternating Dat-Nom verb in Icelandic.

6.3.3 Clause-bound reflexivization

As discussed in Section 1.3 above, clause-bound reflexivization is not an easy subject test to use in Icelandic, since both subjects and objects may bind reflexives within their minimal clause. This, however, does not mean that there are no differences between subject and object binding or that these differences cannot be used to distinguish between these two grammatical categories, subjects and objects.

As a matter of fact, the differences between subject and object binding in Icelandic involve binding of reflexives vs. personal pronouns. That is, subjects may only bind reflexives, while objects may bind either reflexives or personal pronouns (cf Thráinsson 1976, 2007: 462–464; Maling 1986; Jónsson 1996: 74–76). What this means is that objects turn out to have a choice regarding whether they bind reflexives or personal pronouns within their minimal clause. In German the difference between subject and object binding is even clearer, since objects tend to only bind personal pronouns and not reflexives, according to my informants, as is shown in the examples below (although some differences between speakers seem to exist, see the discussion in 4.2.2 above).

German
Subject binding
(306) a. **Der Troll**$_i$ hat eine sehr hässliche Statue von
the.NOM troll has a.ACC very ugly statue of
sich$_i$ /*ihm$_i$ gesehen.
REFL him seen
'The troll saw a really ugly statue of himself.'

Object binding
b. *Ich   habe   **den   Troll**$_i$ getötet mit dieser hässlichen*
   I.NOM have   the.ACC troll   killed with this   ugly
   *Statue von   *sich$_i$ /**ihm**$_i$.*
   statue of   REFL   him
   'I killed the troll with this ugly statue of himself.'

Icelandic
Subject binding
(307) a. ***Trölli**$_i$ sá   hræðilega ljóta styttu$_i$ af   **sér**$_i$ /*honum$_i$.*
         troll.NOM saw   horribly ugly statue.ACC of   REFL   him
         'The troll saw a really ugly statue of himself.'

Object binding
b. *Ég   drap   **Trölla**$_i$ með   þessari   hræðilega ljótu*
   I.NOM killed troll.ACC with this   horribly ugly
   *styttu$_i$ af   **sér**$_i$ /**honum**$_i$.*
   statue.ACC of   REFL   him
   'I killed the troll with this horribly ugly statue of himself.'

The (a) examples in (306–307) above represent subject binding, while the (b) examples instantiate object binding. The subject is nominative, *der Troll* and *Trölli*, in the (a) examples and this nominative subject can only bind the reflexive in the adnominal prepositional phrases, *von sich* and *af sér*. These (a) examples are of course fully grammatical with personal pronouns, but not if such personal pronouns refer back to the subject, only if they refer to a different referent than the subject, external to the clause.

For the accusative objects, *den Troll* and *Trölla*, in the (b) examples above, these are perfectly grammatical with either a reflexive or a personal pronoun referring back to the object in Icelandic, while only being acceptable in German with a personal pronoun referring back to the object. These examples therefore demonstrate a clear difference between the binding properties of subjects and objects in that subjects may only bind reflexives, while objects may bind reflexives, as well as personal pronouns in Icelandic, while in German objects may only bind personal pronouns. For these reasons, distinguishing between subject and non-subject behavior, with regard to reflexivization, is far from beyond the bounds of possibility.

Turning now to dative subjects in German, observe that either the dative or the nominative subject of *gefallen* 'like, please' and *Spanish vorkommen* 'find strange' may bind reflexives within their minimal clause.

German
Dat-Nom
(308) a. **Dem König**$_i$ *gefiel die Marmorstatue von* **sich**$_i$
the.DAT king likes the.NOM marble.statue of REFL
/*ihm$_i$ *besonders gut.*
him particularly well
'The king particularly liked the marble statue of himself.'

Nom-Dat
b. **Der Volvo-Käufer**$_i$ *gefällt* **sich**$_i$ */*ihm*$_i$ *in der*
the.NOM Volvo-buyer likes REFL.DAT him in the
Vorreiterrolle.
pioneer.role
'The Volvo buyer likes himself in the role of a pioneer.'

Dat-Nom
(309) a. **Dem König**$_i$ *kam die Marmorstatue von* **sich**$_i$
the.DAT king came the.NOM marble.statue of REFL
/*ihm$_i$ *etwas Spanisch vor.*
him somewhat strange for
'The king found the marble statue of himself somewhat strange.'

Nom-Dat
b. **Die Band Caminho**$_i$ *kommt* **sich**$_i$ */*ihr*$_i$ *spanisch*
the.NOM band Caminho comes REFL.DAT /her strange
vor, sie feiert sich und die eineinhalb Jahrzehnte
for it celebrates REFL and the one.one.half decade
ihres Bestehens in 15 Kurzkonzerten...
of.its existence in 15 short.conserts
'The band Caminho feels awkward, celebrating itself and the decade and a half of its existence with 15 short concerts...'
(https://www.musik-in-dresden.de/author/michael/page/78)

The example in (308a) demonstrates *gefallen* with the Dat-Nom argument structure, while (308b) shows *gefallen* with the Nom-Dat argument structure. Both the dative in the Dat-Nom construction and the nominative in the Nom-Dat construction may bind reflexives within their minimal clause. The same is true for the dative and the nominative of the Dat-Nom and Nom-Dat constructions with *Spanisch vorkommen* in (309) above.

What is more, the dative and nominative subjects of *gefallen* 'like, please' and *Spanish vorkommen* 'find strange' may only bind reflexives within their minimal clause and not personal pronouns, as is shown with the asterisk in front of the personal pronouns *ihm* 'him' and *ihr* 'her' in the examples above. Note that these examples are of course grammatical if the personal pronoun is not bound by the subject, but refers instead to someone else external to the clause, although that is of no relevance for the present discussion.

Exactly the same binding properties are found with the Icelandic cognates of *gefallen* and *Spanisch vorkommen*, i.e. *falla í geð* og *koma spánskt fyrir sjónir*. These two predicates are known from the Icelandic literature to be alternating (cf. the list of Icelandic alternating verbs in Section 3.2.1 above), as is shown in (310–311) below:

Icelandic
Dat-Nom
(310) a. **Konunginum**$_i$ *féll marmarastyttan af sér$_i$ /*honum$_i$*
king.the.DAT fell marble.statue.NOM of REFL him
alveg sérstaklega vel.
fully particularly well
'The King particularly liked the marble statue of himself.'

Nom-Dat
b. **Bílkaupandinn**$_i$ *fellur viðskiptafélaga sínum$_i$ /*hans$_i$*
car.buyer.NOM falls business.partner.DAT REFL.DAT his
vel í geð.
well in mind
'The car buyer is much to his business partner's liking.'

Dat-Nom
(311) a. **Konunginum**$_i$ *kom marmarastyttan af sér$_i$ /*honum$_i$*
king.the.DAT came marble.statue.NOM of REFL him
etthvað spánskt fyrir sjónir.
somewhat strange for vision
'The king found the marble statue of himself somewhat strange.'

Nom-Dat
b. **Bílkaupandinn**$_i$ *kom viðskiptafélaga sínum$_i$ /*hans$_i$*
car.buyer.NOM came business.partner.DAT REFL.DAT his
etthvað spánskt fyrir sjónir.
somewhat strange for vision
'The car buyer appeared somewhat strange to his business partner.'

Observe that the binding pattern is exactly the same as in the German examples in (308–309) above in that either the dative of the Dat-Nom construction or the nominative of the Nom-Dat construction may bind a reflexive within its minimal clause. Corresponding examples with personal pronouns are ungrammatical on a bound reading but grammatical on an unbound reading.

Compare now the Icelandic examples of *falla (í geð)* 'like, please' and *koma spánskt fyrir sjónir* 'find strange' in (310–311) above with corresponding examples of the non-alternating verbs *líka* 'like' and *leiðast* 'be bored':

Icelandic
Dat-Nom
(312) a. **Konunginum**$_i$ líkaði   marmarastyttan   af **sér**$_i$
          king.the.DAT   liked   marble.statue.the.NOM   of REFL
          /*honum$_i$ alveg   sérstaklega   vel.
            him   fully   particularly well
          'The king particularly liked the marble statue of himself.'

***Nom-Dat**
   b. *****Bílkaupandinn**$_i$ hafði   líkað   viðskiptafélaga   **sínum**$_i$
       car.buyer.NOM   had   liked   business.partner.DAT   REFL.DAT
       /hans$_i$ vel.
        his   well
       Intended meaning: 'The car buyer was much to his business partner's liking.'

Dat-Nom
(313) a. **Konunginum**$_i$ leiddist   þessi   marmarastytta   af
          king.the.DAT   was.bored   this.NOM   marble.statue.NOM   of
          sér$_i$ /*honum$_i$ alveg   afskaplega   mikið.
          REFL   him   fully   unbelievably   much
          'The king was unbelievably bored with this marble statue of himself.'

***Nom-Dat**
   b. *****Bílkaupandinn**$_i$ hafði   leiðst   viðskiptafélaga
       car.buyer.NOM   had   been.bored   business.partner.DAT
       sínum$_i$ /hans$_i$ mikið.
       REFL.DAT   his   much
       Intended meaning: 'The car buyer was incredibly boring for his business partner.'

As these examples demonstrate, only the dative of the Dat-Nom construction may bind reflexives in Icelandic with the verbs *líka* 'like' and *leiðast* 'be bored'. By the same token, the examples in (312b) and (313b) are ungrammatical since *líka* 'like' and *leiðast* 'be bored' cannot instantiate the Nom-Dat argument structure construction in Icelandic.

In sum, there is a clear difference between the binding properties of syntactic subjects and syntactic objects in both Icelandic and German; syntactic subjects may only bind reflexives and not personal pronouns in both languages, while syntactic objects have a choice between binding reflexives or personal pronouns in Icelandic. In German it appears that, although some speaker internal variation seems to exist, objects may only bind personal pronouns. It turns out that both the dative of Dat-Nom verbs and the nominative of Nom-Dat verbs behave consistently as syntactic subjects in both languages, as both bind reflexives within their minimal clause. Thus, the most reasonable analysis is that the relevant verbs are alternating verbs, vacillating between the two argument structures, the Dat-Nom and the Nom-Dat constructions. This analysis is further confirmed by the fact that an additional set of verbs in Icelandic deviate from this pattern, with only the dative of Dat-Nom behaving systematically as a subject, while the nominative behaves systematically as an object. These are the so-called non-alternating Dat-Nom verbs in Icelandic. In conclusion, binding facts in German confirm the existence of alternating verbs in that language, something that so far has already been established for both Icelandic and Faroese in the existing literature (cf. the references in Sections 3.2.1 and 3.2.2 above).

6.3.4 Raising-to-subject

As is explained in Sections 3.2.1 and 4.2.4 above, raising-to-subject is found with verbs that do not select for a subject of their own. These can be modal auxiliaries, aspectual verbs expressing beginning or concluding phases of events, verbs of seeming, etc. What they all have in common is that they are semantically so weak that they do not select for a subject of their own. In this sense, raising-to-subject verbs are like auxiliaries, as the syntactic subject of raising-to-subject verbs belongs semantically to the lower verb. This behavior is particularly pertinent in case languages, since the case marking of the subject of the raising-to-subject verb is the same as the case marking of the lower verb when it is finite. For verbs selecting for oblique subjects, the "raised" subject occurs in the same oblique case, as is selected by the lower verb.

The following examples from German with *misslingen* 'fail', *behagen* 'like, please' and *genügen* 'satisfy, be satisfied' show that either argument of the verb, the dative or the nominative, may take on the subject behavior of the raising-to-subject verb, although of course not at the same time:

German
Dat-Nom
(314) a. *Schien* **dem** **Heimteam** **die** **Mission** *zu*
seemed the.DAT home.team the.NOM mission to
misslingen?
fail.INF
'Did the home team seem to be failing at the mission?'

Nom-Dat
b. *Schien* **der** **Kraftakt** **den** **Gladbachern**
seemed the.NOM tour.de.force the.DAT Gladbachers.DAT
gehörig zu misslingen?
severely to fail.INF
'Did the tour of force really seem to be unsuccessful for the Gladbachers?

Dat-Nom
(315) a. *Scheint nicht* **dem** **Vater** **das** **Thema** **Lissabon**
seems not the.DAT father the.NOM Theme Lissabon
definitiv zu behagen?
definitely to be.satisfied.INF
'Does the father definitely not seem to be satisfied with Theme Lissabon?

Nom-Dat
b. *Scheint nicht* **der** **genannte** **Preis** **unserer** **Kundin**
seems not the.NOM named price our.DAT customer
zu behagen?
to be.to.satisfaction.INF
'Does the asking price not seem to be to our customer's satisfaction?'

Dat-Nom
(316) a. *Scheinen* **allen** **anderen** **diese** **Worte** *zu*
seem.3PL all.DAT others.DAT these.NOM words to
genügen?
suffice.INF
Does everybody else seem to find these words sufficient?

Nom-Dat
    b. *Scheinen* **die** **Vorkehrungen** *gegen* *Brände* *in* *den*
        seem.3PL the.NOM precautions against fires in the
        Gebäuden **dem** **Baurechtsamt** *nicht* *zu* *genügen?*
        buildings the.DAT Building.Code.Office not to suffice.INF
        'Do the precautions against fire in the buildings not seem be sufficient for the Building & Code Office?'

In (314a), (315a) and (316a) above it is the dative of *misslingen* 'fail', *behagen* 'satisfy' and *genügen* 'find sufficient' that behaves syntactically as the subject of the finite *scheinen* 'seem'. Since these examples are formulated as questions, it is clear that it is the dative that inverts with the finite *scheinen* 'seem' in these examples. Note that the same is true for the nominative of *misslingen* 'fail', *behagen* 'satisfy' and *genügen* 'find sufficient' in (314b), (315b) and (316b) above. Here it is the nominative that inverts with the finite *scheinen* in the questions above, thus behaving syntactically as a subject.

To conclude, the raising-to-subject test confirms that *misslingen* 'fail', *behagen* 'satisfy' and *genügen* 'find sufficient' are alternating verbs in German, as either the dative of the Dat-Nom construction or the nominative of the Nom-Dat construction behaves syntactically as a subject, although not at the same time, of course.

Turning to Icelandic, consider now the translational equivalents of the German examples in (314–316) above, involving the verbs *reynast ókleift* 'find undoable, *þóknast* 'suit, satisfy' and *nægja* 'suffice', of which the last one is cognate to its German translational equivalent, *genügen*:

Icelandic
Dat-Nom
(317) a. *Virðist* **heimaliðinu** *ætla* *að* *reynast*
        seems home.team.the.DAT be.about to turn.INF
        ætlunarverkið *ókleift?*
        mission.the.NOM undoable
        'Does the home team seem to be about to fail at the mission?'

Nom-Dat
    b. *Virðist* **þetta** **stórafrek** *ætla* *að* *verða*
        seems this.NOM tour.de.force.NOM be.about to become.INF
        þessu **fólki** *ókleift?*
        these.DAT people.DAT undoable
        'Does this tour de force seem to be about to be unsuccessful for these people?'

Dat-Nom

(318) a. *Virðist **föðurnum** virkilega ekki þóknast **Þema***
 seems father.the.DAT really not be.satisfied.INF Theme
 Lissabon?
 Lissabon.NOM
 'Does the father definitely not seem to be satisfied with Theme Lissabon?'

Nom-Dat

 b. *Virðist hið **uppsetta verð** ekki þóknast*
 seems the asked price.NOM not be.to.satisfaction.INF
 viðskiptavini okkar?
 customer.DAT our
 'Does the asking price not seem to be to our customer's satisfaction?'

Dat-Nom

(319) a. *Virðast **öllum öðrum** nægja **þessi orð?***
 seem.3PL all.DAT others.DAT suffice.INF these words.NOM
 Does everybody else seem to find these words sufficient?

Nom-Dat

 b. *Virðast **varúðarráðstafanirnar** gegn eldi í*
 seem.3PL precautions.the.NOM against fire in
 byggingunum** ekki nægja **Húsnæðis- og
 buildings.the not suffice.INF Housing and
 mannvirkjastofnuninni?
 Civil.Enginering.Institute.DAT
 'Do the precautions against fire in the buildings not seem be sufficient for the Housing and Civil Engineering Institute?'

The predicates *reynast ókleift* 'find undoable, *þóknast* 'suit, satisfy' and *nægja* 'suffice' in Icelandic are all known alternating predicates in the sense that the dative of the Dat-Nom construction and the nominative of the Nom-Dat construction both pass all subject tests, here demonstrated with the raising-to-subject test.

Before leaving the issue of raising-to-subject, consider the following Icelandic examples with *leiðast* 'be bored' and *líka* 'like', which indeed confirm that *leiðast* 'be bored' and *líka* 'like' are not alternating verbs. Instead, both verbs are non-alternating Dat-Nom verbs, as is evident from the fact that the Nom-Dat word order is ungrammatical in raising-to-subject constructions.

Icelandic
Dat-Nom
(320) a. *Virðist* **heimaliðinu** *leiðast* **ætlunarverkið?**
seems home.team.the.DAT be.bored.INF mission.the.NOM
'Does the home team seem to be bored with the mission?'

*Nom-Dat
b. *Virðist **stórafrekið** *leiðast* **fólkinu?**
seems tour.de.force.the.NOM be.bored.INF people.the.DAT
Intended meaning: 'Does the tour de force seem to bore the people?'

Dat-Nom
(321) a. *Virðist* **föðurnum** *virkilega ekki líka* **Þema**
seems father.the.DAT really not like.INF Theme.NOM
Lissabon?
Lissabon.NOM
'Does the father definitely not seem to like Theme Lissabon?

*Nom-Dat
b. *Virðist hið **uppsetta** *verð ekki líka* **viðskiptavini**
seems the asked price.NOM not like.INF customer.DAT
okkar?
our
Intended meaning: 'Does the asking price not seem to please our customer?'

To summarize the findings of this section, the three German verbs under discussion, *misslingen* 'fail', *behagen* 'satisfy' and *genügen* 'find sufficient', are clearly alternating verbs, as either argument, the dative of the Dat-Nom construction and the nominative of the Nom-Dat construction, takes on the subject behavior of the finite verb *scheinen* 'seem, appear'. The same is true for the translational equivalents of these verbs in Icelandic, *reynast ókleift* 'find undoable, *þóknast* 'suit, satisfy' and *nægja* 'suffice'. In contrast, two additional verbs in Icelandic, *leiðast* 'be bored' and *líka* 'like', are clearly non-alternating Dat-Nom verbs in that language, as the Nom-Dat word order with these verbs results in ungrammaticality in raising-to-subject constructions.

6.3.5 Raising-to-object

Raising-to-object turns out to be a more problematic test in Modern German than in Modern Icelandic, as several predicates selecting for oblique subjects appear not to yield grammatical structures when embedded under causatives like *lassen* 'let'. Still, examples with pronouns are relatively easy to come across, and examples from the 18th and the 19th century are found without any greater effort.

Consider now the following two sets of examples, the ones in (322–323) with *einfallen* 'get an idea, come to mind' and *gefallen*, here with the specialized meaning 'put up with sth, accept sth'. Notice that the nominative is realized as an accusative in such constructions, both in German and Icelandic.

German
Dat-Nom (realized as Dat-Acc)
(322) a. Wer zum Kuckuck lässt **sich** **das** einfallen?
who to.the cuckoo lets REFL.DAT this.ACC fall.in.mind.INF
'Who the heck comes up with this?'

Nom-Dat (realized as Acc-Dat)
b. Niemand lässt **es** **sich** einfallen ihn zu
nobody lets it.ACC REFL.DAT fall.in.mind.INF him to
stören.
bother
'Nobody gets the idea to bother him.'

Dat-Nom (realized as Dat-Acc)
(323) a. Doch Vaillant lässt **sich** **dies** nicht gefallen
yet Vaillant lets REFL.DAT this.ACC not like.INF
und handelt.
and acts
'But Vaillant does not accept this and acts.'

Nom-Dat (realized as Acc-Dat)
b. Lode lacht und lässt **es** **sich** gefallen.
Lode laughs and lets it.ACC REFL.DAT please.INF
'Lode laughs and accepts it.'

As these examples show, either the Dat-Nom or the Nom-Dat word order is possible with these verbs. Notice, again, that the nominative is realized as an accusative in raising-to-object constructions of this kind in German. This can be interpreted in two ways, namely either that the "raised subject" receives its case marking from the higher verb, 'let' or that it receives it from the construction itself. Also, consider the following examples with *gefallen* where the original nominative is realized as a nominal and not a pronoun, as in (322–323) above (cf. Barðdal, Eythórsson, and Dewey 2019: 136):

German
Dat-Nom (realized as Dat-Acc)
(324) a. *Ich lasse* **mir** *den schlechten* Wein *nicht*
 I let.1SG me.DAT the.ACC bad.ACC wine not
 gefallen.
 like.INF
 'I will not accept this bad wine.'

Nom-Dat (realized as Acc-Dat)
    b. *Man läßt* **den** *Winter* **sich** *noch gefallen.*
 one lets the.ACC winter REFL.DAT still please.INF
 'One still has to accept wintertime.' (Goethe, *Winter*)

Nom-Dat (realized as Acc-Dat)
    c. ... *oder vielmehr, er läßt* **den** *Helden Pedro*
 or rather he lets the.ACC hero.ACC Pedro
 sich *darin gefallen und schildert die*
 REFL.DAT therein please.INF and describes the.ACC
 Gemeinheit mit Genuß.
 meanness with pleasure
 '... or rather, he lets himself like the hero Pedro in this [story] and describes the meanness with pleasure.'
 (*Zeitung für die elegante Welt*, 1840)

In (324a) the dative *mir* precedes the accusative *den schlechten wein* 'the bad wine', while the order is the opposite in (324b–c). There, the accusatives *den Winter* 'the winter' and *den Helden Pedro* 'the hero, Pedro', precede the dative *sich* 'self'.

It appears that German only allows oblique subject verbs to be embedded under 'let' causatives if the subject of 'let' and the "raised object" are co-referential. In other words, the dative is always reflexive, again ruling out occurrences with the dative realized as a nominal. Irrespective of that, the examples in (324) clearly demonstrate that either the Dat-Nom or the Nom-Dat word orders are grammatical in raising-to-object constructions, which in turn speaks for an alternating analysis of the relevant lower verb in German, *gefallen*.

Before continuing, notice that Icelandic *líka* 'like' also changes its meaning to 'put up with, accept' with causative *láta* 'let', exactly like German *gefallen*:

Icelandic
Dat-Nom (realized as Dat-Acc)
(325) a. *Persinn, Valentínó, lætur **sér** vel líka*
Persian Valentino lets REFL.DAT well like.INF
***greiðslu**, enda vill hann* ...
hair.style.ACC as wants he
'The Persian cat, Valentino, accepts having his hair styled, as he wants ...'

Dat-Nom (realized as Dat-Acc)
b. *að nútímamaðurinn lætur **sér** vel líka*
that modern.man.the lets REFL.DAT well like.INF
hátíðardagana ...
festive.days.the.ACC
'that the modern person accepts the festive days ...'

***Nom-Dat** (realized as Acc-Dat)
c. **að nútímamaðurinn lætur **hátíðardagana** vel líka*
that modern.man.the lets festive.days.the.ACC well like.INF
sér
REFL.DAT
Intended meaning: 'that the modern person accepts the festive days'

The examples in (325a–b) both involve the Dat-Nom argument structure here realized as Dat-Acc, since the nominative receives accusative case from 'let' in structures of this type, exactly as in German. In contrast, the example in (325c) containing Nom-Dat order, is ungrammatical. The reason is simply that *líka* in Icelandic is a non-alternating Dat-Nom verb, as the reader should remember by now, thus the dative has to precede the nominative in the linear order, at least when the nominative is a nominal. In cases where the nominative is a pronoun, both word orders are found in texts, with the two pronouns occurring in the midfield.

Icelandic
Dat-Nom (realized as Dat-Acc)
326 a. *Frumburðurinn lætur **sér** þetta vel líka og* ...
first.born.the lets REFL.DAT this.ACC well like.INF and
'My firstborn appears to accept this and ...'
(https://birgittah.blog.is/blog/birgittah/entry/47027)

Nom-Dat (realized as Acc-Dat)

b. En neytandinn virðist láta **þetta** **sér** vel
but consumer.the appears let.INF this.ACC REFL.DAT well
líka
like.INF
And the consumer appears to accept this.'
(https://www.hugskotid.blog.is/blog/hugskotid/entry/1270672)

The order of pronouns is generally not this free in the midfield in Modern Icelandic with this verb, which leads me to believe that the structure in (326b) may be a relic from earlier periods, perhaps speaking for an alternating analysis of *líka* in Old Norse-Icelandic. However, (326b) is not entirely felicitous in my language.

Continuing with the comparison with German, consider now examples with the Icelandic verb *nægja* 'suffice' in (327–328) below, where the first set of examples, (327), contains pronouns, while the second set, (328), has the "raised" accusative occurring as a nominal:

Icelandic
Dat-Nom (realized as Dat-Acc)

(327) a. Hann langafi minn lagði vegi sem lágu víða, fyrir firði, fram dali, yfir fjöll.
Hann lét **sér** **það** nægja, leið best heima,
he let REFL.DAT it.ACC sufice.INF felt best home
langaði ekki neitt.
'My great grandfather laid roads that lay far and wide, inside fjords, out valleys, over mountains. He let himself be satisfied with that, felt best at home, did not want to go anywhere.'

Nom-Dat (realized as Acc-Dat)

b. Davíð lét **það** **sér** nægja, að borða rúsínur
David let it.ACC REFL.DAT sufice.INF to eat raisins
og vera plötusnúður.
and be.INF disc.jockey
'David let it be enough for him to eat raisins and be a disc jockey.'

Dat-Nom (realized as Dat-Acc)

(328) a. Hún lætur **sér** ekki nægja **eina** **tegund**
she lets REFL.DAT not sufice.INF one.ACC type
tónlistar.
music.GEN
'She does not let one type of music be enough for her.'

Nom-Dat (realized as Acc-Dat)
b. *E. Skúlason   lætur   **engan   venjulegan   hjólatúr***
   E. Skúlason   lets   no.ACC   ordinary.ACC   bike.tour.ACC
   *nægja   **sér***   heldur.
   sufice.INF REFL.DAT either
   'Eggert Skúlason doesn't let an ordinary bike tour be enough for him either.'

The examples in (327–328a) confirm that either word order, Dat-Nom and Nom-Dat, is grammatical with the Icelandic verb *nægja* 'suffice, be enough'. This word order variation is not confined to pronouns, as in (327), but is also found when the "raised" subject is a full NP, as in (328). This full NP follows the infinitive in (328a), *eina tegund tónlistar* 'one type of music', while the dative immediately follows the finite 'let'. In contrast, in (328b), it is the dative that follows the infinitive, while the full NP, *engan venjulegan hjólatúr* 'no ordinary bike tour', immediately follows the finite 'let'.

Summarizing the content of this section, the word order variation found with Icelandic *nægja* 'suffice, be enough', on the one hand, and German *einfallen* 'get an idea, come to mind' and *gefallen* 'like, please', on the other hand, confirms that the three verbs are alternating verbs in the two languages. In contrast, *líka* 'like' is not an alternating verb in Modern Icelandic, as it only instantiates the Dat-Nom argument structure construction.

6.3.6 Control infinitives

As discussed in Section 2.3.4 above, attested examples of control constructions under which oblique subject verbs are embedded have received mixed ratings in acceptability judgment tasks in general, with some examples rating high in acceptability, while others rate low on the acceptability scale. These findings are valid, not only for German, but also for Icelandic, which is unexpected given that Icelandic has been regarded as the quintessential "oblique subject" language in the syntactic literature during the last forty years or so. This appears to have given rise to the view that there are no semantic or pragmatic restrictions on control infinitives in Icelandic, meaning that, basically, "everything goes" (see, however, Barðdal and Eythórsson (2006: 160–163) and that all verbs in Icelandic may be equally well embedded under control infinitives, which is quite far from the actual truth.

The attested German examples of oblique subject verbs embedded under control infinitives, reported on in Section 2.3.4 above, have in common the fact that they have been regarded as unacceptable by some native speakers, while at the same time they have been considered more or less acceptable by another set of native speakers. It is not my intention to sweep these facts under the rug, but rather to point out that such examples should be of particular interest to theoretical linguistics, due to their alleged ungrammaticality, despite being found in texts composed by native speakers and despite being accepted by a portion of the German-speaking population.

Consider first the following two examples of *gelingen* 'succeed' found in control infinitives where it is clear that it is the referent of the dative subject that is being left unexpressed in the control construction and not the nominative referent:

German
Dat-(Nom)
(329) a. *bezüglich der (Un-)Fähigkeit, die eigene Existenz gegenüber unausweichlichen massiven Irritationen zu sichern und*
sie endgültig zum Gelingen zu bringen, bei
her.ACC finally to fruition to bring with
gleichzeitiger Sehnsucht __ **zu gelingen.**
simultaneous longing PRO.DAT to succeed.INF
'regarding the (in)ability to secure one's own existence in the face of inevitable massive stimuli and to finally bring it [one's own existence] to fruition, *with a simultaneous longing to succeed.*'
(https://univis.uni-bamberg.de/formbot/dsc_3Danew_2Fresrep_view_2 6rprojs_3Dktheo_2Fsyst_2Fmoral_2Frechtf_26dir_3Dktheo_2Fsyst_2 Fmoral_26ref_3Dresrep)

Dat-(Nom)
b. *In dem vorliegenden Buch – Der seelische Organismus – benennt der Autor Ideen, die sich innerhalb der künstlerisch-therapeutischen Begleitarbeit und in zahlreichen Seminaren als Leitthemen der Biografiegestaltung abzeichneten:*
Die Sehnsucht der Seele, __ *aus egenem*
the longing the.GEN soal PRO.DAT through own
Geschehen zu gelingen, um zum Glücken aller Wege
happening to succeed.INF
beizutragen.
'In the present book – The Organism of the Soul – the author names ideas that emerged within the artistic-therapeutic supervision work and in numerous seminars as guiding themes of biography design: *The longing of the soul to succeed through its own efforts*, to contribute to the happiness of all paths.
(http://www.kunstundkommunikation.de/buch.html)

The example in (329a) is from a description of a philosophical project, being carried out at the University of Bamberg, while the one in (329b) is from a website focusing on art therapy and how to communicate art to the general public. In (329a) the relevant part is italicized: *bei gleichzeitiger Sehnsucht zu gelingen*, which means 'with a simultaneous longing to succeed'. Observe that a longing to succeed entails that there is an animate entity involved, the one that experiences the particular longing to succeed. In the argument structure of *gelingen* in German, it is only the dative-marked argument that fulfills the requirement of being able to experience a longing to succeed. Thus, it is excluded that any other argument but the dative is being left unexpressed here, meaning that the dative, in fact, behaves syntactically as a subject.

The example in (329b) is even clearer than the one in (329a), as the relevant part there is: *die Sehnsucht der Seele, aus eigenem Geschehen zu gelingen*, here translated as 'the longing of the soul to succeed through its own efforts'. Clearly, the soul is here construed as a human-like entity with its own will and intentions, in this case the longing to succeed, and not only that, but also to succeed through its own efforts. This, in turn, means that there is even an intention to put an effort into the event of succeeding, an attribute which may only be expected from a referent of the dative argument, as nominative arguments in Dat-Nom constructions are generally inanimate. There can, therefore, be little doubt that it is the dative of *gelingen* that is left unexpressed in the control infinitive in (329b), again confirming the subject behavior of the dative argument.

Before venturing on to further German examples of control infinitives, consider the following example from Icelandic, which is a translation of the German example in (329a) above:

Icelandic
Dat-Nom
(330) a. *Hvað varðar (van)hæfni til þess að vernda eigin tilvist gegn óhjákvæmilega gríðurlegu áreiti og koma henni til farsældar að lokum,*
samsíða   löngun   til   að ___   takast   vel   upp.
along.with   longing   for   to PRO.DAT   succeed.INF   well up
'regarding the (in)ability to protect one's own existence against inevitable massive stimuli and to finally bring it [one's own existence] to fruition, *with a simultaneous longing to succeed.*'

The occurrence of the noun *löngun* 'longing' in (340) above, controlling the embedded purposive infinitive, indeed excludes a nominative analysis of the subject ellipsis in (330), exactly as in (329) above, leaving a dative analysis as the only viable analysis of these structures in both German and Icelandic.

Notice, however, that *gelingen* in German does not allow for intransitive occurrences of either argument structure, although the Icelandic particle verb *takast upp* does.

German
Nom-only
(331) a. ***Der   Nachweis   dieser   Erhitzung   gelingt   gut.***
this.NOM   detection   this.GEN   heating   succeeds   well
'The detection of this heating works well.'

***Dat-only**
b. ***Ihnen   gelingt   *(es)   gut   im   Leben.***
them.DAT   succeedes   it.NOM   well   in.the   life
Intended meaning: 'They did well in life.'

Icelandic
Nom-only
(332) a. ***Þetta   tókst   vel   upp.***
this.NOM   succeeded   well   up
'This worked well.'

Dat-only
b. ***Honum   tókst   vel   upp.***
him.DAT   succeeded   well   up
'He did well.'

The German example in (331b), with only a dative argument and no nominative one, turns out not to be grammatical in Modern German. This is all the more surprising given that the meaning of the control constructions in (329–330) above rules out any other analysis than it being the dative argument that is left unexpressed in these control infinitives. At the same time, there is no expressed nominative found in these examples, behaving as an object.

This raises the question of whether both types of intransitives in (331) may have existed in earlier stages of the German language. The following example from the latter part of the 14th century documents that *gelingen* could well occur only with a dative argument and no nominative:

Early New High German
Dat-only
(333) a. daz **dem**   ğlingt   auf dˢ rais, daz er...
          that the.one.DAT succeeds on   the trip that he
          'that the one did well on the trip, which he...'
                              (Die Gedichte Heinrichs des Teichners, c.1360–70)

This means that the nominative was an optional argument in earlier periods, while it has become obligatory in Modern German. As such, the ungrammaticality of (331b) does not cast doubt on the analysis of the unexpressed argument as being the dative argument in the control infinitives in (329–330).

Examples of control infinitives with *gelingen*, where the nominative is the argument being left unexpressed, are easy to come by in German:

German
Nom-Dat
(334) a. Um   __   zu gelingen, braucht der
          in.order PRO.NOM to succeed.INF needs   the.NOM
          Wandel Moderation und Begleitung.
          change moderation and guidance
          'To succeed, change needs moderation and guidance.'

Nom-Dat
   b. *Die digitale Transformation von Gesellschaft, Wirtschaft und Staat muss inklusiv und partizipativ gestaltet sein,*
       um   __   zu gelingen,
       in.order PRO.NOM to succeed.INF
       'The digital transformation of society, business and the state must be designed to be inclusive and participatory if it is to succeed.'

In (334a) it is the nominative corresponding to *der Wandel* 'the change' that is left unexpressed in the preceding control infinitive with *gelingen* 'succeed' and in (334b) it is the nominative referring to *die digitale Transformation* 'the digital transformation' that is left unexpressed in the succeeding control infinitive, also with *gelingen* 'succeed'. According to the standard story of German, arguments corresponding to nominative subjects, as in (334) above, may be left unexpressed in control constructions, while datives cannot be left unexpressed in corresponding control infinitives. However, what these examples show is that either the dative or the nominative may be left unexpressed in such control infinitives, although embedding nominative subject verbs under control verbs is considerably easier than the embedding of oblique subject verbs, yet, such examples may be found in German texts.

Turning now to another set of examples, this time with the verb *genügen* 'satisfy, be satisfied' in German. The first one, in (335a) below, stemming from the year 1821, exemplifies the Nom-Dat argument structure, while the second one, in (335b), which is an even older example from the year 1541, instantiates the Dat-(Nom) argument structure construction.

German
Nom-Dat
(335) a. *in dazu unerläslicher Ungestörtheit auszuarbeiten; meine Verpflichtung aber gegen die Lesewelt, nach dem Verhältnisse der Theilnehmenden zum Ganzen, nur zu gering war: so erkläre ich hiemit,*

das	ich	__	derselben	mehr	als	**zu**	**gnügen**
that	I.NOM	PRO.NOM	itself.DAT	more	that	to	suffice.INF

glaube indem ich, jenen Hemmungen zum Troz, die, nur ausführlichere, Beendigung des Werkes jeder mir vortheilhafteren Stellung vorziehe; an vorbestimmter Zeit übrigens ungebunden.

'But my obligation to the reading world, according to the proportion of the participants to the whole, was only too small: so I hereby declare that I believe *that I more than satisfy these*, in spite of those inhibitions, by preferring the, only more detailed, completion of the work over any job offer that may be more advantageous to me; including, by the way, non-temporary ones.' (Isis: oder encyclopädische Zeitung, c.1821)

Dat-(Nom)
b. *Nun wiewol gedachter hertzog solchs, das er nit zu thun schuldig*

biß	__	**zu**	**gnügen**	anzeigen	mag,
until	PRO.DAT	to	be.satisfied.INF	indicate	may

ist doch seiner fstl. Gn. meynung [nicht], in eynichen weg mit euerer ksl. noch dem hl. reich in hader oder tayding zu komen, in ansehung, das er Mt. . . .

'Now, although the said Duke may indicate such a thing, which he is not obliged to do, *until being satisfied*, it is nevertheless [not] his intention, to come in any way into conflict or dispute with your Imperial Majesty or the Holy Roman Empire, in view of the fact that he . . .'

(Der Reichstag zu Regensburg, c.1541)

In (335a) the verb *genügen* has the meaning to 'satisfy' as in 'satisfy obligations'. The relevant structure is *ich glaube derselben mehr als zu gnügen*, which is here translated as 'I believe that I more than satisfy these (obligations)'. The form *derselben* 'itself' is here in the dative case, while the nominative is left unexpressed in the relevant control infinitive with *genügen*. In contrast, in (335b), it appears to be the dative of *genügen* that is left unexpressed in the control infinitive, *biß zu gnügen*, 'until being satisfied'. Therefore, the dative behaves syntactically as a subject in this particular example.

These examples show that either argument of *genügen* 'satisfy, be satisfied' behaves syntactically as a subject with regard to control infinitives in (earlier stages of) German. This is true even though examples of the Dat-(Nom) construction are considerably more difficult to find in texts than equivalent examples with the Nom-Dat construction and even though one has to go back in history to detect them. As such, *genügen* clearly behaves as an alternating Dat-Nom / Nom-Dat verb in German.

Before concluding this section, consider first the following two examples of the Icelandic cognate of German *genügen*, namely *nægja* 'satisfy, be satisfied':

Icelandic
Nom-Dat
(336) a. *að   sú   atvinna,   sem   þar   er   að   hafa,*
that this employment.NOM which there is to have
endist   til   að __   nægja   öllum.
lasts for to PRO.NOM satisfy.INF all.DAT
'That the employment found there is enough to satisfy everybody.'

Dat-Nom
b. *en   þrátt   fyrir   að __   nægja   jafntefli   á*
but despite of to PRO.DAT satisfy.INF standoff.NOM at
Nývangi   til   að komast áfram,   ætla   ...
Nývangur in.order to come forward intend
'but despite being satisfied with a standoff at Nývangur Stadium in order to progress, [the team still] intends...'

These Icelandic examples are clear-cut in the sense that it is the nominative of the Nom-Dat construction that is left unexpressed in (336a), while it is the dative of the Dat-Nom construction that is being left unexpressed in (336b). This analysis is further confirmed by the fact that the dative *öllum* 'everybody' is expressed in (336a) and the nominative *jafntefli* 'standoff' is expressed in (336b), again confirming that *nægja* is an alternating Dat-Nom / Nom-Dat verb in Icelandic.

The Icelandic examples in (337) below with *leiðast* 'be bored' show, once and for all, that not all Dat-Nom verbs may allow either argument, the dative or the nominative, to be left unexpressed in control infinitives in that language. This, in turn, confirms that *leiðast* is not an alternating Dat-Nom / Nom-Dat verb in Icelandic. Instead, the verb *leiðast* clearly is a non-alternating Dat-Nom verb, as is evident from the ungrammaticality of (337b):

Icelandic
Dat-Nom
(337) a. mér   finnst   ég   hrikalega   leiðinleg   að   ___
         me.DAT   finds.3SG   I.NOM   horribly   boring   to   PRO.DAT
         leiðast   þetta   svona   mikið.
         be.bored.INF   this.NOM   so   much
         'I find myself horribly boring to be bored so much by this.'
         (https://bland.is/umraeda/vinkonur-olettar/17100965, c.2009)

*****Nom-Dat**
    b. *Það   er   hrikalega   leiðinlegt að ___   **leiðast**
        it.NOM   is   horribly   boring   to   PRO.NOM   bore.INF
        henni.
        her.DAT
        Intended meaning: 'It is it horribly boring to bore her.'

To summarize the content of this section, some existing Dat-Nom verbs in German turn out to be alternating Dat-Nom / Nom-Dat verbs, as they allow either argument, the dative or the nominative, to be left unexpressed in control infinitives, a behavior confined to syntactic subjects, and in this case limited to alternating verbs. The same syntactic behavior is observed for both translational equivalents and cognate verbs in Icelandic. Yet other Dat-Nom verbs in Icelandic do not show the same distribution of the unexpressed subject across the two arguments, only occurring in the Dat-Nom construction and not the Nom-Dat one.

6.4 Modeling subject behavior in German

On the present approach, and the current definition of subject, it is always the first argument of the argument structure, the dative of Dat-Nom verbs and the nominative of Nom-Dat verbs, that is the syntactic subject. For the nominative of Dat-Nom verbs in German, it is certainly not needed to assume that the subject is the second argument, as is implicitly done by, for instance, Wunderlich (2009: 591) and Haider

(2005: 23–24). The reason is that the observed subject behavior of the nominative, noticed in the literature (cf. Section 6.2 above), stems from the fact that the relevant verbs also instantiate the Nom-Dat construction, in addition to the Dat-Nom one.

The theoretical modeling of the syntactic behavior of alternating verbs has already been laid out in Section 3.4 above on the basis of historical material from early Germanic, early Slavic, Baltic, Latin, Ancient Greek, Hittite and Sanskrit. Exactly as for non-alternating Dat-Nom verbs, the assumption is that there is only one lexical entry for each verb in which the list of arguments is unordered. In contrast, the list of arguments in the argument structure itself is, in fact, ordered. Non-alternating verbs merge with the Dat-Nom argument structure construction while alternating verbs merge with either one of the two, the Dat-Nom or the Nom-Dat argument structure construction.

One question that arises relates to how to account for the facts of "restricted ellipsis" in German. There is no doubt that there is such a restriction in both German and Icelandic (as well as in Faroese), even though this ellipsis restriction is considerably more tangible in German than in Icelandic, as is clearly documented in Section 2.3.4 above. Given the present theoretical framework, and the assumption that constructions are not only language-specific but also construction-specific, one way to model this behavior, while staying true to the assumptions of Radical Construction Grammar, is to index nominative and oblique subjects in different ways.

For instance, nominative subjects could be indexed with an i in the argument structure construction, as they are now, while oblique subjects would be indexed with an h in the argument structure construction. The constructions functioning as subject tests, except for the ones involving ellipsis, would then include both indexes, h and i, while the elliptic constructions would only include the i index. The second argument of the argument structure, the object, in these constructions would still be indexed with j, clearly distinguishing between subjects (h and i) and objects (j).

A further question that arises relates to how to account for the inter-speaker variation found for German speakers regarding oblique subjects' ability to be elliptic or not. This inter-speaker variation is easily dealt with in the present model, namely with the subject argument of elliptic constructions being indexed with an h for the grammar of the relevant speakers, as well as with i, exactly as with other subject test constructions in German. The other modeling option is that some speakers of German only employ the i index for subjects, irrespective of whether the subject is oblique or nominative. Whether these two modeling options are notational variants of each other, I leave unsaid at this point.

The final point to be brought up here relates to the question of which factors determine whether an alternating verb occurs in the Dat-Nom or the Nom-Dat construction. So far, the only (non-theory internal) suggestions offered in the literature relate to topicality and/or the foregrounding of one of the arguments over the other (see Barðdal 2001b; Barðdal, Eythórsson, and Dewey 2019). As a native speaker of Icelandic, my intuition does not go further than affirming that the Dat-Nom construction is used when the dative is the topical argument in the discourse, while the Nom-Dat construction is used when it is the nominative argument that is topical. Further research is needed to uncover the intricacies of the choices Icelandic and German speakers face when using alternating Dat-Nom / Nom-Dat verbs in their respective languages.

6.5 Summary

One of the first problems encountered when diving into the issue of argument structure in German is that there is a major inconsistency in the literature regarding subject status and the order of the arguments in the argument structure. For most verb classes, the subject is regarded as the first argument of the argument structure, which is also how the subject concept is defined in this work, while for a subset of verbs, in particular Dat-Nom and Acc-Nom verbs, their subject is regarded as being the second argument of the argument structure. This is a consequence of the fact that the German scholarship still makes use of the traditional Latin school grammar definition of subject, as being in the nominative case and controlling verb agreement, irrespective of whether German scholars use behavioral properties to motivate their subject definition or not. This discrepancy in how subject is defined across verb classes is clearly not only profoundly *ad hoc*, but it also means that grammatical descriptions of German miss out on a major generalization, namely that it is the first argument of the argument structure that passes the subject tests, be it the nominative or the dative.

In addition, several arguments have been put forward in the literature on why oblique subjects cannot be regarded as syntactic subjects in German. These arguments may be divided into two types:
a) arguments in favor of the subject status of the nominative
b) arguments against the subject status of oblique subjects, based on the relevant verbs' lacking ability to be embedded under control verbs and their lacking ability to occur in second conjuncts with the subject left unexpressed

Regarding the first type of argumentation, there is no doubt that the subject behavior of the nominative is, of course, an argument for the subject status of that very same nominative. However, as is discussed in Chapter 4 above, this is not necessarily an argument against the subject status of the dative. As a matter of fact, this does not qualify as an argument against the subject status of the dative at all if the relevant verbs are alternating verbs, i.e., alternating between the Dat-Nom and

Nom-Dat argument structure constructions. On such an assumption, the subject behavior of the nominative clearly involves the Nom-Dat construction and not the Dat-Nom construction. This argumentation is therefore invalid, as it has no bearing on the subject status of the dative.

Turning to the second type of argumentation, namely that oblique subjects cannot be left unexpressed in conjunction reduction and control constructions, I have here introduced examples showing that oblique subjects may certainly be left unexpressed in both types of structures. This, however, does not mean that I question the ungrammaticality judgments of the examples presented in the literature. Instead, it only means that I believe that there may be further restrictions on ellipsis in German than in Icelandic, a topic which I believe is worthy of further investigation, as opposed to simply assuming that oblique subjects are not syntactic subjects in German. This is what I have referred to as the Restricted Ellipsis Analysis as opposed to a "non-subject analysis" already in Section 2.3.3, as well as above.

An examination of how Dat-Nom verbs in German fare with regard to the six subject tests, here applied on both German and Icelandic data, reveals that either argument, the dative or the nominative, passes the subject tests in German. For word order, in particular, I have presented corpus-based frequencies for two sets of verbs, *helfen* verbs and *gefallen/geziemen* verbs. Verbs of the *helfen* type are unambiguous Nom-Dat verbs, with the nominative being the subject and the dative the object. Word order frequencies for *helfen* verbs, based on full NPs only and excluding pronouns, reveal that these verbs occur in the Nom-Dat linear order in 90%–100% of the cases, while the opposite linear order, dative-before-nominative, is found in 0%–10% of the cases, depending on the verb. Therefore, these numbers provide a baseline for how frequent topicalization of full NPs is, i.e. 0%–10%, vs. how frequent neutral word order is. In contrast, *gefallen/geziemen* verbs do not align with *helfen* verbs in German, as their frequencies are more evenly distributed across the two word order constellations (excluding the outlier *nützen* 'be of use'), ranging from 38% Dat-Nom vs. 62% Nom-Dat to 55% Dat-Nom vs. 45% Nom-Dat. Exactly the same kind of a corpus-based study is presented in Chapter 3 for Icelandic, where the baseline for topicalizations of full NPs is only 4%, not 10% as in German. There is no doubt, however, that *gefallen/geziemen* verbs in German show the same kind of word order symmetry as *henta* verbs do in Icelandic. As such, those word order symmetries are only compatible with an alternating analysis of these verbs, excluding topicalization.

The remaining subject tests are conjunction reduction, clause-bound reflexivization, raising-to-subject, raising-to-object and control infinitives. A comparison with Icelandic further lays bare that for a subset of the relevant verbs in that language, either argument passes the subject tests, the dative or the nominative, while for another set of verbs, it is only the dative that takes on the syntactic behavior of subject. These facts support the claim in the existing literature on Icelandic that there are two types of Dat-Nom verbs in that language, non-alternating Dat-Nom verbs and alternating Dat-Nom / Nom-Dat verbs. For German, in contrast, the implicit assumption in the literature has been that Dat-Nom verbs in German are non-alternating, while at the same time it has been recognized that the nominative passes some of the subject tests. This, in turn, has been accounted for through the assumption that the subject is the second argument, i.e. the nominative, of these Dat-Nom verbs.

A considerably more parsimonious analysis for German is that existing Dat-Nom verbs in that language are alternating verbs, vacillating between the Dat-Nom and the Nom-Dat argument structure constructions. Such an analysis is also able to account for the fact that either argument of Dat-Nom verbs, the dative or the nominative, passes the six subject tests in German discussed in this chapter without making recourse to *ad hoc* stipulations. On this analysis, the behavior of German Dat-Nom verbs is no anomaly in the Germanic linguistic landscape, as it patterns instead with analogous verbs in Modern Icelandic and Faroese, as well as with analogous verbs in the history of the Germanic and Indo-European languages.

7 Synthesis

Research on oblique subjects, i.e. verbal arguments which behave syntactically as subjects, has been ongoing ever since before Keenan's seminal article on subjecthood from 1976. As soon as the modern syntactic research community started developing a concept of subject which focused on the syntactic behavior of subject arguments, as opposed to the traditional morphological concept of subject found in Latin school grammar, attention was directed at non-canonically case-marked subjects. These have been referred to as oblique subjects in this study, following (Falk 1997) and Barðdal (1998, 2001 and later work).

Oblique subjects have been documented in language family after language family around the globe. This includes Modern Icelandic and Modern Faroese which belong to the subbranch of Germanic languages, while their closely related cousin, Modern German, has been regarded as not having oblique subjects. This does not mean, in and of itself, that equivalent predicates selecting for potential oblique subjects do not exist in German; they certainly do. This simply means that potential oblique subjects have not been analyzed as behaving syntactically as subjects in German, but have instead been analyzed as topicalized objects (cf. Verhoeven 2015), following a long tradition in the German scholarship.

This discrepancy between Modern Icelandic and Faroese, on the one hand, and Modern German, on the other, raises the question of whether the situation in North Germanic represents the original state of affairs, or whether it is the situation in West-Germanic that should be assumed to be original. This, in turn, brings to the fore the syntactic status of equivalent verbal arguments in the early Germanic languages, as in Old Norse-Icelandic, Old English, Old Saxon Old High German and Gothic, as solid knowledge of their status is instrumental for evaluating the development of the oblique subject construction from the earliest documented Germanic period until modern times.

Historical syntacticians are divided into two camps with regard to the syntactic status of potential oblique subjects in the early Germanic languages. Faarlund (1991, 1992, 2001), Kristoffersen (1991, 1994, 1996), Juntune (1992), Mørck (1992), Askedal (2001), Falk (1997, 2018) and Heltoft (2021) argue that potential oblique subjects were not syntactic subjects in Old Norse-Icelandic, Middle Norwegian, Old Danish or Old Swedish, respectively. In contrast, Rögnvaldsson (1991, 1995, 1996), Zeefranz-Montag (1993, 1994), Allen (1995), Barðdal (1998, 2000a, 2000b), Barðdal and Eythórsson (2003a, 2012a), Hrafnbjargarson (2004), Eythórsson and Barðdal (2005), Fischer (2010), and Jónsson (2018) argue for the subject status of potential oblique subjects in Old Norse-Icelandic, Old Scandinavian, Old English or Old Germanic in general.

The goal of the present study is to review the Early Germanic evidence, in relation to the status of oblique subjects in the modern languages in order to uncover any possible development from the earliest Germanic stages to modern times. This, in turn, requires a proper discussion and explication of the subject concept, in particular a clear outline of how subject is defined in this study. Setting up a baseline for case languages, grounded in how ordinary nominative subjects behave, is the first step in this process.

Taking Modern Icelandic as a point of departure, I use the following established subject properties (Andrews 1976; Thráinsson 1979; Zaenen, Maling, and Thráinsson 1985; Sigurðsson 1989, 1992; Jónsson 1996; and others), to establish a baseline for case languages, built on how nominative subjects in that language behave syntactically:
- Neutral Word Order
- Subject-Verb Inversion
- Clause-Bound Reflexivization
- Long-Distance Reflexivization
- Conjunction Reduction
- Raising-to-Subject
- Raising-to-Object
- Control Infinitives

The baseline is founded on the syntactic behavior of the arguments of two verbs in Modern Icelandic, *drepa* 'kill' and *treysta* 'trust', which select for Nom-Acc and Nom-Dat, respectively. The verb *drepa* 'kill' occurs with a nominative subject and an accusative object, while *treysta* 'trust' occurs with a nominative subject and a dative object. A comparison of the syntactic behavior of the arguments of these two verbs shows, not unexpectedly, that it is the nominative argument that takes on the subject properties, while the accusative and the dative, respectively, behave syntactically in a different manner from nominative subjects. These two, moreover, show a uniform behavior between themselves, a behavior which is also used to establish a baseline for how objects behave. All in all, the behavior of the nominative provides a solid foundation for the nominative subject baseline established here and applied on the behavior of potential oblique subjects in the remainder of this study.

One major problem with regard to the analysis of oblique subjects is that the subject properties themselves have typically been used as an implicit subject definition, while an explicit definition of subject is entirely lacking. This is not only a problem for several studies devoted to the issue of oblique subjects (see below) but this is also typical for textbooks on grammar in different languages (Tallerman 1998; Huddleston and Pullum 2005; Börjars and Burridge 2010; van Gelderen

2010; Aarts 2011; Payne 2011; Aman and Tan 2018; Kim and Michaelis 2020, only to mention a few). This is particularly problematic in cases where different subject arguments behave differently within a language, a topic I return to below.

In addition, considerable methodological opportunism is detected in the early work on oblique subjects in Icelandic and German. The Icelandic school had as its goal to compare the behavior of oblique subjects to the behavior of nominative subjects (Andrews 1976; Thráinsson 1979; Zaenen, Maling, and Thráinsson 1985; Sigurðsson 1989, 1992; and others). This, in turn, excludes the use of the coding properties, as oblique subjects are not in the nominative case and they do not agree with the verb, with this last property being confined to nominative arguments. In other words, since the goal was to identify the syntactic behavior of oblique subjects and compare them with the syntactic behavior of nominative subjects, case and agreement are naturally not included. Thus, these methodological choices are motivated by the exploratory nature of the enterprise, i.e. by a comparison of the syntactic and distributional properties of oblique subjects with nominative subjects.

For the German school (Reis 1982), things proceeded in a different manner. A systematic comparison was made between nominative and oblique subjects and two steps were taken:
i) all constructions involving word order distribution, in particular those shared by both subjects and objects were ruled out as subject behaviors
ii) every behavior shared by both nominative and oblique subjects was also systematically excluded from being viewed as a subject property

Two major methodological problems may be discerned here: First, it is not motivated to exclude all word order constructions shared by both nominative subjects and accusative or dative objects, as German is not a non-configurational language. That is, it may be entirely possible to use intonation patterns to distinguish between neutral word order and word orders which deviate from these basics, due to information structural factors (cf. Barðdal 2006; and Barðdal, Eythórsson, and Dewey 2019 where this is established for oblique subjects and their word order distribution in German). Second, due to the second methodological procedure, only the properties that were confined to nominative subjects were deemed as subject properties. As a consequence, oblique subjects do not exist in German, by definition.

From an outside perspective, it appears as if the earliest methodological choices made by the German school were first and foremost aiming at protecting the traditional definition of subject as being in the nominative case, at the exclusion of every deviation from the nominative subject canon. It is not clear why else all behavioral properties shared by nominative and oblique subjects would be excluded from consideration.

Later work on German has, first and foremost, directed its focus on the syntactic behaviors which differ between Icelandic and German, thus giving priority to exactly these properties (Zaenen, Maling, and Thráinsson 1985; Sigurðsson 1989, 1992; Fanselow 2002; Bayer 2004; Haider 2005, 2010; Wunderlich 2009; Pankau 2016), without any principled discussion of the methodological choices made. This means that the syntactic behaviors which differ between Icelandic and German have been singled out as criterial for subject and through that choice, oblique subjects in German have systematically been excluded from being analyzed as subjects. This is due to an implicit definition of subject through the use of a subset of the subject properties, more specifically a subset of only two subject tests. These are conjunction reduction and control infinitives, while the remaining six subject properties, shared between Icelandic and German, have all been largely discredited in the literature.

As opposed to this, I have suggested here a bottom-up definition of subject, arrived at through a generalization across the established syntactic properties of subject, in particular on the basis of which argument of the argument structure passes the behavioral subject tests. A closer inspection reveals that it is, in fact, the first argument of the argument structure that passes all the subject tests, while the second argument behaves differently in the very same constructions. This, I believe, constitutes the empirical core of subjecthood, which all theoretical frameworks have to account for in one way or the other.

My definition of subject, as the first argument of the argument structure, is further rooted in the causal conceptual structure of verbs and their force-dynamics, which in turn are derivatives of event structure. As is well known, verbs have different lexical semantics, some being causative, others being inchoative, stative, etc. The different semantic verb classes represent different event types and causal chains. Thus, the type of force-dynamics varies from one lexical semantic verb class to the other, with causative verbs entailing that a force is exerted by an initiator on an endpoint, as initiators exist independently of events, while endpoints do not necessarily exist prior to events, but may instead be incrementally created through the event. This means that it is the causal chain that allows for the internal ranking of the participant roles, i.e. their ranking in relation to each other, and thus which participant role maps to the first argument and which one to the second argument of the argument structure.

In contrast, psychological predicates have a choice between different construals. This is particularly relevant for oblique subject verbs for which the following two event construals are of relevance:

i) Experiencer directs his or her attention towards a stimulus (*fear* construal)
ii) Stimulus affects experiencers (*frighten* construal)

In general, psychological verbs are compatible with both construals, as opposed to causative events which are confined to initiators acting upon endpoints. On the former construal listed above, the experiencer is the first argument of the argument structure, and hence the subject, while on the latter construal, it is the stimulus that is the first argument of the argument structure, thus taking on the subject role. The message to take home from this is, *I repeat*, that the internal order of the arguments in the argument structure stems from event structure, which exists independently of language.

The present approach to the subject concept has here been juxtaposed to an approach on which the subject tests function as stand-ins for a proper definition of subject. Needless to say, I have here rejected this "subject-test stand-in" approach, first and foremost because of its lack of methodological rigor and the unrestrained methodological opportunism that may accompany it, an opportunism devoid of any principled manner of choosing between the subject tests. In contrast, on an approach in which the subject is the first argument of the argument structure, problems like the aforementioned may be avoided altogether, as they simply do not arise.

Regarding word order, I claim, following the iconicity principle, that irrespective of whether or not languages are SO or OS languages, the subject is still the first argument of the argument structure. This is unproblematic for SO languages where the subject precedes the object anyway in constructions involving neutral word order. Taking OS languages into the equation, however, I argue that the mapping from event structure to argument structure is the same for both OS and SO languages, with the difference between them stemming from the mapping from argument structure to neutral word order. This means that for OS languages, the second argument of the argument structure, the object, maps to an earlier position in the clause than the subject. In other words, the relation between argument structure and word order is indirect, yielding linear mapping for SO languages but non-linear for OS languages.

For ergative languages, one can still argue that the first argument of the argument structure is the subject. This is because the subject tests in morphologically ergative languages always target the first argument of the argument structure, irrespective of whether this subject is ergative or absolutive, i.e. irrespective of whether the subject is the subject of transitive or intransitive verbs. For syntactically ergative languages, in contrast, it appears that the so-called subject tests, well-known from an array of other languages, are not really subject tests in these languages, but case tests instead. That is, it appears that only arguments that are case marked in the same morphological case are targeted by the tests, irrespective of grammatical relations.

The present definition of subject, as being the first argument of the argument structure, is easily modeled through the indexing of the arguments in an Attributed Value Matrix, which is how grammar is formalized in several versions of Construction Grammar. This involves two representations, one Attributed Value Matrix for lexical entries and another for argument structure constructions (cf. Figure 33). The order of the arguments in the lexical entry is not set, while the order of the arguments in the argument structure is fixed, namely to Nom-Acc for transitive verbs with accusative objects, Nom-Dat for transitive verbs with dative objects, Acc-Acc for accusative subject verbs selecting for accusative objects, and Dat-Nom for verbs such as *líka* 'like' and *leiðast* 'be bored' in Icelandic, to mention a few options.

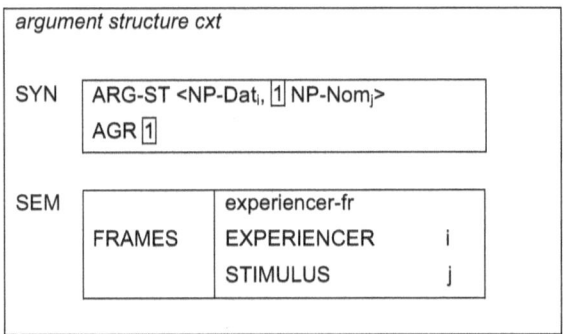

Figure 33: The Order of the Arguments in the Argument Structure.

Further, the first argument of the argument structure is indexed with an *i*, while the second argument of the argument structure is indexed with a *j*. In addition, each of the syntactic constructions which function as a subject test must be modeled, including how the different arguments of the argument structure interact with the remaining structure, as well as with each other. Again, this is modeled via the indexing of the arguments in these constructions. From this modeling, the equivalent subject behavior of both nominative and oblique subjects falls out, as both are indexed with an *i* in their respective argument structure constructions.

All of this entails that subject is not only a language-specific category, but also a construction-specific one, in keeping with Radical Construction Grammar. That is, the subject takes on a specific syntactic role in a given construction as a whole, instead of forming a generalized relation with a predicate, irrespective of the type of construction involved. Such an approach indeed allows subjects of different constructions within a language to show variation in its behavior, which is in principle excluded on the view that the subject forms a generalized relation with its predicate throughout the language, irrespective of constructions.

On a definition of subject as being the first argument of the argument structure, irrespective of the case marking of that argument, oblique subjects not only acquire the right to exist but also become a legitimate subcategory of subject. This, of course, presupposes that it is the first argument of the argument structure that takes on the behavioral properties of subject in the relevant language. And, as I state above, this is a solid generalization for the languages that I have worked on here, i.e. the Germanic languages (see also Barðdal et al. 2023 for similar results in Latin and Ancient Greek).

Given the present definition of subject, a further question that arises is why oblique subjects in German, which are undeniably the first argument of their argument structures, do not conform fully to the baseline provided by nominative subjects in that language. That is, why do oblique subjects in German not behave syntactically as subjects in all respects? It turns out that the differences between nominative and oblique subjects in German involve only two subject behaviors, namely conjunction reduction and control infinitives. These are also the two behaviors which distinguish between oblique subjects in Icelandic and German.

Zaenen, Maling, and Thráinsson (1985) compare the behavior of potential oblique subjects in Modern Icelandic and Modern German across several behavioral subject tests, of which only conjunction reduction and control infinitives are found to differ between the two languages. Nevertheless, Zaenen, Maling, and Thráinsson (1985) argue, on the basis of the outcome of these two subject tests, that there are oblique subjects in Icelandic, but not in German. No argumentation, whatsoever, is provided for the choice of these two subject tests as criterial over the remaining tests that Zaenen, Maling, and Thráinsson discuss. This is a clear example of methodological opportunism, where Zaenen, Maling, and Thráinsson's analysis paved the way for their kowtowers for decades to come.

What is more, no behavioral evidence for an object status of potential oblique subjects in German has ever been provided, neither by Zaenen, Maling, and Thráinsson, nor by any other scholars, as far as I am aware. This means that membership in the category of object is subjected to a much lower standard than membership in the category of subject, with objects basically being treated as a waste-paper-basket category into which any argument that does not behave in all respects according to expectations can be thrown. This is not good linguistic practice and it should not continue.

In the literature on oblique subjects, another way to deal with different behavior of seemingly analogous verbal arguments both within and across languages has been suggested, namely in terms of a prototype approach to subjecthood (Holvoet

2013, 2016; Seržant 2013). Regrettably, the goal of this approach is not to distinguish between subject and object behavior, and thus not to distinguish between syntactic subjects and objects, but rather to uncover which behavioral properties are "more" subject properties and which are "less" subject properties. As a consequence, on this approach an argument may become a "partial" subject, if it only passes a "part" of the subject properties.

The problem with the prototype approach to subjecthood is that due to its built-in concept of "gradience" it is entirely unclear how many and which subject properties a verbal argument must pass in order to be analyzed as a full-fledged subject. That is, which of the behavioral properties of subject should take priority over the others? And, how many subject properties does a verbal argument have to pass in order to be analyzed as a genuine subject? Is it enough to be a 50% "subject" or is it required to be 60% or 75% "subject" in order to qualify as a syntactic subject? Thus, not only does a prototype approach to subjecthood appear as absurd when taken to its logical conclusions, it is also explanatory inadequate, with no evident predictive power.

In order to avoid methodological and theoretical pitfalls of the type discussed above, I have argued in this monograph for an independently applicable subject definition, namely in terms of the order of the arguments in the argument structure. More specifically, I argue that subject is the first argument of the argument structure, as I believe that this is the empirical core of subjecthood from which all subject behaviors are derived. On such a definition of subject, potential oblique subjects in German become syntactic subjects and not waste-paper-basket objects.

Moreover, on a subject analysis of oblique subjects in German, the question arises as to why such verbal arguments do not pass all the same behavioral subject properties as their nominative counterparts do. On a closer inspection of the nature of the behavioral subject tests, a generalization emerges, namely that all the behavioral subject tests which oblique subjects do not pass in German, in fact, involve ellipsis. These are the following:
i) conjunction reduction
ii) control infinitives
iii) deletion in telegraphic style

This suggests that there may be restrictions on ellipsis in German, which are not found in Icelandic, or at least not to the same degree. In addition, playing around with the data, examples of conjunction reduction, for instance, become grammatical with an oblique subject left unexpressed on identity with another oblique subject in the first conjunct, provided that they share the same morphological case. Therefore, oblique subjects do pass the conjunction reduction test, given that the two subjects have identical case marking and that they share the same syntactic roles.

Moving on to control infinitives, there is no doubt that oblique subjects are generally not acceptable in such structures in German, although a few existing examples have been documented, some going back as far as to the 18th century. This includes examples composed by the famous 18th century philosopher, Immanuel Kant, and his contemporaries. Attested examples of this type receive mixed responses in acceptability studies, being judged as grammatical by a portion of the population, marginal by others, and ungrammatical by yet others. There is also considerable variation found between examples. Unexpectedly, corresponding control infinitives in Icelandic, also harvested from texts on the World Wide Web, are judged marginal and unacceptable by some speakers as well, yet grammatical by other speakers. Thus, the same variation between examples as in German is also found in Icelandic, the *quintessential* oblique subject language, the language in which the existence and felicitousness of examples of this type have always been assumed to be above all doubt. Therefore, I conclude that the dichotomy between Icelandic and German, assumed in the literature, is non-existent. At best, the differences between Icelandic and German represent a difference in degree, not a difference in kind.

Note, also, that it is only on a subject analysis of oblique subjects in German that questions like these are asked. On the standard analysis, that these are objects in German, the status of the research has simply been left in a deadlock, without any further questions posed. It is also somewhat of a surprise, and quite a disappointing one, that the scholarship on German appears to find an object analysis of oblique subjects satisfactory, despite the fact that this would entail an almost obligatory topicalization of the alleged object to the front of the clause. Generally, topicalizations are optional. Yet, this situation may, at least in part, be explained by the fact that, for instance, Dat-Nom predicates in German are alternating predicates, which in turn means that not only the dative shows subject behavior, but also the nominative, although not at the same time, of course.

Turning to the historical Germanic material, an important notion of major relevance for the topic of this study is the concept of alternating predicates. These are either simple verbs or compositional predicates which have in common the fact that they occur either with a Dat-Nom or a Nom-Dat argument structure construction. That is, these predicates seem to alternate between two diametrically opposite argument structure constructions, namely Dat-Nom and Nom-Dat.

As a part and parcel of establishing the existence of alternating Dat-Nom / Nom-Dat predicates, I have introduced two predicates from Modern Icelandic, *skiljast* 'gather' and *falla í skaut* 'fall in sb's lap', which happen to behave differently with regard to the behavioral subject tests in Icelandic. The verb *skiljast* 'gather' behaves syntactically in the same way as *líka* 'like' in that the dative always passes the subject tests while the nominative behaves systematically as an object. In other words, *skiljast* 'gather' is a Dat-Nom verb in Icelandic. In contrast, for *falla í*

skaut 'fall in sb's lap', either argument passes the behavioral subject tests, both the dative and the nominative. When the dative behaves syntactically as a subject, the nominative behaves as an object, and vice versa, when the nominative takes on the behavioral properties of subjects, the dative behaves syntactically as an object. This means that *falla í skaut* 'fall in sb's lap' clearly is an alternating Dat-Nom / Nom-Dat predicate in Icelandic. All of this I establish with the use of the following tests:
- word order
- clause-bound reflexivization
- long-distance reflexivization
- raising-to-subject
- raising-to-object
- conjunction reduction
- control infinitives

It has also been argued in the literature that there are alternating predicates in Modern Faroese, Old English, Old Swedish and Old Danish, even though the evidence for the historical languages is considerably more scanty than for Modern Icelandic and Faroese. Allen (1995) argues that *eglian* 'bother, ail', *gelician* 'like', *hreowan* 'pity', *laþian* 'loathe', *lician* 'like', *losian* 'lose, be lost', *mislician* 'dislike', *ofhreowan* 'pity', *oflician* 'dislike', *ofþyncan* 'regret' and *þyncan* 'think, seem' are alternating verbs in Old English on the basis of two tests:
i) word order
ii) conjunction reduction

For Old Swedish and Old Danish, I have argued that the word order distribution of the arguments of *nöghia* 'suffice', *smaka* 'taste' *söma* 'befit, *þykkia* 'think, seem' and *þäkkias* 'like, please' in Old Swedish and *angre* 'pain', *gaghne* 'be of use' and *fortryde* 'regret' in Old Danish, in fact, speak for an alternating analysis of these verbs. This analysis is further corroborated by the fact that the cognates of OSw. *nöghia* 'suffice', *smaka* 'taste' and *söma* 'befit, and ODa. *gaghne* 'be of use' are also alternating predicates in Modern Icelandic. Moreover, variation in the data from the modern Scandinavian languages, involving the argument structure of Sw. *lyckas* / Da. *lykkes* / NNo. *lukkast* 'succeed' and South Sw. *felas* 'lack, miss', can only be explained on the assumption that these were alternating verbs during earlier stages of these languages.

In addition to the data from the early West and North Germanic languages, I have also introduced example pairs from Gothic, Sanskrit, Hittite, Latin, Ancient Greek and Old Russian, all displaying diametrically opposite word order patterns which are typical for alternating Dat-Nom / Nom-Dat predicates. Evidence from

Modern Greek, Modern Lithuanian and Modern Russian has also been presented as corroborating the analysis for the early languages, as this evidence involves either descendent or cognate verbs in the modern languages, showing a clear preponderance for alternation of the type being discussed here.

The difference in behavior between alternating and non-alternating verbs may be modeled such that there is only one lexical entry for, for instance *falla í skaut* 'fall in sb's lap', which then interacts with the two argument structure constructions, Dat-Nom and Nom-Dat, while *skiljast* 'gather' would only interact with one argument structure, i.e. Dat-Nom. This means that lexical entries merge with argument structure constructions, which exist irrespective of the verbs instantiating them. This is shown for *falla í skaut* 'fall in sb's lap' in Figure 34.

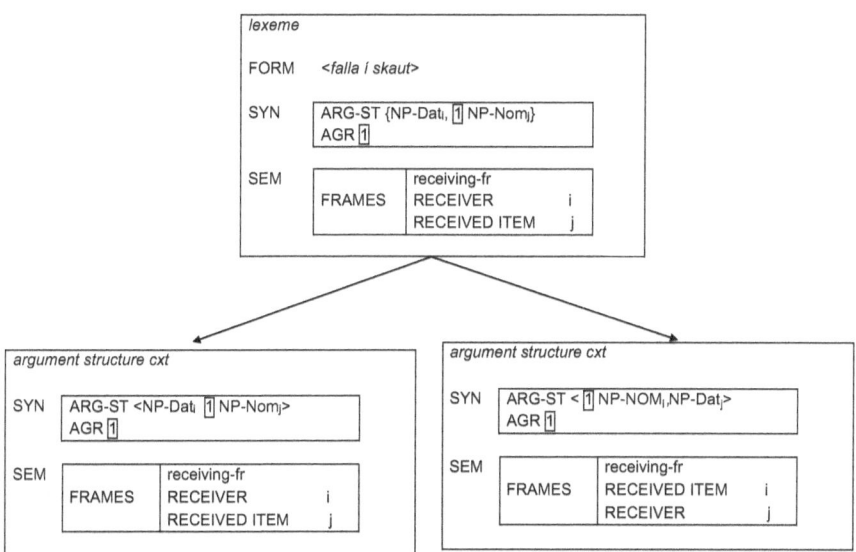

Figure 34: The interaction between the lexeme *falla í skaut* 'fall in sb's lap' and its two Dat-Nom and Nom-Dat Argument Structures.

Contrary to lexical entries, the order of the arguments in argument structure constructions is instead ordered, denoted with angled brackets in the Attributed Value Matrix. This results in non-alternating verbs merging with the Dat-Nom argument structure construction, while alternating verbs merge with either the Dat-Nom or the Nom-Dat argument structure construction. Whether a verb merges with only the Dat-Nom argument structure or with either of the two argument structures is a lexical idiosyncrasy, as several synonymous and near-synonymous verb pairs split across the two patterns, the alternating and the non-alternating one.

At this juncture, I particularly want to draw the readers' attention to a point worthy of being reiterated here, relating to the standard story of the verb 'like' in the history of English. This standard story, originally put forward by Jespersen in 1927, assumes that there was a development from Nom-Dat to Dat-Nom with the verb 'like' in the history of English, with this new Dat-Nom construction then losing its case marking and becoming the default Nom-Acc. Evidence from Gothic (Eythórsson and Barðdal 2005), Old English (Allen 1986, 1995) and perhaps Old Norse-Icelandic (Barðdal 2001b; Sigurðsson and Viðarsson 2020), suggests instead that 'like' was an alternating verb in the earliest Germanic layers. Assuming an alternating analysis for 'like' in Old English would certainly yield a much more parsimonious account of the development of 'like' in the history of English than the one provided by Jespersen's standard story. All that is needed is to assume two argument structure constructions, Dat-Nom and Nom-Dat, of which one fell into disuse, Nom-Dat, while the other, Dat-Nom, adapted to changes taking place later in the morphology of Old/Middle English, thus becoming Nom-Acc.

Another diachronic story, also from the history of English, similar in nature to the story of 'like', is put forward by Harris and Campbell (1995) involving the verb *sēme* 'seem, think, fit'. Harris and Campbell suggest that the existing Nom-Dat construction developed into Dat-Nom, before it started developing into Nom-Obj, then falling into disuse. The greatest problem with their account is that it involves an undocumented swapping of the arguments of the argument structure. Harris and Campbell do not present a convincing chronology documenting their developmental stages and it turns out that both Dat-Nom and Nom-Dat can be documented much earlier in the texts than they presume. Thus, a considerably more parsimonious account of the development is to assume that *sēme* 'seem, think, fit' was an alternating predicate, as its cognate *sœma* 'be proper' still is in Modern Icelandic. Given that, no "swapping" of the arguments within the argument structure needs to be posited. Instead, one of the argument structure constructions falls into disuse, while the other develops with some intermediate steps, into Nom-PP, as it still is in Modern English.

These issues certainly raise the question of the relative chronology of this alternation, especially in relation to non-alternating Dat-Nom predicates. That is, are non-alternating predicates original for Proto-Indo-European, with a Nom-Dat alternant gradually developing for the daughter languages? The problem with this scenario is that alternating predicates appear to be found in most, if not all, early Indo-European languages, as well as in several modern Indo-European languages that have kept their morphological case in tact, like Icelandic, Faroese, German, Lithuanian and Russian. Additional modern Indo-European languages where the dative has changed into a prepositional argument, like Romanian and Greek, also show this alternation.

These issues, in turn, raise the question of whether alternations of this type may be regarded as a shared innovation. I know of no study documenting the emergence of such alternations and I find it highly unlikely that such alternations would arise spontaneously in languages, as this would entail the "swapping" of the arguments in the argument structure. Such an alleged change is radically different from the emergence of case variation, for instance, where a dative subject changes into an accusative subject, or vice versa. Such case variation is easily explained through shared verbal and/or constructional semantics (cf. Barðdal 2009). All things considered, the wide distribution of alternating predicates across the Indo-European phylum rather speaks for inheritance than a shared innovation. Thus, under the second scenario, alternating Dat-Nom / Nom-Dat predicates represent the original state of affairs, with non-alternating Dat-Nom predicates in Icelandic later developing from these through the loss of the Nom-Dat alternant.

I concur with Pooth et al. (2019) who argue that these alternating predicates arose in the development from an active to an accusative system, through the reanalysis of an antipassive-like construction as an active voice construction, here labeled the Extended Intransitive Hypothesis. This antipassive-like construction had only one zero-marked argument, referred to here as absolutive, which later developed into nominative. This intransitive antipassive-like construction could also occur with an extended argument used for experiencers, marked in the locative, which later developed into a benefactive dative. This extended experiencer could either precede or follow the zero-marked absolutive argument in the linear order, due to the non-agentivity of the dative argument and the inanimacy of the absolutive, later nominative, argument.

More specifically, the former agentive -s marker was generalized as a nominative marker throughout different clause types in the language, replacing all zero-marked absolutives during the transition from semantic to accusative alignment. However, this new nominative only bore -s marking in cases of animate nouns, as the zero-marked absolutive continued to be zero-marked in cases where the former anti-agentive argument slot was filled with inanimate neuter nouns. As such, the two word orders, Dat-Nom and Nom-Dat, originate in the transition period between an active system and an accusative system, with the word order variation being motivated by the lack of agentivity found with the relevant verbs. On such an analysis, the alternation between the Dat-Nom and Nom-Dat constructions is indeed reconstructable for Proto-Indo-European.

Turning now to the early Germanic languages, and the syntactic tests used to establish subject behavior in the modern languages, two of the tests in the modern Germanic languages are not conclusive for the old Germanic languages in general. These are conjunction reduction and clause-bound reflexivization. However, Allen (1995), argues that conjunction reduction may, in fact, be used as a subject test for

Old English, taking into consideration different frequencies found for different types of controllers in the main clause. Allen demonstrates that while main clause objects may control the omission of conjoined subjects in 1% of the cases, main clause nominative subjects instead control omission of conjoined subjects in 80% of the cases during the same period in the English language. Oblique subjects control the omission of conjoined subjects in 50–60% of the cases.

While it is certainly true that 50–60% is considerably lower than 80%, these statistics show that the behavior of oblique subjects is considerably more in line with the behavior of nominative subjects than it is with unambiguous objects. However, as long as the restrictions on subject omission in second conjuncts are not known in the 20% of the cases where it does not apply when controlled by a nominative subject, it is impossible to know to which degree these restrictions are at work when oblique subjects control the omission of the subject in second conjuncts. All that can be deduced from this is that even though one cannot draw any conclusions on the basis of individual examples, the statistics confirm that oblique subjects behave syntactically as nominative subjects in Old English with regard to conjunction reduction and do not behave as objects.

Another subject test that is only applicable in a subset of the early Germanic languages is long-distance reflexivization. Examples of reflexives in subordinate clauses being bound by nominative subjects in previous main clauses have been documented in both Gothic (Harbert 1983) and Old Norse-Icelandic (Rögnvaldsson 1996, 2007). This behavior, to bind reflexives in subordinate clauses, is not found with objects. Several examples have been documented in Old Norse-Icelandic where an oblique subject binds a reflexive (Rögnvaldsson 1996, 2007), and one has been found in Gothic (Bucci and Barðdal 2023), indeed attesting to the subject behavior of oblique subjects in these two languages.

Regarding word order, there is no doubt that word order distribution can be used in the modern languages to distinguish between subjects and objects. For the early Germanic languages, things are a bit more difficult, since there are no native speakers to inform us of what counts as neutral word order and what not. Still, quantitative analysis can aid in this task instead. In a study published by Barðdal and Eythórsson (2012), with data ranging from the 11th to the 20th century, it is demonstrated that oblique subjects show, more or less, the same statistical tendencies for word order as nominative subjects do. No real statistical differences are found for different time periods in Icelandic. Also, the reason that oblique subjects have consistently been labeled "psychological" or "logical" subjects in the older literature is because of their word order distribution which has been perceived of as being the same as that of nominative subjects. But due to the non-nominative case marking, a subject analysis was ruled out at the time.

Further subject tests used on the early Germanic languages are raising-to-subject, raising-to-object and control, all involving different types of infinitives. Starting with raising-to-subject, examples of raising verbs with nominative subjects are documented in all the early Germanic languages, indeed corroborating the validity of this test. Examples involving oblique subject predicates, where the oblique subject of the lower verb takes on the behavior of the subject of the finite verb are also documented in all the early languages under investigation, except for Gothic. These languages are Old High German, Old English, Old Saxon, Old Norse-Icelandic, Old Swedish and Old Danish. This property, to take on the subject behavior of the finite raising-to-subject verb, in fact, speaks for the subject status of oblique subjects in the early Germanic languages.

Structures involving raising-to-object also exist in all the early Germanic languages with nominative subjects. Corresponding examples with oblique subjects are also found in Old High German, Old Saxon, Middle English, Old Norse-Icelandic, Old Swedish and Old Danish, but, again, not in Gothic. When accusative subject verbs are embedded under raising-to-object verbs, their "raised" subject occurs in the accusative case, exactly as when nominative subjects are "raised" in such structures. It is, thus, unclear whether the accusative comes from the raising-to-object construction itself, as it does with nominative subjects, or whether it is assigned by the lower verb. In contrast, when dative subject verbs are embedded under raising-to-object verbs, the "raised" subject maintains the dative assigned by the lower verb. This is exactly parallel to the situation in Modern Icelandic and Modern Faroese raising-to-subject constructions, the two modern Germanic languages well-known in the literature for having oblique subjects.

That oblique subjects behave syntactically as objects of raising-to-object verbs, despite maintaining their case marking, is incontrovertible. This is further corroborated by the placement of sentence adverbials in some of the relevant examples, as sentence adverbials demarcate the boundaries of the verb phrase. Since the "raised" oblique subjects are located further to the left than the sentence adverbials, these oblique subjects cannot be analyzed as being within the verb phrase, but must be analyzed as behaving like objects of the finite raising verbs. There is thus no doubt that oblique subjects behave as syntactic subjects in the early Germanic languages with respect to raising-to-object, exactly as nominative subjects do.

Turning to control infinitives, it is well known that control infinitives exist in the early Germanic languages and that nominative subject verbs are frequently embedded in such structures. When that happens, the nominative subject is left unexpressed, while objects in such control infinitives are instead spelled out. This, of course, does not mean that objects cannot be left unexpressed in such structures; it only means that they are not systematically left unexpressed, as opposed to subjects which must be left unexpressed in control infinitives.

In the earlier literature, one example of a control infinitive with oblique subject verbs embedded under a control verb has been documented for Gothic. This involves the Acc-Gen verb 'lust' (see Barðdal and Eythórsson 2012), meaning that the accusative of 'lust' was treated as a syntactic subject when this example was translated from Ancient Greek to Gothic. In contrast, in the Greek original, the relevant verb used is a Nom-Dat verb. This means that when Wulfila translated the Greek Bible to Gothic, he, in fact, equated the accusative of the Acc-Gen case frame of 'lust' with the nominative of the Nom-Dat case frame of the Greek original.

For the other early Germanic languages, two examples of oblique subject verbs embedded in control infinitives are known from Early Middle English, six examples are known from Old Norse-Icelandic and two from Old Swedish. Here I have introduced twelve additional examples, not documented in the earlier literature on oblique subjects in the early Germanic languages. Three of these examples are from Old Saxon, seven are from Old Norse-Icelandic, one from Old Swedish and one from Old Danish. It should be added here that control infinitives in languages like Modern Icelandic, involving oblique subject verbs, are not easy to come by. To tell the truth, this is certainly not what one would expect given the attention such examples have received in the earlier syntactic literature, although finding control infinitives involving oblique subject verbs has certainly become easier with the birth and blossoming of the World Wide Web. Thus, summing up, control infinitives with embedded oblique subject verbs, where the oblique subject is left unexpressed, have now been amply documented throughout the early Germanic languages, indeed attesting to the subject behavior of oblique subjects.

The syntactic behavior of oblique subjects discussed above is summarized in Table 20, which shows that the evidence for a subject analysis of oblique subjects is overwhelming in the early Germanic languages, even though this may be considerably more difficult to document than for modern languages like Icelandic and Faroese.

Table 20: Syntactic Behavior of Oblique Subjects in the Early Germanic Languages.

	Go	O/ME	O/MHG	OS	ON-I	OSw	ODa
Conj. Reduction	n/a	√	n/a	n/a	n/a	n/a	n/a
Long-Dist. Refl.	√	n/a	n/a	n/a	√	n/a	n/a
Subject raising	–	√	√	√	√	√	√
Object raising	–	√	√	√	√	√	√
Control	√	√	–	√	√	√	√
Word Order	√	√	√	√	√	√	√

I now turn to the reconstruction of not only grammatical relations for Proto-Germanic, but also to the reconstruction of oblique subjects, as the evidence from the subject tests in the early Germanic languages certainly justifies such a reconstruction. This procedure entails the following four steps:
i) reconstructing the relevant lexical predicates for the proto-language
ii) reconstructing argument structure constructions for the proto-language
iii) reconstructing the syntactic behaviors that have been identified as distinguishing between subjects and objects
iv) reconstructing the interaction between the two

The very first step, before any syntactic reconstruction can be carried out, is to reconstruct the relevant verbs and predicates instantiating the argument structure constructions that are to be reconstructed. This, however, need not be done here, as this is an enterprise that has already been taken care of by the etymologists during the last two centuries or so. Of the documented oblique subject predicates in early Germanic, there are around fifty or so that may be reconstructed on the basis of the material presented here, stemming from the oldest Germanic languages. These are verbs and predicates that are found in either two or three Germanic branches. Some of these consistently select for the same case frame across the early Germanic languages, while others show some variation, either language-internally or across the early Germanic languages.

In order to demonstrate how argument structure constructions may be reconstructed, the second step in the list above, consider the variation found in the argument structure of 'suffice' in the early Germanic languages. First of all, there turn out to be two 'suffice' verbs, which are etymologically related, even though one is not a direct descendent of the other. The by now extinct primary verb, *ga-nahan, is only documented in Gothic, Old English and Old High German, while the extant one, the deadjectival *ga-nōgjan, is documented in Gothic, Old Norse-Icelandic, Old Swedish, Old Danish, Old Frisian, Middle Dutch, Middle Low and Middle High German.

There is also great variation between the early Germanic languages with regard to the argument structure of these two verbs which makes the choices for reconstruction less than clear-cut. First of all, the Gothic descendant of *ga-nahan occurs with both Acc-Nom and Dat-Nom of which the Greek original only yields Dat-Nom. However, Dat-Nom is found in several of the early daughters, including Old Norse-Icelandic, Old Swedish, Old Danish, Middle Dutch, Middle Low and Middle High German. What is more, the Nom-Dat alternant is also documented in Old Norse-Icelandic, Old Swedish, Middle Low and Middle High German, with ambiguous Dat/Acc examples being found in Gothic and Middle Dutch. These facts certainly motivate a reconstruction of the Dat-Nom / Nom-Dat alternation for Proto-Germanic for *ga-nahan, as is shown in Figures 35–36:

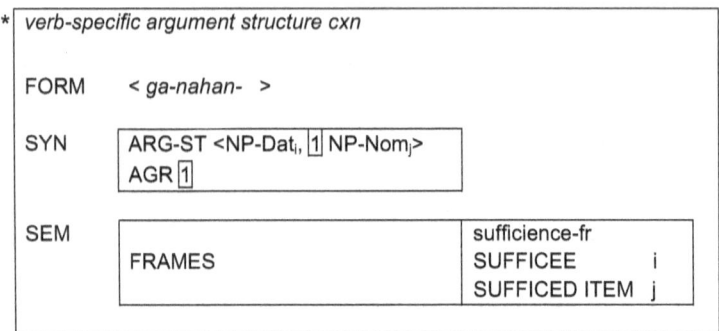

Figure 35: A Proto-Germanic reconstruction of a verb-specific Dat-Nom argument structure construction for *ga-nahan-*.

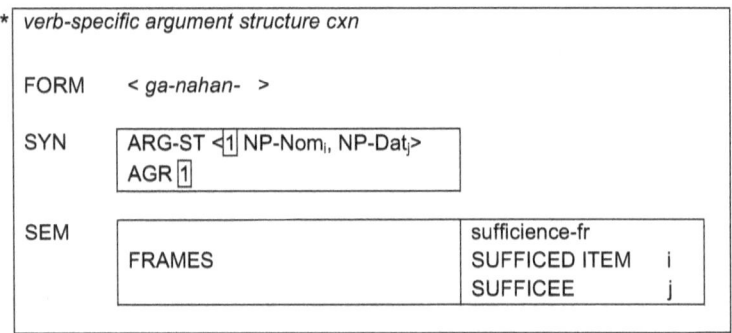

Figure 36: A Proto-Germanic reconstruction of a verb-specific Nom-Dat argument structure construction for *ga-nahan-*.

The reconstructions in Figures 35–37, involve, for the sake of simplicity, a merger between the lexical entries and the argument structure constructions themselves. This, in turn, results in so-called verb-specific argument structure constructions, representing the stage in the grammar after the lexical entry and the argument structure construction have merged.

Returning to the intricate issues of 'suffice', both Acc-Gen and Dat-Gen are documented in Middle High German, and so is an intransitive anticausative Gen-only alternant in Old High German. A further scrutiny of even older layers of Germanic reveals that the later -*jan* verb, *ga-nōgjan*, is attested in ditransitive use in both the Gothic Skeireins and the Old Norse-Icelandic Skaldic poetry from the 10th century, with the meanings 'sate, satiate' and 'endow with'. It turns out that the argument structure in Gothic and Old Norse-Icelandic is exactly the same, i.e. Nom-Acc-Dat, with the accusative being the case for the second argument and the dative the case for the third argument of the argument structure. Due to the existence of this three-place causative verb in both the Gothic Skeireins and 10th century Skaldic poetry, i.e. two out of three branches of Germanic, this argument structure may also be reconstructed for Proto-Germanic, as is shown in Figure 37.

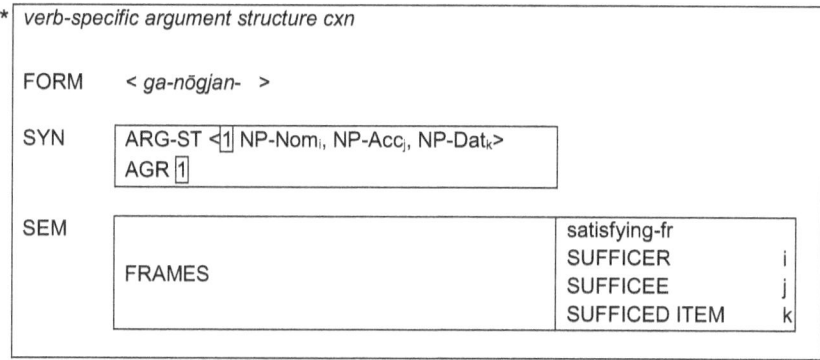

Figure 37: A Proto-Germanic reconstruction of a verb-specific argument structure construction for the three-place *ga-nōgjan-*.

This only leaves Acc-Gen and Dat-Gen in Middle High German behind as unexplained. One possible scenario is that the two-place Acc-Gen and Dat-Gen have arisen through a process of oblique anticausativization, which is a valency-reducing process resulting in the emergence of oblique subject constructions, so far documented in Germanic, Baltic, Slavic, Latin, Greek, Anatolian and Indo-Aryan (cf. Barðdal et al. 2020). Observe, however, that through the process of oblique anticausativization, the reduction in valency should result in an Acc-Dat construction and not an Acc-Gen one.

Be that as it may, a comparison between the case frames found with ditransitive verbs in Old Norse-Icelandic, Old English and Old High German reveals that the Acc-Dat case frame exists in both Old Norse-Icelandic and Old English for the second and the third argument of the argument structure, but is absent in Old High German. Thus, I hypothesize that the ditransitive Nom-Acc-Dat 'satisfy' verb, documented in both Gothic and Old Norse-Icelandic Skaldic poetry, was attracted by the Nom-Acc-Gen construction in the prehistory of German, but not until after the common Germanic period. Due to the shining absence of ditransitive Acc-Dat in Old High German, I assume that this was a general process affecting all Nom-Acc-Dat verbs in the prehistory of German, causing the Nom-Acc-Dat case frame to fall into disuse in that language. The other option, that the ditransitive Acc-Dat arose independently in Old English and Old Norse-Icelandic is not only considerably more difficult to explain, but is also directly contradicted by the Gothic evidence.

Given this, a process of oblique anticausatization targeting the three-place Nom-Acc-Gen 'satisfy' in the prehistory of German would indeed yield a two-place Acc-Gen case frame for the verb 'suffice' in that language. It is also well known from both Old High German and Middle High German that accusative and dative subjects are interchangeable. This variation between accusative and dative subjects might easily have resulted in the emergence of a Dat-Gen frame. Thus, neither of these case frames are reconstructable for Proto-Germanic with this verb, which means that this appears to be a specific inner-German development found with the verb 'suffice'.

The next step, after reconstructing argument structure constructions is to reconstruct the constructions that single out subjects from objects, i.e. the subject tests themselves. Recall that several of the subject tests that are valid for the Modern Germanic languages are not valid for the early languages. For instance, since the early Germanic languages are generally argument-drop languages, it may be difficult to distinguish between ordinary argument drop and omission in second conjuncts, even though there may be major statistical differences between subject omission on identity with subjects or objects in a preceding main clause, as Allen (1995) argues for Old English. For this reason, I do not reconstruct conjunction reduction as a subject test for Proto-Germanic. The same is true for clause-bound reflexivization, in that it varies from language to language whether a reflexive or a personal pronoun is bound by the subject, even within the early Germanic languages. Thus, clause-bound reflexivization is not reconstructed either as a subject test for Proto-Germanic.

Turning to the subject behavior that is reconstructable for Proto-Germanic, this involves neutral word order, raising-to-subject, raising-to-object, control infinitives and long-distance reflexivization. Here I use the notational formalism of Construction Grammar, the Attributed Value Matrix, to model subject behavior for the proto-language.

The first subject test reconstructed here is neutral word order and following that, subject-verb inversion. Figure 38 demonstrates the reconstruction of neutral word order for Proto-Germanic, focusing only on the order between subjects and verbs. The rightmost box represents the slot for the finite verb, while the leftmost box represents the slot for the subject, which is specified as NP_{-i}. Note that since the noun phrase occupying this slot is indexed with i, this results in co-indexation with the first argument of the argument structure of each verb in the language. This co-indexation, thus, is responsible for the interaction between argument structure constructions and different types of clause constructions.

In addition, Figure 39 demonstrates the reconstruction of subject-verb inversion, i.e. the construction in which the order of the subject and the verb inverts, found in topicalizations, questions, narrative inversion, etc. In this case, it is the

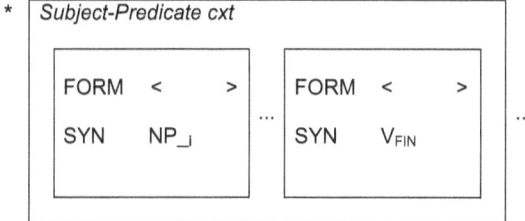

Figure 38: A reconstruction of the Subject-Predicate word order construction for Proto-Germanic.

verb that precedes the subject, hence it occupies the leftmost slot, while the inverted subject occupies the rightmost slot. The subject noun phrase is here indexed with *i*, resulting in co-indexation of the first argument of the argument structure of each verb.

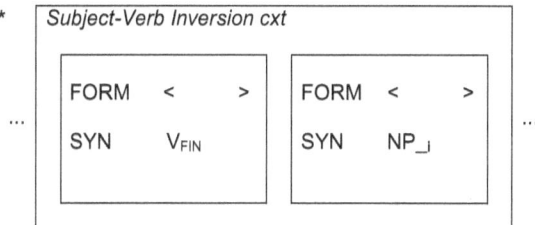

Figure 39: A reconstruction of the Subject-Predicate Inverted word order for Proto-Germanic.

The next subject test reconstructed here is raising-to-subject. For this purpose, I have reconstructed two verb-specific raising-to-subject verbs, 'begin' and 'shall', respectively, as examples. Raising-to-subject verbs do not select for arguments of their own, hence they are only reconstructed with their semantic frames, namely the begin_ and shall_frames, respectively. In addition to the two lexical entries for 'begin' and 'shall', I also reconstruct the larger syntactic raising-to-subject construction, consisting of three definite slots, a subject slot, a slot for the finite verb and a slot for the infinitive, as is shown in Figure 40.

Observe that the finite verb is defined in terms of the two semantic frames discussed above, the begin_ and shall_frames. It is also specified for the subject slot that it is indexed with an *i*, thus yielding co-indexing with the first argument of the argument structure of all verbs in the language, as is shown in Figure 33 above. With this formalism and these specifications, the behavior of raising-to-subject constructions is modeled for Proto-Germanic. This is true for both ordinary nominative subjects and oblique subjects, as both are the first argument of the argument structure and thus both are indexed with an *i*.

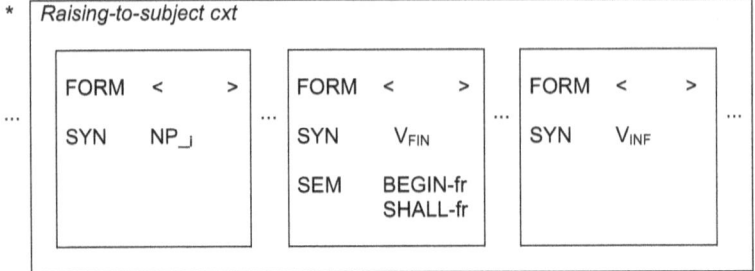

Figure 40: A reconstruction of the raising-to-subject construction in Proto-Germanic.

My reconstruction of the raising-to-object construction is carried out in the same manner as the reconstruction of the raising-to-subject construction, except for the fact that raising-to-object verbs occur with a subject of their own. The relevant verbs reconstructed here are 'let', 'see', 'hear' and 'say', as I have shown that perception verbs occur in the raising-to-object construction in all three branches. The same is true for verbs of saying, which occur in the raising-to-object construction in Gothic, Old Norse-Icelandic and Old High German, contra the literature on, at least, Old High German. As a consequence, I have reconstructed 'let', 'see', 'hear' and 'say' together with the case marking of their nominative subjects for Proto-Germanic. Then, I reconstruct the raising-to-object construction itself, with three slots, one for the finite verb, one for the "raised" subject of the lower verb, and one slot for the lower non-finite verb.

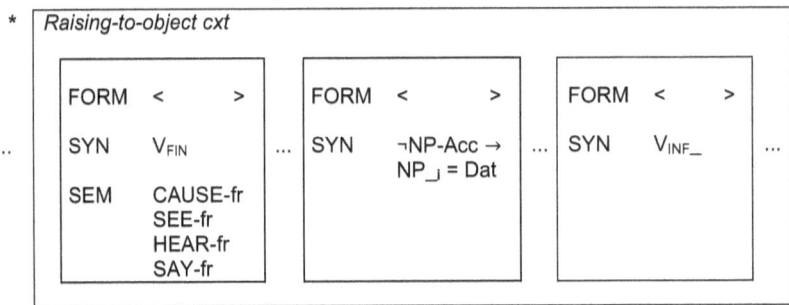

Figure 41: A reconstruction of the raising-to-object construction in Proto-Germanic.

The details of the reconstruction of the raising-to-object construction in Proto-Germanic are laid out in Figure 41, where the first slot specifies the semantic frames of the relevant raising-to-object verbs, namely the cause_frame, see_frame, hear_frame and say_frame. The second slot is the "landing site" of the "raised subject" of the lower verb, which usually occurs in the accusative case, either because the lower non-finite verb is a nominative subject verb receiving accusative case from the construction itself or because the lower verb itself is an accusative subject verb. It is also specified for this second slot that if the subject of the lower verb is in the dative case, this dative case overrides the accusative assigned by the construction. Finally, the third slot of the raising-to-object construction is the slot for the infinitive verb, whose subject turns up as the object of the matrix verb. Note again that the "raised subject" is here indexed with an *i*, thus it is co-indexed with the first argument of the argument structure of all verbs modeled for the proto-language.

Turning to control constructions, these are documented with oblique subject verbs in all three branches of Germanic, including several languages of both West and North Germanic. As stated above, the subject property of control infinitives is to be left unexpressed in such structures. One may of course attempt to argue that this cannot be a convincing test, since the subject argument is omitted anyway, hence one cannot see its case marking. This is absolutely true, but the nature of this test does not hinge upon the visibility of the case marking of the omitted argument in the control infinitive, but rather on which argument of the corresponding finite verb may be left unexpressed and what its case marking is. For ordinary Nom-Acc verbs, it is the nominative that is left unexpressed in control constructions while the accusative is expressed. For predicates selecting for oblique subjects, it is, in fact, the oblique that is left unexpressed. For Dat-Nom verbs, it is the dative that is left unexpressed, while the nominative is not. In that sense, oblique subjects behave in the same manner as nominative subjects do in control infinitives, and that, as a matter of fact, is the test.

An examination of control infinitives further reveals that such infinitives may be embedded under different types of matrix verbs, which is materialized in the fact that the unexpressed subject may be controlled by the subject of the matrix verb, its object, or by none of the arguments of the matrix verb in cases where the matrix verb expresses generic statements. In such cases the unexpressed subject is controlled by an arbitrary controller, retrievable on the basis of the context. For this particular reason, I suggest a partial reconstruction of control infinitives for Proto-Germanic, as is shown in Figure 42. This reconstruction only includes the controlled infinitive and the behavior of its subject argument, as the behavior of any potential objects follows from the modeling of the argument structure of the relevant verb. Hence, this does not need to be modeled for control infinitives *per se*.

Returning to Figure 42, the slot to the right is the slot for the non-finite verb itself, specified as V_{INF}, while the slot to the left is the slot for the unexpressed subject. The specifications for this slot show that the subject argument is unexpressed, namely through the marking [PRO], while at the same time further specifications of this slot involve the indexation of this argument with *i*. This entails a

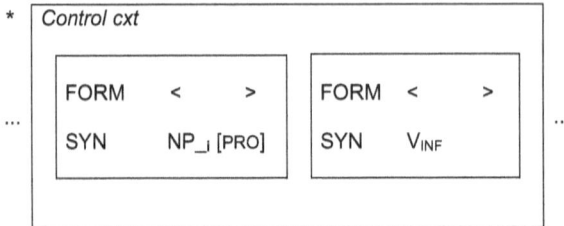

Figure 42: A partial reconstruction of control constructions in Proto-Germanic.

co-indexation of the unexpressed argument in this slot with the first argument of the argument structure, be it nominative or oblique.

Finally, I reconstruct long-distance reflexivization as a subject test for Proto-Germanic on the basis of data from Gothic and Old Norse-Icelandic. Examples of nominative subjects binding a reflexive in a subordinate clause are attested in both languages and the same is true for oblique subjects. Figure 43 shows the indexation between the subject of the matrix verb and a reflexive in a subordinate clause with co-indexation in square brackets. This is done in order not to confuse the reader with the co-indexing of the relation between an argument in the argument structure and the participant roles in the relevant semantic frame.

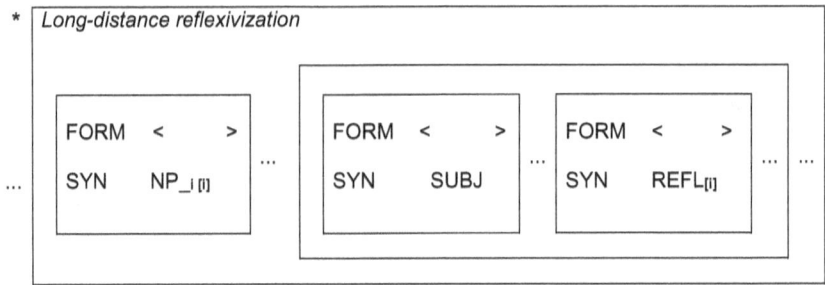

Figure 43: A reconstruction of long-distance reflexivization in Proto-Germanic.

To conclude, through the appropriate modeling of verbs, argument structure and the constructions involving the subject tests, including suitable co-indexing of the arguments in the argument structure and the arguments in the constructions involving the subject tests, grammatical relations simply fall out. The material presented here motivates not only the reconstruction of grammatical relations in general for Proto-Germanic, but also the reconstruction of oblique subjects.

The final issue dealt with here is the situation in Modern German, where it is assumed that potential oblique subjects are not syntactic subjects but are syntactic objects instead. A part of the reason is that in the German scholarship subject is defined as being in the nominative case, which implicitly entails that the subject is the first argument of the argument structure of all verbs except for Dat-Nom and Acc-Nom verbs. For those verb classes, the subject is regarded as being the second argument of the argument structure, as *ad hoc* as that may appear.

In addition to this morphosyntactic definition of subject, another reason that oblique subjects have not been defined as subjects in German is due to the well-documented subject behavior of the nominative in alleged Dat-Nom constructions. However, as I have shown throughout this book, there are Dat-Nom verbs which alternate between two argument structure constructions, namely Dat-Nom and Nom-Dat. Further, if Dat-Nom verbs in German are of this alternating type, then the subject behavior of the nominative would only be relevant for the Nom-Dat alternant and be immaterial for an analysis involving a potential subject behavior of the dative in the Dat-Nom alternant.

A further reason for oblique subjects being analyzed as objects in German is due to them not passing some of the subject tests, something which I discuss at great length in Section 2.3.3 above, where I show, among other things, that some of the subject tests are also case tests. In addition, on the basis of the subject tests that oblique subjects do not seem to pass very easily, I put forward the "restricted ellipsis" analysis, instead of the "non-subject" analysis of the relevant structures in German. This I suggest on the basis of the fact that the subject tests that oblique subject constructions do not pass all involve ellipsis. This is an entirely different analysis, based on a totally different generalization than assuming that the dative in Dat-Nom structures is a syntactic object.

An object analysis of dative subjects in German, more specifically a topicalized object analysis, also makes certain predictions about the behavior of the dative in conjoined clauses containing preposed objects. As I show in Section 6.2, these predictions are not borne out, demonstrating that dative subjects do not behave syntactically as objects in German with regard to topicalization.

Turning to the subject tests in German, it appears that Dat-Nom verbs in German are alternating verbs, as both word orders appear to be neutral for several German verbs investigated here. In order to present independent evidence for the alternating status of these verbs, I present a corpus investigation, based on Somers and Barðdal (2022, 2023) involving 15 Icelandic verbs and 15 German verbs, 30 verbs in total. Of these, five Icelandic verbs are ordinary Nom-Dat verbs like *hjálpa* 'help', five are non-alternating Dat-Nom like *líka* 'like', while five are known alternating verbs. The German dataset also involves five ordinary Nom-Dat verbs like *helfen* 'help', while the remaining ten verbs appear to be of the alternating type.

The statistics could not be more straightforward. It appears that for ordinary Nom-Dat verbs like 'help' that topicalization is found in 4–10% of the cases, at best;

i.e., 4% Dat-Nom word orders are found in the Icelandic dataset but up to 10% in the German dataset when both arguments are full NPs. This means that 96% of the 'help' instances in Icelandic represent neutral word order (Nom-Dat) while 90% of the 'help' instances in German represent neutral word order (Nom-Dat). This is a very clear baseline with which both alternating and non-alternating predicates may be compared. The numbers for non-alternating *líka* types mirror the numbers for 'help' verbs with 4% Nom-Dat word orders and 96% Dat-Nom word orders. These numbers confirm that *líka* verbs are non-alternating Dat-Nom verbs, with 4% of the word orders being topicalizations. For the third verb class, *nægja* 'suffice' verbs, the numbers are very different, involving one outlier but otherwise showing variation between the two linear word orders ranging from 20%–80% for one of the most extreme verbs to 45%–55%. These numbers deviate greatly from the established baseline with 4% topicalizations that it is clear that something totally different is going on. I interpret these numbers as confirming an alternating analysis for these verbs in Modern Icelandic.

The numbers for Modern German are even more striking. For ordinary 'help' verbs, the Dat-Nom word order is found in 10% of the cases, as I mention above, which, in turn, establishes a baseline for how frequent topicalizations are with two-place verbs in German when both arguments are full NPs. For the remaining ten verbs, the numbers are very different ranging from 38%–62% for *zufallen* 'fall to' toward 62%–38% with *reichen* 'suffice'. There is one outlier in the German dataset, *nützen* 'to be of use', with 17% Dat-Nom word order and 83% Nom-Dat word order. Again, the word order differences between the ordinary 'help' verbs and the remaining German verbs supports, as plain as a pikestaff, an alternating analysis for the latter verb class in German.

Returning to the subject tests applicable to German, conjunction reduction also demonstrates that either argument of the argument structure, the dative or the nominative, may be left unexpressed in second conjuncts on identity with the dative or the nominative in the first conjunct, provided of course that the two share syntactic roles. This is true for both German and Icelandic.

Clause-bound reflexivization, unfortunately, is tainted by the fact that not only subjects but also objects may bind reflexives in both Icelandic and German. Nevertheless, distinguishing between subjects and objects is indeed made possible by differences in binding properties of subjects and objects in that subjects may only bind reflexives while objects appear to only bind personal pronouns in German. In Icelandic, objects may bind either reflexives or personal pronouns. A comparison between the binding properties of the two arguments of Dat-Nom verbs in German reveals that either argument, the dative or the nominative, behaves syntactically as subjects, although not at the same time, as either argument may bind a reflexive within its minimal clause. These facts support an alternating analysis for Dat-Nom verbs in German, exactly as in Icelandic.

Raising-to-subject also confirms an alternating analysis for Dat-Nom verbs in German, precisely as in Icelandic, with either the dative or the nominative taking on the subject behavior of the raising-to-subject verb *scheinen* 'seem, appear'. Again, a comparison with Icelandic reveals that German behaves in the same way as Icelandic with respect to alternating verbs, in that either argument takes on the behavioral properties of the subjects of the relevant finite verbs, in addition to Icelandic also having non-alternating verbs. Non-alternating verbs only allow the dative to take on the behavioral properties of 'seem' verbs in Icelandic, with the nominative behaving consistently as a syntactic object, following the infinitive in raising-to-subject constructions.

Regrettably, the raising-to-object test is not as straightforwardly applied in German as it is in Icelandic, since oblique subject verbs do not easily embed under 'let' causatives in that language anymore. Nevertheless, examples with pronouns may be retrieved without difficulty and early examples involving nominals are also relatively easy to detect in earlier historical texts. A comparison with Icelandic confirms that either argument of Dat-Nom verbs may be "raised" to object in German, exactly as in Icelandic, while non-alternating Dat-Nom verbs in Icelandic behave differently in that only the dative takes on the behavioral properties of the "raised" subject, while the nominative behaves syntactically as an object.

The final subject test applied here to German, control infinitives, is a double-edged sword, due to the mixed ratings such examples have received in acceptability judgment tasks. On the one hand, it is possible to present examples composed by native speakers, which should be sufficient to document the subject behavior of oblique subjects in German. On the other hand, if such structures are not regarded as entirely acceptable by all native speakers, the strength of the argument involving the existence of such structures may be severely diminished. Either way, two sets of examples of control infinitives in German are presented here, involving the well-known Dat-Nom verbs *gelingen* 'succeed' and *genügen* 'satisfy, be satisfied', respectively. It turns out that either argument, the dative or the nominative, may be left unexpressed in control infinitives, again supporting an alternating Dat-Nom / Nom-Dat analysis of these two verbs in German. It should also be mentioned here that native speakers deem the *gelingen* examples as sounding old-fashioned, while the *genügen* examples stem from the 16th and the early 19th century.

The Icelandic cognate of *genügen*, *nægja*, exhibits exactly the same behavior, with either argument potentially being left unexpressed in control infinitives, further corroborating an alternating analysis for *nægja* in Icelandic. In contrast, the verb *leiðast* 'be bored' deviates from this pattern in that only the dative may be left unexpressed in control infinitives in Icelandic and not the nominative. These facts show, once and for all, that Icelandic has two types of Dat-Nom verbs, alternating and non-alternating ones, while it appears that German may only exhibit the alternating Dat-Nom type.

In spite of all this, it has generally been assumed in the German scholarship that Dat-Nom verbs in that language are non-alternating Dat-Nom verbs. It has further been assumed that it is the second argument of the argument structure that is the subject, namely the nominative, and that whatever "subject properties" the dative may show is a direct consequence of the animacy and the topicality of the dative (cf. Haspelmath 2001; Verhoeven 2015; among others). One major problem for this standard approach is its *misapplication of the concept of topicalization*. In general, topicalization is an optional movement to the front of the clause, resulting in a clear deviation from neutral word order, with subsequent change in sentence intonation. For Dat-Nom verbs in German, no such change in sentence intonation is found. Instead, both word orders are equally neutral in German, thus speaking for an alternating analysis involving two argument structure constructions, the Dat-Nom and the Nom-Dat constructions, instead of topicalization. The present examination confirms such an analysis, as either the dative or the nominative pass the six subject tests discussed here. As such, German does not pose a problem for the general hypothesis and findings presented in this book that not only are there oblique subjects in the earliest Germanic languages, but also that oblique subjects are reconstructable for Proto-Germanic.

The primary goal of this monograph has been to address the issue of whether North-Germanic or the Irminonic branch of West-Germanic represent the Proto-Germanic situation regarding oblique subjects, given the discrepancy between Modern Icelandic and Faroese, on the one hand, and Modern German, on the other. This discrepancy has given rise to a dichotomy between the two sets of languages, with Modern Icelandic and Faroese being analyzed as exhibiting structures calling for a subject analysis of oblique subjects, while the very same oblique subject structures in German have been analyzed as (topicalized) objects.

Since the relevant structures are inherited from Proto-Germanic, and some perhaps even from Proto-Indo-European, a survey into the status of the earliest stages of Germanic is needed in order to identify the original state of affairs. In short, it has already been shown that there are oblique subjects in Gothic, Old English and Old Norse-Icelandic, and I have documented here that Old Saxon, Old Swedish and Old Danish exhibit the same behavior with regard to the subject tests as Old Norse-Icelandic. Hence, not only the category of subject has shown itself to be reconstructable for Proto-Germanic, but also the category of oblique subjects. These reconstructions are couched in the formalism of Construction Grammar, which in turn allows for reconstructions on the basis of form–meaning pairings.

All of this entails that Modern German does not represent the original situation for Germanic, as it clearly appears that oblique subjects in that language had a wider distribution in earlier stages of German than in the modern language. In addition, the existence of alternating predicates has confused the discussion in the German scholarship considerably, resulting in the assumption that the subject is the first argument of the argument structure for all verb classes except for Dat-Nom verbs, where the subject has implicitly been assumed to be the second argument of the argument structure. However, on an alternating analysis of Dat-Nom predicates in German, the subject behavior of the nominative is easily explained, namely as pertaining to the Nom-Dat alternant of the alternating pair and not the Dat-Nom alternant.

In contrast to most of the scholarship on the status of the subject category, I have here introduced a definition of subject that may be applied independently from the subject tests, i.e., as being the first argument of the argument structure. This definition is bottom-up, arrived at through a generalization of the behavior of the arguments relative to the subject tests. Due to this subject definition, a gradient view of subject may be avoided, with its absurd entailments that an argument may be 40%, 60% or perhaps 75% subject. Also, due to this subject definition, one does not need to rely on a subset of the subject tests, without a principled method of evaluating the relative importance of each of the tests. Instead, with a definition of subject, the questions asked are why a potential subject argument would not pass the tests, as opposed to demoting that argument to object status, as has been widely done in the literature. Consequently, new questions may be asked and new generalizations arrived at, like, for instance, the *restricted ellipsis generalization* for Modern German.

In this monograph I have proposed an alternative view of the historical reality of oblique subjects in the Germanic languages than is standardly assumed and has been assumed since Jespersen (1927), almost hundred years ago. I have presented a wealth of empirical data corroborating this alternative view and speaking against the standard story, all in the hope that the scholarship is ready for a new mindset, with the different world view that complements it.

References

Aarts, Bas. 2011. *Oxford Modern English Grammar*. Oxford: Oxford University Press.
Adger, David. 2003. *Core Syntax: A Minimalist Approach*. Oxford: Oxford University Press.
Allen, Cynthia L. 1986. Reconsidering the history of *like*. *Journal of Linguistics* 22. 375–409.
Allen, Cynthia L. 1995. *Case Marking and Reanalysis: Grammatical Relations from Old to Early Modern English*. Oxford: Oxford University Press.
Allen, Cynthia L. 1996. A change in structural case marking in Early Middle English. In Höskuldur Thráinsson, Samuel David Epstein & Steve Peter (eds.), *Studies in Comparative Germanic syntax II*, 3–20. Dordrecht: Kluwer.
Allen, Kachina, Francisco Pereira, Matthew Botvinick & Adele E. Goldberg. 2012. Distinguishing grammatical constructions with fMRI pattern analysis. *Brain and Language* 123. 174–182.
Aman, Norhaida & Ludwig Tan. 2018. *The Nuts and Bolts of English Grammar*. Singapore: Marshall Cavendish International.
Anagnostopoulou, Elena. 1999. On experiencers. In Artemis Alexiadou, Geoffrey Horrocks & Melita Stavrou (eds.), *Studies in Greek Syntax*, 67–93. Dordrecht: Springer.
Anand, Pranav & Andrew Nevins. 2006. The locus of ergative case assignment: Evidence from scope. In Alana Johns, Diane Massam & Juvenal Ndayiragije (eds.), *Ergativity: Emerging Issues*, 3–25. Dordrecht: Springer.
Anderson, Stephen R. 1976. On the notion of subject in ergative languages. In Charles N. Li (ed.), *Subject and Topic*, 1–23. New York: Academic Press.
Anderson, Stephen R. 1990. The grammar of Icelandic verbs in *-st*. In Joan Maling & Annie Zaenen (eds.), *Modern Icelandic Syntax*, 235–273. San Diego: Academic Press.
Andrews, Avery D. 1976. The VP complement analysis in Modern Icelandic. *North Eastern Linguistic Society* 6. 1–21.
Andrews, Avery D. 1990. Case structures and control in Modern Icelandic. In Joan Maling & Annie Zaenen (eds.), *Modern Icelandic Syntax*, 187–234. San Diego: Academic Press.
Askedal, John Ole. 2001. 'Oblique subjects', structural and lexical case marking: Some thoughts on case assignment in North Germanic and German. In Jan T. Faarlund (ed.), *Grammatical Relations in Change*, 65–97. Amsterdam: John Benjamins.
Avery, John. 1881. On relative clauses in the Rigveda. *Proceedings of the American Oriental Society* 11. 64–66.
Axel, Katrin. 2007. *Studies on Old High German Syntax: Left Sentence Periphery, Verb Placement and Verb-Second*. Amsterdam: John Benjamins.
Axelsdóttir, Katrín. 2014. *Sögur af orðum: Sex athuganir á beygingarþróun í íslensku* [Stories of Words: Six Studies of Morphological Development in Icelandic]. Reykjavík: Háskólaútgáfan.
Barðdal, Jóhanna. 1998. Argument structure, syntactic structure and morphological case of the impersonal construction in the history of Scandinavian. *Scripta Islandica* 49. 21–33.
Barðdal, Jóhanna. 1999a. The dual nature of Icelandic psych-verbs. *Working Papers in Scandinavian Syntax* 64. 78–101.
Barðdal, Jóhanna. 1999b. Case and argument structure of some loan verbs in 15th century Icelandic. In Inger Haskå & Carin Sandqvist (eds.), *Alla tiders språk: En Vänskrift till Gertrud Pettersson november 1999*, 9–23. Lundastudier i Nordisk språkvetenskap A 55. Lund: Institutionen för nordiska språk.
Barðdal, Jóhanna. 2000a. The subject is nominative! On obsolete axioms and their deep-rootedness. In Carl-Erik Lindberg & Steffen Nordahl Lund (eds.), *17th Scandinavian Conference of Linguistics*, 93–117. Odense: Institute of Language and Communication.

Barðdal, Jóhanna. 2000b. Oblique subjects in Old Scandinavian. *NOWELE: North-Western European Language Evolution* 37. 25–51.
Barðdal, Jóhanna. 2001a. The role of thematic roles in constructions? Evidence from the Icelandic inchoative. In Arthur Holmer, Jan-Olof Svantesson & Åke Viberg (eds.), *Proceedings of the 18th Scandinavian Conference of Linguistics 2000*, 127–137. Lund: Department of Linguistics.
Barðdal, Jóhanna. 2001b. The perplexity of Dat-Nom verbs in Icelandic. *Nordic Journal of Linguistics* 24. 47–70.
Barðdal, Jóhanna. 2001c. *Case in Icelandic: A Synchronic, Diachronic and Comparative Approach*. Lund: Department of Scandinavian Languages, Lund University.
Barðdal, Jóhanna. 2002. "Oblique subjects" in Icelandic and German. *Working Papers in Scandinavian Syntax* 70. 61–99.
Barðdal, Jóhanna. 2004. The semantics of the impersonal construction in Icelandic, German and Faroese. In Werner Abraham (ed.), *Focus on Germanic Typology*, 105–137. Berlin: Akademie Verlag.
Barðdal, Jóhanna. 2006. Construction-specific properties of syntactic subjects in Icelandic and German. *Cognitive Linguistics* 17(1). 39–106.
Barðdal, Jóhanna. 2007. The semantic and lexical range of the ditransitive construction in the history of (North) Germanic. *Functions of Language* 14(1). 9–30.
Barðdal, Jóhanna. 2008. *Productivity: Evidence from Case and Argument Structure in Icelandic*. Amsterdam: John Benjamins.
Barðdal, Jóhanna. 2009. The development of case in Germanic. In Jóhanna Barðdal & Shobhana L. Chelliah (eds.), *The Role of Semantic, Pragmatic, and Discourse Factors in the Development of Case*, 123–159. Amsterdam: John Benjamins.
Barðdal, Jóhanna. 2011. The rise of dative substitution in the history of Icelandic: A Diachronic Construction Grammar account. *Lingua* 121(1). 60–79.
Barðdal, Jóhanna. 2012. Predicting the productivity of argument structure constructions. *Berkeley Linguistics Society* 32 (2006). 467–478.
Barðdal, Jóhanna. 2013. Construction-based historical–comparative reconstruction. In Greame Trousdale & Thomas Hoffmann (eds.), *The Oxford Handbook of Construction Grammar*, 438–457. Oxford: Oxford University Press.
Barðdal, Jóhanna. 2014. Syntax and syntactic reconstruction. In Claire Bowern & Bethwyn Evans (eds.), *The Routledge Handbook of Historical Linguistics*, 343–373. London: Routledge.
Barðdal, Jóhanna. 2015. Valency classes in Icelandic: Oblique subjects, oblique ambitransitives and the actional passive. In Andrej L. Malchukov & Bernard Comrie (eds.), *Valency Classes in the World's Languages*, 367–416. Berlin: Mouton de Gruyter.
Barðdal, Jóhanna, Carlee Arnett, Stephen Mark Carey, Thórhallur Eythórsson, Gard B. Jenset, Guus Kroonen & Adam Oberlin. 2016. Dative subjects in Germanic: A computational analysis of lexical semantic verb classes across time and space. *STUF: Language Typology and Universals* 69(1). 49–84.
Barðdal, Jóhanna, Valgerður Bjarnadóttir, Serena Danesi, Tonya Kim Dewey, Thórhallur Eythórsson, Chiara Fedriani & Thomas Smitherman. 2013. The story of 'woe'. *Journal of Indo-European Studies* 41(3–4). 321–377.
Barðdal, Jóhanna, Eleonora Cattafi, Serena Danesi, Laura Bruno & Leonardo Biondo. 2023. Non-nominative subjects in Latin and Ancient Greek: Applying the subject tests on early Indo-European languages. *Indogermanische Forschungen* 128. 321–392.
Barðdal, Jóhanna & Thórhallur Eythórsson. 2003a. The change that never happened: The story of oblique subjects. *Journal of Linguistics* 39. 439–472.

Barðdal, Jóhanna & Thórhallur Eythórsson. 2003b. Icelandic vs. German: Oblique subjects, agreement and expletives. *Chicago Linguistic Society* 39(1). 755–773.

Barðdal, Jóhanna & Thórhallur Eythórsson. 2006. Control infinitives and case in Germanic: 'Performance error' or marginally acceptable constructions. In Leonid Kulikov, Andrej Malchukov & Peter de Swart (eds.), *Case, Valency and Transitivity*, 147–177. Amsterdam: John Benjamins.

Barðdal, Jóhanna & Thórhallur Eythórsson. 2009. The origin of the oblique subject construction: An Indo-European comparison. In Vit Bubenik, John Hewson & Sarah Rose (eds.), *Grammatical Change in Indo-European Languages*, 179–193. Amsterdam: John Benjamins.

Barðdal, Jóhanna & Thórhallur Eythórsson. 2012a. "Hungering and lusting for women and fleshly delicacies": Reconstructing grammatical relations for Proto-Germanic. *Transactions of the Philological Society* 110(3). 363–393.

Barðdal, Jóhanna & Thórhallur Eythórsson. 2012b. Reconstructing syntax: Construction Grammar and the comparative method. In Hans C. Boas & Ivan A. Sag (eds.), *Sign-Based Construction Grammar*, 257–308. Stanford: CSLI Publications.

Barðdal, Jóhanna & Thórhallur Eythórsson. 2018. What is a subject? The nature and validity of subject tests. In Jóhanna Barðdal, Na'ama Pat-El, & Stephen Mark Carey (eds.), *Non-Canonically Case-Marked Subjects: The Reykjavík–Eyjafjallajökull Papers*, 257–273. Amsterdam: John Benjamins.

Barðdal, Jóhanna & Thórhallur Eythórsson. 2020. How to identify cognates in syntax: Taking Watkins' legacy one step further. In Jóhanna Barðdal, Spike Gildea & Eugenio R. Luján (eds.), *Reconstructing Syntax*, 197–238. Leiden: Brill.

Barðdal, Jóhanna, Thórhallur Eythórsson & Tonya Kim Dewey. 2014. Alternating predicates in Icelandic and German: A sign-based construction grammar account. *Working Papers in Scandinavian Syntax* 93. 50–101.

Barðdal, Jóhanna, Thórhallur Eythórsson & Tonya Kim Dewey. 2019. The alternating predicate puzzle: Dat-Nom vs. Nom-Dat in Icelandic and German. *Constructions and Frames* 11(1). 107–170.

Barðdal, Jóhanna & Spike Gildea. 2015. Diachronic construction grammar: Epistemological context, basic assumptions and historical implications. In Jóhanna Barðdal, Elena Smirnova, Lotte Sommerer & Spike Gildea (eds.), *Diachronic Construction Grammar*, 1–50. Amsterdam: John Benjamins.

Barðdal, Jóhanna, Spike Gildea & Eugenio R. Luján (eds). 2020. *Reconstructing Syntax*. Leiden: Brill.

Barðdal, Jóhanna, Kristian E. Kristoffersen & Andreas Sveen. 2011. West Scandinavian ditransitives as a family of constructions: With a special attention to the Norwegian V-REFL-NP construction. *Linguistics* 49(1). 53–104.

Barðdal, Jóhanna & Leonid Kulikov. 2009. Case in decline. In Andrej L. Malchukov & Andrew Spencer (eds.), *The Oxford Handbook of Case*, 470–478. Oxford: Oxford University Press.

Barðdal, Jóhanna & Valéria Molnár. 2003. The passive in Icelandic – Compared to Mainland Scandinavian. In Jorunn Hetland & Valéria Molnár (eds.), *Structures of Focus and Grammatical Relations*, 231–260. Tübingen: Niemeyer.

Barðdal, Jóhanna & Thomas Smitherman. 2013. The quest for cognates: A reconstruction of oblique subject constructions in Proto-Indo-European. *Language Dynamics and Change* 3(1). 28–67.

Barðdal, Jóhanna, Thomas Smitherman, Valgerður Bjarnadóttir, Serena Danesi, Gard B. Jenset & Barbara McGillivray. 2012. Reconstructing constructional semantics: The dative subject construction in Old Norse-Icelandic, Latin, Ancient Greek, Old Russian and Old Lithuanian. *Studies in Language* 36(3). 511–547.

Barkarson, Starkaður, Steinþór Steingrímsson & Hildur Hafsteinsdóttir. 2022. Evolving large text corpora: Four versions of the Icelandic Gigaword Corpus. In *Proceedings of the Language Resources and Evaluation Conference*, 2371–2381. Marseille: The European Language Resources Association.
Barnes, Michael. 1986. Subject, nominative and oblique case in Faroese. *Scripta Islandica* 37. 13–46.
Bayer, Josef. 2004. Non-nominative subjects in comparison. In Peri Bhaskararao & Karumuri V. Subbarao (eds.), *Non-Nominative Subjects*, Vol I, 49–76. Amsterdam: John Benjamins.
Bayer, Josef, Markus Bader & Michael Meng. 2001. Morphological underspecification meets oblique case: Syntactic and processing effects in German. *Lingua* 111. 465–514.
Belletti, Adriana & Luigi Rizzi. 1988. Psych-verbs and θ-theory. *Natural Language & Linguistic Theory* 6(3). 291–352.
Benedetti, Marina. 2013a. Non-canonical subjects in clauses with noun predicates. In Elly van Gelderen, Michela Cennamo & Jóhanna Barðdal (eds.), *Argument Structure in Flux: The Naples–Capri Papers*, 15–31. Amsterdam: John Benjamins.
Benedetti, Marina. 2013b. Experiencers and psychological noun predicates: From Latin to Italian. In Ilja A. Seržant & Leonid Kulikov (eds.), *The Diachrony of Non-Canonical Subjects*, 121–138. Amsterdam: John Benjamins.
Bennett, William. 1950. The Milanese leaves of the Skeireins under ultraviolet radiation. *PMLA* 65(6). 1263–1281.
Bernharðsson, Haraldur. 2004. Um Moldhaugnaháls út í Fjósa og Fjörður: Af áhrifsbreytingum í nokkrum fleirtöluörnefnum [On analogical extensions in some place names]. *Íslenskt mál og almenn málfræði* 26. 11–48.
Bernódusson, Helgi. 1982. Ópersónulegar setningar [Impersonal sentences]. Reykjavík: University of Iceland Master's Thesis.
Bickel, Balthasar. 2004. The syntax of experiencers in the Himalayas. In Peri Bhaskararao & Karumuri V. Subbarao (eds.), *Non-Nominative Subjects* I, 77–111. Amsterdam: John Benjamins.
Bjarnadóttir, Valgerður. 2014a. Dialectal and diachronic distribution of case variation in Lithuanian pain-verb constructions. *Baltic Linguistics* 5. 9–57.
Bjarnadóttir, Valgerður. 2014b. Oblique anticausative in Lithuanian: A comparative approach. *Baltistica* 49(1). 25–39.
Bjorvand, Harald & Fredrik Otto Lindeman. 2000. *Våre arveord: Etymologisk ordbok* [Our Inherited Vocabulary: An Etymological Dictionary]. Oslo: Novus forlag.
Blosen, Hans. 1972. Waz ist bezzer? Zu Walthers Lied 111,22. *Zeitschrift für deutsches Altertum und deutsche Literatur* 101(3). 271–280.
Blöndal Magnússon, Ásgeir. 1989. *Íslensk orðsifjabók* [Icelandic Etymological Dictionary]. [Reykjavík]: Orðabók Háskólans.
Boas, Hans C. 2003. *A Constructional Approach to Resultatives*. Stanford: CSLI Publications.
Boas, Hans C. 2010. The syntax–lexicon continuum in Construction Grammar: A case study of English communication verbs. *Belgian Journal of Linguistics* 24(1). 54–82.
Bobaljik, Jonathan D. & Diane Jonas. 1996. Subject positions and the role of TP. *Linguistic Inquiry* 27. 195–236.
Boon, Pieter. 1979. Der "dativus sympatheticus" in den Werken Thomas Murners: Ein Beitrag zu der Forschung nach dem Wesen des "sympathetischen" Dativs in den indogermanischen Sprachen. *Indogermanische Forschungen* 84. 237–254.
Börjars, Kersti & Kate Burridge. 2010. *Introduction to English Grammar*. 2nd edn. London: Hodder Education.
Brandt, C. J. 1870. *Romantisk Digtning fra Middelalderen*, vol. II. København: Thieles Bogtrykkeri.

Bremmer, Rolf H. 1986. The so-called "impersonal verb"-construction in Old Frisian. *NOWELE: North-Western European Language Evolution* 8(1). 71–95.
Brugmann, Karl. 1925. *Die Syntax des einfachen Satzes im Indogermanischen*. Berlin: De Gruyter.
Bucci, Giacomo & Jóhanna Barðdal. 2023. Dative subjects in Gothic: Evidence from word order. Submitted for publication.
Butler, Milton Chadwick. 1977. Reanalysis of object as subject in Middle English impersonal constructions. *Glossa* 11. 155–170.
Campbell, Lyle & Alice C. Harris. 2003. Syntactic reconstruction and demythologizing 'myth and the prehistory of grammars'. *Journal of Linguistics* 38. 599–618.
Campbell, Lyle & Marianne Mithun. 1980. The priorities and pitfalls of syntactic reconstruction. *Folia Linguistica Historica* 1. 19–40.
Cappelle, Bert. 2005. Particle patterns in English: A comprehensive coverage. Leuven: Katholieke Universiteit Leuven PhD Dissertation.
Castro Alves, Flavia de. 2018. Sujeito dativo em Canela [Dative subjects in Canela]. *Boletim do Museu Paraense Emílio Goeldi: Ciências Humanas* 13(2). 377–403.
Cennamo, Michela, Thórhallur Eythórsson & Jóhanna Barðdal. 2015. Semantic and (morpho)syntactic constraints on anticausativization: Evidence from Latin and Old Norse-Icelandic. *Linguistics* 53(4). 677–729.
Chomsky, Noam. 1957. *Syntactic Structures*. Mouton: The Hague.
Comrie, Bernard. 1973. The ergative: Variations on a theme. *Lingua* 32. 239–253.
Comrie, Bernard. 1978. Ergativity. In Winfred P. Lehmann (ed.), *Syntactic Typology: Studies in the Phenomenology of Language*, 329–394. Austin: University of Texas Press.
Comrie, Bernard, Diana Forker & Zaira Khalilova. 2018. Affective constructions in Tsezic languages. In Jóhanna Barðdal, Na'ama Pat-El & Stephen Mark Carey (eds.), *Non-Canonically Case-Marked Subjects within and across Languages and Language Families: The Reykjavík–Eyjafjallajökull papers*, by 55–82. Amsterdam: John Benjamins.
Cole, Peter, Wayne Harbert, Gabriella Hermon & S. N. Sridhar. 1980. The Acquisition of Subjecthood. *Language* 56. 719–743.
Colleman, Timothy. 2015. Constructionalization and post-constructionalization: The constructional semantics of the Dutch *krijgen*-passive in a diachronic perspective. In Jóhanna Barðdal, Elena Smirnova, Lotte Sommerer & Spike Gildea (eds.), *Diachronic Construction Grammar*, 213–255. Amsterdam: John Benjamins.
Conti, Luz. 2008. Synchronie und Diachronie des altgriechischen Genitivs als Semisubjekt. *Historische Sprachforschung* 121. 94–113.
Conti, Luz. 2009. Weiteres zum Genitiv als Semisubjekt im Altgriechischen: Analyse des Kasus bei impersonalen Konstruktionen. *Historische Sprachforschung* 122. 182–207.
Conti, Luz & Silvia Luraghi. 2014. The Ancient Greek partitive genitive in typological perspective. In Silvia Luraghi & Tuomas Huumo (eds.), *Partitive Cases and Related Categories*, 443–476. Berlin: De Gruyter Mouton.
Corbett, Greville G. 1991. *Gender*. Cambridge: Cambridge University Press.
Cristofaro, Sonja. 2009. Grammatical categories and relations: Universality vs. language-specificity and construction-specificity. *Language and Linguistics Compass* 3(1). 441–479.
Croft, William. 1993. Case marking and the semantics of mental verbs. In James Pustejovsky (ed.), *Semantics and the Lexicon*, 55–72. Dordrecht: Springer.
Croft, William. 1998. Event structure in argument linking. In Miriam Butt & Wilhelm Geuder (eds.), *The Projection of Arguments: Lexical and Compositional Factors*, 1–43. Stanford: CSLI Publications.

Croft, William, 2001. *Radical Construction Grammar: Syntactic Theory in Typological Perspective*. Oxford: Oxford University Press.
Croft, William. 2003. Lexical rules vs. constructions: A false dichotomy. In Hubert Cuyckens, Thomas Berg, René Dirven & Klaus-Uwe Panther (eds.), *Motivation in Language: Studies in Honour of Günter Radden*, 49–68. Amsterdam: John Benjamins.
Croft, William. 2005. Logical and typological arguments for Radical Construction Grammar. In Jan-Ola Östman & Mirjam Fried (eds.), *Construction Grammars: Cognitive Grounding and Theoretical Extensions*, 273–314. Amsterdam: Benjamins.
Croft, William. 2012. *Verbs: Aspect and Clausal Structure*. Oxford: Oxford University Press.
Croft, William. 2022. *Morphosyntax: Constructions of the World's Languages*. Cambridge: Cambridge University Press.
Croft, William & D. Alan Cruse. 2004. *Cognitive Linguistics*. Cambridge: Cambridge University Press.
Culicover, Peter W. & Ray Jackendoff. 2005. *Simpler Syntax*. Oxford: Oxford University Press.
Dal, Ingerid & Hans-Werner Erom. 2014. Kurze deutsche Syntax auf historischer Grundlage. 4th edn. Berlin: De Gruyter.
Danesi, Serena. 2014. Accusative subjects in Avestan: 'Errors' or noncanonically marked arguments? *Indo-Iranian Journal* 57(3). 223–260.
Danesi, Serena, Cynthia A. Johnson & Jóhanna Barðdal. 2017. Between the historical languages and the reconstructed language: An alternative approach to the gerundive + "dative of agent" construction in Indo-European. *Indogermanische Forschungen* 122. 143–188.
Daniels, Don. 2015. *A Reconstruction of Proto-Sogeram: Phonology, Lexicon, and Morphosyntax*. Santa Barbara, Ca.: University of California, Santa Barbara, PhD Dissertation.
Daniels, Don. 2017. A method for mitigating the problem of borrowing in syntactic reconstruction. *Studies in Language* 41(3). 577–614.
Daniels, Don. 2020. *Grammatical Reconstruction: The Sogeram Languages of New Guinea*. Berlin: Mouton De Gruyter.
Dattner, Elitzur, Liron Kertes, Racehli Zwilling & Dorit Ravid. 2019. Usage patterns in the development of Hebrew grammatical subjects. *Glossa: A Journal of General Linguistics* 4(1). 129 doi: https://doi.org/10.5334/gjgl.928.
Delbrück, Berthold. 1878. Die altindische Wortfolge aus dem Çatapathabrāhmana dargestellt [Syntaktische Forschungen III]. Halle: Verlag des Waisenhauses.
Delbrück, Berthold. 1988. *Altindische Syntax*. Halle: Verlag der Buchhandlung des Waisenhauses.
Delbrück, Berthold. 1893–1900. Vergleichende Syntax der indogermanischen Sprachen. Strassburg: Trübner.
Delbrück, Berthold. 1907. *Synkretismus: Ein Beitrag zur germanischen Kasuslehre*. Strassburg: Trübner.
Delsing, Lars-Olof. 1991. Om genitivens utveckling i fornsvenskan [On the development of the genitive in Old Swedish]. In Sven-Göran Malmgren & Bo Ralph (eds.), *Studier i svensk språkhistoria* 2, 12–30. Göteborg: Acta Universitatis Gothoburgensis.
Delsing, Lars-Olof. 1995. Prepositionsstrandning och kasus i äldre svenska [Preposition stranding and case in Older Swedish]. *Arkiv för nordisk filologi* 110. 141–178.
Delsing, Lars-Olof. 1999. Från OV-ordföljd till VO-ordföljd: en språkförändring med förhinder [From OV word order to VO word order: A language change with delay]. *Arkiv för nordisk filologi* 114. 151–232.
Demske, Ulrike. 2008. Raising patterns in Old High German. In Thórhallur Eythórsson (ed.), *Grammatical Change and Linguistic Theory: The Rosendal Papers*, 143–147. Amsterdam: John Benjamins.

Denison, David. 1990. Auxiliary + impersonal in Old English. *Folia Linguistica Historica* 9(1). 138–166.
Denison, David. 1993. *English Historical Syntax: Verbal Constructions*. London: Longman.
Dewey, Tonya Kim & Stephen Mark Carey. 2018. Accusative sickness? A brief epidemic in the History of German. In Jóhanna Barðdal, Na'ama Pat-El & Stephen Mark Carey (eds.), *Non-Canonically Case-Marked Subjects: The Reykjavík–Eyjafjallajökull Papers*, 213–238. Amsterdam: John Benjamins.
Diewald, Gabriele & Elena Smirnova. 2010. *Evidentiality in German: Linguistic Realization and Regularities in Grammaticalization*. Berlin: Walter de Gruyter.
Dixon, R. M. W. 1972. *The Dyirbal Language of North Queensland*. Cambridge: Cambridge University Press.
Dixon, R. M. W. 1979. Ergativity. *Language* 55(1). 59–138.
Dixon, R. M. W. 1997. *The Rise and Fall of Languages*. Cambridge: Cambridge University Press.
Dixon, R. M. W. 2009. *Basic Linguistic Theory Volume 1: Methodology*. Oxford: Oxford University Press.
Dixon, R. M. W. 2010. *Basic Linguistic Theory Volume 2: Grammatical Topics*. Oxford: Oxford University Press.
Dixon, R. M. W. 2012. *Basic Linguistic Theory Volume 3: Further Grammatical Topics*. Oxford: Oxford University Press.
Donohue, Mark. 2008. Semantic alignment systems: what's what, and what's not. In Mark Donohue & Søren Wichman (eds.), *The Typology of Semantic Alignment*, 24–75. Oxford: Oxford University Press.
Drinka, Bridget. 1999. Alignment in Early Proto-Indo-European. In Carol F. Justus & Edgar C. Polomé (eds.), *Language Change and Typological Variation: In Honor of Winfred P. Lehmann on the Occasion of his 83rd Birthday*, Vol II, 464–500. Washington, DC: Institute for the study of Man.
Dryer, Matthew S. 2006. Descriptive theories, explanatory theories, and basic linguistic theory. In Felix Ameka, Alan Dench & Nicholas Evans (eds.), *Catching Language: The Standard Challenge of Grammar Writing*, 207–234. Berlin: Mouton de Gruyter.
Dunn, Michael, Tonya Kim Dewey, Carlee Arnett, Thórhallur Eythórsson & Jóhanna Barðdal. 2017. Dative sickness: A phylogenetic analysis of argument structure evolution in Germanic. *Language* 93(1). e1–e22.
Elmer, Willy. 1981. *Diachronic Grammar: The History of Old and Middle English Subjectless Constructions*. Tübingen: Niemeyer.
van Emde Boas, Evert, Albert Rijksbaron, Luuk Huitink & Mathieu De Bakker. 2019. *The Cambridge Grammar of Classical Greek*. Cambridge: Cambridge University Press.
Engberg-Pedersen, Elisabeth. 2018. Svar til spørger: *jeg lykkedes med at* vs. *det lykkedes mig at* [A response to an inquirer: *I succeeded in* vs. *It succeeded [Me] in*]. *Mål & Mæle* 39(2). 6–8.
Eythórsson, Thórhallur. 1995. Verbal syntax in the Early Germanic languages. Ithaca, NY: Cornell University PhD dissertation.
Eythórsson, Thórhallur. 2001. Dative vs. nominative: Changes in quirky subjects in Icelandic. In Arthur Holmer, Jan-Olof Svantesson & Åke Viberg (eds.), *Proceedings of the 18th Scandinavian Conference of Linguistics*, Vol 2, 37–52. Lund: Department of Linguistics and Phonetics.
Eythórsson, Thórhallur. 2002. Changes in subject case marking in Icelandic. In David Lightfoot (ed.), *Syntactic Effects of Morphological Change*, 196–212. Oxford: Oxford University Press.
Eythórsson, Thórhallur & Jóhanna Barðdal. 2005. Oblique subjects: A common Germanic inheritance. *Language* 81(4). 824–881.
Eythórsson, Thórhallur & Jóhanna Barðdal. 2011. Die Konstruktionsgrammatik und die komparative Methode. In Thomas Krisch & Thomas Lindner (eds.), *Indogermanistik und Linguistik im Dialog: Akten der XIII. Fachtagung der Indogermanischen Gesellschaft vom 21. bis 27. September 2008 in Salzburg*, 148–156. Wiesbaden: Reichert Verlag.

Eythórsson, Thórhallur & Jóhanna Barðdal. 2016. Syntactic reconstruction in Indo-European: State of the art. In J. Gorrochategui, C. García Castillero & J. M. Vallejo (eds.), *Franz Bopp and his Comparative Grammar Model (1816–2016)*, a special monographic volume in *Veleia* 33. 83–102.

Eythórsson, Thórhallur & Jóhannes Gísli Jónsson. 2003. The case of subject in Faroese. *Working Papers in Scandinavian Syntax* 72. 207–232.

Faarlund, Jan Terje. 1990. *Syntactic Change: Toward a Theory of Historical Syntax*. Berlin: Mouton De Gruyter.

Faarlund, Jan Terje. 1992. The subject as a thematic category in the history of Scandinavian. *Folia Linguistica* 26. 151–170.

Faarlund, Jan Terje. 2001. The notion of oblique subject and its status in the history of Icelandic. In Jan T. Faarlund (ed.), *Grammatical Relations in Change*, 99–135. Amsterdam: John Benjamins.

Faarlund, Jan Terje. 2004. *The Syntax of Old Norse*. Oxford: Oxford University Press.

Falk, Cecilia. 1995. Lexikalt kasus i svenska [Lexical case in Swedish]. *Arkiv för nordisk filologi* 110. 199–226.

Falk, Cecilia. 1997. Fornsvenska upplevarverb [Old Swedish Experiencer Verbs], Lund: Lund University Press.

Falk, Cecilia. 2018. From impersonal to reflexive verb. *Working Papers in Scandinavian Syntax* 100. 1–19.

Fanselow, Gisbert. 2002. Quirky subjects and other specifiers. In Ingrid Kaufmann & Barbara Stiebels (eds.), *More than Words: A Festschrift for Dieter Wunderlich*, 227–250. Berlin: Akademie Verlag.

Farrell, Patrick. 2005. *Grammatical Relations*. Oxford: Oxford University Press.

Fedriani, Chiara. 2014. *Experiential Constructions in Latin*. Leiden: Brill.

Ferraresi, Gisela. 2005. *Word Order and Phrase Structure in Gothic*. Leuven: Peeters.

Ferraresi, Gisela & Rosemarie Lühr. 2010. The role of information structure in language change: Introductory remarks. In Gisela Ferraresi & Rosemarie Lühr (eds.), *Diachronic Studies in Information Structure: Language Acquisition and Change*, 1–13. Berlin: De Gruyter.

Fillmore, Charles J. & Paul Kay. 1993. *Construction Grammar Course Book, Chapters 1 thru 11 (Reading materials for Ling. X20)*. University of California, Berkeley, Unpublished Ms.

Fillmore, Charles J., Paul Kay & Mary Catherine O'Connor. 1988. Regularity and idiomaticity in grammatical constructions: The case of *let alone*. *Language* 64. 501–538.

Fillmore, Charles J., Russell Lee-Goldman & Russell Rhodes. 2012. The FrameNet Constructicon. In Hans. C. Boas & Ivan A. Sag (eds.), *Sign-Based Construction Grammar*, 283–299. Stanford: CSLI Publications.

Fischer, Kerstin & Maria Alm. 2013. A Radical Construction Grammar perspective on the modal particle–discourse particle distinction. In Liesbeth Degand, Bert Cornillie & Paola Pietrandrea (eds.), *Discourse Markers and Modal Particles: Categorization and Description*, 47–88. Amsterdam: John Benjamins.

Fischer, Olga. 1990. Syntactic change and causation: Developments in infinitival constructions in English. Amsterdam: University of Amsterdam PhD Dissertation.

Fischer, Olga C. M. 1999. Changes in infinitival constructions in English. In Fritz-Wilhelm Neumann & Sabine Schulting (eds.), *Anglistentag 1998, Erfurt*, 7–27. Trier: Wissenschaftlicher Verlag.

Fischer, Olga C. M. & Frederike van der Leek. 1983. The demise of the Old English impersonal construction. *Journal of Linguistics* 19. 337–368.

Fischer, P. 1924. Zur Stellung des Verbums im Griechischen. *Glotta* 13. 1–11.

Fischer, Susann. 2010. *Word-Order Change as a Source of Grammaticalization*. Amsterdam: John Benjamins.

Foley, William A. 1993. The conceptual basis of grammatical relations. In William A. Foley (ed.), *The Role of Theory in Language Description*, 131–174. Berlin: Mouton De Gruyter.

Foley, William A. & Robert D. Van Valin, Jr. 1984. *Functional Syntax and Universal Grammar*. Cambridge: Cambridge University Press.

Fox, Anthony. 1995. *Linguistic Reconstruction: An Introduction to Theory and Method*. Oxford: Oxford University Press.

Franco, Irene. 2008. V1, V2 and criterial movement in Icelandic. *Studies in Linguistics* 2. 141–164.

Fried, Mirjam & Jan-Ola Östman. 2005. Construction Grammar and spoken language: The case of pragmatic particles. *Journal of Pragmatics* 37(11). 1752–1778.

Friedrich, Paul. 1975. *Proto-Indo-European Syntax: The Order of Meaningful Elements*. Washington, D.C.: Institute for the Study of Man.

Frotscher, Michael, Guus Kroonen & Jóhanna Barðdal. 2022. Indo-European inroads into the syntactic–etymological interface: A reconstruction of the PIE verbal root *menk^w-* 'lack' and its argument structure. *Historische Sprachforschung* 133(2020). 62–96.

Fuss, Eric. 2003. On the historical core of V2 in Germanic. *Nordic Journal of Linguistics* 26(2). 195–231.

van der Gaaf, Willem. 1904. *The Transition from the Impersonal to the Personal Construction in Middle English*. Heidelberg: Carl Winter. [Reprinted 1967, Amsterdam: Swets & Zeitlinger.]

Gabelentz, Georg von der. 1869. Ideen zu einer vergleichenden Syntax: Wort und Satzstellung. *Zeitschrift für Völkerpsychologie und Sprachwissenschaft* 6: 376–384.

Gamon, David. 1997. The grammaticalization of grammatical relations: A typological and historical study involving Kashaya Pomo, Old English, and Modern English. Berkeley, Ca: University of California, Berkeley, PhD Dissertation.

García-Miguel, Jóse M. 2007. Clause structure and transitivity. In Dirk Geeraerts & Herbert Cuyckens (eds.), *The Oxford Handbook of Cognitive Linguistics*, 753–781. Oxford: Oxford University Press.

Garrett, Andrew. 1990. The syntax of Anatolian pronominal clitics. Cambridge, Ma.: Harvard University PhD Dissertation.

van Gelderen, Elly. 2010. *An Introduction to the Grammar of English*. Revised Edition. Amsterdam: John Benjamins.

van Gelderen, Elly. 2018. *The Diachrony of Verb Meaning: Aspect and Argument Structure*. New York: Routledge.

Giacalone Ramat, Anna. 2017. Passives and constructions that resemble passives. *Folia Linguistica Historica* 38(1). 149–176.

Gildea, Spike. 1992. Comparative Cariban morphosyntax: On the genesis of ergativity in independent clauses. Eugene, Or.: University of Oregon PhD Dissertation.

Gildea, Spike. 1998. *On Reconstructing Grammar: Comparative Cariban Morphosyntax*. Oxford: Oxford University Press.

Gildea, Spike. 2000. On the genesis of the verb phrase in Cariban languages. In Spike Gildea (ed.), *Reconstructing Grammar: Comparative Linguistics and Grammaticalization*, 65–106, Amsterdam: John Benjamins.

Gildea, Spike & Jóhanna Barðdal. 2022. From grammaticalization to Diachronic Construction Grammar: A natural evolution of the paradigm. *Studies in Language*. Advance online publication: https://doi.org/10.1075/sl.20079.gil.

Gildea, Spike, Eugenio R. Luján & Jóhanna Barðdal. 2020. The curious case of reconstruction in syntax. In Jóhanna Barðdal, Spike Gildea & Eugenio R. Luján (eds.), *Reconstructing Syntax*, 1–44. Leiden: Brill.

Gillon, Brendan & Benjamin Shaer. 2005. Classical Sanskrit, "wild trees", and the properties of free word order languages. In Katalin É Kiss (ed.), *Universal Grammar in the Reconstruction of Ancient Languages*, 457–484. Berlin: Mouton de Gruyter.

Goldberg, Adele E. 1995. *Constructions: A Construction Grammar Approach to Argument Structure.* Chicago: University of Chicago Press.

Goldberg, Adele E. 2006. *Constructions at Work: The Nature of Generalization in Language.* Oxford: Oxford University Press.

Goldberg, Adele E. & Giulia M. L. Bencini. 2005. Support from language processing for a constructional approach to grammar. In Andrea Tyler, Mari Takada, Yiyoung Kim & Diana Marinova (eds.), *Language in Use: Cognitive and Discourse Perspectives on Language and Language Learning*, 3–18. Georgetown University Round Table on Languages and Linguistics.

Gonzálvez García, Francisco. 2006. Passives without actives: Evidence from verbless complement clauses in Spanish. *Constructions*: SV1-5/2006.

Gray, Russel & Quentin Atkinson. 2003. Language-tree divergence times support the Anatolian theory of Indo-European Origin. *Nature* 426. 435–439.

Greenberg, Joseph H. 1966. Some universals of grammar with particular reference to the order of meaningful elements. In Joseph H. Greenberg (ed.), *Universals of Language: Reports of a Conference Held at Dobbs Ferry, New York, April 13–15, 1961*, 73–113. Cambridge Ma: MIT Press.

Grimshaw, Jane. 1990. *Argument Structure.* Cambridge Ma: MIT Press.

de Haan, Germen J. 2001. Why Old Frisian is really Middle Frisian. *Folia Linguistica Historica* 22(1–2). 179–206.

Haider, Hubert. 2005. How to turn German into Icelandic—and derive the OV–VO contrast. *Journal of Comparative Germanic Syntax* 8. 1–53.

Haider, Hubert. 2010. *The Syntax of German.* Cambridge: Cambridge University Press.

Hale, Mark. 1987a. Notes on Wackernagel's law in the language of the Rigveda. In Calvert Watkins (ed.), *Studies in Memory of Warren Cowgill (1929–1985): Papers from the Fourth East Coast Indo-European Conference*, 38–50. Berlin–New York: Walter de Gruyter.

Hale, Mark. 1987b. Studies in the comparative syntax of the oldest Indo-Iranian languages. Cambridge, Ma.: Harvard University PhD Dissertation.

Hale, Mark. 1998. Diachronic Syntax. *Syntax* 1. 1–18.

Hale, Mark. 2014. The Comparative Method: Theoretical issues. In Claire Bowern & Bethwyn Evans (eds.), *The Routledge Handbook of Historical Linguistics*, 146–160. London: Routledge.

Harbert, Wayne E. 1978. Gothic syntax: A relational grammar. Urbana-Champaign, Il.; University of Illinois, Urbana-Champaign, PhD Dissertation.

Harbert, Wayne. 1991. Binding, SUBJECT, and accessibility. In Robert Freidin (ed.), *Principles and Parameters in Comparative Grammar*, 29–55. Cambridge, Ma: MIT Press.

Harbert, Wayne. 2007. *The Germanic Languages.* Cambridge: Cambridge University Press.

Harkness, Albert. 1869. *Elements of Latin Grammar for Schools.* New York: D. Appleton and Company.

Harris, Alice C. 1973. Psychological predicates in Middle English. Paper presented at the Annual Meeting of the Linguistic Society of America, San Diego.

Harris, Alice C. 1985. *Diachronic Syntax: The Kartvelian Case.* New York: Academic Press.

Harris, Alice C. 2008. Reconstruction in syntax: Reconstruction of patterns. In Gisella Ferraresi & Maria Goldbach (eds.), *Principles of Syntactic Reconstruction*, 73–95. Amsterdam: John Benjamins.

Harris, Alice C. & Lyle Campbell. 1995. *Historical Syntax in Cross-Linguistic Perspective.* Cambridge: Cambridge University Press.

Harrison, S. P. 2003. On the limits of the Comparative Method. In Brian D. Joseph & Richard D. Janda (eds.), *The Handbook of Historical Linguistics*, 343–368. Oxford: Blackwell.

Haspelmath, Martin. 2001. Non-canonical marking of core arguments in European languages. In Alexandra Y. Aikhenvald, R. M. W. Dixon & Masayoki Onishi (eds.), *Non-Canonical Marking of Subjects and Objects*, 53–83. Amsterdam: John Benjamins.

Haspelmath, Martin. 2004. Does Linguistic explanation presuppose linguistic description? *Studies in Language* 28. 554–579.

Haspelmath, Martin. 2007. Pre-established categories don't exist: Consequences for language description and typology. *Linguistic Typology* 11. 119–132.

Haspelmath, Martin & Sandro Caruana. 2000. Subject diffuseness in Maltese: On some subject properties of experiential verbs. *Folia Linguistica* 34(3–4). 245–265.

Haugan, Jens. 2001. Old Norse word order and information structure. Trondheim: NTNU Trondheim PhD Dissertation.

Havers, Wilhelm. 1911. *Untersuchungen zur Kasussyntax der indogermanischen Sprachen*. Strassburg: Trübner.

Hawkins, John A. 1986. *A Comparative Typology of English and German: Unifying the Contrasts*. London: Croom Helm.

Helbig, Gerhard & Joachim Buscha. 2001. *Deutsche Grammatik: Ein Handbuch für den Ausländerunterricht*. Berlin: Langenscheidt.

Hellan, Lars & Christer Platzack. 1995. Pronouns in Scandinavian languages: An overview. *Working Papers in Scandinavian Syntax* 56. 47–69.

Heltoft, Lars. 2012. Zero expression of arguments in Old Danish. *Acta Linguistica Hafniensia* 44(2). 169–191.

Heltoft, Lars. 2021. The typology of Old Norse revisited – The case of Middle Danish. *NOWELE: North-Western European Language Evolution* 74(2). 242–277.

Hendriks, Jennifer. 2012. Case marking (accounts) in collapse: Evidence from Early Modern Dutch egodocuments (1572–1573). In Maia Ponsonnet, Loan Dao & Margit Bowler (eds.), *Proceedings of the 42nd Australian Linguistic Society Conference – 2011*, 123–151. Canberra: Australian National University.

Hentschel, Elke. 2010. *Deutsche Grammatik*. Berlin: De Gruyter.

Hermann, Eduard. 1895. Gab es im Indogermanischen Nebensätze? *Zeitschrift für vergleichende Sprachforschung auf dem Gebiete der Indogermanischen Sprachen* 33(4). 481–534.

Hermon, Gabriella. 1985. *Syntactic Modularity*. Dordrecht: Foris.

Hiietam, Katrin. 2003. Definiteness and grammatical relations in Estonian. Manchester: University of Manchester PhD Dissertation.

Hilpert, Martin, 2014. *Construction Grammar and its Application to English*. Edinburgh: Edinburgh University Press.

Hinterhölzl, Roland & Ans van Kemenade. 2012. The Interaction between syntax, information structure and prosody in word order change. In Terttu Nevalainen & Elizabeth Closs Traugott (eds.), *The Oxford Handbook of the History of English*, 803–821. Oxford: Oxford University Press.

Hinterholzl, Roland & Svetlana Petrova. 2010. From V1 to V2 in West Germanic. *Lingua* 120(2). 315–328.

Hjartardóttir, Thóra Björk. 1987. Getið í eyðurnar: Um eyður fyrir frumlög og andlög í eldri íslensku [Filling the gaps: On subject and object gaps in Older Icelandic]. Reykjavík: University of Iceland Master's Thesis [Published in 1993 by Málvísindastofnun Háskóla Íslands].

Hock, Hans Henrich & Elena Bashir. 2016. *The Languages and Linguistics of South Asia: A Comprehensive Guide*. Berlin: De Gruyter Mouton.

Hoenigswald, Henry M. 1978. The annus mirabilis 1876 and posterity. *Transactions of the Philological Society* 76(1). 17–35.

Hoffner, Harry A. & Craig H. Melchert. 2008. *A Grammar of the Hittite Language. Part 1: Reference Grammar*. Winona Lake, IA: Eisenbrauns.
Hole, Daniel. 2014. *Dativ, Bindung und Diathese*. Berlin: De Gruyter.
Holvoet, Axel. 2013. Obliqueness, quasi-subjects and transitivity in Baltic and Slavonic. In Ilja A. Seržant & Leonid Kulikov (eds.), *The Diachronic Typology of Non-Canonical Subjects*, 257–282. Amsterdam: John Benjamins.
Holvoet, Axel. 2016. Argument marking in Baltic and Slavonic pain-verb constructions. In Axel Holvoet & Nicole Nau (eds.), *Argument Realization in Baltic*, 83–106. Amsterdam: John Benjamins.
van der Horst, Joop. 2008. *Geschiedenis van de Nederlandse syntaxis*. Leuven: Universitaire Pers.
Hrafnbjargarson, Gunnar Hrafn. 2004. Oblique subjects and stylistic fronting in the history of Scandinavian and English: The role of IP-Spec. Aarhus: Aarhus University PhD Dissertation.
Hualde, José I. 1988. Case assignment in Basque. *ASJU: International Journal of Basque Linguistics and Philology* 22(1). 313–330.
Huddleston, Rodney & Geoffrey K. Pullum. 2005. *A Student's Introduction to English Grammar*. Cambridge: Cambridge University Press.
Ilioaia, Mihaela. 2021. Non-canonical subjects in Romanian: The status and evolution of the *MIHI EST* construction. Ghent: Ghent University PhD Dissertation.
Ilioaia, Mihaela & Marleen Van Peteghem. 2021. Dative experiencers with nominal predicates in Romanian: A synchronic and diachronic study. *Folia Linguistica Historica* 42(2). 255–290.
Ingason, Anton Karl, Einar Freyr Sigurðsson & Joel C. Wallenberg. 2011. Distinguishing change and stability: A quantitative study of Icelandic oblique subjects. Paper presented at DIGS 13, University of Pennsylvania, 2–5 June 2011.
Jackendoff, Ray. 1972. *Semantic Interpretation in Generative Grammar*. Cambridge, Ma: The MIT Press.
Jackendoff, Ray. 1990. *Semantic Structures*. Cambridge, Ma: The MIT Press.
Jackendoff, Ray. 1997. Twistin' the night away. *Language* 73. 534–559.
Jacobi, Hermann. 1897. *Compositum und Nebensatz*. Bonn: Cohen.
Jakubíček, Miloš, Adam Kilgarriff, Vojtěch Kovář, Pavel Rychlý & Vít Suchomel. 2013. The TenTen Corpus Family. In Andrew Hardie & Robbie Love (eds.), *7th International Corpus Linguistics Conference*, 125–127. Lancaster: University of Lancaster.
Janda, Richard D. 2001. Beyond "pathways" and "unidirectionality": On the discontinuity of language transmission and the counterability of grammaticalization. *Language Sciences* 23. 265–340.
Jeffers, Robert J. 1976. Syntactic change and syntactic reconstruction. In William M. Christie, Jr. (ed.), *Current Progress in Historical Linguistics: Proceedings of the Second International Conference on Historical Linguistics*, 1–15. Amsterdam: North-Holland Publishing.
Jespersen, Otto. 1894. *Progress in Language: With Special Reference to English*. London: Swan Sonnenschein. [Republished in 1993 by John Benjamins, Amsterdam.]
Jespersen, Otto. 1927. *A Modern English Grammar on Historical Principles*. Vol. 3. London: Allen & Unwin.
Johnson, Cynthia A., Peter Alexander Kerkhof, Leonid Kulikov, Esther Le Mair & Jóhanna Barðdal. 2019. Argument structure, conceptual metaphor and semantic change: How to succeed in Indo-European without really trying. *Diachronica* 36(4). 463–508.
Jolly, Julius. 1872. *Ein Kapitel vergleichender Syntax: Der Conjunktiv und Optativ und die Nebensätze im Zend und Altpersischen*. Munich: Ackermann.
Jónsson, Jóhannes Gísli. 1996. Clausal architecture and case in Icelandic. Amherst, Ma.: UMass Amherst PhD Dissertation.

Jónsson, Jóhannes Gísli. 1997–98. Sagnir með aukafallsfrumlagi [Verbs selecting for oblique subjects]. *Íslenskt mál* 19–20. 11–43.

Jónsson, Jóhannes Gísli. 2000. Case and double objects in Icelandic. *Leeds Working Papers in Linguistics* 8. 1–94.

Jónsson, Jóhannes Gísli. 2003. Not so quirky: On subject case in Icelandic. In Ellen Brandner & Heike Zinsmeister (eds.), *New Perspectives on Case Theory*, 127–163. Stanford: CSLI Publications.

Jónsson, Jóhannes Gísli. 2013. Two types of case variation. *Nordic Journal of Linguistics* 36(1). 5–25.

Jónsson, Jóhannes Gísli. 2018. Word order as a subject test in Old Icelandic. In Jóhanna Barðdal, Na'ama Pat-El, & Stephen Mark Carey (eds.), *Non-Canonically Case-Marked Subjects: The Reykjavík–Eyjafjallajökull Papers*, 135–154. Amsterdam: John Benjamins.

Jónsson, Jóhannes Gísli & Thórhallur Eythórsson. 2003. Breytingar á frumlagsfalli í íslensku [Changes in subject case marking in Icelandic]. *Íslenskt mál og almenn málfræði* 25. 7–40.

Jónsson, Jóhannes Gísli & Thórhallur Eythórsson. 2005. Variation in subject case marking in Insular Scandinavian. *Nordic Journal of Linguistics* 28. 223–245.

Josefsson, Gunlög. 1992. Object shift and weak pronominals in Swedish. *Working Papers in Scandinavian Syntax* 49. 59–94.

Juntune, Thomas W. 1992. Subject and reflexive in Old Icelandic. In Rosina Lippi-Green (ed.), *Recent Developments in Germanic Linguistics*, 60–79. Amsterdam: John Benjamins.

Kachru, Yamuna, Braj B. Kachru & Tej K. Bhatia. 1976. The notion 'subject': A note on Hindi-Urdu, Kashmiri and Punjabi. In Manindra K. Verma (ed.), *The Notion of Subject in South Asian Languages*, 79–108. Madison: University of Wisconsin.

Kalkar, Otto. 1886–1982. *Ordbog til det ældre danske sprog* (1300–1700) [A Dictionary of the older Danish Language (1300–1700)]. København: Thieles bogtrykkeri.

Kampen, Jacqueline van. 2020. Discourse-related V1 declaratives in Dutch. In Elena Tribushinina & Mark Dingemanse (eds.), *Linguistics in the Netherlands 2020*, 149–164. Amsterdam: John Benjamins.

Karlsson, Emanuel. 2018. A radical construction grammar approach to construction split in the diachrony of the spatial particles of Ancient Greek. In Evie Coussé, Peter Andersson & Joel Olofsson (eds.), *Grammaticalization Meets Construction Grammar*, 277–311. Amsterdam: John Benjamins.

Kay, Paul. 1997. Construction grammar feature structures (revised). Unpublished ms. University of California, Berkeley.

Kay, Paul & Charles J. Fillmore. 1999. Grammatical constructions and linguistic generalizations: The 'What's X doing Y?' construction. *Language* 75. 1–33.

Keenan, Edward L. 1976. Towards a universal definition of subject. In Charles N. Li (ed.), *Subject and Topic*, 303–333. New York: Academic Press.

Keydana, Götz. 2018. The syntax of Proto-Indo-European. In Jared Klein, Brian Joseph & Matthias Fritz (eds.), *Handbook of Comparative and Historical Indo-European Linguistics*, 2195–2228. Berlin: De Gruyter Mouton.

Kibrik. Andrej A. 2012. What's in the head of head-marking languages? In Pirkko Suihkonen, Bernard Comrie & Valery Solovyev (eds.), *Argument Structure and Grammatical Relations: A Crosslinguistic Typology*, 211–240. Amsterdam: John Benjamins.

Kikusawa, Ritsuko. 2002. *Proto Central Pacific Ergativity: Its Reconstruction and Development in the Fijian, Rotuman and Polynesian Languages*. Canberra: Pacific Linguistics.

Kikusawa, Ritsuko. 2003. The development of some Indonesian pronominal systems. In Barry J. Blake, Kate Burridge & Jo Taylor (eds.), *Historical Linguistics 2001: Selected Papers from the 15th International Conference on Historical Linguistics, Melbourne, 13–17 August 2001*, 237–268. Amsterdam: John Benjamins.

Kim, Jong-Bok & Laura A. Michaelis. 2020. *Syntactic Constructions in English*. Cambridge: Cambridge University Press.

Klaiman, M. H. 1980. Bengali dative subjects. *Lingua* 51(4). 275–295.

Klein, Jared S. 2010. Review of Principles of Reconstruction, ed. by Gisela Ferraresi & Maria Goldbach. 2008. *Language* 86. 720–726.

Kluge, Friedrich. 2012. *Etymologisches Wörterbuch der deutschen Sprache: Etymological Dictionary of the German Language*, 25th edn. Berlin: De Gruyter.

Kluge, Friedrich. 1913. *Urgermanisch: Vorgeschichte der altgermanischen Dialekte*, 3rd edn. Strassburg: Trübner.

Kotin, Michail L. 2021. Der deutsche Dativ genealogisch und diachron: Eine Sprachwandelstudie über den dritten Fall. *Beiträge zur Geschichte der deutschen Sprache und Literatur* 143(1). 55–111.

Krahe, Hans. 1969a. *Germanische Sprachwissenschaft, Vol. 2: Formenlehre*. 7th edn. Berlin: Walter de Gruyter.

Krahe, Hans. 1969b. *Indogermanische Sprachwissenschaft, Vol. 2: Formenlehre*. Berlin: Walter de Gruyter.

Kristoffersen, Kristian E. 1991. Kasus, semantiske roller og grammatiske funksjonar i norrønt [Case, semantic roles and grammatical functions in Old Norse]. Oslo: University of Oslo Master's Thesis.

Kristoffersen, Kristian E. 1994. Passiv i norrønt og nyislandsk – ei samanlikning [The passive in Old Norse and Modern Icelandic – A comparison]. *Norsk Lingvistisk Tidsskrift* 12. 43–69.

Kristoffersen, Kristian E. 1996. Infinitival phrases in Old Norse: Aspects of their syntax and semantics. Oslo: University of Oslo PhD Dissertation.

Kroonen, Guus. 2013. *Etymological Dictionary of Proto-Germanic*. Leiden: Brill.

Lakoff, George. 1987. *Women, Fire, and Dangerous Things: What Categories Reveal about the Mind*. Chicago: University of Chicago Press.

Landau, Idan. 2009. *The Locative Syntax of Experiencers*. Cambridge, Ma: MIT Press.

Landau, Idan. 2013. *Control in Generative Grammar: A Research Companion*. Cambridge: Cambridge University Press.

Lander, Eric T. & Liliane Haegeman. 2014. Old Norse as an NP language: With observations on the Common Norse and Northwest Germanic runic inscriptions. *Transactions of the Philological Society* 112(3). 279–318.

Langacker, Ronald W. 1991. *Foundations of Cognitive Grammar, Vol. II: Descriptive Applications*. Stanford: Stanford University Press.

Langacker, Ronald W. 2008. *Cognitive Grammar: A Basic Introduction*. Oxford: Oxford University Press.

Lapolla, Randy J. 2013. Arguments for a construction-based approach to the analysis of Chinese. In Tseng Chiu-yu (ed.), *Human Language Resources and Linguistic Typology: Papers from the Fourth International Conference on Sinology*, 33–57. Taiwan: Academia Sinica.

Legate, Julie Ann. 2005. Split absolutive. In Alana Johns, Diane Massam & Juvenal Ndayiragije (eds.), *Ergativity: Emerging Issues*, 143–171. Dordrecht: Springer.

Lehmann, Winfred P. 1974. *Proto-Indo-European Syntax*. Austin: University of Texas Press.

Lenerz, Jürgen. 1977. *Zur Abfolge nominaler Satzglieder im Deutschen*. Tübingen: Günter Narr.

Lenerz, Jürgen. 1992. Zur Syntax der Pronomina im Deutschen. *Sprache und Pragmatik* 29. 1–54.

Letuchiy, Alexander. 2009. Towards a typology of labile Verbs: Lability vs. derivation. In Patience
    Epps & Alexandre Arkhipov (eds.), *New Challenges in Typology: Transcending the Borders and
    Refining the Distinctions*, 223–244. Berlin: Mouton De Gruyter.
Li, Charles N., ed. 1976. *Subject and Topic*. New York: Academic Press.
Lightfoot, David W. 1979. *Principles of Diachronic Syntax*. Cambridge: Cambridge University Press.
Lightfoot, David W. 1981. Explaining syntactic change. In Norbert Hornstein & David W. Lightfoot
    (eds.), *Explanation in Linguistics*, 209–240. London: Longman.
Lightfoot, David W. 2002. Myths and the prehistory of grammars. *Journal of Linguistics* 38(1).
    113–136.
Lindqvist, Axel. 1912. *Förskjutningar i förhållandet mellan grammatiskt och psykologiskt subjekt*
    [Derangements in the Relation between Grammatical and Psychological Subject]. Lund: Gleerup.
Lindström, Jan & Susanna Karlsson. 2005. Verb-first constructions as a syntactic and functional
    resource in (spoken) Swedish. *Nordic Journal of Linguistics* 28(1). 97–131.
Lindström, Liina. 2001. Verb-initial clauses in narrative. In Mati Erelt (ed.), *Estonian: Typological Studies
    V*, 138–168. Tartu: University of Tartu.
LIV = Rix, Helmut, Martin Kümmel, Thomas Zehnder, Reiner Lipp & Brigitte Schirmer. 2001. *Lexikon der
    indogermanischen Verben*. 2. Auflage. Wiesbaden: Reichert.
Ljunggren, Carl August. 1901. *Om bruket av* sig *och* sin *i svenskan* [On the use of *sig* and *sin* in Swedish]
    Lund: Gleerupska universitetsbokhandeln.
Loureiro-Porto, Lucía. 2010. A Review of Early English impersonals: Evidence from necessity verbs.
    English Studies 91(6). 674–699.
Los, Bettelou. 1998. Bare and *to*-infinitives in Old English: Callaway revisited. In Jacek Fisiak & Marcin
    Krygier (eds.), *Advances in English Historical Linguistics*, 173–188. Berlin: Mouton de Gruyter.
Los, Bettelou. 2009. The consequences of the loss of verb-second in English: Information structure
    and syntax in interaction. *English Language and Linguistics* 13(1). 97–125.
Malchukov, Andrej L. 2008. Split intransitives, experiencer objects and 'transimpersonal'
    constructions: (Re-)establishing the connection. In Mark Donohue & Søren Wichmann (eds.),
    The Typology of Semantic Alignment, 76–100. Oxford: Oxford University Press.
Malchukov, Andrej L. 2018. Forty years in the search of a/the subject. In Jóhanna Barðdal, Na'ama
    Pat-El, & Stephen Mark Carey (eds.), *Non-Canonically Case-Marked Subjects: The Reykjavík-
    Eyjafjallajökull Papers*, 241–256. Amsterdam: John Benjamins.
Maling, Joan. 1986. Clause-bounded examples in Modern Icelandic. In Lars Helland & Kirsti Koch
    Christensen (eds.), *Topics in Scandinavian Syntax*, 53–63. Dordrecht: Reidel. [Also
    published in Joan Maling & Annie Zaenen (eds.),. *Modern Icelandic Syntax*, 277–287.
    Syntax and Semantics 24. San Diego: Academic Press.]
Marckwardt, Albert H. 1942. The verbal suffix *-ettan* in Old English. *Language* 18(4). 275–281.
Masica, Colin P. 1976. *Defining a Linguistic Area: South Asia*. Chicago: University of Chicago Press.
Matasović, Ranko. 2013. Latin *maenitet me, miseret me, pudet me* and active clause alignment in PIE.
    Indogermanische Forschungen 118. 93–110.
Mathieu, Eric. 2006. Quirky subjects in Old French. *Studia Linguistica* 60(3). 282–312.
van der Meer, Marten Jan. 1901. *Gotische Casus-Syntaxis*. Leiden: Brill.
Mel'čuk, Igor. 2014. Syntactic subject: Syntactic relations, once again. In Vladimir Plungian, Mixail
    Daniel, Ekaterina Ljutikova, Sergej Tatevosov & Olga Fedorova (eds.), *Jazyk. Konstanty, Peremennye.
    Pamjati Aleksandra Evgen'eviča Kibrika*, 169–216. Sankt-Petersburg: Aletejja.
Mendoza, Julia. 1998. Sintaxis. In Francisco R. Adrados, Alberto Bernabé & Julia Mendoza (eds.),
    Manual de Lingüística Indoeuropea III, 141–246. Madrid: Ediciones Clásicas.

Metslang, Helena. 2013. Coding and behaviour of Estonian subjects. *Journal of Estonian and Finno-Ugric Linguistics* 4(2). 217–293.
Michaelis, Laura. 1998. *Aspectual Grammar and Past-Time Reference*. London: Routledge.
Michaelis, Laura A. 2010. Sign-based Construction Grammar. In Bernd Heine & Heiko Narrog (eds.), *The Oxford Handbook of Linguistic Analysis*, 155–176. Oxford: Oxford University Press.
Michaelis, Laura A. 2012. Making the case for Construction Grammar. In Hans C. Boas & Ivan A. Sag (eds.), *Sign-Based Construction Grammar*, 31–68. Stanford: CSLI Publications.
Michaelis, Laura A. & Josef Ruppenhofer. 2001. *Beyond Alternations: A Construction-Based Account of the Applicative Construction in German*. Stanford: CSLI Publications.
Middeke, Kerstin. 2021. *The Old English Case System: Case and Argument Structure Constructions*. Leiden: Brill.
Miller, D. Gary. 1975. Indo-European: VSO, SOV, SVO, or all three? *Lingua* 37. 31–52.
Miranda, Rocky. 1976. Comments on Jeffers. In William M. Christie Jr. (ed.), *Current Progress in Historical Linguistics: Proceedings of the Second International Conference on Historical Linguistics*, 12–14. Amsterdam: North-Holland Publishing
Moore, John & David M. Perlmutter. 2000. What does it take to be a dative subject? *Natural Language and Linguistic Theory* 18. 373–416.
Möhlig-Falke, Ruth. 2012. *The Early English Impersonal Construction: An Analysis of Verbal and Constructional Meaning*. Oxford: Oxford University Press.
Mørck, Endre. 1992. Subjektets kasus i norrønt og mellomnorsk [The case of the subject in Old Norse-Icelandic and Middle Norwegian]. *Arkiv för nordisk filologi* 107. 53–99.
Mörnsjö, Maria. 2002. *V1 Declaratives in Spoken Swedish: Syntax, Information Structure and Prosodic Pattern*. Department of Scandinavian Languages, Lund University.
Müller, Gereon. 2005. Syncretism and iconicity in Icelandic noun declensions: A distributed morphology approach. *Yearbook of Morphology 2004*. 229–271.
Naylor, Paz Buenaventura. 1995. Subject, topic and Tagalog syntax. In David C. Bennett, Theodora Bynon & B. George Hewitt (eds.), *Subject, Voice and Ergativity*, 161–201. London: School of Oriental and African Studies, University of London.
Nilsson, Jan. 1975. *Plurala ortnamn på Island: Morfologiska iakttagelser* [Plural Place Names in Iceland: Morphological Observations]. Umeå: Umeå University.
Nizar, Milla. 2010. Dative subject constructions in South-Dravidian languages. Berkeley, Ca.: University of California, Berkeley, Bachelor Thesis.
Önnerfors, Olaf. 1997. *Verb-Erst-Deklarativsätze: Grammatik und Pragmatik*. Stockholm: Almqvist & Wiksell.
Ottósson, Kjartan G. 1989. VP-specifier subjects and the CP/IP distinction in Icelandic and Mainland Scandinavian. *Working Papers in Scandinavian Syntax* 44. 89–100.
Ottósson, Kjartan G. 1992. The Middle Voice in Icelandic. Lund: Lund University Doctoral Dissertation.
Ottósson, Kjartan G. 2013. The anticausative and related categories in the Old Germanic languages. In Folke Josephson & Ingmar Söhrman (eds.), *Diachronic and Typological Perspectives on Verbs*, 329–382. Amsterdam: John Benjamins.
Östman, Jan-Ola. 2018. Constructions as cross-linguistic generalizations over instances: Passive patterns in contact. In Hans C. Boas & Steffen Höder (eds.), *Constructions in Contact: Constructional Perspectives on Contact Phenomena in Germanic Languages*, 181–210. Amsterdam: John Benjamins.
Pankau, Andreas. 2016. Quirky subjects in Icelandic, Faroese, and German: A Relational Grammar account. In Doug Arnold, Miriam Butt, Berthold Crysmann, Tracy Holloway King & Stefan Müller (eds.), *Proceedings of the Joint 2016 Conference on Head-driven Phrase Structure Grammar and Lexical Functional Grammar, Polish Academy of Sciences, Warsaw, Poland*, 499–519. Stanford, Ca: CSLI Publications.

Pat-El, Na'ama. 2018. The diachrony of non-canonical subjects in Northwest Semitic. In Jóhanna Barðdal, Na'ama Pat-El & Stephen Mark Carey, (eds.), *Non-Canonical Subjects across Language Families: The Reykjavík–Eyjafjallajökull Papers*, 159–184. Amsterdam: John Benjamins.
Payne, Thomas E. 2011. *Understanding English Grammar: A Linguistic Introduction*. Cambridge: Cambridge University Press.
Pedersen, Holger. 1907. Neues und nachträgliches. *Zeitschrift für Vergleichende Sprachforschung* 40. 129–257.
Pesetsky, David. 1995. *Zero Syntax: Experiencers and Cascades*. Cambridge, Ma: MIT Press.
Petersen, Hjalmar P. 2002. Quirky case in Faroese. *Fróðskaparrit* 50. 63–76.
Platzack, Christer. 1985. Narrative inversion in Old Icelandic. *Íslenskt mál og almenn málfræði* 7. 127–144.
Platzack, Christer. 1987. The case of narrative inversion in Swedish and Icelandic. *Working Papers in Scandinavian Syntax* 31. 9–14.
Platzack, Christer. 1999. The subject of Icelandic psych-verbs: A minimalistic account. *Working Papers in Scandinavian Syntax* 64. 103–116.
Polinsky, Maria. 2013. Raising and control. In Marcel den Dikken (ed.), *The Cambridge Handbook of Generative Syntax*, 41–63. Cambridge: Cambridge University Press.
Pooth, Roland A. 2004. Zur Genese der späturidg. thematischen Konjugation aus frühuridg. Medialformen. *Indogermanische Forschungen* 109. 31–60.
Pooth, Roland A. 2014. Die Diathesen Aktiv vs. Medium und die Verbsemantik im Vedischen der R̥gveda-Saṃhitā". Leiden: Leiden University PhD Dissertation.
Pooth, Roland A. 2021. On converse lability and its decline from Vedic to Epic Sanskrit: The verb *juṣ*- 'to enjoy' and 'to please'. *Yearbook of the Poznań Linguistic Meeting* 7. 217–252.
Pooth, Roland, Peter Alexander Kerkhof, Leonid Kulikov & Jóhanna Barðdal. 2019. The origin of non-canonical case marking of subjects in Proto-Indo-European: Accusative, ergative, or semantic alignment. *Indogermanische Forschungen* 123. 245–263.
Pooth, Roland & Verónica Orqueda. 2021. Alignment change and the emergence of the thematic conjugation from Proto-Indo-European to Indo-European: A wedding of hypotheses. *Transactions of the Philological Society* 119(2). 107–151.
Porzig, Walter. 1932. Die Hypotaxe im Rigveda 1: Die durch das Pronomen *ya* charakterisierten Sätze und syntaktischen Gruppen in den ältern Büchern des Rigveda. *Indogermanische Forschungen* 41. 210–303.
Postal, Paul M. 1970. On coreferential complement subject deletion. *Natural Language and Linguistic Theory* 1. 439–500.
Primus, Beatrice. 1994. Grammatik und Performanz: Faktoren der Wortstellungsvariation im Mittelfeld. *Sprache und Pragmatik* 32. 39–86.
Primus, Beatrice. 2012. *Semantische Rollen*. Heidelberg: Carl Winter.
Puckica, Jérôme. 2009. Passive constructions in Present-Day English. *Groninger Arbeiten zur Germanistischen Linguistik* 49. 215–235.
Rákosi, György. 2006. *Dative Experiencer Predicates in Hungarian*. Utrecht: LOT.
Reis, Marga. 1982. Zum Subjektbegriff im Deutschen. In Werner Abraham (ed.), *Satzglieder im Deutschen: Vorschläge zur syntaktischen, semantischen und pragmatischen Fundierung*, 171–211. Tübingen: Gunter Narr.
Ringe, Don. 2006. *From Proto-Indo-European to Proto-Germanic*. Oxford: Oxford University Press.
Rott, Julian A. 2013. Syntactic prominence in Icelandic experiencer arguments: Quirky subjects vs. dative objects. *STUF – Language Typology and Universals* 66(2). 91–111.

Rott, Julian A. 2016. Germanic psych processing: Evidence for the status of dative experiencers in Icelandic and German. In Christel Stolz & Thomas Stolz (eds.), *From Africa via the Americas to Iceland*, 215–320. Bochum: Dr. N. Brockmeyer.

Rögnvaldsson, Eiríkur. 1990. Null objects in Icelandic. In Joan Maling & Annie Zaenen (eds.), *Modern Icelandic Syntax*, 367–379. San Diego: Academic Press.

Rögnvaldsson, Eiríkur. 1991. Quirky subjects in Old Icelandic. In Halldór Ármann Sigurðsson (ed.), *Papers from the Twelfth Scandinavian Conference of Linguistics*, 369–387. Reykjavík: Institute of Linguistics, University of Iceland.

Rögnvaldsson, Eiríkur. 1995. Old Icelandic: A non-configurational language? *NOWELE: North-Western European Language Evolution* 26. 3–29.

Rögnvaldsson, Eiríkur. 1996. Frumlag og fall að fornu [Subject and case in Old Icelandic]. *Íslenskt mál og almenn málfræði* 18. 37–69.

Rögnvaldsson, Eiríkur. 2007. Reflexives in Older Icelandic. Unpublished manuscript, University of Iceland.

Rysová, Kateřina, Jiří Mírovský & Eva Hajičová. 2015. On an apparent freedom of Czech word order: A case study. In Markus Dickinson, Erhard Hinrichs, Agnieszka Patejuk & Adam Przepiórkowski (eds.), *Proceedings of the Fourteenth International Workshop on Treebanks and Linguistic Theories* (TLT14), 93–105. Warsaw: Institute of Computer Science, Polish Academy of Sciences.

Sag, Ivan. 2012. Sign-based Construction Grammar: An informal synopsis. In Hans C. Boas & Ivan A. Sag (eds.), *Sign-Based Construction Grammar*, 69–202. Stanford: CSLI Publications.

Sandal, Catrine. 2011. Akkusative subjekt og antikausativitet i norrønt [Accusative Subjects and Anticausativization in Old Norse-Icelandic]. Bergen: University of Bergen Master's Thesis.

Sapir Edward. 1917. Review of C. C Uhlenbeck: Het Passieve Karakter van het Verbum Transitivum of van het Verbum Actionis in Talen van Nord-Amerika. *International Journal of American Linguistics* 1. 82–86.

Sapp, Christopher D. 2010. The reflexive possessive *sîn* in Old Saxon. *Beiträge zur Geschichte der Deutschen Sprache und Literatur* 132(3). 329–342.

Sarkar, Anoop & Daniel Zeman. 2000. Automatic extraction of subcategorization frames for Czech. In *CoLing in Europe: Proceedings of the 18th International Conference on Computational Linguistics*, Vol. 2, 691–697. Saarbrücken: ACL.

Sasse, Hans-Jürgen. 1978. Subjekt und Ergativ: Zur pragmatischen Grundlage primärer grammatischer Relationen. *Folia Linguistica* 12. 219–252.

Schlesewsky, Matthias & Ina Bornkessel. 2006. Context-sensitive neural responses to conflict resolution: Electrophysiological evidence from subject–object ambiguities in language comprehension. *Brain Research* 1098. 139–152.

Seefranz-Montag, Ariane von. 1983. Syntaktische Funktionen und Wortstellungsveränderung: die Entwicklung "subjektloser" Konstruktionen in einigen Sprachen. Munich: Wilhelm Fink Verlag.

Seefranz-Montag, Ariane von. 1984. 'Subjectless' constructions and syntactic change. In Jacek Fisiak (ed.), *Historical Syntax*, 521–553. Berlin: Mouton.

Seržant, Ilja. 2013. The diachronic typology of non-canonical subjects. In Ilja A. Seržant & Leonid Kulikov (eds.), *The Diachrony of Non-Canonical Subjects*, 313–360. Amsterdam: John Benjamins.

Seržant, Ilja. 2015. Dative experiencer constructions as a Circum-Baltic isogloss. In Peter Arkadiev, Axel Holvoet & Björn Wiemer (eds.), *Contemporary Approaches to Baltic Linguistics*, 325–348. Berlin: Mouton De Gruyter.

Seržant, Ilja & Leonid Kulikov (eds.). 2013. *The Diachronic Typology of Non-Canonical Subjects*. Amsterdam: John Benjamins.

Shariatmadari, David. 2019. *Don't Believe a Word: The Surprising Truth about Language*. London: Weidenfeld & Nicholson.
Sherman, Iohn. 1969. Overt and covert case in the Riustringen dialect of Old Frisian. Ann Arbor, Mi.: University of Michigan PhD Dissertation.
Shibatani, Masayoshi. 1999. Dative subject constructions twenty-two years later. *Studies in the Linguistic Sciences* 29(2). 45–76.
Sigurðsson, Einar Freyr & Heimir van der Feest Viðarsson. 2020. Frá skiptisögn til ósamhverfrar aukafallssagnar: Um *líka* í fornu máli [From an alternating to a non-alternating oblique subject verb: About *líka* 'like' in Old Icelandic]. *Orð og tunga* 22. 39–68.
Sigurðsson, Halldór Ármann. 1983. Um frásagnarumröðun og grundvallarorðaröð í forníslensku ásamt nokkrum samanburði við nútímamál [Narrative inversion and basic word order in Old Icelandic with some comparison with Modern Icelandic]. Reykjavík: University of Iceland Master's Thesis.
Sigurðsson, Halldór Ármann. 1989. Verbal syntax and case in Icelandic. Lund: Lund University Doctoral Dissertation.
Sigurðsson, Halldór Ármann. 1990–91. Beygingarsamræmi [Agreement]. *Íslenskt mál og almenn málfræði* 12–13. 31–77.
Sigurðsson, Halldór Ármann. 1992. The case of quirky subjects. *Working Papers in Scandinavian Syntax* 49. 1–26.
Sigurðsson, Halldór Ármann. 1993. Argument drop in Old Icelandic. *Lingua* 89. 246–280.
Sigurðsson, Halldór Ármann. 2002. Infinitives in Icelandic: A description. Ms. Lund University.
Sigurðsson, Halldór Ármann. 2004. Icelandic non-nominative subjects: Facts and implications. In Peri Bhaskararao & Karumuri V. Subbarao (eds.), *Non-Nominative Subjects 2*, 137–159. Amsterdam: John Benjamins.
Sigurðsson, Halldór Ármann. 2008. The case of PRO. *Natural Language and Linguistic Theory* 26(2). 403–450.
Sigurðsson, Halldór Ármann. 2018. Icelandic declarative V1: A brief overview. *Working Papers in Scandinavian Syntax* 101. 49–55.
Sigurðsson, Halldór Ármann. 2019. Topicality in Icelandic: Null arguments and narrative inversion. In Valéria Molnár, Verner Egerland & Susanne Winkler (eds.), *Architecture of Topic*, 249–272. Berlin: Mouton de Gruyter.
Sigurðsson, Þorgeir. 2019. *The unreadable poem of Arinbjǫrn, preservation, meter, and a restored text*. Reykjavík: University of Iceland PhD Dissertation.
Smirnicka, Olga. 1972. The impersonal sentence patterns in the Edda and in the Sagas. *Arkiv för nordisk fllologi* 87. 56–88.
Smith, Henry. 1994. Dative sickness in Germanic. *Natural Language & Linguistic Theory* 12(4). 675–736.
Smith, Henry. 1996. *Restrictiveness in Case Theory*. Cambridge: Cambridge University Press.
Smitherman, Thomas & Jóhanna Barðdal. 2009. Typological changes in the evolution of Indo-European syntax. *Diachronica* 26(2). 253–273.
Snædal, Magnús. 1998. *A Concordance to Biblical Gothic*. Reykjavík: Institute of Linguistics, University of Iceland, and University of Iceland Press.
Somers, Joren. 2021. Onpersoonlijke datief-nominatiefwerkwoorden in het hedendaagse Duits: Definitie, inventaris en semantische classificatie. *Handelingen – Koninklijke Zuid-Nederlandse Maatschappij Voor Taal- en Letterkunde en Geschiedenis* 75: 211–238.
Somers, Joren & Jóhanna Barðdal. 2022. Alternating Dat-Nom/Nom-Dat Verbs in Icelandic: An exploratory corpus-based analysis. *Working Papers in Scandinavian Syntax* 107. 83–110.
Somers, Joren & Jóhanna Barðdal. 2023. Comparing the argument structure of alternating Dat-Nom/Nom-Dat predicates in German and Icelandic. *Working Papers in Scandinavian Syntax* 108. 1–25.

Somers, Joren, Ludwig De Cuypere, Torsten Leuschner & Jóhanna Barðdal. 2023. The Dat-Nom/Nom-Dat alternation in Present-Day German: Evidence from word order. Submitted.

Sorace, Antonella. 1995. Acquiring linking rules and argument structures in a second Language: The unaccusative/unergative distinction. In Lynn Eubank, Larry Selinker & Michael Sharwood Smith (eds.), *The Current State of Interlanguage: Studies in Honor of William E. Rutherford*, 153–175. Amsterdam: John Benjamins.

Speijer, J. S. 1886. *Sanskrit Syntax*. Leiden: Brill.

Staal, Johan Frederik. 1967. *Word Order in Sanskrit and Universal Grammar*. Dordrecht: D. Reidel Publishing.

Steever, Sanford B. (ed.). 1998. *The Dravidian Languages*. London: Routledge.

Stepanov, Arthur. 2003. On the 'quirky' difference [sic!] Icelandic vs. German: A note of doubt. *Working Papers in Scandinavian Syntax* 71. 1–32.

Streitberg, Wilhelm. 1920. *Gotisches Elementarbuch*. Heidelberg: Carl Winter.

Söderwall, K. F. 1884–1918. *Ordbok öfver svenska medeltidsspråket* [A Dictionary of the Swedish Language of the Middle Ages]. Lund: Berlingska Boktryckeri- och Stilgjuteri-Aktiebolaget.

Tallerman, Maggie. 1998. *Understanding Syntax*. London: Arnold.

Talmy, Leonard. 1976. Semantic causative types. In Masayoshi Shibatani (ed.), *The Grammar of Causative Constructions*, 43–116. New York: Academic Press.

Talmy, Leonard. 1985. Force dynamics in language and thought. *Chicago Linguistic Society* 21. 293–337.

Talmy, Leonard. 1988. Force dynamics in language and cognition. *Cognitive Science* 12(1). 49–100.

Thommen, Eduard. 1905. Die Wortstellung im nachvedischen Altindischen und im Mittelindischen. *Zeitschrift für vergleichende Sprachforschung auf dem Gebiete der Indogermanischen Sprachen* 38(4). 504–563.

Þórhallsdóttir, Guðrún. 1997. *ylgr, heiðr, brúðr*: Saga *r*-endingar nefnifalls eintölu kvenkynsorða [The history of *r*-endings with nominative singular feminine nouns]. In Úlfar Bragason (ed.). *Íslensk málsaga og textafræði*, 41–56. Reykjavík: Stofnun Sigurðar Nordals.

Þórólfsson, Björn K. 1925. *Um íslenskar orðmyndir á 14. og 15. öld og breytingar þeirra úr fornmálinu: Með viðauka um nýjungar í orðmyndum á 16. öld og síðar* [On Icelandic Word Forms in the 14th and 15th Century and their Changes from the Oldest Language: With an Appendix on Neologisms in Word Formation in the 16th Century and Later]. Reykjavík. [Reprinted by Málvísindastofnun Háskóla Íslands, 1987].

Thráinsson, Höskuldur. 1976. Some arguments against the interpretive theory of pronouns and reflexives. *Harvard Studies in Syntax and Semantics* 2. 573–624.

Thráinsson, Höskuldur. 1979. *On Complementation in Icelandic*. New York: Garland.

Thráinsson, Höskuldur. 2007. *The Syntax of Icelandic*. Cambridge: Cambridge University Press.

Thráinsson, Höskuldur & Thóra Björk Hjartardóttir. 1986. Pro-drop, Topic-drop . . .: Where do Old and Modern Icelandic fit in? In Östen Dahl & Anders Holmberg (eds.), *Scandinavian Syntax*, 150–161. Stockholm: Dept. of Linguistics, Stockholm University.

Thráinsson, Höskuldur, Hjalmar P. Petersen, Jógvan í Lon Jacobsen & Zakaris S. Hansen. 2012. *Faroese: An Overview and Reference Grammar*. 2nd edn. Tórshavn: Faroe University Press.

Thurneysen, Rudolf. 1885. Der indogermanische Imperativ. *Zeitschrift für vergleichende Sprachforschung auf dem Gebiete der Indogermanischen Sprachen* 27(2). 172–180.

Tomasello, Michael. 2003. *Constructing a Language: Usage-Based Theory of Language Acquisition*. Cambridge, Ma.: Harvard University Press.

Tomasello, Michael. 2006. Construction Grammar for kids. *Constructions* 1. 1–11.

Tómasson, Sverrir. 2012. Review of *Stjórn*, Vol. I–II, ed. by Reidar Astås. *Maal og minne* 104(2). 121–128.

Trousdale, Greame & Thomas Hoffmann (eds). 2013. *The Oxford Handbook of Construction Grammar*. Oxford: Oxford University Press.
Uhlenbeck, Christianus C. 1901. Agens und Patiens im Kasussystem der indogermanischen Sprachen. *Indogermanische Forschungen* 12. 170–171.
Vaillant, André. 1936. L'ergatif indo-européen. *Bulletin de la Société de Linguistique de Paris* 37. 93–108.
Van Valin, R.D. Jr. 1981. Grammatical relations in ergative languages. *Studies in Language* 5(3). 361–394.
Van Valin, R.D. Jr. 1990. Semantic parameters of split intransitivity. *Language* 66. 221–260.
Vázquez-González, Juan G. & Jóhanna Barðdal. 2019. Reconstructing the ditransitive construction for Proto-Germanic: Gothic, Old English and Old Norse-Icelandic. *Folia Linguistica Historica* 40(2). 555–620.
Venneman, Theo. 2003. *Europa Vasconica – Europa Semitica*. Berlin: Mouton de Gruyter.
Verhoeven, Elisabeth. 2015. Thematic asymmetries do matter! A corpus study of German word order. *Journal of Germanic Linguistics* 27(1). 45–104.
Verma, M. K. & K. P. Mohanan (eds.). 1990. *Experiencer Subjects in South Asian Languages*. Stanford: CSLI Publications.
Viðarsson, Heimir Freyr, 2009. 'Sól gerði eigi skína': stoðsagnir með nafnhætti í fornnorrænu ['The sun did not shine: *Do*-support in Old Norse-Icelandic]. Reykjavík: University of Iceland Master's Thesis.
Viti, Carlotta. 2017. Semantic and cognitive factors of argument marking in ancient Indo-European languages. *Diachronica* 34(3). 368–419.
de Vries, Jan. 1957. *Altnordisches etymologisches Wörterbuch*. Leiden: Brill.
Wackernagel, Jacob. 1892. Über ein Gesetz der indogermanischen Wortstellung. *Indogermanische Forschungen* 1. 333–436.
Walkden, George. 2009. *The Comparative Method in syntactic reconstruction*. Cambridge: Cambridge University M.Phil. Thesis.
Walkden, George. 2013. The correspondence problem in syntactic reconstruction. *Diachronica* 30(1). 95–122.
Walkden, George. 2014. *Syntactic Reconstruction and Proto-Germanic*. Oxford: Oxford University Press.
Wallenberg, Joel C. 2008. English weak pronouns and object shift. In Charles B. Chang & Hannah J. Haynie (eds.), *Proceedings of the 26th West Coast Conference on Formal Linguistics*, 489–497. Somerville, MA: Cascadilla Proceedings Project.
Wallenberg, Joel C. 2015. Antisymmetry and heavy NP shift across Germanic. In Theresa Biberauer & George Walkden (eds.), *Syntax over Time: Lexical, Morphological and Information-Structural Interactions*, 336–349. Oxford: Oxford University Press.
Wallenberg, Joel C., Anton Karl Ingason, Einar Freyr Sigurðsson & Eiríkur Rögnvaldsson. 2011. Icelandic Parsed Historical Corpus (IcePaHC). Version 0.5. Available online at: http://www.linguist.is/icelandic_treebank.
Watkins, Calvert. 1976. Towards Proto-Indo-European syntax: Problems and pseudo-problems. In Sanford B. Steever, Carol A. Walker & Salokoko S. Mufwene (eds.), *Papers from the Parasession on Diachronic Syntax*, 306–326. Chicago: Chicago Linguistic Society.
Watkins, Calvert. 1995. *How to Kill a Dragon in Indo-European: Aspects of Indo-European Poetics*. Oxford: Oxford University Press.
Wechsler, Stephen. 1995. *The Semantic Basis of Argument Structure*. Stanford, CSLI Publications.
Weerman, Fred & Petra de Wit. 1999. The decline of the genitive in Dutch. *Linguistics* 37(6). 1155–1192.
Wichmann, Søren. 2008. The study of semantic alignment: Retrospect and the state of the art. In Mark Donohue & Søren Wichmann (eds.), *The Typology of Semantic Alignment*, 3–23. Oxford: Oxford University Press.

Willis, David. 2011. Reconstructing last week's weather: Syntactic reconstruction and Brythonic free relatives. *Journal of Linguistics* 47(2). 407–446.

Winkler, Heinrich. 1896. *Germanische Casussyntax I*. Berlin: Dümmler.

Winter, Werner. 1984. Reconstructional comparative linguistics and the reconstruction of the syntax of undocumented stages in the development of languages and language families. In Jacek Fisiak (ed.), *Historical Syntax*, 613–625. The Hague: Mouton.

Witzlack-Makarevich, Alena. 2010. *Typological variation in grammatical relations*. Leipzig: University of Leipzig PhD Dissertation.

Wolf, Norbert Richard. 1981. *Geschichte der deutschen Sprache. Band 1: Althochdeutsch – Mittelhochdeutsch*. Heidelberg: Quelle & Meyer.

Wood, Jim & Halldór Ármann Sigurðsson. 2014. *Let*-causatives and (a)symmetric DAT-NOM constructions. *Syntax* 17(3). 269–298.

Wunderlich, Dieter. 2009. The force of lexical case: German and Icelandic compared. In Kristin Hanson & Sharon Inkelas (eds.), *The Nature of the Word: Studies in Honor of Paul Kiparsky*, 587–620. Cambridge, Ma: MIT Press.

Yoon, James H. 2004. Non-nominative (jajor) subjects and case stacking in Korean. In Peri Bhaskararao & Karumuri V. Subbarao (eds.), *Non-Nominative Subjects 2*, 265–314. Amsterdam: John Benjamins.

Zaenen, Annie & Joan Maling. 1984. Unaccusative, passive, and quirky case. In Mark Cobler, Susannah MacKaye & Michael T. Wescoat (eds.), *Proceedings of the Third West Coast Conference on Formal Linguistics*, 317–329. Stanford, Ca: Stanford Linguistics Association.

Zaenen, Annie, Joan Maling & Höskuldur Thráinsson. 1985. Case and grammatical functions: The Icelandic passive. *Natural Language and Linguistic Theory* 3. 441–483.

Name Index

Aarts, B. 9, 329
Adger, D. 219
Allen, C.L. 3, 97, 98, 99, 138, 142, 155, 174,194, 207, 230, 237, 244, 248, 327, 336, 338, 339, 340, 346
Allen, K. 40
Alm, M. 18
Aman, N. 9, 329
Anagnostopoulou, E. 48, 117, 118, 153
Anand, P. 67
Anderson, S.R. 24, 66, 67, 194
Andrews, A.D. 1, 10, 30, 31, 47, 61, 193, 328, 329
Arnett, C. 77, 82, 108, 188, 218, 230, 247
Askedal, J.O. 2, 142, 327
Atkinson, Q. 146
Avery, J. 215
Axel, K. 155, 248
Axelsdóttir, K. 9

Bader, M. 55
Barðdal, J. 14, 16–18, 24, 31, 33, 34, 36, 39, 40, |44, 52–55, 58, 61–64, 71–73, 76–78, 80, 82, 84, 90, 95, 96, 99, 105, 108, 121, 122, 126–128, 132, 135–137, 139–143, 145, 146, 147, 149, 150, 151–153, 161, 162, 168, 183, 187, 188, 190, 193, 196, 198, 199, 203, 204, 205, 207, 209, 2013, 214, 216–223, 225, 227, 230, 233, 234, 238, 239, 242, 244, 246, 247, 248, 250, 254, 267, 278, 288, 289, 293, 294, 312, 315, 324, 327, 329, 333, 338, 339, 340, 342, 345, 351
Barkarson, S. 203
Barnes, M. 1, 16, 61, 94, 95, 138
Bashir, E. 48
Bayer, J. 2, 4, 28, 32, 51, 53, 55, 134, 139, 275, 276, 279, 280, 298, 330,
Belletti, A. 71, 81
Bencini, G.M.L. 40
Benedetti, M. 54
Bennett, W.H 160
Bernharðsson, H. 9
Bernódusson, H. 76, 77
Bhatia, T.K. 47
Bickel, B. 48, 153

Biondo, L. 153, 196, 333
Bjarnadóttir, V. 77, 82, 219, 220, 234, 247, 248
Bjorvand, H. 143, 221
Blosen, H. 135
Blöndal Magnússon, Á. 221
Boas, H.C. 17
Bobaljik, J.D. 204
Boon, P. 135
Börjars, K. 5, 7, 8, 328
Bornkessel, I. 275, 276, 292
Botvinick, M. 40
Bremmer, R.H. 54, 233
Brugmann, K. 212
Bruno, L. 153, 196, 333
Bucci, G. 161, 340
Burridge, K. 5, 7, 8, 328
Buscha, J. 23, 28
Butler, M.C. 142

Campbell, L. 129–133, 213, 214, 217, 218, 338
Cappelle, B. 17
Carey, S.M. 77, 82, 238, 247
Caruana, S. 135, 144
Castro Alves, F. 48, 153
Cattafi, E. 153, 196, 333
Cennamo, M. 150
Chomsky, N. 24
Cole, P. 4, 134, 139–142, 164, 184, 194, 199, 209, 210, 230, 252, 268, 279, 280, 281
Colleman, T. 18
Comrie, B. 24, 48, 66, 153
Conti, L. 54
Corbett, G.G. 54, 147
Cristofaro, S. 34
Croft, W. 17, 18, 33, 34, 40, 41, 42, 44, 51, 71, 72, 220
Cruse, A. 17, 18
Culicover, P.W. 34

Dal, I. 244
Danesi, S. 77, 82, 153, 196, 219, 220, 234, 239, 247, 248, 333
Daniels, D. 220
Dattner, E. 34

De Bakker, M. 177
De Cuypere, L. 292, 293
Delbrück, B. 113, 212, 213
Delsing, L.-O. 103, 178
Demske, U. 262, 263
Denison, D. 125, 162, 164, 252
Dewey, T.K. 34, 40, 44, 52, 76, 108, 121, 122, 188, 218, 219, 220, 230, 234, 238, 247, 248, 278, 289, 294, 312, 324, 329
Diewald, G. 261, 263
Dixon, R.M.W. 39, 66
Donohue, M. 151
Drinka, B. 151, 213
Dryer, M.S. 39
Dunn, M. 108, 188, 218, 230, 247

Elmer, W. 54, 142
van Emde Boas, E. 177
Engberg-Pedersen, E. 110
Erom, H.-W. 244
Eythórsson, Th. 16, 34, 36, 39, 40, 44, 52, 55, 61, 62, 64, 76, 77, 82, 90, 95, 108, 121, 122, 126, 127, 135, 136, 141–143, 149–151, 162, 168, 183, 187, 188, 190, 193, 196, 198, 199, 203, 204, 207, 209, 213, 214, 218–223, 225, 227, 230, 233, 234, 238, 247, 248, 250, 267, 278, 289, 294, 312, 315, 324, 327, 329, 338, 340, 342

Faarlund, J.T. 2, 3, 32, 33, 142, 177, 179, 191, 203, 204, 327
Falk, C. 4, 29, 33, 39, 101, 110, 134, 135, 139, 142, 146, 155, 158, 159, 172, 176–179, 185, 188, 189, 190, 202, 230, 269, 327
Fanselow, G. 2, 32, 51, 53, 280, 281, 284, 298, 330
Farrell, P. 54
Fedriani, C. 81, 219, 220, 234, 247, 248
Ferraresi, G. 155, 159, 160
Fillmore, C.J. 17, 43, 220, 234
Fischer, K. 18
Fischer, O.C.M. 97, 125, 127, 167, 260
Fischer, P. 212
Fischer, S. 142, 327
Foley, W.A. 34
Forker, D. 48, 153
Fox, A. 212
Franco, I. 75

Fried, M. 234
Friedrich, P. 213, 220
Frotscher, M. 220, 234, 247
Fuss, E. 248

van der Gaaf, W. 142
Gabelentz, G.v.d. 200
Gamon, D. 34
García-Miguel, J.M. 34
Garrett, A. 220
van Gelderen, E. 9, 125, 328
Giacalone Ramat, A. 18
Gildea, S. 18, 213, 214, 216, 218, 219, 220, 227, 234
Gillon, B. 113
Goldberg, A.E. 17, 40, 123, 216, 217, 219, 220
Gonzálvez García, F. 18
Gray, R. 146
Greenberg, J.H. 213
Grimshaw, J. 44, 71

de Haan, G.J. 237
Haegeman, L. 155
Hafsteinsdóttir, H. 203
Haider, H. 2, 29, 32, 51, 53, 276, 281, 284, 285, 287, 288, 298, 322, 330
Hajičová, E. 27
Hale, M. 213, 218, 220
Hansen, Z.S. 94, 95, 230
Harbert, W.E. 4, 134, 139–142, 157, 160, 162, 164, 167, 168, 184, 194, 199, 207, 208, 209, 210, 230, 248, 252, 260, 268, 279, 280, 281, 340
Harkness, A. 23
Harris, A.C. 129–133, 142, 213, 214, 218, 338
Harrison, S.P. 216, 218
Haspelmath, M. 34, 39, 81, 134, 135, 140, 143, 144, 289, 354
Haugan, J. 104, 128, 204, 248
Havers, W. 135, 147, 212
Hawkins, J.A. 289
Helbig, G. 23, 28
Hellan, L. 204
Helmut, R. 221
Heltoft, L. 2, 4, 29, 155, 167, 177, 178, 187, 327
Hendriks, J. 237
Hentschel, E. 24
Hermann, E. 212

Hermon, G. 4, 48, 134, 139–142, 153, 164, 184, 194, 199, 209, 210, 230, 252, 268, 279, 280, 281
Hiietam, K. 153
Hilpert, M. 18
Hinterhölzl, R. 248
Hjartardóttir, Th.B. 154
Hock, H.H. 48
Hoenigswald, H.M. 217
Hoffmann, T. 18
Hoffner, H.A. 114
Hole, D. 147
Holvoet, A. 53, 54, 120, 333
van der Horst, J. 199
Hrafnbjargarson, G.H. 178, 186, 327
Hualde, J.I. 29
Huddleston, R. 9, 328
Huitink, L. 177

Ilioaia, M. 48, 153
Ingason, A.K. 204

Jackendoff, R. 17, 34, 44
Jacobi, H. 212
Jacobsen, J.í.L. 94, 95, 230
Jakubíček, M. 79
Janda, R.D. 218
Jeffers, R.J. 213–215, 218
Jenset, G.B. 77, 82
Jespersen, O. 70, 125, 126, 139, 142, 146, 200, 338, 355
Johnson, C.A. 219, 220, 234, 247
Jolly, J. 212
Jonas, D. 204
Jónsson, J.G. 10, 11, 16, 73, 76, 95, 104, 128, 204, 230, 248, 301, 327, 328
Josefsson, G. 204,
Juntune, T.W. 142, 327

Kachru, B.B. 47
Kachru, Y. 47
Kalkar, O. 106
Kampen, J. van 75
Karlsson, E. 18
Karlsson, S. 75
Kay, P. 17, 34, 220, 234
Keenan, E.L. 24, 25, 26, 30, 141, 327

van Kemenade, A. 248
Kerkhof, P.A. 121, 135–137, 139, 141, 151, 152, 207, 219, 220, 234, 247
Kertes, L. 34
Keydana, G. 151
Khalilova, Z. 48, 153
Kibrik, A.A. 39
Kikusawa, R. 210, 214
Kilgarriff, A. 79
Kim, J.-B. 9, 18, 162, 234, 329
Klein, J.S. 212, 219
Kluge, F. 221, 242
Kotin, M.L. 136
Kovář, V. 79
Krahe, H. 227
Kristoffersen, K.E. 33, 90, 128, 142, 167, 168, 216, 217, 244, 260, 327
Kroonen, G. 77, 82, 220, 221, 226, 234, 247, 255
Kulikov, L. 121, 135–137, 139, 141, 142, 152, 207, 219, 220, 227, 234, 247
Kümmel, M. 221

Lakoff, G. 17
Landau, I. 48, 153, 162, 180, 187
Lander, E.T. 155
Langacker, R.W. 40
Lapolla, R.J. 34
Le Mair, E. 219, 220, 234, 247
Lee-Goldman, R. 43
van der Leek, F. 97, 125, 127
Legate, J.A. 67
Lehmann, W.P. 213, 220
Lenerz, J. 289
Letuchiy, A. 152
Leuschner, T. 292, 293
Li, C.N. 24
Lightfoot, D.W. 125, 142, 146, 213, 214, 216, 218
Lindeman, F.O. 143, 221
Lindqvist, A. 200
Lindström, J. 75
Lindström, L. 75
Lipp, R. 221
Ljunggren, C.A. 159
Loureiro-Porto, L. 125
Los, B. 248, 260
Lühr, R. 155

Luján, E.R. 214, 216, 218, 219, 220, 227
Luraghi, S. 54

Malchukov, A.L. 125, 140, 145–147
Maling, J. 1, 10, 11, 30, 31, 48, 49, 51, 53, 59, 61, 68, 150, 275, 281, 283, 298, 301, 238, 329, 330, 333
Marckwardt, A.H. 242
Masica, C.P. 47
Matasović, R. 150
Mathieu, E. 153
McGillivray, B. 77, 82
van der Meer, M.J. 212
Melchert, C.H. 114
Mel'čuk, I. 34
Mendoza, J. 213
Meng, M. 55
Metslang, H. 29, 34, 153
Michaelis, L.A. 9, 17, 18, 162, 234, 329
Middeke, K. 77
Miller, D.G. 213, 220
Miranda, R. 217
Mírovský, J. 27
Mithun, M. 217
Mohanan, K.P. 48, 153
Möhlig-Falke, R. 77
Molnár, V. 18
Moore, J. 48, 153, 179
Mørck, E. 33, 142, 327
Mörnsjö, M. 75
Müller, G. 9

Naylor, P. B. 67
Nevins, A. 67
Nilsson, J. 9
Nizar, M. 47

Oberlin, A. 77, 82
O'Connor, M.C, 17, 220
Önnerfors, O. 75
Orqueda, V. 151
Östman, J.-O. 18, 234
Ottósson, K.G. 150, 191, 204, 239

Pankau, A. 2, 32, 51, 53, 298, 330
Pat-El, N. 48, 153
Payne, T.E. 9, 329

Pedersen, H. 212
Pesetsky, D. 71
Petersen, H.P. 94, 95, 230
Pereira, F. 40
Perlmutter, D.M. 48, 153, 179
Petrova, S. 248
Platzack, C. 75, 76, 204
Polinsky, M. 162
Pooth, R.A. 121, 135–137, 139, 141, 151, 152, 207, 219, 220
Porzig, W. 212
Postal, P.M. 180
Primus, B. 289
Puckica, J. 18
Pullum, G.K. 9, 328

Rákosi, G. 81, 153
Ravid, D. 34
Reis, M. 1, 30–33, 52, 53, 68, 276, 278, 329
Rhodes, R. 43
Rijksbaron, A. 177
Ringe, D. 227
Rizzi, L. 71, 81
Rögnvaldsson, E. 3, 16, 154, 157, 158, 160, 161, 172, 177, 179, 190, 191, 204, 205, 327, 340
Rott, J.A. 76, 289, 293
Ruppenhofer, J. 234
Rychlý, P. 79
Rysová, K. 27

Sag, I. 234
Sandal, C. 239
Sapir E. 145
Sapp, C.D. 159
Sarkar, A. 27
Sasse, H.-J. 24
Schirmer, B. 221
Schlesewsky, M. 275, 276, 292
Seefranz-Montag, A.v. 142, 145, 173, 230, 238, 246, 247, 258, 327
Seržant, I. 53, 54, 81, 135, 140, 142, 147, 334
Shaer, B. 113
Shariatmadari, D. 125
Sherman, I. 237
Shibatani, M. 48, 153
Sigurðsson, E.F. 128, 204, 338

Sigurðsson, H.Á. 1, 10, 14, 28, 30–32, 51–53, 75, 76, 90, 98, 142, 150, 154, 181, 182, 275, 298, 328, 329, 330
Sigurðsson, Þ. 242
Smirnicka, O. 230
Smirnova, E. 261, 263
Smith, H. 142
Smitherman, T. 77, 82, 96, 143, 147, 219, 220, 227, 234, 247, 248
Snædal, M. 126
Söderwall, K.F. 100, 176, 177, 202
Somers, J. 78, 82, 278, 292, 293, 351
Sorace, A. 34
Speijer, J.S. 113
Sridhar, S.N. 4, 134, 139–142, 164, 184, 194, 199, 209, 210, 230, 252, 268, 279, 280, 281
Staal, J.F. 113
Steever, S.B. 48, 153
Steingrímsson, S. 203
Stepanov, A. 2
Streitberg, W. 207
Suchomel, V. 79
Sveen, A. 216, 217, 244

Tallerman, M. 9, 328
Talmy, L. 40, 41
Tan, L. 9, 329
Thommen, E. 212
Thráinsson, H. 1, 10, 11, 14, 30, 31, 47–49, 51, 53, 59, 61, 68, 75, 76, 90, 94, 95, 154, 167, 230, 275, 281, 283, 298, 301, 328, 329, 330, 333
Thurneysen, R. 212
Tomasello, M. 34, 219
Tómasson, S. 241
Trousdale, G. 18

Uhlenbeck, C.C. 212

Vaillant, A. 212
Van Peteghem, M. 48

Van Valin, Jr., R.D. 34, 44
Vázquez-González, J.G. 217, 219, 220, 234, 246, 247
Venneman, T. 221
Verhoeven, E. 135, 328, 354
Verma, M.K. 48, 153
Viðarsson, H.F. 128, 248, 338
Viti, C. 77
de Vries, J. 221, 233

Wackernagel, J. 118, 212
Walkden, G. 220, 226, 227
Wallenberg, J.C. 204, 205
Watkins, C. 213, 220, 221
Wechsler, S. 71
Weerman, F. 237
Wichmann, S. 151, 213
Willis, D. 218, 220
Winkler, H. 212
Winter, W. 213
de Wit, P. 237
Witzlack-Makarevich, A. 34
Wolf, N.R. 262
Wood, J. 76,
Wunderlich, D. 2, 4, 29, 32, 51, 53, 134, 139, 275, 276, 279, 281, 298, 322, 330

Yoon, J.H. 48, 153

Zaenen, A. 1, 10, 30, 31, 48, 49, 51, 53, 59, 61, 68, 150, 275, 281, 283, 298, 328, 329, 330, 333
Zehnder, T. 221
Zeman, D. 27
Zwilling, R. 34

Þórhallsdóttir, G. 9
Þórólfsson, B.K. 9

Language Index

Anatolian, see Hittite
Ancient Greek 20, 27, 112, 117, 120, 127, 138, 153, 229, 239, 323, 333, 336, 342

Baltic, see Lithuanian
Basque 29
Brythonic 220

Cariban 48, 153, 214
Czech 27

Danish
– see Old Danish
Dardic 48, 153
Dravidian 47, 48, 153
– Malayalam 47
Dutch
– see Middle Dutch
– see Old Dutch

East-Germanic
– see Gothic
English
– see Middle English
– see Old English
Estonian 29, 30, 153

Faroese 1–3, 5, 16, 20, 60, 70, 81, 94–97, 99, 133, 138, 141, 278, 306, 323, 326, 327, 336, 338, 341, 342, 354
Frisian
– see Old Frisian

Georgian 140, 209
German 1–5, 12, 19, 21–26, 28–33, 46–60, 62–65, 68, 69, 82, 97, 108, 112, 125, 128, 135, 141, 143, 147, 148, 154–158, 170, 171, 215, 275–324, 327, 329, 330, 333–335, 338, 350–355
– see also Middle High German
– see also Middle Low German
– see also Old High German

Gothic 4, 20, 112, 113, 116, 120, 126, 127, 133, 138, 141, 157–162, 166–168, 183, 198–200, 206–209, 211, 223–230, 233–238, 240–246, 249, 252, 254, 255, 257–260, 263, 267, 270–274, 278, 279, 327, 336, 337
Greek 20, 117, 118, 120, 138, 143, 144, 153, 337

Hebrew, see Semitic
Hittite 20, 112, 114–116, 120, 138, 146, 150, 151, 239, 323, 336, 345
Hungarian 153

Icelandic 1–5, 9–17, 19–21, 22, 26–28, 30–33, 35, 40–45, 46–54, 58–65, 68, 70–93, 94–97, 99–102, 104, 106–109, 111, 113, 121, 122, 125, 127, 128, 132–138, 141, 143, 146, 148–150, 154–158, 166, 168, 170–172, 177, 180, 181, 190–194, 196, 203–205, 209, 225, 254, 271, 275, 278, 285–287, 289, 292–295, 298–302, 304–306, 308–311, 313–315, 317, 318, 321–326, 327–336, 338–342, 351–354
– see also Old Norse-Icelandic
Indo-Aryan, see Sanskrit
Indo-European 5, 20, 22, 24, 47, 52, 60, 70, 77, 78, 82, 97, 98, 112–121, 133–137, 138–139, 145–147, 150–152, 153, 155, 207, 212–214, 220, 221, 238, 239, 247, 326, 338, 339, 354
Irminonic 246, 274, 354
– see also German
Italian 27, 28

Japanese 48, 153

Korean 48, 153

Latin 20, 23, 27, 96, 105, 112, 115, 116, 120, 138, 150, 153, 167, 196, 226, 239, 262, 263, 323, 333, 336, 345
Lithuanian 20, 53, 112, 120, 138, 150, 239, 323, 337, 338, 345

Middle Dutch 230, 232, 233, 234, 236, 237, 238, 343

Middle English 3, 4, 70, 97–99, 125–133, 155, 173, 175, 183, 184, 194, 200, 208, 209, 237, 254, 258, 267–270, 338, 334, 342
Middle High German 174, 230–247, 274, 343–346
Middle Low German 108, 111, 230–238

North-Germanic 2, 94, 108, 109, 167, 168, 222–226, 234, 238, 240, 244, 263, 354
– see also Danish
– see also Faroese
– see also Icelandic
– see also Norwegian
– see also Swedish
Norwegian 100, 109–111, 135, 216, 217
– see also Old Norse-Icelandic

Old Danish 2, 4, 20, 29, 70, 81, 99, 100, 105–112, 113, 135, 138, 157, 158, 162–169, 173, 177–179, 183, 185–188, 194, 200, 202, 206, 209, 230, 233–238, 240, 250–259, 267–270, 278, 327, 336, 341–343, 354
Old Dutch 188, 199
Old English 3, 4, 20, 42, 70, 97–99, 108, 125–133, 138, 141, 155, 159, 162–166, 169, 174–178, 188, 198, 200, 201, 204, 206–208, 211, 225–230, 233, 234, 237–239, 244–249, 252–255, 260, 273, 278, 327, 336, 338, 340, 341, 343–346, 354
Old French 153
Old Frisian 230–237, 343
Old High German, 20, 108, 145, 162–169, 172–174, 178, 188, 198, 201, 206, 208, 225, 226, 230–240, 242, 244–249, 252, 255, 257, 261–263, 273, 274, 278, 328, 341–348
Old Norse-Icelandic 2–4, 20, 21, 32, 33, 95, 104, 105, 108, 128, 141, 145, 154, 157–163, 165, 168–178, 183, 184, 188, 190–196, 199–209, 211, 225, 226, 229, 230, 233, 234, 236, 237, 238, 240–246, 249, 253, 254, 258–260, 267–271, 274, 278, 314, 327, 328, 340–345, 348, 350, 354
Old Russian 112, 118–120, 138, 336
Old Saxon 4, 20, 159, 165, 166, 169, 171, 172, 174, 178, 179, 183, 184, 188, 194–198, 200, 201, 206, 209, 225, 248, 249, 253–261, 267–270, 278, 327, 341, 342, 354

Old Swedish 4, 20, 29, 33, 39, 70, 81, 100–112, 113, 132, 138, 141, 157–159, 162–165, 169, 172, 173, 176–179, 183, 185–190, 194, 200–202, 206–209, 229–238, 250–259, 267–270, 278, 328, 336, 341–343, 354

Polynesian 141, 209–210
Proto-Germanic 2–4, 18–21, 66, 108, 113, 141, 143, 151, 207, 212, 217, 221, 226, 227, 229, 233–237, 240, 242, 245–248, 250–252, 255–257, 263–267, 270–274, 275, 343–350, 354
Proto-Indo-European 136–137, 139, 151–152, 207, 213, 220, 221, 247, 338, 339, 354
Proto-Northwest Germanic 220

Quechuan 48, 153

Romanian 47, 48, 153, 338
Russian 48, 118–120, 138, 153, 179, 337, 338

Sanskrit 20, 112, 113, 114, 116, 120, 138, 146, 150, 239, 323, 336, 345
Semitic 48, 153
– Hebrew 48
Slavic 20, 150, 239, 323, 345
– see also Czech
– see also Russian
– see also Old Russian
Slavonic, see Slavic
South-Asian 47, 48
Spanish 27, 28
Swedish 26, 97, 110, 110, 135, 204
– see also Old Swedish

Tibeto-Burman 48, 153
Tsezic 48, 153

West-Germanic 2, 3, 108, 167, 168, 179, 222–226, 234, 237, 240, 242–246, 257, 263, 274, 327, 354
– see also Dutch
– see also English
– see also Frisian
– see also German
– see also Irminonic

Subject Index

Acceptability judgments 60–65, 315–316, 325, 335, 353
AcI, see Raising-to-object
Agreement, see Verb agreement
Alignment 214
– Accusative 24, 135–136, 139, 151–152, 209, 201, 339
– Ergative 24, 29, 65–67, 209, 210, 212, 331
– Semantic 135–136, 139, 151–152, 339
Alternating verbs/predicates, see Dat-Nom / Nom-Dat verbs
Anticausative Hypothesis 140, 141, 149–150
Anticausativization 148, 149, 150, 236, 239, 241–244
– Oblique anticausativization 149, 150, 241–247, 274, 344–346
Antipassive, see the Extended Intransitive Hypothesis
Argument drop
– see Pro-drop
– see Topic-drop
Argument structure 4–5, 20–21, 29, 33, 37, 39, 40–44, 46, 47, 54, 60, 65–68, 70, 72–139, 140–152, 177–178, 200, 220–247, 250, 251, 252, 256, 266, 272–274, 276–279, 288–326, 330–332–339, 343–355
Argument "Swapping" Analysis 125–133, 139, 338–339
Attributed Value Matrix 40, 43–46, 121–124, 234–236, 245, 246, 250–252, 255–257, 263–266, 270–273, 275, 277, 278, 332, 337, 344–350

Case mergers 94, 106, 132, 152, 178, 236–237, 246–247, 254, 259, 339
Case variation 238–239, 339
Causal chain, see Event structure
Causal conceptual structure, see Event structure
Causatives, see Event structure
Clause-bound reflexivization 10–12, 31, 53, 81, 84, 86–88, 153, 156–159, 207, 301–306, 326, 328, 336, 339–340, 346, 352–353

Cognacy
– Double cognacy 226–227
– Quadruple cognacy 227
– Triple cognacy 227
Cognate argument structure constructions 214, 220–247
Cognate case frames 227
Cognate predicates 42, 100–102–113, 118–120, 125–129, 132–133, 166, 214–216, 222–227, 229, 254, 293, 300, 304, 308, 321, 322, 336, 337, 338, 354
Cognate sentences 213, 214–216
Cognate structures 214
Co-indexation 43, 46, 235, 246, 250, 252, 256, 271–274, 323, 346–350
Comparative Method 212, 213, 220–273
Configurationality 2, 3, 32–33, 177, 329
Conjunction reduction 1–2, 10, 12–14, 20, 21, 25, 31, 33, 48–50, 51, 53–55, 58, 60, 68, 69, 81, 84–85, 142, 153–155, 207, 211, 248, 280, 283, 284–288, 295–301, 325, 328, 330, 333, 334, 336, 339, 340, 346, 352
Construal 42–44, 70, 71–74, 151, 330–331
Construction Grammar 17–19, 34–38, 40, 43–46, 67, 68, 121–125, 149, 163, 164, 170, 178, 216, 219, 220, 234–236, 250, 263–266, 270–272, 275, 277, 278, 323, 332, 337, 344–350, 354
Control construction's identity relation hierarchy 58–59, 63
Control infinitives 1–2, 10, 15–17, 20, 21, 25, 29, 31, 32, 33, 45–46, 48–49, 50–65, 68–69, 84, 93, 95–96, 142, 178–200, 208–209, 267–271, 274, 279, 281–283, 315–322, 325, 328, 330, 333, 334, 335, 336, 341–342, 346, 349, 353–354
Correspondence sets
– Argument structure 228, 234–236, 239, 245, 274
– Lexical 226, 233, 255, 263, 273, 274

Dat-Nom /Nom-Dat verbs 4–5, 19–20, 221, 70–139, 144, 150, 177, 189, 200, 202, 229, 233, 234, 236, 250, 289–326, 335–339, 351–355

Directionality in syntax 21, 217–218, 273
- Local vs. universal 218
Ditransitive 17, 143, 216–217, 241–243, 244, 245–247, 263–266, 270, 271, 272, 274, 344, 345, 347, 348

Ellipsis 1, 7, 8, 11, 13, 15–16, 19, 27, 28, 45, 48–50, 54–55, 58–60, 63, 85, 91, 93, 97, 98, 153–155, 179–183, 186–191, 194, 195, 197–199, 209, 241, 248, 251, 256, 270–271, 279–286, 288, 297–301, 316–325, 334, 340–342, 346, 349–353, 355
Ergative derivation, see Oblique anticausativization
Event structure 40–43, 71–74, 243, 330–331
- Causal chain 41–43, 68, 70–72, 74, 330
- Causal conceptual structure 36, 39–41, 44, 68, 71, 330
- Causative events 9–17, 41–42, 44, 62, 72, 90, 135, 167, 187, 242, 243–246, 260, 274, 312, 313, 331, 345, 353
- Psychological events, see Stative events
- Stative events 9–17, 42–43, 71–74, 81, 83, 217, 330–331
Extended Intransitive Hypothesis 135–137, 151–152, 207, 339

Floating quantifiers 180, 181–183
Force-dynamics 40–42, 66, 70–74, 330
Form–meaning correspondences 17, 21, 35, 212, 216, 219–220, 226, 227, 233, 273, 354
"Free Dative" Hypothesis 135, 136, 140, 141, 147–149

Generative grammar 16, 17, 30, 39, 46, 164, 178, 179, 212, 219–220
Genetic relatedness 214, 216
German–Icelandic dichotomy, see Icelandic–German dichotomy

Icelandic–German dichotomy 1–2, 3, 46, 48–60, 63, 65, 68, 275, 277–279, 327, 335, 354
Imperatives 7, 8, 26, 27, 30, 31, 53, 212
Impersonal detransitivization, see Oblique anticausativization

Jespersen's standard story of *like*, see Semantic Development Hypothesis

Keenan's subject properties
- Coding properties 19, 24–26, 31, 32, 51–52, 68, 329
- Behavioral properties 4, 19, 24, 25, 31, 32, 36, 48, 53, 59, 67, 68, 135, 141–144, 164, 194, 199, 221, 254, 279, 324, 333–336, 353

Logical subject, see Psychological subject
Long-distance reflexivization 10, 12, 19, 30, 84, 88–89, 141, 159–162, 207–208, 211, 271–273, 274, 275, 328, 336, 340, 346, 350

Methodological opportunism 31–33, 51, 52, 54, 68, 329–330, 331, 334

Narrative inversion, see Word order
Neogrammarians 135, 212, 218
Non-compositional meaning, 17, 37, 219
Non-reductionist theories, see Radical Construction Grammar

Object-to-Subject Hypothesis 141–142, 151, 210, 210
Oblique anticausativization, see Anticausativization
Oblique Subject Hypothesis 140, 151, 207, 209
Omission, see Ellipsis
Optimality theory 39

Passives 8, 57, 58, 182, 281
Phrase structure 2, 3, 23, 177, 341
- see also Configurationality
Pro-drop 28
Prototype approach to subject 23, 30, 45, 53–54, 59, 68, 333–334
Pseudo-subject, see Psychological subject
Psychological event, see Event structure
Psychological subject 54, 200, 340

Quasi-subject, see Psychological subject

Subject Index

Radical Construction Grammar 18, 34–38, 332–333
Raising-to-object 14–15, 20, 25, 81, 90–91, 167–178, 179, 180, 187, 188, 191, 197, 208, 209, 211, 225, 257–267, 311–315, 325, 336, 341, 347–349, 353
Raising-to-subject 10, 14, 15, 20, 21, 25, 84, 89–90, 162–167, 174, 177, 179–180, 187–188, 193–194, 196–197, 208–209, 252–257, 263, 266, 267, 274, 306–310, 325, 328, 341, 346–348, 353
Reconstruction, see Syntactic reconstruction
Reflexivization
- see Clause-bound reflexivization
- see Long-distance reflexivization
Relativization 25, 26
"Relocation" Hypothesis 167
Restricted Ellipsis Analysis, see Ellipsis

Semantic Development Hypothesis 125–129, 142–143, 338
Semantic relations 35–38
Semi-subject, see Psychological subject
Similarity metrics 218
Sound laws 217–218
Subcategorization frame, see Argument structure
Subject definition 8–9, 22–25, 29, 39–40, 42, 351, 353
- Construction-specific category 18–19, 33–40, 60, 67, 68, 323, 332
- Language-specific category 30–40, 48, 60, 67, 68, 248, 323
- Part-whole vs. part-part, see Syntactic roles
- Subject tests stand-in 23, 39–40, 53, 331, 328–329, 331
- Traditional grammar 22–24, 30, 327
- Universal category 25–30, 48, 67–68
Subject properties, see Subject tests
Subject tests
- see Clause-bound reflexivization
- see Conjunction reduction
- see Control infinitives
- see Long-distance reflexivization
- see Raising-to-object
- see Raising-to-subject
- see Word order

Subject-verb inversion, see Word order
Symbolic relations 35–38
Syntactic patterns 213–214
Syntactic relations vs. Syntactic roles 18–19, 34–38, 42, 71, 177, 332, 334, 352
Syntactic reconstruction
- Arguments against 212–220
- Arguments for 212–274
Syntactic roles, see Syntactic relations vs. Syntactic roles

Thematic hierarchy 44
Thematic relations, see Semantic relations
Topic-drop 154, 207
Topicality Hypothesis 134–135, 143–145, 354
Topicalization 13, 20, 75–76, 79–81, 100, 101, 102, 106, 108, 113, 119, 135, 144–145, 205–206, 251, 262, 284–288, 292–295, 301, 325, 327, 335, 351–352, 354
Transimpersonal Hypothesis 140, 141, 145–147

Unaccusative derivation, see Oblique anticausativization
Unexpressed argument, see Ellipsis

Verb agreement 6–7, 23–24, 25, 28, 31, 43, 52, 97–98, 192, 195, 196, 285
Verbal semantics 16, 72, 73, 81–84, 95, 98, 313, 330, 339

Waste-paper-basket category 52–53, 333–334
Word order
- Freedom 27, 120, 126, 113, 178, 179, 209, 314
- Narrative Inversion 11, 75, 205, 206, 251, 346
- Neutral 5–6, 10, 74–81, 97, 101–106, 108–121, 200–202, 204–205, 283, 293–295, 328, 351–352
- Questions, see Subject-verb inversion
- Reconstruction 248–252
- SO vs. OS order 65–66, 331
- Subject-verb inversion 6, 10, 75–78, 95, 100–112, 200–203, 206, 250–252, 284–287, 289–293, 328
- SVO vs. SOV order 213

www.ingramcontent.com/pod-product-compliance
Lightning Source LLC
Chambersburg PA
CBHW031750220426
43662CB00007B/347